About the Author

Tom Clynes has a singular passion for travel.

But, after graduating from the University of Michigan, reconciling his wanderlust with a 9–5 job wasn't panning out. He developed a résumé that included market researcher, cook, shell fisherman, mosquito control technician, brewer, and freelance writer.

Through creative time management and 14-hour workdays, Clynes was eventually able to orchestrate a four-months-work/one-month-travel schedule.

A passion for experiencing cultures firsthand has led Clynes across the Americas and throughout Europe and Asia. He was in Greece and in need of an event-focused travel guide a few years ago when he decided to write the book himself.

Wild Planet! is the delightful result of that decision.

Also From Visible Ink Press

Pop Culture Landmarks: A Traveler's Guide

This illustrated, guided tour of 300 roadside attractions from 20th-century American pop culture stops at theaters, restaurants, amusement parks, famous homes, museums, and more. By George Cantor, 6" x 9" Paperback, 400 pages, ISBN 0-8103-9899-0.

North American Indian Landmarks: A Traveler's Guide

This guided tour of more than 300 sites sweeps across the continent, with captivating text, vivid photos, and detailed maps that bring the history and culture of the first Americans to life. Foreword by Native American activist Suzan Shown Harjo. By George Cantor, 6" x 9" Paperback, 464 pages, ISBN 0-8103-9132-5.

Historic Black Landmarks: A Traveler's Guide

Both a travel book and historical narrative, this cross-country tour of 300 landmarks uniquely related to African American history and culture is a tribute to the impact of black culture on our nation's history. Foreword by Robert L. Harris, Jr., of the Africana Studies and Research Center at Cornell University. By George Cantor, 6" x 9" Paperback, 408 pages, ISBN 0-8103-9408-1.

Organized Obsessions: 1,001 Offbeat Associations, Fan Clubs, and Micro-Societies You Can Join

Here are 1,001 groups that give new meaning to the word "unique." Whether it's the National Chastity Association, Bobs International, or Messies Anonymous, *Organized Obsessions* is a great conversation starter or gift idea. By Deborah M. Burek and Martin Connors, 5" x 9.25" Paperback, 288 pages, ISBN 0-8103-9415-4.

WILD PLANET!

1,001 Extraordinary Events for the Inspired Traveler

1,001 Extraordinary Events
for the Inspired Traveler

Tom Clynes

DETROIT
WASHINGTON, D.C.
LONDON

WILD PLANET!

1,001 EXTRAORDINARY EVENTS FOR THE INSPIRED TRAVELER

Published by Visible Ink Press™
a division of Gale Research Inc.
835 Penobscot Building
Detroit, MI 48226-4094

Visible Ink Press is a trademark of Gale Research Inc.

Back cover photo of Peru courtesy of A.S.K./Viesti Associates; back cover photo of the Philippines courtesy of Mark Downey; back cover photo of India courtesy of Jehangir Gazdar/Woodfin Camp & Associates; photo of Tom Clynes courtesy of Walter Wasacz; photo of carnival mask in Italy (page viii) courtesy of Ian Murphy/Tony Stone Images.

Art Director: Pamela A. E. Galbreath
Illustrator: Kyle Raetz

ISBN 0-7876-0203-5
Printed in the United States of America

10 9 8 7 6 5 4 3 2 1

For Maureen

Contents

Eastern Mediterranean & the Middle East

Africa

South-Central Asia

East Asia

Southeast Asia

Australia & the South Pacific

South America

The Caribbean

Mexico & Central America

Canada & the United States

Festival Finder

INTRODUCTION

One year I realized I was a glutton for spectacle. I had spent Easter week in a Mayan village in southern Mexico, setting effigies of Judas ablaze and toasting the resurrection with "holy" Coca-Cola. After that I found myself at a Caribbean music festival in Colombia, dancing with my head on fire in a Cartagena bullring. Then on to Thailand, where a Chinese innkeeper throws a lavish vegetarian banquet for 600 local monkeys. Finally, on a sleepy Greek island, the ferries stopped running and I was stuck—with nothing to do.

A Mediterranean beach is not a bad place to be marooned, I realized, but something was missing. I felt like a tourist, when I had been a participant. And I knew that somewhere on the planet, maybe even on the next island, people were celebrating something. Somewhere they were dancing and drinking, and the rhythms of local life were cranked up to their uninhibited peak. Somewhere, as F. Scott Fitzgerald said, things were "glimmering."

I decided to research and write *Wild Planet! 1,001 Extraordinary Events for the Inspired Traveler* to feed my own fascination for diverse cultures, and to provide access to the world's extraordinary events for travelers who want to participate in the life and culture of the places they visit. You could call this book a collection of the earth's amazing moments: festivals, celebrations, ceremonies, and other gatherings that capture locales when they're at their most brilliant, open, artistic, musical—when they're most alive.

You could go to Cuzco, Peru, any day of the year, and you'll probably have great time. But if you happen to be there during the Inca solstice rituals, you'll experience one of the most dramatic spectacles on earth—and get a glimpse into a culture that spans millennia. And although the good times are never in short supply in southern Louisiana, if you plan your trip to coincide with a zydeco, jazz, or Cajun festival, you'll feel the music—live—in the place it was born.

Celebrations are also a great time to meet local people and make friends, since day-to-day cares are set aside and outsiders are accepted more readily. Locals and visitors temporarily forget passport colors and make connections on a very personal level, sharing drinks, dances, and inspired moments. Transactions become communions. Customers become friends. Chauvinism dissolves and minds open up. Caught in the carnival, you throw away your own rules and expectations, and embrace someone else's. For a few hours or days you become Brazilian, Trinidadian, or Italian.

In the realm of the revel, there's a lot to learn—about other cultures and yourself. You discover new ways to look at things and realize that everyone has his or her own ideas about what this life and this universe are all about. You see (and may do) things that are so far off the scales of your own judgment system that you're forced to reassess your own personal and cultural truths. Why *not* stage an annual beauty contest for burros, like the people of San Antero, Colombia? Why *not* make a funeral into a five-day party, like the Torajan of Sulawesi? And if the Assumption means that the Virgin Mary was reunited with her soul in heaven, why *not* send up a plastic image of her on a homemade rocket, like the Maya of the Guatemalan highlands?

A German traveler remarked that a book like this wouldn't have been relevant until the waning days of the 20th century. Since it's finally feasible to get almost anywhere in the world in a day or two, it's possible to explore the world's ultra-diverse cultures through their celebrations. Even if your vacation is short, you can plan a trip to coincide with unique happenings somewhere in the world, using *Wild Planet!* as a planning tool to match the events with your scheduling windows, interests, and geographic preferences.

I've chosen the events in *Wild Planet!* for their richness, authenticity, variety, and degree of spectacle. You'll find everything from rodeos and carnivals to solstice rituals and reggae festivals. You'll even find some non-human "events," like the great Serengeti migration in Africa, and the penguin hatching season in Antarctica. Whatever you're into—Tibetan Buddhism, American blues, French wine, or Spanish tomatoes—you can access the subjects, dates, and places that strike your fancy.

What you won't find are many exported events (e.g., the "biggest Oktoberfest in Canada"), events contrived solely for tourists, or events that have been substantially coopted by corporate sponsorship. Also, I've omitted the events of extremely fragile or isolated cultures, and respected the wishes of people who have made it known that they don't want outsiders to visit their celebrations.

For the most part, people love to share their traditions with genuinely interested visitors. Still, some will argue that indigenous cultures could be threatened by a book like this, that ancient traditions may be diluted by the influence of outsiders.

I couldn't disagree more. Many folk traditions are in grave danger, and they will only be kept alive if individual travelers take interest in them before they're smothered by the high-gloss, homogenizing influence of the developed world. Outside interest has actually saved many precious events by helping local people discover new markets for their "old-fashioned" hospitality and handicrafts. By visiting the world's nooks and crannies, sensitive travelers can strengthen local traditions so that they can hold their own against the temptations of MTV, McDonald's, and other marauding multinationals.

As a visitor, though, realize that you will always impact the places and people you visit. It's up to you to choose whether this impact will be positive or negative.

You can be a *traveler,* who approaches the travel experience as a chance to participate in the life of the *people* you visit. Or you can be a *tourist,* who approaches travel as a chance to acquire something—cheap goods, exotic snapshots—of the *place* you visit. Tourists deploy from tour buses, snapping pictures or rolling videos of locals in colorful costumes as if they were animals in a zoo. Travelers acknowledge the worth of the person inside the costume, and seek to make a meaningful connection. Tourists contribute to negative stereotypes of their homeland by behaving according to their own cultural norms and expecting hometown standards of service. Travelers get involved in the life of a place, and when in Rome they don't expect more than the Romans do.

Your approach will impact how much the local people will enjoy and benefit from your presence, and how much you'll enjoy yourself. If you take the approach of the traveler, you can't help but make a positive contribution anywhere you go. And you'll have a lot more fun.

Immersing yourself in the noisy, chaotic storm of celebration can give you an energizing rush, but it can also put you fabulously off-balance. The French call this feeling *dépaysement.* You get it when you leave your safe confines and travel to a place that's outrageously different. The assault on the senses is unsettling, but liberating. Successful event-traveling means making friends with uncertainty (and with a certain amount of vulnerability), and realizing that you'll have to make compromises if you arrive on the Big Day. You may not get the most attentively cleaned rooms, the quickest meals, or the privacy you might like. On the other hand, you may receive constant invitations to dance, sing, eat local food, drink local firewater, or get married. The possibilities are huge when the locals are on a binge!

A friendly word of caution is in order: Although each event listed in *Wild Planet!* is established and reasonably predictable, there's always the possibility that something could be rescheduled or even fall off the face of the earth in the time it takes to load paper onto the press. For that reason, be sure to take advantage of the contact information listed at the end of each country chapter to confirm dates and locations before booking your flight or quitting your job. Also, keep in mind that many celebrations do not start on time. Events can be delayed by a cloud obscuring the imam's view of the new moon, by an inauspicious typhoon, or by an elephant stampede. When traveling afar, flexibility is essential.

When I set out on a travel experience, I *expect* something extraordinary to happen: a fascinating acquaintance, a snatch of uninhibited conversation, an outrageously creative spectacle, the honesty that comes from unbridled revelry. My best souvenirs are, of course, memories—sounds, feelings, rhythms, faces—moments when I've found myself smack dab in the middle of something completely fresh and real.

I hope you'll use *Wild Planet!* to help you create your own great moments. This guide is organized by world region, then country within each region; the events themselves are presented chronologically within each country. If you know what country you're going to (or if you just want to browse through the world's exotic places), simply consult the **Table of Contents** and turn to the appropriate country chapter.

Use the **Festival Finders** at the end of the book to find the events in other ways. If you're interested in something special—from animal celebrations to wreath-floating ceremonies—consult the "What's It About?" Festival Finder. If you have a specific date in mind, "When Is It Happening?" shows you what's happening in each country during each month. To find a particular country, world region, or celebration by name, check the "Where Is It & What's It Called?" Festival Finder.

Now choose your event, and hit the road!

Acknowledgments

The 1,001 event descriptions in *Wild Planet!* were gleaned from my own experiences as well as those of travelers I met along the way in gringo hotels, tea huts, cave lodges, cramped buses, and jumbo jets. For providing information about their favorite events, or for helping me in other ways, I'd like to thank Julio Acevedo, Kim Adams, Brenda Arbeláez, Bob and Prudence Baldwin, John Barringer, Marty Blackwell, Gary Christianson, Karen Clynes, Judy Coloneri, Kate Connell, Tressa Crosby, Mike Cullis, Augustine Frimpong-Mansoh, Elaine Glusac, Andreas Göcks, Andy Henry, Steve and Anne Hughes, Robert Katzman, Janet Kauffman, Jaimy Gordon, Ameen Howrani, Steve Lantos, Sarah Lazin, Steve Lengnick, Eliza Manteca, Katie Mikesell, Linda Minteer, Marianne Montague, Susan Montague, Laura Nolan, Dean Olkowski, Heidi Olmack, Meagan O'Neill, Patrick Pantano, Stephan Rau, Mary Robbins, Piet Sabbe, Phil Semisch, La-iet Silanoi, Justin Summerton, Pete Tomey, Dirk and Gabi Weber, Walter Wasacz, Leslie Wirpsa, Bob Zabor, and dozens of other dusty wild-hearts whose names I've forgotten or never knew.

Several people provided the kind of extra support that merits special gratitude. For their various and substantial contributions to *Wild Planet!*, I'd like to thank Melinda Clynes, Steffan Duerr, Bob and Patty George, George Hales, Susan Jolliffe, Kelly Cross, Maureen Mansfield, Don Montague, John Storm Roberts, Pamela Shelton, and Paul Zimmerman.

Thanks also to *Wild Planet!*'s editorial interns from the USA and Canada: Julie Cook, Kristin Cotts, Andrea Kovacs, James Weyer, and Linda Wilson.

Finally, I'd like to acknowledge the witty and hard-working staff at Visible Ink Press, for fine-tuning the concept of *Wild Planet!*, putting it all together, and making me laugh a lot. Special thanks to designer Pamela Galbreath, typesetter Marco Di Vita, and Christa Brelin, Martin Connors, Dean Dauphinais, Diane Dupuis, Barb Eschner, Marie MacNee, Becky Nelson, Jenny Sweetland, Don Wellman, and Julie Winklepleck.

T. C.

WESTERN EUROPE

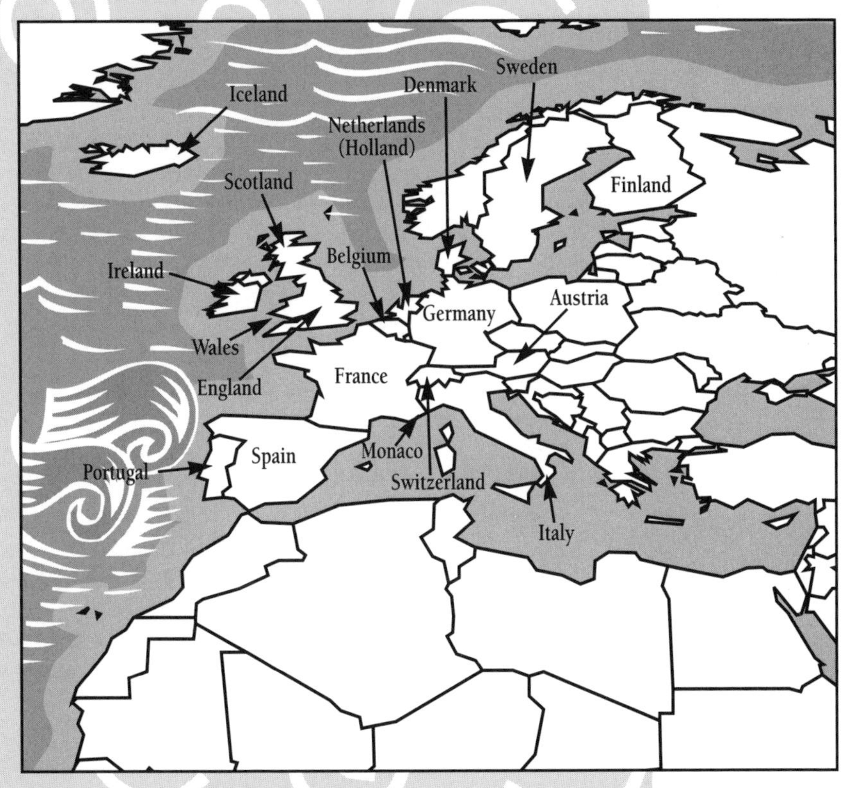

AUSTRIA

The first thing you'll notice about Austrians is their addiction to music, evidenced not only in the dozens of musical festivals in Austria, but in the awesome brood of composers the country has produced. Beethoven, Brahms, Bruckner, Haydn, Mahler, Mozart, Schubert, Strauss—these titans of sound have given modern Austrians a precious musical heritage which they love to preserve and venerate through their many musical events.

Classical music dominates the nation's organized festivals and balls, which take place in beautifully preserved cities like Vienna and Salzburg. Yet to think that Austria is solely a high-brow performance ground would be to pass over the many rustic festivals in mountain villages. Here, the return of the cattle, the grape harvest, or a midsummer night's whim are all cause for celebration. The farmers, fiddlers, and dancers make the Austrian countryside into a welcoming place where wine, beer, and music flow.

VIENNA OPERA BALL

Vienna **February/March**

Vienna, the city that's almost synonymous with the waltz, hosts some 300 spectacular balls between New Year's Eve and the beginning of Lent. Held amidst the incomparable finery of the city's music houses, these expensive affairs are resplendent with elegant gowns, chandeliers, and room after room of dashing couples dancing to Austria's famous waltzes.

The most significant showcase of human vanity is the Vienna Opera Ball, held at the Staatsoper (State Opera House), once the haunt of Mahler, Mozart, and Schubert. Sometimes themed on a particular opera or operetta, it includes a grand entry of 200 debutantes who dance among gold, crystal, and red velvet until 5 a.m. Everyone comes to see and be seen as TV crews scramble to catch the many VIPs in this magnificent, champagne-soaked playground. Although admission is steep, starting at US$220 per person and

The debutantes arrive: The Vienna Opera Ball is Europe's most elegant party. *(Austrian National Tourist Office)*

going up to more than $13,000 for tables for two, spectator (no dancing) tickets are available for less than $50.

DATE: Usually the Thursday before Lent begins. **LOCATION:** Vienna. **TRANSPORT:** Vienna is easily reached by air from anywhere in Europe, Asia, and North America, and by train from all over eastern or western Europe. **ACCOMMODATION:** Vienna offers a wide range of lodging possibilities, although inexpensive rooms are hard to find in the center of town. **CONTACT:** Opern-Büro, Goethegasse 1, A-1010 Vienna, Tel 1-514-44, ext. 2606. Also, Dailey-Thorp Travel, 315 W. 57th St., New York, NY 10019, Tel (212) 307-1555; or the Austrian National Tourist Office (see *Resources*).

Need to Brush Up Before the Ball?

Whether you need to learn to waltz from scratch or just take some of the rough edges off your steps before the big night, you can get lessons from one of Vienna's more than 20 dancing schools. These special "visitors" lessons are attended by the hour on a drop-in basis, and there are no complicated registration formalities. Better still, most schools can give lessons in English, French, German, or Italian. For a list of dance schools, just contact the Vienna Tourist Board (see *Resources*) either before or upon arrival, or the Vienna Association of Dancing Teachers, Gusshausstr. 15, A-1040 Vienna, Tel 1-505-0612.

While you're there ...

- **Ladies' Choice Ball (Rudolfina Redoute), Vienna:** Since 1910, the ladies have chosen their partners and the men have taken to the dance floor with unknown, masked companions. This most intriguing of Austria's balls takes place in the Hofburg's amazing 18th-century halls, and the ladies remain enigmatic until midnight, when the masks are removed and identities revealed. Contact: KÖStV Rudolfina, Singerstr. 12, A-1010 Wien, Austria, Tel 1-512-5375. (February/March; usually the Monday before Lent begins.)
- **Vienna International Festival (Wiener Festwochen), Vienna:** As the premier cultural event in the Austrian capital, the festival spans four or five weeks and includes a varied program of traditional and cutting-edge music, theater, film, and exhibitions. Some of the more than 1,000 events are presented in English. (Early May through mid-June.)
- **Corpus Christi, Nationwide:** Rural Austria celebrates Corpus Christi with colorful processions and religious rituals that vary widely by region. In the Lungau region, the villagers' costumes are fantastic, and on Traun and Halstätter lakes barges and boats are decked out in wild colors for water processions. (May/June.)
- **Shubert Festival (Shubertiade Hohenems), Hohenems:** In the magnificent renaissance castle at Hohenems, and in the nearby medieval town of Feldkirch, the self-doubting composer's symphonies, masses, chamber music, and other songs are featured. Contact: Shubertiade Hohenems, Postfach 100 Schweitzer Strade 1, A-6845 Baden bei Wien. (Two weeks in late June.)
- **Midsummer Night, Tirol and Wachau:** The mountains of Tirol and the riverside region of Wachau go wild during this once-pagan celebration, playing music and traditional sports, and dancing around bonfires until the early morning. (June 21.)

Tickets to Europe's most prestigious summer musical event go fast, but those who book early for the Salzburg Festival can count on seeing the very best in opera, chamber, symphony, and other classical music. *(Bartl/Austrian National Tourist Office)*

Salzburg Festival

Salzburg **July/August**

The birthplace of Mozart is the world's foremost summer pilgrimage site for the very best conductors, musicians, and fans of classical music. Superlatives abound: The city is one of the most beautiful in Europe. The concert halls—the Mozarteum, the Felsenreitschule, the Grosses Festspielhaus and Kleines Festspielhaus—are unsurpassed. The performances—symphonies, operas, ballets, sacred music, and instrumental and lieder recitals—are so phenomenal that the music press talks about them all year long. The cost is enough to keep mere commoners away, with seats for some performances selling for more than US$300. Even at these extraordinary prices, competition for tickets is tight, and many events sell out by the first of the year.

DATE: Late June through late August. **LOCATION:** Salzburg. **TRANSPORT:** Salzburg is easily accessible by air and by train from other major cities in Europe. From America, travelers usually connect in Frankfurt. **ACCOMMODATION:** You'll find a relatively wide range of lodging possibilities in Salzburg, although reservations are a must during the festival. **CONTACT:** To order tickets or a list of tickets still available, write *at least* two months in advance to: Salzburger Festspiele, Postfach 140, A-5010 Salzburg, Austria, Tel 0662-211-1400.

WHILE YOU'RE THERE ...

Summer Szene: This festival started out as an alternative to the pricey, sometimes stuffy Salzburg Festival, but it's grown into a spillover of international music, dance, and theater. Contact: Szene-Büro, Anton-Neumayr Platz 2, A-5010, Salzburg. (Mid-July through mid-August.)

Wiesen Sunsplash/Jazz Festival, Wiesen: Austria's biggest jazz event is followed by its biggest Caribbean and African music event. The tented stage draws performers from all over the world, and spectators from all over central Europe, who camp in a big meadow, Woodstock-style. Contact: Jazz Pub Wiesen, Hauptstrade 140, A-7203. (Mid-July.)

Festival of Early Music, Innsbruck: This old center of European music features Baroque and Renaissance works played on authentic instruments, and a Baroque opera. (Late July through early August.)

Haydn Festival, Eisenstadt: Fans of the composer Joseph Haydn are in for a treat in the first 10 days of September. During the day, walks are scheduled to his home and workplaces (you can see seven organs on which he performed), and at night, concerts of his symphonies, masses, sonatas, and string quartets are given. Contact: Büro Haydnfestspiele, Schlob Esterhazy, A-7000 Eisenstadt. (September.)

Styrian Autumn Festival, Graz: Amid smells of wine grapes and beer hops, the sounds of contemporary music waft through this baroque and medieval city. Lovers of avant-garde music, theater, and art will have all their senses can handle. (October through November.)

Silent Night in Oberndorf: Celebrate the Christmas Eve mass in small chapels north of Salzburg and sing "Silent Night," which Franz Gruber wrote and first performed there in the early 1800s. In processions and inside local churces, the song is sung in various languages. (December 24.)

RESOURCES

In Austria: Austrian National Tourist Office, Margaretenstr. 1, A-1040 Vienna, Tel 1-588660. Vienna Tourist Board, Obere Augartenstr. 40, A-1025 Wien, Austria, Fax 2168492. **USA:** Austrian National Tourist Office, 500 Fifth Avenue, Suite 800, New York, NY 10110, Tel (212) 944-6880, Fax (212) 730-4568. **Canada:** Austrian National Tourist Office, 2 Bloor St. East, #3330, Toronto, ON M4W 1A8, Tel (416) 967-3381, Fax (416) 967-4101. **UK:** Austrian National Tourist Office, 30 St. George Street, GB-London W1R OAL, Tel 71-6290461, Fax 71-4996038. **Germany:** Austrian National Tourist Office, Mannheimerstr. 15, D-60329 Frankfurt, Tel 69-242425, Fax 69-291975. **Australia:** Australian National Tourist Office, 1st Floor, 36 Carrington Street, Sydney, NSW 2000, Tel 2-2993621, Fax 2-2993808.

BELGIUM

Currently the center of action in Europe, Belgium is where Teutonic and Romantic cultures meet. This small, multicultural land has plenty to recommend, yet for some reason Belgium is overlooked by most travelers. The two main cultures, Flemish and Walloon, are generous and tolerant toward outsiders (though not always toward each other), and both have managed to preserve their age-old traditions. The Belgians are also blessed with a great cuisine, an outstanding brewing tradition, and a calendar full of historic pageantry.

Each spring and summer the cities and villages of Belgium erupt with folklore and fun, as long-nosed men swoop across squares, "giants" spin through villages, and cats fly from belfries. The Belgians love to dress up and celebrate, and in the summer it's almost impossible to travel through the country without stumbling upon a festival of some kind. Most of Belgium's colorful events have religious origins that are a sometimes wacky mixture of Christian and pagan tradition. These days, Belgians still acknowledge the festivals' religious roots, but many see the rituals and rites as a vehicle for fun as well as worship. In fact, the beginning of Lent doesn't interrupt the revel; many cities have mid-Lenten festivities, carnivals, and masked balls.

Carnival and Gilles de Binche

Binche **February/March**

Binche's climactic March of the Gilles is one of the world's weirdest sights: Some 600 men dressed exactly alike—in wax masks with surrealistic green shades and thin mustaches, and padded, striped costumes with braided collars and trouser cuffs—throw oranges to the crowd as they march and dance through the streets of Binche to an unrelenting drumbeat. Said to stem from an Inca dance witnessed by the Spanish during the conquest, the dignified dance of the costumed men—who are respected members of various guilds and societies of Binche—has been performed for more than 400 years.

The March of the Gilles is only the final chapter in a three-day carnival that's so robust that it added a word to the English language: *binge*. From Sunday through Tuesday it *is* a binge, as the streets fill with crazed, costumed people dancing to impromptu orchestras of drummers, organists, and horn players. As a preamble, for four Sundays before the main event, drums sound a *soumonce*, or invitation to celebrate, and small dances break out, foreshadowing the main event. This very unusual carnival is one of the world's very best!

DATE: The Sunday, Monday, and Tuesday before Lent begins. **LOCATION:** Binche is located 56 km/35 miles south of Brussels, just east of Mons. Other carnivals take place at Eupen and at Malmedy. **TRANSPORT:** The easiest way to reach Binche is by car or bus. The nearest train station is at Mons. **ACCOMMODATION:** Binche's few lodgings are packed at carnival time, so you may want to do the festival as a day-trip from Brussels. **CONTACT:** Belgian Tourist Office (see *Resources*).

While you're there ...

- **Mid-Lent Carnival, Stavelot:** Long-nosed Blancs Moussis descend on the city. (March 21–23.)
- **Dead Rat's Ball (Bal Rat Mort), Ostende:** One of Europe's most extravagant costume parties gets underway in mid-Lent. (March)

Opposite Page: *Binche: The surrealistic march of the masked Gilles is the highlight of one of the world's most eccentric carnivals. (Joe Viesti/Viesti Associates, Inc.)*

Cat Festival (Kattenwoensdog)

Ypres **May**

Cats are said always to land on their feet, but the citizens of Ypres long ago discovered that if you toss them from a high enough belfry, it doesn't really matter how they land. In this wacky festival the town jester (who else?) is given the job of "casting down the cats." As he climbs to the top of the belfry, the crowd waits in anticipation, and then down they come. Some townspeople try to catch the critters, but others let them flop onto the cobblestones before picking them up.

This peculiar event doesn't use live cats anymore, but it did until 1817. The whole thing started more than 200 years ago, when the town's big fabric hall was inundated with mice that ruined countless yards of cloth. To get rid of the mice, the town brought in dozens of cats, who gorged themselves on the mice and soon multiplied into hundreds and then thousands of cats. The town decided to solve the feline population problem by flinging them from the belfry.

Long live the crusades: Convincingly medieval Bruges stages one of the oldest and most beautiful religious processions in Europe each spring. (Joe Viesti/Viesti Associates)

Nowadays, the cats are made of wool or velvet, and several thousand people show up to try their luck at catching them. In addition to the cat-throwing, there's a parade of floats that feature famous cats from folklore and film.

DATE: Second Sunday in May. The cats are thrown every year, but the floats and surrounding pageant occur only in even-numbered years. **LOCATION:** Ypres (Ieper), West Flanders. **TRANSPORT:** Ypres is 50 km southwest of Bruges, and 60 km southwest of Gent, and can be reach easily by train or road from anywhere on Belgium's coast or interior. **ACCOMMODATION:** During the festival rooms are hard to come by but neighboring towns are often a good bet. **CONTACT:** Belgian Tourist Office (see *Resources*).

Holy Blood Procession

Bruges (Brugge) **May**

One of the oldest and most beautiful religious processions in Europe celebrates the return of the Count of Flanders from the second crusade in 1150. The dramatic parade begins at 3 p.m., with floats and depictions of 27 principal events from the Old and New Testament. Against the backdrop of the medieval city of Bruges, the beautiful costumes seem dramatically authentic. The centerpiece in the solemn procession is the bishop, who carries a medieval reliquary containing the vial of holy blood, which was brought back from the battlefields of the crusade by the count. The blood was said to have been washed from the body of Christ

Ommegang's all-knight revelry: The biggest party of the year in Brussels reenacts the welcome given to Charles V and his court in 1549. Knights on decked-out horses clear the way for musicians, marching giants, and real-life nobility. (Belgian Tourist Office)

by Joseph of Arimathea. Earlier in the day (11 a.m.), a High Mass is celebrated, but, sober Catholicism notwithstanding, the scene in general has a festive air.

DATE: Ascension Thursday, or the 40th day after Easter. **LOCATION:** Bruges. **TRANSPORT:** Trains run hourly from the Gare du Midi in Brussels, and the London-Brussels service stops here as well. Bus excursions from Brussels are another alternative. **ACCOMMODATION:** Bruges offers a variety of lodging possibilities for a wide range of budgets. **CONTACT:** Tel 050-44-86-86. Also, Belgian Tourist Office (see *Resources*).

WHILE YOU'RE THERE ...

- **Giants Ommegang, Zottegem:** Stilt walkers from Belgium and abroad join in this parade of giants, musicians, and local folklore groups. (May/June.)
- **The Brussels Jazz Rally, Brussels:** Outdoor concerts in the Grand' Place accompany gigs and impromptu performances in 60 cafes and pubs around the city. (Late May.)
- **The Battle of St. George and the Dragon, Mons:** Amidst afternoon merrymaking in the town square, St. George squares off against Lumeçon the dragon. The reenactment of the Battle of Lumeçon is the climactic event in a day that features processions of 18th-century carriages, parades of richly costumed women, and other colorful events. Contact: Tel 065-33-55-80. (Trinity Sunday: the eighth Sunday after Easter.)

Ommegang

Brussels **July**

This stately yet rip-roaring nighttime pageant is one of Belgium's true gems, a reconstruction of a welcoming party given by the city magistrate in 1549 in honor of Charles V and his court. This is the biggest and best of Belgium's several *Ommegangs,* which were originally religious marches around large monuments. Eventually, they became more and more ostentatious, incorporating floats, musicians, banners, and horses.

Today's Ommegang in Brussels has grown into the most eagerly awaited event of the year. Amid a full-blown party atmosphere, historic splendor has been maintained in the fantastic costumes of the "nobles," who are played by actual descendants of the original royal families. By 8 p.m., the Grand' Place is packed with people and performers, who parade past in enormous costumes up to seven meters (23 feet) high. Strolling musicians and dancing peasants move ahead of the main procession, clearing the way through the huge crowds for the knights on horseback and the royal family. Afterward, the pubs and cafés of this lively city are crowded with partiers. The Grand' Place (which Victor Hugo called "the most beautiful square in the world") is packed; to ensure a good view, ask your hotel to reserve a place for you.

DATE: The first Tuesday and Thursday in July. **LOCATION:** Brussels. **TRANSPORT:** Brussels's Zaventem Airport is well connected to the United States and the rest of Europe. Brussels is also accessible by the Dover/Oostende Jetfoil and train, and by the Dover/Calais bus and hovercraft. **ACCOMMODATION:** Lodging in Brussels is readily available. **CONTACT:** Tourist Information Board, Hotel de Ville, Grand-Place, B-1000 Brussels; Belgian Tourist Office (see *Resources*).

While you're there ...

Giants Festival, Ath: A folklore procession and a giants' wedding celebrate the marriage of Gouyasse (Goliath) and his wife. On Saturday, the battle between David and Goliath, called *Jeu Parti,* is reenacted. Various costumed "giants" come to celebrate and see Goliath get hitched. (Weekend in late August.)

Breughel Festival, Wingene: More than a thousand participants in 16th-century costumes enact scenes from the paintings of Pieter Breughel, who specialized in depicting peasants. The afternoon parade is followed by a party in the evening with sausages, rice, pancakes, beer, singing, and dancing. (Second Sunday in September.)

The Colorful Beers of Belgium

Belgians regard their beer with a reverence that's reserved for wine in the rest of Europe. In homes and in brasseries, rare bottles are seduced from cellars and respectfully cradled while being opened and poured into special glasses. Many are bottle-conditioned in the *méthode Champenoise*, and the variety of styles is astounding. There are monk-brewed Abbey Ales, spontaneously fermented Lambic beers, fruity White Beers, sour oak-aged Red Beers, and what may be the world's most elegant beers, the raspberry and cherry-flavored Framboise and Kriek.

No other nation has such an idiosyncratic and colorful assortment of beers, or such a highly developed beer culture. Each *streek*, or district, has its own favorite brewery, and each course in a meal has an accompanying beer. Brewers are thought of as individual craftsmen—-heroes even—-and their handmade products continue to fascinate and beguile Belgians, regardless of their ethnicity, creed, or sex.

Resources

In Belgium: Bureau d'Information et d'Accueil Touristiques, Rue Marche aux Herbes 61, B-1000 Brussels, Tel 2-5040390, Fax 2-5136950. **USA:** Belgian Tourist Office, 780 Third Avenue, Ste. 1501, New York, NY 10017, Tel (212) 758-8130, Fax (212) 355-7675. **Canada:** Embassy of the Kingdom of Belgium, 85 Range Rd., Ste. 601, Ottawa, ON K1N 8J6, Tel (613) 236-7267 & (613) 236-7269, Fax (613) 236-7882. **UK:** Belgian Tourist Board, 29 Princes St., London W1R 7R9, Tel 71-629-0230, Fax 71-629-0454. **Germany:** Berliner Allee 47 D-4000 Dusseldorf, Tel 211-326008, Fax 211-134285.

DENMARK

As the most cosmopolitan and liberated of the Scandinavians, the former Vikings now known as Danes are proud of their current reputation as the most peaceful people in Europe. Sophisticated Copenhagen offers the most lively of Denmark's cultural delights, with a summer full of music, fairs, and festivals amid ancient buildings and twinkling amusement parks. Outside the city a different, slower-paced Denmark uses its festivals as an opportunity to re-explore its seafaring and farming past.

Copenhagen Jazz Festival

Copenhagen **July**

Europe has more than 400 major summer jazz festivals, and the problem with most is that they are staid, hands-in-your-lap events. Copenhagen, on the other hand, really knows how to throw a jazz party, with a loose and laid-back format that encourages spontaneity. Each day the festival takes to the streets with an exhilarating afternoon jazz parade. The Strøget (the main retail thoroughfare) is packed with people shopping and bopping to the world's top jazz stars. At the more than 130 concerts the musicians seem amazingly accessible, and 80 percent of the events are at free, open-air stages in the Old Town's major squares.

Copenhagen's night life is another reason to come. The city's jazz clubs are, of course, packed with the festival's overflow, but even joints that don't normally feature jazz become temporary hipsters' hot-spots.

DATE: 10 days in early to mid-July. **LOCATION:** Copenhagen's Old Town. **TRANSPORT:** Copenhagen can be reached by non-stop flights from North America and most of Europe's large cities, by train from anywhere in Europe, and by ferry from nearly anywhere in Scandinavia. **ACCOMMODATION:** Hotels in Copenhagen vary in price. For the most part, they are clean and comfortable. **CONTACT:** Copenhagen Jazz Festival, City Center, Norregade 7A-2, DK-1165 Copenhagen, Denmark. Also, Danish Tourist Board (see *Resources*).

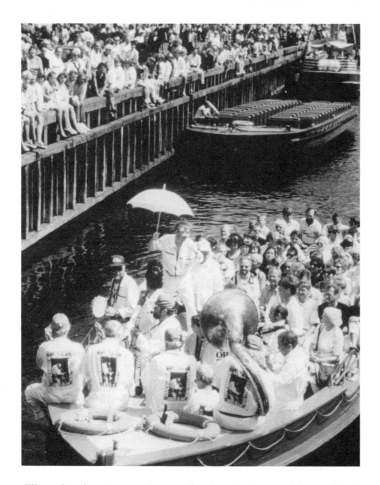

When there's not enough room in the streets, musicians take to the canals during the world's most liberated jazz festival. (Danish Tourist Board)

Roskilde Festival

Roskilde **June/July**

Roskilde draws rock and roll bands and fans from just about everywhere. Staged in a suburb just west of Copenhagen, Roskilde is definitely the biggest, and probably the oldest rock festival in northern Europe. Although mainly a rock fest, its lineup also includes jazz, folk, and world music. In addition to Roskilde's eclectic roster, the festival is known for its ability to identify and book up-and-coming acts before they get too well-known.

Viking Festival: The Danes may be the most politically correct people on the continent, but once a year repressed Viking urges are let loose in a rampage of mock raping, pillaging, and fire-dancing. (AP/Wide World Photos)

DATE: Four days from late June to early July. **LOCATION:** Roskilde. **TRANSPORT:** Roskilde can be reached by train from Copenhagen (about 30 minutes). **ACCOMMODATION:** Although a free campground is provided, it fills up fast and many concert-goers seek accommodation in Copenhagen. **CONTACT:** Danish Tourist Board (see *Resources*).

While You're There ...

- **Skagen Festival, Skagen:** Rock, folk, and jazz performers from Scandinavia and Great Britain grace venues throughout this city by the sea. (Weekend in late June.)
- **Viking Festival, Frederikssund:** Nordic legends come alive at the site of an ancient Viking village, which produces a pageant full of historical reenactments and open-air Viking plays. Lasting 16 days, the festival brings to life the legends of Leif Eriksson and Erik the Red, and features genuine Viking banquets with barbequed meat and barrels of mead. (Late June–early July.)

Midsummer Night

Nationwide **June**

Like the rest of Scandinavia, Denmark celebrates the summer solstice with songs, dances, and torchlight parades. Across the countryside bonfires are lit and everyone celebrates their pagan roots. In Copenhagen, revelers throw dolls into the bonfires to commemorate the witch-burning ceremonies of the "good old days." Funen Island, the childhood home of Hans Christian Andersen, has more castles per kilometer than anywhere else in Europe, and may well be Denmark's most romantic place to spend the longest day of the year. But anywhere in Denmark will do for this joyous, uninhibited celebration.

DATE: June 23 and 24. **LOCATION:** Nationwide. **CONTACT:** Danish Tourist Board (see *Resources*).

Århus Festival

Århus **September**

This is Denmark's biggest event, drawing hundreds of thousands of people for a week of concerts, sports, exhibitions, theater, ballet, opera, art, and more. The entire town of Århus becomes a festival ground, with hundreds of performances that will suit just about any taste. At the Moesgård Museum of Prehistory, a concurrent medieval fair features jousting tournaments, crossbow competitions, and rides on Viking ships, as well as the food, crafts, and drinks of the era. Jesters abound, and inside the museum you can see the squashed body of a prehistoric victim of a sacrifice, preserved in a bog for 2,000 years. As the cultural and student center of Jutland, Århus has plenty of nightlife and cultural activity.

DATE: The week-long celebration begins on the first Saturday of September. **LOCATION:** Århus is located on the east coast of Jylland (Jutland), about 40 km (25 miles) east of Silkeborg. **TRANSPORT:** The Århus airport handles flights from Copenhagen and Oslo, and its harbor handles ferries from Kalundborg. **ACCOMMODATION:** Moderate to expensive hotels can be found in and near Århus. **CONTACT:** Århus Tourist Office, DK-8000 Århus Denmark. Also, Danish National Tourist Board (see *Resources*).

Resources

In Denmark: Denmark Tourist Information; Bernstofsgade 1; DK-1620 Copenhagen V, Tel 33-111325, Fax 33-934969. **USA:** Danish Tourist Board, 655 Third Ave., New York, NY 10017, Tel (212) 949-2326, Fax (212) 286-0896. **Canada:** Danish Tourist Board, P.O. Box 636, Mississauga, ON L5M 2C2, Tel (519) 576-6213, Fax (519) 576-7115. **UK:** Danish Tourist Board, 55 Sloane Street, GB-London SW1X 9SY, Tel 71-259-5958, Fax 71-259-5955. **Germany:** Dänisches Fremdenverkehrsamt, Postfach 10 13 12, D-20008 Hamburg, Tel 49-40-330584, Fax 45-40-337083. **Australia:** Embassy of the Kingdom of Denmark, 15 Hunter St., Yarralumia, Canberra, ACT 2607, Tel 6-2732195, Fax 6-2733864.

ENGLAND

Tradition is the watchword of English festivals, and although they lack the participative spontaneity of festivals on the continent and even in Wales and Scotland, they do bring history alive with demonstrations of dancing, ancient warfare, and nutty games like cheese rolling and woolsack races. Many are costumed events that seek to recreate the regal splendor of England's past, while others honor the country's esteemed literary tradition in birthplaces of wordsmiths like Chaucer, Shakespeare, and Dickens.

Pomp and ceremony reign in the most famous pageants of England, perhaps because the country's royal heritage is so enduring. The royalty are a fixture in legendary sporting events like the Henly Regatta, Ascot, and Wimbledon, but commoners are welcome to attend (of course, proper attire and aristocratic reserve are *de rigueur*).

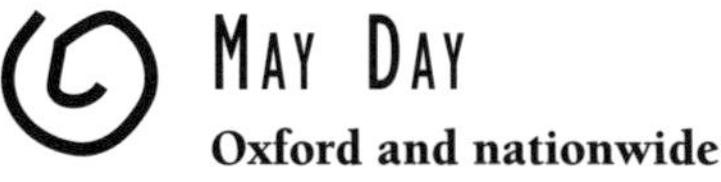

MAY DAY

Oxford and nationwide **May**

Amid the dignified yellow stone of Oxford, one of England's most boisterous rounds of partying ends on a touching note. Everyone from the various colleges fills the streets on May Day Eve for a round of merrymaking that lasts until sunrise. As the revelers stumble into the dawn, the Magdalen College Choir greets the warming spring with madrigals sung from the top of the tower. Below, the bleary-eyed crowd comes to life as a true British miracle unfolds—the pubs open at 7 a.m.! At that point the festivities flourish in the common market, as age-old rituals—morris dancing, beating the bounds, and other games—bolster the argument that summer has indeed arrived.

At Welford-on-Avon, the village green is the site of an age-old custom as children dance and skip around a striped maypole hung with colored ribbons. In Bedfordshire and Buckinghamshire, celebrants gather leaves and flowers in the early morning, then

Morris dancers in Kent take a breather and a brew after a May Day morning rave-up. *(Steve Vidler/Leo de Wys)*

move from door to door with the May garlands they've made. The hobby horse tradition is alive and well in many towns in Cornwall and Devon. In Minehead, villagers deck the Sailor's Hobby Horse with ribbons and dance through the village with it. A similar but more elaborate 'obby 'oss is constructed in Padstow. As the spooky creature moves through the village, he's surrounded by townsfolk who morris-dance in the manner of the pre-Christian people who created the festival to encourage fertility.

DATE: May 1 and the night before. **LOCATION:** Oxford and nationwide. **TRANSPORT:** Trains run from London's Paddington Station to Oxford every hour, and buses run between London's Victoria bus station and Oxford every 20 minutes. **ACCOMMODATION:** Lodging in Oxford ranges from very cheap to expensive. Reservations are strongly recommended. **CONTACT:** British Tourist Authority (see *Resources*).

Aldeburgh Festival

Aldeburgh **June**

Some of the finest performers from all over the world converge at this small fishing town to perform in intimate venues. Music from the 15th century to the present is staged in the Snape Maltings Concert Hall, touted as the best in the country. This quintessential English festival features chamber and symphonic concerts, operas, recitals, exhibitions, and lectures. The town itself is quite fashionable, refined, and expensive, and in addition to the Snape Maltings Concert Hall, many events are held within the traditional confines of old churches.

DATE: Two weeks in mid-June. **LOCATION:** Aldeburgh, Suffolk. **TRANSPORT:** Aldeburgh can be reached via the London tube from Liverpool Street Station to Ipswich. Alternatively, hike across the Blythe Estuary from Walberswick. **ACCOMMODATION:** Accommodation is hard to come by nearby, but with the festival so close to London, finding a place to stay is no problem. **CONTACT:** Aldeburgh Foundation, High St., Aldeburgh, Suffolk IP15 5AX, Tel 728-452935, Fax 728-452715. Also, British Tourist Authority (see *Resources*).

While you're there ...

- **Dickens Festival, Rochester:** Characters from Charles Dickens's greatest novels roam the streets and thousands of people dressed in Victorian garb wander the town as a tribute to the renowned English writer. Street fairs, plays, recitals, and readings are just a few of the events. (Late May.)
- **Malvern Festival, Malvern:** A whirlwind of prestigious musical performances and dramatic events honor British composers at this two-week festival of the arts. Symphony concerts, chamber and choral music, and premieres of modern works highlight this event. The Malvern Festival also has the second-largest "fringe," a local sister festival, in Britain. (Late May or early June.)
- **Nottingham Festival, Nottingham:** The home of Robin Hood and his Merry Men draws tourists to this general arts fair that boasts top artists and venues such as Nottingham Castle, the Robin Hood Statue, and the home of Lord Byron, Newstead Abbey. Part of the festival is geared toward children. (Late May to June.)
- **All England Lawn Tennis Championships, Wimbledon:** The world rarely watches any other tennis event as closely as Wimbledon. Anyone seeking decent seats should apply early. For information contact the All England Lawn Tennis and Croquet Club, Church Rd., Wimbledon, London SW19 5AE, Tel 81-946-2244, Fax 81-947-8752. (Late June.)

Royal Regatta & Henley Festival

Henley-on-Thames **June/July**

Sport and society mingle at this regal rowing affair attended by royalty and Britain's elite. This international event is watched from grandstands or boats along the banks of the Thames, where the most famous annual crew race in the world takes place. The party doesn't stop when the racing is over—the Festival of Music and Arts is held in town immediately following the races. The public is admitted to the regatta enclosure for about US$8. Tickets are usually available by the river, or you can write to the Secretary's Office (see below).

DATE: The festival spans five days in late June or early July. **LOCATION:** Henley-on-Thames. **TRANSPORT:** From London, catch a train at Paddington Station or take a bus from Victoria. **ACCOMMODATION:** Most visitors stay in London. **CONTACT:** The Secretary, Henley Royal Regatta Headquarters, Regatta House, Henley-on-Thames, Oxfordshire RG9 2LY. Also, British Tourist Authority (see *Resources*).

While you're there ...

Royal Ascot, Ascot: The horses are nearly outdone by the hats in this most snooty of equestrian events, but amid all the highbrows and head gear you realize that most everyone's tongue is partly planted in cheek. The royal family is always at hand, but don't expect to get too close—the Royal Enclosure is open only to those with an invitation. Contact: The Secretary, Grandstand Office, Ascot Racecourse, Ascot, Berkshire SL5 7JN. (Late June or early July.)

Great British Beer Festival

London **August**

People who bemoaned the impending death of real ale in Britain 20 years ago may wonder if they've stumbled into the afterlife—a beery heaven of about 300 bitters, milds, stouts, and porters happily gurgling away in a London convention center. This paradise of cask-conditioned ales and other treats is the work of the Campaign for Real Ale. CAMRA, as beer enthusiasts know, is the group that can take much of the credit for the revival of Britain's traditional ales. The group hosts more than 40,000 people, who crowd into the Olympia Grand Hall to sample the creations of British brewing craftsmen. Beers take center stage, but traditional ciders and perries (fermented pear juice) are also featured, all against a backdrop of live entertainment and pub games.

Europe's largest street party takes over Notting Hill for two days of total Caribbean madness. (Trip/G. Pritchard)

DATE: Five days in early August. **LOCATION:** Olympia Grand Hall. **TRANSPORT:** Olympia tube. **ACCOMMODATION:** London has a wide range of hotels in all classes. **CONTACT:** CAMRA, 34 Alma Rd., St. Albans, Hertfordshire AL1 3BW, Tel 0727-867201, Fax 0727-867270.

Notting Hill Carnival

London **August**

Stepping out of the Underground station and into the sunlight, the scene hits you like a Jamaican bobsled. Boom, boom, boom—a huge kettle drum bears down, the drummer spinning and

More than a pint of bitter: Three "alternative" types hold down the turf at Reading. (Trip/Joan Wakelin)

thrashing away like a maniac, almost knocking you over as he whirls past. A float approaches, every square inch of its flat top packed with calypso musicians playing their butts off. They're driven on by 200 dancers who gyrate around the float as it moves down the street. Suddenly a dreadlocked rastaman appears, offering a spliff and pulling you into the skanking mob as it snakes its happy way down the street.

You've just joined Europe's largest street party, an amazing juggernaut of fun that careens down the streets of west London every year in late August. The Notting Hill Carnival wraps up the sights, sounds, and smells of the Caribbean, and although the organizers have recently gone looking for sponsorship, it's still nothing but a big rave-up in England's senior black neighborhood. Reggae, calypso, ska, dub, and dance-hall are featured on moving floats and at stationary stages. Plus, there's food, art, activism, and even dancing policemen.

DATE: Sunday and Monday during the August Bank Holiday (usually the last weekend in August). **LOCATION:** London's Notting Hill area. **TRANSPORT:** Ladbroke Grove tube station. **ACCOMMODATION:** London has plenty of lodging in all classes. **CONTACT:** British Tourist Authority (see *Resources*).

Reading Festival

Reading **August**

If "alternative rock" still has a meaning it can be found at the world's premier showcase of alternative music, the Reading Festival. In a scene that inspired the USA's Lollapalooza, about 45,000 young people converge on a cow field in a commuter town west of London, for three days of music from England, the United States, and elsewhere. Woodstock it ain't—although stoned kids do frolic in the mud, and a now-martyred rock star (Kurt Cobain) did play a tortured version of "The Star-Spangled Banner" in 1992.

The promoters are particularly adept at booking alternative's big and soon-to-be-big players—be they ravaged popsters, agit-hoppers, or slacker grunge-merchants. It's a scraggly scene, especially when it rains and huge clouds of steam rise from the pogoing masses up front. Beer and hard cider are the drinks of choice, and the crowd, although not rough on itself, is fickle enough to boo and pelt performers with debris. These are dyed-in-the-flannel rock and rollers, and they usually respond to anything that's *truly* alternative (i.e., not rock or hip-hop) with a flurry of mud and manure balls.

DATE: Usually the last weekend in August (Summer Bank Holiday weekend). **LOCATION:** Reading. **TRANSPORT:** Reading is located about 65 km/40 miles west of London. Trains leave regularly, and special buses serve the event from central London. **ACCOMMODATION:** Either day-trip or camp. **CONTACT:** Reading Festival organizers: 81 961 5490. Also, English Tourist Board (see *Resources*).

Resources

In the UK: English Tourist Board, Thames Tower, Black's Road, Hammersmith, London W6 9EL. British Tourist Authority, Thames Tower, Black's Road, Hammersmith, London W6 9EL. English Heritage Special Events Unit, 429 Oxford Street, London W1R 2HD. For info on folk and music events, contact the English Folk Dance and Song Society, Cecil Sharp House, 2 Regent's Park Road, London NW1 7AY. **USA:** British Tourist Authority, 551 Fifth Ave, New York, NY 10176, Tel (800) 462-2748. **Canada:** British Tourist Authority, 94 Cumberland St., Ste. 600, Toronto, On M5R 3N3, Tel (416) 925-6326, Fax (416) 961-2175. **Germany:** British Tourist Authority, Taunusstr. 52-60, D-5000 Frankfurt/Main 1, Tel 69-2380711, Fax 69-2380717, **Australia:** British Tourist Authority, 210 Clarence Street, Sydney, NSW 2000, Australia: Tel 2-2674555, 298627, Fax 2-2674442.

Most visitors to Finland are drawn by the neoclassical splendor of Helsinki or the undisturbed natural wonders of the Finnish countryside. The islands and coastal areas are unspoiled paradises for hiking, biking, and sailing, while in the north the boundless wilderness of Lapland is home to the indigenous Sami people.

FINLAND

This tidy, taciturn country doesn't manage to lure boat-loads of visitors, yet in the summer there are plenty of cultural events to get excited about. Among the castles of the lake districts, or in the seaside towns punctuated with lakes and parks, you'll find world-class opera, folk music, and classical concerts. These summertime events are great opportunities to meet the shy Finns who, after a little sunshine and beer, tend to let their inhibitions drop a bit.

MIDSUMMER (JUHANNUS)

Nationwide **June**

Although ethnically and linguistically distinct from their neighbors, the Finns celebrate the summer solstice with variations on the same Scandinavian theme. The Saturday closest to June 24 resembles in many ways a medieval holiday. The festivities are liveliest around university towns like Oulu, where celebrants light a giant tar pit and hold golf and sailing tournaments at midnight. Birch branches are cut to decorate houses, cars, and cattle, thus ensuring future happiness, and no matter where you are, the good times are sure to be a-hoppin'. Most people head to one of hundreds of lakes that dot the interior of the country, where they set up huge stacks of wood to be lit into a bonfire at midnight. The accordions and fiddles come out, as does a seemingly endless supply of expensive beer and spirits. Amid the dancing and drinking, Finns are encouraged to drop their inhibitions and become lost in the revel. Most young people stay up all night, and in the morning cleansing saunas are prepared.

DATE: The Saturday closest to June 24. **LOCATION:** Nationwide. **CONTACT:** Finnish Tourist Board (see *Resources*).

In a magnificent castle deep in the Tsars' lake-district playground, Verdi's Aida *is performed during the Savonlinna Opera Festival. (Finnish Tourist Board)*

Joensuu Song Festival

Joensuu **June**

This eclectic event extends across the border into Russia in a musical marathon that coincides with the midsummer celebrations. For a week there are a variety of rock, jazz, and classical concerts, including several major performances on the huge Laulurinne stage. Clubs and even market squares host performers from as far away as India and Africa, and street performers give the town a carnival atmosphere. On midsummer eve (June 22), there's usually a concert on the Russian side of the border, in the town of Sortavala.

DATE: The week surrounding the summer solstice in late June. **LOCATION:** Joensuu (northern Karelia). **TRANSPORT:** Joensuu's airport is served by flights from Helsinki. **ACCOMMODATION:** Joensuu has a variety of hotels, although competition for rooms at festival time makes advance booking essential. **CONTACT:** Joensuu Festival, Koskikatu 1, FIN-80100 Joensuu, Finland.

Sata-Häme Accordion Festival

Ikaalinen **June/July**

Originally held as a small gathering for folk musicians, the Sata-Häme Accordion Festival has grown into a fairly massive undertaking that packs this rustic town. In the parks and between the old wooden houses, about 800 accordionists get together to squeeze out melodies both kooky and sublime, while some 45,000 listeners mingle and move from stage to stage. Performing ensembles come from all over Europe and even as far away as Brazil, playing more than 70 concerts during the week. Some of the best, though, are from Finland, a country that really takes its "national instrument" seriously. Many concerts are free, open-air events, and if you're an accordion *manqué,* here's your chance to strap one on and cut loose. The Finnish Accordion Institute arranges lessons and workshops—even for beginners.

DATE: Late June through early July (one week). **LOCATION:** Ikaalinen. **TRANSPORT:** Ikaalinen is located about 50 km northwest of Tampere, which has an airport. Buses run from Tampere to Ikaalinen. **ACCOMMODATION:** The town has few hotels, but organizers can often arrange lodging with enough notice. **CONTACT:** Sata-Häme Accordion Festival, Hanuritalo, PO Box 37, FIN-39501 Ikaalinen, Tel 358-73-167-5330, Fax 358-73-167-5320.

SAVONLINNA OPERA FESTIVAL

Savonlinna **July**

There could hardly be a more perfect setting for an opera festival. Deep in the heart of eastern Finland's lake district, the three towers of the medieval Olavinlinna Castle rise dramatically above the rolling hills and lakes. Within the courtyard, the stage offers magnificent operatic experiences, such as Strauss's *Salome,* Mozart's *Magic Flute,* and Verdi's *Aida.*

The stunning venue is home to one of Europe's most important and critically acclaimed opera festivals, a large-scale event with the theme of "quality before quantity." The first-class performances, by both Finnish and international companies, always win critical acclaim, and buttressing the operas are ballets and symphonic concerts. At nearby Retretti Arts Center, concerts are presented within the fantastic acoustics of a deep cave, and on Kasinonsaari Island, an exhibition focuses on the history of the festival, which was first staged in 1912.

DATE: The last three weeks in July. Order your tickets at least six months in advance, or check the status of unclaimed tickets at the box office. **LOCATION:** Savonlinna, about 360 km/225 miles northeast of Helsinki. **TRANSPORT:** From Helsinki, five trains a day serve Savonlinna, and the cities are connected by good roads. **ACCOMMODATION:** Lodging on the lake and everywhere else is very expensive; reserve in advance for the festival. **CONTACT:** Savonlinna Opera Festival, Olavinkatu 35, FIN-57130 Savonlinna, Tel 358-57-514-700, Fax 358-57-21-866.

While you're there ...

Ruisrock, Turku: Thousands of rock music fans gather at the world's oldest regularly scheduled rock-fest in Finland's oldest city. (Weekend in early July.)

Pori Jazz, Pori: The sounds of internationally renowned jazz and blues musicians playing everything from traditional jazz to Dixieland draw more than 60,000 people to this small town 150 miles northwest of Helsinki. (A week in mid-July.)

Kuhmo Chamber Music Festival, Kuhmo: Perhaps the most remote chamber music festival in the world, Kuhmo manages to present an eclectic selection of high quality concerts based on an annual theme. (Two weeks in mid- to late July.)

Lieksa Brass Week, Lieksa: Brass musicians from around the world converge for a week of international brass music at this annual festival. (Last week of July.)

Kaustinen Folk Festival

Kaustinen **July**

The largest folk festival in the Nordic region may well be its most intimate—given the selection of unique venues ranging from small farmhouses to cafés and clubs. In these settings, and in larger halls and open-air arenas, nearly 3,000 musicians and dancers from around the world perform for nine days and nights. Special "theme days" feature family events and provincial Finnish music, and an entire weekend is devoted to folk dances from around the world.

DATE: Mid-July. **LOCATION:** Kaustinen, about 50 km/31 miles southeast of Kokkola. **TRANSPORT:** Kaustinen is located along the road that runs from Jyväskylä northwest to Kokkola. The nearest airport is at Vaasa. **ACCOMMODATION:** Event organizers can assist with lodging, if given enough notice. **CONTACT:** Kaustinen Folk Music Festival, PO Box 24, FIN-69601 Kaustinen, Finland, Tel 358-68861-1252, Fax 358-68-861-1977.

While you're there ...

Olujaiset Beer Festival, Savonlinna: Beer lovers won't want to miss this festival held to foster Olavinlinna Castle's drinking and brewing traditions. Held in the castle's courtyard, the beer flows and music and games spark the party. (Mid-August.)

Helsinki Festival: Scandinavia's largest cultural event fills Helsinki with concerts (classical, pop, and jazz), ballet, theater, opera, and visual arts. (Late August through early September.)

Resources

In Finland: Finland Tourist Information Office, Efelaesplanadi 4, FIN-00130 Helsinki, Tel 0-403011, Fax 0-40301301. **USA:** Finnish Tourist Board, 655 3rd Ave., New York, NY 10017, Tel (212) 949-2333, Fax (212) 983-5260. **Canada:** Embassy of Finland, 55 Metcalf St., Ottawa, ON K1P 6L5, Tel (613) 236-2389, Fax (613) 238-1474. **UK:** Finnish Tourist Board, 30–35 Pall Mall, GB-London SW1Y 5LP, Tel 71-9305871, Fax 71-3210696. **Germany:** Finnish Tourist Board, Darmstadter Landstr. 180, D-60598 Frankfurt 70, Tel 69-968-8670, Fax 89-686860. **Australia:** Embassy of Finland, 10 Darwin Ave., Yarralumla, Canberra, ACT 2600, Tel 6-2733800, 6-2733435, Fax 6-2733603.

FRANCE AND MONACO

Depending on whom you listen to, France either once was or still is the world's capital of culture, cuisine, fashion, and passion. Snobbery notwithstanding, the French have an instinctive flair for everyday life, and within their villages, farms, medieval cities, and metropolises, you can truly find it all.

For festival-goers, the French countryside is especially fertile ground. Everywhere you turn there are food fairs, wine fairs, carnivals, and religious celebrations—many taking place in castles, chateaux, or other stunning settings. From the highbrow theater and opera celebrations of Avignon, to the parades of "giants" in Douai, to the gypsy pilgrimages and bullfights of Provence, every corner of France contributes to the country's age-old cultural stew.

Carnival on the Riviera

Nice **February**

Never at a loss for *joi de vivre,* the capital of the Riviera is turned upside-down with unbridled gusto during its marathon Carnival celebrations. For 21 days, the *Niçois* adopt a single-minded obsession with fun, decking out their city in wild colors and intriguing disguises. Huge papier-mâché characters spin down the street on foot and float, while revelers dance and throw confetti on each other to the sound of thousands of street-corner buskers and full marching bands. In the Place Masséna, huge frescoes represent some 50 carnival motifs, with a backdrop of panels illuminated by more than 100,000 colorful light bulbs. The sounds of laughter and mischief bubble through the city as residents join visitors in masked balls, regattas, torchlight processions, and spontaneous street-corner sessions of bonhomie.

One event that sets the Nice Carnival apart from others is its *Bataille des Fleurs.* This parade/competition features enough flowers to overwhelm even Matisse, and more than 1,000 marching musicians and majorettes. Finally, on Shrove Tuesday, the big-

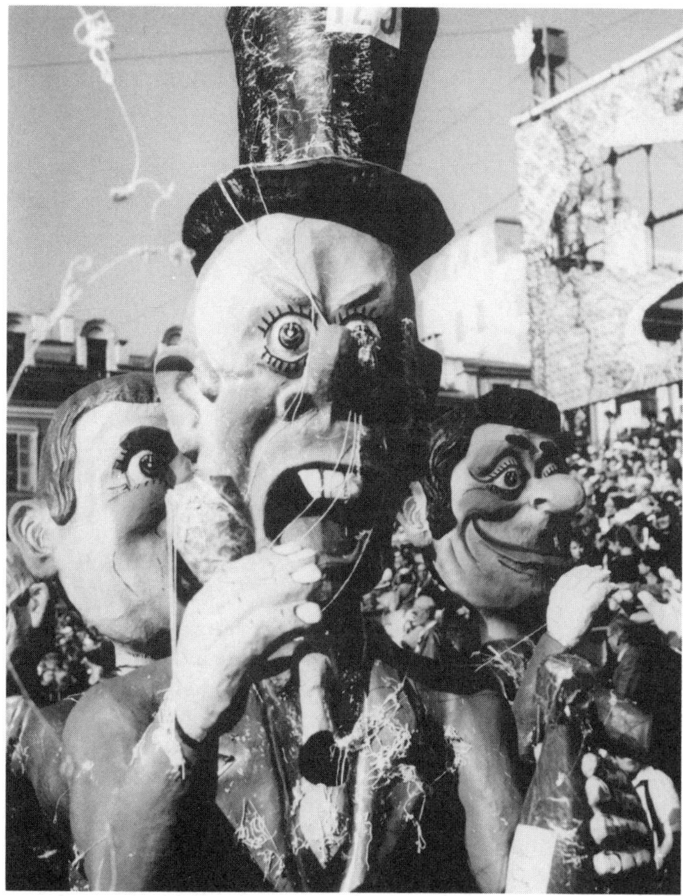

Bring on the giants! Carnival in Nice features hundreds of papier-mâché giants, who spin through the streets provoking general havoc. (Trip/N. Ray)

ger-than-life papier-mâché King Carnival is hauled through the Place Masséna one more time, then taken on his throne to the beachfront to be set ablaze in the sea, bringing Carnival to symbolic close.

DATE: The entire three weeks before Ash Wednesday, culminating on Shrove Tuesday. **LOCATION:** Nice's carnival is the biggest and most famous, but other good ones take place at Cannes, Antibes, Villefranche, and Arles. **TRANSPORT:** The Nice International Airport handles flights from other French cities and around the world. High-speed TGV trains roll into the Gare de Nice from European cities and elsewhere in France. **ACCOMMODATION:** Nice's best-situated hotels are located along the Promenade des Anglais, but there and elsewhere, reservations are necessary for rooms during Carnival. **CONTACT:** Office du Tourisme de la Ville de Nice, 1 Esplanade Kennedy, F-06000 Nice, Tel 93445059. Also, French National Tourist Office (see *Resources*).

- **International Circus Festival, Monaco:** The very best circus acts from around the world perform under the big top at Monaco. (January)
- **Monte Carlo Motor Rally, Monaco:** The world's hottest rods roar through Monaco. (Mid- to late January.)

Gypsy Pilgrimage

Saintes-Maries-de-la-Mer **May**

A colorful, musical frenzy of Gypsy life overtakes this village in the Camargue marshlands, as "traveling people" from all over Europe converge on a small fortress-chapel in honor of the Gypsy patron saint, Sarah. This is the border area that gave the world the Gypsy Kings, and although the group's Romany rock is often heard here, during the festival you're more likely to experience the acoustic Gypsy folk music that inspired them.

The festivities in honor of St. Sarah are definitely *not* tourist-oriented; rather, the Romany people gather in groups and entertain each other with highly spirited outbreaks of singing and dancing. A candlelight vigil in the church features a statue of Sarah, and the festival ends with a procession in which the image is decorated with flowers and brought down to the sea.

DATE: May 23–25. **LOCATION:** Saintes-Maries-de-la-Mer, Provence. **TRANSPORT:** The village is 27 km/17 miles from Arles, which can be reached by high-speed TGV train from Paris. **ACCOMMODATION:** Nearby Arles is your best bet for lodging. **CONTACT:** Syndicat d'Initiative, Ave. Van Gogh, 13460 Saintes-Maries-de-la-Mer, France. Also, French National Tourist Office (see *Resources*).

- **Fête des Gardians, Arles:** This annual rodeo and bullfight brings together the famed *gardian* cowboys of the Camargue, who herd the region's cattle and wild horses. (Early May.)

Mai Musical de Bordeaux, Bordeaux: This well-known event brings a wide variety of classical music and dance to sophisticated, wine-soaked Bordeaux. Contact: Grand-Theatre, Place de la Comédie, 33074 Bordeaux. (Two weeks in early May.)

Cannes Film Festival, Cannes: Sip cappucino in a café next to Marcello Mastroianni, or attend two weeks of star-studded, hyped-up events—if you can get in. (Mid- to late May.)

Monaco Grand Prix, Monaco: The best drivers in the world run the streets of Monaco, which abound with international flair. (Mid-May.)

Festival de l'Ile St.-Louis, Paris: The smaller of the two islands on the Seine hosts a festival of theater, gondola races, and other diversions throughout May. Just walk across the footbridge behind Notre Dame to immerse yourself in the festivities, which are enhanced by the ancient neighborhood. (May/June.)

Festival d'Aix-en-Provence

Aix-en-Provence **July**

One of the world's most exuberant summer music festivals rolls into one of the world's most elegant cities each July. Started in 1948, the Festival d'Aix at first focused primarily on operas, and today at least three are staged, using the Archbishop's Palace Theatre and other venues. The ancient performance halls and other fantastic settings enhance the events to a great degree, and each year the festival's reputation grows as more and more people discover it. Nowadays, in addition to opera, there are chamber and symphonic concerts and recitals in ancient churches, and even street dancing and rock concerts. The promoters do their best to book the world's top performers in each genre, and year after year the critics agree that they've succeeded ... again.

DATE: Mid-July through late July. **LOCATION:** Aix-en-Provence. **TRANSPORT:** To get to Aix from anywhere by train or plane, first you'll need to get to Marseille, then hop down by train or road to Aix. **ACCOMMODATION:** Like the rest of southern France's hot spots, Aix sees stiff competition for its hotel rooms during the summer. **CONTACT:** Festival d'Aix-en-Provence, Place de l'Ancien Archevêché, 13100 Aix-en-Provence, France.

Grand Parade of Jazz

Nice **July**

As the biggest of Europe's hundreds of jazz festivals, the Grand Parade du Jazz brings top performers from America and Europe to Nice for 11 great days of music. About 300 musicians and up to 150,000 fans show up at the two stages of the ancient

Romanesque Cimiez Gardens, and the 5 p.m. 'til midnight schedule leaves plenty of time for the beach. Elsewhere, the live music literally never stops, as Nice's clubs and cafés are packed day and night for jam sessions. In addition to its magnitude, the festival is notable for the quality and quantity of food available to hungry jazz-heads.

DATE: Mid-July. **LOCATION:** Nice. **TRANSPORT:** The Nice International Airport serves the entire Cote d'Azur, with flights from other French cities and around the world. High-speed TGV trains roll into the Gare de Nice from elsewhere in France. **ACCOMMODATION:** The jazz festival just exacerbates the summer shortage of rooms in Nice. Book well in advance. **CONTACT:** Grand Parade du Jazz, 4 rue St.-François-de-Paule, 06000 Nice. Also, French National Tourist Office (see *Resources*).

While you're there ...

- **Recontres Internationales de la Photographie, Arles:** The *crème de la crème* of international photography festivals includes nearly a month of exhibitions, workshops, and fringe shows in cafés in the heart of blue-sky Van Gogh country. Contact: RIP, 16 rue des Arenes, BP 90, 13632 Arles Cedex, France. (July.)
- **Tour de France Finish, Paris:** After more than 2,000 miles, the bicycle race always finishes in the Champs-Elysées, and most of Paris is there to cheer the winner. (July.)

The Giants of Douai

Douai **July**

Like their neighbors in Belgium, the people of the northern regions of France hold spectacular processions that feature giants built by local guilds. As France's biggest "giant festival," the Douai event includes about 100 immense effigies of characters from local legends, who are paraded through the streets and revered as "guests of honor" at celebrations throughout the town.

The Douai giants are among the most unusual folk characters in Europe; some stand more than eight meters (26 feet) tall and require six men to carry. The oldest and most famous is the *Gayant à Douai,* built in 1530. The guilds take great pride in their lasting work, and the entire town goes absolutely wild over their crazy giants as they're carried down the street in a parade accompanied by music and dancing.

DATE: Early or mid-July. **LOCATION:** Douai, Nord-Pas de Calais region. **TRANSPORT:** Douai is about 48 km/30 miles from Lilles, which has an airport and is also served by the TGV train from Paris (less than one hour). The region is accessible by ferry from England, via Calais and Boulogne. **ACCOMMODATION:** The small towns of Nord-Pas de Calais offer many lodging options, especially in Lille. **CONTACT:** Comité du Tourisme de Picardy, 3 rue Vincent Auriol, BP 2616, 80026 Amiens Cedex, France. Also, French National Tourist Office (see *Resources*).

Bastille Day and Eve

Nationwide **July**

In celebration of the French Revolution of 1789, the French go all out with parades, street dances, and fireworks. The entire country takes the day off, though much of the action takes place on the night before. In Paris, the eve of Bastille Day is marked with public *bals*, the most famous being the one sponsored by the Communist Party on the Ile St. Louis. There and elsewhere, class differences dissolve into the night, as Frenchmen and women join together in egalitarian inebriation. There are traditional street dances at the Bastille and at l'Ile de St. Louis, Place de la Contrescarpe, and Hôtel de Ville, and the next morning the military take center-stage with their parade down the Champs-Elysées. On the evening of Bastille Day a massive fireworks display at Montmartre illuminates many of the city's famous landmarks.

The town of Nancy puts on a vigorous show in the Place Stanislaus, and the fortress town of Carcassonne is "set on fire" with carefully placed, moving spotlights. In addition, the Côte d'Azur puts on special balls and fireworks displays. But no matter where you are in France, bands will play, people will dance, fireworks will be lit, and the good times will be ubiquitous.

DATE: Bastille Day falls on July 14. **LOCATION:** Nationwide. **CONTACT:** French National Tourist Office (see *Resources*).

While you're there ...

- **Mosaiques Gitans, Nimes:** Gypsy groups from all over Europe perform in the evenings in various spots around the city. (One week in mid-July.)
- **International Fireworks Festival, Monaco:** The world's best pyromaniacs go wild with exhibitions and technical workshops. (July/August.)
- **Festival of the Pyrenees, Oloron Sainte Marie:** This celebration of friendship between diverse cultures brings the dancers and musicians of France together with performers from dozens of countries all over the world. (Late July and early August.)
- **Festival Interceltique de Lorient, Lorient:** Celtic dancers, artists, writers, musicians, and speakers from Scotland, Ireland, Wales, and the Isle of

Hail the Glorious Grape!

France's wine fairs and grape harvest festivals are great occasions to sample the local vintage, while mixing with the people who grow the grapes and ferment the final product. Some of the most colorful wine fairs include the September festivals in Dijon and Beaune, and the November wine fairs in Meursault, Chablis, and Nuits-Saint-Georges. Many communities hold October grape-picking fairs. Here's a short list of some of the best:

Ile de France: *Nogent-sur-Marne,* June • *Bagneux,* mid-September • *Suresnes,* early October

Alsace: *Guebwiller,* mid-May • *Rodern,* mid-July • *Bibeauville,* late July • *Gueberschwihr,* August • *Colmar,* early August • *Turkheim,* early August • *Bennwihr,* mid-August • *Dambach-la-Ville,* mid-August • *Eguisheim,* late August • *Riquewihr,* mid-September • *Thann,* October • *Barr,* early October • *Obernai,* mid-October

Burgundy: *Mâcon,* mid- to late May • *Dijon,* late August to early September • *Nuits-Saint-Georges,* late October • *Beaune,* third weekend in November • *Clos-de-Vougeot,* third weekend in November • *Meursault (Côte d'Or),* third weekend in November • *Chablis,* fourth Sunday in November

Franche-Comté: *Revermont,* late July/early August • *Andelnans,* early September • *Arbois,* early September

Provence: *Boulbon,* early June • *Cassis,* September

Paris: *Montmartre,* first Saturday in October

Rhône-Alpes: *Ruoms,* mid-August • *Tain-l'Hermitage,* third weekend in September • *Beaujeu,* second Sunday in December

Man are drawn to Lorient to honor and preserve the Breton community. More than 4,500 participants hold concerts, competitions, and parades to entertain the crowds. (First two weeks in August.)

Festival of Avignon

Avignon **July/August**

So many avant-garde *artistes* squeeze into the walled city of Avignon that it sometimes seems as though the town is filling up with hot attitude and rising above the lush vineyards of the Rhône Val-

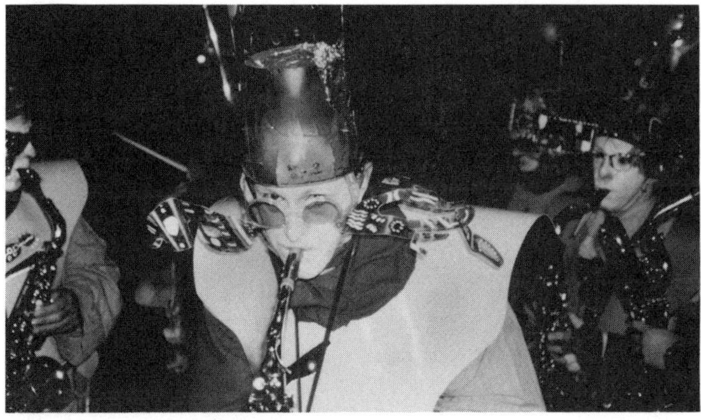

Hipster's delight: Theater, music, wine, and a beautifully random fringe make Avignon's festival a month-long banquet for the senses. (Amos Zezmer/Omni-Photo Communications)

ley. About 150,000 visitors show up during the four-week festival, which gives the city the look and feel of a non-stop celebration. In terms of the cutting edge, this is *the* French theater festival—the quality of the performances is excellent, the venues are diverse and interesting, and the sheer number of simultaneous events is dizzying. Plus, with so much happening on the fringe, it's easy to have a great time even if you're short on funds.

Theater is only part of the action, but it's a big part. The most important of 12 main venues is a spectacular palace built for the pope when he left Rome in the 14th century. World-class directors and well-known actors produce a large body of new work on the massive stage each year. The festival has also spawned a fringe, which turns the entire city into a performance stage. Many of the more than 200 fringe participants are young companies hoping to get noticed by the large number of directors and journalists in attendance.

DATE: Early July through early August. **LOCATION:** Avignon, Provence region. **TRANSPORT:** Although a car trip from Paris takes about eight hours, you can reach Avignon by TGV train in less than four. Avignon has a small airport which handles a couple of flights a day from Paris; the nearest large airport is at Marseilles. **ACCOMMODATION:** Top-end and middle-range accommodation is available inside the walls of the city, within walking distance of everything. Country inns and hotels dot the surrounding countryside. **CONTACT:** Avignon Festival, 66 rue de la Chausée d'Antin, 75009 Paris, France. Also, French National Tourist Office (see *Resources*).

Arles at Christmas: Living nativity scenes spring up at midnight mass in the churches of the Provence countryside. *(Joe Viesti/Viesti Associates, Inc.)*

© WHILE YOU'RE THERE ...

© **Festival of Popular Music and Dance, Dijon:** The living folklore of Europe, Africa, and the Americas is on parade in the cobbled streets of Dijon. Drawing more than 100,000 spectators and performers from 30 countries, the festival brings outstanding color and excitement to beautiful Burgundy. Contact: Cellier de Clairvaux, 27 Boulevard de la Tremuille, 211025 Dijon Cedex. (10 days in early September.)

© **Shepherds' Festival, Provence:** At Christmas midnight mass in Les Baux, Arles, and elsewhere in Provence, living nativity scenes are staged at churches. (December 24–25.)

Resources

In France: Maison de la France, 8 avenue de l'Opera, F-75001 Paris, Tel 1-42961023, Fax 1-42607512, 1-42860894. **USA:** Maison de la France, 610 Fifth Ave., New York, NY 10020-2452, Tel (212) 757-1125, Fax (212) 247-6468. **Canada:** Maison de la France, 30 Saint Patrick St. #700, Toronto, ON M5T 3A3, Tel (416) 593-6427, Fax (416) 979-7587. **UK:** Maison de la France, 178 Picadilly, GB-London W1V OAL, Tel 71-6299376, Fax 71-4936594. **Germany:** Maison de la France, Westendstrasse 47, D-60325 Frankfurt, Tel 69-756083, Fax 69-752187. **Australia:** Maison de la France, B.N.P. Bldg., 12 Castlereagh St., Sydney, NSW 200, Tel 2-2315244, Fax 2-2334576.

In Monaco: Direction du Tourisme et des Congres de la Principaute de Monaco, 2a Blvd. des Moulins, MC-98000 Monte Carlo, Tel 93308701, Fax 93509280. **USA:** Monaco Government Tourist and Convention Office, 845 Third Ave., New York, NY 10022, Tel (212) 759-5227, Fax (212) 754-9320. **Canada:** Honorary Consulate of Monaco, 1800 McGill Gollege Ave., Montreal, PQ H3A 3K9, Tel (514) 849-0589. **UK:** Monaco Government Tourist and Convention Office, 3-18 Chelsea Garden Market, Chelsea Harbour, GB-London SW10 0XE, Tel 71-3529962, Fax 71-3522103. **Germany:** Monaco Touristik Information, PO Box 320131, Gartenstr. 15, D-4000 Düsseldorf 30, Tel 211-4930892, Fax 211-4973194. **Australia:** Honorary Consulate of Monaco, 500 Bourke St., Melbourne, VIC 3000, Tel 3-6023088.

GERMANY

Blessed with an incomparable cultural legacy, Germany is again struggling to define itself while taking center stage in a rapidly changing Europe. Highly developed technology is everywhere, yet outside big cities the castles, monasteries, and ancient villages seem oblivious to the changes. Age-old traditions continue to flourish, and a surprisingly diverse range of rituals, foods, and drinks can be found as travelers move from north to south, or from east to west. In the fairs and historical pageants of small villages, and the huge carnivals of the large cities, Germans approach their celebrations with a great deal of pride. And everywhere, large quantities of beer and wine help to loosen normally taciturn tongues.

Carnival in Cologne (Karneval)

Cologne (Köln) **February**

Latin blood must still be flowing through the veins of the people of Cologne, for the Carnival thrown by this former Roman colony is absolutely over the top in terms of both spirit and spectacle. During the "mad days" leading up to Ash Wednesday, Cologne goes on a world-class binge that is one of the very best in Europe.

The Teutonic tomfoolery begins on the Thursday before Fat Tuesday, with a tradition that will thrill any guy who thought he'd never get a kiss from a German girl. For one night the old market becomes a drunken playground, as women run across the cobblestones, planting kisses (*Bützchen*) on the cheeks of every costumed stranger in sight. This Cologne exclusive is called *Weiberfasnacht,* or women's carnival.

Throughout the week, street parties pop up all over the city, and street stages revive the medieval tradition of puppet theater.

Carnival in Cologne: Cool efficiency dissolves in a masked flurry of Teutonic tomfoolery. (Joe Viesti/Viesti Associates)

The smooth, light *Kölsch* beer flows from taps, and on Sunday the old quarter has a parade of bands, floats, and masked dancers from the carnival clubs. This procession, however, is just a hint of the big things to come the following day. Rose Monday (*Rosenmontag*) features Europe's biggest parade, which serpentines through the packed streets with floats, decorated vehicles, bands, and troupes of masked "fools." The city's normal state of cool efficiency seems far away in this rampage, as everyone dances in the streets, socializes, and tries his or her best to reinforce Cologne's reputation as the most cheerful and spirited city in Germany.

DATE: February (the week before Ash Wednesday). **LOCATION:** Cologne. **TRANSPORT:** Cologne's airport and train station are well

Carnival in Bavaria: With hand-me-down wooden masks and clanging bells attached to lederhosen, the men of Mittenwald dance through town on Fat Tuesday. (AP/Wide World Photos)

connected to just about anywhere in the world. **ACCOMMODATION:** Hotels in the central district are most in demand, and fill up fast. **CONTACT:** Cologne Tourist Office, Unter Fennenhennen 19, D-5000 Cologne 1, Tel 221-221-3369.

CARNIVAL (FASCHING)

Munich, Düsseldorf, Mainz, and elsewhere **February**

In cities around the country, preconceived ideas about the Germans' ability to cut loose are thrown out the window during the "fifth season," also called the "season of fools." Munich is a major carnival center, with its Fasching celebration that begins January 7. In less than two months, there are more than 1,000 balls, parties, and other festivities that keep the waters of the Isar River sparkling with party lights. Some are private, but many are open to anyone wearing the prescribed garb—which can range from black tie to striped underwear, dunce caps, or combat boots.

After two months of preparatory celebrations, Munich reaches a complete frenzy during the final week. Crowds gather to watch the women of the produce market performing wild dances in garish outfits behind the Marienplatz, and on Sunday the parade called *München Harrisch* (mad Munich) winds its seemingly non-stop way through the streets. Costumed celebrants dance and spin between wild groups of staggering musicians, and the Marienplatz witnesses a marathon of drinking, dancing, and music-making. Throughout the week, Munich's famous beer halls are full, and in the Löwenbräu Bierkeller, Fasching appropriately ends with a final ball and "sweeping out" ritual. At midnight a "fool" is put into a mock coffin and carried out amid farewell dousings with beer, while a sweeper follows the crowd into the hall, literally and figuratively sweeping away the trash.

Elsewhere in the southwest, Fasnacht is celebrated by disguised "fools" who run through town making mischief. In Schuddig, they put on red-fringed clothes, traditional masks, and unwieldy hats decorated with snail shells, then run through town whacking people with blown-up hogs' bladders. In Überlingen and Villingen the "fools" crack whips as they race through town wearing smiling wooden masks and fox tails. The "fools" of Rottweil in Württemberg are also known for their vigor, and in the Black Forest, where the carnival is called Fasnet, creepy parades showcase original masks that were developed in the middle ages by craftsmen's guilds. Mainz and Düsseldorf are also known for their excellent parades and parties.

DATE: February (the week before Ash Wednesday). **LOCATION:** Düsseldorf, Mainz, Munich, Überlingen, Villingen, Rottweil, Schudding, and many other cities and towns. **CONTACT:** German National Tourist Office (see *Resources*).

Schützenfest, Hannover: Hannover's Old Town hosts a diverse cornucopia of events ranging from a medieval marksmen's pageant to a huge procession of floats, carriages, and bands from all over Europe. In between there's plenty of carnival-type activities and beer-drinking. (Late June through early July.)

RICHARD WAGNER FESTIVAL

Bayreuth **July/August**

So overwhelming is the experience of the Wagner festival in Bayreuth that many who've attended say they'll never return for fear of diluting their once-in-a-lifetime experience. This is Germany's oldest music festival—devoted wholly to the operas of Wagner—and it's become absolutely the hottest musical ticket in Europe. Like Salzburg, the Wagner festival necessitates planning *at least* a year in advance to get your share of the emotional and artistic energy that emanates from this operatic shrine.

The operas take place in the hall Wagner built as a place to perform his "music of the future." Back then, he saw the quiet hamlet as the perfect setting to stage his operas, but he intended to tear the theater down after the first festival was over. The operas were performed for free, and Wagner saw the festival as a way to put a torch to "the whole of bourgeois civilization, along with its commercialized theater industry."

If only he could see it now! The entire crowd is dressed in evening clothes, and steep prices for tickets, lodging, and food ensure an attendant elitism that eclipses even Salzburg's. The performances are of the highest caliber, featuring the world's top conductors and singers. During the one-hour intermission, you can mingle with the royal and rich who, cynics might argue, reduce Wagner's "revolutionary jubilee" to a celebration of mammon.

DATE: Late July to late August. **LOCATION:** Bayreuth, Upper Franconia. **TRANSPORT:** Bayreuth is connected by train to the rest of Germany. **ACCOMMODATION:** Book hotel rooms as soon as you order tickets. **CONTACT:** Begin preparing to order tickets *at least* one year in advance by contacting Bayreuther Festspiele, Postfach 100262, D8580 Bayreuth 1, Germany. Also, German National Tourist Office (see *Resources*).

Moselle Wine Festival

Bernkastel-Kues **September**

The fountain in the most colorful town of the Moselle Valley actually flows with wine during early September, as more than 200,000 people arrive to pay tribute to the 5,000 vintners in the surrounding hills. The setting, which has illustrated many a calendar, is fantastic. Surrounded by unique half-timbered houses dating from the early 1600s, the old market square is towered over by the ruins of Landshut Castle. You can walk up to it for a great view of the lazy bends of the Moselle, then come back down through the village streets, past houses with elaborately artistic weathervanes. The flow of wine at the festival is fed by town's central cellars, which hold 65 million liters of the white stuff.

DATE: Early September. **LOCATION:** Bernkastel-Kues. **TRANSPORT:** By road, the village is 48 km/30 miles northeast of Trier and 112 km/70 miles west of Mainz. There's frequent train service on the Moselbahn line between Trier and Bullay, and bus service to all Moselle towns is frequent. **ACCOMMODATION:** Bernkastel-Kues and surrounding towns have a wide range of hotels, many of which also serve excellent food and organize activities for wine-lovers. Book early for rooms during the festival. **CONTACT:** Moselle Tourist Board, PO Box 1330, D-5550 Bernkastel-Kues, Tel 6531-2092, Fax 6531-3077.

Dürkheim Sausage Market

Bad Dürkheim **September**

The Dürkheim Sausage Market, one of the world's best wine fairs, is an opportunity for local vintners to maintain a 15th-century tradition of serving pilgrims wine, sausage, and bread on St. Michael's Day. For two weekends, dozens of covered ad-hoc "taverns" serve festival-goers seated on benches at narrow tables. Traditional bands play festive music on stages set up in the larger pavilions, and a nearby amusement park offers rides and curiosities. Local vintners put on parades of decorated floats, and "his royal badness" the Lord Mayor of Bad Dürkheim taps the first cask.

DATE: The second and third weekends in September. **LOCATION:** Bad Dürkheim. **TRANSPORT:** Just 30 km/19 miles west of Mannheim, Bad Dürkheim can be reached by car, bus, or train. **ACCOMMODATION:** Accommodations are available in town, but they fill up fast during the festival; check surrounding villages and towns. **CONTACT:** Bad Dürkheim Tourist Information, Mannheimerstr. 24, D-6702 Bad Dürkheim, Tel 6322-6090.

While you're there ...

- **Kulmbach Beer Festival, Kulmbach:** Some of Germany's very best beer is brewed in this town just south of Coburg, and locals turn out in numbers to sample it. The world's strongest beer, *EKU Kulminator 28,* is brewed and served here.
- **Hop Festival, Wolznach:** In the heart of the world's richest hop lands, the harvest is celebrated with a large beer blast and the crowning of a Hop Queen. (Mid-September.)

Oktoberfest

Munich (München) **September/October**

"It's tapped!" shouts the Lord Mayor of Munich, after opening the keg and drawing the first liter of Oktoberfest beer—the first of six million! Thus begins the world's largest beer blow-out, a 16-day orgy of suds, sausage, *Gemütlichkeit,* and oompah-pah.

Has the Oktoberfest outgrown its quaintness? Most definitely. There's nothing subtle about this massive hurly-burly of carnival rides, food stalls, and 11 huge beer tents, each with its own entertainment. The program begins Saturday morning with a big entry of the Oktoberfest bar owners and brewers, rolling in on the expensively decorated, horse-drawn carriages of all the

Yell for a round and go nuts! There's nothing subtle about Oktoberfest's 16-day orgy of suds, sausage, and song under 11 giant beer tents. (AP/Wide World Photos)

Munich breweries. Behind them come the stereotypically busty waitresses on floats, and the bands that will play in the beer tents. The drinking begins in earnest. In the evening, traditional Bavarian and international bands perform in Circus Krone, and on Sunday morning the huge Costume and Marksmen's Parade brings out marching bands, folk dancers, festooned oxen, and floats from all over Bavaria.

There's much more to Munich than just the Oktoberfest, and consequently, this is Germany's most-visited city. Munich has a great opera and symphony, and its amazing museums present everything from art to aircraft. Green parks and exuberant architecture contribute to its fantastic setting at the foot of the Alps.

DATE: Oktoberfest begins on the second-to-last Saturday in September, and ends on the first Sunday in October. **LOCATION:** Munich. **TRANSPORT:** No problem! Trains and planes from everywhere pull into Munich. **ACCOMMODATION:** Unless you want to sleep in the Englischer Garten (which is both unsafe and illegal), book your room several weeks or even months in advance. **CONTACT:** Tourist Association Munich, PO Box 200929, Sonnenstr. 10, D-8000 Munich 2. Also, German National Tourist Office (see **Resources**).

WHILE YOU'RE THERE ...

Cannstatter Volksfest, Cannstatt (Stuttgart): The other big southern German beer festival takes place in Stuttgart, at about the same time as

Oktoberfest. Here, Stuttgart's three big breweries present *Märzenbier* and other styles in a meadow setting that's a bit more traditional than Munich's. (September/October.)

© **Berlin Festival, Berlin:** Theater, opera, film, art exhibitions, and concerts fill Berlin's many venues from early September through mid-October. (September/October.)

© **Frankenstein Festival, Darmstadt:** Just in time for Halloween, the Frankenstein Castle, which inspired Mary Shelley's novel, is the site of many strange and creepy activities in honor of the famous monster. (Three weekends near the end of October.)

© **Wine festivals, Moselle region:** A list of all the wine festivals in the towns and villages near the river would span four pages. If you go to the Moselle Valley in November, you'll find something going on. (October.)

Resources

In Germany: Deutsche Zentrale für Tourismus e.V., German National Tourist Board, Beethovenstr. 69, D-60325 Frankfurt 1, Tel 69-75720, Fax 69-751903. **USA:** German National Tourist Office, 122 E. 42nd St., Chanin Bldg., 52nd Fl., New York, NY 10168-0072, Tel (212) 661-7200, Fax (212) 661-7174. **Canada:** German National Tourist Office, 175 Bloor St. E., North Tower, Ste. 604, Toronto, ON M4W 3R8, Tel (416) 968-1570, Fax (416) 968-1986. **UK:** German National Tourist Office, 65 Curzon St., Nightingale House, GB-London W1Y 7PE, Tel 71-4953990/1, Fax 71-4956129. **Australia:** German National Tourist Office, Lufthansa House, 12th Fl., 143 Macquarie St., Sydney, NSW 2000, Tel 2-367-3890, Fax 2-367-3895.

ICELAND

Despite having the highest prices in Europe, untrammeled Iceland is currently experiencing a tourist boom. Many visitors are drawn by the country's fantastic, ghost-blown landscapes and geo-thermal wonders. In the primordial wilderness, evidence of nature's power is everywhere: volcanoes, glaciers, and lava flows create weirdly sensational landscapes, and hot springs, geysers, and waterfalls provide whimsical diversion for hikers, bikers, and pony-trekkers. Amid this natural beauty, a thousand-year-old culture flourishes. Durable and self-reliant, the hospitable people of Iceland throw an interesting array of festivals, making the most of their spectacular environments and the midnight sun that prevails during the brief summer.

Thorri Banquet (Thorrablót)

Nationwide **February**

"A feast from hell" could describe this nightmarish midwinter spread of traditional Icelandic delicacies—but don't take anyone's word for it. Instead, bravely pony up to the table and take a hearty helping of ... well, let's see, there's quite a choice here. Maybe you'd like to start off with a bit of pickled ram's testicles? And here's the poor critter's head, nicely singed, boiled, and cut in half, eyes still peering out of sockets. "The eyes are the best," your companion says, brushing you aside and scooping one out with a spoon, then moving on to the *blódmör,* or sheep's blood pudding, rolled in lard and sewn up in the stomach. "It's also called *slátur,*" remarks your friend enthusiastically. "I think that means 'slaughter' in English."

Better get a couple of good belts of "black death" (a potato/caraway schnapps) before getting into the next course, *hákarl.* "Rotten shark" is the literal translation, and yes, it's been buried for three or four months until it looks, smells, and tastes like rubbery road-kill. Wash it down with more black death if you need to. (You will.)

Some of the other delicacies you can expect to see at the Thorri feast are *rjúpa* (ptarmigan in milk gravy), *lundi* (those cute little puffin birds, broiled), and steaks of whale and seal. Finally, there's dessert, a curd concoction called *skyr,* topped with dried wild crowberries. "Even the foreigners like this," your friend says, as he ladles some onto your plate, and—miraculously—he's right. As the band picks up and the dancing starts, you go back for second helpings, comfortable in the knowledge that if you can survive this feast, the rest of winter will be no problem.

DATE: Thorrablóts are presented in February in communities across the nation. Outsiders are welcomed with open arms, but there are no fixed dates, so you'll have to ask at the tourist office for a schedule. **LOCATION:** Nationwide. **CONTACT:** Iceland Tourist Board (see *Resources*).

While you're there ...

Beer Day, Reykjavík and nationwide: In celebration of the day in 1989 when they could finally buy beer stronger than 2.2 percent, Icelanders take to the pubs to toast the hops and malt. (March 1.)

Seamen's Day (Sjómannadagur)

Coastal villages **June**

Seafarers make sure they're in port on this day, which is the biggest party of the year in most fishing towns. The celebration is in honor of the men and women who provide the manpower for the country's most important industry. In each coastal town, festivities are usually sponsored by the Seamen's Union, which organizes tugs of war, mock sea rescues, and swimming tourneys. In addition to ceremonies and sports, there's plenty of socializing and music making, fueled by large quantities of beer and spirits. Foreign visitors (and there aren't many) are welcomed into the villages like family.

DATE: The first Sunday in June. **LOCATION:** Coastal villages nationwide. **CONTACT:** Iceland Tourist Board (see *Resources*).

Independence Day

Reykjavík, Akureyri, and nationwide **June**

The country's biggest festival of the year commemorates the day in 1944 when Iceland gained independence from Denmark. Through-

Independence Day: Iceland's biggest party of the year brings the whole country into the streets for costumed parades, dancing, and music. (Alma/Viesti Associates, Inc.)

out the country people from large and small towns dance, sing, and parade in the streets. Reykjavík hosts big processions of costumed participants, and a variety of street theater. Although the daylight lasts almost all night, the sun, according to tradition, is not supposed to emerge from behind the clouds this day.

DATE: June 17. **LOCATION:** Nationwide, but the most elaborate celebrations take place in Reykjavík. **TRANSPORT:** Reykjavík can be reached directly by air from New York and several points in Europe. Icelandair's New York-Luxembourg flight offers a free stopover in Reykjavík for one to three days. **ACCOMMODATION:** Hostels, guesthouses, and hotels are in high demand during the summer months; consider booking in advance. **CONTACT:** Iceland Tourist Board (see *Resources*).

Thjódhátid and Verslunarmannahelgi

Heimaey, Brekkubaer, and nationwide **August**

When Iceland's constitution was ratified in 1874, the people of Vestmannaeyjar (the Westmann Islands) couldn't attend the mainland celebrations because of bad weather. Not wanting to forego a party, the islanders decided to create their own gig, the Thjódhátid, or "people's feast." It's became so popular that today it draws people from all over Iceland, for three days of partying and dancing around huge bonfires. Among spectacular lava flows and rock escarpments, a camp is set up and Heimaey Island goes into high revel mode, with plenty of music and sports competitions. Barbecued food is plentiful and beer flows by the barrel, but in the more than 120 years since the first festival, the weather hasn't improved much, and the event is often beset by drizzle.

The Verslunarmannahelgi weekend festival at Brekkubaer (near Arnastapi and Ólafsvik) draws New-Agers and others from around the world, many of whom are attracted by the "powercenter" of the Snaefellsjökull Glacier and nearby geo-thermal wonders. At 1,446 meters (4,743 feet) it's possible to climb the glacier in a single day (a guide is necessary). Within walking distance are strange rock formations with exceptional bird life, lava fields, dramatic gashes, and sea caves with remarkable acoustics and bizarre natural light effects. Elsewhere during this long weekend, everyone leaves the cities, and rural Iceland is filled (as filled as it ever gets) with festivals, horse races, and tent cities.

DATE: First weekend in August. **LOCATION:** Heimaey (Vestmannaeyjar, or Westmann Islands) , Brekkubaer (Snaefellsnes Peninsula), and rural areas nationwide. **TRANSPORT:** Heimaey can be reached by air from Reykjavík, or by ferry (often a rough trip). To reach Brekkubaer via Búdir, take a bus from Reykjavík as far as Búdir; from that point either arrange transport at the hotel (an excellent place to stay or dine), or hitch in. Alternatively, take a bus along the north side of the peninsula to Ólafsvik (a New Age center), and enquire in town. **ACCOMMODATION:** In both places there are quite a few hotels nearby, but they fill up fast during the festivals, and most people prefer to camp anyway. The weather is unpredictable in both places, so bring a tent that can withstand rain and high winds. **CONTACT:** Westmann Islands Travel, Kirkjuvegur 65, Heimaey, Iceland. Also: Iceland Tourist Board (see *Resources*).

Sheep Roundup (Réttadagur)

Rettir **September**

For two weeks in September, rural comradery and color are in high supply, as farmers set off on horseback to gather their sheep from the highlands. Throughout the hills and mountains, more than a million sheep have been grazing all summer, and farmers team up to bring them back down. Near the lowland towns the sheep (and some horses) are driven into huge circular pens, where they can be sorted according to owner. Icelandic farmers turn this chore into a community celebration, and once it's completed, singing and dancing breaks out. The festivities are an extremely colorful and exciting way to get a taste of life in rural Iceland.

DATE/LOCATION: September in farming communities nationwide (check with the Tourist Information Center in Reykjavík for the current season's dates and locations). **CONTACT:** Iceland Tourist Board (see *Resources*).

Resources

In Iceland: Tourist Information Center, Upplysingamidstöd Ferdamala, Bankastraeti 2, IS-101 Reykjavík, Tel 1-623045, Fax 1-624749. **USA:** Iceland Tourist Board, 655 Third Ave., New York, NY 10017, Tel (212) 949-2333, Fax (212) 983-5260. **Canada:** Consulate of Iceland, 116 Lisgar St., Ste. 700, Ottawa, ON K2P 0C2, Tel (613) 238-5064, Fax (613) 238-1441. **UK:** Iceland Information Office, c/o Icelandair, 172 Tottenham Court Rd., GB-London W1P 9LG, Tel 71-3885346, 71-3885599, Fax 71-3875711. **Germany:** Iceland Tourist Board, City Center, Carl-Ulrich-Strasse, D-6078 Neu-Isenburg, Tel 6102-254484, Fax 6102-254570. **Australia:** Consulate of Iceland, 4 Wiston Gardens, Double Bay (Sydney), NSW 2028, Tel 2-3271814, Fax 2-3275818.

IRELAND

As Europe's last refuge of the irrational, Ireland brims with a sense of community, spontaneity, and gregariousness that seems somehow out of step with the rest of the world. At festivals and in pubs, the past blends with the cosmopolitan present in spirited music and dance that's very much alive—and constantly changing.

Irish music, especially, is in the midst of a dramatic resurgence. Rather than watching rock and roll chip away at the country's musical traditions, Irish young people have picked up the fiddles and fifes and learned to play the old tunes. In pubs and at musical events across the country, groups of folk musicians play spirited sets—not for tourists, but for their own simple enjoyment.

The cultural revival has spilled over into other arts, too. Nearly every town has come up with an idea for a festival, and at these community events visitors will find that all the clichés about Irish conviviality are true. You can enjoy a good pint and an even better conversation, or ponder just how it is that the Irish have managed to create one of the most interesting, refreshing travel grounds in the Northern Hemisphere.

Note: Events in both the Republic of Ireland and Northern Ireland are covered in this chapter.

Pan-Celtic Week

Galway **April**

The ancient Celts dominated the European continent for centuries before the Roman Empire pushed them to the north and west, into areas that now make up the six remaining Celtic nations: the Isle of Man, Brittany, Ireland, Cornwall, Scotland and Wales. Today, Celtic culture and heritage can be experienced at this multinational gathering, which showcases the great bardic and sporting traditions of the Celts.

Traditional dancing, music-making, and sports make for an extremely colorful event. The hurling matches are particularly vigorous; this lacrosse-like game is played by teams of 15 who thrash at a leather ball with *hurleys* (crooked wooden sticks). At night there are good times aplenty, as participants gather to feast, drink, and indulge in storytelling, poetry, and music.

DATE: One week in early to mid-April. **LOCATION:** Galway City. **TRANSPORT:** Trains and buses run regularly from Dublin and Athlone; connections from other lines can be made at Athlone. **ACCOMMODATION:** A huge variety of accommodations are available, but be wary of crowds in the summer and book ahead. **CONTACT:** Maire Mhic Midhir or Brid Seoighe, Tel 091-68876, Fax 091-68836. Also, Irish Tourist Board (see *Resources*).

While you're there ...

- **St. Patrick's Day, nationwide:** Anyone who's been to New York, Chicago, Boston, or Savannah for St. Patty's Day will be surprised at how low-key the celebrations are in Ireland. On this national holiday most businesses close and there's a big parade in Dublin, followed by the Lord Mayor's St. Patrick's Night Ball. Throughout the week there are horse races, football finals, car rallies, and other sports competitions. (March 17.)
- **Fleadh Nua Traditional Music Fest, Ennis (County Clare):** This colorful festival embodies "the real Ireland" in a mix of traditional music, song, and dance. Thousands come from all over the republic to see and participate in stage shows, competitions, and cultural parades. Contact: Tel 01-280-0295, Fax 01-280-3759. (Usually the third weekend in May.)

Bloomsday

Dublin **June**

June 16, 1904 was the day Leopold Bloom made his way through Dublin in the pages of James Joyce's *Ulysses*. Bloomsday, created in 1954, offers a chance to follow the meanderings of Leopold, Stephen Dedalus, and other characters, alongside thousands of Joyce fanatics who descend upon "dear, dirty Dublin" to cavort among the settings of the novel. Surprisingly, much of Joyce's turn-of-the-century city is unchanged—you'll still find the smoke-filled pubs and soot-covered flats, the dirty lanes and dockside slums. Even many of the bar-flies look like they haven't left their pubstools in a century!

Joyce once remarked that he was "more interested in the street names of Dublin than in the riddle of the universe," yet the writer wasn't well liked in Dublin after he called its row houses "the incarnation of cultural paralysis." In the book, Bloom's meanderings took 19 hours, but the complete path takes most participants about 30 hours, since visits to so many "hot, reeking public houses," tend to slow the trek. The South Bank Restaurant serves a breakfast of kidneys like Leopold ate, and Davy Byrnes' Pub

Dressing the part: On Bloomsday, thousands of Joyce fanatics descend on "dear, dirty Dublin" to follow the meanderings of characters in Ulysses. *(Homer Sykes/Woodfin Camp & Associates)*

serves his lunch of Gorgonzola cheese and burgundy. Hoards of people climb the Martello Tower, walk Sandymount Strand, and stop to read at the National Library.

DATE: June 16. **LOCATION:** Dublin. **TRANSPORT:** Dublin is accessible by air from most major European and North American cities. Ferries are available from England, Scotland, and Wales. **ACCOMMODATION:** Quarters range from hostels to five-star hotels. **CONTACT:** Irish Tourist Board (see *Resources*).

Ballybunion International Bachelor Festival

Ballybunion **June**

Ireland's most eligible bachelors are on display, but ladies, don't expect to take one home with you—they don't like to be seen with a maiden more than once. The beautiful seaside resort town of Ballybunion is the setting for this huge 10-day party that requires the 20 members of the Bachelor Festival Club to have fun, hold their drink, and know how to mingle with women without mingling too long. The bachelors are required to defect from the club and immediately nominate a new member if ever they marry. Although the festival organizers plan a variety of activities for the event, serious partying, with help from lots of music and drink, usually dominates.

Living Literary Dublin

If you don't happen to make it to Dublin on June 16, you can still walk in Joyce's footsteps with the help of a printed or human guide and a few pints of Guinness. Jack McCarthy's *Joyce's Dublin* provides a printed guide to the routes of characters, with maps, photographs, and lots of lore and speculation. The TGI organization (Tel 01-679-4291) offers excellent guided walking tours between May 15 and September 30, with titles like "Ancient Dublin," "Literary Footsteps," and "18th-Century Dublin." These cost about US$8, as does the Dublin Literary Pub Crawl, a beery romp through the pubs that sustained and inspired writers like Beckett, Joyce, Behan, and Kavanagh. The pub crawl meets at the Bailey Pub on Duke Street every Tuesday, Wednesday, and Thursday at 7:30 p.m., June through August. You may also want to check out the Dublin Writers Museum, which has an interesting variety of memorabilia relating to Ireland's greatest gifts to the world.

DATE: Late June. **LOCATION:** Ballybunion, County Kerry. **TRANSPORT:** Buses make the 40 km/25 mile trip from Tralee to coastal Ballybunion, but service is infrequent; consider renting a car or hitching a ride. **ACCOMMODATION:** Hotels are scarce, but bed & breakfasts are usually a good bargain. **CONTACT:** Maria Finuncann, Tel 068-27-293, or Irish Tourist Board (see *Resources*).

While you're there ...

© **Fiddle Stone Festival, Belleek (Northern Ireland):** This small village hosts fiddle players from all over Ireland. (Late June.)

Laytown Strand Races

Laytown **July/August**

When the tide is out the race is on! A world away from the big money and snobbery of Derby Day in Curragh, the small resort of Laytown holds Europe's only official horse race to be run on a beach. Here, the spirit of ancient Ireland's fairs bypasses all modern glamor and pretense, winding up as nothing more than a great day at the races ... and on the beach.

The atmosphere sometimes seems more like a three-ring circus than a race. The track, which had been underwater just a few hours before, is marked on sand with banners. Food sellers, tea rooms, and bars are erected in a field above the officials' quarters. Nearby, horses and trainers fill the paddock, while odds are shouted and boozy predictions are made. On the beach, kids and bookmakers splash through tidal pools while food-hawkers make their rounds. Mounted "huntsmen" in red coats push the crowds away from the track just before race time, when suddenly all eyes turn to the beach ... and they're off!

DATE: The races are usually held in early or mid-August, but it depends on the Irish Sea's tides. Contact the tourist office for the current summer's dates. **LOCATION:** Laytown, County Meath, is located just 50 km (30 miles) north of Dublin. **TRANSPORT:** Laytown is less than an hour from Dublin by car (look for the turn-off from the N1); buses run up the coast. **ACCOMMODATION:** Laytown and nearby Bettystown have several modest resort-type hotels; alternatively you can day-trip from Dublin. **CONTACT:** Irish Tourist Board (see *Resources*).

While you're there ...

- **Galway Arts Festival, Galway:** This wide-ranging festival attracts musical and dramatic groups from all over the republic. (July/August.)
- **Ballyshannon International Folk Festival, Ballyshannon:** The cream of Irish folk and traditional music gathers to sing, dance, and make merry. Contact: Mr. B. McLaughlin, Tel 072-51049. (July/August.)
- **Buskers' Festival, Galway:** Street musicians from all over Ireland and the world converge on Galway for three days of humbuggery. (July/August.)

Puck Fair Festival

Killorglin **August**

One lucky *puck* (male goat) is the reigning king over this long-standing, raucous affair. Festivities are preceded by the capture of a wild goat whose enthronement in the center of town is a symbol of unrestricted merrymaking. Myth has it that the tradition began in 1613 when a bleating goat alerted his shepherd boy to approaching enemy forces, saving the town from siege. The grateful townspeople started a commemorative celebration, and they've been upholding the tradition ever since. This is a real Irish party—complete with pubs that never close, nonstop revelry, and rowdy hijinks. Don't miss the horse and cattle trading on the green, where crusty old men barter over livestock as they have for cen-

One of this bovine's ancestors stole the show in 1613 when he alerted the town to the approach of enemy troops. Still honored at the Puck Fair Festival, the puck (male goat) reigns over the town of Killorglin for three wild days each August. *(Irish Tourist Board)*

turies. For the entertainment-focused, there are open-air concerts and abundant street performances.

DATE: August 10–12. **LOCATION:** Killorglin, County Kerry. **TRANSPORT:** A bus from Killarney leaves twice a day (once on Sunday) in the summer; you can also rent a car or hitchhike. **ACCOMMODATION:** Hotels are scarce, but bed & breakfasts surround the area, as does a hostel and camping site. **CONTACT:** Mr. Declan Mangan, Tel 06661595. Also, Irish Tourist Board (see *Resources*).

© ALL-IRELAND FLEADH CEOIL

Moving venue **August**

The *Fleadh Ceoil* (pronounced "flay kyoh-il") is one of the most colorful and exciting events in Ireland. Drawing the very best singers, whistlers, instrumentalists, and dancers, the focus is mostly on music, but art and other displays of Irish culture add to the color. Towns in Ireland clamor for the chance to host this festival, which draws up to 100,000 people for three days of music and dancing. Day and night, the event is a dream come true for fans of Irish music, many of whom break into spontaneous jigs as the soulful sounds of flutes and fiddles fill the air.

DATE: Three days in late August. **LOCATION:** Moving venue. **CONTACT:** Comhaltas Ceoltoiri Eireann, Belgrave Sq., Monkstown, Co. Dublin, Tel 01-2800295. Also, Irish Tourist Board (see *Resources*).

Rose of Tralee Festival

Tralee **August**

Irish-born girls, girls of Irish parentage, or any of the fair sex with Ireland in their blood are invited to come from all over the world to compete for the rose title. The six-day event is a festive search to find the girl as "lovely and fair as the rose of the summer." This is not your average contemporary beauty contest; the Guinness flows and the atmosphere remains both lighthearted and fun—despite the fierce competition. People roam the streets from early morning to late evening, enjoying pipe bands, carnivals, parades, street dancing, fireworks, and music. There are also robust tug-of-war competitions, and the popular Tralee donkey and greyhound races. The pageant itself is a major media event, televised live on prime-time TV. The winner receives a Waterford Crystal trophy and the illustrious title of "Rose of Tralee."

DATE: Third week in August **LOCATION:** Tralee, County Kerry. **TRANSPORT:** A regular train connects Dublin to Tralee. Buses run from Dublin and between Tralee and Ballybunion. **ACCOMMODATION:** Hotels are scarce and usually open on a seasonal basis. Camping and hosteling are a good option. **CONTACT:** Festival Office, Tel 066-21322, Fax 066-22654. Also, Irish Tourist Board (see *Resources*).

Galway International Oyster Festival

Galway **September**

The International Oyster Festival has been celebrated by the people of Galway and their multinational guests for more than 40 years. This four-day affair of gluttonous feasting is a seafood free-for-all, so prepare to eat whatever comes up from Neptune's watery realm. The bays surrounding Galway are known for their oysters and scallops, and if you haven't developed a taste for these treats of the deep, try washing them down with a pint of Guinness or "black velvet" (Guinness and champagne).

The mayor begins the festivities by cracking open the first oyster of the season, then gulping it down with experienced vigor. Oyster-openers from around the world compete to see who can shuck the most oysters in the least amount of time, but you don't have to be a professional to enjoy the oyster tasting. Other festival activities include yacht racing, golf competitions, and—of course—music, song, and dance. Oyster season is September through December, and at the time of the festival, the bivalves are just waking up in time for dinner.

DATE: Late September. **LOCATION:** Galway. **TRANSPORT:** Trains and buses run regularly from Dublin and Athlone; connections from other lines can be made in Athlone. **ACCOMMODATION:** A huge variety of accommodations are available, but be wary of crowds and book ahead. **CONTACT:** Ms. Anne Flanagan, Tel 091-22066, Fax 091-2728. Also, Irish Tourist Board (see *Resources*).

While you're there ...

- **Clarenbridge Oyster Festival:** The calmer cousin of the Galway festival, this feast takes place in the bayside village of Clarenbridge in early fall. If you want to avoid the raucous revelry of the larger event but still enjoy the palatable jewels of the sea, this festival is a good bet. Festivities include a ladies international oyster opening competition. Contact: Ms. Ann Walsh, Tel 091-96342, Fax 091-96001. (Mid-September.)
- **Belfast Folk Week:** Irish fiddlers and other musicians get together for the weekend in downtown Belfast, for music-making, dancing, and workshops for musicians and songwriters. (Mid-September.)
- **Belfast Festival at Queens:** Hosted by Queens University, this is one of the largest arts festivals in the UK, with three weeks of music, drama, and visual art. Contact: Festival House, 25 College Gardens, Belfast Bt9 6BS, Tel 0232-667687. (November.)

Resources

In the Republic of Ireland: Irish Tourist Information Office, Baggott St., Dublin 2, Tel 1-676-5871, Fax 1-676-4764. **USA:** Irish Tourist Board, 345 Park Ave., New York, NY 10154, Tel (212) 418-0800, Fax (212) 371-9052. **Canada:** Irish Tourist Board, 160 Bloor St. E., Toronto, ON M4W 1B9, Tel (416) 929-2777, Fax (416) 929-6783. **UK:** Irish Tourist Board, 150 New Bond St., GB-London W1Y OAQ, Tel 71 4933201, Fax 71-4939065. **Germany:** Irish Tourist Board, Untermainanlage 7, D-6000 Frankfurt/Main 1, Tel 69-236492, Fax 69-234626. **Australia:** Irish Tourist Board, 5th Leven, 36 Carrington St., Sydney, NSW 2000, Tel 2-2996177, Fax 2-2996323.

In Northern Ireland: Northern Ireland Tourist Board, St. Anne's Court, 59 North St., Belfast BT1 1ND, Tel 232-246609, 232-231221, Fax 232-240960. **USA:** Northern Ireland Tourist Board, 276 Fifth Ave., #500, New York, NY 10001, Tel (212) 686-6250, Fax (212) 686-0861. **Canada:** Northern Ireland Tourist Board, 111 Avenue Rd., Ste. 450, Toronto, ON M5R 3J8, Tel (416) 925-6368, Fax (416) 961-2175. **UK:** Northern Ireland Tourist Board, 11 Berkeley St., GB-London W1X 5AD, Tel 71-4930601, Fax 71-4993731. **Germany:** Northern Ireland Tourist Board, Taunusstr. 52-60, D-6000, Frankfurt, Tel 69-234504, Fax 69-2380717. **Australia:** British Tourist Authority, 210 Clarence St., Sydney, NSW 2000, Tel 2-2674555, 2-298627, Fax 2-2674442.

ITALY

Italy is one of the world's festival kingdoms, the host of an ongoing party fueled by wine, food, and Catholicism. In this land of wild style and stormy politics, contradiction has been elevated to a fine art: On one hand Italy is a harbinger of fashion, a sensual, urban, industrial member of the 20th century. On the other hand, it's a provincial farming country where religion, superstition, and medieval ritual dominate daily life.

The people of Sicily, Piedmont, Turin, or Palermo are unified as Italians only in their extreme embrace of ordinary living. On any given day, hundreds of festivals may be taking place across Italy. At these events—patron saint days, harvest celebrations, sporting competitions—the outlays of beautiful food and wine are lavish, and activities range from subtle to outrageous. Beguiling, tempting, artistic, tumultuous—Italy's celebrations are unmatched anywhere!

CARNIVAL (CARNEVALE) IN VENICE

Venice **January/February**

Mysterious and sophisticated, the Venice Carnival is the world's most romantic and glamorous masked ball. For 10 days, the city falls under the revelers' spell, as lavish balls and parties are staged in old palaces, and fantasy flourishes in exotic 18th-century costumes. On the canals, gondolas ferry Europe's top socialites, while in the shadows masked lovers embrace passionately, knowing they'll part when the party's over.

The final five days before Ash Wednesday are the wildest, as masked balls draw the elite of European society, and cafés are packed with uninhibited amateurs who storm the stage for the night. By Shrove Tuesday, the streets, sidewalks, and canals are teeming with a frenzy of masked, writhing celebrants, and fireworks light up "the finest street in the world," the Grand Canal, in the final hours before everyone settles in for 40 days of Lent.

DATE: The ten days before Ash Wednesday. **LOCATION:** Venice. **TRANSPORT:** Venice's Marco Polo Airport is served by flights from most European cities, and some North American cities. The train station is well connected to all of Italy, as well as Austria, Germany,

Carnival in Venice: Ingenuity and historic flair characterize the world's most sophisticated and mysterious carnival.
(Ian Murphy/Tony Stone Images)

and the former Yugoslavia. **ACCOMMODATION:** Everything in Venice is expensive, and at Carnevale rooms are even more expensive than usual. Book several months in advance. **CONTACT:** Azienda Autonoma di Soggiorno e Turismo, Castello 4421, I-30122 Venezia, Tel 41-5226110, Fax 41-5230399. Also, Italian State Tourist Office (see *Resources*).

Carnival in Ivrea

Ivrea **February**

The Canavese Valley town of Ivrea has a number of amazing events, but the most outrageous are three epic "battles" fought with more than 50 tons of Sicilian blood oranges. As battalions defend the town's five piazzas, invaders relentlessly hurl the fruit, which explodes in flurries against walls, cars, and skulls. Non-fighters express their neutrality with red caps, but at times there's no escaping the crossfire—or the scent of hundreds of thousands of smashed oranges.

Between orange battles, the carnival follows a precise script, involving more than 1,500 people who act out a historical pageant. On Saturday evening the main character, the miller's wife, makes her dramatic entrance on the balcony of the town hall. On Sunday afternoon, Monday, and Shrove Tuesday, costumed figures parade through town. Gargantuan feasts are prepared in the street, and 34 cauldrons work continuously to cook the *tofeja,* a fantastic, French-influenced bean and salami soup.

A Carnival of Italian Carnivals

The Carnival in Venice is Italy's best-known pre-Lenten celebration, by far. But it's only one of a dozen or so major carnivals that erupt in Italy—and every one is packed with good times and outrageous spectacles. Here's a rundown on some of the best.

The traditional Carnival of **Viareggio** (Tuscany) is just as popular as Venice's, and certainly as lively. The highlight is an utterly amazing parade of mechanized floats and monstrous papier-mâché effigies of celebrities. Hotels are usually full in town, so you'll probably have to stay elsewhere along the Rivera della Versilia. Contact: Tel 0584-962233.

In **Oristano** (Sardinia), a medieval tournament called the Sartiglia is reenacted. Horsemen in masquerade try to thrust their swords into a suspended star-shaped object while their horses gallop at full speed. The contest is preceded by a procession of costumed townsfolk. Contact: Tel 0783-74191.

Parades and more parades take over the streets of **Bosa** when costumed citizens mock the faults and idiosyncrasies of fellow townspeople and a group dresses in mourning to improvise a funeral procession searching for milk. Everyone in town will be wearing white and carrying lanterns to acknowledge Carnival. Contact: Tel 0785-373150.

In **Verona** the parade ends with food for all. Gnocchi with piquant sauce waits at the end of the procession of 15th-century-costumed figures representing the Papà del Gnoco. Contact: Tel 045-592828.

Costumed horsemen, riderless horses, floats, and people decked out in the finest brocades parade through the streets of **Ronciglione** in the most important carnival in the Tuscia area of Italy. Contact: Tel 0761-626877.

Some other towns that host excellent carnivals include **Sappada**, **Bagolino**, **Fano**, **Gradoli**, **Modena**, **Aci Reale**, **Cagliari**, **Tempio Pausania**, **Arco**, **Santhià**, **Schignano**, **Ascoli Piceno**, **Milan**, and **Ivrea**.

DATE: The entire week before Ash Wednesday. **LOCATION:** Ivrea, in the Piemonte (Piedmont) Valley of Canavese. **TRANSPORT:** Ivrea is about 40 km (25 miles) northeast of Torino (Turin), along the A5 motorway. It also lies on the rail line between Asti and Aosta. **ACCOMMODATION:** Ivrea has slim pickings for lodging, but Turin is well-stocked with hotels. **CONTACT:** Local Tourist Office: Tel 0125-461-8131. Also, Italian State Tourist Office (see *Resources*).

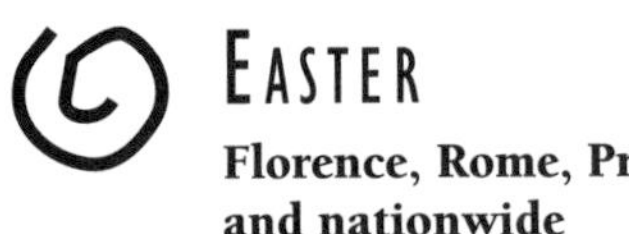

EASTER

Florence, Rome, Prizzi, and nationwide **March/April**

Figuratively, Italians mix fireworks and religion all year, but in Florence's dramatic Easter mass, the two elements come together with a big bang in the main square. During High Mass at the Piazza del Duomo, the resurrection of Christ is announced with ringing bells at noon. At that moment, a blazing mechanical dove is released from the altar, and when it reaches a cart in the middle of the square, it sets off a pyramid of fireworks. Dating back to the Crusades, the ritual is seen as a way of foretelling the city's luck for the coming year: If the bangs are big and bright, the future will be too.

In Rome, the famous Procession of the Cross makes its way between the Colosseum and the Palatine on Good Friday, and the pope blesses the Vatican and the whole world in St. Peter's Square on Easter Sunday. In Prizzi, near Palermo, shaggy gap-toothed devils dance in the main street on Easter Day, while Death, dressed in yellow, runs through the crowds shaking his chains and looking for visitors. These he drags into ad-hoc bars where they must make a donation; then they are given a treat of pastry dough wrapped around a hard-boiled egg, and set free. Finally, the devils and Death are captured by angels as images of the Madonna and Jesus are carried separately through the village, finally reuniting and embracing.

Other interesting Easter rituals are performed at **Taranto** (Apulia), **Chieti** (Abruzzo), **Trapani** (Sicily), **Piana degli Albanesi** (Palermo), **Assisi** (Perugia), and **Sibillo** (Perugia).

DATE: March or April. **LOCATION:** Nationwide. **CONTACT:** Italian State Tourist Office (see *Resources*).

SARDINIAN CAVALCADE

Sassari **May**

The biggest and most extraordinary folklore gathering in Sardinia includes costumed parades, equestrian competitions, and contests of singing, dancing, and music-making. The occasion marks a war with the Saracens at the turn of the millennium, and includes mock battles and acrobatic feats by knights on horseback. The amazingly diverse traditional costumes of the island's hundreds of villages are presented by more than 3,000 participants, many of whom dance or play traditional instruments while parading through the medieval town center.

Screaming through the streets of the City of Silence: Teams of madmen race through town bracing huge candlesticks in an orgy of confusion that honors the town's patron saint, Ubaldo. *(Italian Government Tourist Board, New York)*

DATE: A Sunday in mid- to late May. **LOCATION:** Sassari (Sardinia). **TRANSPORT:** Sassari is connected by bus and train to Cagliari (where the major airport is) and Oristano, Olbia, and Porto Torres. **ACCOMMODATION:** Since the processions get going early, it's advisable to stay either in Sassari or nearby the night before. Unfortunately, hotels are not abundant, so book early. **CONTACT:** Tel 079-233534.

Race of the Candles (Corsa dei Ceri)

Gubbio **May**

The steep, narrow streets of "the City of Silence" explode with noise and energy as three huge wooden candles are raced around town by teams of men. The orgy of confusion begins at dawn when trumpeters call out the structures. Then, teams of about 20 men each (supported by hundreds of identically dressed fans) shoulder the huge wooden "candles" and run through the piazza as if lives depended on their actions. Music blares, people jump up and down, and colorful processions roll through the medieval town.

It's all dedicated to Gubbio's patron Saint, Ubaldo. Feasts of seafood are prepared to fortify the runners, who in the late afternoon surge up Mt. Ingio at a breakneck pace, finally reaching the town's basilica. At dusk, a bit of calm starts to return to this intensely beautiful hillside village.

Costumed pageantry fills the streets of Florence during the Feast of St. John and Gioco del Calcio. (John Garrett/Tony Stone Images)

DATE: May 15. **LOCATION:** Gubbio, Perugia. **TRANSPORT:** Buses run daily from Florence and Rome. The nearest train station is at Fossato di Vico, around 20 km/12 miles southeast of Gubbio. **ACCOMMODATION:** Accommodations are generally expensive, but many locals rent rooms to tourists. You can also day-trip from Perugia. **CONTACT:** Local tourist office, Tel 075-922-0693. Also, Italian State Tourist Office (see *Resources*).

May Music Festival (Maggio Musicale)

Florence **May/June**

You have to be careful when you combine the visual treasures of Florence with a classical performing arts festival of this magnitude—you could get what one French author called "aesthetic overload." With a quality of performance that often equals Salzburg's festival—and a diversity that often surpasses it—the Maggio Musicale packs more events than the month of May can hold. For that reason, it's been extended into June. The architectural wonders of the city that started the Renaissance are used to stage concerts, recitals, ballet, sacred music, and that Italian obsession, opera. A concurrent bonus is the Cricket Festival, held in Cascine Park in late May. Vendors sell crickets in decorated cages, and after a parade of floats the insects are ceremoniously released in the park.

DATE: May and June. **LOCATION:** Florence (Firenze). **TRANSPORT:** Florence's two airports are served by flights from all over Italy and

Europe. **ACCOMMODATION:** Florence has hundreds of hotels in all categories. **CONTACT:** Maggio Micale Fiorentino, Teatro Comunale, Via Solferino 15, 50123 Florence, Italy.

While you're there ...

- **Flower Festival (Infiorata), Genzano (Rome) and Spello (Umbria):** Colorful splashes of flowers carpet cobbled streets on the morning of Corpus Christi. Prepared in a lengthy and painstaking process and arranged in just a few hours, these amazing works are then trampled by religious processions. (Corpus Christi Sunday, in June.)
- **Feast of St. John and Gioco del Calcio, Florence:** Men wearing 16th-century costumes play a soccer-like sport called *Gioco del Calcio.* Only the hardiest athletes participate in this very rough game, but the attendant pageantry appeals to everyone. (June 24 and 28.)

Festival of Two Worlds (Festival dei Due Mondi)

Spoleto **June/July**

This festival in the beautiful hill town of Spoleto was founded by composer Gian Carlo Menotti in 1957, and has become one of Italy's most respected cultural events. Music, opera, and ballet are accompanied by film and theater, making it an indulgent feast for refined senses.

Much of the magic is in the enchanting setting. The dukes of Lombard built Spoleto as their capital in the sixth, seventh, and eighth centuries, situating it on a lush hillside in Umbria. Although small, the town is packed with palaces, art treasures, and hanging gardens. Narrow, crooked streets and lively markets tempt visitors into spending several days or even weeks sniffing around.

Tickets for most performances sell out by March, so make plans early. Alternatively, you can attend one of Spoleto's sister festivals, in **Charleston, South Carolina** (USA) or **Melbourne, Australia.**

DATE: Mid-June through mid-July. **LOCATION:** Spoleto, Umbria. **TRANSPORT:** Spoleto is connected by train and bus to Rome, Ancona, Perugia, Assisi, Monteluco, and elsewhere. If you drive, know that parking can be hellish. **ACCOMMODATION:** The town has many hotels, guesthouses, hostels, and camping grounds, but you'll need to reserve several months in advance to get a space. **CONTACT:** Festival dei Due Mondi, via Cesare Beccaria 18 00186 Roma, Italy.

Palio in Siena provokes several days of riotous street parties culminating in a two-minute bareback race around the city's square. (Stephen Lengnick)

While You're There ...

- **Ardia, Sedilo:** Mellow Sardinia's wild side crops up in this dangerous horse race and carnival in honor of Constantine's victory over Maxentius. Contact: Local tourist office, Tel 0785-333541. (July 6 and 7.)
- **Festa di Noiantri, Rome:** When the posh people have left for vacation and the "real" Romans are left in charge of the city, one of the oldest quarters of Rome sets out a great pagan feast. Food, fireworks, and music fill the Trastevere neighborhood with an air of festivity. (Last half of July.)
- **Feast of the Redeemer, Venice:** To commemorate the 1575 end of a plague that hit Venice, Venetians make their city even more resplendent than it normally is. Boats of all sizes are illuminated with colored lanterns and brought out onto the canals, where passengers enjoy moveable feasts specially prepared for the occasion. Shoreside, people crowd the banks of the Grand Canal to watch the procession and two massive displays of fireworks, followed by music and dancing that continues until dawn. (Third weekend in July.)

Palio delle Contrade

Siena **July/August**

Medieval myth, emotion, and incomparable pageantry combine to create the most dramatic event in Siena's year. The object of all the fuss is a two-minute horse race around the city's main square,

Historical Regatta: "The finest street in the world" is filled with 16th-century splendor, as costumed Venetians race and parade in antique gondolas. (Tony Stone/Tony Stone Images)

every inch of which is packed with spectators. Unless you plan well—or are very lucky—you won't see much of it. But go anyway!

Siena is divided into 17 neighborhoods, or *contrade,* each of which desperately wants to win the *palio,* or winner's banner. Allegiances and rivalries are intense during the multi-day preparations, and by the day before the race, the city is at a fever pitch. Good luck feasts are served in each of the neighborhoods, and washed down with copious quantities of Chianti wine. It's a great party; foreign strangers are often welcomed as family and there's absolutely no shortage of fun.

The three days before the main race feature parades and several trial runs, and on the big morning both horses and riders are brought into neighborhood churches for blessings. In the afternoon people pack the square and grandstands, jostling for space. A cortege of officials and neighborhood residents parades around the plaza in Renaissance costumes to the ring of the bell in the Mangia Tower, and at 6:30 p.m. the race begins. It's a dangerous bareback ride, with 10 horses and riders sprinting three times around a track that's far too narrow. Horses are sometimes knocked down, riders are thrown off, and disputes often erupt into small-scale riots. For the *Sienese,* it's all part of the fun. In less than two minutes, it's over, and the winning *contrade* swarms its jockey, hoisting him on shoulders as the chaos boils over. The triumphant neighborhood becomes a huge teeming party, as wine spurts from fountains and the horse is the guest of honor. The following day, the winners parade through the city.

DATE: The event is held twice a year, on July 2 and August 16. **LOCATION:** Siena. **TRANSPORT:** Trains don't serve Siena directly, so take a bus from Rome or the main cities in Tuscany. **ACCOMMODATION:** Good luck. Unless you've reserved rooms about a year in advance, you'll probably have to stay in surrounding towns. **CONTACT:** Agenzia Viaggi SETI, Piazza del Campo 56, Siena 53100, Italy, Tel 0577-42209. Also, Italian State Tourist Office (see *Resources*).

While you're there ...

- **The Procession of the Thorned Men, Palmi:** "Thorned men" carrying portraits of the French pilgrim Saint Rocco wear cloaks of long, spiky thorns. (Closest Sunday to August 16.)
- **Historical Regatta, Venice:** The Grand Canal comes alive with 16th-century splendor, as gondolas and other vessels race and parade, their occupants dressed in historical costumes. (First Sunday in September.)
- **Human Chess Match, Marostica:** Costumed flesh-and-blood figures move around the great marble chessboard of the Castello Inferiore square on the orders of a herald speaking in a Venetian dialect. The four-day event is a celebration of a match that took place in 1454 between two youths vying for the right to marry the daughter of a lord. (First week of September in even years.)

Resources

In Italy: ENIT/Ente Nazionale Italiano per il Turismo, Via Marghera 2, I-00185 Rome, Tel 6-49711, Fax 6-4463379. **USA:** Italian State Tourist Office (ENIT), 630 Fifth Ave., Ste. 1565, New York, NY 10111, Tel (212) 245-4822, Fax (212) 843-6886; or, 1240 Wilshire Blvd., Suite 550, Los Angeles, CA 90025, Tel (310) 820-0098. **Canada:** Italian State Tourist Office (ENIT), 1 Place Ville Marie #1914, Montreal, PQ H3B 3M9, Tel (514) 866-7667, Fax (514) 392-1429. **UK:** Italian State Tourist Office (ENIT), 1 Princess St., London W1R 8AY, Tel 71-4081254, Fax 71-4936695. **Germany:** Italian State Tourist Office (ENIT), Kaiserstrasse 65, D-6000 Frankfurt/Main, Tel 69-237410, Fax 69-232894.

NETHERLANDS (HOLLAND)

Although old gabled houses still rise over quiet canals, the land of common sense and tolerance is much less inclined toward the traditional than most of Europe. Centuries of vigorous world-wide colonization had the unlikely result of making the Dutch into sophisticated "citizens of the world," and outsiders will note their tolerance for diverse religions and alternative lifestyles—as well as their cheerful accommodation of non-Dutch speakers.

In this land of Rembrandt and jazz, it's not surprising that festivals revolve around art and music. The Dutch love the opportunity to express their cosmopolitan taste by welcoming outside performers to their many jazz and world-music festivals, and the country's open intellectual life continues to attract great minds and artists.

HOLLAND FESTIVAL

Amsterdam and elsewhere **June**

A cutting-edge, contemporary repertoire makes the Holland Festival the high point of the Dutch cultural year. About 100,000 people pack into theaters and concert halls in June to catch theater, classical music, opera, and dance. The world's most adventurous directors and conductors consider it a coup to land an engagement here, but surprisingly spectators find no such competition for seats to most events. Even more surprising is the price—usually less than US$30 per performance. Venues include famed halls like the Royal Concertgebouw and the Het Muziektheater.

DATE: June. **LOCATION:** Throughout Amsterdam, and sometimes the Hague. **TRANSPORT:** Amsterdam is easily reached by air from any major city in the world, and by train from all over Europe. **ACCOMMODATION:** Amsterdam has one of the best selections of lodging in

Breda Old-Style Jazz Festival: In the mellow cafés of Breda, the Dutch herald the spring with traditional jazz from around the world. *(Netherlands Board of Tourism)*

Europe—in all price ranges. **CONTACT:** The Holland Festival, 21 Kleine-Gartmanspantsoen, 1017-RP, Amsterdam.

While you're there ...

Breda Old-Style Jazz Festival, Breda: The world's largest traditional jazz gathering highlights old-time compositions in a historic setting near the Belgian border. (Late March.)

Amsterdam: On the queen's birthday, canals are choked with revelers helping her majesty celebrate. (Esbin/Anderson/Omni-Photo Communications)

◎ **Queen's Day, nationwide:** The Dutch take the day off to celebrate Queen Beatrix's birthday with music, performances, and traditional games. (April 30.)

◎ **Keukenhof Flower Show, Lisse:** In the center of Holland's bulb-growing region, masterfully arranged blossoms form an explosion of color. Other hot spots for springtime flowers are the rural areas around Oegstgeest, De Zilk, Hillegom, and Noordwijkerhout. (April/May.)

◎ North Sea Jazz Festival

The Hague **July**

Many American jazz critics consider North Sea to be the very best jazz festival outside the US. The lineup is the secret of success; year after year the roster reads like a who's who of the international jazz scene. More than 1,000 musicians appear, spread over four days and 14 stages. Incredibly, it all takes place under the single roof of the Congress Hall.

DATE: Early July. **LOCATION:** Congress Hall, The Hague ('s Gravenhage). **TRANSPORT:** Trains from Delft, Rotterdam, and Amsterdam serve The Hague. Ferries run regularly from ports in England. **ACCOMMODATION:** A variety of accommodations are available, but there's not much for the budget traveler. Day tripping from Delft or Rotterdam is a viable option. **CONTACT:** North Sea Jazz Festival, PO Box 87840, 2508-DE, The Hague.

But is it legal?

No. Contrary to what you may see, hear, and smell, drugs are not legal in Holland. Possession of less than 30 grams of hashish or marijuana is subject to fines, and possession of more than this amount is a serious offense. Possession of any quantity of hard drugs is a serious offense.

The reason that so many people come to Amsterdam's coffee houses to buy and smoke openly is that the soft-drug laws usually aren't enforced. Since mellow dope smokers rarely cause anyone any trouble, the ever-pragmatic Dutch government has chosen largely to ignore the soft drug scene. Thai stick, sensimilla, and hashish are sold over the counter in many coffee houses. These bastions of the high life range in atmosphere from mellow to rockin', and are distinguished by plants in the window or the "Rastafarian" colors of red, yellow, and green.

International Zomerfeesten

Nijmegen **July**

World music is everywhere during this week-long festival in one of Europe's oldest towns. Located in the middle of the Dutch countryside, the provincial atmosphere gets overrun by a cavalcade of cosmopolitanism: As the rhythms of merengue and Madagascar fly from the stage, all the languages of Europe can be heard in the squares. At night, fireworks light up the sky and free-spirited dance fests prevail. This one's a hoot!

DATE: Mid- or late July. **LOCATION:** Nijmegen is located 20 km/12 miles south of Arnhem. **TRANSPORT:** Nijmegan can be reached by road or train from Arnhem or Amsterdam. **ACCOMMODATION:** Hotels and hostels are available in Nijmegen, Arnhem, and other nearby cities. **CONTACT:** Netherlands Board of Tourism (see *Resources*).

While you're there ...

- **Mussel Day, Yerseke:** Huge steaming vats of mussels are brought into the town square for an all-you-can-eat feast. (Saturday in mid-August.)
- **Prinsjesdag, The Hague:** In an elaborate display of pageantry, the queen and her prince depart the Palace Noordeinde to open Parliament at the Binnenhof. Thousands of people turn out to watch the military band

escort of the Dutch royalty in a golden, horse-drawn coach. (Third Tuesday of September.)

Brandaris Balkoppenrace, Enkhuizen: Fishing vessels duke it out with a huge tug-of-war on the Ijsselmeer Lake. (Usually the last weekend of September.)

Resources

In the Netherlands: Nederlands Bureau voor Toerisme, Vlietweg 15, NL-2266 MG Leidschendam, Tel 70-3705705, Fax 70-3201654. **USA:** Netherlands Board of Tourism, 355 Lexington Ave., 21st Fl., New York, NY 10017, Tel (212) 370-7360, Fax (212) 370-9507. **Canada:** Netherlands Board of Tourism, 25 Adelaide St. E., #710, Toronto, ON M5C 1Y2, Tel (416) 363-1577, Fax (416) 363-1470. **UK:** Netherlands Board of Tourism, 25-28 Buckingham Gate, GB-London SW1E 6NT, Tel 71-6300451, Fax 71-8287941. **Germany:** Netherlands Board of Tourism, Postfach 270580, D-5000 Cologne 1, Tel 221-2570383, Fax 221-2570381. **Australia:** Netherlands Board of Tourism, 5 Elizabeth St., 6th Fl., Sydney, NSW 2000, Tel 2-2476921, Fax 2-2236665.

PORTUGAL

Caught between the rest of Europe and the Atlantic, Portugal was the first country on the continent to reach across the high seas to the new world. What its adventurers found there—in Africa, Asia, and South America—profoundly altered the course of the country's and the world's history. Even though the 20th century was a period of decline, Portugal continues to be graced by stunning architecture, cuisine, and culture that make it a captivating destination.

This country of discoverers is still undiscovered by travelers—at least relative to the rest of western Europe. In comparison to its Iberian neighbor, Portugal is a working man's country, and a bargain for visitors. Portuguese celebrations—and Portuguese life in general—are much less ostentatious than those of Spain. Yet many similarities remain, including an absorbtion in the mysteries of religion, a love of wine and food (the country has Europe's most highly developed sea cuisine), and a determination to celebrate. There's a different feast day, festival, or market every day of the year in Portugal; all are occasions to meet the country's warm, gentle people amidst the astounding landscapes and simple villages they call home.

HOLY WEEK

Braga **March/April**

Braga tries to outdo the world with its spectacular Holy Week celebrations. Considered Portugal's most pious (or fanatic), the people of Braga take on Holy Week with a fervor that contrasts with their conservative reputation. Black and purple decorations cover the streets, and processions rival even the world-famous Semana Santa parades in Seville. Braga's most elaborate Holy Week processions take place on Monday, Thursday, and Friday, and feature bejeweled floats and masked marchers bearing holy images. Alongside, torches, folk-dancing, and fireworks add color and character to the celebration.

DATE: From Palm Sunday to Good Friday. **LOCATION:** Braga, in the northwest region of Minho. **TRANSPORT:** Trains and buses run regu-

Fátima: In comemmoration of a 1917 apparition of the Virgin Mary, crowds line the huge plaza to witness formal processions during one of the most elaborate religious shows on earth. (Tony Arruza/Bruce Coleman Inc.)

larly from Lisbon. **ACCOMMODATION:** You'll find a plethora of hotels for all budgets. **CONTACT:** Comissao Municipal de Turismo de Braga, Avenida da Liberade 1, P-4700 Braga, Tel 53-22550.

PILGRIMAGE TO FÁTIMA

Fátima **May**

An astounding series of events made Fátima one of the Catholic world's major pilgrimage sites. According to legend, on May 13,

A teenage girl pauses between dances during Costa Verde's Festival of Our Lady of the Roses. (Steve Vidler/Leo de Wys)

1917, as three children tended their sheep, the Virgin Mary appeared in the sky to call for peace and warn against Godless communism. Word of the vision spread throughout Portugal, and Mary appeared several more times that summer, drawing bigger and bigger crowds until an October morning when 70,000 people gathered in the rain. According to witnesses, at noon the sun spun around in the sky several times, then sank toward the earth. When the spectacle was over everything was dry and there was no evidence of the morning's torrential rains.

Regardless of your take on this well-documented "miracle," Fátima's impressive "religious amusement park" is well worth the trip. The basilica dominates a plaza as big as a football field, where a procession with a statue of the Madonna caps off the pilgrimage, and masses are given inside the chapel in six languages. A wax museum has eyewitness scenes of the original events—as well as somewhat more speculative scenes of hell—while another museum re-creates the event in a sound and light show. It's also captured in dozens of variations of postcards for sale, some of which report, "I prayed for you in Fátima."

DATE: The first apparition is commemorated with a big pilgrimage May 12–13, but several more occur throughout the summer, with the final pilgrimage taking place on October 12. **LOCATION:** Fátima. **TRANSPORT:** Fátima lies about 60 km/37 miles east of Nazaré, and 140 km/87 miles north of Lisbon. Buses are frequent from all over Portugal, and trains serve a station about 20 km/14 miles outside town. **ACCOMMODATION:** July and August are the high months and rooms tend to be more expensive and scarce. **CONTACT:** Agencia Peregrianacoes Fatima, Rue Jacinto Marto, Ed. Joao Paulo, 11, P-2495 Fatima, Tel 49-52767.

While you're there ...

Festival of Our Lady of the Roses, Viana do Castelo: In Viana do Castelo and surrounding villages, monstrous flower pageants mark the spring, and women parade through town with beautiful rose tapestries carried above their heads. (May.)

Feast of St. John

Porto (Oporto) and elsewhere **June**

The home of the famous port wine is the most colorful venue for festivities in honor of *São João,* although Braga, Vila do Conde, Évora, and Figueira da Foz also celebrate in high style. In Porto, street corners sprout *cascatas* (religious motifs), and revelers set up bonfires to illuminate their great bouts of all-night singing and dancing. The energy of this attractive harbor town is incredible, and in every corner of the city huge quantities of wine (fortified and otherwise) flow all night. In Vila do Conde the feast is marked by bonfires, arrangements of lights, and processions of women in traditional costumes who lead a candlelight parade to the beach. In Braga, Évora, and Figueira da Foz, the celebrations are similarly devout and spirited.

DATE: June 23 and 24. **LOCATION:** Porto (Oporto), Vila do Conde, Braga, Évora, and Figueira da Foz. **TRANSPORT:** From Lisbon, trains and buses make the five-hour trip to Porto several times daily. **ACCOMMODATION:** Porto's many summer visitors are underserved by hotels and *pensãos;* reserve in advance to be sure. **CONTACT:** Comissao Municipal de Turismo do Porto, Rua Clube dos Fenianos 25, P-4000 Porto, Tel 2-323303, Fax 2-384548.

Festival of the Holy Ghost

Azores Islands **May–July**

Although the Festival of the Holy Ghost has almost disappeared from continental Portugal, it's been celebrated on the Azores Islands since the late 15th century. From Easter through July, the Azores are in almost constant festival mode, with celebrations moving from village to village and usually including folk dances, bullfights, and plenty of singing and dancing.

The *bodos* (banquets) are occasions of great excitement in the villages of the Azores, and in all cases the sacred and the profane are well mixed. Each *bodo* includes huge amounts of food and wine, special masses, fireworks, and the crowning of an

St. Peter's Festival: Children parade through Povoa de Varzim in honor of the patron saint of fishermen. *(Robert Frerck/Odyssey Productions/Chicago)*

"emperor." *Folias,* costumed groups of musicians and singers, attend balls and street parties and sing medieval ballads. Jesters move among the crowds of guests, and special offerings are made in colorful rituals. The village of Rabo de Peixe, on the north shore, hosts one of the most spirited festivals, with local residents leading beautifully trimmed ox carts through the neighborhoods.

DATE: May, June, and July. High points of ritual activity occur on Pentecost and Trinity Sunday. **LOCATION:** Celebrations are scattered through towns and villages in the Azores; for the current year's schedule, contact the SRTA (see below). **TRANSPORT:** The Azores can be reached by air from Lisbon and elsewhere in western

Europe. Scheduled and chartered flights are available from New York and Boston. **ACCOMMODATION:** In the larger towns, hotels, pensions, and residences are available. **CONTACT:** Secretaria Regional do Turismo e Ambiente (SRTA), Edificio do Relogio, Colonia Alema, P-9900 Horta, Ilha de Faial, Azores/Portugal, Tel 96-23286.

St. Peter's Festival, Sintra and Povoa de Varzim: Portugal's biggest agricultural fair brings farmers from nearby villages to Sintra, one of Portugal's oldest and most romantic towns, which features a spectacular castle and dozens of palaces and ruins. In the northern port of Povoa de Varzim, fishermen honor San Pedro with processions and parties. (June 29.)

Vila Franca de Xira **July**

Portugal's answer to Pamplona's Running of the Bulls gets its name from the costumed cowboys who strut down main street, followed by wild bulls. The nightly runs are more tame than Pamplona, since only the "professionals" are involved. Yet this event is more precious in its own way, with a variety of colorful clothing and traditions that haven't come under pressure from hoards of tourists.

The red-vested men are *campinos,* or cowboys who herd the bulls in the nearby pastures. In their waistcoats and green stocking caps, they perform the *Ribatejan Fandango,* a competitive, highly athletic dance for men only. Bullfights are particularly comic, since the bulls (with padded horns) get to take on amateurs and professionals, and the beasts are not killed in the ring, as in Spain. In the afternoons and evenings, special grills are brought into the street to cook deliciously spiced sardines, and everyone participates in wild spurts of nighttime drinking.

DATE: First week in July. **LOCATION:** Vila Franca de Xira, about 40 km/25 miles north of Lisbon on the River Tejo (Tagus). **TRANSPORT:** Buses leave regularly from Lisbon. **ACCOMMODATION:** The town has several hotels and pensions; alternatively, you can day-trip from Lisbon or coastal towns. **CONTACT:** Portuguese National Tourist Office (see *Resources*).

Viano do Castelo **August**

Great name, great festival! For three days, the town of Viano do Castelo is overwhelmed with religious passion—but it never gets

In Sagres and nearby towns, September's Folk Music and Dance Festival is a great time to experience the centuries-old songs and dances of the Algarve region. (Bob Krist/Leo de Wys)

in the way of a great time. This is one of Portugal's most colorful celebrations, and it draws a huge contingent of women from neighboring villages, who march in honor of Our Lady. The music is excellent, and the singing and dancing carries on into the wee hours. An agricultural fair springs up, and carpets of bright flowers are laid down for the main event. Our Lady's statue is carried over the colorful carpet by hundreds of women, who wear matching native costumes of orange, scarlet, and blue. Around each neck are gold necklaces—sometimes dozens—with pendants in the shape of the cross or a heart. After the parade fireworks explode by the riverside.

DATE: The weekend nearest to August 20. **LOCATION:** Viano do Castelo. **TRANSPORT:** Trains serve Viano do Castelo from Vila Nova de Cerveira, Barcelos, Porto, and points in Spain. Buses run daily from Braga and Lisbon. **ACCOMMODATION:** Lodging is generally easy to find—except during this festival. Many private homes offer an alternative to the higher-priced hotels. **CONTACT:** Regiao de Turismo do Alto Minho (Costa Verde), Rua do Hospital Velho, P-4900 Viana do Castelo, Tel 58-822620, Fax 58-829798.

While you're there ...

- **Feast of Our Lady of Monte, Madeira:** The most important religious procession on Madeira follows up pious obligation with a profane outburst of fun. Ukeleles are brought out, and a unique form of singing gossip called *desafio* relates all the news in rhyming form. At night people light special lamps and dance and carouse until dawn. (August 14–15; Assumption Day and Eve.)
- **Festas da Santa Barbara, Miranda do Douro:** Fans of folk dancing will relish this festival and the chance to view the *pingacho* (ethnic ballet), the *Geribalda* (round dance), and the *Mira-me Miguel* (square dance). The event also features dancing sword fighters, who wear flowered hats and aprons. (Third Sunday in August.)
- **Folk Music and Dance Festival, Algarve Region:** This festival is an easy yet rewarding way to experience the centuries-old songs and dances of the Southern Portuguese. All larger towns of the Algarve—Silves, Albufeira, Lagos, and Faro—join in a weekend of celebration that culminates in Praia da Rocha on Sunday night. (Early September.)
- **Vinho Verde Fair, Braga:** If you like your wine tart and fruity, bring your goblet! Highlights of this week-long event include wine-tasting, hosted by many of the area's producers and bottlers of "green wine," named for its age rather than its color. Festivities take place in the Palacio Municipal de Esposicaos. (Late September.)

Resources

In Portugal: Direcção-Geral do Turismo, Avenida Antonio Augusto de Aguiar 86, Caixa Postal 1929, P-1004 Lisbon-Cedex, Tel 1-3155086, Fax 1-3556917. **USA:** Portuguese National Tourist Office, 590 Fifth Ave., New York, NY 10036-4704, Tel (212) 354-4403, Fax (212) 764-6137. **Canada:** Portuguese National Tourist Office, 60 Bloor St. W., #1005, Toronto, ON M4W 3B8, Tel (416) 921-7376, Fax (416) 921-1353. **UK:** Portuguese Trade and Tourism Office, 22/25A Sackville St., GB-London W1X 1DE, Tel 71-4941441, Fax 71-4941868. **Germany:** Portugiesisches Touristik und Handelsbüro, Schafergasse 17, 60313 Frankfurt, Tel 69-234094, Fax 69-231433. **Australia:** Embassy of Portugal, 6 Campion St., Deakin (Canberra), ACT 2600, Tel 6-2852084, Fax 6-2823705.

SCOTLAND

Scotland's unique character and heritage come through loud and clear at Scottish festivals, fairs, and clan gatherings. Here, the exuberant spirit of the countryside can be seen and felt in the games, clothing, and music. Few of these country events are put on for tourists—in fact, at some events tourists are actually discouraged so locals in the tourist trades can skip work to participate.

It would seem impossible to upstage Scotland's stunning lochs, mountains, and valleys, yet many people come to Scotland for its elegant cities where arts festivals are held each summer. Edinburgh in particular demands the spotlight each August, as the international aesthetic community adopts the city as its temporary world capital.

Hogmany and New Year's Day

Comrie, Stonehaven, and nationwide **December/January**

Fireballs ward off ancient evil spirits as the procession makes its way through the crowded city streets, reveling and singing in the new year. At midnight, church bells chime and Scotch whiskey bottles are passed around as the community bursts into the world's most spirited rendition of "Auld Lang Syne."

Hogmany, which begins on New Year's Eve and merges into New Year's Day festivities, is celebrated in different ways from one town to another, although the new year is always welcomed with fire. For instance, Comrie is known for its Flambeaux (torch) procession, whereas participants at Stonehaven are more likely to swing fireballs attached to handles with long wires. It's believed that the fireball tradition finds its roots in a symbolic attempt to call back Mr. Sun—who makes only a few half-hearted appearances in the winter months in the far north. One interesting tradition that has more in common with Asia than the rest of Europe, is the "first-foot." Scots want the first person who crosses their threshold in the new year to be a dark-haired person who brings coal, salt, and a bottle of whiskey—symbols of warmth, food, and merriment for the upcoming year.

Up-Helly-Aa: In remote Lerwick in the Shetland Isles, Guizers *prepare to torch a replica of a Viking ship.* *(Homer Sykes/Woodfin Camp & Associates)*

DATE: December 31 and January 1. **LOCATION:** Comrie, Stonehaven, and nationwide. **TRANSPORT:** Buses out of Edinburgh and trains or buses out of Aberdeen will drop you at Stonehaven, which is on the coast, 20 km/13 miles south of Aberdeen, and just off A92. Comrie, 65 km/40 miles northwest of Edinburgh on the River Earn, can be reached by bus from Edinburgh or Dundee. **ACCOMMODATION:** In the seaside resort town of Stonehaven, you'll find plenty of accommodations, although a larger selection—and more reasonable prices—can be found in Aberdeen. Comrie has hotels and B&Bs, as do many of the surrounding villages. **CONTACT:** Scottish Tourist Board (see *Resources*).

Up-Helly-Aa

Lerwick, Shetland Islands **January**

Scotland's most spectacular flaming extravaganza is held in the remote Shetland Islands. The object of the celebrants' pyromania is a 30-foot model Viking longship, which is brought to the seafront after a proclamation simply called "The Bill" is posted at Market Cross.

Onlookers gather to remember their Norse roots as the "Guizer Jarl," dressed in a spectacular Viking costume, takes the steering oar. Participants then drag the ship to the designated spot, followed by dozens of torch-bearing Guizers, and everyone sings the "Galley Song." After the Guizer Jarl disembarks, a bugle sounds and the fire-bearers throw hundreds of blazing torches upon the ship, engulfing it in flames. The singers then burst into "The Norseman's Home," and celebrations continue through the long northern night.

Unfortunately, you can't just show up as a casual visitor at this festival, since if too many visitors came, the Shetlanders who run hotels and restaurants wouldn't be able to attend the events. You'll need an invitation. If you're serious about seeing this spectacular event, venture to Lerwick some other time of year and make some friends!

DATE: The last Tuesday in January. **LOCATION:** Lerwick, Shetland Islands. **TRANSPORT:** Lerwick can be reached by ferry or airplane from Orkney, Aberdeen, and Bergen, Norway. **ACCOMMODATION:** Hotels and guest houses shut down during Up-Helly-Aa. **CONTACT:** Shetland Islands Tourism, Market Cross, GB-Lerwick, Shetland Islands ZE1 0LU, Tel 595-3434, Fax 595-5807. Also, Scottish Tourist Board (see *Resources*).

While you're there ...

The Burning of the Clavie, Burghead: As if the flaming wonder of Hogmany weren't enough, the Promethean residents of Burghead set the night afire once again on January 11. The Clavie, a tar-filled barrel, is lit by the year's Clavie King, then toted in procession through the streets of Burghead to Doorie Hill. Contact: Moray District Tourist Board, 17 A High Street, GB-Elgin, Moray IV30 1EG, Tel 343-543388, Fax 343-540183. (January 11.)

Common Ridings

The Borders **June/July**

Originally a military exercise to secure the town's defenses, the Common Riding has evolved (devolved?) into a wild, romping town party that lasts anywhere from a weekend to an entire week. The hilly Borders region, which served for centuries as Scotland's last line of defense against invasion, is the setting for main events called "ride-outs." Led by "principals" whose "troops" follow on horseback around the town's outer limits, "ride-outs" symbolically ensure that no rival clans have shifted the stone fences that form local borders.

Other events—the Cornet's Walk, the Proclaiming of the Burgh Officer, and the Snuffing Ceremony, just to name a few—usually begin with a modicum of high ceremony, and degenerate into hilarious exhibitions of Scottish wit. Through it all, the pubs are open almost non-stop, and locals can be counted upon to go "stone mad." If you're anywhere near a common riding, don't miss it!

DATE/LOCATION: Hawick (first or second weekend in June); Selkirk, Peebles, or Melrose (second week in June); Jedburgh (first week in July); Kelso (mid-July); Lauder and Langholm (late July). **TRANSPORT:** There are no trains in the Borders region, but good bus service runs from Edinburgh and from the English town of Berwick-upon-Tweed, which are well connected by train. **ACCOMMODATION:** Hotels and hostels are interspersed throughout the region. **CONTACT:** Scottish Borders Tourist Board, Municipal Building, 70 High Street, GB-Selkirk TD7 4JX, Tel 750-63435, Fax 750-21886.

- **Aberdeen Bon-Accord Week, Aberdeen:** A colorful parade down Union Street marks the start of this week-long event. Grab a brew from the beer garden and enjoy a pleasant selection of musical treats, including an authentic pipe band. (Late June.)
- **Glasgow Folk Festival, Glasgow:** This amicable international festival's roaring array of folklore, music, and dance draws the socially conscious from the UK and everywhere else. (Early July.)

BRAEMAR ROYAL HIGHLAND GATHERING

Braemar **September**

The life and legends of Scotland are presented in this colorful pageant, which features traditional sports, music, and dancing—and big crowds of spectators. One of the largest of the Highland Gatherings, this extravaganza takes place on the rolling hills of Braemar, where highland games have been held for almost 1,000 years.

The "heavy events" draw the most spectators. In the caber toss, a six-meter (19-foot) tree trunk is handed upright to the

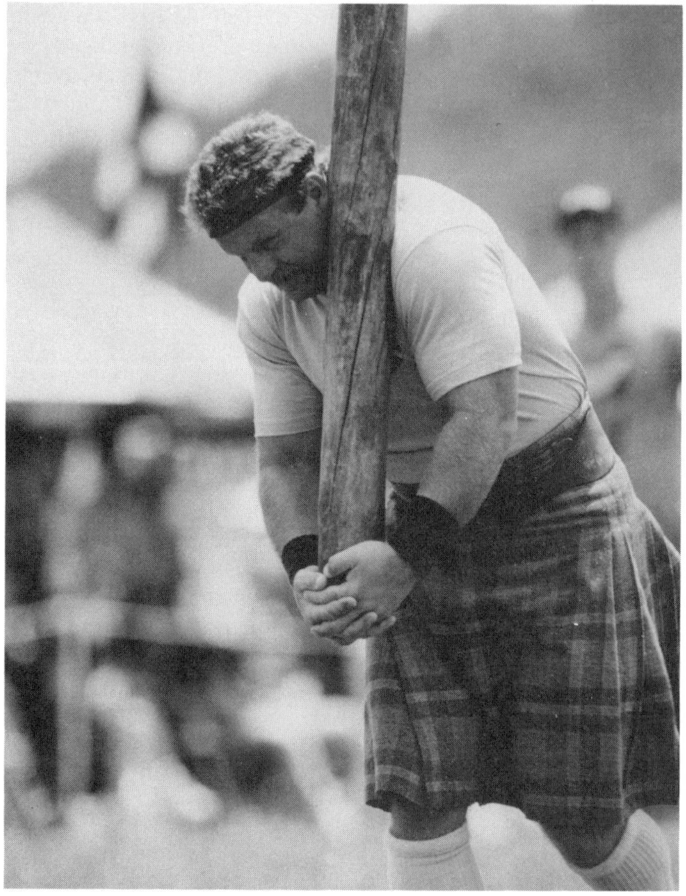

Tossing the caber: This Highland Games event features grunting lads who try to toss the tree trunk the farthest and most stylishly. (Tom Raymond/Tony Stone Images)

squatting competitor, who staggers across the ground with it and finally heaves it as a judge observes his "form." This sport began back when felled tree trunks were thrown into the river and sent downstream to the saw mill.

Hammer-hurling and shot-putting are somewhat different from the Olympic events, and were originally played as a means of selecting the strongest royal bodyguards. The competitors practice and warm up as pipe music floats through the air, and various clans wear their colors on tartan kilts. Dancers twirl around in traditional Scottish garb, performing crowd-pleasers like the Sword Dance, Old Trousers, and the Highland Fling. The Highland

The Highlanders' Wild Games

From early May through mid-September, more than 100 Highland Gatherings are held in Scotland. The big games (Braemar, Cowal, and Oban) offer plenty of spectacle and a chance to see the very best competitors among an international gang of spectators. But the smaller meetings (such as Ceres, or Uist in the Hebrides) can be more rewarding for visitors, since you'll have the chance to mingle with Scots who care more about comradery than glamour.

Some of the most important gatherings include the Aberdeen Games (mid-June); the Atholl Gathering at Blair Castle, Pitlochry (late May); the Inveraray Games (mid-July); the Cupar Games (early July); the Balloch Games (mid-July); the Cowal Gathering at Dunoon (late August); the Argyllshire Games at Oban (late August); and the Isle of Skye Games at Portree (early August).

Games, particularly those at Braemar, have become fashionable and popular in the past few years, drawing about 25,000 people.

DATE: First Saturday in September. **LOCATION:** Braemar, in the Grampian Mountains. **TRANSPORT:** Braemar can be reached via bus from Dundee or Aberdeen. **ACCOMMODATION:** Since the Highland Gatherings bring people from all over the world to the small town of Braemar, plan ahead. Locally run hotels and guest houses are available, as is camping. **CONTACT:** Mr. W.A. Meston, Coilacriech, Ballater AB35 5UH, Tel 03397-55377.

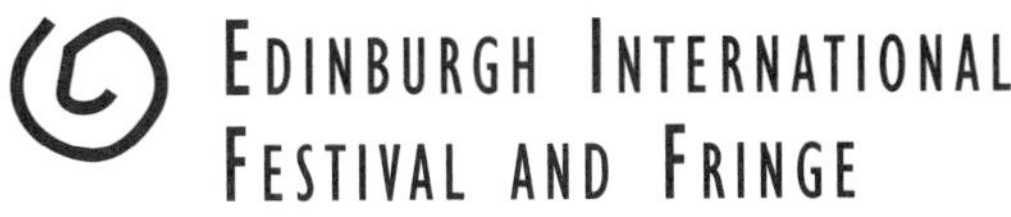

Edinburgh International Festival and Fringe

Edinburgh **August**

In August the eyes of the cultural world turn to Edinburgh. Begun as a series of classical music, opera, dance, and theater performances, the Edinburgh International Festival has been joined, and maybe even bettered, by several other concurrent festivals in Scotland's magnificent capital. For three weeks there's absolutely no possibility of getting bored in Edinburgh, as incredibly diverse events compete for attention and threaten to overload the senses.

The largest of the festivals is the Fringe, which originated as a low-brow alternative to the sophisticated festival. Anyone willing to pay the nominal registration fee may perform, and in the past performers have included experimental and children's theater groups, poetry readers, and mimes. Though the Fringe has generated controversy (as exemplified by the recent spat over a feminist, occasionally nude version of Mozart's opera *Donna Giovanni*) it is now generally accepted—and it sells far more tickets than the original festival. This disturbs those with a yen for the daringly avant-garde, and there have been ongoing attempts to set up a Fringe Fringe Society that offers truly alternative art. In addition to the International Festival and the Fringes, there's even more: a jazz festival, an international film festival, a television festival, and a big military tattoo.

DATE: The last three weeks of August. **LOCATION:** Edinburgh. **TRANSPORT:** Edinburgh is easily reachable by air from cities all over the world and by train from London. **ACCOMMODATION:** Edinburgh has plenty of hotels and other lodging, but they're all booked solid during the festival. Make reservations well in advance. **CONTACT:** Edinburgh International Festival, 21 Market Street, Edinburgh EH1 1BW, Tel 031-226-4001, Fax 031-225-1173. Tourist Information Office, Waverley Market, Princes Street 3, GB-Edinburgh EH2 2QP, Tel 31-5571700, Fax 31-5575118.

While you're there ...

- **The Viking Games, Fairlie:** Brawn and proficiency vie for the prize in these sensational games that pit the Scandinavians against the Scots. Battering ram races, longboat hauling, and McGlashen Stone hurling are part of the competition. (Last weekend in August.)
- **National Mod, Stirling:** Comparable to Wales' National Eisteddfod, the Mod celebrates Gaelic culture with friendly tournaments in music, poetry, and dance. Dating back to 1891, this event is a favorite of most of the country's Gaels. (August.)

Resources

In Scotland: Scottish Tourist Board, PO Box 705, 23 Ravelston Terrace: GB-Edinburgh EH4 3EU Tel 31-3322433, Fax 31-3431513. **Elsewhere in the UK:** Scottish Tourist Board, 19 Cockspur Street, GB-London SW1Y 5BL, Tel 71-9308661, Fax 71-9301817. **USA:** British Tourist Authority, 40 West 57th Street, New York, NY 10019-4001 Tel (212) 581-4700, Fax (212) 265-0649. **Germany:** British Tourist Authority, Taunusstr. 52-60, D-6000 Frankfurt/M 1, Germany Tel 69-2380711, Fax 69-2380717. **Australia:** British Tourist Authority, 210 Clarence Street, Sydney, NSW 2000, Australia Tel 2-2674555, Fax 2-2674442.

SPAIN

After living without many of their beloved celebrations through several decades of dictatorship, the Spanish now seem obsessed with demonstrating their partying prowess to the world. Spain's celebrations are phenomenal outbursts that can involve anything from loose bulls stampeding through streets to papier-mâché fat-heads spinning in squares, to fire-walkers, tomato-throwers, wine-squirters, and "fighting" Christians and Moors.

The residents of Europe's most popular holiday playground hop from one festival to another, preparing and executing extravaganzas with astonishing energy. These extremely lively, sensual events mix the pious and profane in a monstrous, comical whirl that often features statues of patron saints as the center of attention in an orgiastic street-bash. No one—not even the clergy—dares to protest, for after so many stifling years, Spain is unmistakably alive!

Carnival

Cadiz and Santa Cruz de Tenerife February/March

On the mainland, the pre-Lenten carnival scene is liveliest in Cadiz and Sitges. One of the most unusual celebrations takes place in Viana del Bollo, as men in bizarre striped costumes leap up and down while gouging the earth with staffs to encourage fertility. The Canary Islands port of Santa Cruz de Tenerife does Carnival Brazilian-style, with wild rhythms, lavish costumes, and half-nude dancing in the streets. This former "gateway to the Americas," located off the coast of Morocco, spends the week engulfed in flamboyance and abandon, much of it imported by vacationing northern Europeans.

DATE: The week before Ash Wednesday. **LOCATION:** Cadiz on the mainland and Santa Cruz de Tenerife in the Canary Islands have the liveliest carnivals. **TRANSPORT:** Buses serve Cadiz from Seville, Jerez, and Algeciras. Charters and regularly scheduled flights serve Santa Cruz de Tenerife from all over Europe. **ACCOMMODATION:** Carnival puts the squeeze on hotel space in both cities. **CONTACT:** Tourist Office of Spain (see *Resources*).

Carnival: In Cadiz and all over mainland Spain and the Canary Islands, streets explode with music, dancing, and thousands of Carnival revelers. (Daniel Aubry/Odyssey Productions/Chicago)

Fallas de San José

Valencia **March**

The first sparks of spring fever are stoked into a massive blaze at this festival, engulfing Valencia in the flames of hundreds of bonfires. At the center of action are papier mâché effigies of horses and humans, packed with fireworks and set on fire. This grotesque orgy of destruction has a seducing effect, sending Valencians and visitors alike into passionate all-night romps filled with music and romance.

The dramatic week of celebration begins on March 12, when the *ninots* (effigies) are brought out for display. The horse, worshiped in pre-Christian Spain, is the central motif, but celebrities and political figures are also common. Competing "brotherhoods" spend months crafting the enormous, colorful sculptures of wood, cardboard, and papier mâché, knowing that only the single most beautiful *ninot* will be saved. Throughout the week leading up to the night of San José, music fills the streets and the excitement builds. On March 19 the town is crowded with visitors, and everyone takes to the streets and the hills to build huge bonfires. By midnight more than 300 are burning, and the massive sculptures—some five stories tall—are set ablaze.

DATE: March 12–19. **LOCATION:** Valencia. **TRANSPORT:** Trains run from Seville, Madrid, and Barcelona, while buses connect with large cities and many smaller towns. **ACCOMMODATION:** Rooms are generally easy to find in Valencia, but reserve ahead for lodging during

Feria de Abril: A simple horse fair has evolved into a series of full-blown spectacles that celebrate the coming of spring. (Daniel Aubry/Odyssey Productions/Chicago)

the Fallas. **CONTACT:** Dirección General de Turismo de la Generalidad de Valencia, Isabel la Catolica 8, E-46004 Valencia, Tel 6-386-7783. Also, Tourist Office of Spain (see *Resources*).

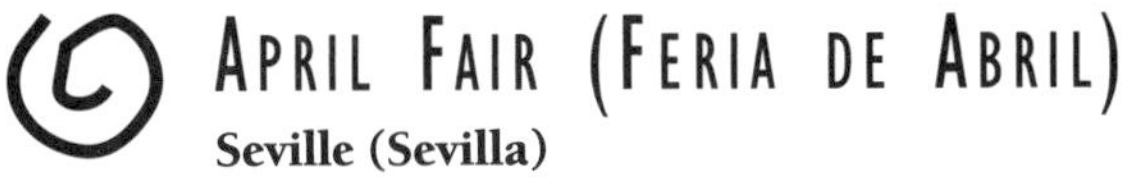

April Fair (Feria de Abril)

Seville (Sevilla) **April**

Seville rewards itself for surviving "winter" by throwing up a bunch of tents and stalls near the river and going on a spree. From a simple horse fair the festival has evolved into a series of full-blown daytime spectacles, featuring parades of horsemen, circuses, and Spain's most important bullfights. Beautiful Andalusian horses trot by with costumed cowboys and swarthy beauties riding sidesaddle in Gypsy dresses.

At night the binge spills into the city. Thousands of lanterns light the night, flamenco groups sing and dance on jasmined balconies, and the aroma of saffron and garlic is everywhere. Wine and sangría flow non-stop, and for six days and nights the Feria continues at an incredible spinning pace, a tireless, sensual blowout in one of the world's impossibly fabulous cities.

DATE: Six days near the end of April (usually two or three weeks after Holy Week). **LOCATION:** Seville (Sevilla). **TRANSPORT:** Seville is easily reached by train, bus, or car, and the airport receives domestic and selected international flights. **ACCOMMODATION:** Prices soar and rooms are almost nonexistent during the April Fair, so book several months ahead. **CONTACT:** Dirección General de Turismo, Avenida Republica Argentina 31-B 2a.p., E-41011 Sevilla, Tel 5-4263610. Also, Tourist Office of Spain (see *Resources*).

Battle of the Moors and Christians

Alcoi (Alicante region) **April**

In Spain's many Moors-and-Christians festivals, the crusades are reenacted in spectacularly costumed and staged battles. Typically the festivities start with a parade, then the cross takes on the crescent moon in a bloodless skirmish. The Moors get to wear the most outrageous costumes, but the Christians always win—sometimes it's close, though.

Alcoi's festival is outstanding. The parades and battles are marched and fought with split-second timing, and great Valencian music blends with fireworks and crowd noise to create a sensual cacophony that continues deep into the night.

A simultaneous Moors-and-Christians Festival takes place in nearby Bañeres. At Onteniente in Valencia (April 20–24), the festival is much smaller, but the costumes are even better. Similar festivals are held throughout southeastern Spain, in Altea (the third Sunday in May), Villajoyosa (July 23–31), and Marcia (September 1–5).

DATE: Alcoi's festival coincides with the festivities in honor of St. George the Martyr, and is held April 22–24. **LOCATION:** Alcoi (also called Alcoy) in Alicante region. **TRANSPORT:** By car or bus, Alcoi is about 45 km/28 miles north of Alicante, and about 100 km/62 miles south of Valencia. Both Alicante and Valencia have airports handling internal flights. **ACCOMMODATION:** The few hotels in town

Preparing for battle: The townspeople of Alcoi disguise themselves as Moors and Christians to re-enact the holy wars. A huge party breaks out after, but only if the "good guys" win.
(Krammer/Tourist Office of Spain)

usually fill up around the festival, but there's always plenty of lodging on the coast. **CONTACT:** Servicio Territorial de Turismo, Artilleros 4, E-03002 Alicante, Tel 6-5123544. Also, Tourist Office of Spain (see *Resources*).

Holy Week (Semana Santa)

Nationwide **March/April**

The death and rebirth of Jesus is celebrated in Spain with unrivaled pageantry that gathers the country's many disparate influ-

During Holy Week in Seville, hooded penitents chant their prayers while carrying tall candles. (Robert Frerck/Odyssey Productions/Chicago)

ences—Christian and pagan, carnal and spiritual, sorrowful and celebratory—and combines them in impressively imaginative and flamboyant events. Wherever you are in Spain, you're sure to see a lot of unforgettable action. Here are some of the hot spots:

Seville is host to the most famous Semana Santa celebration in Spain, where hooded, candle-bearing penitents parade through streets saturated with people. Floats bearing life-sized figures are carried on the shoulders of more than 50 religious brotherhoods. Images of the Virgin (*La Macarena*) and *Jesús del Gran Poder* create a frenzy of excitement as they pass through the streets.

The *tamboradas* or drumbeats of **Teruel** throb through the night to announce the passion and death of Christ. After hours and hours of ceaseless drumming, streams of blood run over the bandaged hands of many men. In **Malaga**, the week is marked by grieving songs and processions of heavy floats carried on the shoulders of rhythmically moving bearers.

On Good Friday in **Murcia**, men in huge hats blow on long *bocina* horns, making a sound that conveys Christ's suffering. **Lorca** marks its celebrations with imaginative extravagance, and as two local guilds compete with each other to put on the best show, the scene become circus-like.

The **Castile** region's austerity shows itself with processions that are grim in comparison to Andalusian celebrations. **Valladolid** is host to a somber procession of hooded penitents and floats bearing wooden figures. The sound of dismally beaten drums and despondent trumpets mark the graveness of **Zamora's** procession.

The people of Spain become Thespians when ancient passion plays are staged by citizens in towns around the country. These plays are based on traditional texts and are usually performed by locals in picturesque surroundings. Some of the best are in **Benetúser, Callosa de Segura, Cervera, Chinchón, Esparraguera, Olesa de Montserrat, Ulldecona, Valmaseda,** and **Verges.**

DATE: The week leading up to and including Easter. **LOCATION:** Nationwide. **CONTACT:** Tourist Office of Spain (see *Resources*).

Romería del Rocio

Almonte **May**

Spain's biggest festival draws up to a million pilgrims to the countryside of Huelva. Some arrive on horses or decorated ox-drawn carts, and many dress in traditional outfits and sleep in the open air. It's a dusty trip across plains and through marshlands; it's also a great opportunity to experience the region's religious fervor, as nighttime processions and celebrations are particularly large and colorful. Around the shrine there's ongoing chaos, as traditional masses, candlelight parades, and lots of music-making give the event the air of a huge, unwieldy family reunion. For many, the religious theme is just an excuse to get out into the country for some wild carrying-on.

DATE: The weekend of Pentecost (50 days after Easter). **LOCATION:** Almonte in the Huelva region is located 60 km (40 miles) west of Seville. **TRANSPORT:** Buses leave Seville for Almonte several times a day, but even with extra buses running, finding a seat can be difficult during the pilgrimage. **ACCOMMODATION:** There's no real accommodation at the site; you should plan to either camp or day-trip

After trekking across the plains in horse-drawn wagons, pilgrims cut loose with music and dance at the Romería del Rocio. (Robert Frerck/Tony Stone Images)

from Seville. **CONTACT:** Oficina de Turismo de la Junta de Andalucia, Vázquez López 5, E-21001 Huelva, Tel 55-7403. Also, Tourist Office of Spain (see *Resources*).

While you're there ...

- **Día de San Juan, Tarragona:** Fireworks and mythical beasts fill the streets, but the big attraction is the competition of "human towers." Teams of men braid their arms together to build human towers as high as 12 meters (40 ft). Crowned with a small boy, these feats of human architecture sometimes come toppling down. (June 23–24.)
- **The Stilt-Walkers of Anguiano, Anguiano (La Rioja):** Costumed stilt dancers are the center of this interesting harvest festival. (June.)
- **The Wine War, Haro (La Rioja):** Bota bags become squirt guns and people hose each other down with Rioja wine. After the battle, whatever's left (there's always plenty) is drunk. (June.)

San Fermín Festival and Running of the Bulls

Pamplona **July**

Both human and bovine testosterone run high at this famous festival, which draws participants from all over the world for nine days of drunken derring-do. The main event is a stampede of bulls to

Machismo overload: During San Fermín Festival, hundreds flirt with calamity during an early-morning jog with the bulls. (Joe Viesti/Viesti Associates)

the bullring every morning; between stampedes, a thousand sideshows feature bullfighting, music-making, dancing, and wine-drinking—all adding up to 24 hours of Hemingway-style mayhem.

Since the publication of *The Sun Also Rises,* the festival has attracted an international crowd, and many "expatriots" couldn't imagine missing the blurring days and nights of Pamplona for even a single year—even if the locals say it's become commercialized. The festivities get going at noon on July 6, with the mayor's declaration of "*Viva San Fermín!*" At that point the corks and fireworks begin to fly, bands begin to play, and people begin to dance in the streets in an orgy of fun that doesn't stop until midnight on the 14th.

Each morning a parade of bagpipers announces the impending release of the bulls. At 8 a.m. a rocket is fired from the town-hall balcony, and the excited animals explode into the streets toward the bullring. The men who run with the bulls (women aren't usually allowed) can carry only a rolled-up newspaper for protection, and as the six leading steers bear down on them, they either run with the herd, or leap atop barricades to get out of the way.

The hardy and foolhardy come to Pamplona from all over the world to pass this traditional test of manhood. The most daring are the *aficionados,* or veteran residents, who wear traditional white pants and shirts with scarlet scarves tied around necks and waists. In incredible displays of *machismo,* they taunt and leap in front of the marauding bulls.

In addition to the *encierro,* or running of the bulls, there are parades of papier-mâché giants (a tradition since the 13th century), ceremonial presentations of matadors, and feisty bullfights at 6:30 p.m. The cafés and balconies are crammed with people at all hours, and revelry pervades Plaza Castillo and every inch of the town. Finally, at midnight on the 14th, a sad candlelight parade laments that the festival is over, and everyone goes home—vowing to return again next year.

DATE: July 6–14. **LOCATION:** Pamplona. **TRANSPORT:** Pamplona's airport handles flights from Barcelona, Madrid, Santander, and Vigo. Trains and buses run regularly from locations around the country. **ACCOMMODATION:** You'll pay around two or three times the regular rates during the San Fermín Festival—if you can find a room. Some people book a year ahead, but two months is usually sufficient. **CONTACT:** Tourist Office of Spain (see *Resources*).

WHILE YOU'RE THERE ...

- **Santiago de Compostela Festival, Santiago de Compostela:** The yearly bash in this pilgrimage center (one of Christianity's three holiest cities) has just about everything during its two weeks: Offerings are made, replicas are burned, costumed stilt-walkers dance in the streets, and witches with brooms sweep people aside. On the saint's day (July 25), the exterior walls of the cathedral are rigged with fireworks. (July.)
- **Near-Death Pilgrimage, Santa Maria de Ribarteme (Pontevedra/Galicia):** "Lucky to be alive" is the spirit of this festival, attended as a pilgrimage by people who narrowly escaped being killed during the past year. Reflecting the region's strong sense of Celtic mysticism, many participants actually arrive in coffins! (July.)

TOMATO BATTLE (TOMATINA)

Buñol **August**

This giant food fight and flirtathon draws about 20,000 young people to the town of Buñol each August. The concept is simple, if unlikely: More than 110,000 kilograms (242,000 pounds) of tomatoes are brought in, to be thrown and smooshed against everyone else. When it's all over, there's a festive clean-up.

Buñol's patron saint festival dates back to the middle ages, but locals say the Tomatina started in 1945 as a symbolic anti-Franco rebellion. Parties and celebrations had been banned, so repressed young people started throwing tomatoes at officials and priests. Now the dictator is gone, but the tomato toss lives on—for a few minutes each year. The (very) ripe tomatoes are used as projectiles, and much drinking, singing, and dancing accompanies the bathing in tomato juice. Much of the action is boy versus girl, and the hormones ooze as thick as vegetable goo. When it's

So you want to run with the bulls?

Your girlfriend tells you it's stupid. Your better judgment agrees. But after four or five nights listening to big bar talk about the thrill of the *encierro,* you start to think seriously about Hemingway and impotence and whether you'd stand a chance with Lady Brett Ashley and then ... suddenly you're lining up for an early morning jog with several tons of horned, hairy steak.

Advice in any language isn't hard to find at Pamplona, but here are a few time-honored tips:

• Definitely look at the fracas a couple of times before you leap into it, and don't make your first run during the weekend—the course is especially crowded with pushing, shoving people.

• You can't outrun a bull. In fact, if you feel one breathing down your neck, you don't even have the extra two seconds it takes to climb the barricade. Hit the street and roll under the planks.

• Avoid hiding in doorways, since there's no escape. Several people have been killed this way.

• The narrow opening at the end of the course is the scene of lots of injuries.

• The bulls try to stay together, and they're predictable when they do. If one gets separated from the herd it means big trouble; confused bulls will charge individuals and even crowds of spectators.

• Finally, remember that San Fermín himself was martyred when he was dragged by bulls through the streets. Each year, some people don't make it and are gored by bulls or run over by people. Although there have only been about a dozen deaths this century, the Spanish Red Cross treats at least 25 injuries each day, many of them serious. If you decide to go for it, don't rely on liquid courage. Do it when you're sober, and celebrate later!

over, there's a big mess to clean up. Huge pumps draw water from the town's ancient Roman aqueduct, and nozzles hose down people and the newly decorated walls.

DATE: The Tomatina coincides with the town's patron saint festival, and is held one day (the date changes each year) during the last week in August. **LOCATION:** Buñol is located in the Valencia region, half-way between Valencia and Requena. **TRANSPORT:** From Valen-

Barcelona ablaze: La Merced features spastic charges through the streets and fiery rituals with roots in pagan times. (Daniel Aubry/Odyssey Productions/Chicago)

cia, go west on highway E-901. After about 45 km/30 miles, look for the turnoff to Buñol to the south. **ACCOMMODATION:** There are no hotels in Buñol, but there are several in nearby Chiva; alternatively you could stay in Valencia or elsewhere on the coast. **CONTACT:** Buñol Tourist Office/Town Hall, 6-250-0151. Also, Tourist Office of Spain (see *Resources*).

While you're there ...

- **Big Basque Week, Bilbao:** The Basque region's big party lasts a week and includes music, theater, fireworks, bullfights, and basque sports. (Mid-August.)

Resources

In Spain: TURESPAÑA, Secretaria General de Turismo, Maria de Molina 50, E-28006 Madrid, Tel 1-4114014, 1-4116011, Fax 1-4114232. **USA:** Tourist Office of Spain, 665 Fifth Ave., New York, NY 10022, Tel (212) 759-8822, Fax (212) 980-1053. **Canada:** Tourist Office of Spain, 102 Bloor St. West Suite, 14th Fl., Toronto, ON M5S 1M8, Tel (416) 961-3131, Fax (416) 961-1992. **UK:** Tourist Office of Spain, 57-58 St. James St., GB-London SW1A ILD, Tel 71-4990901, Fax 71-6294257. **Germany:** Spanisches Fremdenverkehrsamt., PO Box 170547, Myliusstr. 14, D-60323 Frankfurt 1, Tel 69-725033, Fax 69-725313. **Australia:** Tourist Office of Spain, 203 Castlereagh St. #21a, PO Box A-685, Sydney, NSW 2000, Tel 2-2647966, Fax 2-267-5111.

Sweden's spacious landscapes and stimulating cities are the launching pads for midsummer celebrations, crayfish-eating orgies, and water festivals that draw people from all over Europe. Known as some of the continent's shyest people, the Swedes set aside their inhibitions during the long summer days, taking advantage of the sunlight to play music, drink, dance, and otherwise frolic. Stockholm draws the most international visitors, with its world-class music and arts festivals, but dancing and other folkloric traditions are faithfully preserved in the festivals of the villages that lie among Sweden's mountains, lakes, forests, and islands.

Midsummer Eve

Nationwide **June**

Swedes break out the fiddles and accordions to dance traditional jigs around elaborate maypoles erected in the parks and gardens of most towns and villages. This celebration of the summer solstice is a national holiday, complete with more-than-moderate doses of music, games, dancing, and drinking.

Although many northern European countries celebrate Midsummer Eve, the Swedes are famous for centering their festivities around maypoles decorated with birch twigs and bright flowers. Residents also adorn their houses with flower garlands. The event is popular everywhere, but notably merry in the southern villages of Lacunate and Bengtsfors (the Gammelgarden hosts a traditional Midsummer wedding), and in the southwestern town of Sandviken. Fatmomakke in the northern province of Lapland also hosts an array of Midsummer Eve activities.

DATE: The closest Saturday to June 21 or 22. **LOCATION:** Nationwide; Sandviken, Lacunate, Fatmomakke, and Bengtsfors are particularly festive. **CONTACT:** Swedish Travel and Tourism Council (see *Resources*).

Gotland Island's colorful Stånga Viking Olympics could be subtitled "kooky games for big fellows." (Lars Hansson/Swedish Travel & Tourism Council)

While you're there ...

Walpurgis Night, Uppsala, Stockholm, Göteborg, and Lund: This wild night of music and revelry brings out the students in a celebration of the ancient "witches' Sabbath." Torchlight parades and songfests celebrate the death of winter and the birth of spring. (April 31 and May 1.)

Stånga Viking Olympics and Medieval Week

Stånga (Gotland Island) **July**

The subtitle "kooky games for big fellows" could sum up the action, but it would ignore the historical significance of this three-day series of events. The Stånga Games are played as they were in the days when Vikings wandered the world, as a sort of "sister celebration" to Scotland's Braemar Highland Gathering (they exchange athletes). One event, the *stångstörning,* is played by tossing large tree trunks. Another, *varpa,* is like horseshoes, but played with a heavy aluminum "stone." Leg-wrestling, pillow-fighting (while balancing on a log), and *park*—which looks like a curious hybrid of cricket, tennis, and soccer—also take place.

Gotland Island itself is a huge, open-air museum, with cairns, hill-forts, mythical monoliths, and ruins dotting the varied landscapes. The Swedes cherish Gotland Island for its wildlife sanctuaries, meadowlands, and fine beaches. Its size makes it an ideal spot to explore by bicycle, and the numerous medieval churches and fine Viking Historical Museum serve to prolong the spirit of days gone by. In cobblestone villages and medieval monasteries, folk music can be heard on both commonplace and festive occasions.

DATE: Three days in early to mid-July. **LOCATION:** Stånga, on Gotland Island. **TRANSPORT:** Gotland's capital, Visby, is linked to Stockholm by several flights a day. The ferry leaves for Gotland from Nynåshamm, which is linked to Stockholm by bus. Bus transport also links Visby with nearby Stånga. **ACCOMMODATION:** Visby has several hotels and campgrounds, and a campground is set up near Stånga. **CONTACT:** Gotland Tourist Office, Burmeisterska, Strandgatan 9, Box 2081, S-621 12 Visby, Tel 498-10982, Fax 498-78941. Also, Swedish Travel and Tourism Council (see *Resources*).

Crayfish Premier (Kraftskiva)

Nationwide **August**

Bring on the crayfish! If food is your fancy, be sure to catch the festivities that befall on the second Wednesday of August at midnight—opening night of the official crayfish season in Sweden. Travelers shouldn't miss the chance to partake in at least one of the traditional activities—catching, preparing, or consuming the more than three million tons of crayfish caught during the short season.

This ancient Swedish tradition involves nearly the entire Swedish population, with most citizens attending at least one *kraftskiva* (crayfish table) each season. Celebrations abound as friends gather together at outdoor parties to gorge on the Swedish delicacy. Swedes prepare crawfish with a flare, first boiling them with dill, vinegar, and salt, and then chilling. *Nubbe,* a shot of aquavit, is the traditional drink consumed after each crayfish is devoured.

DATE: Second Wednesday of August. **LOCATION:** Nationwide. **CONTACT:** Swedish Travel and Tourism Council (see *Resources*).

While you're there ...

- **Stockholm Water Festival, Stockholm:** This wildly successful festival features more than 1,500 events, including regattas, kayak races, waterskiing, and international fireworks teams. (The second week in August.)

Santa Lucia Day: The shortest, darkest day of the year is brightened with pageants and processions of "Lucias," candle-bearing girls who represent the Queen of Light. (*Joe Viesti/Viesti Associates*)

Santa Lucia Day

Nationwide **December**

Young blond girls are chosen from cities across the country as "Lucias" to brighten one of the longest, darkest evenings of the year with wreaths of candles in their hair. Clothed in long white gowns, they visit restaurants, offices, schools, and factories, singing hymns about Santa Lucia with their "handmaidens" and "stable lads," who carry candles and also wear white robes.

The children performing for the feast of Santa Lucia often stop for snacks of *lussekatter* (saffron rolls contoured like priests' wigs and pigs' snouts) and drinks of *glogg* (mulled wine and cognac mixed with almonds and raisins) while they tour the streets of their cities and villages. The traditional Santa Lucia Day menu involved Swedish peasants eating three breakfasts before dawn to ward off the evil darkness, but the girls don't need to take such drastic precautions, since they're well-fed during the day. In Stockholm, Lucia and her attendants are paraded through the streets in decorated carriages.

DATE: December 13. **LOCATION:** Nationwide. **CONTACT:** Swedish Travel and Tourism Council (see *Resources*).

Resources

In Sweden: Swedish Travel and Tourism Council, P.O. Box 3030, Kungsgatan 36, 5-103 61 Stockholm, Tel 8-725-5500, Fax 8-725-5531. **USA:** Swedish

Travel and Tourism Council, 655 3rd Ave., 18th floor, New York, NY 10017, Tel (212) 949-2333, Fax (212) 697-0835. **Canada:** Embassy of the Kingdom of Sweden, 377 Dalhousie Street, Ottawa, ON K1N 9N8, Canada, Tel (613) 241-8553, Fax (613) 241-2277. **UK:** Swedish Travel & Tourism Council, 73 Welbeck St., GB-London W1M 8AN, Tel 71-487-3136, Fax 71-935-5853. **Germany:** Schweden-Werbung für Reisen und Touristik GmbH, Lilienstr. 19, D-20095 Hamburg, Tel 40-33-0185, Fax 40-33-0599. **Australia:** Consulate General of the Kingdom of Sweden, National Mutual Centre, 18th floor, 44 Market Street, Sydney, NSW 2000, Australia, Tel 2-2991951, Fax 2-2901019.

SWITZERLAND

Although the Swiss love for partying isn't widely known, festivals of all types flourish in the country's mountains and valleys. The nature of these events varies widely by location, reflecting the diverse ethnic landscape of the nation. Many events are tied to the religious calendar, while others celebrate battles and milestones experienced by ancestors. Still others are forums for the modern sounds of jazz, rock, and world music. In rural areas, the coming of summer prompts hundreds of agricultural festivals, including traditional celebrations surrounding the summer cattle drive up to the high pastures.

CARNIVAL (FASNACHT)

Basel **February/March**

In Switzerland, most carnivals are held *after* Lent begins—a onetime Protestant reaction to Catholicism. Basel's carnival is the country's biggest, involving about 20,000 masked participants who march through the streets in three huge processions.

The action starts early on the Monday morning following Ash Wednesday. As the clock strikes 4 a.m., street lights are switched off and costumed fife-and-drum bands begin playing, their head-lanterns swinging through the darkened streets. Next come the *Cliquen,* or Carnival Cliques, wearing imaginative costumes—such as pigs' heads, grotesque caps, and giant leering faces—that correspond to particular themes. Each group is illuminated by transparent, shouldered lanterns, most of which are over three meters (10 feet) high.

The procession is repeated on Monday and Wednesday afternoons, and on both evenings small groups wander from bar to bar, singing and acting out events of the past year. Tuesday evening brings the *Guggemuusige,* or masked musicians, who fill

Carnival has begun: As the clock strikes 4 a.m. Carnival Cliques storm into Basel's streets, declaring an end to sleep and sadness. (Joe Viesti/Viesti Associates)

the streets with improvised musical chaos. On Wednesday night the carnival climaxes with the *Gässle,* a wild, free-form romp through the city center. Masked groups and individuals wander through the narrow streets, following the pipers and drummers until 4 a.m. Thursday morning.

DATE: Carnival begins at 4 a.m. on the Monday following Ash Wednesday. **LOCATION:** Basel is located on the Rhine River, and borders both France and Germany. **TRANSPORT:** Basel is easily reached by train from anywhere in Europe, and although the city has an airport, nearby Zürich handles most international flights. **ACCOMMODATION:** A wide range of hotels are available, but lodging is tight during the festival. **CONTACT:** Tourism Assoc. of Northwest Switzerland, Blumenrain 2, Ch-4001 Basel, Tel 61-255050, Fax 36-225716. Also, Swiss National Tourist Office (see *Resources*).

© WHILE YOU'RE THERE ...

© **Sechselauten, Zürich:** A snowman made of wadding is blown to bits in a symbolic attempt to welcome the long-awaited spring. Colorful parades of bands and costumed guilds on horseback accompany this wintertime symbol to his fiery and explosive end. (Usually the third Monday in April.)

© **Cow Fights, Valais:** The small black Herens cows instinctively organize themselves into a social hierarchy and form their own cowdom. During the month of June, human spectators take to the Alpine meadows with wine and picnics to watch the spontaneous head clashes and horn lockings that will determine who will be the queen cow of each herd. (June.)

Swiss Carnival Cacophony

Swiss Carnival customs are widely varied, although satire always holds a high place in the festivities. Here are some of the highlights of Carnivals around the country:

Huge crowds are attracted to **Lucerne's** colorful Carnival festivities, which include parades and masked balls. Improvised bands play satirical tunes in a burlesque-like fashion on brass and percussion instruments; the bands march in a haphazard formation, making frequent stops and mixing with the crowds.

Solothurn's torchlight parade begins at 5 a.m. on the Thursday before Ash Wednesday, with participants wailing away on brass and percussion instruments while wearing nightshirts and nightcaps. The following afternoons are marked by masked balls, street parades of "fools," and the torching of the *Böögg,* or straw man.

On Carnival Monday in **Zug**, a traditional figure named Greth Schnell parades through the streets with a basket on her back (to put her drunken husband in and carry him home). She's accompanied by seven colorful "fools" who hand sweets to the children as they call out her name.

During Carnival in the valley of **Lötschental**, young singles assume the leathery faces of carved masks and pass from village to village, frightening and playing pranks on passersby. This custom derives from an ancient belief in evil, grimacing-faced spirits that lived in soot-covered chimneys. The Roitschäggätä (masked persons) tradition is mainly upheld in **Wiler**, where competitions for the best masks are held on the Saturday afternoon during Carnival.

Northern Italian Carnival traditions are celebrated on Shrove Tuesday in the towns and villages in the **Ticino** region. In a tradition dating back to the 1860s, a meal of rice is served outside from a huge vat and enjoyed in a festive community atmosphere.

Montreux International Jazz Festival

Montreux **July**

Despite its name, the Montreux festival features more than jazz—much more. In the lakefront casino the atmosphere changes rapidly, as big-name jazz musicians trade the stage with dreadlocked reggae bands, Cuban salseros, and African tribal chanters. Organizers have a keen sense of mood, knowing when to coat the floor with chairs for more subdued acts, and when to whisk them away for the monster dance-fests that break out nightly. The crowd (about 4,000 each night) is a big part of the appeal, as people come from all over the world to enjoy sophisticated rhythms and ultra-cosmopolitan good times. The festival concludes with a 12-hour marathon of world music—a breathless, dancing finale that finally breaks up in the wee, wee hours.

The festival started in 1966 and has become a resounding success. The city's setting—on posh, peaceful Lake Geneva—enhances the mellifluous mood of the event. Known as the "Pearl of the Swiss Riviera," Montreux has an extremely mild climate that actually supports palm trees and tropical flowers along the lakeshore. In addition to Chillon Castle (immortalized by Lord Byron), Montreux has a six-mile lakeside promenade that is center stage for swans, sailors, and sunset watchers. Competition for tickets is hot, so book at least one month in advance.

DATE: Two-and-a-half weeks, usually beginning on the first Monday in July. **LOCATION:** Montreux, on the eastern shore of Lake Geneva. **TRANSPORT:** Montreux is well connected by electric train from all over Switzerland. The nearest intercontinental airport is in Geneva, about 70 km/43 miles away. **ACCOMMODATION:** Montreux is an expensive city within an expensive country. The festival makes the unreserved hotel room an endangered species, and even camping sites and hostels are jam-packed. **CONTACT:** Montreux Jazz Festival, Case Postale Box 97, CH-1820 Montreux. In the USA: Ciao Travel, 2707 Congress St., Suite 1F, San Diego, CA 92110, Tel (619) 297-8112.

While you're there ...

- **Vintage Festival, Lugano:** Little girls throw flowers from blossom-covered floats and oxen pull festooned wagons in a colorful procession through this Italian-flavored Swiss town. The festivities draw up to 35,000 people every year. (First weekend in October.)
- **Aelplerchilbi, Kerns and other villages of Unterwalden Canton:** Dairymen and pasture owners join villagers in a tradition of fun and socializing to mark the end of the Alpine summer. (Late October or the beginning of November.)
- **Klausjagen, Küssnacht am Rigi:** Enormous headdresses cut out of cardboard are lit from the inside and paraded through the village on the heads of men and women. They accompany St. Nicholas through streets that echo with bells, horns, and the sounds of a brass band. (December 5th, the eve of St. Nicholas' Day.)

Silvesterkläuse: Skiing from house to house, the peculiarly costumed men of Appenzell wish their neighbors a happy New Year—twice. (Joe Viesti/Viesti Associates)

Achetringele, Laupen: Maidens are beaten with inflated pigs' bladders until the weapons fall to pieces in a "happy New Year" procession that gets quite rambunctious. Bell ringers clamor large bells, broom men carry poles tied with juniper branches, and the bladder men beat the crowd while parading through the streets in a farewell bid to the old year. (New Year's Eve.)

Silvesterkläuse, Urnäsch: Elaborately costumed figures ski from house to house singing, ringing bells, and wishing families a prosperous year. Intricately designed disguises distinguish three very different groups: the beautiful, the ugly, and the ordinary. The festival is performed on both the Gregorian New Year (December 31), and the Julian New Year (January 13), which local residents have continued to follow since its general demise in 1582.

Vogel Gryff, Basel: Three strange creatures meet for a symbolic dance through the streets in a festive celebration that dates back to the 16th century. An upright lion, a large-beaked bird, and a savage man symbolize the neighborhoods of Kleinbasel and help to strengthen community ties. (Date changes each year: either January 13, 20, or 27.)

Resources

In Switzerland: Schweizerische Verkehrszentrale, Bellariastr. 38, CH-8027 Zürich, Tel 1-2881111, Fax 1-2881205. **USA:** Swiss National Tourist Office, Swiss Center, 608 Fifth Ave., New York, NY 10020, Tel (212) 757-5944, Fax (212) 262-6116. **Canada:** SNTO: 926 The East Mall, Etobicoke, ON M9B 6K1, Tel (416) 695-2090, Fax (416) 695-2774. **UK:** Swiss National Tourist Office, Swiss Centre, New Coventry St., GB-London W1V

8EE, Tel 71-7341921, Fax 71-4374577. **Germany**: Schweizer Verkehrsbüro, Kaiserstrasse 23, D-60311 Frankfurt 1, Tel 69-2560010, Fax 69-25600138. **Australia**: Embassy of Switzerland, 7 Melbourne Ave., Forrest (Canberra), ACT 2603, Tel 6-2733977, Fax 6-2733428.

WALES

Bound by land and politics to their Anglo neighbors, the Welsh cling steadfastly to their Celtic heritage. These days, Welsh traditions are in the midst of a resurgence that goes well beyond bilingual street signs, and visitors find themselves drawn into the rhythms of a culture that has struggled for its very existence for more than a millennium.

The festivals, farm fairs, sheepdog trials, and medieval pageants of Wales present the best opportunities to get to know the hospitable, eloquent Welsh, and to submerge oneself in their poetic lifestyles. These events highlight the Welsh music, literature, and language, and are held amidst some of the world's most captivating landscapes.

International Musical Eisteddfod

Llangollen **July**

Llangollen's week-long *eisteddfod* (pronounced eye-steth-fud) is a jubilee of nations coming together to sing and dance. Founded in 1947 to heal the wounds of war, this amazing one-of-a-kind assembly celebrates worldwide fraternity through music and merrymaking. A very ambitious event, it floods this traditional and picturesque town of 3,000 with more than 150,000 visitors. Town pubs serve typical Welsh specialties, while food booths at the festival serve dishes from around the world.

DATE: Six days in early July. **LOCATION:** Llangollen is located near the English border in northeast Wales. **TRANSPORT:** Buses and trains from London or Birmingham go as far as Wrexham, about eight miles (13 km) from Llangollen. From there, special buses have been set up; hitching is also easy. **ACCOMMODATION:** Accommodations are hard to find in town during the event. The Tourist Office has lists of lodgings in nearby towns, including households accepting guests. For information, check the Tourist Office at Town Hall and Castle Street. **CONTACT:** International Eisteddfod Office, Llangollen, Clwyd, North Wales LL20 8NG, Tel (0978) 860-236. Tourist Office: (0978) 860-838.

The Royal National Eisteddfod

Moving location **July/August**

The hundreds of *eisteddfodau* that dot the Welsh countryside each summer culminate with the National. Unlike the cosmopolitan Llangollen event, this and most other *eisteddfodau* make few concessions to outsiders. Considered a cultural bastion, these country gatherings are usually conducted in Welsh Gaelic, with bucolic contests in literature and music. The events of the National's main pavilion—such as the awarding of the Bardic Crown and Bardic Chair, and contests in Welsh poetry and penillion singing—have intricate rules and rituals that are nearly impossible to understand if you don't speak Welsh (more than three-quarters of the country's population doesn't, by the way).

Outside the main pavilion, the scene is lighter. Stalls spring up selling traditional Celtic clothing, musical instruments, and even Welsh lamb. Everywhere, sporting events and music (traditional, folk, and even Welsh rock) create the atmosphere of a three-ring circus. One main-pavilion ceremony welcomes people of Welsh ancestry who are visiting their homeland, and it's always a high point of the entire event.

DATE: Seven days in late July and/or early August. **LOCATION:** The location moves from village to village every year; write or call in advance for locations and dates. **CONTACT:** Eisteddfod of Wales Office, 40 Parc Ty Glas, Llanishen, Cardiff CF4 5WU, Tel 0222-763777, Fax 0222-763737.

While you're there ...

Festival of Music and the Arts, Swansea: The largest arts festival in Wales incorporates theater, jazz, opera, dance, and literature into a three-week program of events. Contact: North Wales Music Festival Office, High St., St. Asaph, Clwyd LL17 0RD. (Late September to November.)

Resources

In Wales: The Wales Tourist Board publishes an annual listing of events, which is available at the beginning of each year. Wales Tourist Board (Bwrdd Croeso Cymru), Brunel House, 2 Fizalan Rd., GB-Cardiff CF2 1UY, Tel 222-499909, Fax 222-485031. **USA:** British Tourist Authority, 40 West 57th St., New York, NY 10019-4001, Tel (212) 581-4700, Fax (212) 265-0649. **Canada:** British Tourist Authority, 94 Cumberland St., Ste. 600, Toronto, ON M5R 3N3, Tel (416) 925-6326, Fax (416) 961-2175. **UK:** Wales Travel Centre, 12 Regent St., GB-London SW1X 4PQ, Tel 71-

4090969, Fax 71-2871761. **Germany:** British Tourist Authority, Taunusstr. 52-60, D-6000 Frankfurt/Main 1, Tel 69-2380711, Fax 69-2380717. **Australia:** British Tourist Authority, 210 Clarence St., Sydney, NSW 2000, Tel 2-2674555, Fax 2-2674442.

EASTERN EUROPE & RUSSIA

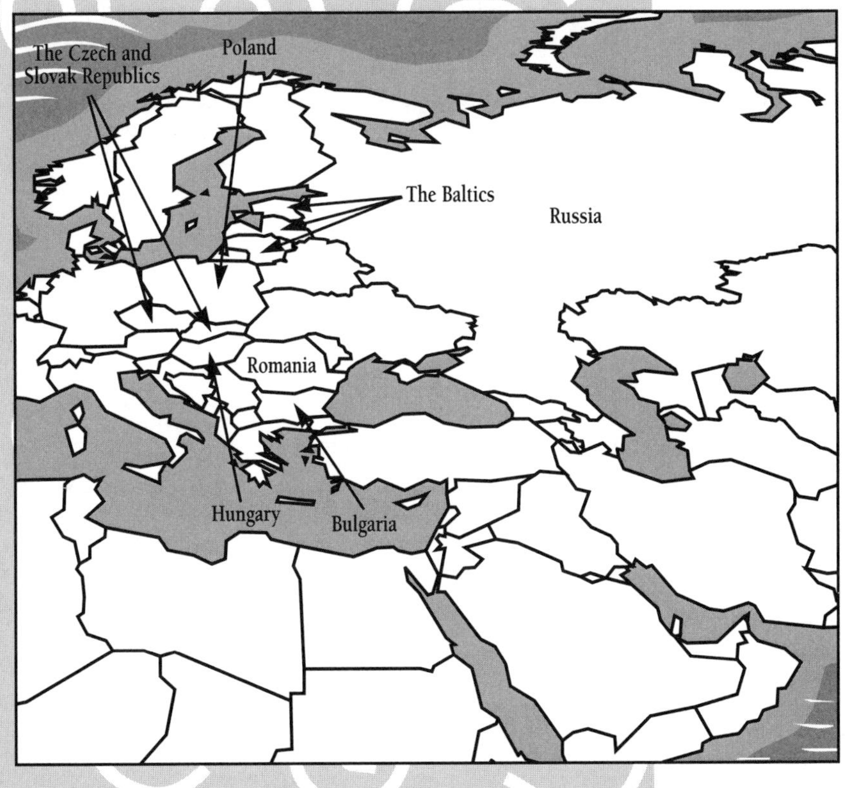

THE BALTICS

The Baltic countries burst into the headlines as leading players in the breakup of the Soviet Union. Before that, the world had heard little of these mythical places, and few outsiders had ventured to visit them. These days, travelers are discovering these three very different nations, each with its own language, culture, and celebrations.

Unlike most of the former Soviet Union, Estonia, Latvia, and Lithuania are brimming with summer festivals of the arts, religion, folk culture, and plenty of music. Under Soviet rule, the festivals allowed people to hold on to their rich artistic traditions. Now, the struggle to rebuild embattled economies is offset by simmering national pride, and even though the fall of the Iron Curtain has meant a loss of funding for artistic work, it's given artists and musicians new freedom. You'll note this spirit of renewal at lively gatherings like the mid-summer celebrations, Baltic Song Festivals, and Baltika Folk Festivals.

Midsummer Night/St. John's Eve

Throughout the Baltics **June**

The longest day of the year inspires the biggest party in the Baltics, as pagan roots re-emerge and people head to the countryside to dance, sing, and celebrate around bonfires. Special beers are brewed, cheeses are made, and pies are baked. In Latvia, houses are decorated with wreaths for good luck—which may come in handy due to the evil spirits that are said to lurk this night! The climax of events always takes place the night before St. John's Day, which is known as *Jaanipäev* in Estonia, *Jānu Diena* in Latvia, and *Rasos* or *Joninės* in Lithuania. Around bonfires across the country, men and women sing to each other, often wearing crowns of oak leaves and wild flowers. Young couples still wander into the woods to seek the magical, mythical fern flower that is said to give the man and woman who see it simultaneously whatever their hearts desire.

DATE: June 23. **LOCATION:** Everywhere in all three Baltic countries. **CONTACT:** (See *Resources.*)

A choir 10,000 strong in Estonia: The music that powered the "singing revolutions" of the Baltics can be experienced at the Baltic Song Festivals. (Paolo Negri/Tony Stone Images)

The Baltic Song Festivals

Tallinn, Riga, Vilnius **June/July**

Music has played an important role in the Baltic region since pre-Christian times, and according to some Baltic texts, songs and storytelling helped to create the world. Under the long period of Soviet dominance, the Moscow-sanctioned Baltic Song Festivals were, ironically, partly responsible for maintaining nationalistic feelings, and the Baltic states' independence struggles were so musical that they became known as the "Singing Revolution."

Today, thousands of people singing and dancing in traditional Baltic dress still create great surges of patriotism. In each capital, performers open the festival with two days of song and dance. The celebration continues with preliminary concerts, an international choir competition, and a parade of singers and dancers who create huge, intricate human designs. A climactic finish includes a choir of up to thirty thousand people singing in the national capital's open-air amphitheater. This powerful combination of music, history, and nationalism can become pretty heavy, although the atmosphere is lightened by children who run onto the stage with flowers for their favorite conductors.

DATE: The festivals range from a weekend up to a week, and are held in late June or early July, depending on the year and place. **LOCATION:** Traditionally, all three countries hold festivals simultaneously, but in the confusion surrounding independence the cycle has been altered. Riga (Latvia) now plans to hold its festival on odd-numbered years. Tallinn (Estonia) plans to hold its next festival in 1999. Vilnius (Lithuania) has scheduled its next festival for 1998. All organizers stress that plans may (and probably will) change, so be sure to call in advance to confirm dates. **CONTACT:** (See *Resources*.)

Baltika

Tallinn, Riga, Vilnius **July**

Baltic folk traditions are showcased in colorful displays of music, art, and dance at this week-long celebration. Exhibitions and parades focus on the region's folk culture, while people wearing traditional Baltic dress add to the festival's flair. The Baltic states take turns holding the festival, which is always centered in the capital city.

DATE: Usually in mid-July. **LOCATION:** Estonia (Tallinn) in 1995 and 1998, Lithuania (Vilnius) in 1996 and 1999, Latvia (Riga) in 1997 and 2000. (Organizers stress that dates are very likely to change, so confirm before booking.) **ACCOMMODATION:** Hotels range from luxurious to filthy. The hostel system is new, but encouraging. **CONTACT:** (See *Resources*.)

While you're there ...

- **Sartu Lake Horse Races, Utena, Lithuania:** The first Saturday in February brings the horses and people out onto the frozen lake for a big day of merrymaking.
- **Carnival (Uzgavenes), Zemaitya, Lithuania:** People masquerade as different animals and birds in Mardi Gras fashion. (February/March.)
- **Birstonas Jazz Festival, Birstonas, Lithuania:** This extremely popular three-day jazz event features top-notch Lithuanian and international musicians. (Late March, even-numbered years.)
- **Skamba Skamba Kaukliai, Vilnius, Lithuania:** A folk music and dance festival is held in the Old Town. (Last week in May.)
- **Rock Summer Festival, near Tartu, Estonia:** International rock, blues, and world musicians along with local favorites perform at the Tallinn Song Bowl in the Baltics' biggest rock fest. (Early July.)
- **Jazz and Blues Festival, Estonia:** This music festival boasts international jazz and blues groups. (Early October.)
- **Vilnius Jazz Festival, Lithuania:** This popular festival focuses on eastern European contemporary jazz. (Autumn, usually October.)
- **Bildes, Riga, Latvia:** This week-long festival features Latvia's top folk, jazz, and rock musicians, as well as visual artists. (October/November.)

Resources

In Estonia: Estonian Tourist Board, Pikk 71, EE-0001 Tallinn, Tel 0142-441239, Fax 0142-440963. **USA:** Consulate General of Estonia, 630 Fifth Ave. Suite 2415, New York, NY 10111, Tel (212) 247-7634. **Canada:** Honorary Consulate General of Estonia, 958 Broadview Avenue, Toronto, ON M4K 2R6, Tel (416) 461-0764, Fax (416) 461-0448. **UK:** Embassy of Estonia, 16 Hyde Park Gate, London, SW7 5DG, Tel 71-589-3428, Fax 71-589-3430. **Germany:** Estonian Tourist Board, c/o Baltisches Reiseburo GmbH, Bayerstr. 37/I, D-8000 Munich 2, Tel 89-596783, Fax 89-525913. **Australia:** Honorary Consulate General, 29 Wentworth St., Point Piper NSW 2027. Baltic Council of Australia, P.O. Box 457, Strathfield, NSW 2135, Tel 02-252505.

In Latvia: Latvian Tourism Board, 4 Pils Sq., Riga LV-1050, Tel 371-2-229945. **USA:** Embassy of Latvia, 4325 17th St. NW, Washington, DC 20011-4203, Tel (202) 726-8213, Fax (202) 726-6785. **Canada:** Baltic Business Council, 151 Young Street, Suite 1402, Toronto, Ontario M5C 2W7. **UK:** Embassy of Latvia 72 Queensborough Terrace, GB-London W2 3SP, Tel 71-727-1698, Fax 71-221-9740. **Germany:** Latvian Tourism Board, c/o Schnieder Reisen GmbH, Dammtorbahnhof, D-2000 Hamburg 36, Tel 40-458097, Fax 40-418615. **Australia:** Consulate of Latvia, PO Box 457, Strathfield, NSW 2135.

In Lithuania: Lithuanian Tourism Association, Ukmerges Str. 20, 2000 Vilnius, Tel 0122-356191, Fax 0122-651385. **USA:** Embassy of Lithuania, 2622 16th St. NW, Washington, DC 20009-4292, Tel (202) 234-5860, Fax (202) 328-0466. **Canada:** Consulate of Lithuania, 235 Yorkland Boulevard, Willowdale, PN M2J 4Y6, Tel (416) 494-4099, Fax (416) 494-4382. **UK:** Embassy of Lithuania, 1937–1588 17 Essex Villas, GB-London W8, Tel 71-9371588, Fax 71-2216164. **Germany:** Embassy of Lithuania, Simrockallee 27, D-5300 Bonn 2, Tel 228-352027, Fax 228-352028. **Australia:** Consulate of Lithuania, 26 Jalanga Crescent, Aranda, ACT 2514, Tel 6-2532062, Fax 6-2532063.

BULGARIA

Bulgaria's festivals reflect the country's continual cultural and ethnic flux, which has introduced influences ranging from Greek to Byzantine and Ottoman. The fall of the Berlin Wall in 1989 brought quick and decisive change to the country of Bulgaria, and relative to other Soviet satellites the transformation from communism to capitalism has been smooth. Still, Bulgaria doesn't get as many tourists as it deserves, with its beautiful Black Sea beaches, its mountain valleys, and people who are among the friendliest in eastern Europe. The country's music and folk festivals are a great chance to hear the esoteric musical traditions of roving "wedding bands," haunting female choirs, and ensembles such as le Mystère des Voix Bulgares.

Rose Festival

Kazanlak & Karlovo **May/June**

The beautiful Valley of the Roses provides the backdrop for this month-long rose harvest festival. Thousands converge on the rose fields to pick the delicate petals at the precise moment of maturity. Performances by national and international stars, along with processions, parades, feasts, and a demonstration of rose-picking rituals, take place throughout the month in Kazanlak and Karlovo. This early summer festival is held in the valley that supplies the world's perfume industry with 70 percent of its rose oil.

Kazanlak, a rather dull and dirty city most of the year, spruces itself up during the festival. Make sure to take a tour of the Museum of Roses, where you'll learn that it takes 2,000 petals to make a single gram of rose oil. You can also tour the rose factory, which produces liqueurs, rose-water, jams, and Turkish Delight candy.

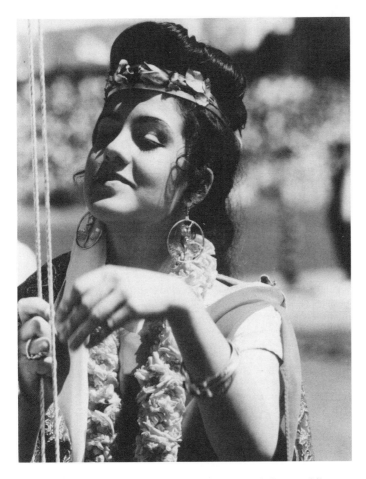

Rose Festival: The women of Kazanlak sing and dance while plucking roses from the vines. (M. Freeman/Bruce Coleman Inc.)

DATE: Mid-May through mid-June. **LOCATION:** Kazanlak and Karlovo in central Bulgaria's Valley of Roses. **TRANSPORT:** Both cities lie on the rail route between Sofia and Burgas. **ACCOMMODATION:** Most of the hotels are expensive and shabby. **CONTACT:** Dolinata na Rozite, 2 Rozova Dolina St., Kazanluk, Bulgaria. Also: Bulgarian National Tourist Office or Balkan Holidays (see *Resources*).

While you're there ...

March Music Days, Rousse: Symphony music, cantatas, oratoria, opera, and chorales are featured in this annual two-week festival. (Late March.)

Sofia Music Weeks, Sofia: World-famous orchestras and soloists add an international flair to this two-month celebration of symphony, chamber, opera, and ballet music. (May 24–June 24.)

Golden Orpheus International Pop Song Festival, Sunny Beach (Sonnestrand): Bulgaria's largest seaside resort is host to the festival named after the mythological Greek poet and musician whose music had the power to move inanimate objects. (First week of June.)

Varna Summer Festival, Varna: This international festival has been held annually for more than 60 years. Performances include operas, ballets, symphonies, and chamber concerts. (July and August.)

Festival of the Arts in Old Plovdiv, Plovdiv: Eclectic tastes are satisfied when art exhibitions are combined with theater, opera, ballet, and music. (September and October.)

Resources

In Bulgaria: Bulgarian National Tourist Office, UUI.Nusiceva 3/1, YU-11000 Belgrade, Yugoslavia Tel 11-331132. **USA:** Balkan Holidays, 41 East 42nd Street. #606, New York, NY 10017, Tel (212) 573-5530, Fax (212) 573-5538. **Canada:** Embassy of Bulgaria, 325 Stewart St. Ottawa, ON K1N 6K5, Tel (416) 232-3215. **UK:** Bulgarian National Tourist Office, 18 Princes Street, GB-London W1R 7RE, Tel 71-499-6988, Fax 71-499-1905. Balkan Holidays Ltd., Sofia House, 19 Conduit Street, GB-London W1R9TD, Tel 71-491-4499, Fax 71-493-2680. **Germany:** Bulgarian National Tourist Office, Stephanstr. 1-3, D-6000 Frankfurt 1, Tel 69-295284, Fax 69-295286. Balkan Holidays, Stephanstr. 3, D-6000 Frankfurt 1, Tel 69-295384, Fax 69-205286.

THE CZECH AND SLOVAK REPUBLICS

Amid Prague's pointed towers, gargoyles, and cathedrals, signs trumpet Seattle-style espresso and fast foods—an indication of the sometimes confused, sometimes crass conversion to tourist capitalism that has widened the inequities between local people and visitors. Yet even the vulgarities of Prague's latest invasion are belittled by the architectural and cultural majesty of this historic city.

Prague is blessed with spring and summer festivals, but so are the rugged mountains of Slovakia and the historic castles and towns of Bohemia and Moravia. In both the Czech and Slovak republics, these events demonstrate the importance of music and folklore to the people, and discerning travelers can learn much about their common history—and significant cultural differences—by spending some time amid eastern Europe's most vital summer festival grounds.

Prague Spring International Music Festival (Prazke Jaro)

Prague **May/June**

The Prague Spring festival starts every year on the anniversary of Bedrich Smetana's death with a procession from his grave to the Obecni dum. There, his composition *Ma Vlast* (*My Homeland*) is performed. After this rousing and patriotic debut, the festival spreads out to Prague's elegant concert halls for three weeks of sublime music from around the world.

Smetana is considered the founder of modern Czech music and is also known for being the teacher of Antonin Dvorák. Like

The Beer Halls of Bohemia

Bavaria's beer halls seem like overpriced practice grounds when compared to the *pivnice* of Bohemia. At more than 1,300 inns and taverns in Prague alone, you can get some of the world's best lagers, brought to your table by grimacing matrons who slam down fistfuls of mugs with a splashy east-bloc *thwack!*

There's no glamour in these ramparts of relief from the post-communist world. Amid a drab, smoky decor, tabs are kept with pencil marks on the long tables, and conversation is loud and lively. The beer (*pivo*) includes world-famous brands like *Plezensky Prazdroz* (the original pilsner) and *Budvar* (the original Budweiser). Beer halls in the center of Prague tend to be crowded with foreigners, but on the city's outskirts and anywhere else in the Czech Republic you can socialize with the Czechs at neighborhood beer halls—where the best beers in the world can be quaffed for about four mugs to the U.S. dollar.

A few favorites: U Fleků is full of young travelers drinking good dark lager, as is the ultra-historic U svatého Tomáse. U Kalicha figured prominently in Jaroslav Hasek's novel *The Good Soldier Schweyk*, and U Pinhasů was the first Prague *pivnice* to serve pilsner. To drink with the locals check out neighborhoods like the Smíchov District or Obranců Míru.

Dvorák's works, the Prague Spring Festival blends classical themes with elements of Slavic and other folk music. Orchestras, ensembles, and singers from all over the world converge on the city, as do music lovers from Europe and elsewhere.

While there, check out the Dvorák and Smetana museums and the Mozart Museum, housed at the Bertramka villa where Mozart stayed during visits to Prague. Beethoven, although he doesn't have his own museum, is an honored guest, and the festival always concludes with a performance of his Ninth Symphony.

DATE: The concerts begin May 12 and continue for three weeks. **LOCATION:** Concert halls all over Prague. **TRANSPORT:** Prague's airport is served by flights from North America, the Middle East and nearly everywhere in Europe, although from points in Europe the train is usually a better bet. **ACCOMMODATION:** There's plenty of variety in Prague, although summer shortages necessitate reservations for inexpensive hotels. Private homes, campgrounds, and bed and breakfasts are reasonably priced. **CONTACT:** Prague Information Service, Staromestiske nam. 22, Stare Mesto, Tel 02-22-44-53. Also, CEDOK (see *Resources*).

Vychodna Annual Slovak Folk Festival

Vychodna (Slovak Republic) **July**

The folk culture of the region around Vychodna is the richest in Slovakia, and this enduring festival is its most important showcase. Groups gather every summer with traditional instruments like the *gajdy* (bagpipes), *fujara* (shepherd's shawm), fiddles, and dulcimers, to lay down old melodies on the main stage and in makeshift performance spaces all around town.

Much of the emphasis is on regional dances; you'll see the polka, the *odzemok* (a shepherd's dance), and the *chorodovy,* which is danced by large groups of women. Traditional songs relate ancient legends from the time of Turkish invasions, and groups from every region of Slovakia come to perform within a format similar to the music festival in Straznice.

DATE: Late July. **LOCATION:** Vychodna (Slovak Republic) **TRANSPORT:** Vychodna is served by bus from Bratislava. **ACCOMMODATION:** Accommodations in town are sparse, but many musicians and visitors prefer to camp or stay in nearby villages. **CONTACT:** CEDOK (see *Resources*).

While you're there ...

- **Bratislava Lyre, Bratislava:** Slovakia's youth converge for a weekend of stadium rock concerts. (May/June.)
- **International Folklore Festival, Straznice:** Folk music groups from Moravia and all over the world perform in stadiums near the castle. The costumes and dancing are great and the crowds are big at one of the world's most prestigious music festivals. (Late June.)
- **Chode Festival, Domazlice:** *Dudy* (bagpipes) and other folk instruments of the culturally independent western Bohemians are highlighted at this weekend concert. (Late August.)
- **Zatec Hops Festival, Zatec:** Beer-drinking and other festivities celebrate the end of the hop season in northern Bohemia. (September.)
- **Bratislava International Jazz Festival, Bratislava:** National and international musicians perform at concert halls throughout the city. (Late October.)
- **Pardubice Steeplechase, Pardubice:** This world-class steeplechase is notorious for its grueling course and competition. (October.)

RESOURCES

In the Republics: CEDOK (the national tourist office), Oanska 5. Na prikope 18, Tel 02-212-71-11. Association of Czechoslovakian Travel Agents *(Asociace ceskych soukromych cestovnich kancelai),* c/o CK Florateur, Novostrasnicka 58, CS-1000 Prague 10. **USA:** CEDOK, 1040 East 40th Street, New York, NY 10016, Tel (212) 689-9720, Fax (212) 481-0597. **UK:** CEDOK, 17–18 Old Bond Street, GB-London W1X 4RB, Tel 71-4994541, Fax 71-4837841. **Germany:** CEDOK, Kaiserstr. 54, D-6000 Frankfurt 1, Tel 69-2740170, Fax 69-235890.

Hungary is a great place to ease into an eastern European adventure. With its great cities, history, sights, and food, the Hungarian experience rivals anything that can be found in the West—at the bargain-basement prices of the East. The country's colorful folklore is evident at its festivals, where gypsy music and violins spice the air while paprika and fine wines spice the palate. In the south, especially, the old folk traditions have persevered in remote villages.

HUNGARY

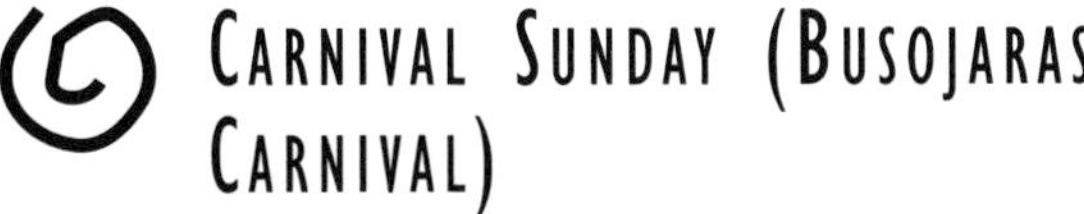

Carnival Sunday (Busojaras Carnival)

Mohacs **February/March**

In this southern Slavic version of Mardi Gras, the streets of Mohacs fill with men waving flaming torches and wearing *buso* (masks), which are made of wood, covered with ox blood, and topped with animal skins and curved rams' horns. They're said to have frightened the Turkish hordes, but in peacetime they're used to frighten away winter and welcome the spring. To this day the masks are passed down from father to son, and on Carnival Sunday the men run through town twirling huge wooden rattles and setting off cannons that shower people with debris.

DATE: The Sunday before the beginning of Lent. **LOCATION:** Mohacs, along the Danube just north of the Serbian border. **TRANSPORT:** By rail, take the main line from Budapest to Belgrade, and change trains at Villány. Alternatively, you can take a bus from Pécs or Villány. **ACCOMMODATION:** Few options are available in Mohacs, but nearby Pécs has a wide range of hotels. **CONTACT:** Hungarian Tourist Board or IBUSZ (see *Resources*).

Budapest Spring Festival

Budapest **March**

Boasting 10 days, 100 venues, and 1,000 events, this festival brings even more excitement to one of the liveliest, most stunningly beautiful cities in the world. Amid the medieval splendor of Castle Hill, a fair pops up with folk art and performance stages, and classical and folk music can be experienced by the banks of the Danube at Vigadó tér. At the dazzling State Opera House and other gilded venues across the city, there are operas, rock operas, theatrical events (both classical and avant-garde), ballets, poetry readings, children's events, and concerts featuring folk, classical, jazz, rock, and much more.

Budapest itself is worth the trip no matter what's going on. Called the "Paris of Eastern Europe" and "Queen of the Danube," this ancient city has a thriving cultural scene that's yet to be "discovered" by much of the world. Unlike Prague (to which it's often compared), Budapest has not priced locals out of the action and fast-food billboards are rare. There are thriving museums, cafés, and theaters, with non-stop action played out atop layers and layers of history, revealed in Roman aqueducts and castles of the Buda district. Since simultaneous spring festivals are held in Sopron, Szentendre, and Kecskemét, this is a fantastic time of year to visit Hungary.

DATE: Approximately the last 10 days of March. **LOCATION:** Budapest. **TRANSPORT:** Budapest is easily reached by air from anywhere in Europe, North America, or the Middle East, and by rail from eastern or western Europe. **ACCOMMODATION:** Budapest has a fine selection of hotels and hostels, but private rooms assigned by the local "travel agencies" are probably the best value. **CONTACT:** Interart Festivalcentre, 1051 Budapest, Vorosmarty ter 1, Hungary, Tel 22-355-099. Also: Hungarian Tourist Board or IBUSZ (see *Resources*).

© While you're there ...

- **Spring Festivals, Sopron, Szentendre, and Kecskemét:** The streets fill with music and dancing as spring is celebrated in conjunction with the Budapest festival. (Last third of March.)
- **Visegrád Palace Games, Visegrád:** Ruins of a 14th-century royal castle are the site of a pageant and equestrian tournaments featuring period costumes. (June.)
- **Sopron Festival Weeks/Festival of Ancient Music and Cave Theater, Sopron:** Folklore displays, theater, and all types of music concerts take place over a three-week period at various locales in Sopron. Many of the concerts and operas are held at the impressive theater carved out of an old stone quarry outside of town. (Roughly June 22–July 14.)
- **Szeged Summer Festival, Szeged:** Opera, theater, dancing, and classical music are staged in an open-air theater where the great towers of the Votive Church serve as a backdrop. (Mid-July to mid-August.)
- **Savaria Autumn Festival, Szombathely:** This celebration of culture features concerts, sports, folk dancing, and exhibits, among other events. (September.)

RESOURCES

In Hungary: Hungarian Tourist Board, Magyar Idegenforgalmi Tajekoztato Kozpont, Vigado utca 6, H-1051 Budapest V, Tel 1-1180750, Fax 1-1184846. Tourist Information Centre, TOURINFORM, Suto u. 2, P.O. Box 185, H-1364 Budapest, Tel 1-1179800, Fax 1-1179578. **USA**: Hungarian Tourist Board, c/o IBUSZ/Hungarian Travel Agency, One Parker Plaza, #1104, Fort Lee, NJ 07024, Tel (201) 592-8585, Fax (201) 592-8736. **Canada**: Embassy of Hungary, 7 Delaware Avenue, Ottawa, ON K2P 0Z2, Tel (613) 232-1711, Fax (613) 232-5620. **UK**: Danube Travel Ltd., 6 Conduit St., GB-London W1R 9TG, Tel 71-4913588, Fax 71-4936963. **Germany**: Hungarian Tourist Board, Berliner Str. 72, D-6000 Frankfurt, Tel 69-20929, Fax 69-292808. **Australia**: Embassy of Hungary, 17 Beale Crescent, Deakin, ACT 2600, Tel 6-2823226, Fax 6-2853012.

POLAND

Charismatic, unpredictable, and yet steadfastly traditional, Poland has baffled everyone from Franklin D. Roosevelt to Joseph Stalin, who once remarked that imposing communism on Poland was like trying to saddle a cow. These days, a popular nationalistic slogan seen spray-painted on walls is Polska dla Polaków *(Poland for the Poles!). It reflects at once the purity, determination, and xenophobia of the Polish people, who are bound together by a common language, ethnicity, church, and history.*

Traditional festivals and fairs in Poland are observed in the same spirit of solidarity reflected by the slogan. Many of the songs and costumes of the Catholic feast days have become representative of national pride, although outsiders are usually welcome to attend. In well-preserved old cities like Kraków, and among the mountains and lakes of the countryside, the traditions come alive with a friendliness and musicality that does justice to the beautiful settings.

Holy Week

Nationwide **March/April**

The week associated with Jesus' crucifixion and resurrection is the most important holiday of the year for the highly religious Poles. Visitors who come to Poland—especially the countryside—during this period can experience the Poles' deeply felt faith through their elaborate and colorful Easter rituals.

On Palm Sunday, palm fronds are carried in processions to and from church. The palm procession at Kalwaria Zebrzydowska is the most famous in Poland, as are the passion plays enacted there over the week. Maundy Thursday is the day zealous Poles take symbolic revenge on Judas Iscariot for his betrayal of Jesus. They hang him, drag him out of the village, flog him, then burn or drown him in effigy.

On Good Friday, villagers visit constructed "caves," as if paying respects to their crucified Lord at the Holy Sepulchre. At Wambierzyce (near the Pope's native village of Wadowice) and at

Kalwaria Zebrzydowksa, the sepulchers are permanent structures. In Warsaw and elsewhere, ad-hoc creations are the rule. Some places, such as Rzeszów, incorporate a bit of symbolism inspired by King Jan Sobieski's victory in the siege of Vienna, by having costumed "Turks" placed in charge of the tomb.

On Holy Saturday, everyone takes painted Easter eggs, sausages, bread, and salt to church to be blessed and sprinkled with holy water. They eat the consecrated food Sunday morning, then go to church for Easter mass. On Easter Monday gangs of children douse people with water, in playful celebration of Christ's resurrection and the coming of spring.

DATE: Palm Sunday to Easter Monday. **LOCATION:** Nationwide. **CONTACT:** Polish National Tourist Office (see *Resources*).

Lajkonik Festival and Days of Kraków

Kraków **June**

Amid Poland's immaculately preserved medieval city of Kraków, this resplendent pageant has the atmosphere of a true folk festival that's so rare in the former east-bloc countries. Commemorating the defeat of Tatar invaders in the 14th century, its central figure is the hero Lajkonik, a brave raftsman who heads a procession through the city dressed in the defeated khan's finery and riding a hobby horse. At Rynek Square he toasts the city's future, then leads revelry that lasts late into the night.

The people of Kraków are strongly attached to the Lajkonik tradition, and they gather in the morning along the route. Boys climb trees, families sit on cars, and balconies and open windows are crowded. The actors in the procession—mostly local factory workers—enter the courtyard of the Norbertine Monastery around 2:30 p.m. wearing the folk costumes of the Kraków region and accompanied by members of a band known as *mlaskoty*, who are dressed in the long gowns and overcoats of the Polish nobility. Lajkonik makes a fanfared entry, a bearded rider in pseudo-oriental dress, mounted on a richly draped wooden horse. Basket in hand, he collects money from the crowd, striking contributors lightly with a baton to distribute good luck. After visiting the nuns and the vicar, he commands the band to strike up a lively tune. Then he leads the procession out of the courtyard onto Zwierzyniecka street, where he eventually slips into a restaurant named in his honor for a rest stop (around 4 p.m.).

He soon returns to the street and is surrounded by greater crowds eager for his shouting and blows. Together, they pop into the Philharmonic and the students' club *(Pod Jaszczurami)* for

Singing and dancing fill the squares of medieval Kraków during the lively Days of Kraków. (Henryk Kaiser/Leo de Wys)

more drinks. Lajkonik's capers continue late into the night until he and his followers file into the old Hawelka (a restaurant near the square) for a hearty meal. Finally, the hero performs a dance for the city fathers in Rynek Square. They reward him with a leather purse full of money and a glass of wine, with which he toasts Kraków's future.

DATE: June, one week after Corpus Christi. **LOCATION:** Kraków, in southern Poland. **TRANSPORT:** Kraków's airport handles flights from London, Paris, Cologne, Frankfurt, Vienna, and Rome. From other departure points it's necessary to change planes in Warsaw. By train or bus, Warsaw is three hours away. **ACCOMMODATION:** Since almost three million tourists each summer scramble for 4,000 beds, be sure to make reservations in advance. **CONTACT:** Polish National Tourist Office (see *Resources*).

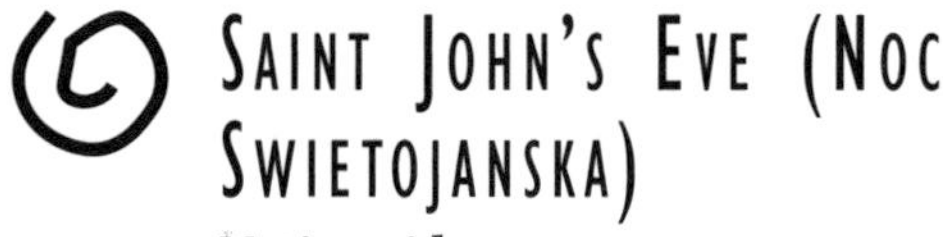

Saint John's Eve (Noc Swietojanska)

Nationwide **June**

Originally a pagan solstice ritual coopted by Christian missionaries, St. John's Eve mixes fire, water, and superstition on the longest day of the year. In Poznan, the marketplace has a week-long medieval fair which exhibits folk arts. There and in Warsaw and Kraków, unmarried women float poetry-laden wreaths of candles, wildflowers, and ribbons down rivers to forecast their romantic futures. Each woman hopes that some pleasing bachelor will pick her wreath out of the water and be inspired by the poem to fall in

The Sounds of Chopin in Poland

A devout nationalist who based much of his music on traditional Polish dance themes, Fryderyk Chopin (1810–1849) is Poland's favorite musical son. In August, pianists flock to the International Chopin Festival in Duszniki Zdroj to give concerts in imitation of the legendary composer, and every five years Warsaw hosts the International Chopin Competition. Throughout the year, Chopin's melancholy, nostalgic themes can be heard at Sunday recitals in Warsaw's Royal Lazienki Park next to the composer's monument. Chopin concerts are also held regularly in his home town of Zelazowa Wola.

love her. If her wreath simply drifts to shore, she takes this to mean that she will never marry, and if the wreath sinks, she's supposed to die before the year ends!

Wreath-floating rituals are also popular in the countryside, where they're typically augmented by singing, fireworks, boat parades, and dancing around lighted bonfires *(sobotke)*. When the last embers cease to glow, the young women retire, and if they go to bed alone they're comforted by the old belief that they'll someday marry the man who appears in that night's dreams.

DATE: The night of June 23. **LOCATION:** Warsaw, Kraków, Poznan, and the countryside. **CONTACT:** National Polish Tourist Office (see *Resources*).

While you're there ...

Juvenalia, Kraków: This three-day student party begins when the mayor presents young people with a "key to the city," which they interpret as a declaration of the state of "anything goes." Events include costumed marches, concerts, plays, and sports. (Last weekend in May.)

Tatra Autumn Festival of Highland Folklore

Zakopane **August/September**

Poland's highest city plays host to a rowdy bunch of highlanders who arrive in their feather-topped hats ready to have a go at vio-

Tatra Autumn Festival: As leaves begin to turn, nearly every mountain village is filled with traditional music. (Joe Viesti)

lins, accordions, and thumping basses. The festival features a surprisingly diverse array of Polish highland groups, including the *górale* bands of the Podhale and Pieniny regions. Each group dresses in its region's traditional attire, and the music is always spirited and authentic.

In addition to the locals, highland performers from all over Europe perform in front of a jury under a tent set up in the Równi Krupowej valley. There are traditional costume shows, parades, art fairs, and poetry competitions, but the real fun is found in the impromptu romps by groups who whoop and holler their way through old mountain melodies. You'll find these groups in both over-touristed Zakopane and the villages of the Podhale and Pieniny regions. Towns like Szczawnica and Kroscienko have a wide range of lively open-air music in August, and the highlanders are fantastically friendly.

DATE: August/September. **LOCATION:** Zakopane, Poland's most popular winter resort, is at the southern base of the Tatra mountain range, next to the Slovak border and about 150 km/90 miles from Kraków. **TRANSPORT:** A car is the preferred mode of transportation to Zakopane, but parking is limited. Local buses provide links to many of the Tatras' valleys. **ACCOMMODATION:** Hotels in Zakopane are crowded through the winter months, but summer lodging is usually less tight. Private lodgings and hospices are also available in Zakopane. **CONTACT:** Tatra Autumn Organizing Bureau, ul. Kosciuszki 13, Zakopane, Tel 669-50. Also, National Polish Tourist Office (see *Resources*).

WRATISLAVIA CANTANS

Wroclaw **September**

Fans of oratory and cantata music will swoon at this outstanding event, which features more than two dozen concerts of Gregorian chants, operas, oratorios, and cantatas. The beautiful music is accentuated by historic venues, which include Wroclaw University's Aula Leopoldina, the lavishly frescoed St. John's Cathedral, and the magnificently ornate town hall. These gothic structures add a significant presence to the performances, and since Wroclaw is Poland's largest university town, there's always something going on. The beautifully restored city has often been compared to St. Petersburg or Amsterdam, with its criss-crossing canals and more than 100 bridges.

DATE: September. **LOCATION:** Wroclaw, Silisia.**TRANSPORT:** Wroclaw has an airport and two train stations served by international and domestic trains. **ACCOMMODATION:** Hotels, hostels, campsites, and private rooms are available. **CONTACT:** Culture and Art Center 50-1-1 Wroclaw, Rynek-Ratusz 24, Poland, Tel 44-28-64. Also: Polish National Tourist Office (see *Resources*).

WHILE YOU'RE THERE ...

- **International Festival of Street Theater, Jelenia Góra and Kraków:** Amateur and professional street groups from around the world perform circus acts, theatrical productions, and concerts. (August.)
- **Music in Old Kraków, Kraków:** Classical concerts are held in churches and squares. (August.)
- **Warsaw Autumn International Festival of Contemporary Music, Warsaw:** This festival, first presented in 1956, showcases classical and avant-garde music, opera, and ballet. (August.)
- **Willa Atma, Zakopane:** Concerts are held all over town in a festival honoring the Polish composer Karol Szymanowski. (September.)
- **All Hallows' Eve/All Saints Day, Nationwide:** On October 31 villagers attempt to strengthen ties with ancestors by visiting cemeteries, lighting candles, and placing food on graves of deceased loved ones.
- **Christmas Creche Competition, Kraków:** In Rynek Square, traditional *szopki,* or nativity cribs, are exhibited and judged. (December.)
- **Vagabonds New Year, Bedzin:** "Vagabonds" pantomime outlandish skits and pranks based on traditional formulas. Dressed in amusing costumes, these rogues perform their way around the entire village from early New Year's Eve until late New Year's Day.

Resources

In Poland: Tourist Information Center *(Centrainy Osrodek Informacji Turystyki)*, ul. Mazowiecka 7, PL-02-052 Warsaw, Tel 22-266539, Fax 22-266204. **USA:** Polish National Tourist Office, 333 N. Michigan Ave., Suite 224, Chicago, IL, 60601, Tel (312) 236-9013, Fax (312) 236-1125; ORBIS (for group tours), 342 Madison Ave., New York, NY 10173, Tel (212) 867-5011, Fax (212) 682-4715. **UK:** ORBIS, 82 Mortimer St., London W1N 7DE, Tel 71 5808028, 71-6374971, Fax 71-4366558. **Germany:** Polish National Tourist Office, Hohenzollerning 99-101, D-5000 Cologne 1, Tel 221-5102240, Fax 221-528277.

ROMANIA

The land of Dracula and Ceausescu is eastern Europe's most bizarre and inexplicable country. An island of Latin culture and language in the midst of Slavs, Romania spent much of its recent history in terror and isolation, which culminated on Christmas Day in 1989 with the nationally televised execution of the dictator and his wife.

Ceausescu's weird legacy left Romanians with bulldozed historical treasures, polluted cities, and dire poverty. No one's predicting a speedy comeback for this country, yet outside the traveler's nightmare of Bucharest and other large cities, an extremely romantic and enjoyable Romania can be found. In the pristine hills and valleys of Transylvania and Moldavia, peppered with historic monasteries, the people live, work, and celebrate in ways that haven't changed since medieval times. The few foreigners who venture to festivals in these out-of-the-way spots can expect to find great music, dancing, and wine, as well as people who are extremely hospitable—once they get over the shock of seeing you there!

Trandafir de la Moldova

Iasi **July**

One of Romania's romantic old cities spruces itself up for three nights of lively music and folk dancing. Couples move around in circles and lines, forming leaping, writhing chains by grabbing each other's belts, while bands play traditional folk instruments like bagpipes, flutes, pan pipes, and violins. The performances are often untraditional and unpredictable, and although locals are indifferent, they're offset by an enthusiastic crowd of international visitors.

Iasi and the surrounding province of Moldavia are an oasis of beauty and civility in one of Europe's most backward countries. The city's great monasteries, cathedrals, and museums were far enough from Bucharest to have survived the Ceausescu era, and as an intellectual center Iasi is a great place to spend a few days exploring and relaxing in cafés or wandering through a countryside dotted with horse farms and interesting monasteries.

DATE: July. **LOCATION:** Iasi, in northeastern Romania's Moldavia region. **TRANSPORT:** Iasi's airport is served by flights from Bucharest and Constanta, and by trains from Bucharest and Kiev. **ACCOMMODATION:** Iasi has five or six hotels and a variety of private rooms. **CONTACT:** Tourism Agency of Moldavia, Casa Studentilor, Calea 23 August, Iasi. Also contact the Romanian National Tourist Office (see *Resources*).

While you're there ...

- **Hora de la Prislop Festival, Prislop Mountain, Maramures district:** This traditional festival and dance contest draws a spirited range of performers from Maramures and northern Moldavia. (Second Sunday in August)
- **Wine Harvest Folk Festival:** The grape harvest is honored in this traditional festival, which takes place at the 500-year-old Odobesti Winery in Vrancea district on the last Sunday in September.
- **Cibinium Festival, Sibiu:** Musicians converge on this sleepy medieval city in the heart of Transylvania for a weekend of music and dance. (September.)
- **Musical Autumn, Cluj-Napoca:** This well-preserved Transylvanian city hosts musicians and dancers who celebrate the changing seasons. (November.)

Resources

In Romania: Carpati Bucuresti S.A., Magheru Boulevard 7, Bucharest 1, Tel 0-145160, Fax 0-156253. **USA:** Romanian National Tourist Office, 342 Madison Ave., Suite 210, New York NY 10173, Tel (212) 697-6971, Fax (212) 697-6972. **Canada:** Embassy of Romania, 655 Rideau St., Ottawa, ON K1N 6A3, Tel (613) 232-5345, Fax (613) 567-4365. **UK:** Romanian National Tourist Office, 83A Marlybone High Street, GB-London W1M 3DE, Tel 71-2243692. **Germany:** Romanian National Tourist Office, Zeil 13, D-60313 Frankfurt 1, Tel 69-295278, Fax 69-292947. **Australia:** Consulate General of Romania, 333 Old South Head Rd., Bondi (Sydney), NSW 2026, Tel 2-305715/8, Fax 2-305714.

RUSSIA

Few countries have generated as many myths about their history, culture, and people as has Russia. Wrapping around almost half the Northern Hemisphere, this vast land has been separated from much of the world by the Iron Curtain for most of the twentieth century. Now that the curtain has lifted, travelers have begun to make their way into the country in search of the truth about Russia. It's a truth that's elusive, and sometimes contradictory: Russia is both an urban country and a rural country, a western country and an oriental country, a country cynical of its politicians' promises and a country deeply faithful in its religions.

No one celebrates revolutions these days, and consequently many of the old Soviet holidays have fallen off the calendar. Russia's illustrious cities still hold exhibitions of the classical arts and music, which often overflow into rambunctious "people's festivals," such as the St. Petersburg White Nights. Religion is at the heart of the rural festivals, and even though the government spent more than seven decades trying to wipe out the church, many Russians have kept the faith and are dusting off the old traditions with vigor. Celebrations in the Russian countryside open doors to understanding the country's past and present way of life. Isolated from Western culture, the native folk traditions have remained pure, often incorporating ancient pagan themes and mythology.

Russian Orthodox Christmas (Rozhdestvo)

Nationwide **January**

The emotional rush and Byzantine splendor of the Orthodox mass was revived in Russia in 1992, and for the first time since the early 1920s the choirs, incense, and liturgies have re-emerged at Russia's great cathedrals. Now both a national and religious holiday, the early January Orthodox Christmas is quickly becoming one of the most popular celebrations of the year. The cathedrals at St.

Christmas in Moscow: Russian children dance with a puppet in Red Square during festivities marking the Orthodox Christmas. St. Basil's Cathedral is in the background. (AP/Wide World Photos)

Petersburg and Moscow are especially enchanting, and whether worshiping or observing, visitors are encouraged to come and go as they please, since the mass starts at midnight and lasts until dawn.

There are no seats in Orthodox churches, but even non-believers are likely to stay longer than they had planned, becoming engrossed by the meticulously organized ritual of the Russian Orthodox mass. Among beautifully colored icons and through air that's thick with incense, the clergy communicates with a mostly elderly congregation through a perfectly memorized series of chants.

Inside the Gogoiavlensky Patriarch Church, a Muscovite places a candle at a side-altar. (Trip/A. Tjagny-Rjadno)

St. Basil's Cathedral, whose twirling onion domes above Red Square is one of Moscow's most recognizable landmarks, spent decades as a museum, but is again functioning as a church. The same is true of Spas no Krovi in St. Petersburg, where Alexander II was assassinated. Both are great locations to take in the murky magic of the Orthodox Christmas.

DATE: Services start just before midnight, January 6, and last until dawn, January 7. **LOCATION:** Spas no Krovi (St. Petersburg), St. Basil's Cathedral and Epiphany Cathedral (Moscow), or other churches and cathedrals throughout Russia. **TRANSPORT:** Moscow and St. Petersburg are served by most major airlines, although many flights require a stopover at a major European hub. Both cities can also be reached by train from Helsinki and eastern Europe. **ACCOMMODATION:** First-class or tourist-class accommodations are available at Intourist hotels, but expensive. Privately run hotels, hostels, and dormitories are just emerging. **CONTACT:** Intourist (see *Resources*).

Winter Festival of Igbi

Shaitli and Kituri **February**

Wearing creepy masks, the young wolf-boys *(botsi)* move into the village, extending long wooden swords so that the woman of each house can put *igbi* (bagels) on it. "Make *igbi*," they chant, "one who does not give *igbi* will be punished." In the square a skit enacts the story of the spirit-custodian of spring called Kvidili, a bizarre creature that, according to legend, came down from the

Big Macs from the McGulag

Directly across from Moscow's Pushkin Ploschad is post-communist Russia's biggest consumer success story. Each day, the world's largest McDonald's serves more than 50,000 customers, many of whom queue up for more than an hour to get their "fast food." Eating or lounging in the more than 800 seats, the customers say one positive part of the Mickey D experience is the smiles on the faces of the Russians working the 27 cash registers—a rare sight in the scowling world of Russian restaurateurs.

Like most hot consumer goods in Russia, McDonald's food has a thriving black market. In peak hours, people line up, purchase the maximum of eight burgers, then walk outside and sell them at a hefty profit. The grounds outside are a festive scene, as kiosks have sprung up selling trinkets and refreshments, and bands play while kids romp and socialize. The McDonald's restaurant workers consider themselves lucky to have a living wage, but in the huge food production complex outside the city, some workers aren't as enthusiastic. The place is so big and efficient that employees have taken to calling it the "McGulag."

mountain on the first day of spring and spoke with the village schoolmaster. The teacher then announced that the Kvidili had come to encourage hard workers and denounce lazy people, drunks, and cheats. Using the schoolmaster as his mouthpiece, the spirit ordered that the best shepherds, dairymaids, students, and dancers be awarded bread and that all miscreants be drowned in the cold river.

In keeping with the story, young people make notes of all the villagers' deeds—positive and negative—and treat the holiday as a day of reckoning. Anyone who has committed some kind of transgression in the past year—drunkenness, for instance—is punished by being immersed up to their ankles in the river, through a hole chopped in the ice. People who have done good deeds are congratulated with igbi. The drama continues through the morning until the Kvidili arrives. This furry creature with a big head, bug-eyes, and copper teeth descends the mountainside clapping his jaws together as villagers look on with respect and mock fear.

Eventually the actor playing Kvidili is picked up and brought to a bridge, where he lays down and a village elder pretends to decapitate him. Several *botsi* lift him out of a pool of fake blood onto a stretcher and carry him off as the rest of the *botsi* shed their wolf costumes and join the other villagers in making merry back at the town center.

DATE: Igbi is usually held in early February, but it can be held at the end of January. In Shaitli, the festival is usually held on the Sunday nearest February 5. **LOCATION:** Shaitli and Kituri, in the Caucasus Mountains of Dagestan (southwest Russia). **TRANSPORT:** Flights from Moscow to the Caucasus generally land in Makhachkala. The area can also be reached by train from Moscow, but the trip may take days. **ACCOMMODATION:** Be prepared to find a shortage of hotels. **CONTACT:** Intourist (See *Resources*).

Spring Festival (Maslenitsa)

Kreshnevo **March**

Winter meets a most violent symbolic death when an enormous effigy of Maslenitsa is raised on stilts, paraded through town, and finally burned under the setting sun. This celebration also features Mardi Gras–like street dances by masqueraders dressed as devils, cats, and goats.

Although the Vesegonsky District of the Tver Region, 250 miles north of Moscow, remains cloaked in snow, the Spring Festival celebrates the imminent warm weather. Women spend the winter sewing huge dolls representing the spirits of winter who, like Maslenitsa, will meet their destiny at the Spring Festival. *Blini* (or pancakes) symbolizing the sun are eaten, and various winter sporting events, such as ski races and skating competitions, take place throughout the festival.

Much of the dancing and singing emphasizes young married couples, who are traditionally associated with the fertility of spring. The word *Maslenitsa* finds its roots in the word maslo, meaning "butter." Milk is poured on the fire to symbolize that dairy products will replace meat during Lent and that, in addition to Maslenitsa, other winter spirits will be destroyed.

DATE: The week before Lent begins. **LOCATION:** Kreshnevo, approximately 250 miles north of Moscow in the Vesegonsky District of the Tver Region. **TRANSPORT:** The Tver Region can be reached from Moscow by train. **ACCOMMODATION:** Since there are no hotels in town, count on camping or the hospitality of villagers. **CONTACT:** Intourist (See *Resources*).

Tun-Payram

Abakan, Khakassia **June**

The villages of this remote Siberian region overflow with festivities celebrating the end of the planting and the opening of summer pas-

Reindeer racing is a highlight of Murmansk's highly participative Festival of the North. (Trip/V. Kolpakov)

tures. Festivities center at first in Abakan, where more than 10,000 villagers gather to partake in traditional dances, sports, and food. Many wear colorful traditional costumes as they romp around to traditional Khakass music. Unlike most of Russia, this region features plenty of great food. You'll find oat biscuits, noodles, yoghurt, tomatoes, melons, and berries, as well as pork and mutton seasoned with onion, garlic, and peppers. The drink of choice is *araka,* distilled from fermented milk. After the festivities in Abakan, the parties move to local villages, and continue for several days.

The fertile Minusinsk Basin and the western Sayan Mountains offer plenty of opportunities for hiking and other recreation. The summer weather is usually great, rivers and lakes are plentiful, and villagers are friendly.

DATE: The first or second Sunday in June. **LOCATION:** Abakan, the capital of the Khakass Autonomous Region. **TRANSPORT:** Abakan's airport is served by flights from Moscow, Krasnoyarsk, Irkutsk, Novosibirsk, and Kysyl. **ACCOMMODATION:** Comfort is a relative term in Siberia, and by Siberian standards Abakan's few hotels are quite comfortable. **CONTACT:** Intourist, 54a Pushkin St., 662200 Abakan, Russia, Tel 66133.

Tibetan Buddhist New Year (Tsagaalgan), Biryatia: The families of Biryatia perform ancient rituals over a fortnight to welcome the new year. (February/March.)

© **Festival of the North, Murmansk:** Visitors flock to Murmansk for winter sports such as a skiing, skating, and reindeer races. Everyone is welcome to either watch or participate. (Last week of March.)

© **Orthodox Easter *(Pashka)*, nationwide:** Energized by a new-found religious freedom, Russia's Orthodox community packs churches and ancient cathedrals to sing, pray, and exchange triple-kisses and painted eggs. (March/April.)

© **Music Spring, St. Petersburg:** Classical music concerts and other performing arts spectacles are staged on Yelagin Island, and half the city gathers on the *strelka* to watch melting ice flows as they drift down the Neva River. (April/May.)

© **Festival of Moscow Stars, Moscow:** A nine-day music festival features the Bolshoi and other nationally renowned drama companies, symphony orchestras, choirs, dance and chamber music groups and soloists, as well as talented young artists. (First week in May.)

© **May Day, Moscow and nationwide:** Less spectacular and more festive than the military parades of old, the Labor and Spring Holiday (its new official name) is still quite colorful in Moscow's Red Square. The tanks and ICBMs are no longer brought out, but a few of the not-so-joyous workers still march past. (May 1.)

© **Pushkin Festival:** Activities honor the great writer Pushkin at Mikhailovskoe (the Pushkin family estate) and surrounding hamlets, near Pushkinski Gori, 130 km/80 miles south of Pskov. (First Sunday in June and two preceding days.)

© St. Petersburg White Nights (Beilyi nochi)

St. Petersburg **June/July**

As the brief twilight descends on one of the world's most northerly cities, the streets and squares acquire an eery but charming ambience. It was this mood that inspired Dostoyevsky's *White Nights*, and it's this mood that inspires revelers to take to the streets and stay up late in a city-wide outburst of celebration.

At present, the city government is short on funds for the concerts, ballets, and other cultural events on Yelagin Island, but the quality of the performances are excellent and residents of St. Petersburg are in high spirits throughout the three-week celebration. Nevskiy Prospekt is packed with revelers, its epic imperial architecture forming a bizarre baroque backdrop for the drunks, gypsies, travelers, teenagers, and merchants who stroll up and down the pot-holed thoroughfare all night, yelling, dancing, and carrying on. Plan to be on the Neva embankment at 1:45 a.m., as the raising of the bridges prompts revelers to pop champagne corks and toast the sun. Boats fill the river, cannons are fired, and fireworks and fountains shoot skyward.

St. Petersburg Raves

On Saturday night in St. Petersburg, people in the know hit the streets for any of the five or six raves that are usually happening in the city. At the bigger, better-known events, foreigners and even Russians often have to pay in dollars or deutsche marks, but the lesser-known organizers usually have better music and more interesting, funky venues. Magic (psilocybin) mushrooms are grown outside the city and have become the drug of choice, and if western fashions are copied, the associated ideologies have somehow gotten lost in the translation: skinheads dance with punks, bikers converse with drag queens, and everyone gets along fine until the Russian Mafia sniffs a success story and tries to get in on the action. Then, organizers are threatened, "protection" money is demanded, and what was once a jolly love-in becomes a rather nervous, expensive night out.

St. Petersburg—formerly Petrograd, formerly Leningrad, formerly St. Petersburg—is a city that's very much alive and filled with an astounding amount of culture and history. You can explore the back streets of the fascinating city when you need a break from the revelry, or spend a white night on a ship sailing out into the Gulf of Finland. Or, check out the fireworks at Petrodvorets, "the town of the fountains," just outside the city.

DATE: Approximately June 22 through July 11. **LOCATION:** St. Petersburg and environs. Other White Nights festivals are held in Vladimir, Suzdal, and Novgorod. **TRANSPORT:** St. Petersburg is served by most major airlines and can be reached by train from Helsinki and Moscow. **ACCOMMODATION:** Hotels are being modernized all the time, but there's still a good deal of variety in both price and quality. **CONTACT:** Intourist, 11 Isakievskaya Sq., St. Petersburg, Russia, Tel 812-3155129. Also: Intourist offices abroad (See *References*).

While you're there ...

Buryat and Russian Folk Festival, Ulan Ude: More than 5600 km/3500 miles from Moscow, Ulan Ude is known as an industrial *and* cultural center. Its world-class operas and ballets are featured at this festival, as are local favorites from this predominately Buddhist region with beautiful scenery and hundreds of carved wooden pagodas. (Early July.)

Ysyakh, Rural Yakutia: Yakutia's thriving shamanist culture boils over in the villages surrounding Yakuts, which welcome the summer with dances, horse races, wrestling, and other games of the Far East. *Kumyss*, made of fermented horse milk, is the drink of choice. (Late July.)

Crimean Dawns, Yalta: Festivities in Yalta pick up for this art and music festival. (August.)

Russian Winter Festival, Moscow, St.Petersburg, Suzdal, Novgorod, Irkutsk: Folk music and dancing, opera, and ballet are performed in concert halls all over each city. In St. Petersburg, *troika* rides appear in Kirov Central Park. (December 25–January 5.)

New Year (Noviy God), St. Petersburg and nationwide: The western Christmas is overlooked in the festive dash to prepare for New Year's Eve. Although New Year is celebrated nationwide, festivities in St. Petersburg are particularly interesting. Torches are set ablaze atop the Rostral Columns, lighting the way for a round of drunken house calls that continues until dawn. Some residents wish their friends and neighbors a happy new year dressed as Uncle Frost and his female sidekick, Snowflake. On New Year's Day, presents are set under the traditional pine tree (*yolka*). (December/January.)

Resources

In Russia: 3 Mokhovaya St., Moscow, Tel 292-3786. **USA:** Russian National Tourist Office, 800 Third Avenue, Suite 3101, New York, NY 10022, Tel (212) 758-1162, Fax (212) 758-0933. **Canada:** Intourist, 1801 McGill College Ave., #630, Montreal, PQ H3A 2N4, Tel (514) 849-6394, Fax (514) 849-6743. **UK:** Intourist Travel Ltd., 219 Marsh Wall, Isle of the Dogs, GB-London E14 9FG, Tel 71 5385966, Fax 71 5383967. **Germany:** Intourist Reisen GmbH, Kurfurstendam 63, 1000 Berlin 15, Tel 30-880070, Fax 30-88-007126.

EASTERN MEDITERRANEAN & THE MIDDLE EAST

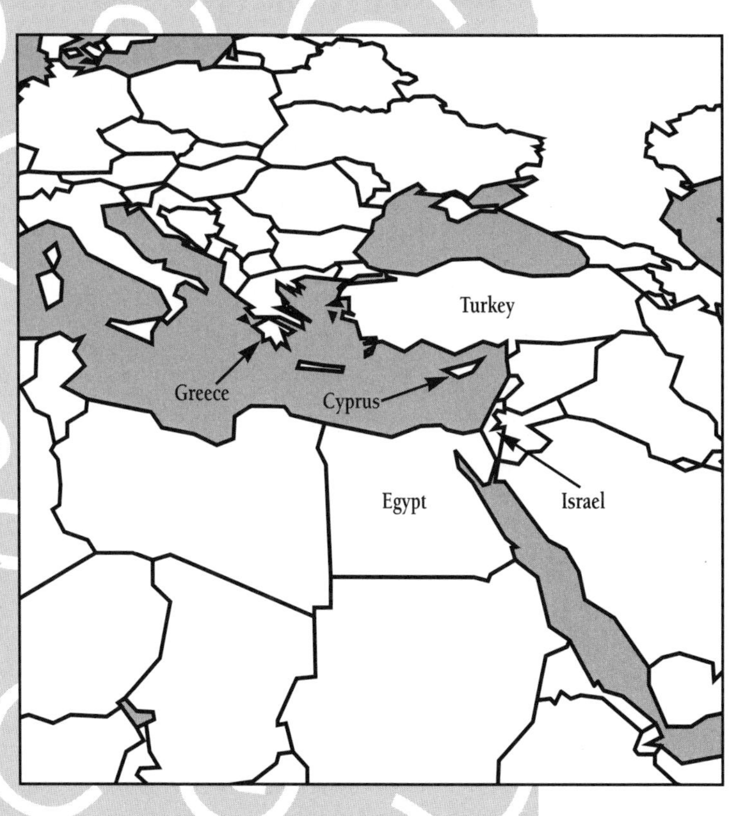

CYPRUS

Straddling the civilizations of both the Orient and the West, Cyprus has been endowed with a rich cultural diversity and vivacity. Its turbulent history—capped by the 1974 Turkish invasion that divided the island—contrasts with the spectacular beauty of its landscapes. Cool cedar forests and orange groves are rimmed by palmy beaches and cliffs, and arid hills support hundreds of native species of wild flowers.

The birthplace of Aphrodite is a romantic setting for the fairs, feasts, and folk dances that are part of everyday life in Cyprus. In the southern (Greek) territory, the celebrations are founded on Orthodox beliefs spiced with pagan and Asian influences. These festivals are steeped in great wine and passionate drama, and are held near beaches and ancient architectural treasures.

Festival of the Flood (Kataklysmos)

Seaside Towns **June**

Only Cyprus celebrates this colorful holiday, which commemorates the salvation of the biblical Noah and the mythical Deukalion—both of whom survived great floods. Coastal towns are filled with street fairs, folk music, and dancing, and harbors host swimming and boat races. Most of inland Cyprus also heads to the coast, for it's good luck to be sprinkled with sea water on this day. The legend arose from the story of Adonis, who is said to rise from death one day each year to rejoin Aphrodite at the seaside. On beaches everywhere, people playfully toss water at each other in a lighthearted rite of purification. Afterward, *Chattismat* (verse arguments) are held, in which two witty contestants exchange quick, rhyming insults.

DATE: The feast coincides with Pentecost; dates can vary from late May to mid-June (contact the Cyprus Tourism Organization for current or coming year dates). **LOCATION:** All the seaside towns of the south hold celebrations. **CONTACT:** Cyprus Tourism Organization (see *Resources*).

Carnival in Cyprus is celebrated with two weeks of costumed parades, feasts, and parties. (*Bill Gleasner/Viesti Associates*)

© While you're there ...

© **Carnival (Apokreo), Limassol and nationwide:** Two weeks of celebrations climax on the Sunday before the beginning of Lent, when the Grand Carnival Parade moves through the streets of Limassol. Nationwide, the Apokreo period is marked by masked balls, parades, satirical songs, feasts, and parties. (February/March. Note that the Orthodox Lent begins about a week later than the Roman Catholic Lent.)

© **Curium Festival, near Episkopi:** Ancient Greek and Shakespearean plays are performed at the ancient Roman amphitheater of Curium, which overlooks Episkopi Bay a few miles west of Limassol. (Six weeks in June and July.)

© **International Folklore Festival, Paralimni:** Cypriot culture is celebrated in this week-long festival, which features open-air theater and other performances. (Early August.)

© **Feast of the Dormition of the Virgin Mary, nationwide:** Towns all over Greek Cyprus—especially those whose patron saint is Mary—go wild with folk music and dancing until early morning. (August 15.)

© Resources

In Cyprus: Cyprus Tourism Organization, P.O. Box 4535, Th. Theodotou St. 18, Nicosia, Tel 2-315715, Fax 2-366744. **USA:** Cyprus Tourism Organization, 13 E. 40th St., New York, NY 10016, Tel (212) 683-5280, Fax (212) 683-5282. **Canada:** High Commission of the Republic of Cyprus, 37 Endeavour St., Red Hill, ACT 2603, Tel 6-2952120, Fax 6-2952892. **UK:** Cyprus Tourist Office, 213 Regent St., GB-London W1R 8DA, Tel 71-7349822, Fax 71-2876534. **Germany:** Fremdenverkehrszentrale Zypern, Kaiserstr. 50, D-6000 Frankfurt 1, Tel 69-251919, Fax 69-250288.

A few highly publicized attacks just about killed Egypt's tourism industry, but for those still willing to make the trip, Egypt offers stunning sites, people, and culture—at bargain prices. Populated Egypt is a fertile strip in the middle of a desert, and a crowded, powerful place where people treat everyday life as a celebration. Festivals include mawlid *(birthdays of religious figures), secular holidays, and festivals honoring the country's architectural wonders.*

EGYPT

Abu Simbel Festival (Celebration of Ramses II's Ascension)

Abu Simbel **February**

The great Ramses II painstakingly angled his temple so that each year on the dates of his birth and coronation, the sun would reach into the structure and illuminate the inner sanctum holding statues of him and of the gods whose company he would join upon death. The rest of the year, the silent images wait in darkness, deep within the temple.

On the morning of February 22 (and again on October 22), people crowd into the temple as the sun rises. The light begins to creep in through strategically placed crevices in the temple's walls, and finally extends the 100 meters (330 feet) from the outer walls to the inner sanctum, to light up Ramses, Ra-Hurakhti, and Amon. Ptah, the Theban god of darkness, fittingly remains in the shadows. After viewing the naturally illuminated gods, the crowd moves outside to celebrate at a special fair which features folk dancing by the Nubian Cobana, Aswan, and Abu Simbel troupes.

The Great Temple of Abu Simbel is the masterpiece of Ramses II, and stands as an enduring self-tribute. Yet one of Egypt's greatest treasures was nearly submersed when the waters of Lake Nasser rose as a result of the Aswan Dam. Egypt and several nations banded together to save Abu Simbel and other archeological sites around the lake. At a staggering cost, the temple was broken up and moved 200 meters (660 feet), then reassembled. After the move the timing of the illumination shifted by one day (February 21 is Ramses II's actual birthday, and October 21 his actual coronation).

DATE: February 22 and October 22. **LOCATION:** Abu Simbel. **TRANSPORT:** Abu Simbel is southwest of Aswan (by about 230 km/150 miles). Air-conditioned buses make the 3 1/2-hour trip in the morning, and return in the late afternoon. Several flights each day also make the trip between the two cities, their timing contingent on demand. **ACCOMMODATION:** There are only two hotels and one campground in town (reservations should be made in advance and confirmed). **CONTACT:** Egyptian Tourist Authority (see *Resources*).

End of Ramadan (Eid al-Fitr)

Nationwide **January/February/March**

After a month of short tempers and tension, the end of the Ramadan fast is signaled by the firing of a cannon at dusk. At that time, Cairo and all of Egypt's cities erupt in a three-day celebration. Wearing new clothes, people take to the streets to visit friends and buy the goods needed to prepare huge feasts. Amusement rides are set up and, although there are no particular "events," the entire country is a festival of cheerfulness and generosity.

DATE: Moving date, according to the Islamic lunar calendar. **LOCATION:** Nationwide. **CONTACT:** Egyptian Tourist Authority (see *Resources*).

While you're there ...

- **The First Day of Spring (Shem al Nessim), Luxor and nationwide:** Egyptian families of all religions observe Shem al Nessim ("sniffing the breeze") by picnicking in the countryside or at the seashore. Traditional foods are *fasik* (a dried, salted fish) and kidney beans. In some villages dancing, singing, games, and storytellers enhance the observance. Luxor has particularly spirited events. (Monday after Coptic Easter.)

The Great Feast (Aid al-Kabir or Eid al-Adha)

Nationwide **April/May**

Excitement is in the air as Egyptians celebrate both Abraham's willingness to sacrifice his son, and the departure for the yearly pilgrimage to Mecca. Streets are festooned with colored lights and banners, and children run around in new clothes, playing drums and riding the makeshift merry-go-rounds set up in streets. The big event in each town is the ceremony of Mahmal, at which pilgrims on their way to Mecca are presented with carpets for the Kaaba at Mecca, and shrouds for the tomb of Mohammed at Medina. Great crowds form at the mosques, and those who are making the pilgrimage assume a high level of prestige, both religiously and socially.

Any family who can afford to will sacrifice a lamb after morning prayer on the fourth day, and distribute more than half of the animal to the poor. This commemorates the commitment that Abraham, who is considered the first Moslem, made to God by sacrificing a sheep, after first offering to sacrifice his own son. Lambs are tethered for sale all over Cairo, and even businessmen in suits can be seen carrying the animals home on their shoulders.

DATE: Moving date, according to the Islamic lunar calendar. **LOCATION:** Nationwide. **CONTACT:** Egyptian Tourist Authority (see *Resources*).

WHILE YOU'RE THERE ...

- **Red Sea Surfing Championship, Hurghada:** Sun, surfers, and seafood can be found above the surface; underwater there's a dizzying array of plant and animal wonders for scuba-dudes and snorkelers. (June.)
- **Prophet Mohammed's Birthday (Maulid an-Nabi), nationwide:** Cairo and all major cities are illuminated and strewn with banners for Mohammed's birthday. Parades and drum shows take place in the streets, and special candy is sold. Muslims outside Cairo celebrate with ritual meals and chants in decorated houses; special tents are set up for male guests. (July/August; moving date according to the Islamic lunar calendar.)
- **International Folkloric Art Festival, Ismailia:** Folkloric troupes from Africa, Europe, and Asia are featured in this international festival of music and dance. The event opens with a parade, then performers in traditional dress take to the stage for a solid week. (Late September.)
- **Celebration of Ramses II's Coronation, Abu Simbel:** This repeat of the February 22 festival honors Ramses II with a natural illumination of his statue and folk entertainment outside the temple. (October 22.)
- **Coptic Christmas, Cairo:** Amid the ancient churches and battlements of Cairo's Christian quarter, the once-dominant Coptic branch of Christianity continues its traditions, with Christmas as its most colorful holiday. (December/January.)

© Resources

In Egypt: Egyptian Tourist Authority Headquarters, Misr Travel Tower, Abbassia Square, Cairo, Tel 02-82351, 02-824858, Fax 02-830844. **USA:** Egyptian Tourist Authority, 630 Fifth Avenue, Suite 1706, New York, NY 10111, Tel (212) 332-2570, Fax (212) 956-6439; 645 North Michigan Avenue, Suite #829, Chicago, IL 60611, Tel (312) 280-4666, (312) 280-4693, Fax (312) 280-4788; **Canada:** Office du Tourisme du Gouvernement Egyptien, 1253 Ave. McGill College #250, Montreal, PQ H3B 2Y5, Tel (514) 861-4420, (514) 851-4606, Fax (514) 861-8071; **Germany:** Agyptisches Fremdenverkehrsamt, Kaiserstrasse 64/A, DW-6000 Frankfurt 1, Tel 69-252153, 69-252319, Fax 69-239876; **Australia:** Consulate of Egypt, 335 New South Head Road, Double Bay (Sydney), NSW 2028, Tel 2-324610.

GREECE

Ancient Greece gave us words and ideas like philosophy, democracy, and hypocracy, but with tourism as the country's largest modern industry, it's fitting that there's no Greek word for "privacy." Much of Greece has been transformed into a hedonistic international colony where the party never stops, and the sunny skies and great beaches often seem to upstage the country's astounding cultural legacy.

Plenty of foreigners in Greece seem to think they invented the drunken, riotous celebration, forgetting that Greece is the home of Dionysus, the god of wine. A trip to more "Greek" areas shows that his legacy is in no danger of dying out. At country fairs and patron-saint festivals, piety is mixed with pleasure in rituals that descend from pre-Christian days, when gods were honored with feasting, dancing, and orgies (even today, Greek villages typically experience mini baby booms nine months after a big feast day). These festivals are great occasions to find villages with their tourist traps disarmed, ready to welcome visitors into the infectious celebrations. Wine and beans are doled out, bandstands are set up in front of the church, and the old ways emanate from the collective unconscious through music, dancing, and other rituals.

Greece's ancient heritage also comes to life in plays and other living spectacles that are presented in well-preserved ancient ruins. Nowhere else on earth can you experience so many of the world's oldest plays performed in the world's oldest theaters—with a perfect open-air setting, perfect acoustics, and dependably perfect weather.

Carnival

Patras and nationwide **January/February**

The revels of Dionysus, the god of wine, are the symbolic origins of the Western world's Carnival, so it's not surprising that Greece, his birthplace, celebrates with an inbred, almost dutiful passion. In most cities the party lasts three weeks. During the first, fattened pigs are slaughtered; during the second everyone feasts on meat; during the third everyone feasts on cheese. The dancing, drinking, and masquerading reaches its peak on the final Sunday before "Clean Monday," the first day of the Orthodox Lent.

Easter on Karpathos: As a priest sermonizes, the men of the village of Olymbos carry religious paintings up the stairs. Massive feasts are prepared to celebrate the resurrection. *(Joe Viesti/Viesti Associates)*

Greece's wildest Bacchanalia can be found in its third-largest city, Patras. The entire town is overcome by insane energy for three weeks, as people of all ages grab their masks and animal skins and come out in the streets to dance the nights away. Macedonia, where Dionysus is said to have been born, is the scene of the oldest surviving Carnival rites. In some towns, men dress up as goats or other animals and parade through the streets. In Naoussa, men dress as damsels, then dance to the main square in groups, accompanied by musicians. In the square the dancing continues, with bystanders pinning drachma notes to the dancers' costumes.

The most unusual celebrations are held on Skyros on the weekend before Clean Monday. In Skyros Town, the *Yeros* (an old man dressed in a heavy cape and goat's mask) festoons his waist with 70 or 80 shepherd's bells. He then leads a wild dance with *Korella,* his "girlfriend," who dresses in women's clothes but wears a sheep's mask. Another member of the party is the *Frangos,* or European, whose 17th-century outfit is designed to provoke as much laughter as possible. The Yeros steps in rhythm, shaking his bells, while the Frangos blows his conch shell. The ensemble works its hilarious way to the monastery of St. George, making as much ruckus as possible as they dance, sing, and imitate the roaring crowd of bystanders.

In Galaxidi, near Delphi, villagers wear masks and costumes and run around the streets whacking each other with sacks of flour until everyone is unrecognizable—a symbolic fracturing of all social conventions. In Thebes a mock peasant wedding is enacted in the streets. Other Carnival hot spots are Cephalonia, Veria, Zante, Kozani, Xanthi, Mesta, Poligiros, Olimbi, Thimiana, Agiassos (Lesbos), Efxinoupolis, Ayia Anna (Evia), Messina, Soho, and Serres.

DATE: The three weeks before the beginning of Orthodox Lent (February–March). **LOCATION:** Patros and nationwide. **CONTACT:** Greek National Tourist Organization (see *Resources*).

While you're there ...

Gynaecocracy, Serres, Kilkis, Xanthi, Komotine: The traditional roles of men and women are reversed at this interesting non-festival. Basically, the men spend the day cleaning house, and the women spend the day socializing and telling fibs in cafés. In the evening, women of child-bearing age bring gifts to the midwife, and the men are allowed to join in the celebrations. (January 8.)

Feast of St. George

Arachova and elsewhere **April**

Three days of festivities surround Arachova's feast in honor of St. George, the knight on the white horse who slew the dragon. The festival fills the town with music, dancing, and bizarre athletic contests.

On the first day, a religious service and procession feature St. George's icon, and dancers move to the sound of traditional bagpipes and drums. The water supply is shut off, since St. George slew the dragon not only to free the princess, but to let the waters run free. During the service old men recite the verse "Dragon, set free the water that the revelers may drink," and the water in the communal tank is allowed to run again. After the service comes a hilarious event that's pretty well summed up by its title, the "Race of the Old Men." All the old men in the village race each other barefoot up a steep slope covered with loose stones; at the top a lamb awaits the winner. The second day is devoted to a jumping contest and the third to wrestling matches.

This relaxing village lies just below the ski center of Mt. Parnassos, and just above the tourist center of Delphi. St. George's day is also celebrated with elaborate feasts and horse races at Kaliopi on Lemnos, and Pili on Kos. At Assi Gonia (near Hania) a religious celebration is followed by a sheep-shearing contest.

DATE: The festival begins on St. George's day, April 23. **LOCATION:** Arachova is located about 10 km/6 miles east of Delphi. **TRANSPORT:** Five buses each day run from Athens or Itea. **ACCOMMODATION:** Both Delphi and Arachova have a wide variety of lodging catering to the many world travelers that inundate the region. **CONTACT:** GNTO (see *Resources*).

While you're there ...

- **Easter Week, nationwide:** On Good Friday, traditional candlelight funeral processions kick off Easter weekend. Processions are also held on Holy Saturday, and feasts follow the midnight mass to celebrate the resurrection. The feasts continue Sunday; spit-roasted lamb and red-dyed eggs are highlights. Afterward, there's usually dancing in the villages. (April/May.)

- **Anastenaria Firewalking Festival, Langada and Ayia Eleni:** Descendants of Thracian refugees continue their pagan/Byzantine ritual of hopping over red-hot coals. In Langada they walk over embers while holding icons of Saint Constantine and Saint Helen, to commemorate the rescue of icons when a church caught fire. In Ayia Eleni a calf is sacrificed in a pre-Christian ritual, and candles are burned in its ears. (May 21.)

- **Athens Festival:** The second-century Odeon of Herodes Atticus on the south slope of the Acropolis is the setting for ancient dramas, operas, music, and ballet performed by the world's top artists. Reserve well in advance. Contact: Athens Festival Box Office, 4 Stadiou Street, Athens. (Early May to late September.)

Wine Festival

Rethymnon` **July/August**

If all the Cretan wine you can drink for about US$2.50 strikes your fancy, bring your own carafe to western Crete and go wild—

The ancient amphitheater at Epidauros: On a warm night you can see for centuries. (*Greek National Tourist Organization*)

you'll have plenty of company! Best of all, you can write your fun off as a historically correct, "educational" venture, since the festival was originally a tribute to Dionysus, the god of wine.

Today, the merchants who benefit from the tourist traffic subsidize the wine and early evening entertainment, which consists of dance groups and *bouzouki* music. You can wander in and out of the festival grounds and explore Rethymnon's narrow, arched streets and small, Venetian-influenced harbor. This quiet, beautiful harbor town is a great place to kick back and relax.

DATE: Two weeks at the end of July and beginning of August. **LOCATION:** Rethymnon, Crete. **TRANSPORT:** Crete's main ferry and air port is Iraklion, but some ferries stop in Rethymnos; buses from Iraklion are frequent (about 1 1/2 hours). **ACCOMMODATION:** The harborside and Arkadiou Street have plenty of lodging. **CONTACT:** GNTO (see *Resources*).

EPIDAUROS FESTIVAL

Epidauros **August/September**

Each summer ancient drama is staged in an ancient theater so acoustically perfect that Henry Miller said he could sense in its confines the beating of the "great heart of the world." Here, each evening, twilight falls and the audience quiets, chilled and humbled by the serene setting—and the notion of watching a play first performed nearly 2,500 years ago.

Plays from the classical Greek canon (written by the likes of Euripides, Sophocles, Aristophanes, and so forth) are performed

The traditional clothing and rituals of the ancient Dorian Greek heritage are faithfully preserved at August's Feast of the Assumption of the Virgin Mary in Olymbos.
(Henneghien/Bruce Coleman Inc.)

by the National Theater of Greece and visiting companies. The ancient tragedies and comedies are known for their excellent quality, but are almost overwhelmed by the setting. Carved out of a quiet rural hillside near the Saronic Gulf (at the sanctuary of the god Asclipius), Epidauros is the best preserved of all Greek theaters. The theater was constructed in the third or fourth century B.C. and was expanded to its current capacity in the second century A.D. Summaries of plays are provided in English—but better yet, bring your own complete translation. And note that children younger than six are not allowed into the theater during performances.

DATE: Friday and Saturday nights from late June through mid-August. **LOCATION:** Epidaurus is about 32 km (20 miles) from Nafplion on the Saronic Gulf in northern Peloponnese. **TRANSPORT:** Special KTEL buses leave Nafplion for Epidaurus at 7:30 p.m., and charters run from Tolo. Nafplion and Tolo are served by frequent buses from Athens. **ACCOMMODATION:** The town of Epidaurus is small and has few accommodations. Most travelers stay in Nafplion or Tolo. **CONTACT:** For tickets and information on performances by the National Theater of Greece, contact Athens Festival Box Office, 4 Stadiou St., Athens, Tel 1-522-3242 or 1-322-1459. In Nafplion tickets can be purchased at Olympic Airways (Tel 274-56) or Bourtzi Tours (Tel 226-91).

While you're there ...

- **Hippokrateia Festival, Kos:** Medical types will dig the costumed reenactment of the first swearing of the Hippocratic Oath. The father of medicine is a native son of Kos, and is honored at this festival, which also includes ancient drama performances, musical evenings, and a flower and art show. (August.)
- **Feast of the Assumption of the Virgin Mary, Olymbos and Tinos:** This festival on the island of Tinos and in the hillside village of Olymbos honors the Virgin's death and ascent to heaven. The island is home to the Orthodox church's most sacred relic, the Icon of the Annunciation, and is mobbed by about 30,000 pilgrims who crawl up from the sea to the shrine on their knees. The evenings are filled with dancing and revelry, and in the mornings the docks, sidewalks, and gardens are coated with sleeping people. (August 15.)
- **Feast of St. Demetrius, Salonika:** Heavy drinking and dancing honors the saint and the season's new wine. (October 26.)

Resources

In Greece: Ellinikos Organismos Tourismou, 2 Amerikis St., GR-10110 Athens, Tel 1-3223111, Fax 1-3222841. **USA:** Greek National Tourist Organization, 645 Fifth Ave., Olympic Tower, 5th Fl., New York, NY 10022, Tel (212) 421-5777, Fax (212) 826-6940. **Canada:** Greek National Tourist Organization, 1300 Bay St., Toronto, ON M5R 3K8, Tel (416) 968-2220, Fax (416) 968-6533. **UK:** Greek National Tourist Organization, 4 Conduit St., GB-London W1R DOJ, Tel 71-7345997, Fax 71-2871369. **Australia:** Greek National Tourist Organization, 51–57 Pitt St., Sydney, NSW 2000, Tel 2-2411663, Fax 2-2352174. **Germany:** Greek National Tourist Organization, Neue Mainzer Str. 22, D-6000 Frankfurt, Tel 69-236562, Fax 69-236576.

ISRAEL

With so many religions claiming Israel and the occupied territories as their spiritual home, it's not surprising that the Israeli festival scene is dominated by religious events. Understandably, most are Jewish holidays, and although they're celebrated in the home and temple, a few are extroverted events that can be enjoyably experienced by any visitor with an open mind. In addition to the Jewish festivities, Israel is packed with pilgrims during Christian holidays, and the resident Palestinian population conducts its own low-key Islamic events. Secular events in Israel often revolve around music, the arts, and sports.

Purim (The Festival of Lots)

Nationwide **February/March**

Most holidays in Israel are celebrated at homes and temples, but Purim—which commemorates the Jews' refusal to compromise their religion—is celebrated with a tremendous amount of communal pageantry. Streets and pedestrian areas are filled with masquerading people who create a carnival atmosphere at the many nighttime celebrations. Israel is essentially a nation of teetotalers, but this is the one day of the year when everyone who can is encouraged to get blotto. Liquor flies off shelves, and people try to get so drunk that they slur the blessings and curses that traditionally are said this day. Everywhere, carnivals, clowns, and street performances spring up. Special foods include *Oznei haman*, or Haman's ears, a fruit-filled pastry.

DATE: February/March (14th day of Adar). **LOCATION:** Nationwide. **CONTACT:** Israel Government Tourist Office (see *Resources*).

While you're there ...

Id ul-Fitr, Arab areas: Observed at the end of the month-long fast of Ramadan, Id ul-Fitr brings Muslims outside to express their joy. Special prayers are given in open fields, children receive presents, and everyone

Purim: A carnival atmosphere envelops Israel, as Jews commemorate their refusal to compromise their religion.
(Joe Viesti/Viesti Associates, Inc.)

visits friends and family to feast on special foods. (January–March; moving date, according to the Islamic lunar calendar.)

Mimouna, nationwide: At the many street parties and open-houses, everyone's invited to join in these lively celebrations when the country's hospitality is at its peak. North African Jews, who brought the celebration to Israel, celebrate this holiday with particular vigor, wearing colorful costumes and setting up elaborate feasts. (March/April; day after the last day of Passover.)

LAG B'OMER

Meiron (Galilee) **April/May**

Hasidim have a ball on this day, which ends 33 days of mourning with dancing, singing, and other good times. The feast is both a spring celebration and a commemoration of the day when a plague ended. It's observed nationwide by all Jews, but nowhere more spectacularly than at Meiron, the hiding place where Shimon Bar Yochai wrote the Book of Splendor (the holy book of the Kabbalists, or mystic Jews).

Torchlight processions move from the Synagogue Quarter in Safed to Shimon's tomb. These parades are quite a sight, featuring thousands of singing and dancing Hasidic men who, upon arrival at Meiron, burn candles at the tomb and light huge bonfires. The next day, three-year-old boys receive a ceremonious first hair cut, and the cuttings are thrown into the fire as part of an ancient ritual.

DATE: April or May (the 18th day of Iyyar). **LOCATION:** Meiron is located just northwest of Safed in Galilee. **TRANSPORT:** Buses run from Tiberias, Haifa, Tel Aviv, Akko, and less frequently from Jerusalem. **ACCOMMODATION:** Safed's accommodation choices are limited. **CONTACT:** Galilee Tourist Marketing Board, P.O. Box 455, 2 Hayarden St., Tiberias 14100, Tel 6-791981, Fax 6-720372.

While you're there ...

- **Independence Day:** All over the country, parades, picnics, and fireworks mark the day Israel became an independent state. (May 14.)
- **Israel Festival, Jerusalem:** As the top event on Israel's calendar of culture, the festival draws international and Israeli performers. Music includes orchestras, choirs, soloists, chamber groups, opera, and jazz bands. Theater productions include classics, satires, modern plays, and pantomime; dance includes ballet, modern, classical, and tap. (May/June.)

Hebrew Music Celebration

Arad **July**

Started as a celebration of Hebrew folk music, this gathering has grown into a full-scale rock fest that's been called the Israeli Woodstock. Young people mob this Negev Desert oasis each year, and just about every Israeli rock or folk star shows up. In addition to simultaneous concerts in various venues, there are cultural events throughout the city and pre-dawn spectaculars at Masada. The whole town has the air of a youth carnival, with enthralled teenagers camping, milling around the pedestrian mall, and eating in local restaurants (many of which have special prices for the event).

When the festival's not in town, Arad is an uninteresting place that's a good base for treks in the Negev or Judean deserts, or to the Dead Sea (which can be seen in the distance). Many people are drawn by its dry, cool, and pollen-free air.

DATE: Mid-July. **LOCATION:** Arad is located on the road between Beersheba and the Dead Sea, about 25 km/15 miles west of Masada. **TRANSPORT:** Buses from Beersheba to Arad are frequent. **ACCOMMODATION:** Don't bother trying to find a hotel or hostel during the festival. Just bring a sleeping bag and stretch out in one of the several campgrounds set up around Arad. It won't rain. **CONTACT:** Tourist Information Office, 28 Eliezer Ben Yair St., Arad 80757, Tel 57-954109. Negev Tourism Development Authority, 1 Sold St., Beersheba, Tel 057-671539, Fax 057-671538. Also: Israel Government Tourist Office (see *Resources*).

While you're there ...

Klezmer Festival, Safed: Israel's many klezmer players and orchestras set this beautiful, ancient city abuzz with their zany tunes. (July/August.)

International Red Sea Jazz Festival

Eilat **August**

Four stages draw local and international performers to this critically acclaimed festival in Israel's biggest resort. Each day there are 10 performances on the main stages in the port area, and workshops at venues around town. The crowd is cosmopolitan and generally upscale.

Eilat itself is a vacation boomtown set up in the past couple of decades. On one hand, it's an ugly and cynical tourist trap. On the other hand, it's one of the few places in Israel where religion doesn't dominate, a hedonistic playground of sunning, snorkeling, and never-ending nightlife. The weather is always hot, but you can cool off underwater where the coral and fish life is fantastic.

DATE: Mid-July. **LOCATION:** Eilat (also spelled Elat) is Israel's port city on the Red Sea. **TRANSPORT:** Eilat can be reached by air from Jerusalem and Tel Aviv, or by bus from Jerusalem, Tel Aviv, or Beersheba. **ACCOMMODATION:** Although Eilat's lodging caters mostly to upscale travelers, there are several cheap hostels in town and beach-camping is allowed (look out for thieves). **CONTACT:** Festival Organizers: Tel 03-510-0994. Eilat Tourist Information Office, Mercas Ariel Hakhan, Eilat, Tel 7-334353.

While you're there ...

Prince of Peace Music Festival, Dimona: At the self-contained Black Hebrew settlement in Dimona, a small music festival features Gospel, funk, and jazz. The event is held in honor of the founder of the Black Hebrews, who are former African Americans claiming descendance from the original Hebrew Israelites. Contact: Tel 57-55400. (September/October.)

Sukkot, nationwide: Full of both religious and cultural significance, this festive holiday reminds Jews of living in the wilderness after the exodus. Most people erect homemade, beautifully decorated *sukkot* (shelters) of leafy branches on their balconies. Jerusalem's main market is especially festive. (September/October.)

Christmas Midnight Mass

Bethlehem **December/January**

The birthplace of Jesus of Nazareth brims with excitement and piety as pilgrims from around the world come to celebrate his birthday. In Manger Square a huge crowd assembles for a Protestant choir service with participants from around the world wrapped up against the late-December chill. Midnight mass itself is celebrated inside the Church of the Nativity, where space is reserved for practicing Roman Catholics (who must get the free tickets in advance). In a high-tech gesture of accommodation for those who can't get in, the mass is broadcast onto a video screen that's mounted on the police station in the square. The next day a procession wends from Jerusalem's Old City to Bethlehem.

DATE: You have your choice of Christmases in Bethlehem. The biggest event is at midnight December 24/25, but the Orthodox celebrate their big day on January 7, and the Armenians on January 19. **LOCATION:** Manger Square in Bethlehem. **TRANSPORT:** Either hike from Jerusalem (about 2 hours, downhill all the way), or take a frequent bus. **ACCOMMODATION:** Two thousand years later, there's still a shortage of rooms in Bethlehem; most travelers stay in nearby Jerusalem with its wide range of accommodations. **CONTACT:** Apply for tickets to the mass at the Terra Sancta office, Christian Information Center, Old City, Jerusalem. Also: Tourist Information Center, Manger Square, Bethlehem, Tel 2-742591.

Resources

In Israel: Israel Tourism Development Corporation, 36 Keren Hayesod St., Jerusalem 92149, Tel 2-668211. **USA:** Israel Government Tourist Office, 350 Fifth Ave., 19th Fl., New York, NY 10118, Tel (212) 560-0600, Fax (212) 629-4368. **Canada:** Israel Government Tourist Office, 180 Bloor St. W., Ste. 700, Toronto, ON M5S 2V6, Tel (416) 964-3784, Fax (416) 964-2620. **UK:** Israel Government Tourist Office, 18 Great Marlborough St., GB-London W1V 1AF, Tel 71-4343651, Fax 71-4370527. **Germany:** Israel Government Tourist Office, Bettinastr. 62, D-6000 Frankfurt 1, Tel 69-752084, Fax 69-746249. **Australia:** Embassy of Israel, 6 Turrana St., Yarralumla, Canberra, ACT 2600, Tel 6-2732045, Fax 6-2734273.

TURKEY

Straddling two continents, Turkey has spent the last several centuries struggling to decide whether it wants to be part of modern, secular Europe or traditional, Islamic Middle East. The country has far more ancient cities and classical ruins than Greece, and whether you're exploring the world's oldest city or climbing through some of the first Christian settlements, a visit to Turkey is a hands-on history lesson.

Lingering stereotypes continue to hurt tourism (mention you're going here and the movie *Midnight Express* will surely come up), but Turkey is one of the most interesting and comfortable budget travel destinations in the world. A surprising number of traditional festivals abound—especially in outlying areas. At these age-old celebrations, you can watch Whirling Dervishes perform their 700-year-old dance, or see a field full of squirming, oiled men wrestling in a 14th-century ritual that will leave only one standing. What's more, at the end of the day, you can head to some of the Mediterranean's best beaches.

Kirkpinar Oiled Wrestling Championships

Edirne **July**

With their oil-coated skin shining in the sun, the 40 wrestlers move quickly into the sweat-soaked grass before pairing off. "Let Allah guide him of the truest heart to victory" squawks the official, and the matches begin. Clad only in olive oil and leather shorts, wrestlers try to get hand or leg holds on their slippery opponents, then flip them and force their shoulders to the ground. Once a pin is made and acknowledged by the referees, the winner pairs off with another winner, continuing a match that will end only when a single wrestler is left standing.

Big money and big prestige are at stake in these free-for-all finals, which last anywhere from a half hour to three hours. For nearly a week the action continues, in matches that feature six-year-old boys up to heavyweights. *Yagli Güres* (oil-coated wrestling) is held all over the country during the summer, but the matches at this scrub-covered island (once the sultan's private

Slippery: After greasing their bodies with olive oil, wrestlers square off at Kirkpinar's championship match. *(Trip/Trip)*

hunting ground) are the most prestigious. It was here, in 1360, that the sport was invented as a means of whipping troops into shape for raids into eastern Europe. More than 1,000 wrestlers show up, and tens of thousands of spectators cheer them on (or boo them if a match gets boring).

The wrestling itself is quite a spectacle, but outside the arena the huge gypsy fair that springs up is just as colorful. "Traveling people" from all over European Turkey, Greece, and Bulgaria converge on the spot, livening up the action with carnival rides, dancing bears, and games of chance (packs of Marlboros are popular prizes). A Gypsy pipe-and-drum band even provides a spirited soundtrack for the opening parade of wrestlers, and exhibitions of folk dancing round out the evenings.

Edirne itself is an architectural gem that's mostly overlooked by tourists, unless they happen to stop here on an overland trip from Europe to Istanbul. Its many resplendent mosques represent the finest work of the great Ottoman architects, and the town is blessed with a surfeit of mysterious covered bazaars, bridges, and *caravanserais*.

DATE: Six or seven days in July. The date fluctuates substantially from year to year, so check with the Tourism Information Office for dates. **LOCATION:** Edirne is situated about 250 km (155 miles) northwest of Istanbul, near the Bulgarian and Greek borders. **TRANSPORT:** The city can be reached via a comfortable four-hour bus trip from Istanbul. Wrestling takes place at Kirkpinar on Sarayiçi Island, just east of Eski Saray on the Tunca River. **ACCOMMODATION:** As a traveler's refuge since the second century, Edirne has a wide variety of budget and mid-range accommodations, but very little on the top end. **CONTACT:** Turkish Tourism Information Office (see *Resources*).

While you're there ...

- **Camel Wrestling, Selçuk:** A three-day festival highlights camel wrestling, a wild and hairy Turkish exclusive. (January.)
- **Manisa Power Gum Festival, Manisa:** Step right up! This festival celebrates *kuvvet macunu,* or "power gum," the Manisa specialty that can preserve youth and restore potency. Created by the wife of Ottoman Sultan Yavuz Selim, the traditional remedy made from 41 different ingredients is said to bring back vigor, vim, and vitality. (End of April.)
- **Kafkasör Art and Culture Festival, Kafkasör:** Bull wrestling, drinking, and general revelry surround this popular festival in the high meadows around Kafkasör. A mini-city of tents is set up, and tens of thousands of locals spend the week partying. This one's a rustic Turkish delight! (Late June.)
- **Istanbul International Festival, Istanbul:** The world's top symphonies, chamber groups, and pop musicians join with folk dancers, folk musicians, and visual artists in this esteemed festival, which bridges Europe and Asia from mid-June through late July.

Festival of the Whirling Dervishes

Konya **December**

Arms folded, each of the Dervishes passes in front of the *seyh,* who whispers the sacred instructions of Mevlana. The dancer then

The brotherhood of the Whirling Dervishes: Dancing to achieve mystical union with God. *(Joe Viesti/Viesti Associates, Inc.)*

moves out onto the floor with the others, extending his arms and beginning his spinning dance. An orchestra led by reed flutes drives the dervishes, who raise their right arms to receive the blessings of heaven, and lower their left arms to communicate the blessings to earth. Spinning ever faster on their left heels, the Dervishes' white robes begin to fly, and under conical red hats expressions of ecstasy appear. The pious crowd is spellbound as the drums beat faster and the constellation of Whirling Dervishes begins to rotate in a mesmerizing circle. The tempo continues to increase as dancers' faces are lost in a blur of motion, until suddenly the music stops and the dancers kneel, their hearts enlightened and ready to receive the Koran's poetry.

Each December, Whirling Dervishes gather in a local gymnasium for their divine ballet, hoping through the dance to relinquish the earthly life and achieve mystical union with God. Founded in the 13th century by the Islamic poet Mevlana Jelaleddin Rumi, the Dervish Order preached tolerance, enlightenment, and forgiveness. They were outlawed as a religious unit in 1925, but the Dervishes survived as a cultural brotherhood. Today they present their *sema,* or whirling ceremony, each year to hundreds of people who still recognize it as a form of worship, and to thousands who recognize it as one of the world's living cultural treasures.

DATE: Mid-December. **LOCATION:** Konya, the former capital of the Seljuk Empire, is located on the Anatolian plateau, about 120 km/75 miles south of Ankara. **TRANSPORT:** In addition to an airport with twice-weekly flights from Istanbul, Konya's bus station has frequent service from all major Turkish cities. **ACCOMMODATION:** Konya's many budget and mid-range hotels offer exceptional value and clean, interesting surroundings. **CONTACT:** Turkish Tourism Information Office (see *Resources*).

While you're there ...

Cirit Games, Konya: This festival presents two days of *cirit*, the uniquely Turkish sport of horseback javelin throwing. (Late September.)

St. Nicholas Festival, Demre: A festival/symposium is held at the fifth-century Byzantine church that honors Demre's favorite son, known to the West as Santa Claus. The legend began when St. Nicholas, a fourth-century bishop, anonymously dropped bags of coins down the chimneys of the homes of village girls who had no dowry, thus allowing them to marry. (December.)

Selçuk Ephesus Festival of Culture and Art

Selçuk and Ephesus **May**

Carved out of the side of Mt. Pion, the ancient Great Theater at Ephesus is the setting for concerts, plays, and folk dances. From the top seats you can gaze on the entire city and marvel at the theater's acoustics, which are so fine that it's possible to stand on the stage and carry on a conversation with someone sitting in the top row. The theater seats 24,000 and is the scene of the festival's classical plays and other events, but exhibitions of art, handicrafts, and performing arts take place throughout the ancient city of Ephesus, and the not-so-ancient city of Selçuk, four km (two and a half miles) away.

In terms of sheer magnitude, Ephesus is probably the world's premier archeological site. It's filled with well-preserved temples, sacred ruins, grottos, libraries, stadiums, and the first church dedicated to the Virgin Mary (who once lived here, as did St. Paul). Even non-aficionados of ancient ruins can't help being fascinated here, with so much history couched in the verdant countryside. And when you get tired and hot from all the hiking around, you can head to the fantastic Agean beaches.

DATE: First week in May. **LOCATION:** Selçuk and Ephesus are located about 50 km/31 miles south of Izmir. **TRANSPORT:** The nearest airport is located in Izmir, and buses run from there and everywhere else in Turkey. **ACCOMMODATION:** Camping and low- to mid-range hotels are located in Selçuk. **CONTACT:** Turkish Tourism Information Office (see *Resources*).

Resources

In Turkey: Ministry of Tourism/Istanbul Information Office, Turizm Bakanligi/Istanbul Bölge Müdürlügii, Mesrutiyet Caddesi 57/6, Galatasaray, Istanbul, Tel 1-2456875, Fax 1-2524346. **USA**: Turkish Tourism & Information Office, 821 United Nations Plaza 7th Fl., New York, NY 10017, Tel (212) 687-2194, Fax (212) 599-7568. **Canada**: Turkish Embassy, 197 Wurtemburg St., Ottawa, ON K1N 8L9, Tel (613) 232-1577, Fax (613) 232-5498. **UK**: Turkish Tourism & Information Office, 170–173 Piccadilly, 1st Fl., GB-London W1V 9DD, Tel 71-3354207, Fax 71-4910773. **Germany**: Turkish Tourism & Information Office, Baseler Str. 37, D-6000 Frankfurt 1, Tel 69-233081, Fax 69-232751. **Australia**: Turkish Embassy, 60 Mugga Way, Red Hill, ACT 2603, Tel 6-2950227, Fax 6-2396592.

AFRICA

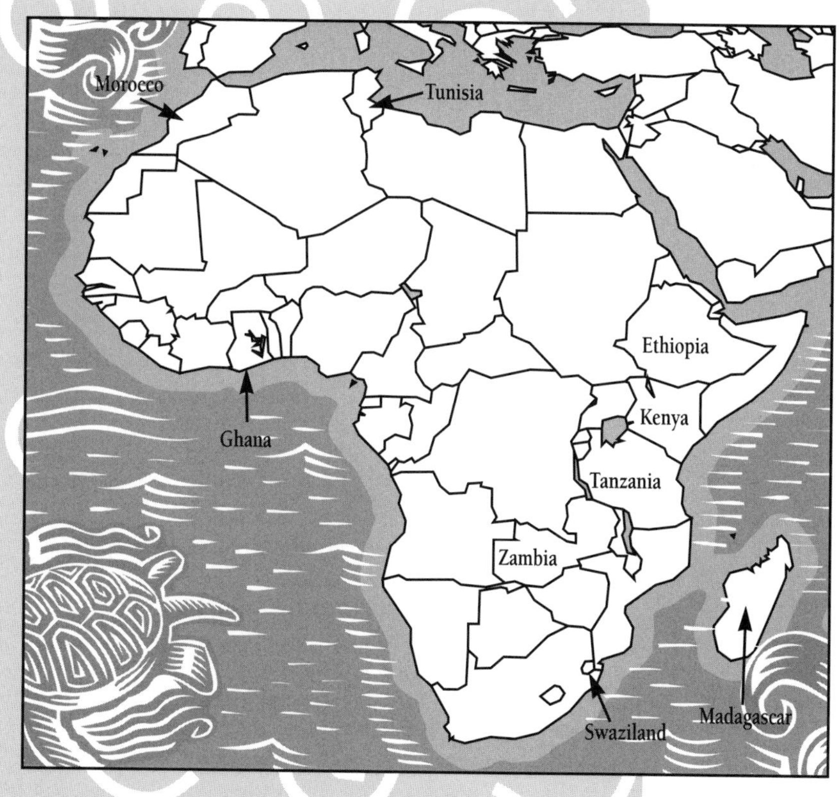
Morocco
Tunisia
Ethiopia
Ghana
Kenya
Tanzania
Zambia
Madagascar
Swaziland

ETHIOPIA

Once fraught with famine and civil strife, Ethiopia is back on its feet. Travelers are rediscovering this beautiful nation with a fascinating culture and a 1,900-year history of nationhood. Its success in staving off European colonizers is unique in Africa, and is complemented by success in staving off the onslaught of Islam, which enveloped the country's neighbors in northeast Africa.

The peculiarly tolerant and ritual-laden Ethiopian Orthodox Church developed in isolation from the rest of the world, and is the driving influence behind most of the country's many unique and spirited festivals. Ethiopian festival origins are often buried deep in pre-Christian pagan ritual, and in many cases they honor gods renamed as Christian or Moslem saints. Impressive in number and spectacle, these feast days serve as colorful landmarks in the lives of ordinary people, and often stretch across religious barriers to draw Christians, Moslems, and tribal animists into special sports, music, and other rituals.

Timket

Nationwide **January**

This very spirited and uniquely Ethiopian affair combines the Feast of Epiphany and the Feast of St. Michael the Archangel, who is Ethiopia's favorite saint. In Christian areas, massive throngs of revelers sing and dance to a cacophony of wildly beating drums while dramatic religious processions move through the streets.

The festivities get going the day before the Epiphany, which, according to Ethiopia's Julian calendar, falls on January 19. In preparation, special *tej* and *tella* (Ethiopian beer and mead) is brewed, bread is baked, and sheep are slaughtered. Everyone dresses in dazzling white except the priests, who wear brilliantly jeweled ceremonial velvets and satins, with sequined velvet umbrellas. The priests emerge from their churches with engraved stone or wooden *tabots* (tablets that represent the Arc of the Covenant and the Ten Commandments) and perform rollicking dances as they bring the *tabots* to a nearby water source. In Addis Ababa, the Jan Meda area assumes a carnival atmosphere as each congregation rolls in, accompanied by ringing bells, blowing

Timket: Amid a flurry of drumming, Ethiopian Orthodox clergy march to Addis Ababa's Jan Meda where they will spend the night performing mass and blessing the water. (Wendy Stone/Odyssey Productions/Chicago)

trumpets, and swinging incense censors. Huge crowds camp in the meadow, eating and drinking by the light of hundreds of fires and torches.

At about 2 a.m. the priests perform mass, and just before dawn the water is blessed by the immersion of a golden cross and a burning consecrated candle. Each priest then sprinkles water on the congregation to commemorate Christ's baptism, and the most fervent members of congregations leap fully clothed into the water to renew their vows. The feasting, singing, and dancing continue in the morning, as processions of people and decorated horses wind through town, the priests leaping and singing alongside their precious *tabots* (which are covered to avoid being desecrated by the gaze of laymen). In Addis Ababa on this afternoon, *feres gug* is played and groups of musicians from all over the country perform their local music throughout the city.

Most of the *tabots* are returned to their home churches on January 19. Tabots belonging to churches dedicated to St. Michael are kept *in situ* until the saint's big day, January 20. Then a huge, writhing crowd surrounds the church, dancing and singing to the sounds of furiously beating drums. Since the marriage season is beginning, enterprising young men use the occasion to spot potential brides, often approaching fathers to make enquiries.

DATE: January 19 (the date, which is set according to the Julian calendar, can fluctuate by a day or two). **LOCATION:** Nationwide. **CONTACT:** Ethiopian Tourism Commission or embassy (see *Resources*).

While you're there ...

- **Genna, Addis Ababa and nationwide:** The Ethiopian Christmas celebration, called Genna, falls on the old Julian date of January 7, and is marked by services at churches nationwide. Priests sing hymns while carrying prayer sticks and rattles, then lead processions with ceremonial drums, poets, and singing. In the late afternoon a hockey-like ball game, also called Genna, is played.

- **Easter, nationwide:** Ethiopia's most solemn festival is accompanied by unique sacred music and dance, and celebrated in moving rituals during midnight mass. (March/April.)

- **Adbar, southern Ethiopia:** In Oromo tribal areas where ancient animist beliefs have not been overrun by Christianity or Islam, sacrifices and blessings are given to the god *Waqa*. Many celebrations include dancing to music played on a traditional one-string fiddle called the *mesenko*. (Approximately May 8.)

- **Festival of Sof Omar, Sof Omar (Bale):** Moslems make a pilgrimage to the river cave that once housed Omar the holy man. The huge cave's natural columns and buttresses resemble a gothic cathedral. (May.)

Maskal

Addis Ababa and nationwide **September**

Maskal fills Ethiopia's Christian areas with dancing, singing, and feasting, fueled by plenty of local beer. Travelers become revelers as townspeople encourage them to join in the merrymaking that harbingers springtime and the season of flowers.

In Addis Ababa a special torch-bearing procession to Maskal Square on the eve of the holiday draws 100,000 spectators and participants. The parade include priests carrying tasseled parasols, school groups, brass bands, soldiers, and floats toting gigantic lit-up crosses. When the procession reaches the square at twilight, priests chant and marchers stack poles decorated with daisies around a large tree. Pilgrims in traditional finery circle the pyramid three times in honor of the Trinity, and finally *chibo* (flaming torches of bundled eucalyptus twigs) are thrown onto the pyramid, setting it ablaze. Dancing around the bonfire continues until around dawn, when the tree at the middle of the pyre is finally consumed by the fire, its fall marking the beginning of spring.

The festival, which has been celebrated in Ethiopia for 1,600 years, is tied to the fourth-century discovery by Empress Helena, the mother of the Roman emperor Constantine, of the cross on which Christ was crucified. *Maskal* means cross, and is

The Feres Gugs

Ethiopia's national pastime is *feres gugs,* an exhibition of wildly brilliant horsemanship demonstrated by teams of warriors wearing lion-mane capes and baboon-hair headdresses. The game descends from the horseback warfare of olden days, when speed, courage, and stamina were needed to survive. These traits are needed to succeed in the game of *feres gugs,* but the crowd also admires good fashion sense. In addition to the dapper riders, horses sport caparisons of velvet and brocade, embossed saddles, and red wooly tassels with glints of silver.

The teams consist of "pursuers" who chase white-clad "fleers" around, attempting to whack them with sticks and throw them off their mounts. The fleers protect themselves with traditional shields of hippopotamus or rhinoceros hide, and as they tear across the plain they dodge and deflect the blows, sometimes falling and immediately remounting in a comic, though painful-looking spectacle.

At Sululta, just north of Addis Ababa, good times to catch *feres gugs* are on or around January 19 (Timket), January 29, September 27 (Maskal), and October 1.

also the name given to the yellow daisies that bloom on the mountains and plains during this time of year.

DATE: September 27 (the date, which is set according to the Julian calendar, can fluctuate by a day or two). **LOCATION:** Addis Ababa and nationwide. **TRANSPORT:** Addis Ababa can be reached from several cities in Africa, Europe, and the Middle East; from North America it's necessary to change planes in Europe. **ACCOMMODATION:** The city's hotel options range from dirty budget to Hilton. **CONTACT:** Ethiopian Tourism Commission or embassy (see *Resources*).

While you're there ...

Ethiopian New Year, nationwide: As the rainy season comes to an end, singing can be heard in villages as groups of children run from door to door with bouquets of flowers. In cities there are processions and hymns. (Approximately September 11.)

Feast of St. Gabriel (Kullubi)

Kullubi **December**

In the massive pantheon of Orthodox Ethiopian saints, St. Gabriel is said to grant more requests than others. With this in mind, thousands come from all over the country on their patron saint's special day to tell him their hopes. This wish-fest draws people of all creeds and races—Orthodox Christians, Moslems, tribal people, Greeks, Armenians—and is a great opportunity to see and meet a cross-section of Ethiopia's populace.

Set in a terraced coffee-growing area, the church at Kullubi is surrounded by thousands of tents as the big day draws near. Many pilgrims walk the final few kilometers, in some cases carrying boulders on their backs to demonstrate their piety. One wish the saint is particularly good at granting is pregnancy; you'll see a good many babies, presumably born through Gabriel's intervention, being carried to the font for baptism. Most will be named Gabriel.

People-watching opportunities are sensational. Many people wear the typical Ethiopian outfit of bright white cotton, but others, especially the nearby Harer tribe, wear brilliant reds, oranges, and purples. The smells from thousands of campfires waft through the air, and vendors sweep through selling peanuts, beer, and candy. Most camps have large pots of *tella* and *tej* (local beer and mead), and above the many radios you'll hear laughter and shouts of joy. The church itself is small, and most people experience High Mass via loudspeakers.

DATE: December 28 (the date, which is set according to the Julian calendar, can fluctuate by a day or two). **LOCATION:** Kullubi is 68 km/42 miles from Dire Dawa, in the Harerge Region. **TRANSPORT:** Don't consider making this journey unless you've arranged transport weeks in advance, since every train, bus, and truck will be completely full. From Addis Ababa, you can take the train or bus as far as Dire Dawa, then you'll need to have prearranged rides to Killubi itself. **ACCOMMODATION:** Most people bring a tent and bed down with the masses. **CONTACT:** Ethiopian Tourism Commission or embassy (see *Resources*).

Resources

In Ethiopia: Ethiopian Tourism Commission, P.O. Box 2183, Meskel Sq., Addis Ababa, Tel 1-517470. **USA**: Embassy of Ethiopia, 2134 Kalorama Rd. NW, Washington, DC 20008, Tel (212) 421-1830, Fax (212) 754-0360. **UK**: Embassy of Ethiopia, 17 Prince's Gate, GB-London SW7 1PZ, Tel 71-5897212, Fax 71-5847054. **Germany**: Embassy of Ethiopia, Bretanostr. 1, D-5300 Bonn 1, Tel 228-233041, Fax 228-233045.

GHANA

As West African budget travel destinations go, no other country inspires raves like Ghana. Crime is low, cities are hopping, beaches and lagoons are beautiful, and people are friendly and sociable almost beyond belief. Along the coast, you can feast on fresh seafood, sleep in old castles and forts, or contemplate the abominable history of slavery amid the many surviving architectural remnants.

The well-educated Ghanaians have long had contact with northern cultures, but they've also recognized the advantages of maintaining their own rich and vibrant cultures. Well-known tribal groups like the Ashanti prosper from handicrafts (kente cloth, carvings, stools, and fertility dolls) and perform elaborate ceremonies in honor of chiefs, ancestors, and fertility gods. These are extremely colorful, the action is diverse and non-stop, and visitors are welcomed with open arms by Ghanaians who are proud to show off their astounding culture.

Addae-Kese

Kumasi **January**

The largest and most important event in the Ashanti culture celebrates the date that the fetish priest Okomfo Anokye magically summoned the Ashantis' Golden Stool from heaven. It's an occasion of incredible pomp and pageantry, with marathon hip-shaking dance-fests, talking drums, and an over-the-top procession in which the Ashanti king is carried on the shoulders of courtiers while he dances.

Elaborate stools play a big part in Ashanti culture. Everyone has a favorite, and after a relative dies the stool is kept in a special spot for ancestor worship. Only one bona fide golden stool ever existed, which is said to have been magically bestowed on the founder of the Ashanti kingdom, King Osei Tutu.

During the festival, the ancestral stools are purified in household ceremonies, and mashed plantains, yams, and eggs are "fed" to the gods and ancestors. The public events feature the precious golden stool and the recipient of its powers, the current Ashanti King. The king and the golden stool sit in state, receiving homage from sub-chiefs and citizens of the Ashanti community, and often the President of Ghana.

Kumasi itself is a vibrant, pretty, highly cultural town that houses the king's palace, an old British fort, a huge market (which is a good place to buy kente cloth and handicrafts), and the National Cultural Centre, where excellent variety shows of African music, dance, and drama are staged on weekends (you can also take courses in drumming and dancing). The museum houses the fake golden stool that the Ashanti used to bluff and humiliate the British, who demanded the golden stool they had never seen after hearing that the Ashanti king got his strength from it. Near Kumasi, thriving, traditional Ashanti villages specialize in weaving, wood carving, and goldsmithing.

DATE: The ritual is held every 40th or 42nd day of the year, but the January celebration is the biggest and most important. The Ghana Tourist Board has the exact date several months in advance. **LOCATION:** Kumasi is situated in the heart of Ghana. **TRANSPORT:** Daily flights are available from Accra and Tamale, as are buses and bush taxis. Trains serve Kumasi from Accra and Takoradi. **ACCOMMODATION:** A variety of accommodations are available in Kumasi, many in old colonial buildings with beautiful terraces and gardens. **CONTACT:** Ghana Tourist Board (see *Resources*).

Deer Hunting Festival (Aboakyere)

Winneba **May**

Ghana's most dramatic cultural tradition is a ceremonious hunt in which two groups of unarmed hunters (*Asafo* companies) move through the woods in separate directions in an effort to find an antelope, the clan totem of the Winneba people. The first group to capture one alive and bring it back to the chief wins.

Festivities begin early in the morning as each *Asofo* company goes to the beach for purification and then marches to the residence of the Penkye Otu fetish to be baptized with herbs. They continue to the palace of the village chief (Omanhene) to greet the royal family, and then they're off to the hunting grounds. Each company has its own colors and flags, so it's easy to identify them as they trek through the hunting grounds, singing war songs and sounding gongs, whistles, rattles, bells, and bugles to scare the deer from hiding. When an animal is caught, a hunter slings it over his shoulder and returns with his group to the chief's palace, singing and dancing all the way.

Members of the winning *Asofo* company are crowned as heroes of the town, since failure to catch a deer would have been considered a bad omen and a curse from gods and ancestors. The animal is sacrificed by the chief and part of it is prepared in a spe-

Hooting at hunger: A drummer hails the harvest, while women look on with plates of kpolpei, *the festival specialty.* *(Robert Frerck/Odyssey Productions/Chicago)*

cial soup, which is extended as an offering to the Penkye Oto fetish. At that point, a round of spirited partying begins that doesn't stop until the early morning. Traditional music is played on drums and bamboo flutes, while native women sing and dance through the streets to cheer the triumphant hunters.

Winneba has a beautiful, peaceful beach—unblemished by tourists—where local fishermen arrive in the morning to pull in their nets. In nearby Senya Beraku, you can stay at an old Dutch fort built on a stunning site overlooking the beach.

DATE: The first Saturday in May. **LOCATION:** Winneba, about 62 km/38 miles west of Accra. **TRANSPORT:** Tro-tro (minibuses), buses, and bush taxis from Accra are both convenient and inexpensive. **ACCOMMODATION:** A variety of accommodations, from inexpensive hotels to resort fare, are available. **CONTACT:** Ghana Tourist Board (see *Resources*).

Hunger Hooting Festival (Homowo)

Accra **August/September**

Celebrated as a way to commemorate an excellent harvest that blessed the Ga people after an ancient exodus, the Homowo Festival also marks the new year for the Ga, who are the original inhabitants of Accra. During the first week, daily drumming reminds ancestors to join their descendants in celebrating the festival and participants shoot guns into the air to drive away any evil that may attempt to disturb the celebration. People begin arriving from out-

Sidetrip: A Seaside Heaven for Music Buffs

Anyone interested in West African music won't want to leave the Accra area without checking out the Academy of African Music and Arts, a combination beach resort, restaurant, concert ground, and music school. Run by master drummer Mustafa Tettey Addy and his German wife, the center offers concerts on weekends and weekday afternoons, featuring visiting musicians from all over West Africa. During the week there are courses in African dancing, drums, kora, and other instruments. Should the music get too hot you can cool off under beach palms, take a dip in the ocean, or eat fresh seafood and fruits. Rooms and beach camping are available.

The Academy is located about 34 km/21 miles west of Accra in Kokrobite. Contact: Sunseekers Tours, Novotel, Accra, Tel 21-667-546, Fax 21-667-533.

lying areas, marching in groups while carrying on their heads baskets holding freshly harvested okra, corn, tomatoes, onions, and peppers.

Processions and dances hail the harvest, and everywhere people shout *Soobi, soobi!* (Thursday people!), to commemorate the Thursday arrival of the settlers. On Friday, special events revolve around twins, who are believed to be a blessing from the ancestors. Mothers smear a whitish clay on their twins and prepare them a special meal of mashed plantain or yam with eggs. These rites are meant to bless their souls and thank the ancestors responsible for providing the family with the twins.

Food is in abundance everywhere, in keeping with the tradition of "hooting at hunger." Throughout town, you can smell huge meals of fish, chicken, corn, yams, and palm-nut soup being prepared. According to the "open house" tradition anyone, stranger or friend, can walk into a house and be served a big meal of *kpokpei,* the festival specialty. Traditional clothing and bare chests are seen throughout the city, as friends visit each other making elaborate call-and-response greetings accompanied by hearty handshakes. At cemeteries priests and elders sprinkle *kpokpei* and alcoholic beverages in tribute to the ancestors.

DATE: The festival usually begins at the end of August. **LOCATION:** Accra. **TRANSPORT:** Accra is served by direct flights from many major European hubs and New York. **ACCOMMODATION:** A large variety of lodging prospects is available. **CONTACT:** Ghana Tourist Board (see *Resources*).

While you're there ...

- **Fishing Festival (Bakatue), Elmina:** The fishing season begins in earnest on the Benya River with this grand celebration. Chiefs parade through the fishing village dressed in their finest garb, accompanied by family members who carry the royal stools and family staffs. They stroll under ornately decorated umbrellas with entourages of singers, dancers, and stilt-walkers. (The first Tuesday in July.)
- **Great Yam Festival (Odiwera), Abron tribal areas:** The Abron people's most elaborate festival combines ancestor worship with first-fruit celebrations lifting the taboo on yam eating. Rituals and dances are performed. (October.)

Resources

In Ghana: Ghana Tourist Board, P.O. Box 3106, Accra, Tel 21-665441. Ghana National Culture Centre, P.O. Box 3085, Kumasi, Tel 31-2822. **USA:** Embassy of Ghana, 3512 International Drive NW, Washington, DC 20008, Tel (202) 686-4520, Fax (202) 686-4527. **Canada:** Embassy of Ghana, 85 Range, Road #810, Ottawa, ON K1N 8J6, Tel (613) 236-0871, Fax (613) 236-0874. **UK:** Ghana High Commission, 104 highgate Hill, London N6 5HE, Tel 71-342-8686, Fax 71-342-8566. **Germany:** Ghana Embassy, Rheinalle 58, D-5300 Bonn 2, Tel 228-352011, Fax 228-363498.

KENYA AND TANZANIA

The variety of Kenya's attractions is amazing, ranging from nature reserves with some of the most abundant wildlife on earth, to mountains, semi-deserts, and unspoiled islands where African-Arab civilizations have flourished for 1,000 years. With so many sights and a well-developed infrastructure, it's no wonder that Kenya draws droves of visitors. Untouristed Tanzania, on the other hand, offers more rustic variety in quintessential African settings. Populated by more than 120 ethnic groups, the country has some of the world's last great expanses of undeveloped wilderness, occupied by an astounding range of wildlife. Tanzania is also home to the continent's highest mountain, deepest lake, and largest caldera (collapsed volcano).

The most spectacular events in both countries are organized by non-humans. Millions of wildebeests and other animals put on one of the most impressive shows on earth when they make their spirited migration between nature reserves in the two countries. Tribal celebrations take place almost constantly in Kenya and Tanzania, but most aren't regularly scheduled. In inland areas where animist religions mix with Christianity, you're likely to come across colorful initiations and other rituals in villages—if you know where to look. On the coast or the islands of Lamu and Zanzibar, the Arab influence is strong, and Moslems celebrate Islamic feast days with a uniquely East African flourish.

Great Serengeti Wildlife Migration

Serengeti National Park (Tanzania) April/May/June

The most spectacular gathering of wildlife in the world begins as the Serengeti rainy season comes to an end. In April, more than

Huge herds of wildebeests raise clouds of dust after crossing a river in the Masai Mara. (Nik Wheeler)

two million wildebeests begin to mass over the southern Serengeti plain. Spread out horizon to horizon, they saturate the air with dust as they mill around in preparation for their migration, making a grunting "he-haw" sound. From time to time they engage in a weird "practice" ritual in which two animals break away and start running, drawing the whole herd after them in single file. Sometimes they stop after a few hundred meters; sometimes they keep going until they're out of sight.

In May the wildebeests begin their migration to the west and north, forming long lines of several thousand animals which stretch for several kilometers in one of nature's most awesome and inspiring rituals. By June, most are racing north toward the Masai Mara in Kenya, drawn by an instinctive knowledge of the lush grasslands waiting there. Accompanying the wildebeests are tens of thousands of zebra, antelope, gazelle ... and opportunistic lions.

The Serengeti National Park consists of four distinct habitats—plain, savanna, woodland, and wooded grassland—which contain the world's highest concentrations of large mammals. In the south you'll see gazelle, topi, zebra, and buffalo. Warthogs scurry around digging for roots, and ostriches and secretary birds run through the grass, joined overhead by more than 500 species of flyers and swampland birds. The woodlands hold more browsers, including elephants, giraffes, impalas, and elands. Lions stalk the forests and the northern slopes, where herds of zebra and buffalo roam.

DATE: April, May, and June. **LOCATION:** Serengeti National Park in Tanzania, near the Kenyan border. **TRANSPORT:** Tanzania's international airport at Dar es Salaam is served by flights from Europe and other points in East Africa. From North America you'll need to

Maulidi: With good-luck currency tucked into kofia *caps and pinned to robes, Moslems sing the praises of the Prophet on his birthday.* (Jason Lauré)

change planes in Europe or in Nairobi, Kenya. Light planes serve the park's landing strips, but service is erratic. Buses and tourist minibuses are available in Dar es Salaam. **ACCOMMODATION:** Wildlife lodges and safari lodges are strategically placed so that visitors may witness migrations and wildlife in general, but they are expensive. There are also nine campsites in the park. **CONTACT:** Serengeti National Park, Box 3134, Arusha, Kenya, Tel Arusha 3471. Also: Tanzania Tourist Board (see *Resources*) or group tour operators.

Maulidi

Lamu (Kenya) **June/July/August**

The birth of Mohammed is celebrated with music and fanfare on the island of Lamu, one of the planet's last living escapees from the 20th century. In beautiful, mellow Lamu Town and throughout the archipelago, mosques are painted and holy men are summoned to read the poetic Maulidi text. Everywhere, you'll see *tarabu,* small groups of musicians playing haunting music to back up the epic lyrics that glorify the birth and life of Mohammed.

Celebrants carry on oblivious to the travelers who drop by with their cameras to see the source of the commotion. Some of the celebrations are private, but others are quite extroverted, with participants standing up and taking turns reciting their own specially prepared poetry praising the Prophet. Even if you don't speak Swahili the story lines are predictable: First, the world before Mohammed is described. Then, when the point of the

Caught in mid-leap: During the migration, safari groups can expect to come across Masai people pogoing up and down in unison. *(Martha Cooper/Viesti Associates)*

Prophet's birth is reached, everyone stands up and sings religious poems and praises.

DATE: Moving date according to the Islamic lunar calendar—check with the Kenya Tourist Office for the current year's date. **LOCATION:** Lamu Island and other nearby islands. **TRANSPORT:** You can reach Lamu's airport (on Manda Island) via Mombasa and Malindi, then ferry across the channel to Lamu Town. Buses run from Mombasa and Malindi, terminating at the ferry jetty to the island. Also, you may be able to hook up with a *dhow* sailing from Mombasa. **ACCOMMODATION:** Lamu is absolutely packed with budget and mid-range accommodations, many of which are in historic houses with beautiful courtyards and verandas. Top-end accommodation is less prevalent, but available. **CONTACT:** Tanzania Tourist Board or embassy (see *Resources*).

Great Masai Mara Wildlife Migration

Masai Mara Game Reserve (Kenya) — **July–September**

One of the world's most spectacular events includes humans only as sideline spectators. Each year, up to two million plains animals cross from Tanzania's Serengeti to Kenya's Masai Mara in search of lush grass. Wildebeests in long, single-file lines lead the migration, and are closely followed by zebras. Behind them come the predators, including migratory lions who have no problem putting fresh meat on their tables every night. The experience is staggering, and for most people, humbling.

No matter when you visit the Masai Mara Game Reserve, you'll see an incredible amount of wildlife. Lions are everywhere, and this is the best place on earth to see cheetahs and leopards (although they're shy), along with elephants, buffaloes, hippos, giraffes, gazelles, impalas, topis, baboons, wart hogs, hyenas, and jackals.

DATE: The animals start arriving in Kenya in June, and by July the migration is in full swing. They stay through July and August, and into September. The most photogenic time to visit Masai Mara is probably mid-August through late September, as the animals are massing up to leave. Most are gone by mid-October. **LOCATION:** Masai Mara Game Reserve. The western end of the park, with the Oloololo Escarpment, has the highest concentrations of game, but is swampy and sometimes inaccessible. Most safaris stay on the eastern end of the park. **TRANSPORT:** The Masai Mara is served by light-plane flights twice each day from Nairobi. Nairobi's airport is served by flights from New York, Toronto, and most Western European capitals. Buses run from Nairobi to Narok, but there's no public transport to or within the park, so you'll need to rent transport or arrange for a safari. **ACCOMMODATION:** Within the reserve lodging prices are outrageous but the settings are great. Lower-end accommodation is found just outside the gates; alternatively you can camp, but in some sites security is an issue. **CONTACT:** Masai Mara Game Reserve, Box 72, Narok, Tel Narok 4. Also: Kenya Tourist Office (see *Resources*) or tour operators.

© While you're there ...

- **Luhya Circumcision Ceremony, around Kakamega:** The 18 or more tribes who farm the area northeast of Lake Victoria hold complex, colorful initiation ceremonies for teenage boys. The area is heavily forested, with plenty of hiking trails, and few safari minibuses venture out this way. (August.)
- **Cultural Celebration, Bagamoyo (Tanzania):** A celebration of traditional culture is presented by the Bagamoyo College of Arts. (September.)
- **Camel Derby, Maralal (Kenya):** The weirdly captivating safari center of Maralal puts on a race and pageant featuring the star of many a safari around here, the camel. Surrounded by the Maralal National Sanctuary, the town has good facilities, friendly people, and an exciting, wild-west atmosphere. (October.)

Resources

In Kenya: Ministry of Tourism and Wildlife, P.O. Box 30027, Utalii House, Uhuru Highway, Nairobi, Tel 2-332030, Fax 2-217604. **USA:** Kenya Tourist Office, 424 Madison Ave., New York, NY 10017, Tel (212) 486-1300, Fax (212) 688-0911. **Canada:** Kenya High Commission, 141 Laurier Ave. E. #600, Ottawa, ON K1N 6R4, Tel (613) 563-1773. **UK:** 25 Brooks Mews, London W1Y 1LG, Tel 71-3553144, Fax 71-3236717. **Germany:** Kenya Tourist Office, Neue Mainzerstr. 22/IV, D-6000 Frankfurt 1, Tel 69-232017, Fax 69-239239. **Australia:** Kenya High Commission, P.O. Box 1990, 33–35 Ainslie Ave., Canberra, ACT 2601, Tel 6-2474788.

In Tanzania: Tanzania Tourist Board, IPS Bldg., Maktaba St., P.O. Box 2485, Dar-es-Salaam, Tel 51-26680, Fax 51-46780. **USA:** Embassy of the United Republic of Tanzania, 2139 R. St., NW, Washington, DC 20008, Tel (202) 939-6125, Fax (202) 797-7408. **Canada:** Tanzania High Commission, 50 Range Rd., Ottawa, ON K1N 8J4, Tel (613) 232-1509. **UK:** Tanzania Trade Centre, 78/80 Borough High St., GB-London SE1 1LL, Tel 71-4070566, Fax 71-4032003. **Germany:** Zanzibar Tourist Office, Bahnhofstr. 41, D-6200 Wiesbaden, Tel 611-375013, Fax 611-309043.

MADAGASCAR

Although considered part of Africa in a geographical sense, the world's fourth-largest island is distinct in all other ways—including a general lack of tourists. Madagascar occupies its own tectonic plate, a condition which allowed its many endemic species—lemurs, panther-like fosas, and huge chameleons—to develop independently from those on mainland Africa or anywhere else. This unique flora and fauna thrive among geological oddities like rock forests, whaleback domes, and a rapidly disappearing tropical forest.

Madagascar's people are descended mostly from Malay-Polynesian sailors who came across the island 1,500 years ago and developed a culture with a distinct religion, music, and arts. In the highlands, you can see the music and storytelling spectacles called *hira gasy,* or the lively, colorful reburial rituals known as *famadihana,* or "turning of the bones." Everywhere, you'll hear the hearty Malagasy singing and dance rhythms played on traditional instruments.

Turning of the Bones (Famadihana)

Antananarivo and environs **August/September**

The Famadihana is a rollicking occasion that does the Irish wake at least one better. From time to time, the Merina people decide to dig up a dead ancestor to hold a family reunion. No expense is spared in showing the guest of honor a good time, and living relatives go wild for a day or two of eating, drinking, and—quite literally—dancing with the dead.

The custom stems from the Merina belief that relatives remain spiritually with the family after they die. The Famadihana is just one of the great lengths taken to ensure a happy afterlife, but it's the most dramatic. You'll see them taking place throughout the Malagasy winter, and, since a stranger's presence is an auspi-

The Rhyming, Rhythmic Rhetoric of Hira Gasy

Music, dancing, storytelling, and costumes combine in the highland spectacles known as *hira gasy.* These popular extravaganzas feature troupes of 25, and begin with an eloquent, elaborate *kabary,* or discourse, by an elder. After the speech, other members of the group set about exuberantly and dramatically reinforcing the theme, which is usually a simple moral virtue like honesty or respect for elders. Trumpets and clarinets provide an aural backdrop as dancers leap into the fray and singers perform specially composed songs in their wild, colorful outfits. Usually, several troupes will compete in a day, each trying to outdo the other with the most exciting performance or best costumes. The winner is decided based on audience response. *Hira gasy* performances take place all over the country on weekends, and a regular Sunday-afternoon performance is held at Isotry (near Tana).

cious omen, there's a good chance you'll be invited to one if you make friends with Merina people (though it's bad form to just drop in).

It's an amazing experience. The men of the family, dressed in matching clothing, go into the tomb and bring up the shrouded body, which is then washed and neatly rewrapped (in many cases it's no more than dust and bones). At that point, the celebration begins with vigor. The band lays down a lively tune while the people set about dancing with each other and visiting with the guest of honor—consulting him, singing to him, hugging him, and at times even taking him for a twirl on the ad-hoc dance floor.

Zebu cattle are slaughtered and huge feasts are prepared for the celebration, which lasts either one or two days. An *ombiasy* (healer-priest) can often be seen running around orchestrating rituals that will secure earthly help from the ancestor. Finally, a farewell ceremony is undertaken, and the body is showered with gifts and returned to the tomb.

DATE: August or September (the Malagasy winter) is the high season for Famadihana. **LOCATION:** The Merino people are located in the central highlands, around the city of Antananarivo. **TRANSPORT:** About 15 km/10 miles from Antananarivo, the international airport at Ivato handles flights from Africa (Nairobi and the Comoros) and Europe (Paris and Zürich). From other places, you'll need to connect in Europe or Africa. **ACCOMMODATION:** The town of Antananarivo isn't known for posh or even clean accommodations, but there are several decent places to stay. Alternatively, you can stay in surrounding towns like Ambatolampy or Ambohimanga. **CONTACT:** Madascar Embassy (see *Resources*).

Resources

In Madagascar: Direction du Tourisme, Boite Postale 610, Rue Fernand Kassanga, Tsimbazaza, Antananarivo 101, Tel 2-26298, Fax 2-26719. **USA:** Madagascar Embassy, 2374 Massachusetts NW, Washington DC 20008, Tel (202) 265-5525, Fax (202) 986-6271. **Canada:** Madagascar Honorary Consulate, 335 Walson Ave., Toronto, ONT, Tel (416) 845-8914. **UK:** Madagascar Honorary Consulate, 16 Lanark Mansions, London W12 8DT, Tel 81-746-0133, Fax 81-746-0134. **Germany:** Teutsch-Madegassische Gesellschaft, Schmalholt 4, D-2301 Achterwehr, Tel 4342-86917, Fax 431-552413. **Australia:** Madagascar Honorary Consulate, 92 Pitt St., Sydney, NSW 2000, Tel 2-221-3007.

MOROCCO

Morocco breaks the low-key, puritanical mold of most Islamic countries, with extroverted national and local festivals that put a premium on entertainment and feasting. Several of these take place in Morocco's legendary cities—Casablanca, Fès, Marrakesh, Tangier—but many more can be found in remote, mysterious villages of the High Atlas or Rif mountains. At these festivals, and in the everyday experience of Morocco's exotic souks, *or markets, travelers are overwhelmed by a feast of color, noise, aroma, and ubiquitous touts, all of which conspire to create an unforgettable travel experience.*

Modern Morocco presents a hospitable, profoundly seductive mix of African, European, Arab, Berber, and Islamic influences. Like their Spanish neighbors, Moroccans honor ancient events and local patron saints (Muslim, in this case) with festivals known as *moussems* or *amouggars*. In Berber villages, these festivals are the events of the year, with religious ceremonies, folk music, traditional dancing, and even marriage arrangements adding up to an extremely lively scene.

Marrakesh Festival of Popular Arts

Marrakesh **June**

Few destinations tug on travelers' imaginations like Marrakesh. For centuries a metropolis for Saharan nomads and for decades a Mecca for free-spirited world travelers, Marrakesh is a feast of fantasy and legend that's matchless in terms of atmosphere, energy, and location.

With the snow-covered High Atlas peaks towering dramatically in the background, dancers, musicians, and other entertainers from all over the country fill the Ksar el Badi Palace, producing an enormous variety of colors, movements, and rhythms. On

At the Marrakesh Festival of Popular Arts, you can experience Morocco's many diverse folk traditions. Here, a Berber dancer wears her traditional headdress. (Wolfgang Kaehler)

paper, the Marrakesh Festival of Popular Arts looks suspiciously like a contrived tourist event. Upon closer inspection, it *is* a contrived tourist event—one of the best in the world. Unlike other "tourist festivals" scattered throughout the country, you'll find a great many Moroccan spectators here, reuniting with the traditions of their not-so-distant homelands, or checking out the performing styles of the nation's many other ethnic groups.

At no other event can you experience so many styles of Moroccan folk tradition. The traditional costumes are the stuff from which fantasies are born, either huge and garish, or sublimely subtle. You'll hear classical "Andalusian" guitarists from

Snake charming with a pair of deadly cobras is about the tamest stunt you'll see any night at the Djemaa el Fna. (Blaine Harrington)

northern cities, popular Arabic bands, and Berber musicians who play the breathtaking rhythms of the countryside on the *Bendir* (a wooden frame over which goat skin is stretched). Dances include the *ahaidous*, in which bejeweled women and stately costumed men beat out complicated rhythms on the ground, and the *tissint* dagger dance, performed by women cloaked in indigo blue. Other dances include the virile *taskiouine* warriors' dance, and the magico-religious *gnaouas*.

You'll also encounter hundreds of people who make their living preying on tourists and travelers. Be ready: shopkeepers, street

The Nightly Medieval Pageant at Marrakesh

Washington Square in New York City looks like a cub scout meeting compared to the spectacle of Marrakesh's Djemaa el Fna. Night after night, this square has to be the weirdest, consistently wildest performance ground on earth.

The bustle—and extreme hustle—is continuous. Filled with markets selling flowers and spices each afternoon, the square becomes a romping melee once the air cools at sunset. Food and juice stalls are thrown up in minutes, and almost immediately you'll see acrobatic dancers leaping through the air over here while trained monkeys make the crowd guffaw over there. A lunatic might foam at the mouth in one corner while a snake charmer sits next to him hypnotizing both serpents and spectators. Spin around and you could see nomadic Berbers listening to a traditional storyteller, or a Swede getting his pocket picked. Teams of jugglers whip machetes at each other, while the scent of exotically spiced couscous or *harira* tempts travelers to take a time-out in a café overlooking the action. On a mellow rooftop you can sip mint tea, serenely detached from a nightly pageant that seems to get its energy from another century.

touts, and "guides" are incredibly aggressive and, in contrast to subdued Fès (which never had a rock and roll song written about it), Marrakesh has been beset and almost magnificently corrupted by world travelers for more than 900 years. During the festival—and the rest of the year as well—Marrakesh is a remarkably lively, vibrant, thieve-ridden place (although violent crime is rare).

DATE: Ten days; usually the first and second weeks in June. **LOCATION:** Marrakesh. **TRANSPORT:** Buses and trains serve Marrakesh from everywhere, including the ferry port at Tangier, and the international airport at Casablanca. **ACCOMMODATION:** Marrakesh is well-endowed with budget, mid-range, and luxury hotels, and even a Club Med. **CONTACT:** Moroccan Tourist Office (see *Resources*).

While you're there ...

Fête du Trône, nationwide: This three-day celebration commemorates the king's accession. In towns and villages extraordinary war exercises

Spirited precision: During the Fête du Trône, extraordinary war exercises called fantasias *feature riders who charge back and forth, whooping and throwing their muzzle-loaders into the air.* *(Joe Viesti/Viesti Associates)*

called *fantasias* are held. These feature men on horseback raising huge clouds of dust as they race back and forth, shrieking, throwing muzzle-loaders into the air and catching them as they ride. As the horses come to an abrupt halt, riders fire their weapons simultaneously. (March 2–4.)

© **Fête des Roses (Rose Festival), Kelaâ des M'Gouna (Dadès Valley):** This *amouggara* in celebration of a successful rose harvest features *zaine* music, which derives from Arabic musical modes but uses the Berber language and intervals. The percussion is particularly interesting, often making use of unusual instruments like automobile wheels. (April/May.)

© **Goulimine Moussem, Asrir:** Although the Saturday-morning "Camel Souk" in Goulimine has become a sham set up purely for tourists, the *moussem* in Asrir (10 km/6 miles southeast of Goulimine) features hoards of camels, Touareg nomads, and *guedra* dancing. (Early June.)

© **Moussem of Moulay Ibrahim, Asni:** One of Morocco's largest *moussems* takes place in the High Atlas range, amidst spectacular scenery and near the hikeable beauty of North Africa's highest peak, Mt. Toubkal (4,165 meters/13,744 feet). (June/July.)

© **Tan-Tan Moussem, Tan-Tan:** This desert outpost draws nomadic "Blue Men" from neighboring tribes for prayer, *Guedra* dancing, and the ritualistic slaughtering of she-camels. (July.)

© **Sidi Allal el Hadj Moussem, near Chaouen:** This excellent *moussem* features handicrafts and the unusual culture of the Djebala people, amid a relaxing area rich in ancient Andalusian architecture and climatic delights. (August.)

A caravan of nomadic "blue men" arrives at the Tan-Tan Moussem. (Henneghien/Bruce Coleman Inc.)

Moussem of Moulay Idriss

Fès **September**

Taking place in the Arab world's most hauntingly beautiful medieval city, this *moussem* honors Fès's founder and patron saint, Moulay Idriss. The residents of Morocco's cultural capital proudly turn out in numbers to celebrate not only Moulay, but their city's remarkable history. Merchants and shoemakers join blacksmiths, tanners, and other craftsmen in processions and gatherings throughout the city, making offerings of big, decorated candles. Cattle and oxen are sacrificed in rather bloody spectacles, and special markets, music, and traditional entertainments spring up in the cramped streets and squares of the old city. Everywhere there's a sense of timeless chaos.

Fès itself is the embodiment of a traveler's dreams, a city whose very existence seems impossible at the end of the 20th century. With its clocks set permanently in an ancient time zone, Fès seduces visitors—at least those with flexibility—into overstaying their planned visits by days, weeks, sometimes years. A metropolis of golden stone surrounded by sunburned hills, Fès is impossibly tangled with unmapped, narrow streets and maze-like passageways. One minute you're in the street of hammering blacksmiths, the next you're overpowered by scents and sights of saffron glowing in purple shadows. Take a right turn and you may or may not find the hidden source of chanting schoolchildren, or a *muezzin* calling the faithful to prayer. With its ancient bazaars and some of the Arab world's best-preserved architecture, Fès offers travelers discovery after discovery.

DATE: Mid-September. **LOCATION:** Fès. **TRANSPORT:** Fès can be reached by air from Casablanca and Marrakesh (but this is only necessary if you're really short on time), and by bus or train (the train's your best bet) from Tangier, Marrakesh, Casablanca, and Rabat. **ACCOMMODATION:** Bottom-end accommodations are centered around the entrance to the Old City. Most don't have showers, but there are many *hammam* (bath houses) nearby. Top-end lodging is generally located in the New City. **CONTACT:** Moroccan Tourist Office (see *Resources*).

Engagement Festival

Imilchil **September**

Morocco's most famous moussem draws upwards of 20,000 tribespeople to arrange marriages and generally have a ball. Although tourist operators have discovered the festival (and shuttle in groups from Marrakesh), the event is still an extravagant, lively, traditional affair. The approach to picking a life-mate looks, to the outsider's eye, a lot like choosing a horse on which to bet. There's all kinds of shouting and cajoling, papers are waved, negotiations are made, and young people are set down to sign marriage contracts, California-style. Markets spring up, selling everything from food to handicrafts. Can't-live-without-it items include white rocks which, when put into a fire, "will reveal the face of one's secret enemy." Much of the action takes place in the town's excellently preserved Kaidal kasbah.

DATE: Three days; approximately the third week in September, but varies some years (check with the Moroccan Tourist Office). **LOCATION:** Imilchil is located in the Er Rachidia Province, about 65 km (40 miles) north of Âït Hani, on the road between Midelt and Bénni-Mellal. **TRANSPORT:** Special tourist buses run from Marrakesh, but you can usually flag down trucks, which will take you (for a fee) from Âït Hani, Midelt, or Er Rachidia. **ACCOMMODATION:** There are no hotels in town, but many villagers will rent rooms; also, you can camp beside one of the two small lakes near the town. **CONTACT:** Moroccan National Tourist Office (see *Resources*).

While you're there ...

- **Fêtes du Cheval (Horse Festival), Tissa:** Horses are rounded up and in addition to many equestrian events there's music and dancing. (October.)
- **Fêtes des Dattes (Date Festival), Erfoud:** The date harvest is celebrated with music and dance. (October.)

Resources

In Morocco: Office National Marocain du Tourisme, 31 Angle Avenue Al Abtal et Rue Oued, Fès, Rabat-Agdal, Tel 7-775171, Fax 7-777437. **USA:** Moroccan Tourist Office, 20 East 46th Street, New York, NY 10017, Tel (212) 557-2520, Fax (212) 949-8148. **Canada:** Moroccan Tourist Office, 2001 Rue Universite, #1460, Montreal PQ, H3A 2A6, Tel (514) 842-8111. **UK:** Moroccan Tourist Office, 205 Regent Street, GB-London W1R 7DE, Tel 71-4370073, Fax 71-7348172. **Germany:** Moroccan Tourist Office, Graf-Adolf-Str. 59, D-4000 Düsseldorf 1, Tel 211-370551, Fax 211-374048. **Australia:** Moroccan Tourist Office, 11 West Street, North Sydney, N.S.W. 2060, Tel 2-9576717.

SWAZILAND

Swaziland is often touted as "Africa's Switzerland," but in truth the small country is much more diverse, offering a nearly complete sampler of African landscapes (all that's lacking is desert). Europeans and Americans don't hear much about Swaziland, but it has a thriving tourist industry, fueled mostly by South Africans who are drawn to the country's casinos and its calmer social and political climate.

One reason for Swaziland's relative stability is its enduring monarchic tradition, one of the few remaining in Africa. The royalty runs the show here, and a series of colorful festivals are staged in honor of the royal family. Many other vestiges of traditionalism, such as *Sibhaca* dancing and communal singing, continue to flourish in rural Swaziland. Unlike most of Africa, drums are not in great use, and dancers often accompany themselves vocally, occasionally using flutes and musical bows.

Reed Dance (Umhalanga)

Lobamba **August/September**

Unmarried Swazi women and girls from all over the country show respect for the Queen Mother during this very traditional coming-of-age ceremony, which includes processions, singing, and complicated dancing. The maidens first set out to selected areas to collect long reeds, which will serve as wind breakers for the queen's *kraal,* or palace. Upon their return they form groups, and set to the task of building the windbreakers, singing hymns while they work.

On the evening of the fifth day women and girls prepare dance costumes and perform the difficult Reed Dance, tossing reeds high in the air in a performance before the Queen Mother. Their costumes of bead skirts and beautiful jewelry are elaborate yet skimpy enough to serve the dance's original purpose—to demonstrate nubility to the King and his courtiers, who were on hand to choose brides from among the maidens. A traditional ceremony for young men, called the *Timgoma Temabhace,* follows the Reed Dance.

In a colorful coming-of-age ceremony, Swazi girls perform a dance for the Queen Mother of Swaziland. (Jason Lauré)

On the afternoons of the sixth and seventh days, the girls and women attend a ball honoring the royal family, then the Umhlanga is concluded with feasting and more reed dancing.

DATE: A week in late August or early September (contact the tourist office in Swaziland for the exact date each year). **LOCATION:** Lobamba. **TRANSPORT:** Flights into Swaziland are available from Johannesburg, Durban, Dar-es-Salaam, Harare, Lusaka, Nairobi, and Maputo. **ACCOMMODATION:** There are few accommodations in Lobamba, but hotels are scattered throughout the valley between Mbabane and Manzini. There's also a nature reserve within an hour's driving distance of Lobamba with camping facilities. **CONTACT:** Swaziland Dept. of Tourism or embassy (see *Resources*).

Festival of the First Fruits (Incwala)

Mbabane region **December/January**

The Incwala ceremony is the most sacred and colorful of all Swazi ceremonies, serving to renew communal strength and unity, and to sanctify the kingship that binds the nation. This extremely elaborate festival also recognizes the royalty as a source of fertility—a role underscored by the fact that the late King Sobhuza II had more than 600 children by dozens of wives.

Two main festival periods occur over a span of nearly three weeks, culminating in a final six days which are called the Big Incwala. The ceremony begins at the new moon with a journey by the Bemanti clan to the Indian Ocean to collect the foam of waves, which is believed to hold mystic powers. Their return to the King's *kraal* (palace) is celebrated as Little Incwala or Small Incwala. For two days the people chant sacred songs and wear traditional outfits, but the king remains in seclusion.

During the week between the Small Incwala and the Big Incwala, villages mark the time with daily singing and dancing. When the moon is full the Big Incwala begins. Young men from all over the country are ordered to hike from Ngabezweni to Egundvini (a distance of some 40 km/25 miles) that same afternoon and night. Their mission is to gather branches from the sacred *lusekwane* tree by the light of the full moon. (If any of them has ever seduced a married woman or made a girl pregnant, he shouldn't participate, since his branches will wither and the "pure ones" may attack him.)

When the young men return, elders use the branches to construct a sacred bower next to the King's cattle stable. A black ox is driven out of the enclosure, captured, then slaughtered. The next day excitement is high as warriors and guests assemble in the King's yard, singing sacred songs and drinking traditional beer while wearing animal skins, woven skirts, and other traditional clothing. The climax approaches as the warriors dance around the sacred bower, surging back and forth in an attempt to persuade the king to return to the people. The king feigns reluctance, then finally emerges, his face smeared with paint, head plumed, boots covered with grass, and waist tied with a belt of silver monkey fur.

The warriors go wild as the king performs his sacred dance before his people and eats the first pumpkin to be harvested, thereby leading the way for the consumption of new crops. When he's done, his majesty tosses the rind and the crowd breaks out in special songs and dances.

No one works on the fifth day, which is intended for rest and meditation. On the sixth day a huge bonfire is built for the burning of articles which represent the year just passed. To mark the new year, participants beseech their ancestors' spirits to extinguish the fire with rain—this actually happens with amazing regularity. The Incwala ends and the nation's new year begins with feasting, singing, and dancing.

DATE: December/January. Actual dates set by tribal astrologers; the Swazi tourist office or embassy obtains the dates several months in advance. **LOCATION:** The various royal *kraals* where the ceremonies occur are in the vicinity of Mbabane and Lobamba. **TRANSPORT:** Flights into Swaziland are available from Johannesburg, Durban, Dar-es-Salaam, Harare, Lusaka, Nairobi, and Maputo. From Europe, the Americas, and elsewhere, a change in one of the above-mentioned cities is usually necessary. **ACCOMMODATION:** Hotels are spread across the Ezulwini valley from Mbabane to

Manzini. There's also a nature reserve with camping facilities within an hour's driving distance of Lobamba. **CONTACT:** Swaziland Dept. of Tourism or embassy (see *Resources*).

Resources

In Swaziland: Ministry of Tourism, P.O. Box 338, Mbabane, Tel 43201, Fax 42442. Malolotja Nature Reserve, P.O. Box 100, Lobamba, Tel 61179, Fax 61875; Mlilwane Wildlife Sanctuary, P.O. Box 33, Mbabane, Tel 61591; Hotel Associations of Swaziland, P.O. Box 762, Mbabane, Tel 42218, Fax 44246. **USA:** Embassy of the Kingdom of Swaziland, 3400 International Drive, Suite 3M, Washington, D.C. 20008, Tel (202) 362-6683, Fax (202) 244-8059. **Canada:** High Commission of the Kingdom of Swaziland, 130 Albert Street, Suite 1204, Ottawa, ON K1P PG4, Tel (613) 567-1480, Fax (613) 567-1058. **UK:** Southern Africa Regional Tourism Council (SARTOC), P.O. Box 675, GB-Gerrards Cross, Bucks SL9 8YS; High Commission of Swaziland, 20 Buckingham Gate, London SW1E 6LB, Tel 71-630-6611, Fax 71-630-6564. **Germany:** Swaziland Department of Tourism, c/o STR Touristic Promotions KG, Leerbachstr. 118, D-6000 Frankfurt 1, Tel 69-550640, Fax 69-598933.

TUNISIA

The vast majority of Tunisia's visitors come for the country's excellent Mediterranean beaches, yet those who wander farther inland than the golf course will experience the best of this country, with its rich cultural and social heritage. Just an hour away from the ocean resorts lie some the world's most extensive and least visited Roman ruins, while a little farther north are the rugged Khroumier Mountains and the lush Medjerda Valley. Beautifully preserved Arab and French cities, and vast expanses of Saharan desert can easily be seen in a week in Tunisia.

The people of Tunisia, with their European-influenced Islamic culture, celebrate harvests and commemorate the doings of local saints with spirited festivals. In the north, you'll find that grapes are actually intended for drinking as well as eating (an Islamic anomaly), and in the south, the mysteries and colors of the desert unfold at oasis festivals and markets.

Festival of the Sahara

Douz **December**

Ten days of *fantasias,* horse-racing, and camel charges shake up this normally quiet Saharan market oasis, drawing more than 50,000 villagers, nomads, and tourists. The action is great, both at the organized events and at the attendant markets, where bartering men form a sea of bobbing white head-cloths in the beautiful square. In terms of both people watching opportunities and organized attractions, the Douz Festival is one of Tunisia's classics—despite the fair numbers of tourists who attend.

The *fantasias* are the most popular spectacles. These former military exercises are basically precision cavalry charges with dozens of men. Dressed to the nines, they charge across the sand on horseback, shrieking and hollering while throwing their muzzle-loaders into the air, catching them on the run and then simultaneously blasting them skyward while skidding to a dusty stop. There are also camel, horse, and greyhound races, and traditional poetry, music, and wedding ceremonies. Since the event coincides with the date harvest, fresh dates and *lagmi* (the fermented juice of the date palm) are sold in the market. Other commodities include camels, copper handicrafts, Berber tapestries, bird cages, incense, ebony, and desert flowers.

Douz is the last major settlement along the paved road into the Grand Erg Oriental desert, and holds a lively Thursday market throughout the year. When you arrive in town, you'll find a jumbled maze of sand-colored houses and winding, narrow streets with tranquil lines of palm trees and slow-moving donkey carts. Completely surrounded by the desert, the town wages a daily battle against the blowing sands, which would bury Douz if not removed by donkey cart each day. From Douz or Kebili, you can set up expeditions deeper into the desert, to the very isolated oasis villages of Zaafrane, Nouil, Toulba, or El Faouar.

DATE: Ten days in mid-December. The timing varies depending on the harvest. **LOCATION:** Douz, about 32 km/20 miles south of Kebili. **TRANSPORT:** Daily air-conditioned buses run from Tunis and Gabes, and local transport runs from Kebili. **ACCOMMODATION:** There are several hotels in town, but most are booked by tour groups. Reserve well in advance or stay in Kebili. **CONTACT:** Tunisia embassy or National Tourist Office (see *Resources*).

© While you're there ...

- **Berber Festival, Tarouine:** Traditional festivities of this minority tribal group include excellent displays of equestrian prowess. (March.)
- **Festival of the Sparrow Hawk, El Haouaria:** Drums beat and trumpets blare as locals make their way to this town on the rugged coast. Falcons, which had been taken from cliff-side nests and trained to hunt quail, rabbits, and partridge, compete in this colorful, very traditional event. The birds are set free again in the fall. (May/June.)
- **Siren Festival, Kerkennak:** Often alluding to the Greek wanderer Ulysses, this island celebration of traditional wedding customs features boating events as well. (July/August.)
- **International Festival of Carthage, Carthage:** Tunisia's entry in the glamorous world of international arts festivals features theater, ballet, music, and folklore. The traditional music is always interesting, as are the fusions of Tunisian music and jazz. (July/August.)
- **International Festival of Hammamet, Hammamet (Nabeul region):** Drama, folk music, dancing, and art fill out this smaller festival, which features both Tunisian and international performers. (July/August.)
- **Desert Festival of Tozeur, Tozeur:** This festival features folklore, dancing, camel races, and *fantasias*. (December/January.)

Resources

In Tunisia: Office National du Tourisme Tunisien, 1 Avenue Mohamed V, 1001 Tunis, Tel 1-341077, Fax 1-350997. **USA**: Tunisia Embassy, 1515 Massachusetts Avenue NW, Washington DC 20005, Tel (202) 862-1850, Fax (202) 862-1858. **Canada**: Tunisia Embassy, 515 Oscannor St., Ottawa, ON K1S 3P8, Tel (613) 237-0330, Fax (613) 237-7939. **UK**: Tunisia National Tourist Office, 77a Wigmore St., London W1, Tel 71-224-5598, Fax 71-224-4053. **Germany**: Fremdenverkehrsamt von Tunesien, Am Hauptbahnhof 6, D-6000 Frankfurt 1, Tel 69-231891, Fax 69-232168. **Australia**: Tunisia Consulate, Australia Square 48th Floor, Sydney, NSW 2000, Tel 2-2477231.

ZAMBIA

Sparsely populated Zambia is a place where traditional rituals are still very much alive. Throughout the countryside, people of vastly different ethnic origins mark the seasons and appease ancestors with elaborate ceremonies involving swords, masks, and tufted headdresses. Zambia's tremendous range of traditional dances is particularly astounding, as is the physical ability, rhythmic sense, and stamina of its dancers, considered by neighboring countries to be the region's best.

Few visitors to Zambia miss one of the natural wonders of the world, Victoria Falls. Twice as tall and twice as wide as Niagara, the falls plummet down from a plateau high enough to bless the country with a spring-like climate, despite its tropical latitude. Zambia's two major game parks lie along rivers abounding in hippos, crocodiles, and large birds. In the plains beside the rivers are elephants, rhinos, lions, rare giraffes, and most other species of big game.

N'CWALA

Mutenguleni **February**

On the day in 1835 when the Ngoni tribe crossed the Zambezi River into what is now Zambia, they had a ceremonious beer rave-up of such magnitude that locals tell stories of the occasion to this day. Later that day there was a blackout, caused not by alcohol but by a total eclipse of the sun.

The N'cwala ceremony gives thanks for this Zulu-descended tribe's good fortune since then, with a round of partying that rivals the original. Fortunately for visitors, there's much more than just drunkenness, for Southern Africa's most notorious beer drinkers also happen to be the region's best dancers. Appearances are typically made by the masked Nyau cult dancers, whose intricate routines require years of practice and phenomenal physical endurance. Also seen is the Vimbuza dancer, who is generally regarded—even by other tribes—as the best dancer in Zambia.

Ku-omboka: In a ceremonious evacuation of the royal court, men propel the zebra-striped royal barge while chanting the hymns of the Ku-omboka. (Jason Lauré)

The peak of the ceremony comes when the chief tastes the year's first fresh produce, signaling that the harvest can begin. Then the dancing, drumming, feasting, and merrymaking continue through the night.

DATE: February 24. **LOCATION:** Mutenguleni, about 15 km/10 miles southwest of Chipata. **TRANSPORT:** Mutenguleni is located along the main road between Lusaka and Chipata. You can rent a car or catch a bus to Chipata, and get out 15 km/10 miles short of Chipata. Or you can fly to Chipata and bus the short distance to Mutenguleni. **ACCOMMODATION:** Chipata offers several hotels and guesthouses. **CONTACT:** Zambia National Tourist Board (see *Resources*).

Ku-omboka

Lealui and Limulunga **February/March**

Each year, torrential rains swell the flood plain of the Zambezi River, where centuries ago the Litunga, or chief of the Lozi tribe, established his headquarters. The site, now called Lealui Knoll, is in the center of a land mass that becomes completely submerged during the annual floods, necessitating a very ceremonious annual evacuation of the royal court to higher ground.

When the Litunga makes his decision to leave, the drums send out the signal and people begin packing their household goods in canoes. At the appointed hour the flotilla pulls away, headed by the Litunga's fantastic zebra-striped royal barge, the *Nalikwanda*. Thirty men dressed in swank, matching outfits with tufted headdresses propel the boat with their black and white paddles while chanting the songs of the Ku-omboka, which means "getting out of the water." The *Nalikwanda* is followed by a similar vessel carrying the Litunga's wife, the Moyo, and hundreds of other boats and canoes. The procession takes five or six hours to reach the new tribal headquarters, Limulunga, where a crowd is waiting to welcome the new arrivals with traditional dancing and singing that lasts until the wee hours.

DATE: February or March. The actual departure date depends on the rains. The less elaborate return trip, called the *Kufulehela,* is made in July. **LOCATION:** The procession departs from Lealui and makes its way along the waterway to Limulunga. Both places are just north of Mongu in the Western Province. **TRANSPORT:** Mongu has an airstrip served by flights from Lusaka and Livingstone. The town can also be reached by bus from both cities, or by rental car from Lusaka. **ACCOMMODATION:** Lodging is limited to low-range hotels, camps, and rest huts. **CONTACT:** Zambia National Tourist Board (see *Resources*).

While you're there ...

- **Umutomboko, Luapula Province:** The senior chief of the Lunda people performs his ancestral war dance, the Mutomboko, in an arena by the Ng'ona River. (July 29 or the nearest weekend.)
- **Likumbi Lya Mize, Zambezi Boma:** The Luvale people of the North Western Province come together to celebrate their cultural heritage with singing, dancing, and displays of handicrafts. The rituals take place at Mize, about 7 km/4 miles west of Zambezi Boma. Nearby attractions include a beach, Chavuma Falls, fishing on Lake Mwange, and boating on the Zambezi River. (July/August.)
- **Shimunenga, Maala (Kafue Flats):** The Lla people express their devotion to their divine ancestors at this traditional ceremony held at the Ba-lla. (Full moon in September or October.)

Resources

In Zambia: Century House, Lusaka Square, P.O. Box 30017, Lusaka, Tel 1-229090, Fax 1-225174. **USA:** Zambia National Tourist Board, 237 E. 52nd St., New York, NY 10155, Tel (212) 308-2155, Fax (212) 758-1319. **Canada:** Zambia High Commision, 130 Albert St. #1610, Ottawa, ON K1P 5G4, Tel (613) 563-0712, Fax (613) 235-0430. **UK:** Tourist National Tourist Board, 2 Palace Gate, Kensington, London W8 5NG, Tel 71-589-6343, Fax 71-581-1353. **Germany:** Tourist National Tourist Board, Mettelstr. 39, D-5300 Bonn 2, Tel 228-376-568, Fax 228-379-536. **Australia:** Tourist National Tourist Board, 68 Pitt St. Level 12, Sydney, NSW 2000, Tel 2-231-2172.

SOUTH-CENTRAL ASIA

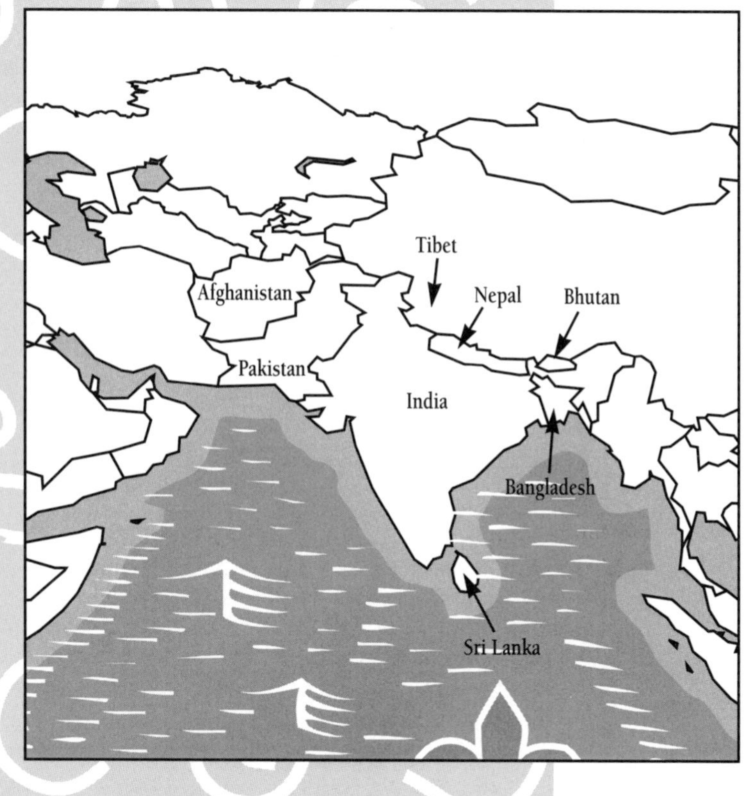

Lying astride the ancient silk routes between Asia and the Middle East, Afghanistan has long been shaped by the forces of trade and migration, while resisting would-be conquerors. Most recently, Soviet troops with advanced weaponry fought for nine years to subdue the country's low-tech horsemen before being forced to retreat in defeat.

AFGHANISTAN

Although sporadic internal hostilities continue to flare, Afghanis are sprucing up their drab landscapes with brightly decorated buses, animals, and even people. Festivals, such as Nawroz, are great occasions for experiencing first-hand the vitality of a culture that has so often persevered in the face of daunting challenges. Afghanistan offers few tourist amenities, but its people excel in rustic hospitality and friendliness, and they approach their feasts, festivals, and folklore with great enthusiasm.

New Year's Day (Nawroz)

Kabul, Mazare Sharif, Kunduz, and nationwide — **March**

The Afghanis had the good sense to locate the first day of their year on the first day of spring. This is a fantastic time to be in the Afghan countryside, as farm families dress up and travel to nearby towns to attend livestock fairs. Starting on March 21 (also called Farmer's Day), the festivities are usually extended into a two-week celebration of rural life. While Nawroz is observed throughout the country, the north is particularly colorful, as many Afghanis make pilgrimages to towns such as Mazare Sharif, Kunduz, and the capital, Kabul.

In addition to the outrageous sporting spectacle known as *Buzkashi,* a Nawroz highlight is the decorating of cows. Paper flowers and garlands are the norm, but many families go to extremes, painting cattle hides with bright designs in a bid to outflash the gaudy Afghan buses. In Kabul, the annual agricultural fair is where the action is. Wearing turbans, flowing trousers, and long shawls slung over their shoulders, farmers show up with an extended family of children, sheep, cattle, and horses. After the exhibitions people celebrate in bazaars and in open fields, where

On New Year's Day (March 21), thousands of men scramble to kiss a sacred pole erected at a mosque in Kabul. (AP/Wide World Photos)

they fly and fight kites. These homemade masterpieces are cut out and painted to resemble birds, bees, and butterflies, and as the bright creations are maneuvered above the drab expanses of sand and rock, there's hearty gambling on the winners below.

In Mazare Sharif, the northern town famous for its traditional Turkmen carpets, pilgrims converge for the raising of a huge religious banner called the *Janda.* Here and in Kabul, a pole is erected in the courtyard of many mosques, and thousands of men scramble to kiss it to ensure a lucky year. In the *attan* dance, groups of 20 or more men revolve around a stake or fire to the rhythm of *tabla* drums and reed flutes. The dance begins slowly and sedately, then gains momentum as the circle widens and the

Buzkashi—The World's Roughest Sport?

Spend some time watching this mounted mayhem, and you'll understand why Soviet troops were no match for the Afghan horsemen. *Buzkashi* reflects the boldness and ferociously competitive spirit of the Afghan people, and their great equestrian tradition that extends back to the time of Alexander the Great.

Buzkashi is a blustery free-for-all involving a couple of dozen riders on horseback and the headless carcass of a goat or calf. It begins with two (sometimes three) teams of at least 10 horsemen forming a starting circle in a dusty field. After a few ceremonious gestures, the carcass is dropped and all hell breaks loose. The teams charge in, whooping and lashing their horses and colliding in a torrid mass resembling a mounted rugby scrum. Men lean over the sides of their mounts, clawing the stony ground for the dead beast and tugging it away from each other, while being rammed, broadsided, and generally abused by the opposing team. After a ferocious struggle, someone eventually succeeds at picking up the carcass and slinging it across his saddle, then he gallops off at full speed with the competition in hot pursuit. The object is to carry the carcass around a flag at least 15 meters (50 feet) away, then get back to a scoring circle near the starting point. The other team will, of course, do anything to prevent this.

Buzkashi lasts about 90 minutes, and each minute is breathless chaos. The men and horses (both bred in northern Afghanistan), show the exceptional endurance, courage, and physical strength that has helped them beat back invaders from the time of Genghis Khan. At times there are huge pile-ups, with tangled limbs of beasts and men squirming to rise and play on. At other times riders are tackled off their horses at full speed. Spectators scramble as horses skid out of control and into the crowd, and riders fly heads over heels. Bruises are common, and broken bones are barely noticed.

Buzkashi is played throughout northern Afghanistan, on holidays such as Nawroz and at many other celebrations during the winter and early spring. Kabul and Kunduz are good spots to catch matches.

men begin to fling swords and guns. The pace keeps increasing as both dancers and musicians chant the songs, punctuating them with clapping, shouting, and weapon-clanging. The dance finally climaxes in a frenzied blur of sound and motion.

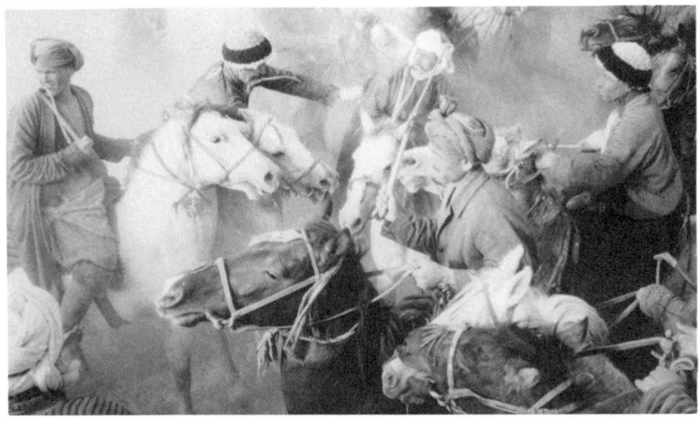

Buzkashi: What may be the world's roughest sport brings out the bold and ferociously competitive spirit of the Afghan horsemen. (R. & S. Michaud/Woodfin Camp & Associates)

DATE: New Year celebrations begin on the first day of the Afghan calendar, March 21. **LOCATION:** Regional capitals throughout the country, especially Kabul, Kunduz, and Mazare Sharif in the north. **TRANSPORT:** Kabul can be reached by air directly from Europe and the Indian subcontinent. From Kabul by bus or truck, Kunduz is 370 km (230 miles), and Mazare Sharif is 437 km (271 miles). **ACCOMMODATION:** Both Kunduz and Mazare Sharif have basic guest houses. **CONTACT:** Afghan Tourist Organization (see *Resources*).

While you're there ...

- **Id-ul-Fitr, nationwide:** Three days of feasting, visiting, and festive new clothes mark the end of the month-long fast of Ramazan. (January–March; moving date according to the Islamic lunar calendar.)

Resources

In Afghanistan: Afghan Tourist Organization, Ansari Watt, Sar-e-Naw, P.O. Box 281, Kabul, Tel 93-30323. **USA:** Embassy of the Republic of Afghanistan, 2341 Wyoming Avenue NW, Washington, DC 2008, USA, Tel (202) 234-3770, Fax (202) 238-3516. **UK:** Embassy of the Republic of Afghanistan, 31 Prince's Gate, GB-London SW7 1QU, England, Tel 71-589-8891. **Germany:** Embassy of the Republic of Afghanistan, Liebfrauenweg 1a, D-5300, Bonn 1, Germany, Tel 228-251927.

BHUTAN

Hidden in the high Himalaya, the "Land of the Thunder Dragons" is an isolated mountain paradise rarely visited by Westerners. Those who do venture there find spectacular scenery, peaceful villages, and a treasure trove of mystical traditions that come alive during religious festivals. Bhutan is expensive, but for many it's worth the price to visit a place where television is officially banned and people live, work, and worship in ways that haven't changed since medieval times. White prayer flags still flutter on hilltops, and stunning monasteries cling to rocky outcrops. A one-day trek can bring you from subtropical valleys to high pastures, or to any of dozens of virgin peaks and forests full of leopards, tigers, rhinoceroses, monkeys, and battalions of huge butterflies.

Bhutan may be "the last Shangri-la," as visitors have called it, but the country's local name, Druk Yul (Land of the Thunder Dragons,) better sums up its mysterious appeal. This identity is rendered graphically in Bhutan's great seal, which features a diamond scepter that symbolizes eternal wisdom and indestructible selfhood, and two dragons that symbolize two-fold strength and invincibility.

You'll see the seal in the great monastery/fortresses called *dzongs,* where the religious festivals called *tsechus* are held. These exceptional displays of Tantric wizardry have changed little since their beginnings in the eighth century, when Mahayana (Tantric) Buddhism was introduced. The Drukpa (Red Hat) sect, which presents these mystical masked dance-dramas, believes that dramatic depiction of spirits and the evil parts of human nature are necessary to help people recognize and combat them. Thus, the dancers play their parts in a living tradition, capturing the imaginations of local people and anyone else who wanders into this mountain kingdom that has lain undisturbed for more than a thousand years.

© New Year's Archery Tournament (Losar)

Lhasa, Paro, and elsewhere **February**

The advent of the Bhutanese New Year is an occasion for feasting, masked dancing, and that ever-popular Bhutanese pasttime and obsession, archery. At times resembling the great game, at times a spontaneous comedy skit, Bhutanese archery is a rich blend of sport, superstition, and high jinks. Spectators don't typically see the preparatory rituals in which gods are evoked to help the team's performance, and shamans are employed to decide the shooting sequence. Players born under the sign of the dog are typically chosen to start the competition, since a dog is a good guide. Team members sleep away from home the night before the match, in an effort to foil opposing spies who may trail them and try to "spiritually foul" their surroundings by leaving female underwear draped on nearby tree branches.

The games themselves are full of revelry, shouting, and dancing, and people show up in their best attire. Amid lavish feasting and socializing, the sharpshooter takes his aim at targets 140 meters (240 feet) away, chanting his personal lucky mantra. Teammates stand near the target, urging him on and dodging stray arrows. When someone makes a strong shot, they often celebrate by dancing, singing, and drinking either *chang* (an unhopped beer mixed with eggs and butter), *marua* (a beer made from fermented millet), or distilled *arak*.

In the heat of the competition, a monk-astrologer may come disguised as a mere spectator, signaling changes in strategy with secret signs or making on-the-spot offerings to the team's patron gods. Women are sometimes brought in to divert the sharpshooters, and any form of distraction short of physical contact is permitted. You'll witness hilarious acts of imitation, name-calling, dirty jokes, and even cross-dressing—a favorite means of making the crowd laugh and throwing the shooter off-balance.

Preceding page photo: *At the Thimphu Tsechu, masked dance-dramas reveal the secrets of a mystical culture that has lain undisturbed for more than 1,000 years. (Brian Vikander)*

DATE: Archery can be seen at the New Year celebrations in February, and in many towns on any Sunday. **LOCATION:** Nationwide, but especially in Thimphu. **TRANSPORT:** Thimphu is Bhutan's capital, and is accessible by 90-minute bus from Paro airport, which has flights from Kathmandu, Delhi, Calcutta, and Bangkok. **ACCOMMODATION:** In addition to the Bhutan Tourism Corp., several private operators have set up good, well-managed hotels catering to upscale travelers. **CONTACT:** Tour operators listed in *Resources*.

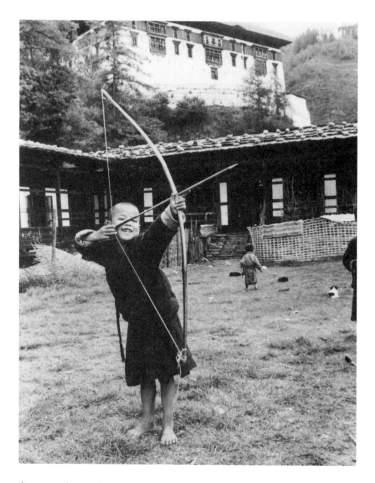

A young boy takes aim at a target 140 meters (240 feet) away. Archery is Bhutan's national obsession, and is played most fervently during New Year celebrations. (AP/Wide World Photos)

Paro Tsechu

Paro **March/April**

Set in one of the world's most peaceful, beautiful valleys, the Paro Tsechu begins with the blare of brass horns three meters (10 feet) long, followed by crashing cymbals. Villagers in bright robes and pixie-style haircuts fix their attention on the courtyard where, for the next two days, they'll be held spellbound by masked monks depicting monkey men, giant beaked bird-men, horned devil-dogs, and beautiful gods.

Bhutan's *tsechus* offer spectacular insights into the wild reaches of the imagination of the *lamas* (monks) of the Drukpa sect. Their inspiration is rooted in the teachings of Guru Rinpoche, the Tantric saint who brought the Buddhist Dharma from Tibet to Bhutan.

The *cham* dances take place amid cloth flags designed to carry the teachings on the winds in every direction. Because most people are illiterate, the dances have long served as a vehicle to teach religion. The moral is usually the triumph of good over evil, or the short duration of material values. In the spectacular Dance of the Black Hats (*Shanang*), an evil Tibetan king is killed by a monk who hides bows and arrows in the huge sleeves of his robe. The victory is celebrated by the "Black Hat" dancers who beat drums and leap through the air. In the Dance of the Fearsome Gods (*Tungam*), dancers prevail over an evil spirit by executing it with ritual daggers, thus redeeming consciousness from body. A rare treat is the ancient Sword Dance, in which men clad in ancient armor and rhinoceros skin feign battle with swords and buckler shields.

The setting, Paro Dzong, dominates the skyline of this beautiful valley, and is one of the most striking of the eight major *dzongs* in Bhutan. A seven-story tower shares the courtyard with a giant prayer wheel, which is turned by crank, ringing a bell at each turn. Like most Bhutanese *dzongs*, Paro resembles a medieval castle. The *dzongs*, along with about 200 smaller shrines (*gompas*), constitute the architectural legacy of Bhutan, and usually command imposing positions on mountain spurs. Inside, beautiful wooden balconies and galleries are precision-butted together using no nails. Beams are often painted in wild variations of blue, orange, and gold, with carved dragons and bronze castings tucked between hanging helmets, swords, matchlocks, and hundreds of flags and silk scarves.

DATE: March/April (check with a tour operator listed in *Resources* for exact dates). **LOCATION:** Paro, 30 km (19 miles) from the capital, Thimphu. **TRANSPORT:** Paro has the county's only airport, with flights from Kathmandu, Delhi, Calcutta, and Bangkok. **ACCOMMODATION:** There's only one hotel in town, so most visitors stay in Thimphu, 90 minutes away. **CONTACT:** Tour operators listed in *Resources*.

Thimphu Tsechu

Tashichho Dzong, Thimphu **September/October**

As a single long note blares from a horn fashioned from a human thigh bone, a commotion breaks out at the edge of the crowd of villagers. A monk in a bright robe appears and begins cutting a

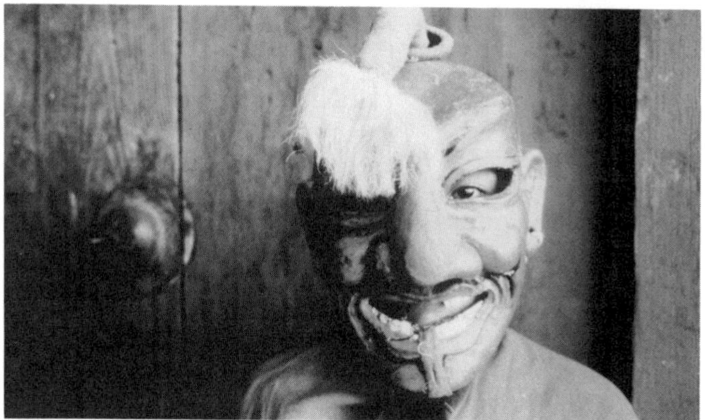

Mysteries of Bhutan: A young child poses wearing a devil mask between dances at the Heypu Tsechu. (Network Aspen)

path through the audience with his whip. Whipping the ground—as well as monks and spectators, who consider it a lucky blessing—he clears and purifies a path for the abbot, who is then mobbed by blessing-seekers.

So begins the Thimphu *Tsechu*, a spectacular three days of shamanistic magic, rituals, and masked dancing that packs enough color and symbolism to last the entire year. Many of the villagers have walked for days to get here, to picnic and make merry while catching a glimpse of the heaven envisioned by the founders of Mahayana Buddhism. It's a heaven drained of earthly worries and filled with dancing heros in glittering crowns, leaping into the air and forming rainbow-arcs with long, colorful scarves. Also, there are glimpses of a hell occupied by fearsome demons with skeleton faces and three-sided daggers.

Most of the *cham* dances performed at the *tsechus* carry lessons in desired behaviors here on earth, and how they affect the afterlife. Many of the stories are highly moralistic, such as the Dance of the Stag and the Hunting Dog, or the wildly imaginative Dance of the Judgment of the Dead. Other dances have a deeper function, that of influencing the actions of the spirits, or purifying sacred ground. But whenever the seriousness starts to get out of hand, a legion of red-masked clowns runs in to provide witty diversion.

The Dance of the Drummers from Dametsi is the best known and perhaps most colorful of all the *cham* dances. It's believed to have been composed by a 16th-century saint who had a dream-vision of the heavenly palace of Guru Rimpoche. Twelve men dance in yellow skirts and animal masks, beating decorated

How to visit the "Land of the Thunder Dragon"

Due to the Bhutanese government's isolationist policies and a near total lack of transportation and tourist amenities, Bhutan has been one of the world's most difficult places to visit. Recently the government has slowly begun to open the country to outside visitors, aware of the devastating impact that large incursions of foreigners could have on the ancient culture and religious traditions.

Tourism is very tightly controlled, with only about 5,000 foreigners admitted each year in groups of no fewer than six. The government dictates that visitors must spend a minimum of about US$200 daily—effectively ruling out Bhutan for anyone but affluent Western tourists traveling in officially organized groups. If you want to visit Bhutan, your best bet is to contact a tour operator in your own country (see *Resources*).

drums and spinning through the courtyard to celebrate the victory of religion. Their complicated steps and leaps evoke the spirit of the afterlife, in which gods and spirits romp all day, pausing only to eject demons from their paradise.

Some performances feature elaborate symbolism, such the Dance of the Masters of the Cremation Grounds (*Durdag*). A patch of human skin (yes, it's real) is set down in the middle of the courtyard, and four "skeleton dancers" begin to step out a complicated exorcism ritual. Suddenly *gings*, or celestial beings, appear in the audience. A flurry of drumming breaks out and the *gings* are everywhere, beating on drums, window sills, and even human heads to drive out evil spirits and bless the recipient.

At times the crowd—in handwoven silks and silver jewelry—is captivated by the performance; at other times they socialize and reach into their baskets for handfuls of red rice mixed with chilis and yak cheese. The men typically sport long robes with sashes and high boots; the women wear robes held by silver broaches, a *togo* (short jacket), and flowery ceremonial scarfs to cover their hair.

DATE: September/October. **LOCATION:** Tashichho Dzong, Thimphu. **TRANSPORT:** Thimphu is Bhutan's capital, and is accessible by 90-minute bus from Paro airport, which connects with Kathmandu, Delhi, Calcutta, and Bangkok. **ACCOMMODATION:** In addition to the Bhutan Tourism Corp., several private operators have set up good, well-managed hotels catering to upscale travelers. **CONTACT:** Tour operators listed in *Resources*.

Sacred dream-visions of heaven and hell are played out in the courtyard of the Thimphu Dzong. (Mark Chester/Leo de Wys)

RESOURCES

In Bhutan: Tourism Authority of Bhutan, P.O. Box 126, Thimphu, Bhutan, Tel 975-22854, Fax 975-22479. Yod Sel Tours, P.O. Box 574, Thimpu, Bhutan, Tel 975-23912, Fax 975-23589. Bhutan Tourism Corporation Ltd. P.O. Box 159, Thimphu, Tel 975-22479, Fax 975-23392. **USA:** Tourist Information Section, Bhutan Permanent Mission to the United Nations, 2 UN Plaza, New York, NY 10017. Bhutan Travel, 120 East 56th St. Suite 1130, New York, NY 10022, Tel (212) 838-6382, Fax (212) 750-1269. Mountain Travel, 6240 Fairmount Ave, El Cerrito, CA 94530, Tel (415) 527-8100. **UK:** Himalayan Kingdoms, 20 The Mall, Clifton, Bristol BS8 4DR, Tel 0272-237163. Worldwide Safaris, Chelsea Reach, 2nd Fl., 79–80 Lots Rd,

London SW10 ORN, Tel 071-351298. **Germany**: Marco Polo Reisen GmbH, P.O. Box 1320, Dettweilerstr. 15, DW-6242 Kronberg/Ts., Tel 6173-79070. Bhutan-Hamalaya Club e.V., Schaafenstr. 7, D-7000 Köln, Tel 221-249516.

INDIA

In terms of festivals, no single country can approach India's splendor, pageantry, and diversity. Whenever and wherever you are in India, you're likely to encounter festivals, carnivals, fairs, and bazaars, each erupting with music, dance, fireworks, and epic processions. The fact that there's a festival every day somewhere in India is a tribute to the country's ongoing vitality and the astounding diversity of its population. With at least seven religions and thousands of deities, saints, and prophets, there's plenty of worshiping to be done.

Each temple has its own festival, occasions when god-images are taken out and bathed, anointed, fussed over, reunited with spouses, or dragged through the streets at breakneck speeds. Religion has an impact on every aspect of Indian life, and while Hindu is the majority's faith, it's only one of many. With some 70 million Muslims, India has one of the largest Islamic populations in the world. In addition, there are some 16 million Christians, 13 million Sikhs, five million Buddhists, and smaller contingents of Jains, Zoroastrians (Parsis), and tribal animists. This religious diversity is further compounded by widely differing ethnicities, languages (more than 800 languages and dialects are spoken), and landscapes ranging from desert and jungle to high Himalaya.

India is famous for its overcrowded urban areas, yet its population is in fact mostly rural. Outlying areas offer some of the country's most rewarding travel experiences, with villagers carrying on within social and religious structures that defined their cultures 4,000 years ago. In the countryside, India's festivals—especially major celebrations like Dussehra, Diwali, and Holi—are most rewarding; visitors often prefer the friendly interaction of the small town festivals to the epic scale of the events in large cities. But no matter where you choose to experience the festivals of India, you'll find yourself enveloped in pageantry that retains remarkable links to the past. Whether you're covered in colored water, draped with flower garlands, or dodging a passing parade of elephants, India will leave an indelible, unforgettable imprint on all your senses.

As trumpets blare, the lamas (monks) of Spituk prepare to bring the esoteric gods and spirits of Tibetan Buddhism to life. *(Bill Cardoni)*

Spituk Festival

Spituk **January**

Across the windswept mountain kingdom of Ladakh, ancient trade routes zig-zag through the harsh brown landscape. Nomad families move slowly through this majestic panorama which, although geopolitically in India, is almost completely Tibetan in culture. Once each year, these wanderers descend into the alpine oasis of Spituk to watch the esoteric gods and spirits of Tibetan Buddhism as they come to life in the bright mask dances of the Spituk *gompa*, or monastery.

The Spituk Festival is smaller but similar to the well-known Hemis festival, and is organized by the *lamas* (monks) of the Gelukpa order of Tibetan Buddhism, whose members include the Dalai Lama, and who wear special hats during the festival. Also present is a statue of the goddess Kali, whose face is revealed only once a year during this event, and the imaginative *Jelbagh* masks which hang on the dark walls inside the *gompa*. Downstairs, through passages lit by yak-butter lamps, there are shrines to the sinister god Vajra-Bhairav, and the goddess Tara, whose 23 manifestations are captured in elaborate imagery. The temple is open to visitors, but you'll find few Westerners here at this winter festival.

DATE: Early to mid-January. **LOCATION:** Spituk is located on the banks of the Indus, just outside Leh on the road to Kargil, in the Ladakh region of the Jammu and Kashmir state. **TRANSPORT:** Leh has an airport with flights from Delhi, Jammu, and Candigarh, and an often-canceled flight from Srinagar. There are also buses to Leh from Srinagar and Manali, but roads are open only during the summer. **ACCOMMODATION:** There are no hotels in Spituk. Leh has a few basic-but-comfy hotels and guest houses, but many are closed during the winter. Supplies of electricity and water (cold only) are sporadic. **CONTACT:** Director of Tourism, Jammu & Kashmir, Gulab Bhavan, Srinagar 190001, Jammu & Kashmir, India; also Government of India Tourist Office (see *Resources*).

Pongal (Makara Sankranti or Bihu)

Throughout southeast India **Mid-January**

The harvest season is wrapped up during this Tamil festival which offers the bounties of the gods back to them for approval. Festivities begin with a mellow housecleaning and bonfires fueled by discarded goods. Flavored rice is offered to the sun god Surya, and a pot of *pongal* (milk, rice, sugar, and dhal) is put on the stove. As it begins to boil over, this symbol of prosperity is marked by bellows of conch-shell horns and cries of "pongal, pongal!" Candies of sesame seed and molasses are exchanged with the greeting, "Have a sesame sweet and say only sweet things."

On *Mattu Pongal* day, the villagers go cow-crazy. Cattle are washed, fed pongal, and decorated with paints, flowers, garlands of mango leaves, colored lights, bells, and anything else that shines or makes noise. As drums beat and music blares, the animals are paraded through the village streets. In the deep south, the cattle are stampeded in a rodeo of sorts, in which village boys try to grab bundles of cash from the horns of bulls. The festival is called Bihu in Assam, and Sankranti or Makara Sankranti in other parts of South India.

DATE: The first three or four days of the Tamil month of Thai (mid-January). **LOCATION:** Throughout the states of Tamil Nadu and Karnataka; also in many villages of Andhra Pradesh. **CONTACT:** Govt. of Tamil Nadu Tourist Office, 180 West Veli Street, Madurai, Tamil Nadu, India; Karnataka Government Tourist Office, 9 St. Mark's Road, Bangalore 560001, Karnataka, India; also GITO (see *Resources*).

Kite Festival

Ahmedabad **Mid-January**

This gathering of international and local kite enthusiasts coincides with the Makara Sankranti festivities in Ahmedabad, in the Gujarat State of Southwest India. The whole city is domed with colorful kites, which can be purchased in the markets at Tankshala Kalupur and Manek Chowk. Many enthusiasts coat their strings with ground glass and rice-flour glue, then send the kites up to do battle. The festivities continue after dark, as thousands of kites are outfitted with cylindrical paper lamps, filling the sky with brightly flickering stars. The festival is heavily promoted by the government, and hence is a bit touristy, but there are many sideshow exhibitions of folk dancing, crafts, and cuisines from all over India. The tourist authority even sets up a tent city called *Patand Nagar* (Kite Town).

DATE: Mid-January. **LOCATION:** Ahmedabad (sometimes spelled *Ahmadabad*), Gujarat state. **TRANSPORT:** As one of India's major industrial cities, Ahmedabad is easily reached by air, rail, or road from throughout the country. **ACCOMMODATION:** A wide range of accommodation is available, from luxury to budget. **CONTACT:** Gujarat Tourism Development Corporation, Head Office Block No.1, 2nd floor, Old Sachivalaya, Gandhinagar 382010, Gujarat, India; also GITO (see *Resources*).

Elephant March

Trivandrum and Thrissur (Trichur) Mid-January

Dozens of elephants and hundreds of tourists show up at this festival, created especially for international visitors. Although the festival was contrived by the Tourist Office, it does offer the chance to travel all over Kerala on the back of the giant pachyderm. The tours are tightly organized, and include stops to sample local cuisine, watch music and dance shows, and shop for crafts. Prices, although astronomical by Indian standards, are still a bargain for Westerners.

DATE: Mid-January. **LOCATION:** Trivandrum and Thrissur (until recently called Trichur), Kerala state. **TRANSPORT:** Trivandrum has international flights from Colombo and Male, and domestic flights from Madras, Bombay, and Bangalore. The railroad serves Trivandrum from the above points plus Delhi, Calcutta, Quilon, and Mangalore, and there are many bus connections. Thrissur has rail connections with the Kerala coast, as well as Kochi and Madras. Direct buses come from Bangalore, Mysore, Madras, Madurai, and Palani. **ACCOMMODATION:** Lodging options are most extensive in Trivandrum. **CONTACT:** Kerala Tourism Development Corp., P.O. Box 46, Elenjikal Bungalow TC26/342, Trivandrum 695001, India; also GITO (see *Resources*).

Republic Day

New Delhi January

One of the few festivals thrown according to the Gregorian calendar, Republic Day celebrates the day (January 26, 1950) when

India declared itself a republic independent from Great Britain. Even if you hate parades, don't miss this one if you're anywhere near Delhi—it's as spectacular and ostentatious as they get. You'll see column after column of soldiers in the absolute swankiest of outfits, plus tanks, floats, elephants, and camels parading down the Rajpath in a brilliant display of pride, color, and finery. The military is followed by schoolchildren and bands of musicians and dancers from around the country.

The parade and the following two-day festival are a great opportunity to get an all-in-one-place sampling of the country's extraordinarily diverse range of music, dance, dress, and ethnicities. The celebration winds up at dusk on January 29, with the "Beating of the Retreat" at Vijay Chowk. In this impressively precise performance, camels stand like statues as military bands weave intricate patterns to the martial tunes. Tickets cost approximately US$3 and are available through travel agents and most hotels.

DATE: January 26–29. **LOCATION:** New Delhi. **TRANSPORT:** New Delhi, India's capital, can be reached by air from all major gateways in Asia, Europe, Australia, and America. **ACCOMMODATION:** Lodging ranges from the most luxurious centrally located hotels to the cheap guest houses around Janpath and Paharganj. **CONTACT:** GITO (see *Resources*). For tickets, contact major hotels or travel agents.

FLOAT FESTIVAL (TEPPAM)

Madurai **January/February**

South India's lively temple town of Madurai rolls out the rafts in late January or early February, as it honors its 17th-century ruler, Tirumali Nayak. The site is the Mariamman Teppakkulam Tank (reservoir) and the illuminated, many-tiered island temple at its center. On the night of the full moon, fantastically dressed and jeweled images of the goddess Meenakshi and her consort Sundaresvara are floated on rafts decorated with flowers and hundreds of oil lamps. Along the shore the Tamil crowd chants hymns, as a bevy of bands thumps encouragement. While in town, be sure to visit the riotously elaborate Shree Meenakshi Temple, where sportive displays of piety are common.

DATE: Mid-January to mid-February (full moon in the Tamil month of Thai). **LOCATION:** Madurai, in the southern part of the Tamil Nadu State. **TRANSPORT:** Easily reached by air from Madras, Bangalore, or Tiruchirappalli (Trichy); train from Madras or Trichy; or bus. The tank is located on the riverbank just east of the city. Take the #4 bus from the State bus stand. **ACCOMMODATION:** A full range of hotels and guest houses are available, with better hotels lying north of the river. **CONTACT:** Government of Tamil Nadu Tourist Office, 180 West Veli Street, Maduri, Tamil Nadu, India; also GITO (see *Resources*).

The Desert Train to Jaisalmer

The traditional way to arrive in Jaisalmer is via the *Jaisalmer Express* from Jodhpur. The night train offers comfort in its sleeper berths, with a classic dawn arrival. The day train is a marathon of desert sightseeing, Rajput people-watching, and a spectacular sunset roll-in at Jaisalmer. The overnight train is the most popular, but during the high season (January–March) it fills up fast, so be sure to book as soon as you arrive in Jodhpur.

If you choose the day train, prepare for the 10-hour trip by packing plenty of water and fruit. You also may want to bring a book, although you'll probably be well stimulated by the combination of world travelers and stay-put Rajput villagers. The latter seem to board the train directly from another century, fantastically attired in traditional outfits. The tall, thin men stand proud in fancifully tied white *dhotis,* with scarlet turbans and sparkling earrings. The women are adorned with silver jewelry from head to toe. A married woman is identified by her *chaori,* a bone bracelet that stretches from the shoulder to the wrist. At times, itinerant musicians will board the trains to play *ragas* to the crowd's delight. As you pass through the flat Thar Desert (the name means "abode of death"), you'll see nomadic camels walking among gnarled trees, and *paniharis,* or female water carriers, near the villages. As dusk approaches, the trip nears its climactic end. Jaisalmer comes into sight on the horizon, bathed in ethereal light, one of India's—and the world's—most dramatic and unforgettable sights.

If you're a big spender, it's possible to make the trip in one or both of the Maharaja of Jodhpur's white carriages, fully decked out and emblazoned with his coat of arms. These include ornate coupés, dining quarters, cooks, butlers, and escorts from the Umaid Bhawan Palace. The price for the six-person carriage is about US$450; for the 14-person carriage about US$1800. Contact Indian Railways directly (Railway Information Office, New Delhi Railway Station, New Delhi, India), or through a travel agent.

Desert Festival

Jaisalmer **February/March**

Floating on the edge of the Thar Desert, the medieval fortress-city of Jaisalmer is remote, romantic, and completely unspoiled. The place—even more than the event—rewards the substantial effort it takes to get there, with its maze of sun-sheltered lanes and carved sandstone dwellings, and spectacular sunsets that endow the city with golden evening hues.

What the Desert Festival lacks in authenticity (it's a government-sponsored tourist event), it makes up with atmosphere and action. Legions of puppeteers, acrobats, and folk dancers add splashes of color, and sometimes corniness, to the haunting scene. Camel races and camel polo are big attractions, as are turban-tying competitions and the "best-dressed Rajput" contest. Nomads trek across the desert to sell woven goods, silver jewelry, and black-market items at the bazaar. Hotels set up camel safaris for eager tourists. And don't miss the music of the Manganiyars, who live in neighboring villages. You'll hear their ancient, haunting desert ballads; you'll see them sitting with clip-on backstage passes! On full-moon night the festival closes with a cheesy sound and light show in the sand dunes outside the city walls.

DATE: The full moon and preceding two days in late February or early March (the Hindu month of Phalgun). **LOCATION:** Jaisalmer, Rajasthan State. **TRANSPORT:** The nearest large airport is in Jodhpur, 287 km (178 miles) away, although Vayudoot Airlines flies light aircraft to the small Jaisalmer airstrip from Delhi, Jaipur, and Jodhpur. Buses run from Jodhpur and Bikaner, but the long trip across the desert is hellish. The train from Jodhpur is recommended. During the festival rail and air bookings can be difficult; reserve well in advance. **ACCOMMODATION:** The town is a bit of a zoo at festival time, and rooms in any price range are hard to come by. A large "tourist village" with tents, restrooms, and showers is erected beneath the fort. Also, many hotels offer the pleasant option of sleeping under the desert moon and stars on rooftop mattresses. **CONTACT:** Rajastan Tourist Information Bureau, Kota, Rajastan, India; also GITO (see *Resources*).

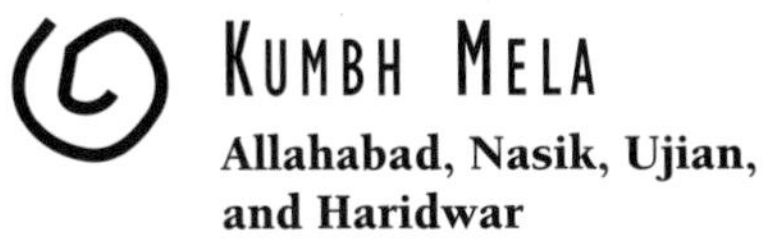

Kumbh Mela

Allahabad, Nasik, Ujian, and Haridwar — **January/February**

Although not an annual event, the Kumbh Mela merits mention in any description of Indian festivals. Known as the "greatest religious show on earth," the Mela begins when priests announce that the positions of the sun and moon are most auspicious, causing holy rivers suddenly to run with life-preserving nectar. Millions of pilgrims and thousands of holy men (*sadhus*) converge to take a holy dip that will cleanse their souls of sin. The action is non-stop: Naked ascetics perform miracles, brahmins bless (for a fee, of course), itinerant performers fill the air with music, and gurus in leopard skins rant and rave in front of audiences large and small. The authorities do their best to control the crowds, but because

It's a living: Cash donations lie near the single foot that holy man Latkani Baba has stood on continuously for more than 10 years. The Kumbh Mela, known as the "biggest religious show on earth," draws millions of saints, charlatans, and pilgrims. (Reuters/Bettman)

there are precise times for especially holy dips, stampedes do occur; in 1986, 50 people were trampled or drowned in a mad dash for the water.

The Kumbh Mela is held every three years in one of four places: Allahabad, Nasik, Ujian, or Haridwar. The event at Allahabad, occurring every 12 years, is the holiest of all, since the city lies at the sacred confluence of the Ganges and Yamuna rivers. At its peak day in 1989, an estimated 15 million people were gathered, making it the world's largest human assembly—ever.

DATE: Every three years according to astrological projections, throughout the month of *Magha* (January/February). **LOCATION:** Nasik (Maharashtra) in 1995, Haridwar (Uttar Pradesh) in 1998, Allahabad (Uttar Pradesh) in 2001, and Ujian (Madhya Pradesh) in 2004. **CONTACT:** GITO (see *Resources*).

Festival of Color (Holi)

Throughout northern India **February/March**

As the brief spring warms the landscape, northern India cuts loose for a day of high jinks and general hilarity. Holi, or the Festival of Color, is closely linked with a variety of age-old Hindu legends, but in modern times it's an excuse for Indians to shed inhibitions and caste differences for a day of spring fever and big fun. Teenagers spend the day flirting and misbehaving in the streets, adults extend the hand of peace, and everyone chases everyone else around, throwing brightly colored powder (*gulal*) and water over each other.

Holi is a great time to be in northern India—especially small towns—because it's India at its most playful and coquettish. The festival's preamble begins on the night of the full moon. Bonfires are lit on street corners to cleanse the air of evil spirits and bad vibes, and to symbolize the destruction of the wicked Holika, for whom the festival was named. The following morning, the streets fill with people running, shouting, giggling, and splashing. Western tourists are favorite targets, so bring old clothes and an interesting water-shooter and you'll be a big hit! Marijuana-based *bhang* and *thandai* add to the uninhibited atmosphere.

Promptly at noon, the craziness comes to an end and everyone heads to either the river or the bathtub, then inside to relax the day away and partake of candies. In the afternoon an exhausted and contented silence falls over India. Although Holi is observed all over the north, it's celebrated with special joy and zest at Mathura, Vrindavan, Nandgaon, and Barsnar. These towns once housed the divine Krishna, the handsome flautist whose beauty enchanted all the cowherd girls of the village. On Holi, his favorite festival, he danced with all the girls—especially his beloved Radha—then pranked around, drenching the girls with colored water and stealing their clothes while they bathed.

Each area celebrates Holi differently; in large cities it's often an excuse for youngsters to misbehave (women stay indoors to escape pinching and pawing). Traditions are more rustic, less jaded, and better for travelers in smaller towns and villages. One option is to check out the unique celebrations and garb of the Bhil tribesmen of western Madhya Pradesh, who've retained many of their pre-Hindu customs. Another is to travel to rural Maharash-

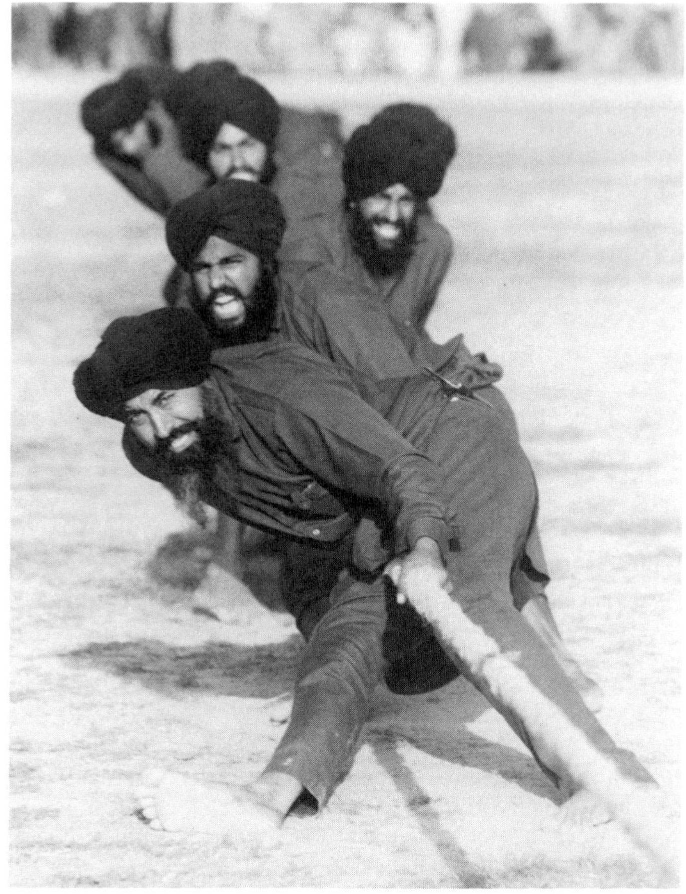

Hola Mohalla: Ancient orders of Sikh warriors square off in a tug-of-war at Kila Raipur's annual fighting festival. Similar war games are held at Anandpur Sahib. (Reuters/Bettman)

tra State, where the festival is known as *Rangapanchami* and is celebrated with dancing and singing. In the towns of Rajasthan—especially Jaisalmer—the music's great, and clouds of pink, green, and turquoise powder fill the air. The grounds of Jaisalmer's Mandir Palace are turned into chaos, with dances, folk songs, and colored-powder confusion.

DATE: Full moon in the month of Phalgun (late February or early March). **LOCATION:** Everywhere in northern India. Holi is also celebrated in Nepal and parts of Sri Lanka and Indonesia (see *Resources*).

Hola Mohalla

Anandpur Sahib **February/March**

In a remote part of the Punjab, the town of Anandpur Sahib puts a Sikh twist on the Holi festivities, as notoriously fierce Sikh warriors converge at the foothills of the Himalaya for a day of war games. The action takes place just below the shrine to Sikh guru Govind Sagar, and includes mock battles on horseback with ancient weapons, and games such as archery, fencing, and tent-pegging. It's all organized by the *Nihangs* (the Order of the Blue-Clad Farmer-Warriors), who descend from two ancient orders of Sikh fighters. They welcome spectators, but they also warn that they can't be responsible for your safety if you get in the way. Take their advice to heart—these boys play hard!

DATE: The day after Holi (late February or early March). **LOCATION:** Anandpur Sahib, Punjab State. This tiny village is located about 60 km (37 miles) northwest of Chandigarh. Another similar festival is held in Kila Raipur village. **TRANSPORT:** Buses serve Anandpur Sahib from Amritsar and Chandigarh. Amritsar has air and rail connections with Delhi. **ACCOMMODATION:** Choices are slim around the village, so the event is best done as a day trip; Amritsar is a much better bet for lodging. **CONTACT:** Punjab Government Tourist Office, SCA No. 183–85, Sector 22, Chandigarh, Punjab, India; also GITO (see *Resources*).

While you're there ...

- **Khajuraho Dance Festival, Khajuraho (Madhya Pradesh State):** Many of the country's best dancers, representing all kinds of ethnic groups and religions, perform amidst the ancient Chandella Temples. (February/March.)
- **Carnival, Panaji and elsewhere in Goa:** A full-blown Latin carnival in Asia? Yes! In India's small coastal state of Goa, this remnant of Portuguese colonialism is still celebrated with parades, music, and beach parties, under the approving eye of King Momo, the Lord of the Revel. (February/March; the four days before the start of Lent.)
- **Ganguar, throughout Rajasthan:** Women and girls have the spotlight during this event, wearing their finest clothes and taking to the streets with offerings of flowers and song. Many villages feature musicians and dancers, as well as ornamented elephants, camels, and horses. (February/March.)

Karaga Festival

Bangalore **March/April**

Death by sword is the penalty for bad balance or an unlucky sneeze during the Karaga Festival's dramatic procession. Starting

Sweet Dreams of the Nectar of Immortality

Although most Westerners aren't aware of the invitation, everyone's invited to stay for up to three nights in one of the most amazing religious structures in India, the Golden Temple. This holiest shrine of the Sikhs sits in the middle of the Pond of the Nectar of Immortality, its roof of pure gold suggesting an inverted lotus flower. Not only is it the most interesting place to stay in Amritsar, it's also the cheapest—it's free (although nearly everyone provides a small donation for temple upkeep).

The Sikhs have a tradition of hospitality to pilgrims, and if you don't happen to be a Sikh, you're welcome just the same. Inside the temple compound, which was rebuilt after being partially destroyed by the Indian Army in 1984, there are shrines, a museum, kitchens (where volunteers fix 10,000 meals each day), the Sikh Parliament, and the *gurdwara* (temple).

Bedding and shared showers are provided. For more luxury—a double room with private showers—there's a fee of about half a US dollar. When you enter, be sure to remove your shoes and cover your head, and don't smoke or drink alcohol. And be sure to pick up a copy of the English-language booklet entitled *Human Hair: Factory of Vital Energy!* It's available in the information office.

at the Dharmaraja Temple, a clay pot called the *karaga* is balanced upon a chosen devotee's head, while his hands are occupied by staff and sword. The pot embodies Shakti, the mother-goddess of primal strength, and it must not be dropped during the duration of the 20-kilometer (12-mile) procession to the Sampangi Reservoir. The lucky one's colleagues from the *Thegala* gardeners' caste accompany him, swords brandished and ready to carry out the consequence of a bobbled *karaga*. Should the sacred pot break, they are sworn to fall on their friend with their swords and stab him to death. As the procession moves through town the sword-bearers chant encouragement while others drum out a beat. Upon a safe arrival at the tank, the *karaga* is immersed and the honored devotee (and his family) can breathe a sigh of relief. The festival also features a variety of feats of balance, such as stacking multiple clay pots on heads and limbs of devotees to test strength of character.

DATE: Late March or April. **LOCATION:** Bangalore, Karnataka State. **TRANSPORT:** Although there are no international flights, Bangalore has excellent air, rail, and bus connections to all of India's big cities. **ACCOMMODATION:** Many of the luxury and mid-range hotels in

Bangalore have courtyards tastefully arranged to hold up Bangalore's reputation as India's "Garden City." There are also plenty of budget digs. **CONTACT:** Karnataka Government Tourist Office, 9 St. Mark's Road, Bangalore 560001, Karnataka, India; also GITO (see *Resources*).

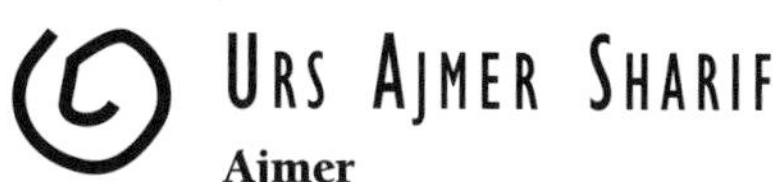

Urs Ajmer Sharif

Ajmer **February/March/April**

The Urs (death anniversary) of Sufi saint Khwaja Moinuddin Chisti is one of India's most festive and colorful Islamic events. Spanning six days, it draws pilgrims from all over south Asia and the Middle East, who arrive to pray at the marble pavilions of the Dargah shrine, built on the edge of a 900-year-old man-made lake. They fill the narrow, winding streets with music and ceremony as stalls spring up to sell baskets of marigolds, roses, embroideries, and veils of velvet and gold thread. Feasts are cooked in tureens so large that they are danced in when empty, and the continuous worship is backed by a soundtrack of eery and beautiful *quwwali* music. On the last day women use their own hair as mops to wash the rose-covered tomb, then squeeze the rose water into bottles for later use in anointing the sick.

Ajmer, India's most important Islamic pilgrimage center, lies in the middle of predominately Hindu Rajasthan and features the Adai-din-ka-Jhonpra mosque, a tribute to the destructive power of religious passion. The mosque was built in just two days by Muhammed Ghori's army, using the remains of 30 Hindu temples razed in an orgy of destruction.

DATE: The first through sixth of Rajab, the seventh month of the Islamic calendar. **LOCATION:** Ajmer, Rajasthan State, 198 km (123 miles) east of Jodhpur, and 130 km (80 miles) west of Jaipur. Pushkar is only 11 km (seven miles) away (see the **Pushkar Mela**). **TRANSPORT:** Ajmer has no airport, but trains come from Delhi, Agra, Ahmedabad, and Jaipur. Also, there are buses from Jodpur, Bikaner, Udaipur, and Chittaurgarh. **ACCOMMODATION:** Hotels range from luxury to budget. **CONTACT:** Rajastan Tourism Development Corp., 100 Jawajarial Nehru Marg, Jaipur 302004, Rajasthan, India; also GITO (see *Resources*).

Hindu New Year (Baisakhi)

Throughout India **March/April**

Baisakhi has special significance for two of India's major religious groups. For Hindus, it's the start of the New Year, and is celebrated

The Looting of the Deg

The Ajmer Dargah's most unusual event is the "looting" of two huge cauldrons called *deg*. Rice is donated by pilgrims on a continuous basis. When enough has been given to fill the two deg (the largest, more than nine feet in diameter, can hold nearly 4,500 kg/10,000 lbs), the rice is cooked with a mixture of raisins, nuts, and milk. After the names of donors have be ceremoniously announced, an exciting free-for-all breaks out. Professional "looters" scramble for the rice, some even jumping into the boiling cauldrons to scrape the bottom. The sanctified rice (*tabarukh*) is then sold by the looters to pilgrims. Since the Looting of the Deg occurs only when enough rice has been donated to fill the cauldrons, it's impossible to predict the event's timing; if you happen to be in the area, just show up and check the status of the deg, or ask at the Dargah for a prediction of the next looting.

with requisite bathing, partying, and worshiping. It's believed that the goddess Ganga descended to earth thousands of years ago, and in her honor many Hindus gather along the sacred Ganges River for ritual baths. The action is centered in the holy cities along the Ganges in north India, or in Srinagar's Mughal Gardens, Jammu's Nagbani Temple, or anywhere in Tamil Nadu. Hindus plant poles wrapped in flags of god-embroidered silk in front of their homes, and hang pots of brass, copper, or silver on top. Children wear garlands of flowers and run through the streets singing "May the New Year come again and again!" In Kerala the festival is called *Vishu,* and includes fireworks, shopping for new clothes and interesting displays called *Vishu Kani.* These arrangements of flowers, grains, fruits, cloth, gold, and money are viewed early in the morning, to ensure a year of prosperity. In Assam, the festival is called *Bohag Bihu,* and the community organizes massive feasts, music, and dancing.

Sikhs assign quite a different meaning to Baisakhi, and if you happen to be in a Punjabi village to catch the men performing the wild *bhangra* dance, you'll get the picture. This strenuous dance tells the story of the agricultural process, from tilling the soil through harvesting. As the *dholak* (drum) changes beats, the dancing sequence progresses, dramatizing plowing, sowing, weeding, reaping, and finally celebrating. Baisakhi also commemorates the day in 1689 when Guru Gobing Singh founded the Khalsa, the fighting Sikh brotherhood that donned the distinctive Sikh outfits. Sikhs visit temples, such as the Golden Temple in Amritsar,

Adorned in gold and jewels, dozens of elephants await the start of the Pooram procession in southwest India's Kerala State.
(Jehangir Gazdar/Woodfin Camp & Associates)

where the holy *Granth* is read, commemorating the day on which the guru asked five volunteers to offer their lives, then took them one at a time into a tent. He emerged each time with a bloody sword, although he had in fact sacrificed a goat. In honor of the "Beloved Five," a series of parades take place in which sets of five men walk in front of the holy book with swords drawn. When the ceremony is over, a round of feasting, music-making, and dancing begins, amid the blossoming flowers and harvested grain.

DATE: The first day of the month of Baisakh in the Hindu calendar (April/May). **LOCATION:** Throughout India. **CONTACT:** GITO (see *Resources*).

Pooram

Thrissur (formerly Trichur) **April/May**

Thrissur's streets erupt with noisy pageantry during this temple festival, which includes dozens of elephants and a fireworks display that many consider to be the best in Asia. It all starts at the peculiar pagoda-shaped entrance to the Vadakkunathan Temple, as images of deities are brought out in procession. The earth shakes as 30 giant "tusker" elephants start to move, their heads decorated with magnificent gold and jeweled caparisons, their brilliant white tusks gleaming in the sun. On the elephants' backs, Brahmin priests in *dhotis* sit under bright silk umbrellas and yak-hair pom-pons. The day-long parade moves through the streets to the beat of temple drums and the blaring of ancient instruments called *panchavadya*. When the sun sets, the partying continues with a wildly elaborate fireworks display that lasts until dawn.

DATE: April/May (the Hindu month of Baisakh). **LOCATION:** Thrissur (the name was recently changed from Trichur) in southwest India's Kerala State, 80 km (50 miles) from Cochin. **TRANSPORT:** Thrissur has no airport, but good rail and bus connections from coastal cities in Kerala. **ACCOMMODATION:** Only very basic rooms are available in Thrissur. **CONTACT:** Kerala Tourist Information Centre, Park View, Palayam, Trivandrum 695003, Kerala, India; also GITO (see *Resources*).

Chitra Festival (Meenakshi Kalaynam)

Madurai **April/May**

Every day's a festival at the Meenakshi Temple, but the 10-day celebration of the wedding of its "fish-eyed" patron goddess cranks up the pomp and splendor to phenomenal levels. About 100,000 people show up to attend the divine marriage of Meenakshi and Sundereswara (an incarnation of Shiva), re-enacted in the courtyard. According to legend, Meenakshi, the daughter of a Pandyan king, was born with three breasts. The king was told that the extra breast would disappear when his daughter met the right man. On Mt. Kailas, she ran into "Mr. Right" in the form of Shiva. She returned to Madurai, and, eight days later, Shiva arrived in the form of Lord Sundereswara to claim his bride. After the marriage ceremony, the deities are taken out in a high-energy procession through town in the temple chariot.

The temple itself is one of the most fabulously excessive displays of architecture on earth. Outlandish even by Indian standards, it is absolutely mind-blowing to Western visitors. Nine towering *gopurams* and thousands of pillars are covered from top to bottom with some 30 million (!) colorful carvings and stucco images of gods, demons, and animals (both real and imagined). Each of the columns in the "hall of 1,000 pillars" is elaborately carved, and the temple walls hold cloisters, sacred tanks, and even a carved "encyclopedia of dances."

Although the temple is a phenomenal piece of religious history, it is very much alive. Daily, up to 10,000 devotees worship, get married, attend classes, eat, and sleep. Almost non-stop revelry fills the bizarre courtyard; as music blares, children dance around dressed as gods, priests chant, and pilgrims devote themselves to worship of all kinds. Outside the temple walls the scene is just as active. Something is always happening in the "City of Honey," one of India's liveliest mid-sized towns.

DATE: Late April or early May (Hindu month of Baisakh). **LOCATION:** Madurai, in Tamil Nadu State. **TRANSPORT:** Madurai is easily reached by air from Madras, Bangalore, or Tiruchirappalli (Trichy); train or bus from Madras or Trichy. **ACCOMMODATION:** A full range of hotels and guest houses are available, with better hotels lying north of the river. **CONTACT:** Government of Tamil Nadu Tourist Office, 180 West Veli Street, Madurai, Tamil Nadu, India; also GITO (see *Resources*).

◎ Buddha Jayanti (Buddha Purnima)

Bodhgaya and Sarnath **April/May**

Buddhists from all over the world converge on Bodhgaya and Sarnath to commemorate the Buddha's birth, enlightenment, and death. Sarnath has a colorful fair and procession of relics, at a temple on the site where the Buddha preached his first sermon. Although the town of Bodhgaya is more interesting, the festivities are lower-key. It was here that Prince Guatama attained enlightenment to become the Buddha. The spot is marked by a red sandstone slab, shaded by a bo (pipal) tree believed to have grown from a sapling descended from the original. Worshipers tie brightly colored strips of cloth to the branches when they come to meditate. As Buddhism's most important pilgrimage site, Bodhgaya has many monasteries and lots of activity. In addition, many of the centers for meditation and study welcome students from around the world.

DATE: April/May (full moon in the month of Baisakh). **LOCATION:** Bodhgaya in Bihar State, Sarnath in Uttar Pradesh. The holiday is also observed in other Buddhist holy places in India, such as Sanchi (near Vidisha) and Kusinagar (near Gorakhpur). **TRANSPORT:** Bodhgaya is 13 km (8 miles) from Gaya. Buses run from

Gaya and Patna. Sarnath is 10 km (6 miles) northeast of Varanasi. Although buses make the trip, auto-rickshaws are more frequent and convenient. **ACCOMMODATION:** There are quite a few decent hotels, and many of the monasteries offer accommodation for voluntary contributions. **CONTACT:** Bihar State Information Centre, Fraser Road, Patna, Bihar, India; Uttar Pradesh Government Tourist Office, Hotel Gomti Complex, 6 Sapru Marg, Lucknow, Uttar Pradesh, India; also GITO (see *Resources*).

Dhungri Forest Festival

Near Manali **May**

After a pleasant walk through the dense cedar forest just outside of Manali, a clearing reveals a small temple. Here, hill women arrive in their colorful garb to dance and worship the goddess Hadimba, wife of Bhima in the epic *Mahabharata.* The festivities take place just outside the simple wooden temple, with its multi-tiered roof and carved doorway. According to legend, the king who commissioned the temple was so happy with the results that he cut off the craftsman's right hand to prevent him from duplicating it elsewhere. Unfazed, the artist used his left hand to build the even finer Triloknath Temple at Chamba. Again, the work was highly admired, and to prevent the creation of a rival, the craftmen's head was cut off.

DATE: May (check with the Government of India Tourist Office for exact dates). **LOCATION:** Hadimba Temple (also known as Dhungri or Doongri Temple), just outside of Manali, Himachal Pradesh State. **TRANSPORT:** The temple lies at the end of a footpath about 2.5 km (1.5 miles) from Manali's Tourist Office. Manali is at the north end of the Kulu Valley, about 40 km from Kulu. There are frequent buses from nearby Kulu, and from Shimla (10 hours), Dharamsala (13 hours), and Delhi (16 hours). **ACCOMMODATION:** Manali has become very touristy, but it does offer a wide range of acommodation, ranging from budget digs to luxuriously peaceful log huts. **CONTACT:** Himachal Pradesh Tourist Development Corporation, The Mall, Ritz Annexe, Simla 171001, Himachal Pradesh, India; also GITO (see *Resources*).

Hemis Festival

Hemis Gompa **June/July**

Hidden in a deep gorge near the roof of the world, the Hemis *Gompa* (monastery) hits you suddenly as you round the mountain. It clings precariously to the spur, dignified and dramatic with tall pillars and prayer flags that wave visitors into the courtyard.

Hemis Festival: Each summer mild-mannered monks are transformed into demons as they play out scriptured battles in the Hemis Gompa's courtyard. (John Elk III)

Families of Ladakhis begin arriving from all over the valley, their ornate festival clothing revealing a Tibetan, rather than Indian, heritage. The men tie their quilted coats with bright cummerbunds, and many women wear the *perak*, an elaborate headdress with woven strips of beads and turquoise, silver dangles, and upright ears of braided yak hair. Each family carries a savovar of yak-butter tea, and a canister of *tsampa,* a roasted barley flour.

The dances are heralded by the weirdly discordant cry of brass trumpets three meters (10 feet) long. Suddenly, the *lamas* (monks) are transformed into demons and gods. Horned devil-masks and padded brocade outfits come to life as they play out

Anticipation rewarded: Pilgrims react as the enormous thangka *embroidery is unfurled, an event that takes place every 12 years at the Hemis Festival.* (Patrick Morrow)

the scriptured battles between good and evil spirits. *Lamas* with red robes and tall tufted hats bang on drums and crash cymbals together as others gyrate and leap to fight off demons.

This two-day festival is a dance-homage to the birth anniversary of Guru Padmasambhava, and the largest and best of the Tibetan Buddhist *gompa* festivals in Ladakh. The *lamas* themselves offer conflicting interpretations as to the meanings of the dances, but no matter—it's food for the imagination of both the Ladakhis and visitors from afar. Desire and anger are often destroyed by good, and the solemn dramas are often interrupted by interludes of comedy. At the climax a human effigy made of *tsampa* dough is dismembered, symbolically purifying the individual soul of desire.

DATE: June or July. **LOCATION:** Hemis is 40 km (25 miles) southeast of Leh, on the opposite side of the Indus River. **TRANSPORT:** Buses from Leh are frequent in the summer. The airport in Leh handles flights (often delayed because of unpredictable weather) from Delhi, Srinagar, and Chandigarh. If you're fit, consider trekking in—you'll get a true feel for the majesty of the mountains and the timeless dignity of the Ladakhi people and their culture. **ACCOMMODATION:** Leh's many hotels offer an array of options ranging from near-luxury to low-budget. **CONTACT:** Director of Tourism Jammu & Kashmir, Gulab Bhavan, Srinagar 190001, Jammu & Kashmir, India; also Government of India Tourist Office (see *Resources*).

Gompa Protocol

You'll find that the Ladakhis are among the most tolerant, hospitable, and courteous people anywhere, but keep in mind that their *gompas* are places of worship, and that the secret treasures of Tibetan Buddhism should be viewed with appropriate respect and reverence. The religious structures should be navigated in a clockwise direction. Bring a flashlight for the dark temple corridors, but be careful to observe restrictions on flash photography, and don't smoke anywhere on the temple grounds. Finally, be prepared to see many images that are extremely surreal and amusing, but save any wisecracks or laughter for later.

Chariot Festival (Rath Yatra)

Puri **June/July**

This holy city and seaside resort works itself into a religious frenzy during the full moon, as gigantic images of Lord Jaganath and his siblings are rolled through the streets on huge chariots. If you can brave the heat, humidity, and humanity, you'll experience one of India's epics, the spectacle that brought the word *juggernaut* into the English language.

Lord Jaganath is an incarnation of Lord Krishna, "the formless one" in whose eyes all castes are equal. The festival commemorates his journey from Gokul to Mathura to visit his aunt. In the weeks before the procession, the huge image is ritually cleaned at the temple. His clothes are changed, his face anointed, and his teeth brushed by more than 6,000 "servants" who have dedicated their lives to him. These ceremonies, and the temple itself, are off-limits to non-Hindus.

On Rath Yatra Day Jaganath goes public, as hundreds of thousands of devotees, pilgrims, and travelers swarm into the streets to watch him make the journey from the temple to his summer vacation home, the Gundicha Mandir (Garden House). His black-faced brother, Balbhadra, and his yellow-faced sister, Subhadra, come along. The three *raths* (chariots) are bigger than houses, with decorated pavilions and brocade cushions on which the gods sit. The largest (Jaganath's) is 14 meters (45 feet) tall and is supported by 16 wheels, each of which is taller than a man.

Once the chariots get moving they are nearly impossible to stop or turn—they are true juggernauts (this is the way the Eng-

Heat, humidity, and humanity: Each of the three chariots will be pulled by 4,200 men, who honor Lord Jaganath in the epic that brought the word juggernaut *into the English language. The Chariot Festival (Rath Yatra) takes place each summer in Puri. (Dinodia Picture Agency/Bombay)*

lish heard the word *Jaganath*). As dictated by a ritual that extends from the 10th century, each wagon is pulled by four horses and 4,200 men, who sweat and strain at the thick ropes. They move to the beat of thousands of cymbal smashers, drum beaters, and horn blowers, and tens of thousands of rice-throwers, totem bearers, and shaven-headed women who have dedicated their locks to Lord Jaganath. This is India at its chaotic best, with masses of pilgrims pressing forward to offer blessings of marigolds and coconut shards. Very occasionally—resist the temptation—someone will throw himself under the wheels to be crushed to death in Jaganath's sight.

When the gods get to the Gundicha Mandir, they're unloaded for a week-long summer vacation. Then they're reloaded for a replay of the procession in reverse, back to the Jaganath Temple. The chariots are dismantled and used for firewood in the temple kitchens, and for sanctified funeral-pyre fuel. The dismantling process commences another round of chaos, as huddles of devotees fling themselves upon every scrap.

Puri itself is a interesting pilgrimage center and seaside town with a fine beach (although there is a dangerous current). At dawn the fishermen drag their unique fleet of fishing boats out into the surf. These are made of carved tree trunks and are enormously heavy and bulky. Another of Puri's quirks is that marijuana is legal, and sold in government-sponsored *bhang* shops.

Snake charmers are in big demand on Naag Panchami, as the deadly hooded cobra is worshiped and doted over. (Jagdish Agarwal/Dinodia Picture Agency/Bombay)

DATE: June or July (check with the tourist office for exact dates each year). **LOCATION:** Puri (Orissa State). **TRANSPORT:** Puri is easily reached by train from Calcutta, Madras, Bhubaneswar, and Delhi (32 hours), or by bus from Konark, Berhampur, and Taptapani. **ACCOMMODATION:** As a seaside resort, Puri has an extensive selection of hotels, many of which have views of the beach. **CONTACT:** Government of Orissa Tourist Office, 5 Jayadev Nagar, Bhubaneswar 751002, Orissa, India, Tel 674-50009; or GITO *Resources*).

© Naag (Naga) Panchami

Nationwide **July/August**

Snake charmers are in big demand during this festival, which pays homage to Ananta (Naga), the 1,000-headed serpent whose coils supported Lord Vishnu as he contemplated and created the universes. The cobra is especially venerated, and women devotees fast and offer milk, sweets, and flowers to live cobras and cobra images in the shrines. Small crowds gather around the deadly hooded serpents as they sway to the hypnotic sound of melodies performed on the *pungis* (double-reed pipes) and *kanjira* (small wooden drum).

At Jodhpur, people erect giant images of Naga, and women seeking fertility dote on the many visiting snake charmers. Snakes are also believed to have some control over the rainfall, and to keep evil from homes. Thus at the Shiva temples at Ujjain, Vaidyanatha, and the "eternal city" of Varanasi, hundreds of

Amarnath Yatra: Pilgrims walk for four days through the rugged Kashmir Himalaya for a glimpse of Lord Shiva's sacred phallic symbol. (Gordon Wiltsie)

cobras are brought by trappers to the temple grounds to be released before Shiva. Worshipers then pour milk over the heads of the serpents, in the belief that by doing so they will never be harmed by a snake. At the end of the day, the snakes are released into the fields.

DATE: Fifth day of Shrawan, brightening fortnight (July/August). **LOCATION:** All over India, but best in Jodhpur (Rajasthan), Ujjain (Madhya Pradesh), and Varanasi (Uttar Pradesh). **CONTACT:** GITO (see *Resources*).

Amarnath Yatra

Near Pahalgam **July/August**

The high Kashmir Himalaya is the setting for this four-day pilgrimage, which takes place throughout the warm months of July and August. The destination is a mountain cave containing a sacred phallic symbol (*lingam*), made of ice and said to wax and wane with the moon. It's impressive, but—as is often the case of pilgrimages—most of the fun is in the journey.

The trek sets out to cries of "Jai Amarnath!" from the resort village of Pahalgam, more than 2,150 meters (6,988 feet) above sea level. The climbing is tough, but most pilgrims do it on foot. Some use mules, and the very old are shouldered on special litters called *palkis*. People from all walks of life and all parts of India are here, their saris and dhoties presenting a colorful human collage.

The trail winds through fields of blooming saffron and high alpine meadows that have hosted a nomadic lifestyle unchanged for centuries. Some villagers open their summer homes to offer sips of buttermilk. There are three campsites and a few rest sites along the way, bustling with food stalls and beverages (so it's not necessary to pack food, only water-treatment gear). One windy site overlooks the legendary Shashnag Lake, which changes color from deep blue to sapphire, and is surrounded by seven peaks.

The route climbs over Mahagunis Pass, which at over 4,218 meters (13,800 feet) is snowbound even in mid-summer. It then descends into a luxuriant meadow with a bustling outpost. Around the cave temple there are brahmins, hermits with matted hair, and people from all over India. The food is free, offered by wealthy Hindus, but the religious icons, postcards, and *bhang* (marijuana) are for sale. It's a long way to walk for a meal, but the food isn't bad and there's plenty of it.

And Lord Shiva's sacred *lingam?* Inside the cave, once your eyes adjust to the low light, you'll see it rising out of the ground. Slightly taller than a man, the icy phallic symbol stands all by itself, waxing and waning perhaps just a little too slowly for the mortal eye to see.

DATE: July/August. **LOCATION:** The pilgrimage begins at Pahalgam, 96 km (60 miles) from Srinagar, in the Jammu and Kashmir State. **TRANSPORT:** Buses from Srinagar (4.5 hours). **ACCOMMODATION:** Although you will be camping along the way, Pahalgam's hotels offer a broad range of lodging. **CONTACT:** J & K Tourism, 202 Kanishka Shopping Plaza, 19 Ashok road, New Delhi, India; also Government of India Tourist Office (see *Resources*).

JHAPAN (MANASA) FESTIVAL

Vishnupur **August**

Snake charmers converge on this town of ornate terra-cotta temples to pay homage to the goddess Manasa, daughter of Shiva and divine leader of the fertility cult of snake worship. You'll see more snakes than a lifetime of nightmares could ever invoke. Woven baskets are unloaded carrying pythons, rat snakes, kraits, and even flying snakes, all of which are trained to do tricks and magical feats. But it is the deadly cobra who draws the biggest crowds, and you'll see dozens wheeled up in decorated carts. As the charmers begin their songs, the revered killer begins to sway gently, and devotees in wild outfits break into dance, sometimes entering trances and exhorting the snakes to bring fertility to ovaries or fields. If you tire of the snake charming, Vishnupur's market is a great place to find pottery, silk, metalwear, clothes, and conch-shell jewelry.

DATE: August. **LOCATION:** Vishnupur (Bishnupur), West Bengal State, located 160 km northwest of Calcutta. **TRANSPORT:** By bus from Calcutta, 4.5 hours; by train, 3.5 hours. **ACCOMMODATION:** Bishnupur has very limited and shabby lodging; consider day-tripping. **CONTACT:** West Bengal Government Tourist Bureau, 3/2 Binoy Badel Dinesh Bagh (East), Calcutta 700001, West Bengal, India; also GITO (see *Resources*).

While you're there ...

- **Phiyang Gompa Festival, Phiyang (near Leh):** This summer *gompa* festival rivals that of Hemis for local color and attendance, although it doesn't draw nearly as many Westerners. Like its better-known cousin, it features masked dancers and colorful locals, in one of the most winsome villages in Ladakh. The *gompa* itself is a very well-lit temple with excellent religious paintings, and a collection of 14th-century Kashmiri bronze images. (July.)
- **Raksha Bandhan (Narial Purnima), throughout northern India:** In a charming reaffirmation of the bonds between siblings, sisters tie *rakhis* (colorful threads or amulets) on their brothers' wrists. Brothers give their sisters gifts, and make a promise to protect them. In some coastal areas, Varuna (the Vedic sea god) is honored with coconuts thrown into the sea. (Month of Srawan: July/August.)
- **Teej, throughout Rajasthan:** In honor of the onset of the monsoon and the goddess Parvati, specially decorated swings are hung from trees and posts. In the streets, images of the goddess are paraded to singing, dancing, and spontaneous poetry welcoming the rains and hailing the goddess. (Month of Srawan: July/August.)

Janmashtami

Throughout India **August/September**

Krishna's birthday is celebrated with a cheerful spirit that would please this mischievous god, known alternately as naughty child, cowherd, Casanova, and destroyer of evil. Many devotees fast until midnight, and an astounding number of rituals, ceremonies, and prayers are conducted at temples dedicated to Krishna. Images of the infant god are bathed and placed in silver cradles, and devotees bring truckloads of toys to the temples to present to him. At midnight, when his birth is announced, his cradles are rocked.

This is a national holiday, but it's presented most fervently at temples in Brindavan, Bombay, Agra, and Krishna's birthplace, Mathura. In Maharashtra, the festival is called Govinda and is celebrated with a reenactment of an episode from Krishna's childhood. Young men climb on each others' shoulders, forming human pyramids in an effort to break pots suspended on wires over the street. These are filled with curds and butter (Krishna's favorite foods), and money.

DATE: August or September (Hindu month of Bhadon). **LOCATION:** Nationwide, but especially Brindavan, Bombay, Agra, and Mathura. **CONTACT:** GITO (see *Resources*).

Tarnetar Mela

Tarnetar **August/September**

This fair draws tribal people—Kolies, Bharwads, and Bararis—to the Trineteshwar Mahadev Temple for three days of worshiping, marketing, and bride-shopping. They arrive on camels or on foot, to celebrate the ancient marriage of Draupadi to Arjuna, the hero of the *Mahabharata.* The tribal people wear traditionally woven costumes, and make special *chatris* (umbrellas decorated with mirror work and embroidery). The men are laden down with a fascinating array of jewelry. According to scripture, Arjuna once danced at Tarnetar; in that vein, you'll hear plenty of music and see many spontaneous folk dances—the *garba,* the *ras,* and the *haro*—in the streets.

In this predominately Jain area, the vegetarian food is excellent, and all-you-can-eat *thali* restaurants offer a huge variety of meatless food. Nearby are the last Asian lions (in the Gir Forest), and the amazing architecture of Ahmedabad, Vadodara (Baroda), and Surat.

DATE: August/September. **LOCATION:** Tarnetar, in the Saurashtra region of Gujarat State (65 km northeast of Rajkot). **TRANSPORT:** Tarnetar is just outside of Rajkot, which can be reached by air from Bombay; rail from Bombay, Ahmedabad, Vadodara, and Porbandar; and bus from all main towns in Gujarat. **ACCOMMODATION:** Tarnetar has no hotels, but Rajkot offers basic lodging. **CONTACT:** Gujarat Tourism Development Corporation, Block No. 1, 2nd floor, Old Sachivalaya, Gandhinagar 382010, Gujarat, India; also GITO (see *Resources*).

Onam Harvest Festival/Nehru Cup Snakeboat Race

Alappuzha (Allepey) and throughout Kerala **August/September**

As beautifully decorated snakeboats race through Kerala's stately backwaters, its shorelines come alive with 10 days of feasting and

Onam: Snakeboats, each with up to 100 rowers, celebrate the Kerala region's warring and seafaring traditions in the annual Nehru Cup race. (Jehangir Gazdar/Woodfin Camp & Associates)

harvest celebrations. Onam is a great time to be in this southwest Indian state, as the region combines a celebration of its warring and seafaring traditions with festivities honoring the ancient Asura King Mahabali.

According to legend, the gods were jealous of the king and sent him into exile in the netherworld, permitting him to return to his people only once each year, during Onam. An over-the-top welcome is prepared in every town. Dances and songs proclaim the munificent reign of the king, and elaborate carpets of flowers and colored powder are laid out on floors and streets.

Although snakeboat competitions are held throughout the region, the most famous is the Nehru Cup regatta in Alappuzha. Snakeboats are dugouts of over 30 meters (100 feet), with elaborately carved prows and bright silk umbrellas providing shade. In each, up to 100 rowers surge to a chanted rhythm of traditional boat songs, while thousands of spectators line the shore shouting themselves hoarse.

You can find tickets for the Alappuzha race at numerous stalls around the lake. Budget seating (less than a US dollar) is on rickety bamboo stands which offer an excellent view that becomes crowded after the start as youngsters without tickets swarm in. A more posh option (around three to four US dollars) is the Rose Pavilion, a stand built in the middle of the lake. In both spots, be sure to bring your own refreshments, as there is surprisingly little food or drink available at the site. In Aranmula, the race is held on the river Pamba, on the final day of Onam. Other races are held in Haripad, Champakulam, Cochin, and Kottayam. At Payipad (near Haripad), the races last for three days, in association with the festivities at the temple of Lord Subramaniya.

DATE: August/September. **LOCATION:** Alappuzha (formerly named Allepey) is located in southwest India's Kerala State, 83 km (52 miles) along the coastal road north of Kollam (Quilon). **TRANSPORT:** There are airports to the north at Kochi (Cochin), and to the south at Trivandrum, and trains and buses run regularly from both points. But the most fascinating way to arrive is by ferry from either Quilon or Kottayam. **ACCOMMODATION:** Although better accommodation is found in larger towns, many of Kerala's villages have hotels and guest houses. **CONTACT:** Kerala Tourist Information Centre, Park View, Palayam, Trivandrum 695003, Kerala, India; also GITO (see *Resources*).

Ganesh Chaturthi

Maharashtra **August/September**

The cities and towns of the Maharashtra State explode with activity and possibility in honor of the elephant god Ganesh, son of Lord Shiva and remover of obstacles. You'll see Ganesh everywhere, sitting with his potbelly on lotus-petal cushions, or being wheeled through the streets waving his multiple arms. Cities and towns begin preparing months in advance, vying to create the biggest, most impressive idols. Even in small villages, shrines are erected and small clay Ganesh idols installed.

Lord Ganesh is many things: the god of intelligence, the symbol that all things are one, the witty and extravagant provider

Ganesh, the potbellied elephant god, is rolled through the streets as everyone in Maharashtra goes wild in his honor. *(H. Mahidmar/Dinodia Picture Agency/Bombay)*

of prosperity. As such, Ganesh Chaturthi is considered the most auspicious day of the year (although one should not invite bad luck by looking at the moon on this day, in remembrance of Shiva's curse).

In Bombay, thousands of processions bring traffic to a standstill. Plaster statues, some three stories tall, are carried through the teeming streets to Chowpatty Beach, and amid devotees' fervent drum beating, dancing, and singing, Ganesh is immersed in the Arabian Sea. In Pune, street stalls are decorated with electric lights, tinsel, and crepe paper, as the scent of curry and coconut oil wafts through the air. Visitors are honored with flower garlands and red curry paste. Fireworks explode everywhere and at all hours. In addition to processions, the festival features elaborate lighting and decoration, and a variety of cultural events in most large towns.

DATE: Late August or early September. The final and most climactic day of the week-long festivities is Ganesh Chaturthi, the fourth day of the Hindu month Bhadon. **LOCATION:** Bombay, Pune, and elsewhere in Maharashtra and Tamil Nadu. **CONTACT:** Maharashtra Tourism Development Corp., Express Tower, 9th Fl., Nariman Point, Bombay 400021, Maharashtra, India; also Government of India Tourist Office (see *Resources*).

While you're there ...

- **Pang Lhabsol, throughout Sikkim State:** This Buddhist/animist festival features masked warrior dances with helmets, shields, and swords. (Month of Bhadon: August/September.)
- **Ramdevra Fair, Ramdevra Temple, near Jaisalmer:** As drums beat out fierce rhythms, the *Tera-Tali* dancers flip around acrobatically, swinging swords, throwing oil lamps, and smashing cymbals. A treat! (Month of Bhadon: August/September.)

Dussehra (Ram Lila)

Throughout India **September/October**

This spectacular 10-day festival caps off months of preparation with a fabulous outflowing of *joie de vivre*. It celebrates two divine victories: that of Rama over the 10-headed demon-king Ravana, and that of the warrior-goddess Durga over the buffalo-demon Mahishasura. The latter legend represents the female deity's pre-eminence over the male gods who failed to destroy the demon.

India's nearly 700 million Hindus go absolutely wild for Dussehra, staging an orgy of noise, color, and movement that will stun the senses. Everywhere you look cars, homes, offices, and people are decorated with marigolds, and deities are paraded through the streets past richly illuminated palaces and houses. The smell of incense and food is everywhere, as is the sound of music and incessant fireworks.

Exactly what you see will depend on where you are. In Mysore, richly caparisoned elephants parade through the streets, leading a procession of members of Karnataka's royal family. Ahmedabad also has a spectacular parade. In Delhi and elsewhere in North India, multi-headed effigies of Ravana and his brothers are exploded and set aflame, while special food stalls and spontaneous markets are erected.

Dussehra is high season for performing episodes from the ancient Hindu epic *Ramayana* on street stages. Since the *Ramayana's* introduction states that "He who reads and repeats this holy life-giving *Ramayana* is liberated from all his sins and exalted with all his posterity to the highest heaven," there's no shortage of performers. In Ramnagar, the *Ramayana* is famous for its length, spectacular staging, and religious feeling.

In Kulu (Himachal Pradesh), the festival takes place about a week later and spans 10 days (see the **Festival of the Gods**). In Gujarat the festival is called Navratri, the Festival of Nine Nights, with folk dances in recognition of the battle between the goddess Devi and the demon Mahisasur. In Bengal and Nepal, it's known as Durga Puja, and includes 15 days of music, dance, and drama, commemorating the homecoming of the 10-armed goddess Durga. Durga and her four children are carried through the city on hundreds of *pandals,* or beautifully illuminated marquees of bamboo and cloth. Calcutta's notorious traffic stops completely as makeshift altars to Durga spring up in the street; these become arenas for all kinds of performing, blessing, and dancing. On the final day the city works itself into a frenzy as residents bring the clay images to the river for a "Durga-dunking" ceremony.

DATE: Dussehra's 10 days of festivities begin on the first day of the Hindu month of Ashwin (September/October). **LOCATION:** Throughout India. **CONTACT:** GITO (see *Resources*).

Festival of the Gods

Kulu **September/October**

This festival brings a magnificent gathering of deity images from temples all around the "Valley of the Gods," to pay homage to the local patron god, Raghunathji. Added to this is a nightly cacaphony of torchlight processions, music, dancing, and revelry, spurred on by the local rice beer, *chang*.

The Festival of the Gods is actually the Dussehra festival with a Himalayan twist, and is held in honor of Raghunathji, whose image resides at the Raghunathpura mountain temple. Raghunathji and the other gods wait outside town until the event's host, the goddess Hadimba, arrives from Manali on the evening of Vijay Dashmi. Since she is said to enjoy high speeds, she's pulled as fast as possible through the valley on her wooden *rath,* or chariot.

When Hadimba has arrived, Raghunathji can be brought down. Surrounded by about 200 other important gods and hung with elaborate garlands, he looks absolutely splendid. First, brahmins and VIPs circle the *rath*. Next, there's a mad scramble as everyone tries to help pull it to the other side of the *maidan* (open field), since this privilege is considered a symbol of good fortune. Then the music, dancing, and drinking begin, with the festivities lasting far into the first night, and at least seven nights more. Music is played on distinct hill instruments such as the *karnal, dhoi,* and *narsinghas,* and the nightly folk-dancing competitions are excellent. On the final day Raghunathji's *rath* is taken to the river bank, and a clump of grass is burnt to symbolize Ravana's destruction.

The Kulu Valley—considered by many to be the most beautiful alpine valley in the world—provides a stunning setting for this event. The cool Beas River flows through its center, past apple orchards, elaborately carved wooden temples, and flocks of sheep. White Himalayan peaks form a phenomenal backdrop. The people of the valley are friendly and prosperous, and the women are known for their exceptional beauty, which is accentuated with silver jewelry and homemade wool clothing. The men wear wool jackets, moccasins, and the one-of-a-kind Kulu cap, a pillbox with a front flap in which wildflowers are often tucked.

DATE: The 10 days of festivities begin on the first day of the Hindu month of Ashwin (September/October). **LOCATION:** Kulu is located in the Himachal Pradesh State. **TRANSPORT:** Kula's Bhuntar airport is 10 km (six miles) out of town, and is served by flights from Delhi, Chandigarh, and Shimla. Buses travel from Chandigarh, Shimla, Dharamsala, and Delhi. The scenery is tremendous, but the journey is long and rough and features perilous cliffs and road signs such as "Arrive late in this life, not early in the next!" **ACCOMMODATION:** Kulu is well-served by a wide range of hotels, but during the festival the better rooms are scarce. **CONTACT:** Himachal Pradesh Tourist Development Corp., The Mall, Ritz Annexe, Simla 171001, HP, India; also Government of India Tourist Office (see *Resources*).

Festival of Lights (Diwali/Deepavali)

Nationwide **October/November**

Diwali illuminates the houses, streets, and businesses of Hindu India to welcome Lakshmi, the fastidious goddess of well-being and prosperity. This is probably the most aesthetically pleasing of

Spirituality, compassion, and common sense—the Dalai Lama can be visited at his home-in-exile near Dharamsala. (Robert McElroy/Woodfin Camp & Associates)

the major Indian festivals, coming three weeks after the chaos of Dussehra.

On the day of a new moon, townspeople clean and whitewash their homes, make sweets, and compose elaborate designs of colored powder on thresholds. At sunset, oil lanterns and garlands of candles are lit to beckon the goddess. Fireworks and sparklers are particularly in demand, since it's believed that the goddess is pleased by flashes of light and loud noise.

Diwali is a multi-purpose holiday. It celebrates the return-from-exile of Lord Rama, the hero of the epic Ramayana, and it marks the beginning of the new financial year. To that end, you'll

How to meet the Dalai Lama

If you're planning a trip to Himachal Pradesh, it's possible to arrange an audience with Tibetan Buddhism's Deity of Universal Compassion, the Dalai Lama. His holiness is, without a doubt, the most accessible major religious leader on earth, a man who welcomes and values the presence of commoners and travelers as much as he welcomes and values the many world leaders who demand his attention.

You can't just drop in to his residence-in-exile near Dharamsala. Instead, send a friendly note about a month in advance (address below), mentioning the dates you'd like to visit. Depending on the Dalai Lama's travels and other scheduling issues, there's a good chance you'll be granted an audience.

The Dalai Lama fled Tibet at the age of 16, after an uprising against the invading Chinese in 1959. For the past 30 years, the spiritual leader has worked for the liberation of his occupied homeland. He was awarded the Nobel Peace Prize in 1989 for his pacifist approach to the world's political and personal conflicts. Those who have met him have noted the friendly, genuine way he looks into the eyes of the visitors he meets, and his thoughtfulness in listening and responding to questions. In addition to his deep compassion, he's known for an unusual blend of spirituality and common sense, and a keen sense of humor.

The Tibetan settlement just outside of Dharamsala is called McLeod Ganj, although it's sometimes referred to as "Little Lhasa." Over the past 30 years it's taken on the spirit of the thousands of Tibetan refugees who have made it their home away from home, carrying on with their traditions while working to free Tibet. In the streets, you can hear the prayer wheels turning, smell the *thukpa* (noodle soup), and see the monks and red-cheeked children hurrying about beneath fluttering prayer flags. If you're interested in studying Tibetan Buddhism, meditation, or language, Dharamsala and McLeod Ganj are the places to be. Courses are offered by individual monks (inquire at monasteries), at the McLeod Ganj library, and at the nearby Tushita Retreat Centre.

To request an audience with the Dalai Lama, write to: Private Office of the Dalai Lama, McLeod Ganj/Dharamsala, Himachal Pradesh, India.

see commemorative gold and silver ornaments, and rampant gambling on the streets and in homes (it's considered an auspicious occasion to test one's luck for the coming year). The materials

Just before sunset, three girls ready candles to beckon Lakshmi, the goddess of well-being and prosperity. (Dinodia Picture Agency/Bombay)

used in various professions are honored and doted over. Carpenters, metalsmiths, and craftspeople sharpen and polish their tools and place flowers on them. Artists and writers give praise to their brushes, pens, typewriters, and ink pots. Merchants pay their respects to account books and cash registers.

DATE: October/November (three weeks after Dussehra in the Hindu month of Kartik). **LOCATION:** Nationwide. **CONTACT:** Government of India Tourist Office (see *Resources*).

PUSHKAR CAMEL FAIR (PUSHKAR MELA)

Pushkar **October/November**

This ancient, secluded village spills over with visitors during late October and early November, as caravans converge from all around the desert state of Rajasthan for the world's largest camel fair. The event is a once-in-a-lifetime treat for the senses and spirit, with all the color, beauty, and diversity of legendary Rajasthan stretched out across a spectacular fairground just west of town.

Starting a week before the full moon, the Rajasthani men begin arriving with livestock. The scene is chaotic and colorful, as camels, cattle, horses, and brightly dressed people move in and out of the encampments. Animals are bought, sold, and shown in an ever-changing scene. Sporting events include camel polo, tent-pegging, and bizarre camel races in which up to 10 men clamber onto the backs of the beasts. Usually, most end up sprawled on the sand.

Pushkar: The world's largest camel fair is a once-in-a-lifetime feast for the senses and spirit. (Joe Viesti/Viesti Associates)

The women arrive three days before the full moon, wearing spectacular handmade outfits. Most have several children in tow, who gape at the wonders of this huge fair while their mothers make rounds buying and selling bangles, beads, embroidered shoes and clothes, brass wear, and mirrored camel saddles.

At night the history, legends, and religion of the region come alive in music and dance. Pushkar itself is a holy city, a maze of more than 400 ninth-century temples built along the shore of Anasagar Lake. On the night of the full moon (Kartik Purnima), devotees go to one of the lake's 52 *ghats,* or stepped landings, for bathing. Hindu legend describes Pushkar as the place where Brahma, Lord of Creation, killed a demon with a lotus flower. Where one of the petals fell, Anasagar Lake emerged. At Varah Ghat (where Lord Vishnu is believed to have appeared in the form of a boar), a married woman can bathe to absolve both her and her husband. (Note that photography is not permitted on the *ghats.*)

DATE: October/November (month of Kartik). **LOCATION:** Pushkar, Rajasthan state, 11 km (7 miles) from Ajmer. **TRANSPORT:** Buses leave Ajmer for Pushkar frequently; both buses and trains serve Ajmer from Delhi, Jaipur, Marwar, or Ahmedabad. **ACCOMMODATION:** With more than 200,000 extra people (and 50,000 camels) showing up at this town of 11,000, it's not surprising that accommodation is hard to come by during the fair. The tourist office erects a special tent city for visitors, which may be your best bet. In town, lodging is very basic. **CONTACT:** Rajasthan Tourism Development

Two men haggle over the price of an elephant at Asia's largest livestock fair and market. (Dinodia Picture Agency/Bombay)

Corp., 100 Jawaharlal Nehru Marg, Jaipur 302004, Rajasthan, India; also Government of India Tourist Office (see *Resources*).

Sonepur Livestock Fair

Sonepur **November/December**

Hey buddy, want to buy a used elephant? There's a deal waiting for you at Asia's largest livestock fair. For anywhere from US$350 to US$3,000, you can set yourself up with the unwieldy pachyderm (but there's no guarantee your mom will let you keep him). You'll also find camels, cattle, buffalo, goats, and anything else that moos, bleats, snorts, or makes a mess.

This month-long event at the confluence of the Ganga and the Sandak rivers begins with a religious splash on the full moon of Kartik Purnima. Merchants arrive in festive moods, their animals sporting bells and newly painted hides of red, yellow, and purple. Dances, magic shows, and tests of horsemanship and elephantmanship liven up the afternoons and evenings, and plenty of stalls spring up selling woven goods and handicrafts, such as that special mirror-inlaid camel saddle you've always been looking for.

DATE: The entire month beginning the first full moon after Diwali (Kartik Purnima), usually in October or November. **LOCATION:** Sonepur, 25 km (15.5 miles) north of Patna in the Bihar State. Other large-scale livestock fairs are held at Pushkar (see **Pushkar Camel Fair**), Naguar, and, in Uttar Pradesh State, at Bateshwar and Mukteshwar. **TRANSPORT:** Bus from Patna. To Patna, air from Delhi, Calcutta, Ranchi, and Lucknow; rail or bus from Varanasi, Delhi, Calcutta, and Gaya. **ACCOMMODATION:** Hotels range from very basic to three-star. **CONTACT:** Bihar Tourism Development Corp., Beerchand Patel Path, Patna, Bihar, India; also Government of India Tourist Office (see *Resources*).

© RESOURCES

In India: Government of India Tourist Office (GITO), 88 Janpath, New Delhi 110001, Tel 11-332-0005, Fax 11-371-0518. **USA:** 30 Rockefeller Plaza, Suite 15, North Mezzanine, New York NY 10112, Tel (212) 586-4901, Fax (212) 582-3274. GITO, 230 N. Michigan Avenue, Chicago, IL 60601, Tel (312) 236-6899. GITO, Wilshire Blvd., Suite 204, Los Angeles CA 90010, Tel (213) 380-8855, Fax (213) 380-6111. **Canada:** GITO, 60 Bloor Street West, #204, Toronto, ON M4W 3B8, Tel (416) 962-3787, Fax (416) 962-6279. **UK:** GITO, 7 Cork Street, London W1X 2AB, Tel 71-437-3677, Fax 71-494-1048. **Australia:** Level 1, 17 Castlereagh St., Sydney, NSW 2000, Tel 2-233-7579, Fax 2-223-3003. **Germany:** Kaiserstr. 77/111, D-6000, Frankfurt 1, Tel 69-235-423, Fax 69-234-724.

NEPAL

Sandwiched between India and China, the "rooftop of the world" could just as easily be called the "peak of partying." This cultural crossroads is home to a vigorous mix of ethnicities that has contrived a fascinating array of festivals. Although the most important events are covered here, there's always something going on in Nepal, and a visit to the Kathmandu Valley is almost certain to coincide with at least one festival.

The festivities—and daily life—take place in a land of stunning beauty and simple charms. With both the world's highest mountain and its deepest gorge, the grace of Nepal's endlessly changing landscapes is matched by the allure of its temples and villages—landmarks of a history that spans millennia. This timeless place has seduced Western travelers for hundreds of years, inviting them to wander in the shadow of Everest or relax and festival-hop in the Kathmandu Valley.

For better and for worse, tourism has for the past half-century strongly influenced the economy of one of the world's poorest countries. As a result, getting away from the four-star set and the backpacking throngs demands a bit of creativity. On the positive side, the increase in tourism has necessitated a well-developed infrastructure of lodging and transport. As Third World countries go, Nepal is fairly comfy and hassle-free.

MACCHENDRATH RATH JATRA

Patan **March/April**

This month-long festival is a three-ring circus of gymnastic dancing, parades, and animals that are ridden, raced, and sacrificed. Best of all, it lasts an entire month, so if you happen to be in Kathmandu anytime between mid-March and mid-April, you're liable to catch some of it. Patan itself boasts great architecture and a lively atmosphere. Located just outside Kathmandu, its main square is packed with a fantastic array of temples, many centuries old.

DATE: The month of Chaitra (March/April). **LOCATION:** Patan, a "suburb" of Kathmandu. **TRANSPORT:** Buses from Kathmandu will drop you off at the Lagankhel bus stand, which is about a 15-minute walk from the centrally located Durbar Square. Cycling from Kathmandu

is also a viable option. **ACCOMMODATION:** You'll find both reasonable and top-of-the-line hotels, but it's just as easy to stay in nearby Kathmandu. **CONTACT:** Nepal Department of Tourism (see *Resources*).

WHILE YOU'RE THERE ...

- **Basant Panchami, Kathmandu:** On the fifth day after the new moon in Magha, parades and ceremonies at Hanuman Dhoka Palace celebrate the approach of spring in the valley. Because the festival takes place in honor of Saraswati, the goddess of learning, school children play an important part in this festival. (Month of Magha: January/February.)
- **Tibetan New Year (Losar):** Three days of revelry welcome the Tibetan New Year in the town of Baudha, as well as in Tibetan refugee settlements near Kathmandu and Pokhara, and Buddhist highland areas. (New moon of Falgun; February/March.)
- **Shiva's Night (Maha Shivaratri/Shiva Raatri):** Shiva's birthday, though honored in all Hindu areas of Nepal, brings throngs of pilgrims and *sadhus* (holy men) to Pashupatinath. The bright colors and hordes of people displaying their deep devotion to the god present a spectacular sight. (New-moon day of Falgun; February/March.)
- **Chaitra Dasain/Sweta Machhendranath, Kathmandu:** Also called "little Dasain," this holiday honors the goddess Durga with sacrificial buffaloes and goats. It falls on the full moon of Chaitra and signals the beginning of the Sweta Macchhendranath Festival. Over the course of four evenings following Chaitra Dassain, worshipers tote the image of Sweta Macchendranath south from the Kel Tole Temple to Lagankhel. (Month of Chaitra: March/April.)

Preceding page photo: Mani Rimdu: A venture to the outer reaches of Asian culture. (Andy Selters/Viesti Associates)

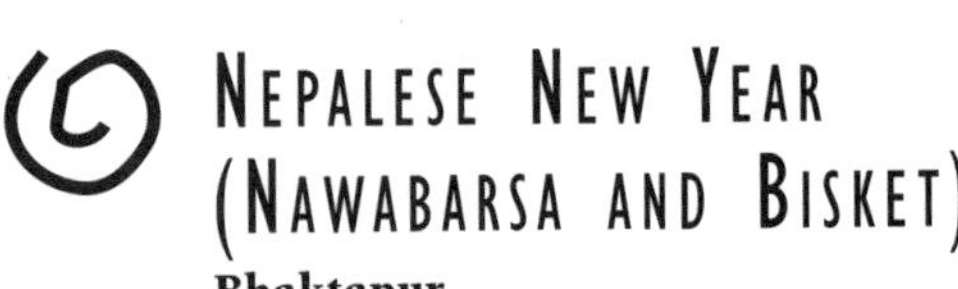

NEPALESE NEW YEAR (NAWABARSA AND BISKET)

Bhaktapur **Mid-April**

Against the Kathmandu Valley's backdrop of uncommon civility and quiet tolerance, the Nawabarsa and Bisket festivals display the look and feel of consummate anarchy. People of vastly different ethnic origins converge on these two villages just east of the capital, cutting loose with spectacular parades, races, tugs-of-war, and torch-lit street dances. The overflowing exuberance of the celebrations is underlain by thousands of years of religious tradition, making for a highly rewarding experience—whether you engage in simple revelry or a deeper exploration of the drama and mystery of Himalayan culture.

As the Nepalese king radios his annual message of goodwill, thousands make the journey overland to these two villages of spired temples and tile-roofed houses. The Nawabarsa Festival in Bhaktapur commemorates the ancient slaying of two serpent demons in the Hindu epic *Mahabharata*. According to legend, the god Kala Bhairab was spending his first night with the goddess Bhadra Kali. As she slept, two snakes emerged from her nose and tried to kill him, just as they had killed her many previous lovers. Kala Bhairab was waiting with his sword drawn, and after a bloody bedroom battle he emerged victorious.

The party begins three days before the Hindu New Year. A huge three-tiered chariot, loaded with figurines depicting the god and goddess, is pulled from the Bhairab Temple square as cheering, worshiping crowds fill the narrow streets. When the chariot reaches the top of a sloping square a tug-of-war ensues: the men of the lower sections of town pull against the men of the upper neighborhoods, jostling and wobbling the top-heavy chariot in a precarious struggle for good fortune in the coming year.

Four nights of non-stop celebration follow. Gifts and offerings—rice, flowers, lighted oil candles, holy water, and sacred red powder—are deposited at the temples. Celebrants wheel effigies of gods and goddesses through the streets with accompanying drummers and worshipers, and masked dancers bid the blessings of divinities whose spirits are believed to descend on the town, attracted by the music and the light of the torches. Separate parades honor Brahmayani, the wife of Lord Brahma; Ganesh, the elephant god of success; Maha Kali, the great goddess of terror; and Mahalaxmi, the goddess of wealth.

On New Year's Eve, chariots are pulled to an open area on the lower outskirts of the city. Here the *lingam*—a carved, 80-foot tree trunk—is raised in a sometimes comic, sometimes dangerous operation. As hundreds of men strain to hoist the giant phallic symbol, the tense, nail-biting silence gradually develops into roaring cheers from the crowd. Sometimes it takes hours; sometimes men are crushed under the *lingam* as it crashes back to earth. When the *lingam* is erected (and it *is* erected, because failure is a dark omen that could bring disaster on the entire nation), banners unfurl from the top, signifying the male and female snake demons. The cheering mob swarms forward with sacrifices of flowers, lights, and bloody animals, and adventurous devotees shimmy up the guide ropes, swaying over the crowd with garlands of good fortune.

On New Year's Day, rivers of people fill the town's streets, windows, balconies, and rooftops. Another tug-of-war ensues, this time to bring the *lingam* down. Two teams strain at the ropes as the pole teeters and sways. When it finally plunges toward the ground, everyone runs for his or her life. A roar of approval goes up, for now the new year can begin! The old year, and the evil snake demons, are dead.

DATE: Hindu New Year (1st of the month of Baisakh: mid-April). **LOCATION:** Bhaktapur (also called Bhadgaon) is located just east of Kathmandu. **TRANSPORT:** Take the east road out of Kathmandu. The distance to Bhaktapur is 13.5 km (about eight miles). Buses leave Kathmandu every few minutes. **ACCOMMODATION:** There are several reasonable guesthouses in Bhaktapur, but most visitors will seek (and find) better lodging in Kathmandu. **CONTACT:** Department of Tourism (see *Resources*).

Bal Kumari Jatra

Thimi and Bode **Mid-April**

Two miles west of Bhadgaon, in the village of Thimi, the Nepalese New Year brings a spectacular "gathering" of deities. Outside the Bal Kumari Temple in the evening, the flames of ceremonial oil torches light the rooftops of nearby houses and temples. The heat of the torches is said to drive the winter away and bring the favor of the gods. The most pious penitents lie in the temple garden all night, using cow dung to glue flaming oil lamps to their foreheads, chests, and limbs.

On the second day of the new year, tradition dictates that no person—visitors included—may refuse an invitation of any kind. At dawn 32 teams of men—bearing ornate, ceremonial canopies called *khats*—charge through the weedy streets to the Bal Kumari Temple. On the way they coat everything and everyone with clouds of brilliant orange-red powder. The scene gets out of hand when the *khat* with Ganesh, the elephant-headed god, is brought out. Several hundred men run alongside, carrying flaming torches overhead and showering vermilion powder. Troupes of musicians keep time at first, then finally surrender the beat to a bedlam of drums and crashing cymbals. The *khats* gain speed, veering toward buildings and scattering spectators at the wild parade's climax. When it's over, the sacrificial blood of chickens and goats drenches the idol of Bal Kumari.

On New Year's Day in the village of Bode (just across the highway from Thimi), the central activity is a religious tongue-boring ceremony that the squeamish should avoid. The principal participants are a penitent, who has gone through a four-day cleansing ceremony, and a priest, who holds the volunteer's extended tongue in a piece of cloth and thrusts a long metal spike through the center. The penitent then shoulders a bamboo platform and walks the lanes of Bode, tongue and spike sticking out so that all may observe his piety. When the penitent returns to the temple, the priest removes the spike and fills the wound with mud from the temple floor, which is thought to have special healing powers.

DATE: Hindu New Year (1st of the month of Baisakh: mid-April). **LOCATION:** Thimi and Bode are located about 10 km (six miles) east of Kathmandu. **TRANSPORT:** Buses leave Kathmandu every few minutes. **ACCOMMODATION:** Seek lodging in Kathmandu. **CONTACT:** Nepal Department of Tourism (see *Resources*).

While you're there ...

- **Buddha Jayanti, Buddhist areas:** The birth, enlightenment, and death of the Buddha are remembered on the full-moon day of Baisakh, especially at the Swayambhunath, Bodhnath, and Patan stupas near Kathmandu. A constant wave of Buddhists pushes toward Swayambhunath, the center of activity. Musicians play as the *lamas* dance around the stupa. (Full-moon day of Baisakh: April/May.)
- **Cow Festival (Gai Jatra), Kathmandu:** Cows, thought to lead humans to Yama, the ruler of the underworld, are paraded through the city for the benefit of those who have died in the past year. Where cows are lacking, little boys dressed as cows stand in. People dress in outlandish costumes to commemorate the "cheering up" of a 17th-century queen mourning the loss of her youngest son. (The day following full-moon day of Srawan: July/August.)
- **Naga Panchhami, Kathmandu Valley:** *Nagas,* or snakes, are honored and appeased when pictures of them are pinned over doors and bowls of milk and rice are left out for them. Snakes are regarded with respect and fear for their magical powers, particularly their ability to influence monsoons. (Fifth day after the new moon: July/August.)
- **Night of the Devil (Ghanta Karna), Newar villages:** The demon Ghanta Karna is also known as "Bell Ears," because he rang his bell earrings in an attempt to drown out the Lord Vishnu. This festival celebrates the destruction of this evil spirit by burning Ghanta Karn in effigy. (Fourteenth night of the dark fortnight of Srawan: July/August.)

Bada Dasain/Durga Puja

Kathmandu, Patan, and elsewhere — **September/October**

Apart from the sheep, goats, and buffaloes sacrificed in Kot Square, everyone has a great time at this giant 10-day festival, the largest and most important of the year. In Patan, there are masked dances in Durbar Square, and throughout town bamboo swings are erected and kites are flown. In Kathmandu, the first six days are celebrated mostly in the home and at riverbanks, with special plantings and bathing in holy rivers. The seventh day (*Fulpati*) opens up the public celebrations, with a reception at Hanuman Dhoka Gate for the sacred flowers that have been sent from Gorkha Palace. The eighth night is "black night" (*Kalratri*), and

The Sherpas

The Sherpas are an ethnic group you'll surely encounter if you do any guided trekking or hiking in Nepal. Inhabiting the high valleys of the Solu Khumbu region near the south approach to Everest, the Sherpas were poor farmers until the arrival of European expeditions in the 1930s. Their courage and skill in high terrain earned the respect of explorers and climbers such as Sir Edmund Hillary, who later set up a foundation for Sherpa schools and hospitals. Although many are now cosmopolitan and Westernized, and speak excellent English, Sherpas do not have last names. To satisfy Western protocol, many take the name "Sherpa" as a surname.

Some cultural points: Don't whistle in a Sherpa home, as this is believed to attract the spirits of the dead. Also, you'll notice that Sherpas are very concerned with the spiritual hygiene of what they eat and drink, so never touch the food of a Sherpa (or any Nepali). If you offer a Sherpa guide a drink from your water bottle, he will likely pour it into his mouth without letting it touch his lips. Finally, Sherpa manners dictate that offers be declined twice before acceptance. Thus, if you offer a Sherpa food or drink and he or she refuses, offer it twice more. *Tuche* means "thank you."

includes complicated and bloody rituals in which buffaloes, sheep, and goats are slaughtered. On the ninth day there are mass sacrifices at the Taleju Temple. Hindus only are permitted on this day, but outside you'll see many people sprinkling the sacrificial blood on cars and trucks, in the hope that the goddess Durga will prevent accidents. Day 10 (*Vijaya Dashami*) celebrates Rama and Durga's victory over evil. Elders apply a *tikka* of rice, curd, and vermilion on foreheads, to encourage health and happiness.

DATE: Starts fifth day of Ashwin, in September/October. **LOCATION:** Kathmandu and Patan. **TRANSPORT:** Kathmandu can be reached easily by air from Asia, Europe, or North America. **ACCOMMODATION:** In Kathmandu or Patan, hotels and guesthouses are available in any class or price range. **CONTACT:** Nepal Department of Tourism (see *Resources*).

While you're there ...

© **Teej Brata, Kathmandu Valley:** Women wear scarlet and gold and bathe at the Bagmati River to honor their husbands and pray to Parvati for a

Not for the squeamish: The 10 days of Bada Dasain are filled with ritual sacrifices. In Phulbari, in the Kathmandu Valley, one man interrupts a water buffalo's final meal while another stands ready with a tray for the animal's head. (Patrick Morrow)

happy married life. Teej Brata lasts three days and ends with a ritual bathing at the confluence of the Bagmati and Vishnumati rivers to wash away all "female sins." (August/September; second to fifth days following the new moon of Bhadra.)

◎ **Ganesh Charturthi, nationwide:** Processions in honor of the elephant god Ganesh take place on the day of the full moon. This day commemorates a heated argument between Ganesh and the moon goddess, and at night, the Nepalis protect themselves from moonlight to avoid an ancient curse. (September/October; full moon of Ashwin.)

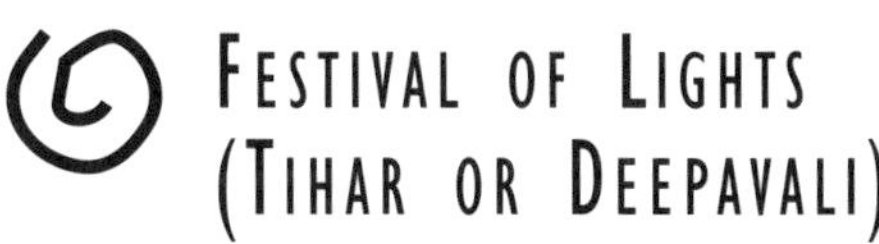

Festival of Lights (Tihar or Deepavali)

Nationwide **October/November**

Much like Diwali in India, this festival illuminates the Nepali night to welcome prosperity. On the first night, thousands of lamps are lit and families take part of their meals outside to feed to the crows, which are associated with Yama, the god of death. The second night is dedicated to man's best friend; dogs are decorated with *tikkas* (colored marks) on their foreheads. On day three (*Lakshmi Puja*) cows are decorated and worshiped, and Lakshmi (the goddess of well-being and prosperity) is welcomed to homes with tiny lamps and candles. Fireworks are everywhere. The fourth day is the Newari New Year, and it spurs family get-togeth-

Festival of Lights: The Nepali month of Kartik (October/ November) illuminates squares, markets, and houses in Kathmandu and throughout Nepal. (Joe Viesti/Viesti Associates)

ers in Newari villages. The fifth day (*Bhai Tika*) symbolizes the bond between brother and sister. Sisters draw colorful *tikas* on their brothers' foreheads, and in return brothers pledge their allegiance and give gifts.

DATE: Month of Kartik (October/November). **LOCATION:** Nationwide. **CONTACT:** Nepal Department of Tourism (see *Resources*).

Mani Rimdu

Thyangboche **November/December**

You trek for days to get here, sharing the mountains with snow leopards and sheep, and watching the culture change as the landscape rises from the Hindu middle hills to the Tibetan Buddhist high Himalaya. In the courtyard of the Thyangboche *gompa* (monastery), a huddle of masked dancers quietly enters as the full moon starts on its path through the night sky. Surrounded by prayer flags and towering white peaks, they begin to act out a Buddhist epic 1,000 years old.

Combined with a trek to the Everest base camp, *Mani Rimdu* is a once-in-a-lifetime venture into the outer reaches of nature and Asian culture. To get here, you'll need to be very fit and spend at least six days walking in the mountains, either camping or stopping at tea huts. In addition to the cultural attractions, the scenery is stunning. At Thyangboche, if the weather's good, get up at dawn and you'll catch a wrap-around glimpse

Worth the trek: Isolated in the high Himalaya, monks prepare to act out a Buddhist epic 1,000 years old during the Mani Rimdu Festival. (Gordon Wiltsie)

worth 10 times the price of your trip. Starting in the southwest and moving toward the east, there's Kwangde (6,187 meters/ 20,417 feet), Tawachee (6,542 meters/21,589 feet), Everest (8,848 meters/29,198 feet), Nuptse (7,855 meters/25,921 feet), Lhotse (8,616 meters/28,432 feet), Ama Dablam (6,856 meters/ 22,625 feet), Kangtega (6,779 meters/22,371 feet), and Thamserku (6,608 meters/21,806 feet). In addition, the *gompa* located near the Everest base camp claims to have the hand and scalp of a *yeti* (abominable snowman), while the *gompa* in nearby Khumjung claims the man-beast's skull.

This festival is also held at the Thami monastery in May or June. Recently, the organizers in both places have started charging admission to foreigners.

DATE: The full moon of Mangsir (November/December). **LOCATION:** Thyangboche. **TRANSPORT:** Your feet, mostly. This is the planet's highest and most popular trekking ground, and you have at least two options. One is to take a bus from Kathmandu to Jiri (8–12 hours), then trek for 10 days to Thyangboche, and either hike back out or fly out of Lukla. The other is to fly into Lukla (where landing at the STOL airstrip resembles a dive-bombing mission), then trek for four days to Thyangboche. Many visitors hike in and fly out. **ACCOMMODATION:** The best places to lodge and dine on Nepal treks are the *bhattis* or tea huts along the way. You'll get at least a place on the floor and a wooden pallet or camp bed. Some *bhattis* even offer a room and shower. **CONTACT:** Nepal Department of Tourism (see *Resources*).

Resources

In Nepal: An annual calendar of events is available from the Department of Tourism, H.M. Government of Nepal, Tripureswor, Kathmandu, Tel 1-211293. There are no official government tourist agencies overseas, but embassies provide tourist information. **USA:** Tourist Information/Visa Section; Embassy of Nepal, 2131 LeRoy Place N.W., Washington, DC 20008, Tel (202) 667-4550, Fax (202) 667-5534. Nepal Travel Bureau, 15 E. 40th St, Suite 1204, New York, NY 10016, Tel (212) 532-4440, Fax (212) 532-4440. **Canada:** Royal Nepal Consulate, 310 Dupont Street, Toronto, ON M5R 1V9, 416 9687252. Canada Nepal Friendship Assoc., 886 Ivanhoe Ave., Ottawa, NO K2B 5S5. **UK:** Embassy of the Kingdom of Nepal, 12a Kensington Palace Gardens, London W8 4QU, Tel 71-229-1594. Promotion Nepal (Europe) Ltd., 3 Wellington Terrace, Bayswater Rd., London W2 4LW, Tel 071-299-3528. **Australia:** Nepal Travel Centre, 29 Cavenagh St., Darwin NT 5790, Tel 89 814466. **Germany:** Embassy of the Kingdom of Nepal, Im Haag 15, D-5300 Bonn 2, Tel 228-343097, Fax 228-856747. German-Nepal Friendship Assoc., P.O. Box 190327, D-5000, Köln.

PAKISTAN

This land of huge contrasts in people and landscapes has much to offer to the somewhat daring traveler. Most visitors are drawn to the adventurous lands of Karakoram and Hindu Kush, home of the highest concentration of great mountains on earth. Although a predominately Islamic nation, Pakistan's position as a cultural crossroads has endowed it with a jumble of ethnicities, many of whom have retained their colorful traditions within the constraints of Islam. The country also has a small yet vital concentration of tribal people who continue to reject repeated attempts at conversion.

Although Pakistanis are on the whole a hospitable people, the security situation in outlying areas of Pakistan is often extremely unstable, and potentially dangerous. A few things that conspire to make travel in some parts of the country a dicey proposition are ongoing family and village feuds, violence between Shia and Sunni Muslims, gangs of *dacoits* (bandits), separatist violence, border skirmishes, and even rowdy Pashtuns firing their guns into the air at weddings. To avoid being caught in the crossfire, be informed! Hot spots include rural areas of Sind and Baluchistan, the NWFP, and northern areas.

Shahi Durbar

Sibi **February**

You won't see many foreigners at this annual fair, which occurs during the "cool" season in one of the hottest places on earth. This *durbar* (royal gathering) is a multi-purpose event. It includes an agricultural fair (cattle, camels, horses, goats, etc.), sporting events, exceptional handicraft markets, minstrels, and spirited politics, all in the middle of "the dump where Allah shot the rubbish of creation," as locals refer to their barren, hostile home.

People from all over Baluchistan flock here, creating a colorful mix of different tribal groups, each with distinct turbans and outfits. Although the outside world is rapidly changing, they've been able to maintain their traditional lifestyles, mainly because no one else can stand the environment long enough to bother them. Many have unusually shaped foreheads hidden under giant floppy turbans, a result of infantile casting with heavy bandages to encourage a pointed, rather than round, skull shape. The wandering Baluch tribe is especially interesting. You'll see them in their long, pleated smocks, carrying on conversations of incredible duration called *has,* in which participants relate all that has happened to them since the last time they met. If the interlude between meetings was long, the conversation can last for hours.

Horse racing is an obsession, and, when challenged, riders will spontaneously whip their horses across the desert, whooping and hollering as they raise big clouds of dust. Other activities include tent-pegging, wrestling, and cockfighting. Unusual embroidery, silk, and leather handicrafts are for sale, as are high-quality wicker items woven from the distinct pish-palm. There's plenty of meat on grills and in makeshift restaurants; try the tasty *Sajji,* a marinated, grilled leg of lamb.

The Durbar has 15th-century origins as a *jirga,* or council of tribal elders, and it's still a forum for political debate. The speeches and shouting matches are vigorous, although participants, who have been described as "people who would need overcoats in hell," are not prone to physical violence. Luckily, this event takes place just before the hot season kicks in, and temperatures during the fair hover just below 38 degrees Celcius (100 degrees Farenheit). If you can't take the heat, just remember the Urdu word for ice: *barf.*

DATE: Early to mid-February. **LOCATION:** Sibi, in the Baluchistan Province, along the road (and railroad) from Shikapur to Quetta and the Afghan border. **TRANSPORT:** Trains from Karachi leave daily for the 18-hour journey. Buses run from Quetta, Ziarat, Hanna Lake, Fort Munro, and Loralai. **ACCOMMODATION:** Simple hotels and guesthouses with fans but no air conditioning. **CONTACT:** PTDC (see *Resources*).

WHILE YOU'RE THERE ...

© **Id-ul-Fitr, nationwide:** These three days of celebrations mark the end of fasting during the month of Ramadan, with visits to families and friends, banquets, gift-giving, and alms to the poor. (January–March; moving date according to the Islamic lunar calendar.)

The most flamboyant vehicle on earth—the Pakistani bus. (Bill Cardoni)

© **Nauroz, northern areas:** This pre-Islamic spring festival features several days of dancing and music. There are large polo matches in Gilgit and the northern areas. (March 21–23.)

© **Basant, Lahore and Kasur:** Similar to the Vasant/Basant Panchami festivals in India and Nepal, this springtime event brings out kites and inspires many rooftop picnics. (Usually March.)

© **Baisakhi, Hasan Abdal (near Rawalpindi):** Sikh pilgrims journey from India to celebrate at the Panja Sahib shrine. (April 13–15.)

© **Mountain Polo Tourney and Gathering, Shandur Pass:** On the high pass between Gilgit and Chitral, a very active four-day festival includes polo matches, dancing, and other indigenous activities of the Hindu Kush. (July/August.)

Artful People Movers

On your way to Pakistani festivals, you'll probably spend some time aboard some of the most flamboyant vehicles in the world—Pakistani buses. These "motorized camels" are amazing beasts. Typically, they're decked out with everything from flashers on top and amulets dangling from bumpers, to side-paintings of gaudy peacocks, mythical animals, or Rambo locked in combat. Interiors look as though drivers have spent a million bucks—five cents at a time. If you're a woman traveler, you'll be amused by the frenzied rearrangements made to ensure your segregation from the male passengers, while you make your way through an elaborate array of shrines, good luck charms, flowers, beaded curtains, and plastic daisy chains.

Kalasha Winter Solstice Festival (Chaumos)

Hindu Kush region **Late December**

The Kalasha winter solstice rituals are an anthropologist's dream, a highly orchestrated 12-day series of dances, animal sacrifices, and other rituals of regeneration, fertility, and unification. These are acted out in three small valleys in the Hindu Kush region. Here, an isolated community of *kafirs* (pagans) stubbornly maintains its complex prehistoric religion and culture, surrounded by an often-hostile Islamic world. Their festivals are living relics of a mysterious ancient culture that, because of its isolation and some accidents of history, has been able to maintain its independence and uniqueness ... so far.

The great Winter Solstice Festival of Chaumos takes place over 10 days in the valleys of Birir, Bumburet, and Rumbur, at an altitude of about 2,500 meters (8,250 feet). The first and second days of the solstice festival begin with the lighting of juniper fires to anoint the sacred goat houses around the valley. At night there are dances driven by singing and hand-clapping (drum beats are forbidden during the entire festival). On the third day there's a ritual "war of words" between teenage girls from up-valley, and those from down-valley. The groups of girls exchange insults (many are crude and sexual in nature) in a ceremony that actually serves to dissolve tension and create friendships.

On the fourth day, bread is baked in animal forms and left on shelves in houses to extract the spirit of the animals from the home. Over the next few days, in a series of private seance-like ceremonies, the dead are communed with, as are the animals, fairies, and deities living in the mountains. During the day, women gather around small fires lit to purify the low fields. On the eighth day a sad female chant starts before dawn, and continues as the men from all the settlements lead goats to the central shrine of the god *Sajjigor.* A blessing is sung, and the goats' throats are slit. After throwing cupped handfuls of blood into the fire, the men return to the village and are welcomed with an erotic dance by the women (a tease, since all sex is banned during the celebration). There's more dancing and sexual jokes, then wood is stacked for the upcoming "night of the torches."

As a holy man leads a torchlight procession around the valley, the chanting and singing group breaks into a frenzied dance when it reaches the site of the bonfire. Teenagers jump around wildly as the women turn circles in their spectacular outfits, often in a trance-like state. The *dehar* (shaman) begins a whirling, possessed gyration, crashing into the crowd and eventually fainting, then awakening with a prophecy. There's much dancing and hand-clapping, with a great celebration that continues into the morning hours, its pace changing according to an esoteric, seemingly instinctual script. On the next night, some couples swap clothes and dance for hours to the hand-clapping and singing of everyone. This represents the pimordial unity of the sexes, the "perfect humanity" thought to have existed in another age.

Several other Kalasha festivals include music, dancing, and often animal sacrifice. Joshi celebrates the spring for five days in mid-May. Uchau, which lasts several weeks, celebrates the summer's wheat and barley harvests with dancing at night in the villages (July). Pul celebrates the walnut and grape harvests (one of Pakistan's few wines is sweet and drunk diluted), with three to four days and nights of dancing and singing (September/October, Birir Valley only).

DATE: The Winter Solstice Festival runs from mid-December through late December. **LOCATION:** Settlements (there are no villages) in the Birir, Bumburet, and Rumbur valleys of the Hindu Kush region. **TRANSPORT:** These valleys can be reached through Ayun, which is 15 km south of Chitral. Since the roads are often closed and there is no public transport, you'll have to hike in. **ACCOMMODATION:** There are some very spartan hotels, with no running water or toilets. Camping may be your best option. **CONTACT:** PTDC (see *Resources*), although they may not be helpful, since most Pakistanis view the Kalasha as *kafirs* (pagans).

Resources

In Pakistan: Pakistan Tourism Development Corporation, Head Office: House No. 2, Street 61, F-7/4, Islamabad, Pakistan. Tel 51-828814, Fax 51-824173. **USA:** PTDC, c/o Lan-Si-Aire Travel Inc, 305 5th. Ave, #508, New York, NY 10016, Tel (212) 889-5478. **Canada:** PTDC, c/o Bestway Tours & Safaris, Ste. 202-2678, W. Broadway, Vancouver, BC V6V 263, Tel (604) 732-4686. **UK:** PTDC, c/o T&T Marketing Services, Holborn Hourse #433, 52-54 High Holborn, GB-London WC1V 6RL, Tel 71-242-3131, Fax 71-242-2838. **Germany:** Walji's Travel c/o Tiger Tops Mountain GmbH, Kastanienstr. 21 D-6242 Dronberg, Tel 6173-6926.

SRI LANKA

"The finest island in the world" was how Marco Polo described Sri Lanka—and the modern explorer will likely agree. This ancient land in the Indian Ocean offers great beaches, spectacular jungle scenery, historic cities, rare wildlife, great food, low costs, and friendly people—all in a compact, easy-to-navigate package.

Although small, Sri Lanka boasts a concentrated richness of culture, manifested in masked demon dances, caparisoned elephants, and the spectacular religious processions known as *peraheras*. Peraheras are public acts of worship, but they also are determined to delight the eyes and ears with a mix of the sacred and secular. Every full moon is a holiday in Sri Lanka, and every temple and shrine seems to be constantly busy preparing or orchestrating one kind of festival or another.

Because of violence between Tamil separatists, Sinhalese extremists, and the Sri Lankan government, parts of the island are uneasy. The Colombo and Kandy areas are relatively safe, but violence has put areas north of Anuradhapura and much of the east coast off-limits.

Duruthu Perahera

Colombo **January**

Elephants, dancers, musicians, and thousands of devotees dressed in white march from the Kelaniya Raja Maha Vihara Temple's hollow *dagoba,* to commemorate the Buddha's visit to Sri Lanka. Costumed characters move down the street enacting familiar episodes from religious lore. One popular character is the *veddah,* or wild man, who leaps around with a grotesque mask. This *perahera* is second in importance to the well-known Kandy Perahera.

DATE: Full moon in January. **LOCATION:** Kelaniya Temple in Colombo. **TRANSPORT:** Colombo is the main entry point for travelers, who can fly directly from Asia, Australia, Europe, and the Middle East. Flyers from the Americas or Africa will need to change planes. **ACCOMMODATION:** Colombo offers a wide array of accommodations, ranging from inexpensive hostels to expensive motels complete with all the conveniences of home. **CONTACT:** Sri Lanka Tourist Board (see *Resources*).

National Day: Hundreds of drummers march in traditional costume through the streets of Colombo and other cities.
(Reuters/Bettman)

WHILE YOU'RE THERE ...

- **National Day, nationwide:** Throughout the country, spirited commotions break out in celebration of Sri Lanka's independence from Britain. Traditional games, parades, and dancing are among the highlights of the day. (February 4.)
- **Navam Perahera, Colombo:** Held at the February full moon, this procession includes about 100 elephants, who march around Beira Lake and Viharamahadevi Park. (February/March.)

VESAK (WAISAKKA)

Nationwide **May**

Although often overshadowed by the Kandy Perahera, this "Festival of Lights" is actually the most important religious date in the Buddhist calendar. It marks the birth, enlightenment, and death of the Buddha, and brings out wildly imaginative illuminations and spirited street theater. Every Buddhist home fires up lanterns during the two nights of Vesak, and many go much further.

You'll see hundreds of people gathered around complicated arrays of electric lights on towering, elaborately decorated billboards known as *thoranas*. These amazing monstrosities blink, change color, and cyclically highlight painted panels that tell the main episodes of legends in an interesting comic-strip fashion. Many stories from Buddhist scripture are told, especially the

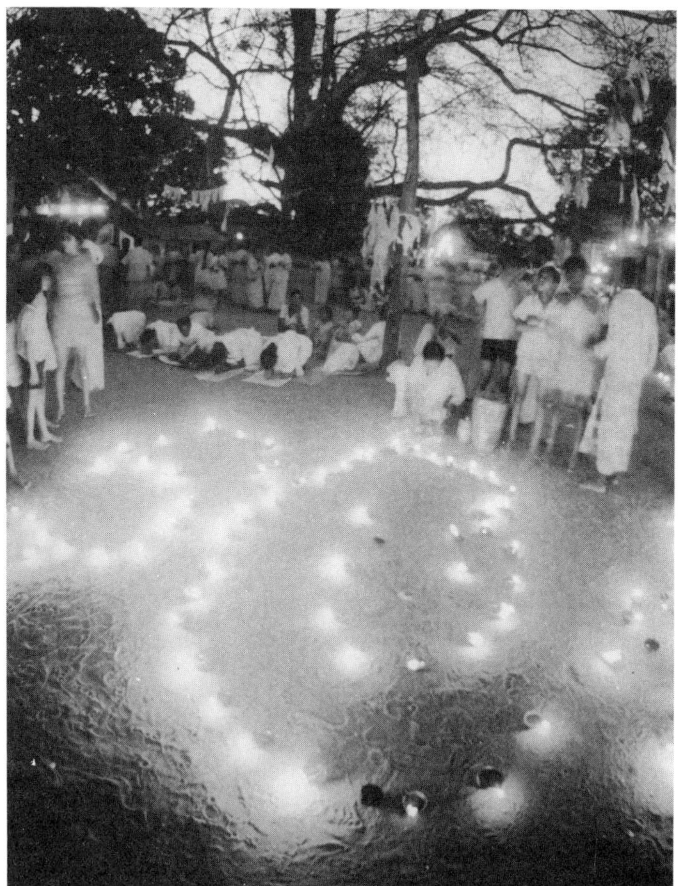

Vesak: Wildly imaginative illuminations and street theater mark the birth, enlightenment, and death of the Buddha. (Joe Viesti/Viesti Associates)

Jataka, or birth stories of the Buddha. With a loud soundtrack including voices of main characters, narration, and music, the *thorana* is a multi-media extravaganza that satisfies both religious sentiment and the public's taste for large-scale spectacle.

The *Jataka* stories are also popular subject matter for street theater and mime performances staged on tall platforms throughout the cities and towns, usually to a pre-recorded soundtrack. The dramas are straightforward enough for even non-Sinhala speakers to get the gist. In addition, more "cutting edge" street theater has recently developed in Sri Lanka, offering a critical commentary on social, cultural, political, and even religious issues. These are often done without stages, and take place spontaneously on streets and sidewalks during Vesak.

DATE: May (full-moon day and the day after). **LOCATION:** Nationwide. **CONTACT:** Sri Lanka Tourist Board (see *Resources*).

While you're there ...

Poson Perahera, Anuradhapura and Mihintale: Although celebrated nationwide, the main sites are Anuradhapura and Mihintale, where Mahinda met and converted the Sinhalese king to Buddhism. You'll see skits acting out the occasion, and pilgrims climbing the 1,840 granite stairs to the top of Mihintale. (April: Poson full-moon day.)

Kandy Esala (Dalada) Perahera

Kandy **July/August**

The English language doesn't hold enough superlatives to describe the scale and splendor of this event. Its 15 days seem to have everything: thousands of dancers in elaborate costumes moving to the beat of thousands of drums ... cracking whips, waving banners, temple chieftains, golden palanquins ... swordsmen, flame dancers, acrobats, tens of thousands of barefoot pilgrims ... and finally, a parade of more than 50 magnificently decorated elephants, led by one of the largest creatures on earth, the sacred Maligawa Tusker.

The Kandy Esala Perahera is quite simply one of the most invigorating pageants a human could experience—in Asia, in the world, in a lifetime. The object of all this fuss is a single tooth, a sacred molar that is believed to have belonged to the Buddha himself. It was brought to Sri Lanka in the third century A.D., hidden in a princess's hair. Since then it has remained the most prized possession in the nation, an object that defines, for many, the Buddhist Ceylonese identity.

The Relic, as the tooth is known, is enshrined in the Dalada Maligawa, or Temple of the Tooth. It's here that the festival begins, slowly, with five nights of foreshadowing. On the sixth night, the *peraheras* start, setting out from each of Kandy's four shrines for the Temple of the Tooth. On the seventh night, *randolis* bearing the deities' consorts join in, each borne behind emblemed elephants. The *peraheras* increase each night in grandeur and size, climaxing on the 14th night with a procession that fills the streets with elephants, dancers, drummers, and seemingly everything else under the sun. The procession's cen-

Kandy Esala Perahera: In preparation for one of the most invigorating pageants on earth, the sacred Maligawa Tusker is led over a carpet of white linen. (Joe Viesti/Viesti Associates)

terpiece is the Maligawa Tusker, who carries the golden casket of the Relic (the real Relic is considered too precious to leave the temple) under a large canopy. Decorated from head to toe with colorful cloth and tiny electric bulbs, the Tusker walks on a carpet of white linen laid in front of him, his feet never touching the bare earth.

On the morning after the climactic parade, a "water-cutting" ceremony is held to purify the Kataragama deity's sword. At the river just south of the city, the water is parted with a circular sweep of the sacred sword. The final and only daylight *perahera* begins at noon, as the replica of the Relic is returned to the temple.

Kandy is the cultural and spiritual capital of Buddhist Sri Lanka, a relaxed, pretty city situated in Sri Lanka's lush central hills. In the center, a jumble of shops specializes in antiques and gems; there are plenty of accoutrements for visitors.

DATE: Full moon in the Sinhalese month of Esala (July or August). **LOCATION:** Kandy. **TRANSPORT:** There are several trains from Colombo to Kandy each day (3 1/2 hours), and several buses (3 hours). Arrive at the roadside by 2 p.m. to ensure a seat at the biggest *perahera.* **ACCOMMODATION:** Hotels fill up fast and prices go up as the procession grows. There are many hotels near the town center, and several popular guesthouses near the edge of town along Anagarika Dharmapala Mawatha Road. **CONTACT:** Sri Lanka Tourist Board (see *Resources*).

Sidetrip: Elephant Orphanage

Near Kandy, an "elephant bath" has been set up solely for the purpose of milking visitors. A far more interesting alternative is the Pinnewala Elephant Orphanage, near Kegalle (90 minutes outside of Kandy). Usually about a dozen abandoned or orphaned wild elephants are in residence. Meal time for the calves (some so small that they drink milk from baby bottles) is 1 p.m.; bath time is 11 a.m. and 2 p.m. The orphanage also runs a breeding program for the Sri Lankan sub-species of elephant.

While you're there ...

- **Vel, Colombo:** Held on the Esala full moon, this Hindu procession features the god of war—in all his regalia—being hauled from a temple in Pettah to one in Bambalapitiya. (July/August.)
- **Hindu Thaipusam Festival, Kataragama:** Heavily laden with ritualistic masochism, this may be one festival that you choose to watch rather than join. Those who do take part can be seen doing such things as piercing their own bodies with skewers or hooks that they then use to tow heavy loads. The ritual continues with a barefoot fire-walk across a steaming bed of coals. As the walk is taking place, other pilgrims make the trek from Batticaloa to Kataragama. (July/August.)

Pilgrimage to Adam's Peak

Dalhousie **December–April**

Both those strong of body and those seeking strength of spirit are drawn to Sri Lanka's most interesting site of religious pilgrimage, Adam's Peak. For over 1,000 years devotees have bravely climbed to the top, where, legend has it, one can find a footprint believed to mark the first step of Adam on earth. Others believe the footprint belongs to the Buddha, St. Thomas, or Lord Shiva. Today, a large stone tablet with another footprint carved into it covers the original. Local tradition maintains that a woman who successfully maneuvers her way to the the top will be born a man in her next life.

Guided by moonlight and streams of lanterns, the travelers make their way up the hillside. Don't be fooled by the early gentle slopes; soon they give way to rugged terrain that necessitates use of the built-in safety steps and bridges. If you arrive at the break of dawn you'll be welcomed by cascading sunbeams breaking to the east and growing triangles of shadow cutting into the western coastline. The view is vast and breathtaking. Colombo, at a distance of 65 km (40 miles), can be seen on a clear day.

There are two routes to the summit of Adam's Peak. The first and fastest takes about three hours, while the second takes about seven hours and stretches from Ratnapura via the Carney Estate. Both paths are well lit and refreshments are available periodically along the way. You'll notice a change in the temperature at the summit, which can get quite windy, so be sure to take along some warm clothes.

DATE: The season begins on Poya (December), and runs until the Sinhalese and Tamil New Year (April). **LOCATION:** Dalhousie. **TRANSPORT:** Buses run from Kandy (the Nuwara Eliya bus stand), Nuwara Eliya, and Colombo in peak season. Alternatively, you can first get to Hatton, which offers seasonal buses direct to Dalhousie via Maskeliya. The road offers plenty of excitment with a plethora of tight corners and unguarded drops. **ACCOMMODATION:** In Dalhousie a few tea shops (some open all night) supply refreshment and reserves for the journey, as well as a place to grab a few hours of sleep. **CONTACT:** Sri Lanka Tourist Board (see *Resources*).

Resources

In Sri Lanka: Sri Lanka Tourist Board, 76–78 Stuart Place, Colombo, Sri Lanka, Tel: 1-437-059/060. Fax 1-549-280. Ceylon Travel Information Center, 321 Galle Rd., Colombo 3, Sri Lanka. **USA:** Embassy of the Republic of Sri Lanka, 2148 Wyoming Avenue NW, Washington, DC 20008, Tel (202) 483-4025, Fax (202) 232-7181. **Canada:** Embassy of Sri Lanka, 85 Range Road, The Sandringham, Suites 102-104, Ottawa, ON K1N 8J6, Tel (613) 233-8440, Fax (613) 238-8448. **UK:** Ceylon Tourist Board, 13 Hyde Park Gardens, London W2 2LU, Tel 71-262-5009, Fax 71-262-7970. **Australia:** Ceylon Tourist Board, 439 Albany Highway, Victorial Park, WA 6100, Tel 9-362-4579. **Germany:** Ceylon Tourist Board, Allerheiligentor 2-4, D 6000 Frankfurt 1, Tel 69-287734.

TIBET

The Tibetan people and culture have been under assault since 1950, when the Chinese army marched in and occupied Tibet. Since then, more than 1.2 million Tibetans have been killed, another 100,000 forced into exile, and thousands imprisoned. Recently, the Chinese have discovered that Tibetan culture is a tourism/hard currency draw, but the loss to the world in human and cultural terms is incalculable: hundreds of monasteries have been destroyed, statues mutilated, and religious treasures more than a thousand years old have been sold as bullion or scrap metal.

Yet outside the cities, among the highest mountains on earth, sturdy nomads continue with their lives as they have for thousands of years, pitching tents and starting fires in what Giusseppe Tucci called a "temporary halt in an eternal wandering." Tibetans are remarkably resilient, and even in urban enclaves like Old Lhasa, the visitor gets the feeling that even if many of the Tibetans' external icons are gone, their culture is essentially intact. The spirit of this culture can be found at the many festivals that are beginning to spring back to life. You'll see it in the sparkling eyes of dancers who find a bridge to a happier past—and future—in the music and mysteries of Tantric Buddhism.

Tibetan New Year (Losar)

Lhasa, Shigatse, Tashilhumpo, and throughout Tibet — **February/March**

As colorful new prayer flags are hung out over each home, the smell of incense wafts through the villages. At dawn on New Year's Day, Tibetans visit monasteries, shrines, and *chortens* to make offerings. Then families venture out to drink the New Year's *chang* (unhopped beer) with friends, to picnic in the parks and meadows, or to watch an archery tourney. Devotees journey to the Jokhang temple in Lhasa to donate yak butter that keeps the lamps burning well into the year. At Barkor Plaza the giant incense burners work overtime to handle hundreds of people queued up

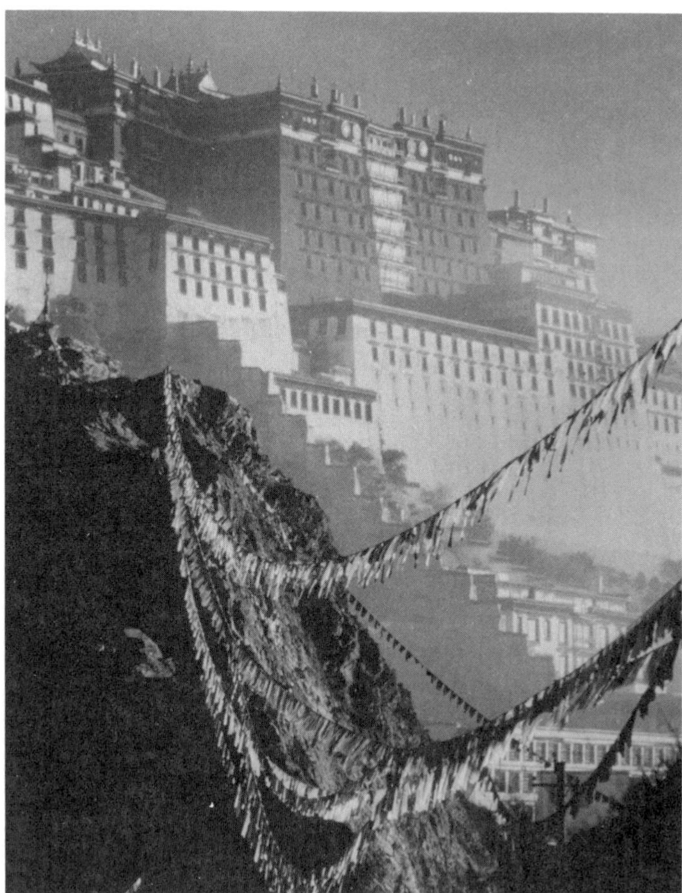

Lhasa: Under siege for decades, the spiritual home of Tibetan Buddhism now receives visitors. (Gordon Wiltsie)

to throw in their offerings of juniper branches. New sculptures of yak butter and *tsampa* (roasted barley flour) are displayed. Made by the *lamas* (monks), the sculptures depict deities and Buddhist scenes, and will be unveiled at the **Butter Sculpture Festival** at the first full moon of the year (15 days after New Year's Day).

New Year's Eve is *Lu Yugpa,* an opportunity to banish evil spirits from the old year and clear the way for starting the New Year right. A frenzied housecleaning chases away the evil spirits to let the good ones in. Some houses make a ritual soup for the spirits, which is put outside on a bed of burning straws. In the monasteries at Lhasa and Shigatse, *lamas* walk in procession with *tsampa* dough dolls. Their destination is the monastery forecourt, where, amid much chanting, the images are burned and the spirits driven away. At Tashilhumpo monastery on this last day of the year, the *lamas* perform masked dances to symbolize the triumph of good over evil.

DATE: Celebrated the last day of the year through the third day of the Tibetan calendar (February or March). **LOCATION:** Although the festivities are large-scale in Lhasa, you'll find a lot of activity in any town or village in Tibet. **TRANSPORT:** You can reach Lhasa by air from Kathmandu or Chengdu (with connections from Beijing and Canton). There are land routes from Kathmandu (one of the world's most dramatic roads) and, for the durable traveler, from Chengdu or Golmud. **ACCOMMODATION:** Although there's a Holiday Inn in town, expect most accommodations to be Spartan by Western standards. Tibetan-run hotels are centrally located near the old town, and rooms are usually dormitory style with shared bath and no hot water. Chinese-run hotels usually have hot water available in the evening, though most don't have room heaters. **CONTACT:** China National Tourist Office (see *Resources*).

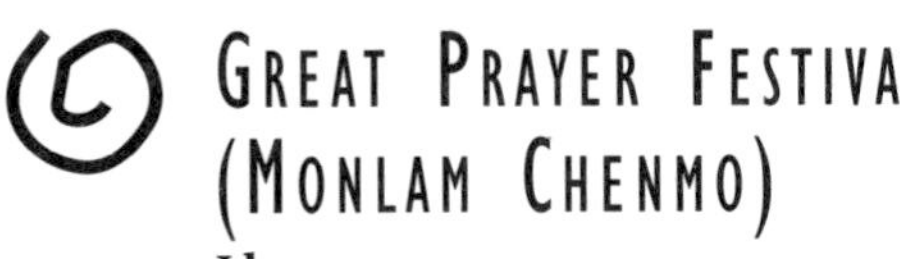

GREAT PRAYER FESTIVAL (MONLAM CHENMO)

Lhasa **February/March**

Like many festivals in Tibet, the Great Prayer Festival has seen more vital days. It was started in 1409 by Tsong Khapa, as a way of commemorating the Buddha's victory over his six opponents. A victim of Chinese contempt for religion and large public gatherings, the festival was suspended in 1959, but recently has achieved a bit of a comeback. More than 1,000 Gelukpa *lamas* now make the trip to Lhasa's Jokhang Temple for public and private prayer celebrations, chanting, music-making, and theological debates.

On the eve of the full moon, huge sculptures made of colored yak butter and *tsampa* dough are erected around the Barkor. As an orchestra of *lamas* in festival finery plays conch-shell horns and other traditional instruments, a line of pilgrims files past the sculptures. Thousands of butter lamps assist the moon, lighting the way for pilgrims who keep coming until just before dawn, when the sculptures are finally removed.

DATE: February/March (first month, days 8–15 of the Tibetan calendar). **LOCATION:** Jokhang Temple, Lhasa. **TRANSPORT/ACCOMMODATION:** See above. **CONTACT:** China National Tourist Office (see *Resources*).

Gyangzê Horse Racing Festival (Tamang)

Gyangzê **May/June**

Gyangzê is one of Tibet's gems, an undamaged medieval town towered over by the Gyangzê *Dzong* (castle). Winding lanes shaded by willow trees host pony carts and horsemen gearing up for journeys. Amid this low-key splendor, the four-day Horse Racing Festival is an astounding showcase for the Tibetans' remarkable horsemanship and yakmanship. In addition to beautiful horses and yaks driven by madly disheveled riders, it's a good chance to see traditional mask-dancing, and to stroll among the tents and picnic areas of Tibetans who have traveled from small towns to attend the festival.

The festival's first day is devoted to traditional mask dances and operas, performed by the *lamas* in the Kumbum courtyard. Kumbum's 112 chapels (23 of which are open to the public) and multi-tiered stupas are exceptional, with many built in the 15th century. A 14th-century *thangka* (long cloth painting) is hung from the monastery's wall before sunrise on the third morning. Nearby is the restored Pelkor Chode, which has brilliant murals, hanging masks, *thangkas,* and ancient weapons hung from the ceiling.

The rest of the four-day festival is dedicated to sport on horseback. At full gallop, mounted archers shoot arrows at targets and snatch up ceremonial *katas* (scarves), which are placed on the ground at intervals. Yaks are ridden and raced. The festival commemorates history's highest battle, in which the Tibetans emerged victorious against invading British troops led by Colonel Younghusband.

DATE: The fourth month, days 15–18 of the Tibetan calendar (May or June). **LOCATION:** Gyangzê lies on the trade route to Sikkim and Darjeeling, about 200 km (124 miles) southwest of Lhasa. **TRANSPORT:** Travel outside of Lhasa can be difficult to arrange individually, but it's possible to hook up with tour groups to arrange bus trips. **ACCOMMODATION:** There are only two hotels in town, the Gyangtse Hotel and the Gyantse Hotel (note the subtle spelling difference). The former has both Chinese and Tibetan-style rooms, and hot water, but no heat. The latter is Tibetan-style, and very spartan. **CONTACT:** China National Tourist Office (see *Resources*).

While you're there ...

Tshurphu Monastery Festival, Tshurphu: The monastery's *lamas* perform mask dances. (May/June; fourth month, 10th day of Tibetan calendar.)

Buddha's Enlightenment and Ascent to Heaven (Saga Dawa), throughout Tibet: Throughout the fourth Tibetan month (and especially at full moon), offerings are brought to monasteries. (May/June.)

Samye Dholdhe Festival, Samye: This gathering of monks and pilgrims celebrates the descendence of the Buddha and features mask dances. (May/June.)

World Incense Day (Zabling Chi Sang), nationwide: Tibetans dress up and smile on this day as a hedge against evil spirits. It's believed that the spirits descend in search of sad people, who can more easily be possessed. So if you're in Tibet, be happy (as if you needed an excuse!). Also on this day, Tibetans pray for world peace and climb holy mountains. (June/July; 15th day of the fifth month.)

Wheel of Dharma Festival (Chhokor Duchhan/Drukpa Sewa Shi), Lhasa, Shigatse, and Gepel Ri Mountain (near Drepung): Pilgrims climb Gepel Ri and other mountains to hang prayer flags and make offerings of incense. Pilgrimage circuits are made in cities. This is also called the Six/Four Festival, because it falls on the sixth month and fourth day of the Tibetan calendar. (June/July.)

Ganden Thangka Festival (Ganden Khi-khu), Ganden: The founder of the Gelukpa sect is honored by traditional music and a huge *thangka,* which is hung from a special wall. (June/July.)

Yogurt Festival/Tibetan Opera Festival (Zhuedun), Norbulingha, Lhasa: A *thangka* is hung and mask-dance/opera troupes from around Tibet perform in this week-long festival. (August/September; seventh month, days 1–7.)

Looking Around the Fields Festival (Ongkor), Zetang: Horse racing, archery, and dances ensure a good harvest. (September/October.)

Tsong Khapa Death Anniversary (Ganden Ngamchu), throughout Tibet: Special foods are prepared to symbolize sadness; houses and monastery rooftops and windows are illuminated with yak-butter lamps. (November/December; 10th month, 25th day.)

Resources

In Tibet and China: Tibet Tourism Bureau, West Beijing Road, Lhasa, Tibet Autonomous Region, People's Republic of China (PRC), Tel 891-24484. National Tourism Administration, A-9 Jiangoumennei Dajie, Beijing 100740, PRC, Tel 1-513-8866. **USA:** China National Tourist Office, Lincoln Building, #3126, 60 E. 42nd St., New York, NY 10165, Tel (212) 867-0271. **UK:** CNTO, 4 Glentworth Street, GB-London NW1, Tel 71-935-9427. A pocket calendar with dates of Tibetan festivals is printed annually by the Rigpa Fellowship, 44 St. Paul's Crescent, London NW1 9TN, England. **Australia:** CNTO, 11th Floor, 55 Clarence Street, Sydney, NSW 2000, Tel 2-299-4057. **Germany:** CNTO, Ilkenhansstr. 6, D-6000 Frankfurt 50, Tel 69-520135.

EAST ASIA

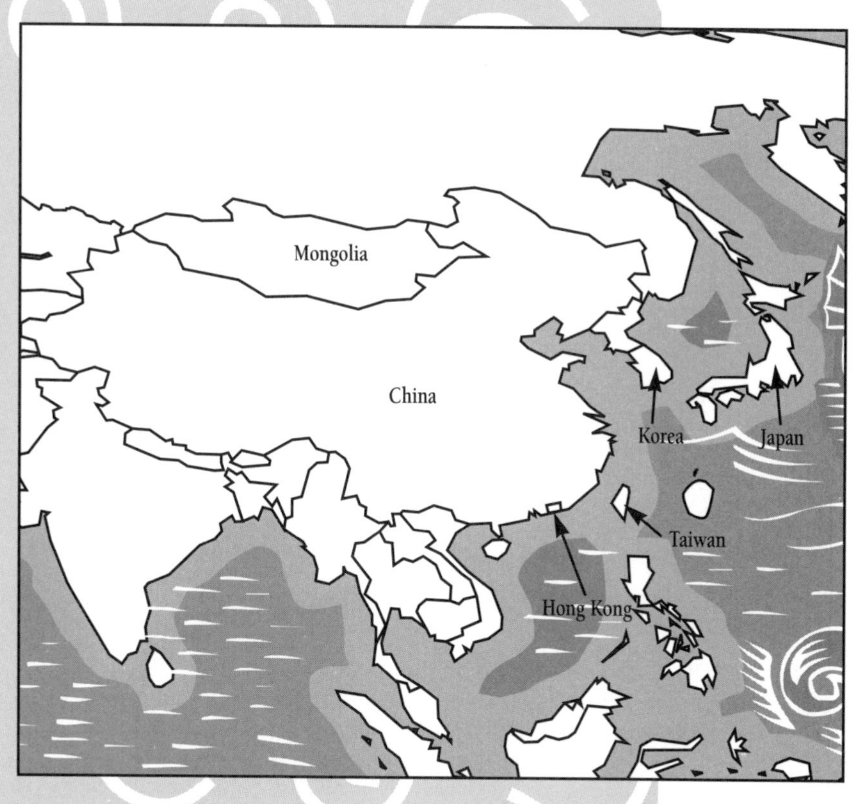

CHINA

The world's longest enduring civilization has spent much of its history isolated by natural or political barriers, but today China beckons Westerners to explore what's left of its culture. Unfortunately, the world's largest populace doesn't have scores of festivals commensurate with its size. Like many of the physical remains of China's past, many religious celebrations were wiped out by the Cultural Revolution.

During the festivals that *have* survived, the Chinese people and culture are at their most vital. Temporarily distracted from the primitive capitalism that's been adopted as their new religion, the modern Chinese use celebrations as an opportunity to embrace their rich history, morals, and traditions. During the festivals, China's roots emerge from its collective unconscious, and neighborhoods are temporarily transformed into ritual grounds that are vigorously and colorfully alive. These spirited parties echo the past and seek to influence the future with activities, foods, and props that can be traced to the folkloric tales and primitive rituals that form the fabric of Chinese celebrations.

Note: Tibet, which was invaded by China in 1950 and has been occupied since then, is covered in the *South-Central Asia* section.

Lantern Festival (Yúanxiāo Jié)

Xi'an and nationwide **February**

As the yellowy moon shines above, the cities and villages of China are aglow with the light of millions of colorful lanterns. For the last 2,000 years, Chinese people have fashioned these lanterns into countless shapes resembling vegetables, fish, men, animals, swords, and hundreds of other objects. Today the craftsmanship is phenomenal, and starting several days before the full moon, parks and squares in cities all over the country are beautifully decorated. The evenings draw people out to stroll among the ingenious designs and eat rice dumplings called *yúanxiāo*.

In the historical city of Xi'an a lantern market springs up; it's packed with children who can hardly wait until nightfall to

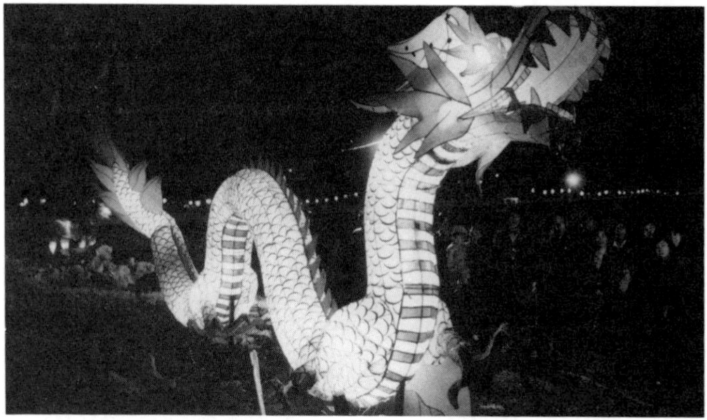

The display of huge, immaculately crafted lanterns is a tradition that lights up the night in cities and towns all over China. *(John Roberts/The Stock Market)*

light their own lanterns and carry them outside. The wall around the old city is decorated with hundreds of thousands of lanterns, and for 10 days the top of the wall is filled with people who walk around admiring the lanterns, trying to solve the riddles that are written on some. In old Xi'an's narrow, cobbled lanes, lanterns illuminate the mud-brick houses and Taoist temples that are unique to this city.

In Xi'an and elsewhere, festivals spring up with parades of people walking on stilts and performing lion dances. The one-person dance is called *Shaoshi,* or "lion-cub dance." The "master-lion dance," or *Taishi,* is done in an elaborate two-person suit, and always wows the crowds. Other dances include *Hanchuan* (boating on land) and *Paolu* (donkey running).

DATE: The full moon in February. **LOCATION:** Xi'an and nationwide. **TRANSPORT:** Xi'an is easily reached from nearly everywhere in China by plane or train. In addition, there are charter flights from Hong Kong. **ACCOMMODATION:** As a major tourist destination, Xi'an is well outfitted with hotels of all classes. **CONTACT:** China National Tourist Office (see *Resources*).

WHILE YOU'RE THERE ...

© **Chinese New Year, nationwide:** The sad truth is that the Chinese New Year is much better experienced nearly anywhere else but China. Although some customs have survived (see **Hong Kong, Taiwan,** and **Singapore**), most people in the PRC spend three days loafing, visiting, gam-

In the days before the New Year, Beijing's parks are filled with music and traditional performing arts. (ChinaStock/Argus Photoland)

bling, and watching the big New Year's Eve show on Chinese Central TV. Beijing has several fairs, but since nobody wants to work, many hotels and restaurants are closed and it's impossible to book transport.

© **Ice Lantern Festival, Harbin:** This dazzling event features ice and snow sculptures in the shapes of people, pavilions, trees, and animals, sculpted with exceptional skill and craftsmanship. The festival is held January through early March at Zhaolin Park in this cold, cold city near the Russian border.

© **Flower Festival, Chengdu:** Apart from the fantastic displays of flowers, the festival features all kinds of cultural events, including theater, music, and opera, held in the shadow of the Taoist Ching Yang Palace. (March; beginning on the 15th day of the second lunar month.)

Frolic with an Ancient Army

Standing in ghostly silence near Xi'an, more than 6,000 terra-cotta soldiers and horses are ready to defend their emperor's nearby tomb. Only discovered in the early 1970s, the army and tomb are one of the world's most astounding archaeological sites and one of China's greatest attractions. For unstated reasons, no photography of any kind is allowed, but the site shouldn't be missed. In life-sized relief, there are legions of crossbow bearers, spear-holders, axe-swingers, and chariot drivers, each one differing in facial features and expression. Emperor Qin Shi Huang Di's mausoleum is yet to be excavated, and experts believe that the best treasures are yet to be uncovered.

Water-Splashing Festival

Xishuangbanna **Mid-April**

With mountains towering over subtropical jungles and waterfalls falling into thousands of creeks and rivers, the Xishuangbanna area is one of China's most beautiful and pristine regions. Yet this area's natural splendor is surpassed by the cultural wonders created by the stately Dai people. Continuing to practice their traditional Buddhist rituals in beautiful temples and shrines, they display a nonchalant disregard for the authority and anti-religious sentiments of the Chinese government.

The Water-Splashing Festival is an exceptional cultural treasure, and attending it is a great way to meet the Dai people and observe their customs. During the festival the old year's dirt and demons are washed away, and the happiness of the New Year is welcomed. Activities take place in the town of Jinghong, and in villages like Manjing, Menghai, and Menghun—although virtually every Dai settlement has something going on. The first day of the festival is dedicated to colorful and large markets, in which tribal women sell earrings, bracelets, headdresses, and leggings. On the second day there's dragon-boat racing along the Mekong River (the biggest races are in Jinghong), and swimming and rocket-launching competitions. On the morning of the third day, the water-splashing begins in earnest. The scene is similar to the water-splashing events across the border in Burma; everyone hoses down everyone else in a hilarious romp that often targets travelers for good-natured drenchings.

Each night giant balloons made of paper are launched; hot air is provided by fires lit on platforms hung under the balloons.

Dai racers relax in their dragon boat after a race during the Water-Splashing Festival in Jinghong, Xishuangbanna. A women's team paddles by in the background. (Trip/J. Moscrop)

People watch the glowing balloons rise and drift out of sight, while on the ground the festivities are non-stop. Many Dais get married during this period, and expressive performances of song and dance are common (the Peacock Dance is especially colorful). The many temple paths are a pleasant way to get from village to village, since the lush hills hold many native species of plants and dwindling numbers of tigers, leopards, wild elephants, and golden-haired monkeys.

DATE: Mid-April. **LOCATION:** Jinghong and surrounding villages in the Xishuangbanna Dai Autonomous Prefecture, Yunnan Province, near the border with Laos and Burma. **TRANSPORT:** Jinghong's airport handles flights from Kunming, and the town is also served by bus from Kunming (a grueling three-day journey). The airport at Simao is sporadically open. Transport is tight during the festival, so book early. **ACCOMMODATION:** Jinghong has the most hotels (all basic), but rooms are scarce during the festival. There are also hotels in Simao, Menghai, and Menghan. **CONTACT:** China National Tourist Office (see *Resources*).

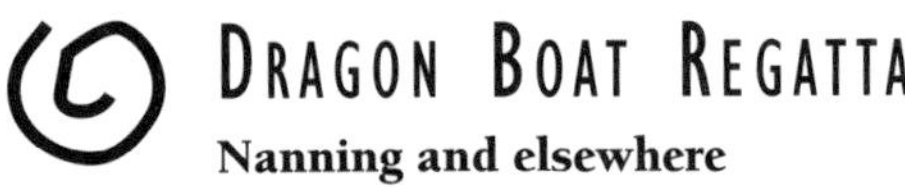

Dragon Boat Regatta

Nanning and elsewhere **May/June**

More than a millennium ago, Tang Dynasty poet Zhang Jianfeng wrote the following account of the Dragon Boat Regatta in Nanning: "Dragon boats with fluttering red flags plunge into action on the third beat of the drum, the oars cut water like so many

Fish Lip Soup and Other Delicacies

Famines are a not-so-distant memory for the Chinese; consequently they tend to make delicacies out of things that Westerners either discard or keep as pets. A trip through a Chinese market can be a trauma for the squeamish; skinned dogs and live rats seem to lurk around every corner, and a misinterpreted gesture can put you in a situation like that experienced by a French woman in Shanghai. As she admired some finches chirping away in a cage, the proprieter arrived and handed her one. After petting it, she carefully handed it back to him. "You like bird?" he smiled, and she nodded, "Yes, I like it." He beamed and quickly snapped off the tiny creature's head, squeezed its blood into a small glass, and handed it to her.

Some other Chinese delicacies you may not want to miss: Fish Lip Soup • Armadillo in the Shell with Tail Handle • Baby Pig's Ears • Cat and Snake Meat Stir-Fry Combination • Jellied Red Duck's Feet with Garlic • Crispy Sea Slugs • Black Chicken with Head Attached • Rendered Pork Fat Back • Pig Face Soup • Bear Paws Braised in Brown Sauce • Eggs Soaked in Horse Urine • Live Rat Embryos with Soy Sauce Dip

swords, and amid thunderous rolls of drums the dragons dart toward the finish line."

This 2,000-year-old festival—interrupted only during the Cultural Revolution—continues to be one of the biggest, most colorful events in China. Although it's celebrated in other cities in the region (most notably Chengdu, Sichuan, and Guangxi), the festivities on Nanning's Yong River are the most elaborate, with more than 250,000 spectators cheering dozens of men's and women's teams.

The basics of the competition haven't changed since Zhang's time. The long, thin boats are elaborately decorated, with bows and sterns shaped like dragons' heads and tails. Some boats hold more than 100 oarsmen, exhorted by gong players and drummers sitting in the middle and rear. The races are tests of will and stamina, accompanied by a thunderous soundtrack of cheers and firecrackers. There are prizes for the fastest and best-decorated boats, yet there's no clearly defined finish line, and there are no official judges. Arguments and fistfights sometimes occur, but the event always ends happily—and drunkenly.

The Dragon Boat tradition started in the third century B.C., with the death of the great poet and statesman Qu Yuan. Banished from his home city of Cheng, Qu wrote the classic poem *Li Sao,* which means "Departure and Sadness." Upon learning that his beloved city had been destroyed, he went to the Miluo River, stuffed his sleeves with rocks, and hurled himself into water. The town's fishermen raced to the scene to rescue him, but they were too late, so they rowed through the night to keep river demons away from his body. With the first anniversary of his death the tradition of offerings to Qu's spirit began, and today his writings continue to have a great impact on Chinese literature and spiritual life.

Preparations for the regatta begin weeks in advance, as the boats are decorated and safeguarded against disaster with appropriate charms and spells. Some parents paint their children with wine or red pigment to dispel evil. Since this is the time of year when days and nights are nearly equal, a tremendous struggle takes place between Yang, the force of light and warmth, and Yin, the force of darkness and cold. The race is said to assist in equalizing the Yin-Yang forces and maintaining balance.

A Chinese festival is incomplete if it lacks a special edible. For this celebration the focus food is *zongzi*—a glutinous rice dumpling wrapped in bamboo or reed leaves and shaped like a pyramid. Sometimes enhanced with dates or bean paste, *zongzi* is a modern version of the rice and bamboo sections that were thrown into the river as a sacrifice to the spirit of Qu Yuan, or perhaps to distract the river dragons from his body. Other local specialties include turtle, lizard, snake, and dog.

DATE: Late May or early June (the fifth day of the fifth month in the lunar calendar). **LOCATION:** Nanning is China's southernmost large city, located along the main route to the Vietnamese border. The festival is also celebrated at other lakeside or riverside cities in China, particularly those along the Miluo River in Hunan Province (the site of Qu Yuan's death), and at Chengdu, Sichuan, and Guangxi. **TRANSPORT:** A pleasant way to arrive is by boat from Wuzhou or Guangzhou. There are flights from Beijing, Guangzhou, Kunming, and Guilin, and trains from Zhanjiang, Kunming, and Guiyang. **ACCOMMODATION:** Only a few hotels in town are approved for foreign tourists and these fill up fast; for best results reserve or arrive early. **CONTACT:** China National Tourist Office (see *Resources*).

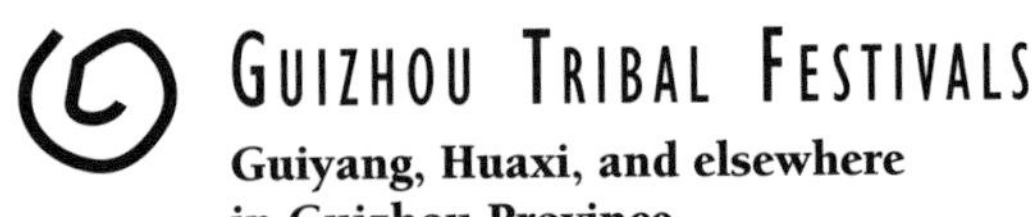

GUIZHOU TRIBAL FESTIVALS

Guiyang, Huaxi, and elsewhere in Guizhou Province — **July**

Far away from the big cities where China's economic miracle is in top gear, the ethnic minorities of the Guizhou province continue

Miao girls dance around the courtyard of the village of Longde. During the sixth lunar month, ethnic minorities in the Guizhou Province hold hundreds of festivals, which are great opportunities to experience their colorful and esoteric traditions. (Michele Burgess)

with lifestyles that have changed little since ancient times. These tribes—the Miao, Dong, Bouyi, Yi, and several more—celebrate hundreds of festivals each year, which are opportunities to experience their colorful and often baffling cultural traditions.

Dong villagers have erected mysterious drum towers and graceful covered bridges that have fascinated anthropologists for decades. Amid these and other settings, the July celebrations are small-scale but high-energy extravaganzas featuring bamboo pipe music, dragon boat races, and mass courting rituals. In addition, the tribal groups perform singing contests and sophisticated comic opera. Sports include unique bullfights and horse races.

At the festivals you'll notice how little life has changed for these cultures—which is truly amazing, considering the mad rush the majority of Chinese have made for the consumer culture. Yet these isolated groups show no signs of discarding their cultural identity. Many live in caves and eschew television, radio, and even electricity, finding their rewards in the preservation of customs that range from elaborate architecture to distinctively woven clothing and exquisite handicrafts.

DATE: The sixth lunar month (usually in July) is a peak time for tribal festivals, and several usually occur simultaneously. Other peak times are the first and fourth lunar months (around February and May). **LOCATION:** Throughout Guizhou Province. Key towns and villages are Guiyang, Kaili, Zhenyuan, Danxi, Qingman, Lei Gongshan, Xijiang, and Panghai. **TRANSPORT:** Guiyang's airport is served by flights from Beijing, Shanghai, Guangzhou (Canton), Chengdu, and Haikou. You can reach the train station from Nanning, Kunming, Guilin, and Chongqing. **ACCOMMODATION:** Guiyang is the largest town around and has several tourist-class hotels. **CONTACT:** CITS/Guiyang, No. 7 Yan'an Zhong Road, Guiyang, PRC. Asian Pacific Adventures, 826 S. Sierra Bonita Avel, Los Angeles, CA 90036. China National Tourist Office (see *Resources*).

Mid-Autumn/Moon Festival

Nationwide **September/October**

With the moon at its fullest and the harvest in full swing, moon cakes tempt the taste buds at every turn. The Mid-Autumn Festival, also called the Moon Festival, brings city dwellers into the parks to dance, sing, eat, tell fortunes, watch puppets, and moon-gaze. In the countryside the hills are alive with moon vigils, rooted in ancient rituals in which the moon was worshiped and asked for favorable weather for the coming harvest. Today, people simply admire the moon and contemplate the Taoist tenet of the union of man and nature.

At midnight, parks across the country are wonderlands of sweet lunacy, as families bearing colorful candlelit lanterns gather to enjoy the full moon. The 1,000-year tradition of preparing and eating moon cakes is still crucial to the event. These pastries, filled with lotus and sesame seeds, reveal round yellow "moons" inside when cut open. Many people also put squares of paper inside each moon cake to commemorate the moon-cake messages that carried a mandate for the uprising that ended Mongolian rule in the 14th century.

DATE: September/October (15th day of the eighth lunar month). **LOCATION:** Nationwide. **CONTACT:** China National Tourist Office (see *Resources*).

While you're there ...

- **Torch Festival, Stone Forest (near Kunming):** Amid a strange landscape of eroded limestone pillars and classical pavilions, the minority Sani people hold bullfights, dances, wrestling competitions, and equestrian events. (June 23–25.)
- **Birthday of Confucius, Qufu, Shandong Province:** Celebrate the birth of the sage and enjoy the scenery of his hometown. The Confucius Temple is impressive in size and in contents. A spectacular fair with a 2,000-year tradition springs up in honor of Qufu's favorite son. (September.)

Double Ninth Festival, nationwide: Although the wearing of mugwort leaves has been abadoned, the thousand-year-old traditions of climbing hills, eating rice cakes, and drinking chrysanthemum wine remain. The ancient Chinese considered it an unlucky day but the modern Chinese revere the festival as a day to aspire to lofty heights.

Tan Ta, Xishuangbanna villages: The minority Dai people hold 10 days of celebrations which include temple rituals, hot-air balloons, and special rockets that explode and shower good-luck amulets. (Late October or early November.)

Resources

In China: China International Travel Service, Head Office, 103 Fuxingmennie Avenue, Beijing 100800, Tel 1-6012022, Fax 1-6012021, 6012013; National Tourism Administration, A-9 Jiangoumennei Dajie, Beijing 100740, Tel 1-5138866, Fax 1-5122096. **USA:** China National Tourist Office, Lincoln Building, #3126 60 East 42nd St., New York, NY 10165, Tel (212) 867-0271, Fax (212) 599-2892. **Canada:** China Travel Service, P.O. Box 17, 999 West Hastings St., Vancouver, BC V6C 2W2, Tel (604) 684-8787, Fax (604) 684-3321. **UK:** China National Tourist Office, 4 Glentworth St., GB-London NW1, Tel 71-9359427, Fax 71-4875842. **Australia:** China National Tourist Office, 11th Floor 55 Clarence St., Sydney, NSW 2000, Tel 2-2994057, Fax 2-2901958. **Germany:** China National Tourist Office, Ilkenhansstr. 6, D-6000 Frankfurt 50, Tel 69-520135, Fax 69-528490.

HONG KONG

The ultimate capitalist society may look Western on the surface, but Hong Kong's heart and soul are emphatically Chinese. Even though high tea and cricket are enduring options, the noises and smells of the markets are unmistakeably oriental, and Hong Kong's intense, stylized festivals are celebrated with a vigor and high regard for chaos that no one would mistake for British.

These celebrations feature dragons dancing, dancers whirling, lanterns swinging, and boats streaming through the breeze. Although most of Hong Kong's festivals were established in China several millenia ago, they've evolved into celebrations that have a distinctly local character. For instance, you'll notice right away that festivals are notably quieter here than in other Chinese areas, because fireworks have been forbidden since the Red Guard political riots of 1967. Thus, evil spirits must be driven away by other means. One such way is clearly in keeping with the consumerist, forward-looking mentality of Hong Kong: Luxury items such as Rolls-Royces and 747s are constructed of papier mâché, then set ablaze in order to enrich the existence of those living in the spirit world.

Lantern Festival

Throughout Hong Kong **February**

The Lantern Festival is smaller but much more interesting for visitors than the Chinese New Year. At full moon the streets are filled with families carrying beautiful lanterns shaped like rabbits, dragons, foods, or pop-culture icons. Victoria Park and Morse Park are spectacular with thousands of traditional lanterns, and "lantern carnivals" spring up on almost every beach. And because this is the Chinese equivalent of Valentine's Day, you'll see lovers strolling everywhere.

The modern-day festival evolved from the belief that celestial spirits could be seen flying around in the light of the year's first full moon. To see them better (and avoid them), people lit lanterns and carried them around after dark. These days, restaurants, homes, and temples are splendidly lit with traditional lanterns in the shapes of butterflies (the symbol of longevity), lobsters (mirth), and carp (power, wisdom, and courage). Children throng to the spontaneous lantern markets all over the territory, harrassing their parents into buying lanterns shaped like rockets, boats, and even tanks.

DATE: Mid- to late February (the full moon 15 days after the New Year). **LOCATION:** Throughout Hong Kong, and especially at Victoria Park and other parks. **TRANSPORT:** As East Asia's major gateway, Hong Kong is exceptionally easy to get to, with direct flights from nearly every industrialized country. **ACCOMMODATION:** Hong Kong's hotels and guest houses aren't cheap, but they are plentiful. **CONTACT:** Hong Kong Tourist Assn. (see *Resources*).

While you're there ...

Chinese New Year, throughout Hong Kong: As Hong Kong's biggest festival, the Chinese New Year brings all work and transportation to a crawl. The entire territory is decorated to the hilt, but unless you're invited into a home, you probably won't see many of the interesting rituals intended to scare off bad spirits and welcome good ones. Victoria Park is packed with people, and huge flower fairs spring up. Occasionally there are lion dances in the street. (Late January/early February.)

Bun Festival

Cheung Chau Island **May**

The former pirate's lair of Cheung Chau Island is the scene of one of the most unusual festivals in Asia. Among its weird features are extraordinarily colorful costumes, children who appear to "float" above crowds, and bamboo scaffolding covered with edible buns.

The Bun Festival is a spirit-placating ritual, but it's questionable whose spirits are being placated. Some say they're the spirits of people killed during a plague that swept the island earlier in the century, or people killed by the notorious pirate Cheung Po Chai. Others mention the bones disturbed by residents when they were constructing houses. Maybe it's all of these and more; at any rate, no one wants to chance failing to appease the spirits, thereby inviting a disaster such as a typhoon.

In addition to placating the human spirits and deities, the crowd makes offerings to the spirits of the animals and fish who provide food. In their honor all food is vegetarian; the priest at the Pak Tai Temple reads a decree that during the festival no animal or fish will be killed or eaten on the island. The third day of the festival is most interesting, and features a grand procession of stilt-walkers, costumed dancers, and floats depicting the various human virtues and vices. Children ride the floats, playing key characters in extraordinarily colorful costumes while kneeling or doing handstands. The "floating children" are probably the most fascinating. They appear to hover over the crowd, although they are in fact strapped into hidden supports on top of poles and carried through the streets by adults.

At midnight on the third day, a symbolic offering of *pao,* or buns, takes place. These are mounted on bun towers—bamboo scaffoldings up to 20 meters/66 feet high. In earlier times a mad scramble up the towers took place, since the buns from higher up the towers are believed to hold the best *joss,* or good luck. Since 1978, when a major accident occured, the buns have been simply handed down from the towers.

Cheung Chau Island itself is a living postcard. The harbor is jammed with fishing junks (it's estimated that up to 20 percent of the population lives off-shore), and the island retains its calm and rural demeanor even though it's become a popular weekend getaway spot. The Bun Festival's four days draw big crowds, and extra ferries are needed to get everyone back and forth.

DATE: The festival begins on the eighth day of the fourth moon (usually early May). **LOCATION:** Cheung Chau Island (in the Outlying Islands). **TRANSPORT:** Ferries depart from Outlying Islands Ferry Pier in Hong Kong, and from Lantau Island. **ACCOMMODATION:** Although the island has several hotels, these are extremely expensive and usually filled during the festival (and on any weekend). It's much easier to stay on Hong Kong Island. **CONTACT:** Hong Kong Tourist Assn. (see *Resources*).

© Tin Hau Fisherman's Festival

Taoist Tin Hau temples **May**

Seeking the blessings of Tin Hau, the mother-goddess of the sea, the boat people of Hong Kong set off at dawn, filling the territory's waterways as they head for one of the many temples dedicated to the goddess. The scene is astoundingly colorful: junks, sampans, and lighters are decked out with multi-colored pennants that stream behind as the boats motor and sail in long lines through the harbors, every inch of deck space crammed with people.

The favorite destination is the Tai Miu Temple at Joss House Bay, which draws massive crowds offering fruits and pink dumplings to the goddess. Outside the temple, there are lion dancers, fortune tellers, and Chinese Opera players. At some temples, the boat people carry their on-board shrines to shore to be

Tin Hua Fisherman's Festival: Young girls in traditional dress bring offerings to the mother-goddess of the sea. (Jeffrey Aaronson/Network Aspen)

blessed by priests; at others, the image of the goddess is paraded through the streets.

DATE: May (the 23rd day after the third moon). **LOCATION:** Tai Miu Temple (Joss House Bay) has the biggest celebration, but Yuen Long in the New Territories also puts on a great show. Other large Tin Hau temples are at Stanley (Hong Kong Island), and Sok Kwu Wan (Lamma Island). **TRANSPORT:** No roads go to Tai Miu, but special ferries run during the festival. **ACCOMMODATION:** See above entries. **CONTACT:** Hong Kong Tourist Assn. (see *Resources*).

© While you're there ...

© **The Clear and Bright Festival (Ching Ming), throughout Hong Kong:** The Chinese spend a festive day in the cemeteries picnicking, communing with ancestors, and caring for graves (sometimes they even scrub the bones!). Incense and money are burned, and food and wine are offered. (April; 106 days after the winter solstice.)

© **The Buddha's Birthday, Lantau Island:** Although celebrated sedately, the rituals associated with the Buddha's birth, death, and enlightenment are quite interesting in Hong Kong. Buddha images are ceremoniously bathed with scented water, and the water is then drunk by participants. Po Lin and other monasteries on Lantau Island are active, as are the temples at Shatin and Lam Tei in the New Territories. (Late May; the eighth day of the fourth moon.)

© **Dragon Boat Festival, various locations:** Like the dragon boat festivals of mainland China, Taiwan, and Singapore, the Hong Kong event commemorates the death of the poet and statesman Qu Luan, who threw himself into the river in protest of a corrupt government. Local races, in boats with bows and sterns carved in the shapes of dragon heads and tails, are held at Aberdeen, Stanley, Yaumati, and Tai Po, and on Cheung Chau and Lantau islands. The international competion is held the following week. (June; fifth day of the fifth moon.)

© **Festival of the Hungry Ghosts, throughout Hong Kong:** This Chinese equivalent of All Soul's Day commemorates the lunar month when ghosts are released from purgatory to roam the earth. To forestall spirit-mischief, paper models of cars, houses, and food are burned so the ghosts can take them back to the underworld. Colorful scenes break out on the streets and sidewalks. (Late August; the 15th day of the seventh moon.)

© **Mid-Autumn (Moon Cake) Festival, throughout Hong Kong:** The Chinese have spent millennia worshiping the moon, but during this festival the moon is only admired. Also commemorated is a 14th-century uprising against the Mongols, which was announced by plans hidden in moon cakes. Today, the cakes (*yuek beng*) are still eaten, and in Hong Kong, they are probably the best and most diverse in the Chinese world. Fillings range from coconuts, dates, and sesame, to egg and lotus seeds. A huge display of traditional lanterns lights up Victoria Park, and everyone heads for the hills to watch the moon rise and eat the cakes. (September; the 15th day of the eighth moon.)

© Resources

In Hong Kong: Hong Kong Tourist Association, 11th Floor, Citicorp Centre, 18 Whitfield Road, North Point, Hong Kong, Tel 852-807-6543, Fax 852-806-0303. **USA:** Hong Kong Tourist Association, 590 Fifth Avenue, New York, NY 10036-4706, Tel (212) 869-5008, Fax (212) 730-2605; or, 10940 Wilshire Blvd., Suite 1220, Los Angeles, CA 90024, Tel (310) 208-4582, Fax (310) 208-2869. **Canada:** Hong Kong Tourist Association, 347 Bay Street, Suite 909, Toronto, ON M5H 2R7, Tel (416) 366-2389, Fax (416) 366-1098. **UK:** Hong Kong Tourist Association, 125 Pall Mall, 5th Floor, London SW1Y 5EA, Tel 71-9304775, Fax 71-9304777. **Australia:** Hong Kong Tourist Association, Level 5, Harrington St., The Rocks, Sydney, NSW 2000, Tel 02-251-2855, Fax 02-247-8812. **Germany:** Hong Kong Tourist Association, Humboldtstr. 94, D-60318 Frankfurt, Tel 069-95-91-29–0, Fax 069-59-78-05–0.

JAPAN

Visitors who are afraid that there's nothing traditional left in Japan need only venture beyond the outskirts of Tokyo or Kyoto. Here, modernity is known, but it hasn't made much of an impact on the farmers and others who live among the ancient shrines and castles that dot the countryside. These people look to religion as a practical extension of daily life and turn to it whenever necessary, performing simple rituals designed to beseech the kami *spirits for fertility and abundant crops. You'll see these activities, and the beautiful portable shrines called* mikoshi, *at the local festivals that take place throughout the countryside.*

Tradition and progress are not seen as opposing forces in Japan, and city people often take time out from their focus on the 21st century to reconsider their ancestors' traditions at the many picturesque and joyful festivals. The festivals are scheduled according to the Gregorian calendar (which makes planning easier for Westerners), but time-honored traditions serve to strengthen the sense of a distinctly Japanese community. Perhaps ironically, the Japanese are most gregarious and open toward outsiders when they are in festival mode, dusting off the old rituals and embracing them with a self-assured vitality that seems to surprise even the participants.

Snow Festival (Yuki Matsuri)

Sapporo and throughout Hokkaidō **February**

One of Japan's friendliest cities celebrates the winter with a mass display of ice sculptures. This is Sapporo's main event of the year, and the featured scuptures and other entertainments are sensational. The action centers at Odōri Kōen Park and along Sapporo's main thoroughfare, where elaborate snow and ice figures are lined up. Some are intricate buildings several stories tall, and many feature sublime internal lighting.

The city's permanent architecture and other sights aren't very interesting, but the residents of Sapporo are a fun-loving

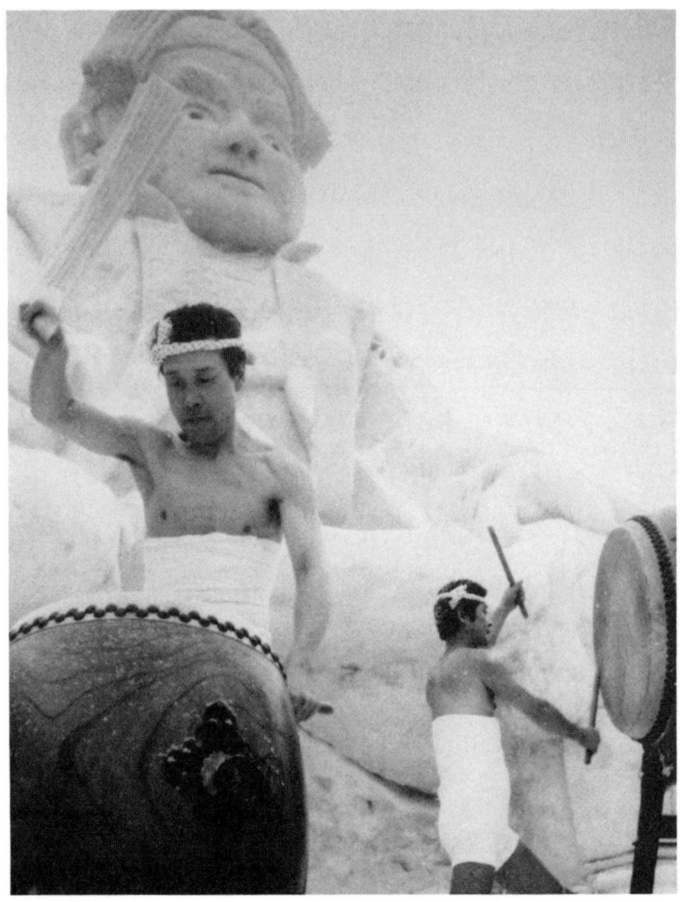

As the snow continues to fall, half-naked drummers pound away in front of an enormous snow sculpture. Elaborate ice sculptures line the streets of Sapporo, one of Japan's friendliest cities, during the annual Snow Festival. (Joe Viesti/Viesti Associates)

bunch that is very open and receptive to outsiders. In addition to checking out the best nightlife scene north of Tokyo, you can take a side trip to Japan's first brew-house, the Sapporo Brewery. Founded in 1878, the brewery offers free tours and reasonably priced food and drink, but reservations are required.

DATE: February 5–11 (or, if the 11th falls on a Saturday or Sunday, the festival moves to the 6th through 12th). **LOCATION:** Sapporo stages the most popular snow festivals, but similar festivals are held in districts throughout Hokkaidō Island, including Asahikawa, Mombetsu, Abashiri, and Obihiro. **TRANSPORT:** Sapporo

Setsubun: Priests toss packages of roasted beans, which will be used to cast devils from homes and encourage good luck. (David Ladd Nelson)

can be reached by air from Tokyo, or by a combination of train and ferry. **ACCOMMODATION:** Rooms at Sapporo's many hotels are tightly booked during the festival; reserve well in advance. **CONTACT:** Sapporo City Tourism Dept., City Office, Nishi-2chome, Kita-5jo, Chou-ku, Sapporo. Also, Japan National Tourist Organization (see *Resources*). Make reservations for the Sapporo Brewery tour (English guides available) by calling 11-73104368 a day or two in advance.

WHILE YOU'RE THERE ...

- **Toka Ebisu, Osaka:** A gathering of thousands witness a parade of colorfully kimonoed women who move through the street in a session of prayer for a year of successful business ventures. (January 9–11.)
- **Grass Burning Ceremony on Wakakusayama Hill, Nara Prefecture:** In a scene reminiscent of the traditional burning of the hill, nighttime fireworks set the slope aglow. Centuries ago the first fires marked the end of a land dispute by two temples in Nara. (January 15.)
- **Niramekko Obisha, Komagata-jinja Shrine, Ichikawa-shi, Chiba:** This festival involves two competitors who drink *sake* while conducting a staring contest. The one to keep from laughing is the winner. (January 20.)
- **Yah-Yah Matsuri Festival, Owase:** This "quarreling festival" vents frustrations with fiery yelps of "Yah! Yah!" (February 1–5.)
- **Lantern Festival of Kasuga Taisha Shrine, Nara:** More than 3,000 ancient bronze and stone lanterns are lit, and a *bugaku* dance is held in the Apple Garden. (February 2–4.)

Setsubun (Bean Throwing), major temples nationwide: The vast crowd gathers with wild chants of *"Fuku wa uchi, oni wa soto,"* which translates into "In with good luck, out with the devils." The ritual bean throwing, *mame-maki,* is done by the most respected citizens, such as priests, actors, and *sumo* wrestlers, who aim directly at the congregation. Once the devils have successfully been warded off, some people go home to eat the number of beans that corresponds with their age as a measure to ensure good luck. (February 3.)

Eyo Festival of Saidaiji Temple, Saidaiji, Okayama Prefecture: Partially dressed young men vie for a pair of sacred wands released into the darkness surrounding the temple. (Third Saturday in February.)

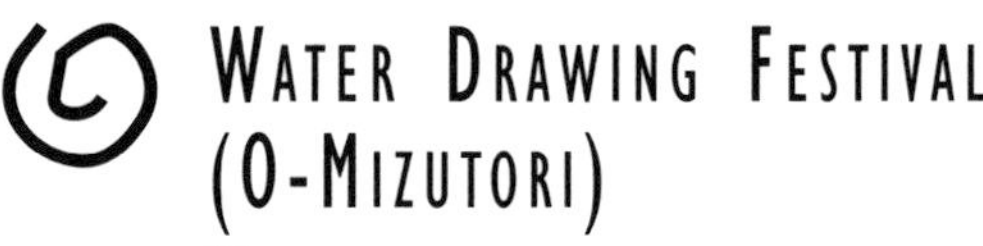

Water Drawing Festival (O-Mizutori)

Nara **March**

Shrouded in mystique and lore, the traditional drawing of the water has, since the eighth century, served to bless the crops and help humans fight the onslaught of aging. Even today, many Japanese believe that a few sprinkles of the heavenly liquid of youth can endow humans with something of the eternity that's normally the prerogative of the gods.

This beautiful nighttime ritual takes place at the monastery of Tôdaiji, on the balcony of a vast hilltop structure called the Pavilion of the Second Moon. Twelve monks converge, guided by huge torches, to honor Kannon, the *bodhisattva* of infinite compassion and mercy. For 15 nights they return, marching around the balcony while chanting hymns and raining embers down on pilgrims who collect them as talismans. Behind the marching monks, through a transparent veil of linen, the oversized shadows of praying monks are visible.

A Tôdaiji monk named Jitchû is said to be the first to have drawn water in the year 752. When he reached the Buddhist paradise occupied by Kannon and the other *bodhisattvas,* he witnessed the ceremonies of the gods and wanted to replicate them for humans. But since the life of man proved vastly too short to accommodate the celestial ceremony (a day and a night there correspond to 400 human years), the ceremony had to be shortened considerably. Thus, the monks gradually speed up the ceremony on some nights, and their circumambulations become a strange, frantic race around the altar until the climax, when the veil of linen is lifted to reveal the spendor of the praying monks' rituals within. At this point, a lone monk sprints to an adjoining room where he flings himself toward the spring-loaded "plank of prostration," and strikes it with his knee. The other monks follow, one by one.

On some nights, the gods themselves come to visit and dance, disguised as monks who skip around showering the prayer room with lustral water, embers, and grains of rice. They leap to the noisy rhythms made by rattles, conch shells, and bells, brandishing sabres and willow rods to drive away offending spirits.

As the dance continues, pilgrims line up to receive sprinklings of water drawn from a nearby holy spring by the "master of esoteric rites." Only the master and a hermit layman actually go to the spring, at 2 a.m. (although following at some distance are the monks and an orchestra playing ancient music). The source of the water is said to be a gift from the god who owned the river Onyû; it was given to compensate for being late for the ceremony.

DATE: The first two weeks of March. **LOCATION:** Monastery of Tôdaiji at Nara. **TRANSPORT:** Osaka Itami is the nearest airport; rail connects Nara to Osaka and Kyoto. **ACCOMMODATION:** Hostels, pensions, hotels, and other options are packed at festival time, but the Nara City Tourist Center keeps lists of accommodation options. **CONTACT:** Nara City Tourist Center, 23–4 Kami-Sanjo-cho, Nara City, Japan, Tel 742-223900. Also, Japan National Tourist Organization (see *Resources*).

While you're there ...

- **Tagata-jinja Honen Matsuri, Tagata-jinja Shrine, Komaki-shi, Aichi:** Large wooden phalluses are toted about town in acknowledgement of the treasure of life and procreation. (March 15.)
- **Gōhan Shiki, Nikkō:** These days, samurai lords have been replaced by ordinary pig-men, who are forced to eat huge quantities of rice as a tribute to the gods of the rice harvest. Priests perform sacred dances. (April.)
- **Cherry Blossom Festival, nationwide:** Geishas perform the Cherry Dance at sight of the cherry blossoms, which occur at different times throughout Japan. Interesting performances take place in Tokyo, Osaka, Arashiyama, and Kiyomizudera in Kyoto, and in Yoshino near Nara. (April.)

Tōshō-gō Shrine Festival

Nikkō **May**

The spirit of a time long past is captured in this celebration, which features thousands of people parading through the streets masquerading as Tokugawa warriors, sacred lions, monkeys, and more. Joined by horseback archers and Buddhist priests who perform sacred dances, participants render a truly epic reenactment of the delivery of the body of Tokugawa Ieyasu, who founded the Tōshōgō Shogunate. This is one of Japan's most spectacular events, and it takes place at one of the country's most spectacular structures.

Multiple-Choice Religion

What religion do the Japanese practice? If you answered materialism, you're a cynic—and only half right. For although the Japanese are notorious consumers, most turn to religion often in their everyday lives. And most have no qualms about double-dipping into the ideological pools of two religions: Shintoism and Buddhism.

With typical practicality, the Japanese turn to whichever religion covers the spiritual area in question at any given time. Matters of life here and now are covered by Shintoism. Matters of the afterlife are governed by Buddhism. That means that marriages in Japan are typically Shinto rituals, while funerals are Buddhist. To further confuse things, Japan's ethical and social order is heavily influenced by Confucianism.

The Tōshōgō Shrine itself is an ancient multimedia experience. More than 15,000 artisans were recruited to create an ornate, complicated array of images, including dancers, mythical beasts, and a dragon that roars when you clap your hands under it. And if you've been looking all over the world for the origin of the famous "hear no evil, see no evil, speak no evil" threesome of monkeys, look no further—it's on the wall of the shrine's Sacred Stable. Nearby are misty, cedared mountainsides and the beautiful Kegon Waterfall, which has the distinction of being Japan's favorite suicide spot.

DATE: May 17–18. **LOCATION:** Nikkō. **TRANSPORT:** The best route from Tokyo is via the Tobu Nikkō train line from Asakusa station. Express trains take nearly two hours; JR trains require a train switch midway. **ACCOMMODATION:** As one of Japan's prime tourist attractions, Nikkō has a wide variety of lodging in nearly all price ranges (book in advance at festival time). **CONTACT:** Japan National Tourist Organization (see *Resources*).

While you're there ...

- **Hakata Dontaku, Fukuoka, Fukuoka Prefecture:** Flutes and drums accompany participants posing as gods and riding horses through the streets. (May 3–4.)
- **Cormorant Fishing (Ukai), Nagara River, Gifu Prefecture:** Night fishers use trained, playful cormorant birds to catch river trout, which is a great

Every corner is an epic, as a legion struggles to turn one of nine huge hoko *floats in Kyoto's Gion Matsuri Yamaboko parade. The parade is part of a massive three-week pageant originally organized to thank the gods for ending a plague that had ravaged the city.* (Orion Press/Pacific Stock)

delicacy in Japan. Seats on riverboats can be reserved for cheering the fishermen, sipping sake, and eating grilled trout. (May 11–October 15.)

© **Hollyhock Festival (Aoi Matsuri), Kyoto:** One of the most spectacular of Kyoto's festivals, Aoi includes an ornate royal procession of messengers, courtiers, standard bearers, and guards in authentic costumes. (May 15.)

© **Chagu-Chage Umakko, Morioka, Iwate Prefecture:** This festival, named for the sound of harness bells, features festooned horses ridden by children and paraded to Sozen Shrine, where their owners pray for the horses' long lives. (June 15.)

© **Tsuburosashi, Sugawara-jinja Shrine, Hamochi-machi, Niigata:** A *kagura* sacred dance is performed by a woman playing a musical instrument and a man holding a wooden phallus. The idea is to charm a good harvest out of the gods. (June 15.)

© Gion Matsuri Yamaboko

Kyoto **July**

This very unusual parade dates back to the ninth century, when it was organized by the priest at Kyoto's Yasaka Shrine as a means to ask the gods to end a plague that had laid the city low. Now it is one of the the world's great urban festivals, a long parade in which huge two-story "houses" called *hoko* are hauled through the streets on massive wheels by teams of 20 men.

The *hoko* are magnificent works of craftsmanship that remind the huge crowds of Japan's long and unbroken history and culture. Representing regions of the country and other themes, some have dancers and entire orchestras mounted on top, playing a flute and drum music unique to the festival. Each *hoko* takes about four hours to complete the circuitous route through the city, and since the turns are particularly spectacular, try to position yourself at a corner. The wheels of these juggernauts are fixed, necessitating a bizarre turning operation in which small changes in course are effected by fearless attendants who push blocks under the leading wheels while they move. Major turns call for more extreme and time-consuming efforts, negotiated by teams who pull sideways after the front wheels have been bound by ropes and jammed with bamboo.

The *hoko* are alternated with smaller *yama,* which are carried on the shoulders of men or on small wheels. These depict scenes from Japanese and Chinese history and mythology, and in the weeks before the great parade the *hoko* and *yama* are displayed in neighborhoods. During the final few days before the parade, bright paper lanterns light up the city. Many residents of Kyoto allow visitors into their old houses, displaying kimonos, antiques, screens, and other family treasures in an art and antique lover's dream come true.

DATE: The Gion Matsuri festival covers at least three weeks before the *yamaboko* (parade), which falls on July 17. **LOCATION:** Kyoto's main streets. **TRANSPORT:** Kyoto is connected by air from Tokyo and points abroad, but high-speed trains are your best bet if coming from Tokyo. **ACCOMMODATION:** Accommodations during the festival are extremely tight; book well in advance. **CONTACT:** Kyoto Cultural Affairs and Tourism Bureau, Kyoto Kaikan, 13 Osazaki Saishoji, Sakyo-ku, Kyoto 606. Also, Japan National Tourist Organization (see *Resources*).

O Bon Festival

Nationwide **July/August**

The magic of the spirits descends on Japan during these few days when lanterns and dances tempt departed ancestors back to earth. This ancient Buddhist festival is a great time to be anywhere in the country. On rivers and bays lighted paper lanterns are floated to symbolize the return of departed ones to the netherworld. Everywhere there are rites and ceremonies, many using fire to purify surroundings and commemorate departed souls. Nearly every temple in Japan has a candle-lighting ceremony.

The timing of events changes from place to place, but the Japan National Tourist Organization has up-to-date information on event schedules and locations. In Tokyo, exceptional Bon Odori folk dances are held at Yasakuni Shrine. In Kyoto, the Rokukaramitsu Temple is beautifully illuminated and paper lanterns are sent down the river near Arashiyama. An enormous bonfire is lit on the slopes of Mt. Nyogatake, in the form of the Chinese character *dai* (large). At Nachi Shrine in Katsura (Wakayama Prefecture), priests in white robes light 12 huge torches. Other exceptional festivals are held at Tobata and Kita-Kyushu City in Fukuoka Prefecture.

DATE: The traditional O Bon Festival is is held July 13–16, but these days many towns wait until vacation season in mid-August to hold the festivities. **LOCATION:** Nationwide. **CONTACT:** Japan National Tourist Organization (see *Resources*).

While you're there ...

- **Summer Festival of Warei Shrine, Uwajima City (Ehime Prefecture):** Bullfights, fireworks, and a dramatic river crossing are the high points of this festival. (July 23–25.)
- **Wild Horse Festival (Soma Namaoi), Haranomachi (Fukushima Prefecture)** History comes alive as a thousand riders clad in ancient garb shoot across the playing field on horseback, struggling to possess three shrine flags. On the second day the "warriors" drive wild horses toward men in white suits who attempt to catch the animals. (July 23–25.)
- **Tenjin Matsuri of Temmangu Shrine, Osaka:** Sacred boats drift down the river chaparoned by other boats carrying historically significant images. Land events and sky events (fireworks) follow. (July 24–25.)
- **Peace Ceremony, Hiroshima Peace Memorial Park:** Thousands of glowing lanterns are carried off with the Ota River water in memory of atomic bomb victims and in hopes of world harmony. (August 6.)
- **Awa Odori, Tokushima, Tokushima Prefecture:** This participative event includes 10,000 people, both Japanese and foreigners, precision-dancing through the streets with simple straw hats decorated with paper flowers. Accompanied by musicians, the kooky parade is heaps of big-time fun! (August 12–15.)
- **Nakizumo, Ikiko-jinja Shrine, Kanuma shi, Tochigi:** Sumo wrestlers hold babies and await the first cry. The wrestler holding the infant who wails first is victorious. (September 19.)

Nebuta Matsuri

Aomori and Hirosaki **August**

The festivals of remote Tohoku are some of the most spectacular in the country, serving to highlight the simplicity and unpreten-

Nebuta Matsuri: In remote Aomori, processions of huge papier-mâché images provoke a rare sight in Japan—spontaneous dancing the streets. (David Ladd Nelson)

tious beauty of villages where the heart of old Japan still beats. During the Nebuta Matsuri, the ancient, mystical face of Japan shows up on the *nebutas*, or huge papier-mâché images of warriors and animals that are carried through the streets.

The origin of these figures is an eighth-century battle in which a warlord tricked local rebels by using *nebutas* to make his forces look larger. These days the pageants serve to beseech the spirits for a bountiful harvest. At night, the image of hundreds of beautifully painted *nebutas* lit by candles from within is priceless. Each evening the procession takes a different route through town, the eerily bobbing *nebutas* accompanied by drummers and flautists.

The festival in Hirosaki is more subdued than Aomori's, but both are absolutely stunning, and both draw large crowds from the big cities. Tohoku, as northern Honshu is often called, is one of the main island's most interesting areas, combining the shrines, temples, and culture of classical Japan with the natural beauty of rugged mountains and forests, and—according to both ancient and modern legend—the most beautiful women in Japan.

DATE: Aomori, August 2–7; Hirosaki, August 1–7. **LOCATION:** Aomori and Hirosaki, in Aomori Prefecture, Tohoku (northern Honshu). **TRANSPORT:** Aomori can be reached by air from Tokyo, Osaka, and Sapporo, and by train from Tokyo, Morioka, and Hokkaidō. Hirosaki can be reached by train from Aomori. **ACCOMMODATION:** Hotels and hostels are plentiful most of the year, but fill up fast during festival time. **CONTACT:** Japan National Tourist Organization (see *Resources*).

Star Festival (Tanabata Matsuri)

Sendai and nationwide **August**

Forbidden love is the theme of this precious festival, which brings lovers together under the stars. Young people are permitted to spend the evening together unchaperoned, and the Japanese are encouraged, for this one night, to speak their hearts' feelings.

Tanabata's origins lie in the consumation of an ancient forbidden love between a princess and a peasant boy. They met under a similar rendezvous between the celestial lovers Vega and Altair. Throughout the country (and especially in the north), people write love poems on banners and hang them out for display, and children copy poems onto colorful streamers.

The town of Sendai goes all out for this festival. Doorways, trees, and everything else are decorated with vibrant bamboo branches, and large, colorful balls called *tanabata* are hung to frighten evil spirits. Everywhere, bright paper streamers cascade throughout the streets, blowing in the breeze and decorating the many parades and fireworks exhibitions.

DATE: August 6–8. **LOCATION:** Sendai, Miyagi Prefecture, Tohoku (northern Honshu). **TRANSPORT:** Sendai's airport connects with Sapporo, Osaka, Komatsu, and Okinawa. The high-speed railway connects with Tokyo (two hours), Fukushima, and Morioka. **ACCOMMODATION:** Hostels and inns are booked solid during this festival, so you may want to treat it as a day-trip from Tokyo or elsewhere. **CONTACT:** Sendai Tourist Information Office, Sendai Station, 1–1 Chou, Aoba-ku, Sendai City, Japan. Also, Japan National Tourist Organization (see *Resources*).

Festival of the Ages (Jidai Matsuri)

Kyoto **October**

This epic fashion show celebrates the founding of the ancient capital of Kyoto in the year 794. More than 2,000 people dress in costumes of the historical epochs of the city, and parade from the Imperial Palace to the Heian Shrine. The procession is almost two kilometers (1.4 miles) long and features costumes ranging from the eighth through the 19th centuries, including a beautiful collection of antique kimonos.

If you tire of the festivities in Kyoto (or if you just want to pack another great festival into one day), hop on quick train and head to Kurama Village for the Great Fire Festival (*Kurama-no-Himmatsuri*). Starting at around sunset, the village's narrow streets are lined with blazing torches that were once thought to guide the gods on visits to earth. Young men carry flaming torches and portable shrines through the streets, and at 10 p.m. a priest cuts a ribbon, sending crowds stampeding into the temple.

DATE: October 22, beginning at noon. **LOCATION:** Kyoto and Kurama Village. **TRANSPORT:** Kyoto is connected by air from Tokyo and points abroad, but high-speed trains are your best bet if coming from Tokyo. Kurama Village can be reached via a 30-minute train from Kyoto's Eki Station. **CONTACT:** Kyoto Cultural Affairs and Tourism Bureau, Kyoto Kaikan, 13 Osazaki Saishoji, Sakyo-ku, Kyoto 606. Also, Japan National Tourist Organization (see *Resources*).

While you're there ...

- **Marimo Matsuri, Lake Akan, Hokkaidō:** The Ainu are the only non-Oriental race of Japanese natives, and their traditional dances and ceremonies are wildly different from those of the rest of Japan. This unusual event includes a traditional lakeshore dance, and ceremonial tossing of the *marimo* (a green weed) into the lake on the 10th. (October 8–10.)
- **Rooster Fair (Tori-no-ichi), Tokyo:** At shrines throughout the city (especially Otori Shrine at Asakusa), good-luck bamboo rakes are decorated and sold with much fanfare. Each time a purchase is made a rousing hand-clapping ceremony sends the buyer off to hang the rake in shop or home. (November; held on "Cock Days" according to the Zodiacal calendar.)
- **Chichibu Yo-matsuri, Chichibu City, Saitama Prefecture:** This affair is one of the grandest float festivals in Japan, and features six immense floats glorified with shining lanterns. The third day is filled with a *Kabuki* play, a grand parade, and an evening fireworks display. (December 2–3.)

Resources

Japan National Tourist Organization provides an up-to-date booklet entitled *Annual Events in Japan*. **In Japan**: Japan National Tourist Organization, 2-10-1, Yurakucho, Chiyoda-ku, Tokyo 100, Tel 3-3216-1902, Fax 3-3214-7680. **USA**: Japan National Tourist Organization, 630 Fifth Ave., New York, NY 10111, Tel (212) 757-5640, Fax (212) 307-6754; JNTO, 401 N. Michigan Ave., #770, Chicago, IL 60611, Tel (312) 222-0874, Fax (312) 222-0876. **UK**: Japan National Tourist Organization, 167 Regent Street, London W1R 7FD, Tel 71-7349638, Fax 71-7344290. **Australia**: Japan National Tourist Organization, Level 33, Chifley Tower, 2 Chifley Sq., Sydney, N.S.W. 2000, Tel 2-2324522, Fax 2-2321494. **Germany**: Japan National Tourist Organization, Kaiserstr. 11, 60311 Frankfurt 1, Tel 69-20353, Fax 69-284281.

Korea was once known as the "hermit kingdom," but the treasures of this fascinating, enigmatic nation are slowly becoming known to the outside world. With its rich, mountainous countryside, low travel costs, and fun-loving people, South Korea is starting to attract visitors, although a Western face outside the capital is still a rarity.

KOREA

Korean culture, sometimes dismissed as a pale reflection of Japan or China, is actually completely distinct in terms of character and identity. The music, dance, and sports events that make up the city and country festivals reflect the Koreans' deep fascination and appreciation for their culture and history. For the visitor, the festivals offer a spellbinding education in a culture that spans five millenia, packaged in an unmistakeably Korean mix of spectacle, enthusiasm, and fun. In contrast with their Chinese and Japanese neighbors (who have spent most of the past 2,000 years trying to absorb Korea), the Koreans are spontaneous, gregarious, and extroverted. In fact, as you'll quickly realize walking down any street, Koreans hardly need the excuse of a festival to break into song and dance.

Tano Festival

Kangnung and nationwide **May/June**

As the event of the year in rural Korea, this festival welcomes the spring with wrestling matches, swinging contests, silent mask dancing, and shamanistic rituals. The fishing town of Kangnung holds the largest and most elaborate festivities, which go on for 20 days or more. Batches of *shinju* (divine liquor) are brewed, and female shamans are called upon for a variety of rituals designed to drive away evil spirits and encourage deities to bestow good crops, good health, and long life. Villagers believe that the fifth day of the fifth month is the day the celestial bodies gather overhead, creating positive cosmic forces and auspicious opportunities for prayer. Many shamans enter trances to establish communication between gods and people, reporting human wishes and relaying divine instructions.

Events of interest include *ssirum* wrestling, which resembles Japanese *sumo* and requires contestants to throw each other down using a limited repertoire of moves. In the *kwanno* mask drama, performers mime their messages, spinning wildly around the stage in oversized masks of wood or papier mâché, as a battal-

An epic parade is only one part of the Tano Festival in Kangnung; there's also wrestling, fireworks, dance dramas, floating lanterns, entranced shamans, and the divine liquor called shinju. *(Korea National Tourism Corp.)*

ion of drummers drives them on. On the final day the *taemaji kut* ritual is performed to make sure local guardian deities have watched and enjoyed the festivities.

All villages and cities in South Korea make a big deal out of this festival. Circuses spring up and special markets sell chestnuts, liquor, and clothes. In Seoul, the banks of the Han River are active with folk dances and shaman ceremonies.

DATE: Late May or early June (the festival culminates on the fifth day of the fifth month). **LOCATION:** Kangnung City (Kangwondo Province) on Korea's east coast, and nationwide. **ACCOMMODATION:** Kangnung, Kyogp'o (with a nice beach), and Yongch'on have a variety of tourist hotels. **TRANSPORT:** Air from Seoul to Sokch'o; bus from Seoul (3.5 hours) and Soraksan (2 hours). **CONTACT:** Kangnung Institute of Culture, Tel 0391-648-3014. Also, Korea National Tourist Corporation (see *Resources*).

P'UNGNAM FESTIVAL

Chonju **May/June**

Perhaps unique among East Asians, Koreans break into songs and dances spontaneously, whenever and wherever the urge overtakes them. The P'ungnam Festival's mass dance carnival is a chance to experience this trait in its extreme form, in the town where the *P'ansori* (traditional narrative song) was invented.

Korean Spirit-Toasting

The two cardinal rules of Korean drinking are "never drink alone," and "always drink until drunk." There's no social stigma attached to public inebriation, and moderation is actually discouraged in the many Korean social and business drinking customs.

If you're drinking with Koreans, remember never to pour your own glass—unless you want to be considered arrogant and greedy. Instead, wait until a cup is offered to you (it will be—often), then hold it with both hands while your companions fill it to the brim. After drinking it, return the cup with both hands to the person who offered it to you, then grab the bottle with both hands and fill his or her cup. Get a new bottle if there's less than half a glass left, since half a pour indicates that the recipient will have daughters—and sons are very important in Korea. If you're in a group, remember that a person who's given up his or her cup can't drink until the recipient has returned it, or until someone else has offered a cup. Thus, whoever has received a cup is obligated to chug it down without delay and pass it on. The big challenge is to get your hosts to stop pouring you drinks when you've had enough; this can be accomplished (usually) by leaving your cup full.

Drinking has been an important part of religion and culture since the early Korean dynasties, and today it continues to have a big role in many rituals. Korean wedding custom dictates that if the alcohol runs out, the guests may hang the groom upside down and beat him. Funerals are seen as a time to raid the deceased's liquor cabinet. To help the family forget their grief, friends and relatives visit the home of someone who has just died to drink, sing, and gamble until dawn.

Starting at Chonju Station, a huge lantern parade through the city is led by a farmers' dance band. The mass dancing takes place at the Soch'ongyo Bridge, hung for the occasion with hundreds of homemade lanterns. (If you climb as many stairs as your age on this bridge, it's believed that you will enjoy a long life without sickness.)

The P'ungnam Festival is also a good chance to see a wide variety of Korean folk arts, dances, and sports. *Chonju Taesasup Nori* is a series of competitions in nine categories of folk arts and games, including *P'ansori* (dramatic vocal performances), *Nongak* (folk songs), and *Kayagum Pyongch'ang* (played on 12-stringed zither with vocal accompaniment). Sporting events include archery and a national *ssirum* wrestling championship. Chonju is

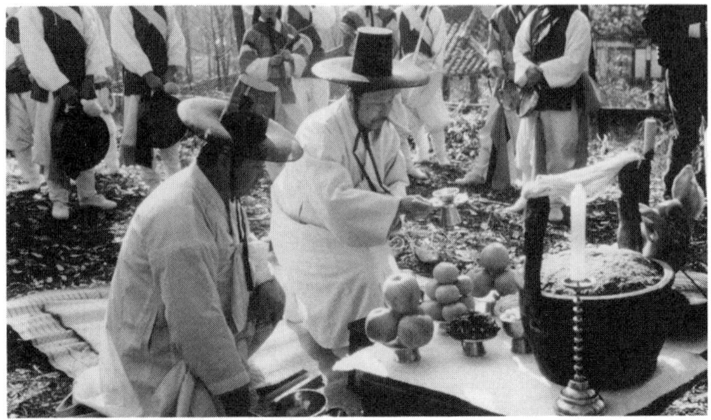

Tongshin-je: Intimate, elaborate fertility rituals welcome the Lunar New Year in rural Korea. (*Korea National Tourism Corp.*)

also one of the few places where traditional Korean handmade paper is still made.

DATE: Late May or early June (the festival culminates on the fifth day of the fifth month). **LOCATION:** Chonju City, Chollabuk-do Province, 93 km/56 miles south of Seoul. **TRANSPORT:** Bus or train (three hours) from Seoul. **ACCOMMODATION:** As a provincial capital, Chonju has a variety of lodging available. **CONTACT:** P'ungnam Festival Organizing Committee, Tel 0652-85-5151. Also, Korea National Tourist Corporation (see *Resources*).

WHILE YOU'RE THERE ...

- **Tongshin-je, rural villages:** For those willing to travel to the Korean countryside, this festival features shaman fertility rites and Lunar New Year celebrations. (February; 15th day of first lunar month.)
- **Farmer's Day:** Celebrate with folk dancing and music on this day at rural farmers' festivals nationwide. (June 15.)

SHILLA CULTURAL FESTIVAL

Kyongju **October**

One of Korea's most exuberant festivals provides a glimpse into the Buddhist culture and Hwarang spirit that flourished during the Shilla period of the first century A.D. The ancient capital of the Shilla kingdom is bedecked with flags and lanterns for three days of music, dance, sports, and parades.

The gods want to play!

If you hear a cacaphony of drums, cymbals, and shouting resounding from a side street in a Korean town, follow it to its source. You'll probably encounter a *mudang,* recognizable by her flowing robes of hemp and cock-feather head dress. She'll be leading a *kut,* or all-night exorcism ceremony, and since *kuts* are more effective when there are more people, she'll probably invite you inside to participate.

The *mudang,* or shaman, is part witch doctor, part priestess, and part folk therapist, and even Koreans who deny that shamanism exists in modern Korea will call on a *mudang* if a household situation turns desperate. To repair the family's relationship with the gods, the *mudang* may announce that "the gods want to play," in which case a *kut* will be scheduled.

The entire family, plus friends and neighbors, will be asked to attend, since it takes a lot of noise to successfully urge angry gods and ancestors to feast and thereby vent their malevolence. When they do come down, the *mudang* becomes a medium, and the women of the household will talk back. Sometimes unruly ancestors make an appearance through the *mudang,* talking rudely, spasming and jerking crazily, or gorging themselves on food and wine. When it's over in the morning, everyone joins in a loud song and dance as the *mudang* and her assistants beat drums outside the house to cast lingering ghosts away.

The week of *Tano* (late May or early June) is an opportune time to come across a *kut.* In Seoul, the Kuksadang shrine (above Sajik Park) is often rented by *mudangs* for clients who can't hold the ritual in their own home.

The *Kil-nori,* or opening parade, is a highlight of the festival, and exceptional in that spectators become participants in a historic drama, joining with masked personalities from Shilla history to dance and sing in the streets. The costumes and floats are excellent, and include a golden dragon-snake more than 40 meters (130 feet) long. The festivities include Buddhist dances, farmers' folk music contests, and *ch'ajon'nori,* or "war of the dragons." In this epic sporting spectacle warriors try to throw each other to the ground while mounted on large wooden structures supported by dozens of men.

DATE: The first or second weekend in October. **LOCATION:** Kyongju City, Kyongsangbuk-do Province. **TRANSPORT:** Train or bus (about 4.5 hours) from Seoul; air to Taegu (one hour away from Kyongju).

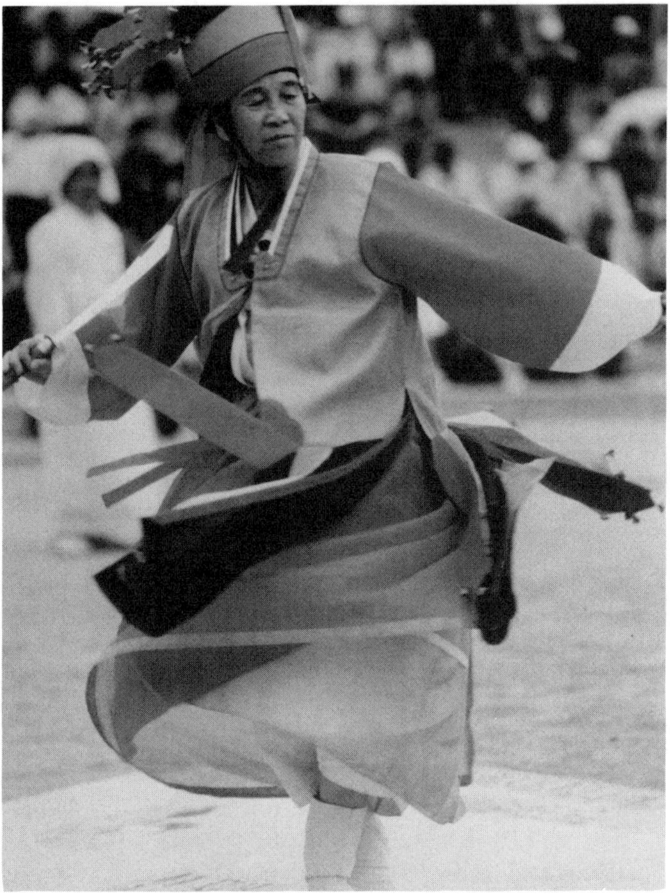

Shaman priestess: A mudang *in flowing robes performs a ritual. (Korea National Tourism Corp.)*

ACCOMMODATION: Kyongju has many hotels ranging from super-deluxe to budget, but book well in advance. **CONTACT:** Kyongju City Hall, Tel 0561-748-9037. Also, Korea National Tourist Corporation (see *Resources*).

While you're there ...

Andong Folk Festival, Confucian Academy, Andong: Similar to Shilla's spectacle, hordes of huge men carry battling warriors on frames in the *ch'ajon'nori*, or "war of the dragons." (September 28.)

Korean drummer/dancers fire up the spirits at the Andong Folk Festival. *(Joe Viesti/Viesti Associates)*

Paekche Cultural Festival, Kongju and Puyo (alternates): One of Korea's three main cultural festivals, the Paekche Festival celebrates the royalty and heroes of the influential Paekche culture. (October 13.)

Halla Cultural Festival, Cheju: The island rings loudly with bells and whistles to kick off this festival, which includes art exhibitions and folk music. (October 18–20.)

Kaechon (National Foundation) Arts Festival, Chinju, Kyongsang-nam-do Province: This festival features exciting sword-dancing with drums, and a variety of exhibitions. Artists compete in calligraphy, painting, and drama events. (November; third day of 10th lunar month.)

Resources

In Korea: Korea National Tourism Corporation, 10, Ta-dong, Chung-gu, P.O. Box 903, Seoul 100, Tel 2-7299600, Fax 2-7575997. **USA:** Korea National Tourism Corporation, Two Executive Drive, 7th Floor, Fort Lee, NJ 07024, Tel (201) 585-0909, Fax (212) 585-9041. 3435 Wilshire Blvd., Suite 350, Los Angeles, CA 90010, Tel (213) 382-3435, Fax (213) 480-0483. 205 N. Michigan Ave, Suite 2212, Chicago, IL 60601, Tel (312) 819-2560, Fax (312) 819-2563. **Canada:** Korea National Tourism Corporation, 480 University Ave, Suite 406, Toronto, ON M5G 1V2, Tel (416) 348-9056, Fax (416) 348-9058. **UK:** Korea National Tourism Corporation, 20 St. George St., London W1R 9RE, Tel 71-4092100, Fax 71-4912302. **Germany:** Korea National Tourism Corporation, Mainzer Landstr. 71, D-60329 Frankfurt, Tel 69-233226, Fax 69-253519. **Australia:** Korea National Tourism Corporation, Tower Building, #1714, Australia Square, George St., Sydney, NSW 2000, Australia, Tel 2-2524147, Fax 2-2512104.

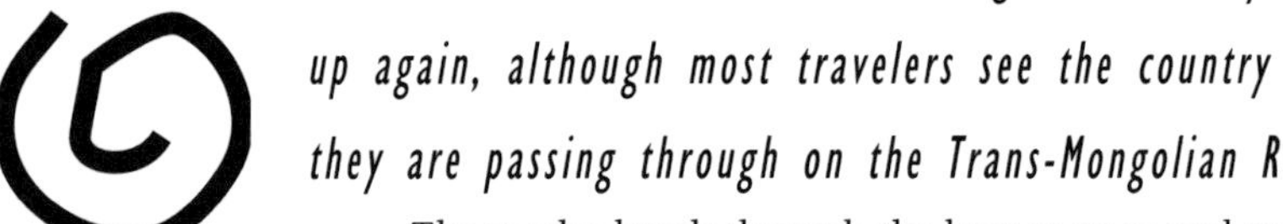

Few places on earth are more remote, traditional, and insanely difficult to travel than this isolated land of huge deserts, mountain lakes, and untouched forests holding some of the most abundant wildlife in Asia. Although Mongolia once had much contact with the West (mostly by invading it), the country has been almost completely isolated since the Marxist revolution of 1921. Now, Mongolia is slowly opening up again, although most travelers see the country only as they are passing through on the Trans-Mongolian Railway.

Those who break through the bureaucracy and manage to step off the train or plane during the summer will get to know Mongolia at its festive peak. The country's two major events can be supplemented with once-in-a-lifetime excursions into the Gobi Desert, the Hangai Mountains, and other harsh climates that have bred tough animals and people like Genghis Khan, Attila the Hun, and the still-wandering nomads of the Siberian steppes.

Ovoo Worship Festival

Nationwide **June**

This rural event honors Mongolia's many shamanistic shrines called *ovoos*, which were denounced by the communists but have made a recent comeback with the pro-democracy movement. At first glance, an *ovoo* appears to be a pile of debris with a flag on top. Stones, tin cans, and animal bones are piled around a cavity in which offerings of coins, milk, or vodka are placed to ensure prosperity and safety while traveling.

In June, villages and towns turn out to honor the *ovoos* with horse races, feasts, offerings, and prayers by Tibetan Buddhist monks. The festivals also serve to welcome the spring and provide an opportunity to pray for an abundant agricultural season. You'll see people splashing milk and vodka on the *ovoos* and, in the tradition of the shrines of Tibet, circumambulating the structures three times in a clockwise direction.

Horse racing is one of Mongolia's Three Manly Sports, yet the children's division is the big crowd-pleaser. (AP/Wide World Photos)

DATE: Weekends in June (dates vary by location). **LOCATION:** Nationwide (rural areas). **TRANSPORT:** Mongolia only has one truly international airport (in Ulaan Baatar), which handles direct flights from Beijing, Moscow, and Irkutsk. By train you can come from either Beijing or Moscow, although tickets are tight during the summer and the visa process is complicated. **CONTACT:** JUULCHIN/Mongolia National Tourist Organization or tour operators (see *Resources*).

NAADAM

Ulaan Baatar and nationwide **July**

Naadam is Mongolia's one and only big event, a summer fair featuring traditional sports, foods, and folk dancing accompanied by cymbals, horns, and drums. The festivities take place in nearly all provincial capitals, although the event is liveliest in the national capital, Ulaan Baatar. Some provinces schedule their fairs the week after Ulaan Baatar's so inhabitants can attend both.

As you might expect of a people who produced Attila the Hun and Genghis Khan, the festival is dominated by warrior-type activities, including the *Eryn Gurvan Nadom,* or Three Manly Sports: wrestling, archery, and horse racing. The wrestling is quite different from Western versions of the sport. Contestants wear tight briefs and a vest that covers the shoulders and upper arms, but leaves the chest bare. This unusual outfit is worn to make it clear that both contestants are indeed men, since centuries ago, a champion wrestler was discovered to be a woman (to the great

Big boys of Ulaan Baatar: Ever since a female imposter embarrassed the men centuries ago, Mongolian wrestlers have made manliness conspicuous with bare-breasted vests and tight briefs. (Nik Wheeler)

embarrassment of the men she had defeated). The wrestlers first swoop into the ring in imitation of the Garuda bird of Buddhist lore. When the referee signals the start, each tries to topple the other; the first to touch the ground with anything more than the soles of his feet loses. Then the loser must kneel while the winner makes a victory sign over his head.

Both women and men compete in the archery events, using short compound bows (which may have been invented by the Mongolians). Some events are stationary, while other events have the riders on moving horses, shooting at traditional leather targets. Mongolian horse racing is similar to a Western steeplechase, conducted over a cross-country course at least 20 km/12 miles long. There are races for all riders and both sexes, but the crowd-pleaser is the children's division. In rural Mongolia, most children begin to ride in infancy, and their almost instinctive skill in horsemanship is clearly apparent. The children's race features boys and girls ages 7–12, wearing colorful traditional costumes. Other horse races include blindfolded scrambles (by adults).

Mongolia's resurgent nationalism combines with cash prizes to inspire vigorous competition. Symbols of Genghis Khan are everywhere. Warriors kneel and kiss a braided horse tail dedicated to him, and a white Genghis figure rides around the stadium mounted on a horse. Accommodation at Naadam in rural areas is strictly bring-your-own, as families simply dismantle and bundle up their *gers* (circular dwellings made of canvas), then re-erect them outside the grounds.

DATE: July 11–13. **LOCATION:** Ulaan Baatar has the biggest festival, but Naadam is held in provincial capitals nationwide. **TRANSPORT:** See **Ovoo Worship Festival.** **ACCOMMODATION:** Ulaan Baatar offers several budget and "tourist class" hotels, but don't expect much for your money. **CONTACT:** JUULCHIN/Mongolia National Tourist Organization, or tour operators (see *Resources*).

While you're there ...

White Moon/Mongolian New Year (Tsagaan Sar), nationwide: A religious celebration coopted by the communists into a collective agriculture celebration, the White Moon's religious roots are now being resurrected. This winter festival features the "Three Manly Sports" of archery, wrestling, and horse racing. (January/February.)

Resources

Because of the difficulty of arranging paperwork for travel to Mongolia, many travelers enroll in an organized tour, then stay longer to travel independently. Several tour companies are listed here, in addition to the state tourist office.

In Mongolia: Mongolia National Tourist Organization, Avenue Khuvisgalchid 11, Ullan Bator 11, Tel 20163. **USA:** JUULCHIN, Mongolian Tourism Corporation, c/o Klingeburger Worldwide Travel, 3627 First Avenue South, Seattle, WA 98134, Tel (206) 343-9699, Fax (206) 632-8868. Embassy of Mongolia, 1020 Iron Gate Rd., Potomac, MD 20854, Tel (301) 983-1962, Fax (301) 983-2025. Blue Sea Travel Service Inc., 8929 Wilshire Boulevard, Suite 420, Beverly Hills, CA 90211-1953, Tel (310) 659-4438, (800) 441-8288, Fax (310) 659-4518. **Canada:** Canada-Mongolian Society, c/o Far Eastern Studies, University of Saskatchewan, Saskatoon, S7N OWO. **UK:** Regent Holidays Ltd., 15 John St., GB-Bristol BS1 2HR, Tel 272-211711, Fax 272-254866. **Germany:** Mongolia Tourist Information Service, Dudenstr. 78, D-1000 Berlin 61, Tel 30-7865056, Fax 30-7865596.

TAIWAN

Many pleasure travelers think Taiwan is all business, and pass up this island in favor of its higher-profile neighbors. Yet the images of Taiwan's factories, ports, and crowded cities are balanced by enduring natural and cultural wonders that prompted the Portuguese to name it Ihla Formosa, *or "beautiful island." Taiwan has great food and beaches, thick forests, and spectacular mountains. Its people are among the friendliest in Asia, and its culture blends Taoism, Buddhism, and Confucianism.*

Taiwanese culture reaches its colorful peak during ancient festivals that draw island inhabitants together to worship, dance, drink, and socialize. *Pai-pai* festivals, dedicated to popular "city gods," occur nearly every day in Taiwan; devotees indulge in parades, joss-sticks, and lavish feasts that are first offered to the gods before the humans are allowed to gorge themselves. All in all, Taiwanese festivals represent some of the best opportunities in East Asia to see and participate in ancient rituals, while being wholeheartedly accepted by modern locals.

Lunar New Year (Sang-Sin)

Nationwide **January/February**

The New Year is the biggest celebration of the year for the Chinese. Cities and villages are decked out in red and everyone's mood is festive. Unfortunately for visitors, most of the celebrations take place in the home, or at the homes of friends and family. On the 24th day of the previous month, the household gods are "seen off" with a series of sacrifices. Firecrackers are lit, paper money is burned, and banquets are prepared, since it's in the humans' best interest to ensure that the spirits are in a good mood when they go to heaven to report on the activities of the mortals to the Jade Emperor. On the last day of the old year, each family lays a banquet at their ancestral shrine, and the greater the abundance of food, the more rewards a family can expect in the coming year. Once the ancestors have had their fill (determined by the family matriarch), the food is re-warmed for the humans, and as it's eaten, only the most inspiring talk is allowed.

Lantern Festival: The dragon prepares to dance through the streets of Taipei, and bearers prepare to dodge the many firecrackers that will be thrown at their feet. (Dave Bartruff)

At midnight the entire country erupts in an orgy of fireworks, and people in temples and houses light fuses to frighten evil spirits from the threshold (the Chinese invented gunpowder 1,000 years ago for this purpose). After daybreak guests begin to arrive, bringing New Year's greetings and gifts of money for the children. Guests are offered sweets, then thank the hostess with the wish *Hō lí si hāu si*, or "May you give birth to a boy."

DATE: Late January or early February. **LOCATION:** Nationwide. **CONTACT:** Taiwan Visitors Assn. (see *Resources*).

Lantern Festival (Yúanxião Jié)

Nationwide **February**

The people of ancient China believed that celestial spirits could be seen flying around in the light of the year's first full moon. To help spot them (and thus avoid them), they made special torches, which evolved into an incredible array of elaborate lanterns of every size, shape, and color. Today, this three-day cultural blowout attracts millions of visitors and is Taiwan's largest mass gathering.

Events vary from town to town, but wherever you go, count on lots of fireworks, dances, processions, and lanterns shaped like swords, rabbits, snakes, monkeys, and even Chiang Kai-shek. Yenshui, Luerhmen, and Peikang are popular spots to catch the festivities, and in Hakka-dominated towns like Miao Li, dragon dances are performed in the streets. These consist of dragons made of cloth strung over bamboo poles, carried by eight to 10 men. The dragons dance around chasing a red pearl held by a member of the group, and bystanders hurl firecrackers under their feet to make them "dance."

In Taipei, the festival takes place in the square opposite the Chiang Kai-shek memorial. The entertainment is almost constant, with lion and dragon dances presented by children and adults, demonstrations of folk arts, mock bullfights, and ceremonial processions. The acrobatic performances are great, and include stilt dancing (some of the performers use only one stilt). On the final night a giant figure of the year's zodiac character (dog, rabbit, etc.) is illuminated with bright lights, and more than a million spectators parade around the square with colored lanterns.

DATE: February (15th day of the first moon). **LOCATION:** Nationwide, but particularly in Taipei, Miao Li, Yenshui, Luerhmen, and Peikang. **TRANSPORT:** Taiwan is easily reached by air from anywhere in the world, although a stop in Hong Kong is often necessary. **ACCOMMODATION:** Although Taiwan is well endowed with hotels for any budget, accommodation gets scarce around this festival. **CONTACT:** Taiwan Visitors Assn. (see *Resources*).

BIRTHDAY OF CHENG HUANG

Taipei **June**

As far back as the Hsia Dynasty (about 2200 B.C.), people went out of their way to worship local deities who were believed to have the power to protect and reward cities. Today, more than 100 very popular "city gods" are commemorated at colorful celebrations called *pai-pai*. Taipei's is the largest, of course, and at the City God Temple there's plenty to see and photograph.

The action starts with a lavish feast of food and wine, prepared for the city god. Once it's clear that he has had his fill, the people dig in. Wine flows freely as the city god's icon is mounted on a pedestal and paraded through the streets; many devotees show up dressed as dragons and lions and dance in the streets, past offerings of cooked pigs and cows stretched on bamboo poles. The entire city is jubilant (and most of it is at least half-drunk) as people take time off work to go out with friends.

DATE: June (check with the Taiwan Visitors Assn. for the current year's dates). **LOCATION:** City God Temple, No. 61 Ti Hua St., Sec. 1, Taipei. **TRANSPORT/ACCOMMODATION:** See above entries. **CONTACT:** Taiwan Visitors Assn. (see *Resources*).

WHILE YOU'RE THERE ...

Birthday of the Sea Goddess, shrines nationwide: Matsu, the patron goddess of fishermen, is worshiped with elaborate sacrificial rites, parades, puppet shows, and dragon dances at the more than 300 temples dedicated to her. Fairs are set up with watermelon stalls and sling-shot ranges, and devotees make sacrificial offerings of roast pigs and incense. (April/May; 23rd day of the third moon.)

Dragon Boat Races, Taipei and coastal villages: Taipei and other cities hold races of boats with bows carved in the shapes of dragons to commemorate the Chinese poet Qu Yuan (see **Dragon Boat Regatta**, China). In addition, sweet rice dumplings are made and mugwort plants are stuck on doorposts to terrify evil spirits. Children sport necklaces made with chunks of incense formed into the shapes of the "five harmful things" (wall-lizards, toads, centipedes, spiders, and snakes). (Late May or early June; the fifth day of the fifth moon.)

HUNGRY GHOST FESTIVAL

Nationwide **August/September**

On this day the gates of hell are opened, and souls suffering in purgatory are allowed to roam freely on earth. Taoist temples are a good place to see processions of deities, who are carried around to see that the ghosts don't misbehave. You'll also see the guardians of the gates of hell, generals Fan and Hsieh, who are left in various spots around the cities to serve as "ghost policemen."

Although many Chinese are afraid of the ghosts, and do not travel for the entire month they are believed to be on earth, many others feel sorry for these poor souls and try to release them from their torments by performing elaborate rituals. For instance, people who died unnatural deaths or who had no family to bury them correctly are condemned to wander the earth until they are properly conducted into heaven by the living. To encourage the souls' journey to paradise, mortals lay food out in front of their houses, and burn paper money and incense. Lanterns are floated on rivers and carried along river banks, to conduct drowning victims to their final resting place.

DATE: August/September. The main festivities take place on the 15th day of the seventh lunar month, but rituals are performed on the first and throughout the month. **LOCATION:** Nationwide. **TRANSPORT:** Since many people are afraid to travel this month, it's an especially good time for visitors to get seats on the normally crowded trains and buses. See above entries for specifics on getting to Taiwan. **ACCOMMODATION:** With fewer travelers, rooms are much easier to come by this entire month. **CONTACT:** Taiwan Visitors Assn. (see *Resources*).

While you're there ...

- **Double-yang, mountains and hills nationwide:** On the ninth day of the ninth lunar month (a lucky combination), people give banquets and picnics and go for walks in the hills. It's said that the day's main purpose is to "drink wine and enjoy from a mountain top." (September/October.)
- **Winter Solstice:** Celebrants make offerings and prepare "solstice balls" of rice dough boiled in sugar syrup. (December 22.)

Resources

In Taiwan: Taiwan Visitors Association, 5th Floor, 9 Min Chuan East Rd., Section 2, Taipei, Tel 2-5943261, Fax 2-5943265. **USA:** Taiwan Tourism Representative, 1 World Trade Center, Suite 7953, New York, NY 10048, Tel (212) 466-0691, Fax (212) 432-6436. **Canada:** Taipei Economic and Cultural Office, Suite 805, 123 Edward St., Toronto, ON M5G 1E2, Tel (416) 964-9213. **UK:** Taiwan Visitors Association, 4th Floor Dorland House, 14–16 Regent St., GB-London SW1Y 4PH, Tel 71-9309553, Fax 71-3210043. **Germany:** Taiwan Tourism Bureau, Dreieichstr. 59, D-6000 Frankfurt 70, Tel 69-610743, Fax 69-624518. **Australia:** Far East Trading Co. Pty. Ltd., MCL Center, Suite 1904, Martin Place, Sydney, NSW 2000, Tel 2-2316942, Fax 2-2337752.

SOUTHEAST ASIA

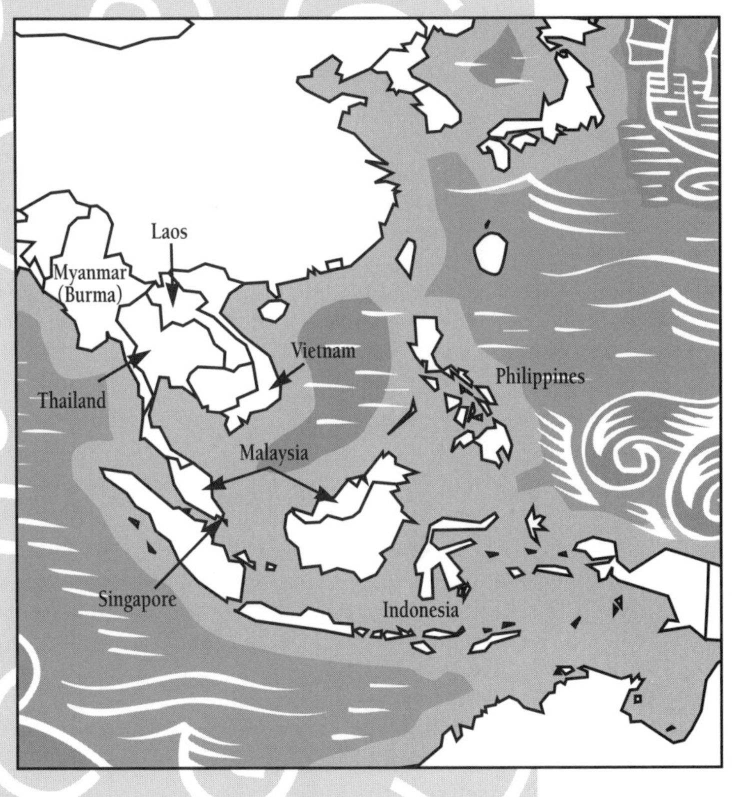

LAOS

Laos is one of the last bastions of Southeast Asia as it was, an underdeveloped and seldom-visited land where peasants carry on as they have for centuries. Having survived decades of war, the countless ethnic groups of Laos have retained most of their ancient beliefs in the powers of shamans, sorcerers, and earth-spirits called phii. *These animistic traditions are mixed and matched with Buddhism and other* isms*—including communism, which is now part of the curriculum for monks—to form the basis of modern-day religion in Laos.*

This religious/political syncretism drives many of the festivals in Laos. The majority of events take place in *wats* (temples) around the full moon, and often begin with a *sukwan* ritual, to call back the "wandering soul of man." Following the lead of the Vietnamese, the Lao government is opening up the country to tourism and commerce, allowing the Lao people to demonstrate their legendary hospitality and curiousity. Nevertheless, some areas are still being fought over by ethnic insurgents, and tourism is fairly tightly controlled.

Lao New Year

Luang Prabang and nationwide **Mid-April**

When astrological signs point to light and prosperity, and life-giving rains are expected to put an end to the hot, dry season soon, it's time to celebrate the Lao New Year. For three days the country's business comes to a standstill, as processions, prayers, and festive water fights break out in the streets. The temple city of Luang Prabang has the most elaborate celebrations, with processions of royal elephants and colorful releases of birds and animals.

All over the nation dances (some masked) commemorate the ancestors of the Lao, and *wats* receive fruits, flowers, vegetables, and candles as offerings. In the *wat* courtyards, sand castles and elaborate arrangements of stones are erected. After prayers and offerings, people take to the streets to throw water on each other—a welcome relief, since this is the hottest time of year.

DATE: Mid-April (the official holiday runs April 16–18). **LOCATION:** Nationwide, but with particular vigor in Luang Prabang. **TRANSPORT:** Luang Prabang can be reached by air or river boat (2–3 days) from Vientiane. The two-day road trip is not recommended, since anti-government insurgents are active near Kasi. **ACCOMMODATION:** The few hotels in town don't offer particularly great facilities for the money. **CONTACT:** Tourism Authority of L.P.D.R. (see *Resources*).

Rocket Festival (Bun Bang Fai)

Vientiane and nationwide **May**

This is one of the wildest festivals in Laos, with plenty of music, dancing, parades of carved wooden phalluses, and bamboo rockets. The latter are sent blasting off toward the heavens in a pre-Buddhist tradition meant to prompt the gods for rain.

Monks are the original rocket makers, and are still known as the best. They traditionally stuffed bamboo stalks with gunpowder, sealed them at the top, and added bright streamers. On full-moon morning, they would wheel wagon-loads of rockets to Vientiane, and set them off on the banks of the Mekong River. These days, the launching pad hasn't moved, but the competition has expanded into the lay community. Vientiane and villages throughout the entire country become temporary powder kegs as neighborhood teams and civic and military groups arrive with rockets and more rockets. Most are homemade, which adds to the randomness of the event.

Toward dusk, participants gather in long lines with their rockets. When the sun goes down the rockets go up, one after another, with fiery blasts accompanied by wild cheering and heavy betting. In Vientiane a judges' grandstand is erected near the river, and the fastest, highest, and prettiest rockets receive silver bowls.

Prizes are also given for the best processions from surrounding *wat* communities, and people go to great lengths to win. Since the festival is connected with ancient fertility rites, erotic songs and dances are common. In one part of the procession, women carry carved wooden phalluses in imitation of the men, who are often costumed. The *mâw lám*, a uniquely Lao art form of drama and verbal repartee, is performed on makeshift stages.

DATE: The full moon in May. Bun Bang Fai is celebrated at the same time as the more religious Visakha Bu-saa festival in Laos and northeastern Thailand. **LOCATION:** Vientiane and throughout the country. **TRANSPORT:** Vientiane can be reached by air from Bangkok, Phnom Penh, Hanoi, Ho Chi Minh City, and Moscow. **ACCOMMODATION:** First class or dog's class, Vientiane has it all. **CONTACT:** Tourism Authority of L.P.D.R. (see *Resources*).

That Luang Festival: Young monks in saffron robes receive alms and flowers on the morning of the first day of That Luang. (Joe Viesti/Viesti Associates)

The Festival of the Waters (Bun Nam and Awk Watsa)

Nationwide **October/November**

General rejoicing marks the end of the monks' three-month retreat, and after confessing their evil and careless thoughts, monks leave the *wat* for pilgrimages. Villagers make sure they are well taken care of by making ceremonious offerings of robes, begging bowls, and sleeping mats. Processions are made to the *wats*, and houses are decorated and cleaned to sweep out evil *phii* spirits that lurk during the rainy season. In addition, there are boat races at riverside towns such as Vientiane and Savannakhet.

DATE: October or November. **LOCATION:** Nationwide. **CONTACT:** Tourism Authority of L.P.D.R. (see *Resources*).

While you're there ...

- **Magha Puja, nationwide:** *Wats* throughout the country are circumambulated in candlelight processions, to commemorate a sermon given by the Buddha. This is especially elaborate at the Wat Phu ruins near Champasak, and in Vientiane. (Full moon in February.)
- **Sisakha Bu-saa, nationwide:** *Wats* light up with ceremonies and candlelight processions to celebrate the Buddha's birth, enlightenment, and death. (Full moon in May.)

That Luang Festival, Vientiane: This week-long festival includes fireworks, processions, and music. On the first day, monks receive alms and flowers; on the final night, there are candlelight circumambulations of That Luang. (Full moon in November.)

Bun Pha Wet, nationwide: Males are ordained into the monkhood and the *Jataka* is recited during this *wat* festival, held on staggered days so that friends and relatives from nearby towns can attend. Villagers offer hospitality by staging banquets and cockfights, and in the *wat* courtyards *mâw láms* are staged. In the That Luang temple outside of Vientiane, special rites commemorate Lao origins and historical events. The temple is reported to house a relic of the Buddha. (December/January.)

Resources

In Laos: Tourism Authority of L.P.D.R., Boite Postale 2912, Quartier Nahadiao, Vientiane, Tel 856-6343. Also, La Société Nationale Lao Tourism, Boîte Postale 2912, opp. FAO Building. Vientiane, Tel 856-5898, Fax 856-5025. **USA:** Embassy of the People's Democratic Republic of Laos, 2222 S Street NW, Washington DC, 20008-4014, Tel (202) 332-6416/7, Fax (202) 332-4923. **Australia:** Embassy of the People's Democratic Republic of Laos, 1 Dalman Crescent, O'Malley (Canberra), ACT 2606, Tel 6-2864595. **Germany:** Embassy of the People's Democratic Republic of Laos, Am Lessing 6, D-5220 Königswinter 1, Tel 2223-21501, Fax 2223-3065.

INDONESIA

Forming a necklace of 13,677 islands, the world's largest archipelago stretches along the equator for some 4,800 km (3,000 miles). Visitors can see fiery tropical sunsets, erupting volcanos, bird-sized butterflies, and prehistoric Komodo dragons. These natural experiences are awesome enough, but in terms of human culture, Indonesia teeters at the very edge of the earth.

Indonesia's phenomenal cultural diversity continues to fascinate and baffle anthropologists, who have been probing around the country for more than 100 years. Speaking more than 300 very different languages, Indonesians range from cosmopolitan city dwellers to sea gypsies and head hunters. Millions of people continue to observe rituals that haven't changed since the dawn of time, and almost every event in an Indonesian's life is celebrated with some kind of colorful ceremony. Each of the archipelago's thousands of ethnic groups has distinct festivities connected with birth, marriage, and death, and many hold huge religious festivals—some of which rank among the most extraordinary and dramatic events on the planet.

Best of all, Indonesia is so big that there's still plenty of room for each visitor to have his or her own private Indonesian experience. Whether you hit the wild festival islands of Bali and Lombok, or the Indonesian sections of primative Borneo and New Guinea, plan to see—and feel—plenty of magic!

Balinese Caka New Year (Nyepi)

Bali **March/April**

While Nyepi Day itself is a very quiet, stay-at-home occasion, the night before Nyepi is the noisiest night in Bali, and maybe in all of Asia. Festivities start a few days before the New Year, as temple icons are brought to the seacoast for ritual bathing. At major crossroads in villages and cities all over Bali, elaborate exorcism rituals are held just before noon. Priests can be seen luring evil spirits (*buta* and *kala*) into large offerings shaped like an eight-pointed star (*mecaru*), surrounded by villagers who scream and beat drums to drive the spirits back into the heavens. Huge food offerings, rit-

Village girls dance to welcome the deities at a temple festival in Asak. *(Nik Wheeler)*

ual sacrifices, gambling, and mantra-chanting are all part of the commotion intended to exorcise the demons of the old year.

As night falls, a series of demon-raising processions begins. Gongs, cymbals, and drums are brought out and clanged through all corners of the family compound to chase away evil spirits. Once the spirits have been chased away inside, it's time to make a commotion in the streets. People light torches and run through the villages with effigies as the smashing and clanging continues until everyone is confident that all lingering spirits have been sent packing.

The next day Bali is completely silent. The hope is that the malicious spirits roused the night before will find Bali completely barren of life and leave the island. No one may light fires, do work, or even venture out into the streets.

DATE: The spring equinox is the last day of the year in the Caka calendar (March/April). **LOCATION:** Throughout Bali, but most vigorous and colorful in Denpasar. **CONTACT:** Dipara Bali (Bali Tourist Office), Nita Mandala Civic Centre, Jalan S Parman, Renon, Denpasar 80235, Indonesia. Also, Indonesia DGT (see *Resources*).

Galungan and Kuningan

Bali **Moving dates**

This 10-day festival is the most important in the Balinese year, marking the creation of earth, the victory of religion, and the return of gods and ancestors to earth to feast with friends and relatives.

The Temple Festivals of Bali

On holy days, the temples of Bali come alive with drama and dance to welcome deities and ancestral spirits that descend from heaven to visit their offspring. Each temple has a major festival at least once a year, and since the Balinese year is 210 days long (and most villages have three or more temples), there's no doubt that you'll see a festival or two if you spend any time at all on Bali. The full moons of April and September/October are particularly active festival seasons.

Like all other religious activities in Bali, the temple festivals are a whole lot of fun. The all-night marathon of spirited socializing and worship usually begins with cock fights. Men gamble on roosters whose spilled blood will protect the temple from evil spirits, while women arrive with fantastically arranged offerings of flowers, fruit, and other foods. These are stacked on tops of heads in colorful pyramids as the women move through the crowds of gamblers, dancers, musicians, charlatans, and salesmen.

Inside the temple, priests bid the gods to come down and join in the fun, and women supplement the request by dancing the *pendet,* a slow, beautiful series of body and hand motions. Through the thick incense special seats for gods and ancestral spirits are visible, and villagers often fall into trances. When this happens, the entranced person is believed to be a medium possessed by a deity, and everyone gathers around to ask advice (through the priest) or look for auspicious signs and divine gestures. Once the messages are passed, the medium is awakened with prayers and gentle dousings of holy water. Toward dawn the festivities get sleepier, and the final dances are performed to bid the deities farewell. Then everyone leaves the temple to spend the new day lounging and sleeping.

Unlike the Hindu temples in India, those in Bali don't exclude non-Hindus from entry. There are only a few rules of etiquette. First, although it's not usually necessary to remove shoes, you'll need to be conservatively dressed and put on a temple scarf, which is worn as a sash tied around the waist. These can be bought cheaply or rented at the larger temples. You should not, at any time, stand on a higher plane than the priest, and you should make a small donation. Also, many temples have signs requesting that women not enter the temple during menstruation.

According to legend, the demon-king Mayadanawa was defeated by the people, with the help of the god Indra and other deities. After the great battle, the people were free again to worship their ancestors and deities according to the Agama Hindu Bali religion.

On Kuningan Day, devotees bring offerings of food for gods and ancestors who return to earth to feast with friends and relatives. All over Bali, temples are spendidly decorated, and over the 10-day holiday you'll see a near-continuous array of processions, songs, and costumed dancers who leap from temple to temple. (Nik Wheeler)

On Galungan Day, the Supreme God (*Sanghyang Widi*) comes down to the temples of Bali to feast, followed by other gods and ancestral spirits. For 10 days they are entertained by an almost continuous array of processions, songs, and dances, and fortified by thousands of offerings. Pigs are slaughtered, feasts are prepared, and bamboo poles called *penjor* are erected and laden with fruits and flowers. These are planted at the gates to houses, arching up over the roads as symbols of prosperity. The shaggy half-lion, half-man Barong dancers leap from temple to temple, and perform spontaneous roadside versions of their mystical dance-dramas. They're often accompanied by the evil witch-queen Rangda, who puts the supporting dancers into a trance, causing them to stab themselves with daggers. All in all, this is a spectacular time to be on Bali (actually, any time is), as the entire island is alive with temple festivals, celebrations, and parades. The final day of the festival cycle is Kuningan, when celestial spirits and ancestors are bid farewell with a variety of offerings and events. At the holy springs of Tirta Empul (Tampaksiring), devotees bathe to purify themselves.

DATE: This festival is an annual event in the 210-day *wuku* calendar, which is divided into 30 seven-day weeks. Thus, there are usually two Galungans each Gregorian year. For upcoming years, the festival will start on the following days: 1995, May 31 and December 27; 1996, July 24; 1997, February 19 and September 17; 1998, April 15 and November 11. **LOCATION:** Throughout Bali. **TRANSPORT:** Bali's Denpasar International Airport handles flights from Australia, New Zealand, and throughout East and Southeast Asia. From Europe and North America it's necessary to connect in either Jakarta, Hong Kong, Singapore, or Bangkok. **ACCOMMODATION:** With its long tradition of hosting travelers from all over the world, Bali offers plenty of lodging, and at low prices. Options range from four-star beach hotels to the family-run *losmen* guest houses, many of which offer clean and pleasant surroundings for US$3–5 per night. **CONTACT:** Diparda Bali (Bali Tourist Office), Jl. S. Parman, Niti Mandala, Denpasar 80235, Indonesia, Tel 0361-22387. Also, Indonesia DGT (see *Resources*).

WAISAK

Borobudur (Java) **May**

The world's largest Buddhist monument is a fitting place to celebrate the Lord Buddha's birth, enlightenment, and death. On full-moon day a serene procession of monks winds its way from Mendut to Pawon, then to Borobudur. With saffron robes and offerings of flowers and candles, the hundreds of monks cut a sublime image as they enter the grounds. As the moon comes up to light the ancient complex, candles are lit and the monks begin praying, meditating and chanting well into the evening.

The stunning structure, built in the eighth and ninth centuries, seems to have been conceived as a representation of the cosmos in stone. The pilgrim's walk, which covers five miles, takes you past a detailed, carved textbook of Buddhist doctrine. On the lower levels is the conscious world. The elaborate stone carvings depict people caught up in their everyday lives, trapped by desire

Mix & Match Religion

Although each of the four great "world religions" (Islam, Christianity, Hinduism, and Buddhism) is practiced extensively in Indonesia, the vast majority of inhabitants are Muslims. In fact, with 140 million people practicing the Islamic faith, Indonesia is by far the largest Islamic country in the world. Nevertheless, a Muslim from the Middle East might bristle at the sight of a self-declared Muslim Indonesian making offerings to Hindu gods, eating through Ramadan, or burning incense to convince local spirits to stave off disaster.

Mostly, the big religions serve as a veneer over enduring local animist customs. Like Muslims, Indonesian Hindus (who reside mostly on Bali) share their faith between some Hindu deities and a host of native Balinese spirits, ancestors, and gods of mountains and rice fields. Christians and Buddhists also incorporate local elements into the mainstream orthodoxy, much to the consternation of religious purists. One example is the image of the "Black Virgin," which is worshiped in the Easter procession of Larantuka.

Religion in Indonesia is complex, sometimes contradictory, and constantly changing. The big four religions rarely clash with each other, but occasionally their efforts to convert "savages" have had less than miraculous results. Missionaries on Irian Jaya still talk about the four Dutch families who, in 1974, tried to convince Dani headhunters to stop enhancing their village's prosperity with their neighbors' noggins. The families apparently thought they were making some progress when they were invited to a Dani village for Christmas dinner, but they hadn't realized that "white meat" would be on the menu. They were eaten by the natives on Christmas Day.

and passion, while those who follow the Buddhist path are rewarded by reincarnations into higher forms of life. You'll see more than 400 images of the Buddha, as well as processions of elephants, dancers, warriors, ships, and kings. Finally, the structure spirals up to depict *nirvana*, the absence of suffering and the Buddhist idea of heaven.

DATE: Full-moon day in May. **LOCATION:** Borobudur, in central Java. **TRANSPORT:** Bus from Yogya (1.5 hours), where there's an airport and train station. **ACCOMMODATION:** There are several places to stay in Borobudur village and in nearby Mendut. **CONTACT:** Diparda Tk. I Jawa Tengah (Central Java Tourist Office), Jl. Imam Bonjol No. 209, Semarang, Indonesia, Tel 024-510924. Also, Indonesia DGT (see *Resources*).

In the courtyard of an ancient temple, Kecak *dancers act out the Hindu epic* Ramayana. *(Steve Vidler/Leo de Wys)*

Easter Parade

Larantuka (Flores) **March or April**

Larantuka's Easter-week rituals reflect the influence of both the Portuguese, who colonized the area, and pre-Christian animists. Among the highlights is a Good Friday procession in which a statue of a black Virgin Mary is carried through the streets to the accompaniment of songs sung in Latin. The statue is said to have washed ashore at a cove designated by a mysterious, beautiful woman who appeared in a villager's dream.

Like Seville's similar procession, ominous-looking men dressed in white outfits with towering red hats carry Jesus' black coffin through the streets during the day and again at night, stopping along the way for prayers and songs. Each year, a statue of Jesus is washed, and the water, believed to have magical powers, is used in difficult childbirths and to cure sick children. As further evidence of the syncretism of Catholicism and animism, many of the traditional *kada* houses in nearby villages have beams carved with serpents and life-sized men and women, sometimes interpreted by the occupants as Jesus and Mary, sometimes as Father Sun and Mother Earth.

DATE: Easter week (March or April). **LOCATION:** Larantuka, on Flores Island. **TRANSPORT:** Air from Kupang, Lewoleba, and Lembata. Bus from Maumere. Boat from Kupang, Adonara, Solor, and Lembata. **ACCOMMODATION:** There are several tidy, basic inns in town. **CONTACT:** Indonesia DGT (see *Resources*).

The Sacred Dance-Dramas of Bali

Dance, music, and drama are nearly synonymous in Bali, and since they're happening all the time everywhere on the island, finding performances is no problem. Temple festivals, weddings, and birthdays are all occasions for dramatic entertainment, and even outside of tourist areas the performances are usually open to anyone.

The *Kecak* (Kechak) dance is probably the best-known, with its circle of up to 100 bare-chested men who act out the Hindu epic *Ramayana.* While chanting non-stop, these players go through highly coordinated movements, swaying back and forth, raising hands, fluttering fingers, and rising to eerily exciting crescendos. At some times they depict a forest, at other times a legion of monkeys (hence the nickname "monkey dance").

The *Kecak* is unique in Balinese dance, in that the men provide the music, a chanting choir of "chak-a-chak" sounds. In all other dances, the music is provided by a *gamelan* orchestra, which serves up a highly dramatic sound track of abruptly shifting tempos and dynamics that move between near-silence and crashing, seemingly chaotic noise. The *Barong and Rangda* dance makes superb use of music to present a classic battle between good and evil, fought by two figures from the netherworld. The good guy, the *Barong,* is a fun-loving, mischievous cross between human, sheep dog, and lion. With the support of the *keris* dancers, the *Barong* protects the village from the wicked witch *Ragda,* a horrible figure with fangs, wagging tongue, and entrails draped around her neck. At one point during the performance she puts the supporting dancers into a trance, causing them to stab themselves with daggers.

The *Wayang Kulit* is a sacred shadow-puppet play. The leather puppets are holy objects, manipulated by a *dalang* (puppeteer) who has priestly powers to speak for the gods and consecrate offerings. His skill is astounding: during a typical five-hour play (with no breaks) he will handle more than 100 puppets, conduct musicians, and give each character a distinct voice in any one of three different languages.

There are dozens of other dance-dramas in Bali, including the *Pendet,* danced while presenting offerings, and the *Sanghyang,* in which young girls enter trances to connote spirit possession. In the sophisticated *Legong,* girls present a very stylized ancient story, and in the martial *Baris,* men prepare for battle and then meet their make-believe enemies with energetic prowess.

As part of the Usaba Sambah celebration, Tenganan boys do ritual battle with sharp-edged pandanus leaves, trying to scratch each others' backs until blood is drawn. (Mary Altier)

While you're there ...

- **Pagerwesi Day, Bali:** All over the northern part of Bali, ritual offerings are made to stave off evil forces. The rites are devoted to the deity Sang Hyang Pramesti Guru, creator of the universe. (January/February.)
- **Lomban, Jepara, Central Java:** The fishermen of this community drift offerings offshore and hold races of colorfully decorated boats. They also stage a "war" between fishermen and "pirates," and display extremely well-crafted carved wooden items. (March/April.)
- **Art Festival, Pontianak, West Kalimantan (Borneo):** This festival pulls together the dance, music, and fashion of many of the cultural groups in West Kalimantan, for a harvest thanksgiving. This is a good opportunity to become acquainted with the Dayak culture before heading to the interior for treks or river trips. (March/April.)

Usaba Sambah

Tenganan, Bali **June/July**

This festival's ritual fistfights and hand-powered Ferris wheels are only a couple of many strange phenomena taking place in Tenganan—a town that's considered eccentric even by Balinese standards. The unique, walled village has its own calendar, and each day begins with 21 throbbing drumbeats that bring the villagers to life. Tracing their origins via a divine book, the resident Bali Aga tribe believes they were selected by a god to administer the surrounding lands and keep them pure. This concept of territorial integrity and purity enters most of the many festivals and exorcisms of the Bali Aga people, and although other Bali Aga villages are extremely conservative to the point of being hostile to outsiders, Tenganan is friendly and welcomes visitors. In fact, duing the festival they set up stalls to sell *tuak bayu* palm beer and the village's prized fabrics.

Makare battles pit the village's healthiest young men against one another. As an orchestra of iron-keyed metallophones called *gamelan selunding* strikes up, fists are wrapped with sharp-edged pandanus leaves. These are used as weapons, with the object of scratching the opponent's back with the thorns until blood is drawn. After the battles, a mixture of turmeric and vinegar is applied to the wounds to prevent scarring.

Women and girls wrap themselves with the spectacular "flaming cloth" called *kamben geringsing,* and crown themselves with flowered, golden headdresses. The *kamben geringsing* are the product of double *ikat,* an intricate process of dyeing and weaving known only to the Tenganan people. Because both crosswise and lengthwise threads are dyed before weaving, single pieces of cloth can take up to five years to complete. As the fabric shimmers in the sunlight, the women perform ritual offering dances called *rejang.* Unmarried women ride the creaky wooden Ferris wheels built and powered by the men, in an ancient ritual that represents the unification of sun and earth.

DATE: June or July. **LOCATION:** Tenganan lies on Bali, just inland from Padangbai (the port for the Bali-Lombok ferry). Similar ritual battles occur on the island of Sumba. **TRANSPORT:** From Padangai or Candidasa, take a bus to the turnoff to Tenganan, then either walk or take a motorcycle taxi up the hill. **ACCOMMODATION:** Since visitors are supposed to leave Tenganan at night, your best bet is to stay at the beach resort of Candidasa or the picturesque port of Padangbai. **CONTACT:** Dipara Bali (Bali Tourist Office), Nita Mandala Civic Centre, Jalan S. Parman, Renon, Denpasar 80235, Indonesia. Also, Indonesia DGT (see *Resources*).

Caci Whip Duels

Ruteng (Flores) **August**

Outfitted with head-wrappings and upturned, horned helmets, the Manggarai combatants circle one another warily. One warrior has a buffalo-hide shield and a long whip; the other has a thick cloth wrapped around his arm and a short stick. Each loudly boasts of his bravery, trying to overcome the spiritual defenses of his opponent, while a band of gongs and wooden drums beats out

Caci Whip Duels: The blood from the impending whip wounds will be used to placate the spirits of ancestors; the scars will be admired by the women of Ruteng. (Tony Halford/American Landscapes)

a martial rhythm. The warrior with the whip strikes first, lashing out at the other, who tries to protect himself with his stick. If the blow is deflected the round continues; if it connects with the body, the two exchange weapons and go into the next round, pausing while the dripping blood is collected to be used as an offering to the spirits of ancestors. The resulting welts and scars are much admired by the women of Ruteng.

Ruteng's inhabitants, the scruffy Manggarai hill people, survive by farming, raising miniature horses, and weaving high-quality fabrics. This normally quiet settlement lies in an extremely picturesque area of sculpted slopes, low volcanoes, rice paddies, and small Christian shrines that often have animist motifs.

DATE: Although whip duels are a part of weddings and other ceremonies throughout the year, the only time you can be sure to see them is during Independence Day celebrations August 17. **LOCATION:** Ruteng, Western Flores. **TRANSPORT:** Air from Bima, Kupang, and Laguhanbajo. Bus from Labuhanbajo, Bajawa, and Ende. **ACCOMMODATION:** Ruteng has several decent, clean hotels. **CONTACT:** Diparda Nusa Tenggara Barat (West Nusa Tenggara Tourist Office), Jl. Langko 70, Ampenan 83114. Also, Indonesia DGT (see *Resources*).

While you're there ...

Bali Arts Festival (Pesta Kesenian Bali), Denpasar: This festival brings together the very best performing arts groups and individuals from all over Bali. The opening parade is particularly spectacular, with more than

40 ensembles of musicians playing a huge variety of musical styles. (June/July.)

© **Sekaten, Yogyakarta and Surakarta (Central Java):** For the entire month before Prophet Mohammed's birthday, these two cities are packed with thousands of Javanese. Massive carnivals are set up, and sacred *gamelan* music is played in mosques. On the final day, a procession includes noblemen, dancers, musicians, and a variety of nattily dressed officials. (July/August; moving date according to the Islamic lunar calendar.)

© **Musi Festival, Palembang (South Sumatra):** In celebration of Indonesia's Independence Day (August 17), boat races are staged in watery spots all over the country. Palembang's are probably the most unusual, featuring canoes shaped to resemble animals and animal heads. Each canoe can hold 40 paddlers. There are also exhibitions of handicrafts and cultural performances. (August 17–18.)

© **New Guinea Cultural Festival, Wamena:** Traditional dances and music are the draw at this outpost on the Indonesian half of New Guinea, the world's most primitive island. The July/August date often changes, so be sure to check with Indonesia DGT (see *Resources*).

© Torajan Funeral Feasts

Tanatoraja District (Sulawesi) **September**

If the Torajan tradition of scheduling festive funerals months in advance sounds strange to Westerners, imagine what the Torajans must think of our tradition of burying family members in gloomy, hastily prepared ceremonies. These Christian inhabitants of south-central Sulawesi believe that a person is dead only after an elaborate, expensive funeral feast. Until then the deceased is just "ill," and the corpse is kept in the southern end of the house (facing west), visited and fed as if still living. The ancestor will not pass to the afterworld, or bestow blessings upon the living, until a funeral feast has been held in his or her honor.

The feasts are scheduled in advance because they are outrageously expensive. Families often work for months, and even years, to set aside enough resources to send their kin off in a manner consistent with their earth-bound status, thereby impressing the gods with their importance. The feasts are held throughout the year, but August through October is harvest time, and the additional wealth funds more funerals. September is the peak month.

The funerals, which last about a week, are organized by a "funeral director" called a *tomadalu*. Since these are festive rather than somber occasions, visitors are usually welcome, especially if gifts of soap, clove cigarettes, or food are brought to assist the family. The ritual begins with dances and chants. Buffaloes and pigs are slaughtered and food and palm wine (*tuak*) are offered, as the corpse is moved to face north, now officially dead. Relatives wear black as the body is placed in a wooden coffin shaped like a house,

Tanatoraja: Life-sized effigies of the dead sit on balconies and gaze over the lush valleys of their homeland, and the friends and family they left behind. (Cory Langley)

and work begins on a life-sized wooden effigy (*tau-tau*) of the deceased. A funeral tower (*lakkian*) is constructed, and the body is brought out in a colorful death shroud, as more pigs and buffaloes are slaughtered.

The corpse and guests arrive at the village's ceremonial field, which is decorated with beautiful banners surrounding the funeral tower. After the body has been installed in the tower, relatives and villagers cavort late into the night, dancing, singing, and eating great quantities of food. As the departed presides from his or her elevated abode, the pageant continues with kick-boxing (*sisemba*), cock fights, buffalo fights, and sometimes reenactments of the deceased's life-story. The next day dances, such as the *makatia* and *maranding,* are performed, to remind everyone of their friend or relative's generosity and heroism.

Finally, a massive sacrifice of water buffaloes takes place. The souls of these animals—the Tanatoraja symbols of wealth and power—will accompany their masters into the next life. If an important community member is being bid farewell, dozens of the beasts will be killed, each with a single sword-stroke to the neck. Family members collect the blood to be cooked with the meat, and what can't be eaten at the feast is distributed among guests. There's great excitement as the coffin is brought from the ceremonial field to the graveyard. Long streamers are unwrapped, and with a great deal of yelling the coffin is run up to the cliff-side, which serves as the high-rise Torajan graveyard. The coffin is hoisted up the cliff and interred in a hollowed-out section, then the effigy is set on a "balcony" alongside the other family members. Reunited in death, they stand behind the railing, gazing out over their homeland of terraced slopes and lush valleys, and the friends and family they left behind.

DATE: Although funerals take place throughout the year, the high season is the harvest (August through October); September is the peak month. **LOCATION:** Villages of the Tanatoraja region in south-central Sulawesi. **TRANSPORT:** Ujung Pandang on Sulawesi's south coast handles flights from major Indonesian cities. From there, light aircraft serve Makale (just south of Rantepao). There are regular buses from Ujung Pandang to Rantepao (and the 10-hour ride goes through some stunning scenery). There are also air-conditioned taxis which can be set up at the Ujung Pandang airport. If hiking in, you can put away the compass, since all homes (*tongkonans*) face north, and all rice barns face south. **ACCOMMODATION:** Most travelers stay in Rantepao, where there is a wide range of good-value hotels and even some luxury digs. **CONTACT:** In Rantepao, ask your hotelier for information on funeral ceremonies. Soon, someone will appear who can get you to one—for a price, of course. Also, Diparda Sulawesi Selatan (South Sulawesi Tourist Office), Jl. Sultan Alauddin 105B, Ujung Pandang; or Indonesia DGT (see *Resources*).

ERAU FESTIVAL

Tenggarong **September**

Short of mounting a serious expedition into the deep heart of Borneo, this is probably your very best opportunity to hang out with some of the most primitive and colorful people on earth. The Erau Festival is a three-day extravaganza of dancing, feasting, boat racing, and ritual battles featuring Dayak warriors from surrounding villages, dressed in full battle regalia. As the Dayaks go through their dances and sports, you'll see chains of beads around heads, bear claws and boar tusks through noses, studded belts, woven shields, and incredibly complicated headpieces of hornbill feathers and inlaid beads.

Villages situated only a few kilometers away from each other sport dramatically different clothing and customs. This diversity is due in part to the impenetrable jungle, and in part to the fact that just a few years ago the contact between villages was limited to brawls and raiding parties. One group would set out to bring back its neighbors' heads, along with women and children to be used as slaves. These days, the headhunting raids are reenacted with all the attendant ritual and preparations. Simulated battles often draw blood, but heads stay firmly attached. In between, there are sporting events such as top throwing and blow-gun target shooting. At the very end of the festival a ritual dragon is low-

The Erau Festival provides an opportunity to experience the fashions and lifestyles of the people of Borneo. (Cory Langley)

ered into the Mahakam, Indonesia's largest river. Its decorative head is removed, and its body set adrift toward the open sea. At the moment the head is cut off a free-for-all water fight breaks out. Everyone on the riverbank participates in the event's final battle by dousing each other with buckets of river water, and boats open fire on each other with huge water cannons.

The splendor and spectacle of the Dayaks' fantastic costumes and customs bring this otherwise dull town to life. In addition to Erau, the Dayaks hold elaborate harvest festivals in March, April, and August. These occur in villages throughout East Kalimantan, and, although they're not announced to the outside world, there's a chance you may stumble upon one in all its prehistoric splendor if

The otherworldly customs of Asmat region of New Guinea come alive in the dance performances of the Asmat Cultural Exposition. (Wolfgang Kaehler)

you happen to be "way upriver." Although this takes some effort, the bizarre war dances of the Modang, Kenyah, and Bohau tribes are worth it. Their rituals and dances are designed to preserve and enhance the fertility of both land and people. Although headhunting probably no longer exists in Kalimantan, human skulls still hang in wooden baskets in some remote longhouses, protecting the villagers with their powerful magic.

DATE: September. **LOCATION:** Tenggarong, on the Mahakam River in East Kalimantan (Borneo). **TRANSPORT:** Balikpapan has a large airport, and Samarinda a small one. From Samarinda, riverboats can take you up the Mahakam River. Buses and motorcycles to Tenggarong are available from both towns. **ACCOMMODATION:** Only four or five grungy hotels are available. **CONTACT:** Diparda Kalimantan Selatan (East Kalimantan Tourist Office), Jl. Pangeran Samudra 92, Banjarmasin 70111, Kalimantan, Indonesia. Also Indonesia DGT (see *Resources*).

While you're there ...

Asmat Cultural Exposition, Agats/Merauke (Irian Jaya): Dance performances, a rowing competition, and an art exhibition are part of this remote outpost's cultural show. The date often changes, so be sure to check with Indonesia DGT (see *Resources*).

Resources

In Indonesia: DGT/Directorate General of Tourism, Jalan Kramat Raya 81, P.O. Box 409, Jakarta 10450, Tel 021-310-3117, Fax 21-310-1146. **USA:** Indonesia Tourist Promotion Board, 3457 Wilshire Bloulevard, Los Angeles, CA 90010, Tel (213) 387-2078, Fax (213) 380-4876. **Canada:** Embassy of Indonesia, 287 McLaren Street, Ottawa, ON K2P OL9, Tel (613) 235-7403, Fax (613) 563-2858. **UK:** Embassy of Indonesia, 157 Edgware Road, London W2 2HR, Tel 71-4997661. **Australia:** Indonesia Promotion Office, Level 10, 5 Elizabet St., Sydney NSW 2000, Tel 02-233-3630, Fax 02-233-3629. **Germany:** Indonesia Tourist Promotion Office, Wiessenhuttenstr. 17, D-6000 Frankfurt 1, Tel 69-233-677, Fax 69-230-840.

MALAYSIA

Modern Malaysia is an often-confusing land of contrasting images. Around the corner from golden-domed mosques are steepled churches; just outside huge cities are peaceful riverside villages built on stilts; and butting up against tangled rain forests are tidy tea plantations that ship their crops to historic colonial ports. Malaysia is a mainland country, and it's an island country. Although it's officially an Islamic country, Malaysia guarantees freedom of religion.

Malaysia's religious and ethnic minorities include Hindus, Christians, Buddhists, and animist tribespeople of Borneo. As is usual in Islamic countries, the minorities are responsible for staging the most interesting festivals, although Malaysia's Islamic tradition is by no means staid.

THAIPUSAM

Kuala Lampur **January**

Outlawed in the land of their origin (India), spectacular masochistic acts of religious fervor are the main event at this Hindu festival. Devotees honor the birthday of Lord Subramaniam by ritually torturing themselves and carrying *kavadis*, huge decorated frames supported by spikes that pierce the chests and backs of the carriers.

The first of three days is dedicated to preparing the temple statues of the deity, which are decorated with jewels and finery, and set on huge chariots. The chariots are made of carved wood and plated with silver images of gods, goddesses, and animals, then decked out with streamers, flags, and tinsel, and hitched up to several bullocks. On the morning of the second day, processions make their way from the temples through the city and up Ipoh Road to the Batu caves.

The third day, the extensive caves and surrounding grounds are inundated by 200,000 people, most of whom are making the pilgrimage in fulfillment of a prior vow to Lord Subramaniam,

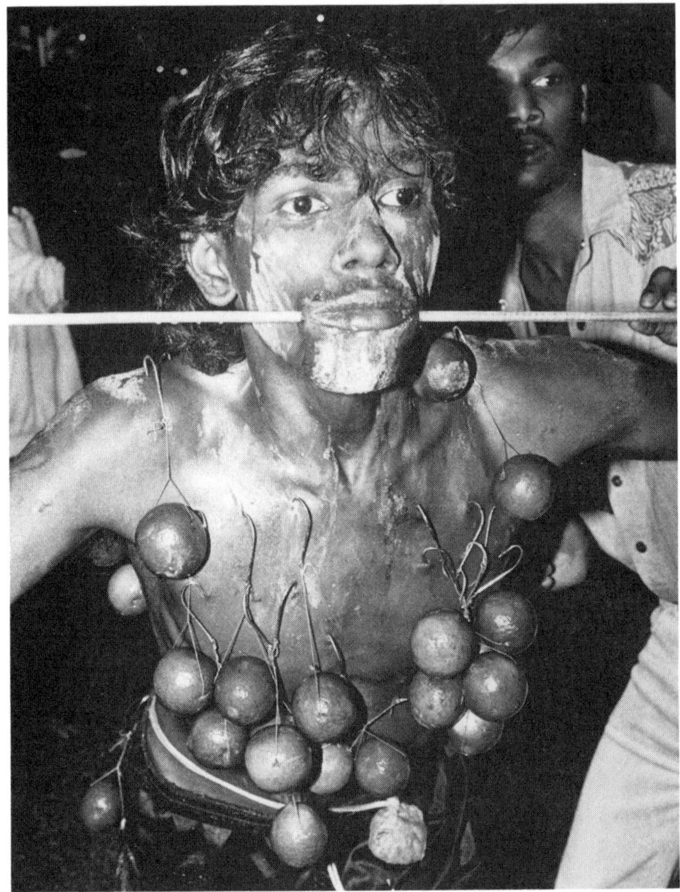

Once he has attained the proper spiritual mood, the devotee feels no pain and bleeds little as he fulfills his vow. During Thaipusam, thousands of Hindus perform spectacular masochistic stunts that horrify the squeamish and glorify the devout.
(Reuters/Bettmann Newsphotos)

such as, "If I have a baby/don't lose my job/recover from cancer, I will torture myself at Thaipusam." The modes of devotion are many and varied. Some penitents dance the route like dervishes. Others thrust skewers through their tongues and cheeks, or pierce their bodies with hooks and needles attached to friends or relatives who guide the entranced devotee.

The most extreme form of devotion is the carrying of the *kavadi*. The carriers have prepared themselves spiritually by following a vegetarian diet and abstaining from physical pleasures for about two weeks. At the shrine a ceremony is performed to put each carrier into the proper spiritual mood, and the entranced penitents leave to supporters' shouts of *vel-vel, vetri-vel.*

They move through the town and up the hill with the *kavidis* cutting into their flesh. Hanging from the structures are colorful arrays of peacock feathers, streamers, fruit, and even pots of milk. The carriers, in a state of religious ecstasy, appear to feel no pain. At the caves the *kavadis* are deposited at the feet of the deity's image. Their penitence accepted, the devotees relax, bodies full of holes but faces serene and still showing no sign of pain.

DATE: Late January. **LOCATION:** The Batu Caves just outside Malaysia's capital of Kuala Lumpur are probably the most interesting venue, but Thaipusam is also celebrated at Penang's Nattukotai Temple on Waterfall Road. (See also the **Singapore** chapter). **TRANSPORT:** Kuala Lumpur is peninsular Malaysia's hub for air, rail, and bus traffic, and is fairly easily reached from any major city in the world. **ACCOMMODATION:** Kuala Lampur has plenty of hotels and hostels in every price range. **CONTACT:** Malaysia Tourism Promotion Board (see *Resources*).

Birthday of Chor Soo Kong

Penang **January/February**

According to divine legend, the number of snakes at the Temple of the Azure Cloud multiplies on the birthday of Chor Soo Kong. The snakes—poisonous Wagler's pit vipers—are sprawled all around the ornate temple, hanging from the ceiling, wrapped around vases and chandeliers, and even draped across the altar. Presumably, the heavy incense in the air keeps the snakes happy and slightly doped, since they never lunge at visitors. Special ceremonies are undertaken this day, and attendants are happy to drape live snakes over visitors' shoulders and take pictures at no charge—although a donation for the temple's upkeep is appreciated.

The island of Penang is the oldest British settlement on the Malay Peninsula, an uncomplicated place where time seems to have stopped in the colonial age. The main city of Georgetown is a great place to spend several days just wandering around; there's always something going on in the streets and in the Chinese- and European-style buildings. The entire island is known for its beaches, architecture, and outstanding food.

DATE: January/February (six days after the Chinese New Year). **LOCATION:** Penang's Temple of the Azure Cloud, on the road out of Georgetown just before the airport. **TRANSPORT:** Airport bus or

Fire-walking is part of the ritual during Panguni Uttiram, an occasion celebrating the marriages of several Hindu deities.
(AP/Wide World Photos)

rented car or motorcycle from Georgetown. Penang's airport is served by flights from throughout Malaysia, and from elsewhere in Europe, Asia, and Australia. **ACCOMMODATION:** Georgetown has a variety of budget and mid-range hotels, and the Batu Ferringhi area caters to luxury travelers. **CONTACT:** Malaysia Tourism Promotion Board (see *Resources*).

© While you're there ...

- **Chinese New Year:** This new beginning is marked by open houses, businesses clearing debts, children receiving *ang pows* (red packets of money), and the spectacle of a dancing dragon and villager parades. Cheerfully try out your Chinese as you wish others a *Kong hee fatt choy!* (Happy and prosperous New Year!). (January/February.)
- **Masi Magham, Malaka:** The Hindu Chetty community holds a two-day festival of oratorical contests, stage dramas, and street processions, in Malaysia's most historically interesting city. (February/March.)
- **Panguni Uttiram, Bukit Mertajam and other Hindu areas:** The marriages of several Hindu deities are celebrated with processions, fire-walking, and, in Bukit Mertajam, a musical procession following a devotee who dances all the way with a clay pot balanced on his head. (March/April.)
- **Birthday of the Monkey God:** Clairvoyants enter trances then rupture their cheek and tongue flesh so that the blood may be used to write special messages. (March/April.)

Kota Belud Tamu Besar

Kota Belud (Sabah) **May/June**

This huge open-air market and tribal gathering is a photographer's dream. As one of Borneo's largest and most interesting events, it features traditional ceremonies, native dances, and a never-ending cavalcade of characters, ranging from herbal medicine men to Bajau cowboys riding their caparisoned horses. The latter are known all over the "wild east" for their exceptional horsemanship, and at the Tamu Besar they dress up in outfits resembling medieval knights' costumes, demonstrating their riding skills in a variety of special events.

Even if you miss the annual Tamu Besar, Kota Belud is a happening place every Sunday. The weekly *tamu* is a giant open-air market and much more. It gets hopping by 7 a.m., as people arrive from the nearby hills, forests, and rice paddies, dressed in a colorful array of traditional clothing. Stalls are set up to sell batik clothing, saltfish, exotic fruit, and consumer goods brought in by Chinese and Indian traders. For many, the market is an excuse to see old friends and family, gossip, and watch cock fights or buffalo races.

The Malay fishing village of Mengkabong lies above the water on stilts a few miles from Kota Belud, its thatched houses connected by ingenious wooden catwalks. A couple of hours away is Mt. Kinabalu (4,101 meters/13,455 feet), Southeast Asia's highest peak and the legendary Kadazan tribal home for the spirits of the departed. From the top on a cloudless morning, you can see all the way to southern islands of the Philippines. The park also is a great area for trekking and hiking.

DATE: Late May or early June. **LOCATION:** Kota Belud is in the Sabah state of East Malaysia, the northern part of the island of Borneo. **TRANSPORT:** Flights to Kota Kinabalu from peninsular Malaysia, Hong Kong, and Manila. The minibus from Kota Kinabalu to Kota Belud takes about 1.5 hours. **ACCOMMODATION:** There are two hotels in town. **CONTACT:** Sabah Tourism Promotion Corp., Mail Bag 112, 88000 Kota Kinabalu, Sabah, Malaysia. Also, to arrange a climb of Mt. Kinabalu, contact the Park Warden, Box 626, Kota Kinabalu, Sabah, Malaysia.

Gawai Dayak

Sarawak **May/June**

Along the remote rivers of Sarawak, the longhouses of the Dayak and Iban tribes come alive to celebrate the rice harvest with ritu-

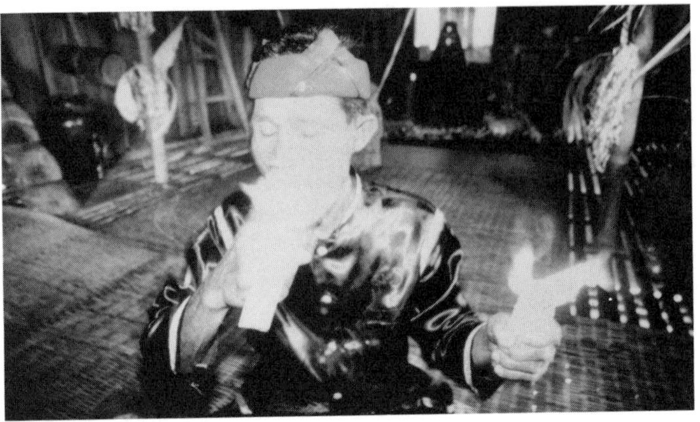

Up-river in Sarawak: In a longhouse in the Sarawak cultural village of Kuching, a Melanau witch doctor demonstrates the art of eating fire. (Jeff Greenberg/Omni-Photo Communications)

als of drinking and dancing. Travelers are particularly welcome during this period, as tribal people drop their inhibitions while consuming large quantities of *arak* and *tuak* (rice and palm wine).

The farther you go inland from Kuching, the more authentic the experience will be. If you play your cards right, you'll be welcomed with open arms, invited to sleep in the longhouse with the chief's family, and asked to demonstrate your own tribe's ceremonial gyrations at the wild dance parties that break out after the sun goes down.

In Dayak areas, war dances, cock fights and blow-pipe target shooting events go on during the day. In Iban areas, the men look fantastic in their tatoos and rare-feathered crowns, performing warrior dances and demonstrating how to shoot their short blow-guns while the women look on, beautifully done up in ceremonial head-dresses. Often the *ngajat* is performed, which originally celebrated successful head-hunting exhibitions.

DATE: Late May and early June. **LOCATION:** Longhouses along the Rejang, Balleh, Belage, Balui, and Baram rivers. **TRANSPORT:** Kuching can be reached by air from Kuala Lumpur, Singapore, Pontianak, and Jakarta. Transport up-river can be arranged in Kuching, both independently and through tour operators. **ACCOMMODATION:** Along the Rejang River there are hotels in Belaga, Kapit, Kanowit, and Song, but you will most likely stay at longhouses. **CONTACT:** Sarawak Tourist Assoc., P.O. Box 887, 1–3 Temple Street Ground Floor, Specialist Centre, Kuching 93718, Sarawak, Indonesia. Also, Malaysia Tourism Promotion Board (see *Resources*).

While you're there ...

Kadazan Harvest Festival: The *sumazau* Kadazan dance is performed by the Kadazan farmers of Sabah during this harvest festival. (May 10–11.)

Tuaran Tamu Besar, Tuaran: Bajau horseriders, boat races, and other events mark this annual market event. (July 29.)

Return of the Leatherback Turtles

East peninsular Malaysia **August**

Shortly after midnight the first turtles usually become visible, swimming quickly through the breaking surf. When they reach shore their waterborn speed and grace becomes an awkward crawl, as each female drags her more than 600 kilograms (1300 pounds) up the beach. Past the point of high tide, she begins to dig holes for the eggs, which are laid in clutches of about 120. "Tears" stream from her eyes (to wash away sand), as she huffs and puffs, often digging a decoy hole and filling it before digging the real one. Then she lays the eggs, fills the hole and smooths it over, and lumbers slowly back to the sea. Upon reaching the water the giant amphibian is back in her preferred element, stroking gracefully through the surf to resume the speedy wanderings that take her as far away as the Atlantic Ocean.

The seven species of giant leatherback turtle reach lengths of three meters (nearly 10 feet), and can be seen coming ashore to lay eggs in June, July, and August along the beaches of Malaysia's east coast. The eggs are often scooped up by crabs, birds, fish, or humans (they're a Malaysian delicacy) as soon as they're laid, although government controls and special hatcheries ensure that several thousand baby turtles are returned safely to the sea after their 55-day incubation period.

DATE: June through September, but August is peak season. **LOCATION:** Malaysia's east coast, between 35 and 150 km north of Kuantan. Tioman Island, with its jungled mountains and splendid beaches (at Kampung Nipah, Juara, and Pulau), is a great place to turtle-watch. Other hot spots include Chendor Beach and Rantau Abang (where a large black stone resembling a turtle is thought to beckon the real ones). **TRANSPORT:** The nearest airport is at Kerteh, which is served by flights from Kuala Lumpur, Kuantan, and Terangganu. **ACCOMMODATION:** Lodging ranges from guesthouses to bamboo huts to ritzy hotels. **CONTACT:** Turtle Information Center, Rantau Abang, Malaysia. Also, Malaysia Tourism Promotion Board (see *Resources*).

Longhouse Etiquette

If you're going up-river in Sarawak, a stay at a Dayak or Iban longhouse will be a highlight of your visit. Longhouses are communal residences that may hold a few people or crowds of several hundred. They're built on stilts of ironwood, with roofs of palm leaves and floors of split bamboo. The most interesting and remote longhouses are several days by longboat from Kuching.

Usually you'll need an introduction to visit a longhouse, but during the harvest season this requirement is relaxed. When you arrive, ask for the *rumah*, or chief. He'll usually invite you to dinner and offer a place to stay in the longhouse with his family, unless there is a *pemali*, or ritual prohibition in force because of a death or accident. In exchange for the hospitality, gifts of alchohol and cigarettes are appreciated (i.e., expected).

Before you enter the longhouse, wait to be explicitly invited, and take off your shoes. A drink of *tuak* is usually offered, which you should accept. When you sit (on the floor) to eat, tuck your feet under your body and be sure to eat at least some of the food (usually it's bland meat of some kind). You may want to supplement the meal with food of your own, which you should divide and offer to your hosts.

After sunset the *tuak* comes out, which is drunk from a glass a whole shot at a time. The Dayaks and Ibans get pretty loose when they party, and they love to dance and sing. They'll usually expect you to participate actively, and when you do you'll generate lots of laughter with your odd, unpredictable Western ways. Throw inhibitions out the window, try to speak the local language, and you'll be a big hit!

While you're there ...

- **Sri Krishna Jayanti:** The hot spot for celebrating the major events in the life of Krishna is the Laxmi Narayan Temple in Kuala Lumpur. Festivities last for 10 days, climaxing on Krishna's birthday on the eighth day. (July/August.)
- **Papar Tamu Besar, Papar:** This annual market is held in Sabah, an area known for its pretty Kadazan women. (September 15–20.)
- **Thimithi Fire-Walking Ceremony, Melaka:** At the Gajah Berang Temple, radiant coals are braved by devout Hindus as a sign of their faith. (September/October.)

© **Pesta Pulau, Penang:** Dragon boat races and other water events are featured during this month-long carnival on Penang Island. (December/January.)

Resources

In Malaysia: Malaysia Tourism Promotion Board, 24th–27th Floor, Menara Dato' Onn, Putra World Trade Centre, 45 Jalan Tun Ismail, 50480 Kuala Lumpur, Tel 3-2935188, Fax 3-2935884. **USA:** Malaysia Tourism Promotion Board, 818 West 7th Street, #804, Los Angeles, CA 90017, Tel (213) 689-9702, Fax (213) 689-1530. **Canada:** Malaysia Tourism Promotion Board, 830 Burrard Street, Vancouver, BC V6Z 2K4, Tel (604) 689-8899, Fax (604) 689-8804. **UK:** Malaysia Tourism Promotion Board, 57 Trafalgar Square, London WC2N 5DU, Tel 71-9307932, Fax 71-9309015. **Australia:** Malaysia Tourism Promotion Board, 65 York Street, Sydney NSW 2000, Tel 2-2954441, Fax 2-2622026. **Germany:** Malaysia Tourism Promotion Board, Rossmarkt 11, D-6000 Frankfurt 1, Tel 69-283782, Fax 69-285215.

Moving to the ancient rhythms of Theravada Buddhism, this rich land of golden pagodas and cheerful people is still only sparsely visited by outsiders. Those who do manage to make the trip find a country endowed with rich natural and religious treasures, and friendly and hospitable people who celebrate full moons by partying all night.

MYANMAR (BURMA)

Myanmar hasn't changed much since the British "settled" the land and named it Burma, after its majority ethnic group, the Bamar. Called Myanmar since 1990, the country is relatively untouched by both the lifestyle changes and the cynicism that have accompanied the "economic miracles" in neighboring Thailand and China. Traditions of close family ties, respect for elders, and simple native dress have persevered, as have the festivals that form the center of Myanmar social activities. As is usual in Buddhist countries, the sacred and the secular mix, and amid activities dedicated to guardian spirit-gods called *nats*, you'll find food stalls, magic and puppet shows, and unique dramas called *pwes*.

Although the vast majority of Myanmar is quite peaceful, the government isn't fully in control in outlying areas, and never has been. Some 67 ethnic groups and 25 insurgent armies continue to vie for power, and restrictions on foreign visitors are tight in terms of both length of stay and "approved" areas to visit. Nevertheless, these restrictions are easing up somewhat, and foreign travelers have had few problems in Myanmar.

THINGYAN WATER FESTIVAL

Nationwide **Mid-April**

A lighthearted, boisterous spirit prevails during this four-day festival ushering in the Myanmar New Year. The year's biggest party marks the arrival on earth of Thagyamin, king of the *nats*, who bears a water jar symbolizing prosperity and peace for the coming year. This visitation is greeted with an explosion of celebrations:

Thingyan Water Festival: The only way to escape the barrage of water is to pose as a monk. (Photobank/Viesti Associates)

there are parties, parades, and music, and water is everywhere—hurled from buckets, sprayed from hydrants, thrown in balloons, and poured from balconies.

Coming at the height of the dry season, the water-throwing is a welcome relief from the heat, figuratively serving to wash away the grime of the old year. In Yangon (Rangoon), the great Shwe Dagon Pagoda is the center of attention at dawn on the first day (*kyo nay*), with the rising sun reflecting off its gold-leafed, diamond-studded spire. Offerings of fruit, rice, jasmine, flowers, and incense are made to the many Buddha images, who also receive the first splashes of scented water as they are ceremoniously bathed by devotees. While adults remain in the pagodas to pray, children venture outside to begin spraying and pouring water on passersby.

Early the next day, the water-throwing is ubiquitous. Barrels of water line the streets, fire hydrants are opened, and groups of boys and girls drench each other. Pranksters are everywhere. Foreign tourists receive special attention, and only monks and fasting devotees (distinguished by prayer beads) are spared. Cars and trucks with platforms carrying bands move through the streets, and spontaneous wet dancing breaks out everywhere. Teams of girls try to capture boys, who, if caught, are bound, smeared with soot, and led around humiliated.

In the larger towns, you'll see an interesting verbal contest called *thingyat,* in which political or satirical slogans are hurled from one group to another. The rhymes get raunchy at times, but the contests end with characteristic smiles as one group concedes victory to the other. During the chaos of the festival, all revelers find a quiet moment each day to visit a pagoda and make an offering.

The third night (New Year's Eve) brings the merrymaking to a climax. The water-throwing continues as drum orchestras move through the streets on brightly decorated floats, and the dancing is non-stop. Prizes are awarded for the best floats, the best dancing, and the best *thingyat,* and many people stay up through the night to welcome the dawn of *a tet nay,* the New Year. Cattle and fish are decorated and set free, in dramatic processions led by drummers and dancers.

The festival winds up at home, with a family hair-washing, since Myanmar Buddhists believe that the head—the noblest part of the body—should be clean for the New Year. Elders are given special attention; nails are trimmed and hair is washed with perfumed shampoos. Monks visit homes to collect rice and gifts, and many people visit pagodas to offer gold leaf as decoration.

DATE: March/April. The first three to four days in the month of *Tagu* (the festival length is determined each year by astronomers). **LOCATION:** Nationwide. **CONTACT:** Myanmar Hotels and Tourism Service, or Myanmar Embassy (see *Resources*).

© While you're there ...

- © **Independence Day, nationwide:** Fairs spring up all over the country, including a big one at Yangon's Royal Lake. (January 4.)
- © **Kason Festival, nationwide:** In honor of the birth, enlightenment, and death of the Buddha, processions of dancers and musicians converge at local pagodas, where scented water is poured over the sacred *bo* (banyan) tree, under which the Buddha gained enlightenment. (Full moon in May.)

© Taungbyon Spirit Festival

Taungbyon **August**

Medieval miracle plays, ritual dances, and hundreds of costumed locals going wild are just some of the wide range of uniquely Myanmar phenomena encountered at this celebration. At times resembling a three-ring circus, at times an international bazaar, this event honors two god-spirits called the Taungbyon Brother Lords.

Perhaps no other event gets closer to the pre-Buddhist animist traditions of the Myanmars. Assemblies of shamans are widespread, and images are annointed and paraded through the crowds

In conjunction with the beginning of the Buddhist Lent, young boys dressed as princesses walk in procession.
(Jeffrey Aaronson/Network Aspen)

as people strain to touch them between bouts of eating, gambling, and frenzied socializing. The festival honors two 11th-century brothers who were executed for laziness, only to rise after death to the status of *nats*, or spirit-gods.

DATE: The festival begins eight days before the full moon in August. **LOCATION:** Taungbyon, 20 km (30 miles) north of Mandalay. **TRANSPORT:** Buses from Mandalay are frequent. **ACCOMMODATION:** Mandalay has plenty of budget hotels, but few upscale lodgings. **CONTACT:** Myanmar Hotels and Tourism Service, or Myanmar Embassy (see *Resources*).

While you're there ...

- **Beginning of Lent, nationwide:** This day commemorates the Buddha's first sermon and is the beginning of the three-month Buddhist Lent. At the pagodas, much pomp and pageantry accompanies the offerings of new robes made to monks; young people gather flowers to offer at the pagodas. (June/July; Waso full-moon day.)
- **Lot-Drawing Festival, nationwide:** Names of local monks are drawn by households in the community, who then feast their chosen monk. One lucky household will draw the name of Guatama Buddha. (July/August; month of Wagaung.)

Phaungdaw Oo Festival

Inle Lake **September/October**

Inle Lake's "floating" villages provide an exotic locale for the Phaungdaw Oo Festival's unique water processions and boat races. Amid calm waters and even calmer tribal people, this peaceful and pleasant place comes to life to pay homage to the Buddha images of the Phaungdaw Oo Pagoda.

The images, covered with gold leaf, are taken out only once a year, and placed on the royal barge called the *Karaweik* (Mythical Bird). Starting at the Phaungdaw Oo Pagoda (at Ywama), the raft makes its way around the lake, and as it calls out at each village a festival of music, dancing, and boat races erupts. The races feature the highly original local style of "leg-rowing." Rowers stand in the stern on one leg and wrap the other leg around the oar. By standing above the water, they're able to navigate the boats around the many thick patches of vegetation that float in the lake.

These patches of weeds are called *kyunpaw,* and are gathered and anchored to form floating islands on which vegetables and flowers are grown. Surrounded by floating fields, the village of Ywama (where the Phaungdaw Oo Pagoda is located) is navigated via canals, like Venice. In its floating market, you'll find colorful Shan woven goods and *khamouts,* or conical straw hats. All the surrounding towns, and especially Taunggyi, have extremely diverse and colorful populations of hill tribespeople.

DATE: September/October. **LOCATION:** The villages of Inle Lake hold the Phaungdaw Oo Festival, although boat races are held in many areas of Burma, since rivers and lakes are freshly filled by the monsoon. **TRANSPORT:** Transport can be complicated. There's an airstrip in nearby Heho, with flights from Yangon, Pagan, and Manealay, and buses to Shwenyaung and Taunggyi are available. The train from Thazi to Shwenyaung is a spectacular eight-hour

The Burmese Pwe

If you attend any festival between November and May, you're sure to encounter the everyday Myanmar theater called *pwe*. These remarkable mixtures of dance, drama, comedy, and music are some of the true gems of Asian theater, and are performed not only at festivals and fairs, but at weddings, funerals, and even boxing matches.

Pwes often go on all night, taking the audience to heights of hysteria, sorrow, laughter, and even sleep. The plots are often as simple as American soap operas, and even if you don't speak Burmese, it's easy to follow along with the characters. You'll see handsome princes and ravishing princesses, dancers in dazzling costumes, and acrobatic clowns. Meanwhile, the orchestra pounds out unnerving melodies on drums, gongs, and other instruments. Lacking a chromatic scale, the music is as esoteric to most locals as it is to foreigners; legend has it that a 12th-century king was told the secret of the Bamar tonal system when he encountered Thagyamin, king of the *nats,* under a rose-apple tree at the end of the world.

The most popular form of *pwe* is the *zat pwe*, a hodgepodge of drama, dance, and music. Other forms include the *yein pwe,* a singing and dancing ensemble; *anyein pwe,* a folk theater presenting scenes from everyday life; and *yokethe pwe,* a highly skilled performance using huge puppets. For more information on *pwes* that might be happening in Yangon or outlying areas, contact a local office of Tourist Myanmar.

journey through the mountains. On the lake, Tourist Burma runs boats from Yaunghwe. **ACCOMMODATION:** The village of Yaunghwe has a couple of bamboo lodges that offer decent accommodation; alternatively, the interesting smuggler's hangout of Taunggyi (the westernmost point that foreigners can officially visit) has a more substantial range of lodging. **CONTACT:** Myanmar Hotels and Tourism Service, or Myanmar Embassy (see *Resources*).

Festival of Lights (Thadingyut)

Nationwide **October**

This festival marks the month in which the Buddha descended to earth along a path lit by many lights. Coming at the end of the Lenten period of fasting and retreat, and the end of the rainy season, Thadingyut illuminates the entire country with beautiful oil lanterns, fire balloons, and tiny lighted rafts that are set adrift in rivers. On full-moon night, most people try to stay up all night to enjoy the festive atmosphere.

For three days, pagodas, shops, and homes are illuminated to beckon the Buddha. The entire family visits their local pagoda, taking food to the monks and offering gifts of woven robes and other items, beautifully arranged. The father buys a packet of gold leaf and makes an offering by rubbing it on an image. The mother visits the corner in the temple that corresponds to the day of the week she was born, where she lights candles and offers fresh lotus flowers.

DATE: Mid-October (Full moon of Thadingyut). **LOCATION:** Nationwide. **CONTACT:** Myanmar Hotels and Tourism Service, or Myanmar Embassy (see *Resources*).

Tazaungdaing Festival

Taunggyi and nationwide **Mid-November**

The full-moon night of the month of Tazaungmon brings another festival of lights, accompanied by all-night speed weaving competitions. In the Shan states, the festival is celebrated with particular zest, and in Taunggyi and Tavatimsa, there are spectacular send-offs of fire balloons. These are large bamboo frames covered with homemade bark paper. At the bottom, under the open mouth of the balloon, torches and other flammable materials are piled on a wooden platform. The balloon is tethered while the fuel is lit, and gradually the balloon, with its heated air, begins to pull on the stays. When the strain is sufficient, the stays are cut, sending the balloon skyward at an amazing rate. Often fireworks are attached, and when they detonate huge explosions light up the sky and rock the earth.

At the pagodas, unmarried girls sit under the full moon, working diligently but lightheartedly through the night to produce new robes for the monks. At dawn they ceremoniously present their finished products, which will replace the soiled robes worn during the monsoon.

DATE: Mid-November (full-moon day of Tazaungmon). **LOCATION:** Nationwide, but the fire balloons are best at Taunggyi and Tavatimsa, and throughout the Shan states. **CONTACT:** Myanmar Hotels and Tourism Service, or Myanmar Embassy (see *Resources*).

While you're there ...

Spirit Festivals, nationwide: At the full moon, nearly every village dedicates a celebration to a particular *nat*, or spirit-god. (November/December; month of Nadaw.)

Resources

In Myanmar: Myanmar Hotels and Tourism Services, 77–91 Sule Pagoda Road, Yangon, Myanmar, Tel 77571, Fax 82535. **USA:** Embassy of the Union of Myanmar, 2300 S Street NW, Washington, DC 20008, Tel (202) 332-9044, Fax (202) 332-9046. **Canada:** Embassy of the Union of Myanmar, 85 Range Road, #902–903, The Sandringham, Ottawa, Ontario D1N 8J6, Tel (613) 232-6446. **UK:** Embassy of the Union of Myanmar, 19 A Charles Street, London W1X 8ER, Tel 071-629-6966. **Australia:** Embassy of the Union of Myanmar, 22 Arkana Street, Yarrulumla, Canberra, ACT 2600, Tel 273-3811.

PHILIPPINES

Although tourism is on the increase in the Philippines, the world seems still poised to discover this traveler's paradise. With more than 7,000 islands, the Philippines' tropical treats include exotic landscapes, churches, beaches, and tremendously friendly people. Filipinos have been called the "least Oriental of the Orientals," and, given 400 years of Hispanization, they often seem to have more in common with Mexicans than with their Malay-Polynesian ethnic brethren.

Festival hoppers are in for a big time in the Philippines. During national holidays or the patron-saint days in villages, the country's boisterous version of Catholicism takes to the streets for processions, music, beauty contests, and some of the world's most creative costumes. No expense is spared as everyone—even people who can ill afford the binge—splurges on musicians and entertainers. Food and drink are offered with boundless generosity, and travelers who are lucky enough to wander into the fray are welcomed like family, treated like royalty, and bid farewell like old friends.

Ati-Atihan

Kalibo (Panay Island) **January**

Masked lion dancers shimmy with drunken cowgirls; a King Kong drummer whacks out rhythms while dancing the *merengue* with a tipsy burlesque queen; soot-faced cultural "warriors" stop in mid-battle with Spanish *conquistadores* to guzzle wine while a salsa band kicks up on the corner. Everywhere, people are shouting the Ati-Atihan communal mantra *"Hala Bira, Puera Pasma!"* ("Keep on going, Keep on!").

Ati-Atihan is inevitably compared to Mardi Gras, but the soot-blackened, drunken revelry of this event reaches extremes of confusion and humbuggery that even New Orleans would have trouble matching. Anyway, comparisons are worthless; Ati-Atihan is a uniquely Filipino ceremony that dates back to the 13th century, when 10 Datu families fleeing Borneo successfully bartered

Like Mardi Gras on acid: Ati-Atihan reaches extremes of soot-faced, jubilant weirdness. (Joe Viesti/Viesti Associates)

with the Panay residents for a piece of land. To celebrate the real-estate deal, the refugees threw a feast for their new neighbors, and blackened their faces with soot in an affectionate imitation of the *Negritos*. The newcomers assumed their "black" identities once again a few years later, to deceive and resist hostile Muslims. Thus the ritual of disguise became part of the yearly harvest celebration.

Religion was injected into Ati-Atihan a few centuries later by Spanish Friars, who persuaded the Christianized islanders that the child Jesus (*Santo Niño*) had appeared and driven off an attack by marauders. In a ritual nod to this event, black-faced revelers stumble into church the third day, throbbing hangovers echoed by church bells, for the ritual *patapak*. The priest touches all parts of

On Sinulog Sunday, the costumed crowd dances its way through Visayas. (Mark Downey)

their flagging bodies with a healing symbol of the Christ Child and, once cleansed, the masses file back out into the streets for the culturally bonding finale, a massive, blurry sing-along of religious hymns.

On the weekend after Ati-Atihan, the towns of Ibajay and Iloilo also have big festivals (the latter is called Dinagyang). While Iloilo's event is subdued, the partying at Ibajay is less touristy but no less vigorous. On Iloilo, the highlight is the Paraw Regatta, in which outrigger sailboats race across the Iloilo Strait between Iloilo and Guimaras Island.

DATE: Third week of January for celebrations in Kalibo and Aklan; fourth week of January for celebrations in Ibajay. The Dinagyang takes place the weekend after the Ati-Atihan. **LOCATION:** Kalibo, Aklan, Ibajay, and Iloilo are all on Panay Island, in the Visayas Islands chain. **TRANSPORT:** Panay can be reached by ferries from other Visayas Islands. Iloilo has an airport, which handles flights from Manila. **ACCOMMODATION:** Each town is well-served by hotels and attractive guesthouses. Most travelers stay in Iloilo. **CONTACT:** Visayas Islands Tourist Information Center, Fort San Pedro, Cebu City, Philippines; also, Philippines Dept. of Tourism (see *Resources*).

SINULOG

Cebu City and Kabankalan **January**

The week-long festival of Pasundayag sa Sinulog comes to a climax on Sinulog Sunday, when revelers assemble around the capitol buildings in brilliant costumes. At noon, the procession starts, and the crowd marches and dances its way through the city shouting *"Pit Señor!"* ("Long live the Christ Child!") in celebration of the Christianization of their community.

The traditional *Sinulog* dance was inspired by the river's current and is performed daily by elderly women in front of Magellan's Cross and the Basilica Minore del Santo Nino. On Sinulog Sunday, everyone gets into the act, surging, weaving, and flowing down the street to the peculiar steps. The week-long celebration is held in both Cebu City and Kabankalan, on the island of Negros. Both locations include feasts, processions, and horse fights.

DATE: The week leading up to the climactic third Sunday in January. **LOCATION:** Cebu City (island of Cebu) and Kabankalan (island of Negros). **TRANSPORT:** Cebu City can be reached by boat or plane from a number of Visayas islands. Negros can be reached by ferries from other Visayas islands. Kabankalan has an airport handling flights from Manila. **ACCOMMODATION:** Cebu City has quite a few hotels and pensions to choose from. Kabankalan has a few inns. **CONTACT:** Visayas Islands Tourist Information Center, Fort San Pedro, Cebu City, Phillippines, Tel 91503; or Philippines Dept. of Tourism (see *Resources*).

WHILE YOU'RE THERE ...

© **Procession of the Black Nazarene, Quiapo District of Manila:** The Quiapo District of Manila is mobbed by crowds during this fanatical ritual. Thousands jostle for the chance to help carry a life-sized image of Christ, carved from blackwood, in the Philippines' largest procession. (January 9.)

Yep, it's real: A penitent goes the distance on Good Friday.
(Mark Downey/Viesti Associates)

Holy Week

Nationwide **March/April**

Easter week explodes in the Philippines with a dramatic fervor rarely seen outside Latin America. All over the country, Christ's last seven days—his passion, death, and resurrection—are relived in all their gory and glorious detail. The sensational processions, decorations, and reenactments are heartful and authentic, and feature many uniquely Filipino twists that syncretize pre-Christian animist traditions with the now-dominant religion of the Spanish conquerors.

From Palm Sunday through Holy Saturday, death and piety are in the air. Marinduque's colorful Moriones Festival focuses its Passion Play on the fate of the Roman soldier Longinus, who stabs Jesus and suddenly is able to see out of his blind eye. Fantastic carved masks blend tropical sensibilities with the fierce features of the Roman centurions.

Good Friday ceremonies are especially elaborate in Pampanga and Nueva Ecija, where women kneel and wail a translation of the sung gospel of Seville, and passion plays spring up in the plaza. Wearing white hoods with crowns of vines, *flagellantes* beat their bare backs bloody with glass-spiked leather thongs, and some fulfill vows by taking the masochism an incredible step further—at high noon they actually have themselves crucified! In fact, in the past few years, the crucifixions have been so common that they've become tourist attractions.

Holy Saturday is completely still, but at midnight the church bells ring and the strength of a perpetually dying and resurrecting god is reaffirmed. Priests in bright yellow vestments remove the mourning shrouds from saints and begin a joyous midnight mass. In the morning fireworks and bells ring out as separate mother and son processions called *salubong* dramatize Christ's reunion with his mother. Little girls dress as angels and run through the streets as huge feasts are prepared.

DATE: March or April. **LOCATION:** Nationwide. The most colorful Good Friday rituals (and most of the crucifixions) take place in Manila, Antipolo (Rizal Province), San Fernando (Pampanga Province), and Jordan (Gulmaras Island). **CONTACT:** Philippines Dept. of Tourism (see *Resources*).

Carabao

Pulilan, San Isidro, and Angono **May**

Carabao is a two-day festival that honors San Isidro Labrador, the patron saint of farmers—and which features water buffalo as you've rarely (or never) seen them before. On the first day, the buffalo are bathed, shaved, oiled, and ornamented with frangipani and hibiscus. Off they march to the church square, where they are bid to kneel en masse to receive blessings from the priests. On the second day, the water buffalo compete in races, and in Quezon the saint is honored with special displays of fruits and vegetables.

DATE: May 14 and 15. **LOCATION:** Pulilan (Bulacan), San Isidro (Nuevo Ecija), and Angono (Rizal). **TRANSPORT:** Pulilan (Bulacan Province) is about 60 km/40 miles from Manila, and can be reached by bus (or take a train to Malolos, and bus onward to Pulilan). Angono is about 150 km/90 miles from Manila, and can be reached by bus. **ACCOMMODATION:** Day trips from Manila to these small communities are recommended, especially for this festival. A wide range of lodging is available in Manila. **CONTACT:** Philippines Dept. of Tourism (see *Resources*).

Fertility Rites

Obando **May**

In the town of Obando on the Bulacan River, an ancient fertility rite has been co-opted into a celebration honoring a trio of saints. Devotees dance and patronize San Pascual Baylon if they need a wife, Santa Clara de Assisi if they need a husband, and *Virgen de Salambao* (Virgin of the Fishing Raft) if they need a child. The dancers move through the streets, pushing carved wooden carts with images of the saints, and participants break now and again into bawdy ballads to Santa Clara. At the church the celebration gets chaotic, as participants grab bystanders and bring them up on the altar for wild, whirling fandangos.

Suntan sans squeal: In Balayan, a roast suckling pig is dressed up in beach clothing and paraded through town in honor of St. John the Baptist. (AP/Wide World Photos)

DATE: Third week in May. **LOCATION:** Obando, Bulacan. **TRANSPORT:** Obando is within 30 km/20 miles of Manila, and can be reached by road. **ACCOMMODATION:** Your best bet is to stay in Manila, where there are plenty of hotels. **CONTACT:** Philippines Dept. of Tourism (see *Resources*).

While you're there ...

Flores de Mayo and Santacruzan, nationwide: Beautiful young Filipino girls in white dresses shower statues of the Virgin Mary with flowers.

Parades with women dressed as female figures from the Bible take place throughout the Phillippines. (May 1–30.)

© **St. John's Pig Parade, Balayan:** Dozens of fully clothed roast suckling pigs are carried around town in a parade held in honor of St. John the Baptist. In commemoration of the baptism ceremony, this unique celebration also features huge water fights and dousings of unsuspecting passersby. (June 24.)

© **Penafrancia Festival, Naga City, South Luzon:** A colorful boat procession down the Naga River is part of the ceremonies to honor the Blessed Virgin of Penafrancia. (Third weekend of September.)

© **Zamboanga Hermosa, Zamboanga:** The city's celebration includes religious and cultural ceremonies, regattas, and the Miss Zamboanga contest. (October 7–12.)

© **All Saints' Day (Undas):** Families spend a festive day and night at the graves of their dead. Cemeteries are beautifully decorated with candles, lamps, and flowers, and games of bingo and *mahjong* break out. (November 1.)

© **Grand Canao, Baguio, North Luzon:** The hill people of Baguio sacrifice water buffaloes, pigs, and chickens during this festival. Dancing and rituals honor local warriors. (November/December.)

© **Giant Lantern Festival, San Fernando, Pampanga Province:** This is the best parade of lanterns in the country. It takes huge tractors to pull the largest of the colorful paper lights, and a contest for the most beautiful is held after midnight mass. (December 24.)

© **Christmas Week, nationwide:** The season officially begins December 16, and Filipinos rally around the rituals of carols, processions, and night masses.

© RESOURCES

In the Philippines: Philipine Dept. of Tourism, P.O. Box 3451, Agrifina Circle, DOT Building, Rizal Park, T.M. Kalaw, Manila, Tel 2-599031, Fax 2-501567. Philippine Convention and Visitors Corp., P.O. Box EA-459, 10–17 Legaspi Towers 300, 4th Floor, Roxas Road, Manila, Tel 2-575031, Fax 2-5216165. **USA:** Philippine Dept. of Tourism, 556 Fifth Ave., New York, NY 10036, Tel (212) 575-7915, Fax (212) 302-6759. **UK:** Philippine Dept. of Tourism, 199 Piccadilly, GB-London W1V 9LE, Tel 71-7346358/9/0, Fax 71-2874115. **Australia:** Philippine Dept. of Tourism, Highmont House, Level 6, 122 Castlereagh St., Sydney, NSW 2000, Tel 2-2672695, 2-2672756, Fax 2-2831862.

SINGAPORE

Singapore is Asia in a nutshell—an astounding mix of Chinese, Malays, Indians, Pakistanis, Europeans, Eurasians, Arabs, Indonesians, Thais, Filipinos, and Japanese. In this former British colony turned affluent city-state, a polyglot patchwork of people clings to individual traditions, arts, foods, and festivals. The small country is pretty much crime-free (if a bit oppressive), and travelers find that it's easy to get around, easy to find lodging, and easy to spend a small fortune!

The one thing you can do in Singapore both cheaply and exquisitely is eat. In restaurants, at festivals, and in the streets, Singapore is rightly called the food capital of Asia. At celebrations shaded by skyscrapers and centuries-old red roofs, Singapore's ethnic chefs create their masterpieces in the open air, feeding the throngs who flock to experience the lively, colorful traditions of their home regions.

THAIPUSAM

Little India **January**

This awesome spectacle of body-skewering usually temporarily horrifies, then awes, those who gather along Serangoon Road to watch. The participants are Hindu penitents, who fall into trances and walk three kilometers carrying huge steel frames called *kavadis*. The weight of these decorated contraptions is concentrated on a torturous array of spikes and hooks, which are driven into bodies in the most inconvenient of places. Amazingly, devotees shed little blood, even from holes pierced in their cheeks, tongues, foreheads, and chests.

Celebrations start several days before the actual event. Along Serangoon Road, stalls offer an eye-popping array of elaborate paraphernalia that can be used to make offerings or embellish the frame of a *kavadi*. You'll see flowers (for people or gods), spices, peacock feathers, and can't-find-it-anywhere-else goodies, such as sandals of nails or plastic images of the boy-god Muruga riding on his peacock. On Thaipusam Day Hindus flood the area,

Bearing the weight of the kavadi, *an entranced, skewered devotee exits the Sri Srinivasa Perumal Temple.* *(Tettoni, Cassio & Assoc. Photobank/Viesti Associates)*

partaking in free drinks that are offered courtesy of wealthy Hindus who want to earn merit points. Inside the temple (closed to non-Hindus this day), the *kavadis* are blessed and then set on the human carriers with much ceremony. As they walk out into the street they're joined by supporters who loudly chant, beat on tin cans, and yell "Vel, Vel," helping the devotees concentrate and thus ease their load.

DATE: January (usually late in the month—check with the STPB for details). **LOCATION:** Little India. The procession starts at the Sri Srinivasa Perumal Temple on Serangoon Road, and ends at the Sri Thandayuthapani Temple on Tank Road. Route maps are published in daily newspapers, or are available from the STPB. **TRANSPORT:** Getting to Singapore is no problem at all. At least 35 airlines serve the small country, hundreds of passenger and cargo ships dock there, and rail and bus lines run from Malaysia and Thailand. **ACCOMMODATION:** Luxury, luxury, luxury is the triple-watchword for Singapore's thousands of hotels, although budget accommodations can be found. **CONTACT:** Singapore Tourist Promotion Board (see *Resources*).

Lunar New Year

Chinatown and elsewhere **January/February**

Singapore's majority Chinese population rolls out the lucky red carpets, scrolls, and banners for 15 days to welcome the New Year.

This is one of the most colorful, vibrant, and entertaining festivals on the Singapore calendar, a time of year when the streets are full of smiles and wishes of *kong hee fatt* (a happy and prosperous New Year). Although the entire city is in a festive spirit, special events center around the Singapore River and Chinatown. At the river, stages are set up featuring music and dance companies, and a night market pops up selling handicrafts, food, and souvenirs guaranteed to bring luck and prosperity. Late in the festival, Chinatown strings up colored Chinese lanterns and other traditional decorations over the crowds that flock into the streets.

The Chingay Parade is a multi-cultural event organized in 1973 to sustain the festive spirit of the Chinese New Year. Crowds line the route early to catch views of stiltwalkers, lion dancers, bands, and performers from all around Southeast Asia.

DATE: Late January or early February (two weeks). **LOCATION:** Chinatown, the Singapore Riverside, and elsewhere. **TRANSPORT/ACCOMMODATION:** See **Thaipusam** entry. **CONTACT:** Singapore Tourist Promotion Board (see *Resources*).

Birthday of the Monkey God

Monkey God Temple **September**

During the Tang Dynasty, the emperor needed a courier to fetch the Buddhist *Sutras* (scriptures) from India. A pilgrim monk was dispatched, and was helped out along the way by the Monkey God, whose bravery and resourcefulness made him one of the most famous and popular characters of Chinese mythology. At Singapore's Monkey God Temple, a sedan chair is carried on shoulders of devotees, rocking and jerking as if possessed by the spirit of the crafty creature. He leads a colorful procession of mediums, who move through the courtyard in a trance, distributing paper charms to devotees. Many perform feats such as skewering tongues and cheeks, and writing good-luck charms in their own blood.

DATE: September (the 16th day of the eighth moon) and February/March. **LOCATION:** Monkey God Temple, Seng Poh Road, opposite the Tiong Bahru Market. **TRANSPORT/ACCOMMODATION:** See **Thaipusam** entry. **CONTACT:** Singapore Tourist Promotion Board (see *Resources*).

Festival of the Nine Emperor Gods

Kiu Ong Yiah Temple **September/October**

This nine-day festival includes *wayangs* (Chinese Operas), and parades of decorated floats and precision flag-bearers. Honored are the Nine Emperor Gods, who grant longevity and good fortune,

Singaporeans light joss-sticks in celebration of the Chinese New Year. (Bob Krist)

and cure all ailments when they come down to earth during the festival. At the climax of the celebration, worshipers gather to watch images of the nine gods parade past in elaborate sedan chairs carried by eight men. As soon as the chairs leave the temple, they begin to sway and jerk. The carriers then charge into the crowd, running back and forth as devotees are bathed in the smoke of hundreds of joss-sticks. Some people open their wallets and handbags, fanning in the holy smoke to encourage financial success.

DATE: September/October. **LOCATION:** Kiu Ong Yiah Temple, Upper Serangoon Road, Hougang (opposite the Singapore Crocodile Farm). **TRANSPORT/ACCOMMODATION:** See **Thaipusam** entry. **CONTACT:** Singapore Tourist Promotion Board (see **Resource**).

WHILE YOU'RE THERE ...

- **Dragon Boat Festival:** Races take place at Marina Bay, in the style of the great dragon boat races of China (see **Dragon Boat Regatta**, Nanning, China). Teams show up from all over the world, inspiring a carnival aura among the 30,000 spectators lining the shore. (May/June.)
- **National Day:** Three or four days of festivities culminate with an August 9 parade that gets bigger and more impressive each year. (July/August.)
- **Thimithi Festival, Sri Mariamman Temple:** Fire-walking is the main attraction of this festival, held in honor of Drapadi, the heroine of the Hindu epic *Mahabharata*. Thousands watch incredulously as barefoot devotees defiantly walk across white-hot embers, showing no signs of pain. The festival starts in the early afternoon, and coals are laid down around 5 p.m. Get there early to get a good spot. (October/November.)

Singapore's Caged Choir

Singapore's most talented vocalists gather each Sunday along Seng Poh and Tiong Bahru roads, to warble their melodies from carved wooden cages atop bamboo poles. The bird concert usually begins around 8 a.m., and the participants—merobok jambols, thrushes, sharmas, mata putehs, and others—put on a show that adds a blissful flourish to the Singapore experience. The birds' owners provide an interesting visual accompaniment as they sit on stools below, sipping coffee, trading notes, and listening in rapture whenever their pampered pets break into song. Bird doctors, food sellers, and cage makers weave in and out of the orchestra, and sometimes judges grade the birds on vocal quality, repertoire, looks, and showmanship.

Resources

In Singapore: Singapore Tourist Information Centre, Raffles City Tower #36–04, 250 North Bridge Road, Singapore 0617, Tel 65-396622, Fax 65-3300431. **USA:** Singapore Tourist Promotion Board, 590 Fifth Avenue, 12th Floor, New York, NY, USA, Tel (212) 302-4861, Fax (212) 302-4801. **Canada:** Singapore Tourist Promotion Board, 175 Bloor Street East, Suite 1112, North Tower, Toronto, ON M4W 3R8, Tel (416) 323-9139, Fax (416) 323-3514. **UK:** Singapore Tourist Promotion Board, 1st Floor Carrington House, 126/130 Regent Street, London W1R 5FE, Tel 71-4370033, Fax 71-7342191. **Australia:** Singapore Tourist Promotion Board, Westpac Plaza, Suite 1604, 60 Margaret Street, Sydney NSW 2000, Tel 2-24133771/2, Fax 2-2523586. **Germany:** Singapore Tourist Promotion Board, Poststr. 2–4, D-6000 Frankfurt 1, Tel 69-231456, Fax 69-233924.

Thailand's remarkable range of scenic and man-made beauty encompasses deep jungle valleys sheltering caves and ruins, as well as ancient but still-living cities. On dreamy beaches the full moon draws travelers and locals who stay up all night, sampling the delights of one of the world's classic and most diverse cuisines. All this is wrapped up in a package that's safe, friendly, inexpensive, and easy to traverse.

THAILAND

As a low-risk, high-reward introduction to the fascinations of Asia, Thailand is especially attractive to first-time Asian travelers. The Thais, always smiling (a cliché, yes, but an accurate one), seem to genuinely enjoy meeting *farang* (foreigners). Their living Buddhist traditions are presented through the many festivals that take place throughout the year. A well-organized tourist authority promotes these events, but travelers to Thailand often find that their most precious moments are found in the details everyone forgot to mention. As with most of Asia, the beauty is in the surprises.

SONGKRAN WATER FESTIVAL

Nationwide **April**

The traditional Thai New Year is a great time to be anywhere in the country (unless you're hydrophobic), as the normally poised Thais cut loose in wild revelry. Water was traditionally sprinkled to bless monks and elders and to induce rain, but today the festival is a free-for-all of dousings with cups, buckets, squirt guns, hoses, and anything else locals can find to wet down friends, family, and—especially—foreigners. Since it's really hot in Thailand this time of year, the best approach is to hit the streets in old clothes and make a big splash.

The religious side of the festival includes visits to the *wat* (temple) to bathe Buddha images and present special foods to the monks. Monks and elders still receive special treatment; instead of being splashed over the head, their hands are sprinkled with

A Songkran procession winds its way through the countryside near Lampang. (Tettoni, Cassio & Assoc. Photobank/Viesti Associates)

perfumed water. Many children bring colored sand to the *wat* compound to build miniature *chedis* (stupas), and some people release fish from their bowls, or birds and other animals from their cages. Although small villages offer the most personal Songkran experiences, the festival is celebrated particularly enthusiastically at touristy Chiang Mai, where it's accompanied by parades and beauty contests. At Sanam Luang, which fronts the Grand Palace in Bangkok, the beautiful Phra Buddha Sihing image is displayed and ceremoniously bathed.

DATE: April 12–16. **LOCATION:** Nationwide. **CONTACT:** Tourism Authority of Thailand (see *Resources*).

While you're there ...

Dragon and Lion Parade, Nakhon Sawan: In honor of the golden dragon god (and in a bid to profit from his benevolence), processions fill the streets of this predominantly Chinese city. It's a lively, crowded event, with marching bands and costumed dancers depicting venerated deities. (Three days in late January.)

Chaiyaphum Elephant Roundup, Chaiyaphum: Smaller and less touristy than the high-profile roundup at Surin, this event features dozens of elephants and their rider-trainers, who demonstrate their skills at log-pulling and other forestry tasks. In addition there are tugs-of-war, processions, and reenactments of elephant-back warfare with elephants outfitted in full medieval garb. (January 10–12.)

Straw Bird Festival, Chainat: Local villagers construct superbly crafted straw birds—some eight meters/26 feet high with realistic chirps and flapping wings—and parade the brightly colored creatures through the streets. Many of the 85 species in the Chai Nat Bird Park are represented, and local handicrafts and foods are featured. (Late January/early February.)

Chao Mae Lim Ko Nieo Fair, Pattani: Pattani comes to life to pay homage to Chao Mae Lim Ko Nieo, a goddess who is believed to possess a formidable capacity for magic deeds. This is a favored venue for the region's living "wizards," who descend on Pattani's San Jao Leng Ju Kieng Shrine for seven days of wild stunts. (Late February/early March.)

Rocket Festival (Bun Bang Fai)

Yasothon, Ubon, and Nong Khai **May**

Villagers in the remote northeast part of the country spend weeks making rockets of bamboo stuffed with gunpowder, then send them skyward with great amounts of ceremony, humor, and general commotion. Parades with traditional clothing are held the first day and rockets take off the second, but there's pretty much never a dull moment in this festival, which is intended to convince the heavens to send rain to fuel the coming rice season. Yasothon has the biggest rockets (some several meters long) and the biggest festival, but in Ubon and Nong Khai there's also plenty going on. In fact, the entire northeast part of the country moves into high-revel mode, with folk dancing, stage shows, "roasts" of political figures, and hilarious beauty contests.

Thailand's northeast provinces are a bit off the beaten tourist track and heavily rain-forested, which makes them excellent places to visit for those who have tired of the Chiang Mai/Mae Hong Son/Ko Samui circuit. The culture and food are exceptionally interesting, with many influences of Lao/French, Khmer, Chinese, and hill tribes.

DATE: Full moon in May (two days). **LOCATION:** Throughout the northeast, but particularly in Yasothon, Ubon, and Nong Khai. **TRANSPORT:** Ubon has daily flights from Bangkok, overnight sleeper-train service from Bangkok, and no shortage of bus routes. Yasothon can only be reached by bus (100 km/62 miles) from Ubon or Khorat. Border-town Nong Khai is at the end of the US/Thai-built Friendship Highway, and can be reached by rail (with sleeper service) from Bangkok, or by bus from Ubon and elsewhere. **ACCOMMODATION:** Ubon and Nong Khai are well-hoteled, but accommodations are much more sparse in Yasothon. **CONTACT:** Tourism Authority of Thailand (see *Resources*).

Phi Ta Khon Festival

Loei **June**

This festival is one of Thailand's most precious living relics, a "spirit dance" in which devotees of the Buddha suit up in flamboyant costumes and masks to dance for him. The dancers reenact a traditional Buddhist tale in which a host of spirits emerged to welcome the Buddha to his hometown in his final incarnation. Young men in Loei's Dan Sai district are the primary participants; in their outrageously creative and colorful ghost-masks they parade a sacred Buddha image and run through the crowds teasing villagers. Meanwhile, monks recite the story of the Buddha's last great incarnation before attaining enlightenment.

DATE: Late June. **LOCATION:** Loei is in northeast Thailand near the border with Laos. **TRANSPORT:** Buses from Udon or Phitsanulok (six hours), or Bangkok (10 hours). **ACCOMMODATION:** Plenty of hotels and guesthouses are available. **CONTACT:** Tourism Authority of Thailand (see *Resources*).

Vegetarian Festival

Phuket **October**

Posh Phuket plays host to an unlikely combination of religious piety, black magic, merry-making, and food-eating, all staged by the Chinese community. The Vegetarian Festival is quite a bit livelier than the name would suggest: In addition to enormous piles of vegetarian food, there are Chinese opera performances, unique offerings at temples, and a five-day extravaganza of fire-walking, knife-blade climbing, and other acts of self-mortification.

Interestingly enough, there's no evidence that masochistic rituals were any part of the vegetarian festivals of traditional China. More likely they were imported from India, where self-mortification was once common in Hindu ritual. During the festival, the island's Chinese residents go on a 10-day vegetarian diet, believing that abstaining from meat will purify the body and mind, avert disaster, and generate good fortune. Many also believe that the supernatural powers of the "nine spirits" temporarily on earth are transferred to purified humans, enabling them to endure self-inflicted ordeals without pain during or after. Both gods and people are offered a huge array of food at the five Chinese temples on Phuket, which are sanctified with joss-sticks and specially decorated for the occasion. The rituals are staggered, so there's plenty of time to enjoy almost all the action.

It's hard to believe that the skewers, swords, knives, and axes on display at each temple will eventually be used by participants—on themselves. Yet, sure enough, the purified believers walk calmly over hot beds of coals, force sharp spikes or tree branches—or even umbrellas—through their cheeks, and scale ladders that have rungs of razor-sharp blades. Skeptics in the crowd are welcome to try, and although the call for participants sends a nervous murmur through the crowd, the lack of volunteers is conspicuous.

Processions through the streets pass by shops where mini-altars have been set up, offering food, drink, and flowers to the human "soldiers of the gods," who are believed to be temporarily possessed by spirits. The mediums stop to pick up items and pass them to bystanders (an auspicious blessing), then move on through the frenzy of firecrackers, dancing, and the entranced movements of bloody, pain-free vegetarians. On the final night, the nine spirits are sent off with a huge party in the city.

DATE: Mid-October (Phuket's TAT office prints a detailed schedule of events during the 10-day festival). **LOCATION:** Phuket City and several other towns on Phuket Island and around southern Thailand. **TRANSPORT:** Getting to Phuket is no problem, with air connections from several cities in Thailand, and as far away as Kuala Lumpur, Singapore, Taipei, Hong Kong, and Sydney. Bus, tour bus, shared taxi, and boat are other options. **ACCOMMODATION:** Phuket still has a few budget accommodations, but they are slowly giving way to the luxury digs that have come to dominate the island. **CONTACT:** Tourism Authority of Thailand (see *Resources*).

Chon Buri Buffalo Races

Chon Buri **October/November**

The dusty streets of Chon Buri resemble a cross between Pamplona and Cheyenne, as water buffaloes are prodded, galloped, and tackled in this "wild east" rodeo. One of the Thai farmer's main tools, the ubiquitous Thai water buffalo spends most of the

Loi Krathong: Near Lop Buri, a woman prepares to launch her krathong *into the river with a wish for the Mother of the Waters. (Tom Clynes)*

year dragging plows through fields, but this is his (or her) chance to go for the glamour. Chon Buri is turned into a race course, with riders leaping atop the huge beasts and driving them toward the winning post. Other attractions include a "Miss Water Buffalo" beauty contest and buffalo-wrestling rodeos.

DATE: October. **LOCATION:** Chon Buri. **TRANSPORT:** Buses leave from Bangkok and nearby areas every few minutes. **ACCOMMODATION:** Hotels are available, but aside from the festival there's not much happening in Chon Buri, so it's best to treat this as a day-trip from Bangkok or a stop on the way to points further along the coast. **CONTACT:** Tourism Authority of Thailand (see *Resources*).

Loi Krathong

Nationwide **November**

Loi Krathong is one of the most enchanting festivals you are likely to encounter in Thailand, in Asia, or anywhere in the world. On this night, Thais gather at riversides throughout the country to launch tiny candle-boats into the water as they make wishes and ask for blessings from the Mother of the Waters.

The ritual's beginnings in the 13th century are unclear. Some say a young queen floated a small boat laden with candles and incense downriver to the spot where her husband was meeting with friends. Others contend that the ritual is performed to atone for the boats which move over any footprints of the Buddha that may be embedded in the sand. Still others believe that it's a way to thank the Mother of the Waters for her life-giving qualities, and to apologize for polluting her in daily life.

No matter what the meaning is, Thais love Loi Krathong. Everywhere, houses and *wats* are decorated with streamers and lights. In villages where there isn't a waterway, lamps are made in the shapes of birds, dragons, and other animals. Some people road-trip to the nearest waterway, even if it's just an irrigation ditch. In smaller villages, the *loi krathong* (literally, floating leaf-cups) are made by families from folded banana leaves; in the larger towns they are made and sold by vendors. Recently, a few plastic *krathongs* have been seen, and though they're not in wide use, their introduction into the waterways is an ironic pity.

At temples near the riverbanks, there's plenty of commotion. Food stalls and stages for musicians are set up, and elaborate ceremonies take place. At Wat Yang Na Rungsi Sao Kho, near Lop Buri, an ancient tree is honored with offerings of pigs' heads and whiskey, and comedic boat races are held. In Sukhothai the ruins of the ancient capital come alive with fireworks and a spectacular light and sound presentation. In Chiang Mai (where the festival is called Yi Peng), lanterns light up homes and shops, and candle-lit hot-air balloons are launched to bear away the troubles of the earth-bound.

DATE: November (three days). **LOCATION:** Nationwide, but especially northern Thailand. **CONTACT:** Tourism Authority of Thailand (see *Resources*).

Surin Elephant Roundup

Surin **November**

If you've ever wanted to see lots and lots of elephants, this is your festival. Unfortunately, they're accompanied by lots and lots of

Surin: The world-famous elephant pageant draws more than 100 elephants and many more humans. (Nik Wheeler)

tourists. Thousands of visitors (mostly foreign) converge on this provincial capital to see the feats of more than 100 elephants, and ride them, too. In addition to a parade of pachyderms outfitted for medieval warfare, the festival features log-pulling, wild elephant hunts, and elephant soccer. One great event is a tug-of-war between a huge elephant and 100 men (the elephant usually wins).

DATE: Late November. **LOCATION:** Surin, capital of the Surin Province, 450 km/280 miles northeast of Bangkok. **TRANSPORT:** Train or bus (special charters run during the festival) from Bangkok. **ACCOMMODATION:** Surin has several hotels, but unless you book ahead, don't count on finding rooms during the roundup. **CONTACT:** Tourism Authority of Thailand (see *Resources*).

Vegetarian Banquet for Monkeys

Lop Buri **November/December**

The guests of honor behave like animals at this resplendent banquet, arriving late, leaping on the tabletops, and fighting over food. When they've had their fill they show their gratitude by stealing cans of Coca-Cola and swinging from the chandeliers (tree branches), laughing and throwing food at their hosts.

Lop Buri hotelier and banquet organizer Yongyuth Kijwattananuson has come to expect bad manners from his 600 guests, who live in the trees and ruins around the city's 13th-century temples and shrines. Yongyuth started the fête in 1988 as a way of expressing gratitude for his prosperity. Gratitude to the monkeys?

Elephant School

Most of the elephants that participate in the Elephant Roundup at Surin are trained at the Ban Tha Klang Elephant School, about 40 km (25 miles) north of Surin. Here, and at the Young Elephant Training Center in Lampang (164 km/102 miles south of Chiang Mai), you can take a peek at the process of training and caring for elephants.

Elephants typically begin intensive training at age four or five, and spend the next four years learning how to move teak logs around forests (Thailand supplies much of the world's legally logged teak). Elephant masters are also trained in how to bid the beasts to kneel, pick up logs, and push and drag felled trees.

"Yes, they really give the town much of its character, so I treat them once a year to a big day of fun."

The rest of the year the monkeys—long-tailed macaqués—beg and steal food from visitors and townspeople. But today, they get a spread that makes thousands of human mouths water. Dozens of chefs and servers work for two days to prepare the vegetarian delicies that are beautifully arranged on tables covered with red cloth. There's *thang yod* (a Thai sweet), pumpkin, sticky rice, tropical fruit salads, and much more. When the monkeys arrive (and it sometimes takes a while, since they're often scared off by the loudspeakers, onlookers, and scores of press photographers), they soon reduce the arrangments to a mess that would make a human toddler proud.

Most of the monkeys live in Lop Buri, where residents grate their windows to keep them out of houses, and travelers guard earrings and food as they walk among the temples. But some monkeys are rumored to travel great distances to attend the banquet. "Some come from as far away as Sukhothai or Chiang Mai," says Yongyuth. "You can see them getting off the trains the morning of the banquet."

DATE: Late November/early December. The banquet is served at 10 a.m., noon, and 2 p.m. **LOCATION:** Lop Buri is 115 km (71 miles) north of Bangkok. **TRANSPORT:** Lop Buri lies along the main Bangkok-Chiang Mia rail line, and is easily reached from anywhere in central Thailand. **ACCOMMODATION:** There are a number of comfortable hotels in town; alternatively, the banquet can be done as a day-stop on the way north or south. **CONTACT:** Yongyuth Kijwattananuson, Lopburi Inn, 28/9 Narai Maharach Rd., Lopburi

Eating like animals: Hundreds of monkeys are treated to a gourmet banquet once a year in Lop Buri. *(Tom Clynes)*

15000, Thailand, Tel 036-412300. Also, Tourism Authority of Thailand (see *Resources*).

While you're there ...

- **Narathiwat Fair, Narathiwat:** Traditional southern Thai music and dance, artisan displays, dove-singing contests, and boat races bring in visitors from all over, including the King and Queen of Thailand. (Last week of September.)
- **Wan Phra Jao Prot Lok, Nakhon Phanom:** In honor of the Buddha's ascent to heaven, "fire boats" are launched on the Mekong River, carrying offerings of food and flowers. It's an exceptionally beautiful event. (November/December.)

Resources

In **Thailand**: Tourism Authority Of Thailand, 372 Bamrung Muang Rd., Bangkok 10100 Tel 02-226-0060, Fax 02-224-6221. **USA & Canada**: Tourism Authority of Thailand, 5 World Trade Center, Suite 3443, New York, NY 10048, Tel (212) 432-0433, Fax (212) 912-0920. **UK**: Tourism Authority of Thailand, 49 Albemarie Street, London WIX 3 FE, Tel 071-499-7679, Fax 071-629-5519. **Australia:** Tourism Authority of Thailand, 12th Floor, Royal Exchange Bldg., 56 Pitt Street, Sydney 2000, Tel 02-247-7549, Fax 02-251-2456. **Germany**: Thailandisches Fremdenverkehrsbüro, Bethmannstr, 58 D 6000 Frankfurt M.1, Tel 069-295-704, Fax 069-281-468.

VIETNAM

To many Westerners, Vietnam brings to mind only a tragic land ravaged by war. But as the country begins to open its doors to the world, first-time visitors may be shocked at what they find: a stunningly beautiful land of lush green mountain rainforests, tranquil beaches, verdant rice paddies, and friendly villages that move to the rhythm of a past millenium. They also find a highly civilized people, whose rich and unique customs are again flourishing.

Hundreds of ancient folk festivals have been resurrected in Vietnam, as the country begins to find its way back to the roots of its culture. Many rituals and customs had not been practiced since the 1940s, when they were banned during the war against French colonists. Some saw a brief resurgence in the 1950s, but were halted when war again broke out, only to resume in 1988, when social and religious controls were relaxed. Most festivals have their roots in ancient animism, ancestor worship, and Confucian ritual, mixed and matched with elements of Taoism, Hinduism, and, most conspicuously, Buddhism.

TET

Nationwide **January/February**

Tet, the Vietnamese New Year, is like Chanukah, Christmas, and New Year's Eve combined. It's time to deck the halls with plum tree blossoms, look sharp, and be on one's best behavior with friends, family, and creditors. No matter what a Vietnamese does or believes during his or her modern existence, Tet immerses everyone in an identity based in traditions that are singularly Vietnamese. The whole country is united at Tet, devoting full creative energy to preparing for it and experiencing it.

Tet kicks off the new lunar calendar and the start of spring. It officially lasts a week—although festivities go on much longer—and is an attempt to set the proper tone for the coming year. Pre-Tet ceremonies are performed to clear the way for fun and spiritual safety: Clay trees are made to ward off evil spirits,

Tet: In Ho Chi Minh City, people offer New Year's incense at a temple. (Naomi Duguid/Asia Access)

and lime dust is spread around houses to gain additional protection from the Buddha. To appease the *Tao Quan,* or gods of the hearth, devotees make a ceremonial offering of food, paper models, a robe, and boots (but no pants—these were burned when the *Tao Quan* got too close to the fire!). Followers ask the *Tao Quan* to put the Emperor of Jade in a good mood when they visit him in heaven, and they prepare special food and decorate their homes.

On New Year's Eve and New Year's Day, fireworks are set off to the accompaniment of a gong and drum chorus, to frighten away the devil Na A and his wife, who hate light and loud noises. Listening in between bursts of fireworks, Vietnamese try to detect the first sounds of the New Year. A barking dog means that confidence and trust can be expected; a buffalo's bellow foretells hard work; an owl's hoot means impending sickness. Like the first sound, the first visitor to the household on the first day of Tet is believed to indicate the kind of luck the family can expect for the rest of the year. Consequently, charming, successful, and happy-go-lucky people receive many invitations.

Vietnamese "visit" and pay respects to dead ancestors, and engage in many other religious ceremonies. On the seventh day the *Tao Quan* are believed to return to earth to protect the Vietnamese people, and the real partying can begin! Over the next month fairs and festivals happen throughout the country, and a mood of generosity and gratitude prevails. People put on exotic costumes and masks, and ferocious dragons shake through the streets with discrete, athletic operators serving as the beasts' backbones and legs.

DATE: January/February (starting on the 23rd day of the 12th lunar month, and continuing for at least a month thereafter). **LOCATION:** Across Vietnam, with Hanoi, Ho Chi Minh (Saigon), and Hue doing it best. **TRANSPORT:** Ho Chi Minh or Hanoi can be reached from a growing number of international airports. Most frequent flights are from Bangkok and Manila. **ACCOMMODATION:** Hanoi and Ho Chi Minh City have lots of hotels, but reservations for Tet should be booked well in advance. **CONTACT:** Vietnam Tourism (see *Resources*).

While you're there ...

- **Mai Dong, Hai Ba Trung district, Hanoi:** This festival, which pays homage to the great general Lady Le Chan and the Trung sisters' army who battled the Chinese in 40–43 AD, features wrestling matches. (February/March; fourth through sixth day of the first lunar month.)
- **Chu Dong Tu Festival, Da Trach village, Hai Hung Province:** Processions of villagers in traditional clothing bring gifts of incense, flowers, food, and candles to the temple in honor of Chu Dong Tu, an immortalized 16th-century fisherman. (February/March.)

Huong Tich/Lac Long Quan Festival

Huong Tich mountain range February/March/April

The Huong Tich Buddhist pilgrimage, starting from the Thien Tru Pagoda on the shore of the Yen Vi Stream, makes an extremely photogenic ascent through the low mountains west of Hanoi, moving past temples, shrines, and pagodas. The destination is the Huong Tich Grotto, which many regard as the most beautiful spot in all of Vietnam. The limestone carvings and luscious jungle form a perfect, serene setting, while inside the huge cave, the Pagoda of Perfumes (Chua Huong Thich) can be explored by foot or boat.

The pilgrimage starts with a car or bus ride from Hanoi to the Day River, and a boat ride though the Yen Vi Stream's valley of jungles, rice paddies, and limestone hills. After reaching the Thien Tru Pagoda, a two-hour walk up a steep path winds past countless shrines and pagodas, until reaching the Huong Tich Grotto. Rest and refreshment stops line the trail up the "Mountain of Perfume," and at Huong Tich Grotto, the main religious festivities take place amid stalagmites and stalagtites, shrines, banners, and the smokey haze of countless joss-sticks.

You may want to plan the pilgrimage for late March or early April, to coincide with the six-day Lac Long Quan Festival in Binh Minh, a village on the way to the Huong Son commune. This festival is dedicated to the man who is considered the "ancestor" of the Vietnamese people, Lac Long Quan. His wife, Au Co, is said to have miraculously laid 100 people (hen-style, that is) in Ha Son Binh region, and thus populated the area. Homage is paid to Au Co and her husband, and the Buddha is the "guest of honor" during the festival. The narrow streets are filled with teenage girls carrying sanctified platters of beautifully arranged fruit and flowers. These are strategically placed around town, so that old men wearing bright silk robes can lay food, wine, and other presents on them for the Buddha, to the accompaniment of traditional music.

DATE: The Huong Tich pilgrimage season starts in February, and continues through spring. The Lac Long Quan Festival falls in late March or early April (the first through sixth days of the third lunar month). **LOCATION:** Near Binh Minh, Than Oai district, Ha Son Binh Province. **TRANSPORT:** From Hanoi, an hour's bus or car ride gets you to the Day River, where a boat can be hired to float you along the Yen Vi Stream to the Thien Tru Pagoda. From there, the path is easy to find (just follow the other pilgrims). **ACCOMMODATION:** Unless you wish to sleep under the stars, the trip is probably best made as a long day-trip from Hanoi. **CONTACT:** Vietnam Tourism (see *Resources*).

THAY PAGODA FESTIVAL

Quoc Hai **March/April**

Of variable length, this festival features many traditional forms of entertainment, including firecracker competitions, folk singing, rowing contests, and mountain-climbing events. One highlight is the unique water puppetry (*mua roi can*), an exclusive of the Vietnamese Red River Delta dating from the eighth century. Puppeteers stand chest-deep in the water, behind a screen, and manipulate the puppets' bamboo rods from beneath the surface, letting the puppets use water for a stage floor. The festival is dedicated to Dao Hanh, a respected Buddhist monk and teacher who was master of the Ly Dynasty, and a big fan of water puppetry.

DATE: March/April (seventh day of the third lunar month). **LOCATION:** Quoc Hai, Ha Son Binh Province. **TRANSPORT:** Transport is probably best arranged through Vietman Tourism (see below). **ACCOMMODATION:** Consider staying in Hanoi and day-tripping to Quoc Hai. **CONTACT:** Vietnam Tourism (see *Resources*).

WHILE YOU'RE THERE ...

Holiday of the Dead (Thanh Minh), nationwide: Families visit the graves of deceased relatives and make offerings of food, flowers, votive papers, and incense. (March/April; fifth day of the third lunar month.)

Buddha's Birth, Enlightenment, and Death, nationwide: Buddhists decorate their temples, pagodas, and homes with lanterns, and hold evening processions. (May; eighth day of the fourth lunar month.)

Summer Solstice Day (Doan Ngu), nationwide: The God of Death is always looking for soldiers to staff his army. On Doan Ngu, people burn humans in effigy to placate him, and make offerings to spirits and ghosts. (June; fifth day of the fifth lunar month.)

The Feast of the Wandering Souls and Hungry Ghosts (Trung Nguyen)

Nationwide **August/September**

The souls of the damned can be found wandering around Vietnam during Trung Nguyen, looking for something to eat. Luckily, they can count on the generosity of the Vietnamese, who kindly provide for them on their annual 24-hour leave from hell. Assortments of cooked meat, fruits, sweet rolls, and vermicelli soup are lavishly laid out in pagodas and public places, to feed the poor starving souls who are thought not to eat the rest of the year. Earnest prayers for their absolution are lobbied, and cash and clothes fashioned out of votive papers are burned, to help the dead either escape from purgatory or cope better upon their return.

DATE: August/September (full-moon day of the seventh lunar month, traditionally, but celebrated in different places at different times during the seventh month). **LOCATION:** Nationwide. **CONTACT:** Vietnam Tourism (see *Resources*).

Mid-Autumn Festival (Trung Thu)

Nationwide **September/October**

The mid-autumn festival isn't just for kids; they merely star in it. During the Duong Dynasty (so the legend goes), Emperor Minh-Hoang took his empress to Thai Dick Lake on full-moon night to admire the moon, and to recite his inspired moon-poetry. Nowadays, the mooning is done by adults, not so much over the moon as over their children. Moon cakes with unusual fillings, sold in colorful boxes for gift-giving, are part of the bounty for youngsters. Children also receive colorful lanterns depicting dragons, butterflies, cars, and boats, which they swing around on sticks. On the night of the festival, boys and girls form a dance-procession with their candle-lit lanterns, interpreting various "unicorn dances" to the delight of all.

DATE: Mid-October (the 15th day of the eighth lunar month). **LOCATION:** Nationwide. **CONTACT:** Vietnam Tourism (see *Resources*).

© RESOURCES

In Vietnam: Vietnam Tourism (*Du Lich Viet Nam*), 69–71 Nguyen Du Street, Hanoi, Socialist Republic of Vietnam, Tel 90772. **USA:** Permanent Mission of the Socialist Republic of Vietnam to the United Nations, 20 Waterside Plaza, New York, NY 10010, Tel (212) 725-4680, Fax (212) 686-8534. Vietnam Resource Group, 955 L'Enfant Plaza North, SW, Suite 4000, Washington, DC 20024, Tel (202) 651-8007, (800) 871-8626. Fax (202) 484-4899. **UK:** Embassy of the S.R. of Vietnam, 12–14 Victoria Road, London W8 5RD, Tel 71-937-1912, Fax 71-937-6108. **Germany:** Embassy of the S.R. of Vietnam, Konstantinstr. 37, D-5300, Bonn 2, Tel 228-357021, Fax 228-351866. **Australia:** Embassy of the S.R. of Vietnam, 6 Timbarra Crescent O'Malley, Canberra, ACT 2606, Tel 6-286-6059, Fax 6-286-45341.

AUSTRALIA & THE SOUTH PACIFIC

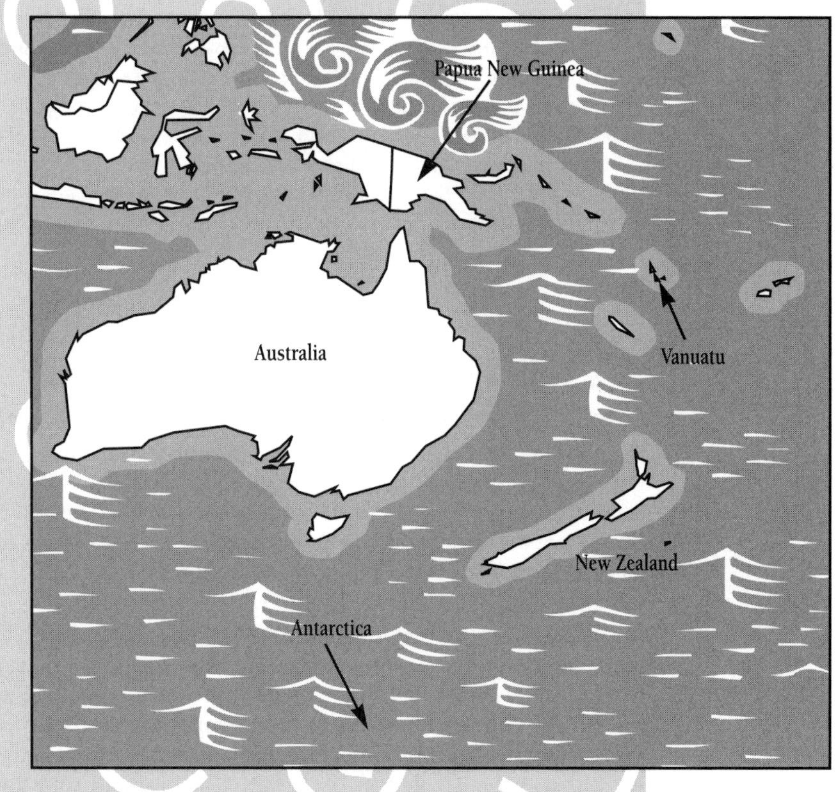

Frozen and inhospitable most of the year, Antarctica actually brims with life during the "warm" months. There are few human-sponsored events, but the continent shines during the Austral summer with the round-the-clock antics of whales, seals, flying birds, and penguins—who put on some of the most spectacular performances on earth.

ANTARCTICA

One nice thing about Antarctica is that nobody technically owns it. The seven countries that once claimed parts of it have signed a treaty relinquishing their claims and giving everyone free access. Thus, there are no passports, visas, borders, or customs to deal with—and the only rules are those that protect wildlife. It should be noted, though, that Antarctica isn't the kind of place where independent travel is practical, and nearly everyone hooks up with a tour operator of some kind.

PENGUIN HATCHING SEASON

Antarctic Peninsula **January**

January is a noisy, active month near the bottom of the world, as the eggs of millions of penguins begin to hatch and the nippers start squawking for food. In coastal colonies of 50,000 or more, busy mom and pop penguins work in shifts, one incubating the chick while the other waddles and slides into the water to gather sustenance.

What's known as the "guard stage" in the reproductive cycle of the penguin is the most interesting and picturesque time of year to visit the Antarctic Peninsula, which reaches up in a long arc toward the southernmost tip of South America. Temperatures reach a bearable 7°C (45°F), and the peninsula's shoreline is teeming with a phenomenal range of species. Whales and leopard seals ply the blue open water, while the sky is filled with masses of birds like the Arctic Tern, which makes a 32,000-kilometer (20,000-mile) migration from the northern polar area each year.

The peninsula's seven varieties of penguins create a lively and amusing spectacle. In a scene that's repeated over and over

Getting mighty crowded: Giant colonies of penguins on the Antarctic Penninsula and nearby islands are a photographer's dream. (Wolfgang Kaehler)

again, you'll see a male come whirring through the water with a full crop of food, then make a flamboyant, hilarious landing. His next task is to waddle through the closely laid lairs of his thousands of neighbors to his own nest. This is harder than it sounds, since bumps, missteps, or dallying are treated as invasions of privacy that often result in a pummeling barrage of beaks. This in mind, he tries to make himself as slim as possible by pulling in his stomach, then "pencil-walking" quickly through the chaotic maze.

Preceding page photo: *Proud parents: A pair of chinstrap penguins admires its newly hatched chicks. (Wolfgang Kaehler)*

Finally, he makes it to his nest, where the baby is fed and the couple trades places. The wife sets out to gather food, knowing that she'll have to deal with the cruel world of high-strung neighbors on land, and the penguin's arch-nemesis—the leopard seal—in the water. Danger also lurks above, and parents who relax for even a moment are making a tempting offer to a skua, a fierce predatory bird that flies around looking for opportunities to snatch babies from nests.

The best thing about the often comical, often brutal world of the penguins is that you can stand as close as 4.5 meters (15 feet) from the edge of the giant hatcheries without disturbing the habitat. Small groups of observers and photographers land on the majestic shores daily in January and February, taking small launches in from the comfortable quarters of larger yachts offshore. Many trips combine excursions to the penguin hatcheries with mountain climbing and fjord cruising in Antarctica or Tierra del Fuego.

DATE: January or early February is the best time to watch penguins in the "guard stage." Adults locate nesting sites in October and November, the chicks hatch in December, and by mid-February the vulnerable chicks are too big for the nest. **LOCATION:** The Antarctic Peninsula is located due south of South America's Tierra del Fuego. **TRANSPORT:** Private tour services stage excursions from Punta Arenas (Chile), Ushuaia (Argentina), and Stanley (Falkland Islands). Excursions approach the other side of Antarctica from Invercargill or Bluff (New Zealand), and Hobart (Australia). **ACCOMMODATION:** Since there's only one land station for non-scientific personnel, most visitors stay in "floating hotels" or yachts just offshore. **CONTACT/RESOURCES:** For a list of tour operators and transportation services, or other information about Antarctica, contact the International Association of Antarctica Tour Operators, 11417 S.E. 215th Street, Kent, WA 98031, USA, Tel (206) 854-7541, Fax (206) 850-3167.

AUSTRALIA

Stimulating, amusing, rowdy, and sometimes perfectly civilized, the world's largest island and smallest continent is a place where variety reigns supreme. In this huge country you can experience great cities and some of the world's last great expanses of empty, sculpted landscape. There are blizzards on Tasmania and sandstorms in the bush; cute critters and sharp-toothed beasts; skiing in July and surfing at Christmas.

Blessed with all this flip-flopped variety and an extroverted, sportive populace, it's not surprising that Australia is an extremely lively festival ground. Ever in search of a spectacle or a spree, Australians have filled their calendar with unlikely events like beer can regattas, cockroach races, and other imaginative opportunities to socialize and knock back a few "tinnies" or "stubbies." In addition to these rousing rave-ups, you'll find highbrow arts festivals, ethnic gatherings, and outback celebrations that accent the sophisticated, mystical culture of the original Australians, the Aborigines.

Albert Aussie Weekend Celebrations

Carara (Queensland) **January**

Coinciding with Australia Day weekend, this monster event has huge helpings of everything Australians love: the outdoors, horses, sports—and just plain having a good time with massive quantities of the "amber fluid." The Carara Sporting Complex on the banks of the Nerang River is stretched to the max with events, including the crowd-riling spectacle of wild cow milking.

Horses figure prominently in bush rodeos, Clydesdale demonstrations, wagon runs, and picnic races. Participants get out of the saddle to test their athletic prowess in an iron man competition, various water sports, and other muscle-bound activities. But if you don't feel like working up a sweat on a hot January weekend, you can just lay back and listen to live bands, or refresh yourself at the Ethnic Food and Wine Fair. Other options include nearby bungee jumping sites or the way-cool happenings at Surfers' Paradise.

DATE: Australia Day Weekend (the weekend closest to January 26). **LOCATION:** The Carara Sporting Complex is located in Carara, 40 km (25 miles) south of Brisbane in Queensland. **TRANSPORT:** From Brisbane, trains and buses make regular runs along the Gold Coast; the trip takes less than an hour. **ACCOMMODATION:** A huge variety of accommodation can be found at Surfers Paradise and along the entire Gold Coast. **CONTACT:** Albert Aussie Day Foundation Inc., P.O. Box 172, Nerang, Queensland 4211, Tel 075-58-0217. Also, Australian Tourist Commission (see *Resources*).

While you're there ...

- **Coominya Grape and Watermelon Festival, Coominya (Queensland):** At this country festival you name it and they do it—with fruit that is. Melons and grapes are thrown, eaten, loaded, or relayed in races. The 20 kilogram Watermelon Marathon and the seed-spitting contest shouldn't be missed (from a distance). Street processions, music, bush dance, and arts and crafts round out the festivities. (Second Saturday in January.)
- **Cockroach Race, Darwin (Northern Territory):** The course is a large map of Australia, where roaches navigate a plastic tube running around the coastline. Unbeknownst to each of the scrambling contestants, their time is running out—the winner will be the first to get gassed by pest controllers at the finish. Contact: Darwin Sailing Club, P.O. Box 89, Darwin, Northern Territory 0801, Tel 089-81-1700. (Australia Day, January 26.)
- **Annual Cockroach Races, Brisbane (Queensland):** Amid a hotel-catered luncheon spread featuring Pig on a Spit, Aussies let loose their BYO roaches in a battle for first place. The event also features live entertainment of the two-legged variety. Contact: Story Bridge Hotel, Tel 07-391-2266. (Monday after Australia Day.)
- **Montsalvat Jazz Festival, Eltham (Victoria):** Australia's biggest jazz festival is held at the charming Montsalvat artists' colony. (January.)

Compass Cup Cow Race

Mt. Compass Oval (South Australia) **February**

Cattle chaos reigns in this kooky outing in the heart of wine country. Daring locals bid on chances to take 10 brown-eyed Bossies for a spin—in whatever direction the unwieldy beasts choose. And while contestants cluelessly meander the course in search of a snack, there's plenty more to do and watch. Hay-bale stacking brings on the brawn, and a rubber-boot marathon has contestants wallowing in water-filled Wellies (Wellington boots). There's a dung fling, and of course that Australian favorite, the Toot Loading competition, which provides a hilarious answer to the question "how many people can squeeze into an outhouse?" If you really want to know, this is the place to find out.

DATE: Second Sunday in February. **LOCATION:** Mt. Compass is about 60 km (37 miles) south of Adelaide. **TRANSPORT:** Buses and scenic-tour trains run through the area from Adelaide. **ACCOMMODATION:** While Mt. Compass is within day-tripping distance from Adelaide, there are accommodations in nearby McClaren Vale. **CONTACT:** Mt. Compass Cup, P.O. Box 47, Mt. Compass, South Australia 5210, Tel 085-56-8263. Also, Australian Tourist Commission (see *Resources*).

© Adelaide Festival and Festival Fringe

Adelaide (South Australia) **February/March**

A biennial event with a split personality, Australia's best-known highbrow arts festival also has a spirited lowbrow side. A week before the city turns into a Mecca of art and culture, the Fringe kicks off with a flamboyant parade introducing the cast of characters: offbeat musicians, dancers, performers, mimes (get 'em!), and exhibitionists. The procession spills into Rundle Street, where stages have been set up to treat observers to the innovative, the extravagant, the irreverent, and the downright bizarre.

Within a week, the Fringe activities are joined by the country's premiere arts festival. The Adelaide Festival attracts talent from all over the world and includes the finest in Australian visual and performance art. Plays, exhibitions, and music are staged within the city's Festival Center, while Writers' Week and Artists' Week allow for lively intellectual exchange. Some years, the festival combines with World of Music and Dance (WOMAD) in playing host to a World Music Weekend near the festival grounds. Like the rest of the festival, such events confirm Adelaide's position at the top of Australia's cultural roster.

DATE: The four-week biennial event is hosted in even-numbered years; mid-February to mid-March. **LOCATION:** Adelaide (South Australia). **TRANSPORT:** Planes, trains, and buses run fairly regularly from Sydney, Canberra, Brisbane, Melbourne, and Perth. **ACCOMMODATION:** Adelaide boasts a variety of accommodations, but with over 600,000 people attending, it's best to book well ahead. **CONTACT:** Adelaide Festival, G.P.O. Box 1269, Adelaide, South Australia 5001, Tel 08-216-8600. Also, Australian Tourist Commission (see *Resources*).

Psychedelic confusion: You name it, you'll probably see it in the Adelaide Festival Fringe. (Australian Tourist Commission)

BINDOON ROCK FESTIVAL

Bindoon (Western Australia) February/March

In the United States, a Woodstock comes along once ... maybe twice ... let's hope not three times. But in Australia, they've ditched the hype and let rock and roll fanatics gather every year for 30 hours of good rockin' fun. There's plenty of beer, serious partying, and music from more than a dozen world-class bands from Australia and overseas.

Amid a beautiful natural setting—a pine forest interspersed with a couple of swimming holes—Australia's answer to Woodstock or Reading features plenty of food and rousing, beery companionship. You can't BYO, but massive bar facilities keep everyone well juiced. The festival officially starts Saturday morning, but fans start showing up Friday to stake out prime campsites and get the party in motion.

DATE: Usually the second weekend in February. **LOCATION:** Bindoon, north of Perth. **TRANSPORT:** If driving, take the Great Northern Highway from Perth through Bullsbrook; make a left onto Gingin Road and follow the signs. Buses from Perth run during the event. **ACCOMMODATION:** To really experience this, you've got to tent it. **CONTACT:** C. C. Promotions, 50 Clavering Road, Bayswater, Western Australia 6053, Tel 09-272-2727. Also, Australian Tourist Commission (see *Resources*).

The Melbourne Municipal Bicycle Band strikes it up during one of the Melbourne Moomba Festival's more than 200 events. (Joe Viesti/Viesti Associates)

WHILE YOU'RE THERE ...

Evandale Village Fair and Penny Farthing Championships, Evandale (Tasmania): The world's largest gathering for enthusiasts of big-wheel bicycles draws competitors and the curious from all over the world. In this low-key Tasmanian village of 19th-century Georgian buildings, events include the Slalom, the Obstacle Race (a crowd-pleaser since 1884), the 200-Meter Sprint, and the Slow Ride, where the last one to finish wins (a real challenge on these top-heavy contraptions). In addition to the biking events, the town hosts a village fair. Contact: Evandale Village Fair

Association Inc., 29 Murray Street, Evandale, Tasmania 7212, Tel 003-91-8223. (Last weekend in February.)

The Great Tasmanian Bicycle Ride, Hobart and throughout Tasmania: This race-and-ride takes riders open-air through Tasmania's beautifully lonely landscapes and historic villages. Sag wagons carry maintenance, camping, and waterproof gear. Register at least one month in advance. Contact: Bicycle Victoria, CPO Box 1961 R, Melbourne, Vic. 3001, Tel 03-670-9911. (Late February.)

Sydney Gay Mardi Gras, Sydney: The costumes are extravagant, the parade is a riot, and the partying along Oxford Street is always spirited. This is the largest event of its type in the world, and includes a month of events large and small. Not to be missed is the "dogs and their owners look-alike contest." Contact: Tel 02-332-4088. (February/March.)

Melbourne Moomba Festival, Melbourne (Victoria): The colorful fireworks that spark the night skies over Melbourne are nothing compared to what's happening in the streets during Moomba. The 11-day party has more than 200 events, including dragon boat racing, a major pop festival, a waterskiing competition, carnivals, and art displays. The highlight of the festivities is a float parade through the city, lorded over by a celebrity appointed "King of Moomba." Be sure to ask the locals what "Moomba" means. (11 days in mid-March.)

Hunter Valley Vintage Festival, Hunter Valley (New South Wales): Whether or not you want to participate in grape-picking or grape-stomping contests, here's a great opportunity to sample Australia's wines. Some 50 wineries present a series of events and tastings in February and March.

Port Fairy Folk Festival, Port Fairy (Victoria): Australia's largest folk music festival attracts music lovers to this tiny coastal town. Music, dancing, storytelling, and handicrafts draw more than 10,000 people. (Labour Day Weekend.)

Festival of Perth: About half a million people attend this major arts festival over its six-week stint. Events include drama, music, opera, dance, film, visual art, and parades, with performers from Australia and all over the world. (Mid-February through mid-March.)

WIND ON WATER

Near Geraldton **March**

Where there's water, you'll find Australians, and where Aussies congregate, you'll find beer. Put those two facts together and you have the Wind on Water festival featuring the Great Canboat Race. Seaworthy vessels made from beer cans maneuver as best they can at the mouth of the Greenough River. Captains of canboats that prove unseaworthy can console themselves by raising a few tinnies to the contestants in the Leaky Boat Race, in which two-man crews row and bail perforated dinghies along an obstacle course on the shallow river. Kiting is also displayed for those who would rather keep their eyes focused on the heavens.

Sidetrip: A Windy, Watery Playground

Windy Geraldtown has a fantastic climate for activities like sailing, windsurfing, and kite flying. Situated along a beautiful stretch of coast, the town specializes in lobster and other fresh-caught seafood. Both Geraldtown and the nearby backpacking center of Kalbarri have alluring coastlines with spectacular gorges and Dutch East India shipwrecks lying offshore. In Kalbarri there's an excellent museum with antiques salvaged from wrecks, and a nearby rainforest has exceptionally diverse bird life.

DATE: First Sunday in March. **LOCATION:** Geraldtown, 421 km/261 miles north of Perth in Western Australia. **TRANSPORT:** Geraldtown's airport handles flights from Perth only; buses serve Geraldtown from Perth and points north along Highway 1, all the way to Darwin. **ACCOMMODATION:** A wide range of hotels, hostels, guesthouses, and campgrounds are available. **CONTACT:** Lions Club of Greenough, P.O. Box 310, Geraldton, Western Australia 6530, Tel 099-38-1479. Also, Australian Tourist Commission (see *Resources*).

Opal Festival

Coober Pedy (South Australia) **April**

One of the harshest regions of the outback surprisingly draws lots of travelers. Most come to check out the lifestyle of the 2,000 people living in subterranean cities to escape temperatures that often exceed 51°C (125°F). They fill up *Kupa Piti* ("White Man's Burrow" in the local Aboriginal language), hoping to strike it rich mining the opal pockets that supply most of these stones to the world.

Opals and mining provide the focus of Coober Pedy's annual festival. To a true Aussie, anything can be reduced to a sport, and hard work is no exception. Events include dump shoveling, winching, and the exciting/igniting gelignite toss. For those who would rather keep a safe distance from the sporting area, the mining events coincide with local craftsmen's displays of zebra stone carving and other handicrafts, while ethnic music and dance shows keep things hopping.

DATE: Easter Saturday. **LOCATION:** Coober Pedy is 820 km (510 miles) northwest of Adelaide via the Stuart Highway. **TRANSPORT:** Several buses make regular stops from Adelaide or Alice Springs; you can also fly in from Adelaide. **ACCOMMODATION:** There are motels available, as well as a local hostel. **CONTACT:** District Council of Coober Pedy, P.O. box 265, Coober Pedy, South Australia 5723, Tel 086-72-5298. Also, Australian Tourist Commission (see *Resources*).

While you're there ...

Barossa Valley Vintage Festival, Barossa (South Australia): In alternate years the valley boasts not only the best scenery of any of the country's wine-making regions, but some of the most spectacular bouts of drinking. Aussified Germans let down their hair and celebrate the bounty of the area's three dozen or so vineyards by eating, stomping grapes, and generally getting "rolling." (Biennial; begins on Easter Monday in odd years.)

Camel Cup

Alice Springs (Northern Territory) **May**

Camels have adapted well to the harsh life in the Northern Territory and Aussies have adopted the camel as part of their culture. That means they've found a way to bet on them. Born of a wager, the first Camel Cup took place on the dry bottom of the Todd River in 1971. Now the race and quite a few other camel events are accompanied by wide-ranging spreads of food and libation that encompass another part of Australian culture: partying hardy. Alice Springs itself is a major jumping-off point for north-south ventures, and many visitors stop here one their way to Ayers Rock and elsewhere in the outback.

DATE: Second Saturday in May. **LOCATION:** Blatherskite Park in Alice Springs. **TRANSPORT:** Alice Springs is accessible by plane from all major cities; buses and trains also make frequent (and long) trips to the city. **ACCOMMODATION:** There's a variety of accommodation in the city, but it's advisable to book ahead for events like this. **CONTACT:** Alice Springs Lions Club, Tel 089-52-4472. Also, Australian Tourist Commission (see *Resources*).

While you're there ...

Keppel Krabtastic World Crab-Tying Championships, Keppel Sands (Queensland): In one of Australia's finer native arts, the barefoot crabber takes ten steps into an arena full of big crabs, grabs one, binds its claws together, then gets the heck outta there. Due to the event's limited participant appeal, it is now joined by crab races (with untied crabs), a tug of war (sans crabs), and live music. Contact: North-West Canoe Club, P.O. Box 475, Mount Isa, Queensland 4825, Tel 077-43-6602. (First Sunday in May.)

And they're off: Camel jockeys goad their unweildy beasts toward the finish line in the Camel Cup at Alice Springs. (Bill Bachman)

- **Baycarna and World Smiling Championships, Pialba Oval (Queensland):** As part of the Baycarna community festival, the World Smiling Championships lure contenders from around the globe with prizes that include toothpaste, T-shirts, and cash. Contact: Tourist Officer, Council of the City of Hervey Bay, P.O. Box 45, Torquay, Hervey Bay, Queensland 4655, Tel 071-28-2544. (First weekend in May.)
- **Melbourne Film Festival, Melbourne (Victoria):** The grandaddy of Australian film events presents flicks from Australia and all over the world. (May/June.)
- **Barunga Sports Festival, Beswick Land Trust (Northern Territory):** The festival, attended by some 40 Aboriginal groups, is a great chance to experience arts and crafts, contests in spear-throwing and firelighting, and *bush tucker* (outback food). Contact: Barunga-Lugularr Government Council, P.M.B. Katherine, Northern Territory 0852, Tel 089-75-4505. (Late May or early June.)
- **Bougainvillea Festival, Darwin:** This week-long festival features concerts, dances, parades, and a picnic in the Botanical Garden. One highlight is the Rock-Sitting Contest at the full moon, in which teams perch on surf-side outcrops, drinking beer. Teams stay out on the rocks for days, each trying to outlast the others and take home the endurance title. (Two weeks in mid-June.)

Cape York Aboriginal Dance Festival

Laura, Queensland **June**

The faint-hearted might want to consider staying back at the hotel. While the festival is only three days long, it takes several

Aussie Tucker

Although not what the French would consider "haute cuisine," Aussie *tucker* (food) has a certain charm of its own. Meat pies and sausage rolls are common fare, and vegemite—a yeasty mixture with a suspicious similarity to congealed motor oil—is fun to eat on a dare or useful for threatening unruly children. For native Australian dining, head to the bush for some of these Aboriginal delights:

Kup maori (meat and vegetables wrapped in banana skins and roasted in an underground oven) • Honey ants • Goanna (roast lizard) • Witjuti (grubs) • Kangaroo tail soup • Emus, possums, or snakes thrown directly on an open fire • Green ants • Water-holding frogs • Moths • Ooliworms (foot-long delicacies drawn out of rotting mangrove trees)

days of hard driving through deserted, unpaved roads just to get there. For adventurous souls, it's well worth a sore derriere to experience the native dancing and music of the Aboriginal tribes in the authentic setting of the Cape York Peninsula outback.

The Cape York festival is one of the few opportunities to engage in Aboriginal traditions in a truly unspoiled setting; the downside is that there's no muscle-soothing Holiday Inn jacuzzi nearby. During the day, you'll see competitions in spear throwing, fire lighting, and boomeranging. Body paint and traditions abound in the competitions, which are judged by respected tribal elders. Nearby, you'll find traditional food and native handicrafts.

At night impromptu parties get going around the campfire (just keep in mind that alcohol is taboo at the festival site). You'll need to bring your own camping gear, but toilets and showers are provided. Nearby, a wealth of rock paintings, some over 13,000 years old, are free for the exploring. You may want to join an organized bushwalk to the beautiful, ancient murals at Giant Horse Gallery, or to sites that feature paintings of hunters, animals, and spirit-men.

DATE: Last weekend in June. **LOCATION:** Laura is 300 tough kilometers (186 miles) north of Cairns on the inland road. The festival site is the Quinkan Reserve, 16 km (10 miles) south of Laura. **TRANSPORT:** Four-wheel-drive vehicles (strongly recommended) can be rented in Cairns for the trip; there are also three-day bus/plane packages available between Cairns and Cooktown. **ACCOMMODATION:** Camping with toilets and showers is available on-site; there are also a few hotels in nearby Cooktown. **CONTACT:**

Drunken devolution: Charles Darwin's namesake city goes wild during the infamous Beer Can Regatta. *(Australian Tourist Commission)*

Queensland Department of Community and Ethnic Affairs, Spence Street, Cairns, Queensland 4870, Tel 070-52-3155. Also, Australian Tourist Commission (see *Resources*).

BEER CAN REGATTA

Darwin **July/August**

If Charles Darwin were to revisit his namesake city in early July, he'd reel at the drunken devolution of the northern Australian branch of the human species. This week of unruly events features concerts, dances, unusual contests, and the main event: a regatta of incredible boats built entirely out of beer cans.

Australia's most extroverted misfits all seem to wind up in Darwin, a tropical outpost on the north coast. The city's tattooed, brawling population hates authority and spends much of its free time defending Darwin's reputation as the beer-drinking capital of the world. (Darwinians annually consume an average of 230 liters of "the amber.")

During the regatta spectators line Mindil Beach, drinking Darwin Stubbies, which, at 2.25 liters (75 ounces), are the world's largest bottles of beer. Everyone cheers as the boats wallow, flounder, and sink. The Regatta's fleet includes 20 or more canoes, speedboats, and giant Viking warships with fire hoses. One year some adventurous participants decided to sail their craft all the way to Singapore. Another year, a boat was launched that was constructed of *full* beer cans, fresh from the brewery. "Not fair!" other contestants cried, "The beer must be drunk!"

On shore, there are landlubbers' competitions like Henley-on-Mindil, a series of races along the beach with bottomless boats. Bathing beauty contests, thong throwing, and other wackiness rounds out the event. For sideshows, don't miss the Rage in the Cage at Lim's Rapid Creek Hotel, or the Gong Show at the Nightcliff Hotel on Bagot Road. At the latter, "anything goes" on a stage protected by a chicken-wire net. When the audience has had enough, performers are pelted with open bottles of beer. Depraved, mate!

DATE: A Sunday in July or August, depending on the tides. **LOCATION:** The Regatta takes place at Darwin's Mindil Beach. Other events are scattered throughout the city. **TRANSPORT:** Air connections are available from all major Australian cities and from many capitals in southeast Asia. The bus is an extremely time-consuming proposition (i.e., 51 hours from Brisbane). **ACCOMMODATION:** Accommodations in Darwin are of decent quality, but they're not especially cheap. For budget travelers, the area around the bus station offers the best bargains. **CONTACT:** Beer Can Regatta Assoc., GPO Box 1496, Darwin NT 0801, Tel 089-81-3837 & 089-32-1876, Fax 089-41-2965. Northern Territory Government Tourist Bureau, 31 Smith St., Darwin, NT 0800, Tel 089-81-6611.

© Mt. Isa Rodeo and Mardi Gras

Mount Isa (Queensland) **August**

Skilled horsemen compete for $85,000 in prize money in the largest rodeo event in the southern hemisphere. The party begins in earnest at Friday night's Mardi Gras, with live entertainment and a parade of 60 decorated floats. An Aboriginal Didjeridoo and Dance Festival features performers from miles around, and during the day the cowboys get down to the task of busting broncs and roping steers. Jackeroos have to get an early start to catch the action, since starting times are as early as 6:30 am.

Mt. Isa is a multi-ethnic, rough-and-ready mining town that's dominated by a huge exhaust stack from a lead smelter. It's in the middle of the sparsely populated outback, and tours are organized daily to isolated sites of Aboriginal rock paintings, old mines, and 15-million-year-old fossils. The three-hour tour in the underground mine (for which you'll put on a miner's suit and hard hat) is also quite interesting. By the way, Mt. Isa is the largest city in the world, covering an area of 41,255 sqare kilometers (16,502 square miles).

DATE: Usually the second weekend in August. **LOCATION:** Mt. Isa, 124 km/77 miles west of Cloncurry in Queensland's outback. **TRANSPORT:** The Mt. Isa airport is served by flights from Cairns, Darwin, Alice Springs, and Brisbane. **ACCOMMODATION:** The town

Spoils of victory: A Mt. Isa Rodeo winner relaxes with the trophy saddle and a cold beer. (*Mike Larder/SPORT*)

has quite a transient population; consequently plenty of hotels are available. **CONTACT:** Inland Queensland Tourism and Development Board, Centenary Park, Maarian St., Mt. Isa, Queensland 4825, Tel 077-43-4611. Also, Australian Tourist Commission (see *Resources*).

WHILE YOU'RE THERE ...

Darwin Cup: The Northern Territory's premier horse racing event revs Darwin up into a carnival frenzy. About 15,000 people pack into the Turf

Club—some dressed to the nines and drinking wine, others wearing thongs and drinking stubbies. Parties, balls, and fashion shows round out the events. Contact: Darwin Turf Club, GPO Box 589, Darwin, N.T. 0801, Tel 089-81-2328. (First Monday in August.)

Darwin Rodeo, Darwin (Northern Territory): This major event includes teams from Australia, New Zealand, and North America. (Mid-August.)

Warana

Brisbane (Queensland) **September**

In a city that definitely knows how to party, this is the biggest. With 17 days of art and literature, Warana (an Aboriginal word meaning "blue skies") makes spring official. Events are held in the Botanic Gardens, King George Square, and Albert Park. Lest the scene get too pretentious, the highbrow events are balanced by rock concerts, beer festivals, a rodeo, and the raucous Concours de Decadence—a noisy spectacle of trucks, cars, motorbikes, rock music, and bizarroids.

Most visitors agree that Brisbane is one of Australia's most pleasant and scenic cities. Tropical houses with wide verandas overlook the winding river, and picturesque bridges and squares are cradled by steep hills. Mountains, beaches, and islands can be reached in easy day-trips.

DATE: Third and fourth weekends in September. **LOCATION:** Brisbane. **TRANSPORT:** Brisbane's airport has frequent arrivals from Asia, Europe, North America, the Pacific, and throughout Australia. Trains and buses serve Australian cities. **ACCOMMODATION:** While finding lodging is generally no problem in Brisbane, the festival increases demand for top-end accommodations, so book ahead. **CONTACT:** Brisbane Warana Festival, ltd., 1st Floor, 169 Mary St., Brisbane, Queensland 4000, Tel 07-221-0011. Also, Australian Tourist Commission (see *Resources*).

Henley-on-Todd Regatta and Beerfest

Alice Springs (Northern Territory) **September/October**

Toss aside your boat shoes and strap on a pair of joggers, 'cause the closest you'll get to water will be the ice coolers at the Beerfest. The original waterless regatta includes a pre-race parade of bottomless craft—sailing boats, speedboats, racing eights, and whatever else trots up—that go on to compete in a dusty tramp along the dry bottom of the Todd River. Crews consist of eight

Careening through the sandy rapids of a dry riverbed, the Henley-on-Todd Regatta is giddy Australia at its best. (Australian Tourist Commission)

men each, and woe is he who stumbles at the helm—clumsy-footed mates have been routinely keel-hauled to the finish line.

Other nautical-inspired events include the Oxford Tubs, where two-man canoes on rails paddle to the finish line with shovels, and the Australia Cup battle between an Aussie team and American challengers from a nearby military base. Not to be missed is the great Sea Battle, a grand finale where scrambled-up four-wheel-drive battleships pummel each other with water cannons and flour bombs. The chaos continues the next day with huge layouts of food, beer, and wine.

DATE: Last Saturday in September or first Saturday in October. **LOCATION:** Alice Springs is in the center of Australia, 1,938 km (1,203 miles) north of Adelaide and 1,525 km (946 miles) south of Darwin. **TRANSPORT:** Alice Springs is accessible by plane from all major cities; buses and trains also make frequent trips to the city. **ACCOMMODATION:** There's a variety of accommodation in the city, but it's advisable to book ahead for events like this. **CONTACT:** Henley-on-Todd Regatta, P.O. Box 1385, Alice Springs, Northern Territory 0871, Tel 089-52-8877. Also, Australian Tourist Commission (see *Resources*).

While you're there ...

Western Australian Folk Festival, Toodyay (Western Australia): Western Australia's biggest festival of folk music and dancing draws thousands. (September.)

All Australia goes topsy-turvy over the finals of the AFL Australian-rules football season. No pads are worn, so there are plenty of injury time-outs—opportunities to fetch more beer. (Martin Philbey/SPORT)

◎ **Australian Football League Grand Finale, Melbourne (Victoria):** More than 100,000 rabid fans attend the roughhouse that marks the end of the AFL Australian-Rules football season. "Footy"—a rugby-like game invented to keep cricketers fit—is punishing play. To watch it in true Aussie fashion, balance a schooner in one hand and a meat pie in the other. (Mid-September.)

◎ **Cecil Plains Bushmans' Carnival, Cecil Plains (Queensland):** Although it's just one of more than 20 events, the World Sand Goanna Championship slithers away with the most press. Entrants cold-bloodedly scurry along a sandy 35-meter track, chased by owners waving branches, fists, or rolled-up copies of the *Australian*. About a dozen Goannas—among the world's largest lizards—are aimed toward a tree at the end of the course, but sometimes one will scale the fence along the track, causing a panic in the crowds. (October.)

© **Australian Bush Music Festival, Glen Innes (New South Wales):** With workshops on everything from beer brewing to didjeridooing, this non-stop country and Aboriginal music festival draws bands from far and wide. Bush Band Championships are held on Saturday; Sunday starts off with a Poets' Breakfast. (Late November; NSW Labour Day Weekend.)

© Resources

In Australia: Australian Tourist Commission, 80 William Street, Level 3, Woolloomooloo, New South Wales 2011, Tel 2-3601111, Fax 2-3316469. **USA:** Australian Tourist Commission, 100 Park Ave., 25th Floor, New York, NY 10017, Tel (212) 687-6300, Fax (212) 661-3340. ATC, 2121 Avenue of the Stars, Suite 1200, Los Angeles, CA 90067, Tel (310) 552-1988, Fax (310) 552-1215. **Canada:** Australian Tourist Commission, 2 Bloor Street West, #1730, Toronto, ON M4W 3E2, Tel (416) 925-9575, Fax (416) 925-9312. **UK:** Australian Tourist Commission, Gemini House, 10–18 Puteny Hill, GB-London SW15 6AA, Tel 81-7802227, Fax 81-7801496. **Germany:** Australian Tourist Commission, Neue Mainzerstr. 22, D-6000 Frankfurt, Tel 69-27400620, Fax 69-27400640.

There's too much to do in New Zealand! That's what most visitors say when they come back from a typically too-short stint, breathless and amazed at the range of adventures packed into this small country. Rainforest hiking, volcano walking, geyser bathing, trout fishing, penguin watching, whitewater rafting, mountain climbing, mountain biking, glowworm caving, Alps skiing, skydiving, bungee jumping—name the outdoor activity, New Zealand's got it.

NEW ZEALAND

Not surprisingly, many annual events revolve around the outdoors and sports. The native Maori culture can be experienced at sports and arts festivals on the North Island, and in the larger cities the austral summer features European-style arts and music events. New Zealanders, also called *Kiwis*, are pioneers at heart, and are characteristically helpful and friendly. You'll find them a bit more innocent and subdued than their Aussie neighbors; consequently you're likely to run into more low-key festivals than beer blasts.

New Zealand International Festival of the Arts

Wellington **February/March (Biennial)**

Just when New Zealanders start feeling a little too removed from the rest of the world, the International Festival of the Arts brings it home to the South Pacific. For three weeks every other year, Wellington is filled with magnificent plays, renowned classical and jazz musicians, and even circus acts.

The festival's goal is to take audiences on a voyage of discovery—of themselves and the world. Performers come from Australia, Polynesia, Asia, Europe, Africa, and the Americas to perform and exhibit their own particular crafts. A New Zealand writer may share his or her masterpiece with readings, while a Russian orchestra may perform one of Bach's concertos and a German opera company may stage one of Wagner's works.

Windy Wellington and the Wilds Nearby

Surrounding a magnificent harbor, Wellington's houses and office buildings cling to precipitous slopes that send near-constant high winds channeling through streets and doorways. From Mt. Victoria you can look out over the capital and its harbor, then descend into a lively arts, culture, and café scene.

Within day-tripping distance from Wellington is the Kapiti Coast, with white sand beaches backdropped by the Taraua Range with its mountain forests. Just offshore, Kapiti Island is a bird sanctuary, and the waters around it form a marine sanctuary with excellent diving opportunities. A few kilometers east of Wellington is the Rimutaka Forest Park, with sandy beaches and bright blue ocean, plus plenty of sheep and seals. The mountain range rises steeply upward, and rivers tumble down furiously. Visitors can take short walks in the bush or along the coast to see the seals, or safari into the park in four-wheel-drive vehicles.

Home-grown attractions include the traditional and contemporary Maori arts, which are currently undergoing a revival. The enduring beauty and resilience of this indigenous culture is celebrated with theater, dance, arts, crafts, fashion, and music. Of particular interest are the traditional Maori *poi* dances, action songs, and martial arts. Exceptional handicrafts, such as bone and wood carvings and basketry, are displayed.

DATE: Three weeks in late February and early March on even-numbered years. **LOCATION:** Wellington. **TRANSPORT:** From Europe or North America, all flights arrive in Auckland, with onward connections to Wellington. From Australia or elsewhere in New Zealand, you can fly directly to Wellington. Both trains and buses run between Auckland and Wellington. **ACCOMMODATION:** Wellington is well-stocked with places to stay in all categories, and has an especially good selection of hostels. **CONTACT:** P.O. Box 10–113, Wellington, New Zealand, Tel 04-473-0149, Fax 04-471-1164.

Baldwin Street Gutbuster

Dunedin **February**

Motorists attempting to drive up the steepest street in the world often lose control and careen backward, but fortunately, cars aren't allowed in the Gutbuster. Instead, participants take on Baldwin Street with skates, skateboards, and their own two feet—anything as long as it doesn't have a motor.

The *Guinness Book of World Records* measured the maximum gradient at 1 in 2.86, but adventurers who dash to the top and back down again will more likely be measuring their air intake. Serious runners can compete for the record in a speed section, but anyone who finishes the course receives a locally made Cadbury's chocolate bar, a certificate, and some serious shin splints. Helmets are mandatory.

Dunedin is one of southern New Zealand's largest towns, a university center with a spirited cultural life. With New Zealand's most active music scene (every young person seems to be in a band), it's a great place to catch a couple of sets by next year's Kiwi rock and roll sensation. Dunedin is a good drinking town (it has both a brewery and a distillery), with an ever-hopping pub and café scene. It's also a staging point for eco-tourism activities on the Otago Peninsula. You can day-trip or trek in to the habitats of northern royal albatross, fur seals, dolphins, penguins, and many other birds.

DATE: Mid-February, during Dunedin's Festival Week. **LOCATION:** Dunedin (South Island). **TRANSPORT:** The Dunedin airport handles direct flights from Auckland, Christchurch, Invercargill, and Wellington. Buses serve the entire South Island, and the city is situated on the Christchurch-Invercargill train line. **ACCOMMODATION:** Dunedin and the Otago Peninsula have a wide variety of hotels, motels, hostels, and campgrounds. **CONTACT:** Dunedin Visitor Centre, 48 The Octagon, P.O. Box 5457, Dunedin, Tel 03-474-3300, Fax 03-474-3311.

WILDFOODS FESTIVAL

Hokitika **February**

If golden-fried hu-hu grubs don't sound appealing, there's always stir-fried possum. Or you could try the marinated goat kebabs, feather-light smoked eel wantons, gumboot milkshakes, or "the biggest whitebait patties in the world." These mouth-watering delights wouldn't be complete without home-brewed beer and South Island vineyard wine.

The beautiful west coast of New Zealand's South Island is filled with rainforests, glaciers, lakes, farms, and roaring rivers, which are home to a huge variety of unusual game and edible vegetation. The Wildfoods Festival showcases these treats, with about 40 stalls of food and drink, drawing up to 5,000 people who stroll between food tents, talk to locals, and enjoy brilliant views of the Hokitika River and snow-covered Southern Alps. When visitors

Maori war canoes race and parade in the historic Ngaruawahia Regatta. (Joe Viesti/Viesti Associates)

find they can't consume another savory bite, there's music, outdoor entertainment, and west-coast bush dancing. Locally known entertainers perform everything from country to funk, while face-painters, jugglers, clowns, and the ever-popular "human fly" amuse the crowd. Nearby there are plenty of outdoor recreation opportunities, including extreme sports like helicopter-access whitewater rafting.

DATE: February. **LOCATION:** Hokitika, in Westland in the South Islands. **TRANSPORT:** Hokitika is a four-hour drive from Christchurch, and air service connects the two cities. Bus service is frequent. **ACCOMMODATION:** Hokitika has several hotels, guesthouses, and hostels. **CONTACT:** Hokitika Public Relations Office, P.O. Box 171, 23 Weld St., Hokitika, Tel 3-7558101.

While you're there ...

- **Whaleboat Rowing Regatta, Kawhia:** Drawing thousands of spectators, this regatta takes place in the spot where the Maori *Tainui* canoe made its landing during the Great Migration of around 1350 A.D. (New Year's Day.)
- **Art Deco Weekend, Napier:** This art-deco town hosts costume parties, dinners, and tours on the third weekend in February.
- **Christchurch Arts Festival, Christchurch:** A cultural void was filled when this two-week festival was introduced in 1965. Both international and native performers and artists focus on ballet, drama, music, opera, literature, crafts, and plastic arts. Special events are held for children. (Even-numbered years, two weeks in March.)

Auckland Festival, Auckland: Culture comes to park-sprinkled Auckland in the form of a visual and performing arts festival dating back to 1949. Music, opera, theater, poetry, art, and dance are featured. The festival is held on even-numbered years, but the Auckland Fiesta Week hosts fireworks and the "Round the Bay Run" every March.

Ngaruawahia Regatta, Hamilton: This regatta features those amazing Maori war canoes. (March/April.)

Golden Shears Sheep Shearing Contest, Masterton: In a country this sheep-crazy, this is a major (and fun) event. (March/April.)

Resources

In New Zealand: New Zealand Tourism Board, P.O. Box 95, 256 Lambton Quay, Wellington, Tel 4-4728860, Fax 4-4781736. **USA:** New Zealand Tourism Board, 501 Santa Monica Blvd. #300, Santa Monica, CA 90401, Tel (310) 395-7480, Fax (310) 395-5453. **Canada:** New Zealand Tourism Board, IBM Tower #1260, 701 W. Georgia St., Vancouver, BC V7Y 1B6, Tel (604) 684-2117, Fax (604) 684-1265. **UK:** New Zealand Tourism Board, New Zealand House, Haymarket, GB-London SW1Y 4TQ, Tel 71-9730360, Fax 71-8398929. **Germany:** New Zealand Tourism Board, Friedrichstr. 10—12, D-6000 Frankfurt 1, Tel 69-9712110, Fax 69-97121113. **Australia:** New Zealand Tourism Board, P.O. Box 614 NSW 2001, Network House, 84 Pitt St., Sydney, NSW 2000, Tel 2-2336633, Fax 2-2350737.

Papua New Guinea was the last inhabited place on earth to be explored by the Europeans, who found incredibly dense mountain jungles inhabited by crocodiles and thousands of tribes of head hunters. Captain John Moresby, who

PAPUA NEW GUINEA

was one of the very first Europeans to sail into what's now Papua New Guinea, asked, "What have these people to gain from civilization?"

A little more than 100 years later, most inhabitants are still living in the stone age, while others are trying to make the jump into the computer age. These days, visitors find an unsettled, unsettling land where women still chop off a finger when family members die. On the down side, Papua New Guinea is an expensive place plagued by serious crime where only a handful of overpriced, shoddy hotels are available. On the up side, visitors can expect to find spectacular jungles and chances to meet and mingle with people whose prehistoric culture is incomprehensibly different than their own. The highland shows, festivals, and *sing-sings* are some of the most exotic events on the planet. And in spite of all the hassles, the most enduring problem most visitors have with Papua New Guinea is that once they've been there, everywhere else is boring!

Yam Harvest Festival

Trobriand Islands **July/August**

The Trobriand Islands have been poked and prodded by anthropologists ever since they were dubbed the "Islands of Love" because of the unusual sexual practices of their inhabitants. Here, both male and female teenagers are encouraged to have as many sexual encounters as they like, with no guilt. And even though the islanders don't believe there's any connection between intercourse and pregnancy, very few children are born out of wedlock. All the experience in pre-marital sex helps everyone decide on a suitable partner for a more or less monogamous marriage,

The Baining fire dancers (wearing spirit masks) often make an appearance at Rabaul's Frangipani Festival in July.
(Wolfgang Kaehler)

although mutually agreed-upon flings are permissable once a year: during the Yam Harvest Festival.

Yams, not sex, are the centerpiece of this complicated annual ritual that helps maintain connections between clans and villages. The size and quality of the family's yams are of extreme importance, since status within the village depends on one's green thumb. When the yams are first dug up, they're displayed in the gardens with a great deal of fanfare. Neighbors come round to admire each others' gardening skills, and great processions head into the villages, with the men carrying the yams and the women forming a front and rear guard. Circular piles of yams clutter the village streets as families display their pride and joy. Celebrations break out, with the women romping around in short grass skirts, and the men admiring each other's yams and yukking it up.

Eventually, the yam houses are ceremoniously filled. These three-story decorated silos stand on stilts, and are filled according to strict priority. The chief's yam house is taken care of first, then those of brothers-in-law and sons-in-law are filled, since in each marriage the wife's clan has responsibility for filling the yam house.

The Trobriands are pretty isolated, with no phones or banks and only one hotel. The people are friendly, but are a bit fed up with the attention they receive from foreigners who want either to study or convert them. There's no violent crime, but *dim-dims* (foreigners) are often the butts of practical jokes.

DATE: July and August (during the yam harvest). **LOCATION:** The Trobriand Islands, Milne Bay Province. **TRANSPORT:** Kiriwina Island's Losuia airport can be reached from Port Moresby, Gurney, and Vivagani. **ACCOMMODATION:** It's possible to stay in homes in the villages on outlying islands, but the Islanders aren't naive, and will charge hotel prices. **CONTACT:** PNG Tourist Office or Air Niugini (see *Resources*).

While you're there ...

- **New Ireland Provincial Government Day:** *Sing-sings* break out across the island, Kavieng has a big show, and Kontu's "shark-callers" get a good workout. (February 22.)
- **Port Moresby Show, Port Moresby:** In mid-June, traditional dancing and other interesting entertainment liven up the city.
- **Milne Bay Government Day, Alotau and throughout Milne Bay Province:** The islands and mainland shore of this remote province come alive with parades of elaborately decorated outrigger canoes and other events. (July 7.)
- **Frangipani Festival, Rabaul:** Celebrating the blooming of flowers, this festival features fireworks and parades, in one of PNG's most pleasant towns. (July.)

Mt. Hagen Show

Mt. Hagen **Late August**

Strolling around amidst this spectacular gathering of clans is an experience unlike anything else on earth. Bearded men wearing bark and string loin-covers whirl in and out of the fray, as women in grass skirts and fur necklaces dance and cavort. Drums pound out non-stop rhythms as dancers covered in face paint and pig

Gathering of the clans: The sing-sing at Mt. Hagen just may be the wildest show on earth. (McConnell/Bruce Coleman Inc.)

grease stomp and chant, their noses pierced with boars' husks, their feathered headdresses swaying above.

Although not as authentic as the smaller, spontaneous *sing-sings* in outlying villages, the Mt. Hagen show has the advantage of being a regularly scheduled gathering that brings some 15–25 very diverse tribes and clans together. Performers compete for prize money, trying to outdo each other with their wild costumes and dances. The highland "shows," such as those at Mt. Hagen and Goroka, were created in the 1950s by the first Europeans settling in the area, as a way to gather the clans together with each other and the settlers in a friendly assembly. Now they're mainly a tourist attraction, but as tourist attractions go, you'd be hard-pressed to find any better.

Try to get to Mt. Hagen the day before scheduled events begin, as clans begin arriving, setting up camps, and dress-rehearsing in front of people who can't afford the admission (US$25) to the main events. These impromptu shows are more playful and generally better than the formal main events, but don't worry—the whole thing is absolutely great.

DATE: Late August (check with the PNG Tourist Office or Air Niugini for exact dates in the current year). **LOCATION:** Mt. Hagen, Western Highlands Province (the show grounds are about 15 km/10 miles outside of town, beyond the airport. **TRANSPORT:** Daily flights from Port Moresby, Madang, Wewak, Goroka, and Babubil. **ACCOMMODATION:** Although there are several guest houses in town, you'll need to book in advance for the show. Be prepared to pay far more than what the rooms and service are worth. **CONTACT:** PNG Tourist Office or Air Niugini (see *Resources*).

The Sing-Sing

In the villages of highland Papua New Guinea, the main cultural events are the local *sing-sings*, protracted affairs that feature innumerable ceremonies and nighttime dance parties. The occasion for a *sing-sing* might be the completion of a bride pay-off, a *moga* ceremony, or any number of other events. Whatever the reason, these get-togethers are a great chance to see and mingle with highland tribespeople while they are dancing, eating, and partying in their splendidly outrageous garb.

Unfortunately, most *sing-sings* are in remote areas seldom visited by outsiders. There's no fixed yearly schedule for these local affairs, so word of mouth is usually the only way to discover them. During the Provincial Government Days held by each of PNG's 20 provinces, many villages hold *sing-sings*. Also, a great many *sing-sings* take place on the weekend of Independence Day (September 16).

Goroka Show

Goroka **September**

As drummers whack out rhythms that rattle the teeth, clan after clan tries to out-flash the competition with eccentric outfits and performances. Western standards are turned upside-down as lips are painted white and faces red. Nasel septa are pierced with quills, sticks, and tusks. Necklaces are worn on foreheads. Men wear wigs of their wives' locks to ensure a good hair day, and women lop off their fingers to appease the spirits of dead relatives. Earlobes stretch to breasts, breasts stretch to navels, and bird-of-paradise crowns stretch to the trees.

The world's most extreme fashions are on display at this, the biggest and most spectacular of Papua New Guinea's "shows." *Sing-sing* groups from all over the highlands come together for a weekend of music, dancing, and showing-off. Most groups are decked out to the nines, but others have more subdued costumes and let their gyrating performances do the talking.

The Goroka Show, even thought it's basically a tourist event, is an opportunity to get an overview of the exceptional cultural diversity of the valleys of the PNG highlands, an area only "discovered" by Europeans in the 1930s. Most of the performances are authentic, although some of the trappings of the rest of the

Mud men at the Goroka Show: Once you've been here, everywhere else could be boring. (Jackie Foryst/Bruce Coleman Inc.)

world have begun creeping in—clans sometimes beat out their rhythms on "drums" of plastic tubing, while some dancers move in a way that looks quite a bit like the twist. In addition to the *sing-sing* groups, the show features handicraft markets, string-band competitions, and exhibitions of livestock and produce.

DATE: Mid-September (usually the weekend nearest September 16, which is Independence Day). **LOCATION:** Goroka, Eastern Highlands Province. **TRANSPORT:** Flights from Port Moresby, Mt. Hagen, Wewak, Lae, Madang, and Vanimo. **ACCOMMODATION:** Goroka sports several budget hotels and one luxury hotel, but you'll need to book early to lock in a room during the show. Keep in mind that all accommodation is overpriced and fairly shoddy. **CONTACT:** PNG Tourist Office or Air Niugini (see *Resources*).

© WHILE YOU'RE THERE ...

© **East Sepik Provincial Government Day:** In this most fascinating area of PNG, men wear penis gourds, and mighty crocodiles rule the rivers. A variety of activities in Wewak and elsewhere mark this day. (September 16.)

© **Malangan Festival, Kavieng and Namatanai (New Ireland Province):** Starting in mid-September, this two-week festival features tree dancers and other entertainment. While you're there, be sure to catch the famous shark-callers of nearby Kontu.

© **Hiri Moale, Port Moresby:** Although a bit commercialized, the festival features the huge Papuan trading canoes. (Mid-September.)

© **Samarai Pearl Festival:** Amid the sorcerers, strange lights, and ghost-planes of China Strait, Samarai Island's shellfish fest draws a crowd. (November/December.)

Resources

In Papua New Guinea: Papua New Guinea Tourism Promotion Board, P.O. Box 1291, Port Moresby NCD, PNG, Tel 675-200-211, Fax 675-200-223. **USA:** Papua New Guinea Tourism Promotion Board, c/o Air Niugini, 5000 Birch St. Suite 3000, Newport Beach, CA 92660, Tel (714) 752-5440, Fax (714) 476-3741. **UK:** Trans Niugini Tours, c/o Travel Contacts, 45 Idmiston Rd., GB-London SE27 9HL, Great Britain, Tel 81-6709411, Fax 81-7666123. **Germany**: Tourism Development Corporation of Papua New Guinea, c/o Air Niugini, Wadmannstr. 45, D-60596 Frankfurt, Germany, Tel 69-634095, Fax 69-6313332. **Australia:** Papua New Guinea Tourism Promotion Board, 100 Clarence St., Syndney, NSW 2000, Australia, Tel 02-290-1544, Fax 02-290-2026.

VANUATU

As tropical paradises go, festival-rich Vanuatu has all the right stuff. On 74 populated islands, black and white sand beaches are sandwiched between peaceful lagoons and vine-covered rainforests. Cool waterfalls cascade down the sides of active, climbable volcanos, and offshore reefs are a snorkeler's heaven of technicolor fish and submerged WWII fighter planes. Then there's the capital, Port Vila, a French colonial gem so captivating and peaceful that many visitors never find any reason to venture outside its limits.

Vanuatu's indigenous culture is a treasure trove of outlandish rituals and some of the world's most surprising, authentic spectacles. Local life is guided by sorcery and taboos, and tradition-minded islanders spend much of their time preparing and performing spirit dances designed to woo and placate ancestors and gods. Visitors who take the time to explore outlying islands will come across rituals with elaborate headdresses, wildly carved masks, and brilliantly artistic slit drums. Each island has its own unique practices, ranging from rituals of drinking kava (a mild narcotic), to land diving (bungee jumping). The latter was originated by Pentecost Islanders, who continue to jump with jungle vines and little margin for error.

Land-Diving

Southern Pentecost Island **April/May**

Once the developed world discovered bungee jumping, it wasn't long before safety experts and insurance companies diluted the action. But on Pentecost Island, the original "land-divers" continue to make their flamboyant, dangerous leaps into oblivion using jungle vines wrapped around ankles. Vine lengths are so perfectly calculated that they stop each jumper just as his hair brushes the ground—thereby fertilizing the soil for the coming year's yam crop.

Young boys begin training to dive as soon as they can walk, and each year the chaotic-looking towers of about 25 meters (82 feet) are erected using tree trunks and branches bound with liana vines. Divers carefully select and cut their own vines from the jungle, so that no one else can be blamed in the event of a mishap. One after another, the village men and boys climb the tower, younger ones starting from lower heights, and more experienced divers moving higher up.

On the ground there's singing, dancing, and whistling as each diver prepares to jump. High above, friends tie a vine to each of the jumper's legs, then secure the other ends to the tower. When the diver raises his arms in a signal of readiness, the crowd becomes silent. He loudly confides his deepest thoughts and problems, often criticizing his wife or other family members gathered below. After a hand clap, he launches himself head-first off the tower. The crowd stands breathless as he free-falls in a frog-like position, stretching the curly vine until it stops him just as his hair connects with the surface. Safe descents meet with rambunctious acclaim as fellow tribe members rush forward to untie the diver and applaud his audacity by dancing in his honor.

The most experienced elder is the last to jump, from the very top of the tower. Having overseen every detail of the construction of the tower, which is built from scratch every year, he checks vines for strength and elasticity, and enforces "safety" taboos, such as keeping women away while the structure is being built. Only rarely are there injuries, and only one death has been recorded; weirdly enough, it happened in front of Queen Elizabeth II at a special off-season jump staged in her honor.

Villagers prohibit outsiders from jumping, but they are quite welcome to watch. It's an expensive proposition, though. The entrance fee for foreigners, which includes the right to shoot a still camera, is about US$70; to shoot video the fee is a whopping $210.

DATE: April, May, and early June (Tour Vanuatu can provide specific dates several months ahead). **LOCATION:** Land dives are held at 10 locations on southern Pentecost Island: Lonorore Airfield, Bay Barrier, Bay Martelli, Bunlap, Panas, Pangi, Poinkros, Rangusus‌u, Varsare, and Wali. In Bunlap the native dress and other customs are more traditional. **TRANSPORT:** Three scheduled flights each day serve Lonorore Airfield from Port Vila. Tour Vanuatu has set up an efficient charter flight operation to bring tourists in and out of South Pentecost from Port Vila (the flights are quite expensive). **ACCOMMODATION:** Most people watch the land diving as a day trip, but camping in villages is also an option. **CONTACT:** Vanuatu National Tourism Office (see *Resources*).

Independence Day

Port Vila and nationwide **July**

Almost any time of year is a great time to be in Port Vila, but during Independence Day celebrations, the colorful town revs into high gear. Groups from many of Vanuatu's islands arrive for exhibitions of custom dancing, and although the setting isn't authentic, the ceremonies certainly are. Food stalls are set up along the seawall, serving specialties like mangrove oysters and *laplap*, a seafood or meat-stuffed roll of yam and manioc dough. At Independence Park there's a military parade, and canoes race in the harbor while landlubbers' sporting events crowd the town.

Port Vila itself is one of the most beguiling towns in the Pacific. Colonial houses rise up from its harbor on gentle hills that overlook two smaller islands. Orchids and tulip trees abound, and the town moves to a lively French rhythm that's especially apparent in the many cafés along the waterfront. At sunset, ceremonies are held in which Vanuatu *kava*, a mild narcotic made from a pepper plant, is drunk. Just outside town, Efate Island is graced with white and black sand beaches, lagoons, lush rainforests, and coconut plantations.

DATE: July 30. **LOCATION:** Port Vila. **TRANSPORT:** Although there are no direct links to Port Vila from America or Europe, you can easily get to either Sydney or Nadi (New Caledonia), and connect from there to Port Vila. **ACCOMMODATION:** From backpackers' dives to top-end digs, Port Vila has plenty of places to stay, both in town and on the outskirts. **CONTACT:** Vanuatu National Tourism Office (see *Resources*).

© Maghe Ceremony and Rom Dance

Ambrym Island **July**

The influence of magic and sorcery is strongest on Vanuatu's volcanic islands, and nowhere more so than on Ambrym, with its fiery twin volcanoes. The Rom dance is part of the Maghe, or grade-taking ceremony, in which village males gain prestige by giving their wealth away in a series of extraordinary rituals.

The Rom costume is spectacularly creepy. Participants don't appear human at all, but rather as giant dancing cones of banana fibers. On top of the mass of fiber covering the entire body, a tall, brightly painted mask is adorned with feathers. The dance itself is deeply steeped in ritual, and as dancers move in a line the local *man blong majik*, or sorcerer, can be seen moving in and out, working his magic. Afterwards, up to 100 pigs are slaughtered and huge feasts are prepared in a show of wealth and generosity intended to gain the hosts new respect and prestige in the eyes of their guests.

Strict taboos surround the making of the Rom costume, and if you happen to see one being put together you will be punished with a fine (usually at least one pig) and a flogging with a poisonous, thorny plant called the *nangalat*, which burns the skin for several days. The Rom costumes represent spirits, and are burned after use so that the spirit doesn't come back to torment the dancer.

Special *tamtams,* or slit drums, are made for each Maghe ceremony. These are man-sized, hollowed-out logs with long sound-slits and at least one carved, grotesque head on top. Canine teeth flank the head, and holes through the nose feature fern leaves during ceremonies. Other handicrafts include carved and painted tree-fern figures, bamboo clubs, and dancing masks, though the latter are usually destroyed after ceremonies. The Ambrym Islanders are also known for their exceptional "temporary art," the elaborate sand drawings that communicate stories, legends, or simple messages, such as, "I'll be back at sunset."

Many of the villages of the northern part of Ambrym Island have resisted conversion by Christian missionaries, and cling steadfastly to their old beliefs and customs. Most men wear *nambas,* or penis wrappers, and women wear grass skirts. *Kava* (a mildly narcotic drink) is very strong here, and the otherworldly atmosphere is enhanced by the presence of two very active volcanoes, which make their presence known through occasional booms, waterspouts, and steam escaping from the jungle floor.

DATE: Throughout the month of August. **LOCATION:** Fanla, Neuwa, and other villages of northern Ambrym Island. Some villages perform the dance and the accompanying Maghe ceremony several times, both in their own villages and at neighboring villages. **TRANSPORT:** There are no airstrips in the northern part of the island, but speedboats meet incoming flights at Craig Cove, and take passengers onward to Ranvetlam, Olal, or other settlements in the north. Also, transport from Port Vila can often be arranged on boats. **ACCOMMODATION:** Very spartan guesthouses can be found in several spots on the island, but in the northern section the only options are village stays or the Catholic mission at Olal. **CONTACT:** Vanuatu National Tourism Office (see *Resources*).

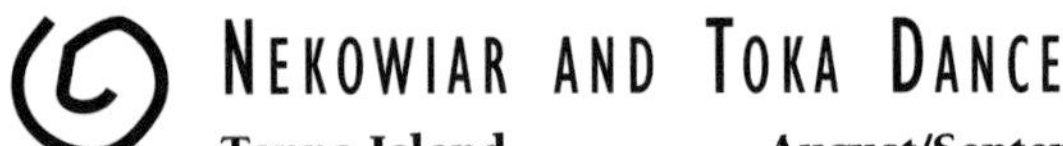

Nekowiar and Toka Dance

Tanna Island **August/September/October**

The Nekowiar Festival is one of the most spectacular pageants in the South Pacific—and the entire world. This three or four-day blow-out features painted faces, grass skirts, pig sacrifices, and a massive burst of testosterone known as the Toka Dance. Held to cement alliances between clans and to revive the traditional rhythms of island life, the festival climaxes with a massive gift-giving ceremony.

In the days before the big event, dances are practiced and islanders of all ages begin to paint their faces red, yellow, and black, inviting the "beauty magic" to possess them. On the first day of the festival, thousands of people from the invited villages arrive in the host village, where the pigs that will be slaughtered are carefully displayed to impress the hosts' wealth upon guests. At night the young men of the host village begin dancing and invite the young women who are watching to join in. The women, wearing face paints and grass suits, eventually respond with a dance that symbolizes their work in the fields.

The next day, things get out of hand as the Toka begins. Women huddle together when the invited men begin an elaborate dance, wearing outrageous costumes of tasseled skirts and feathered, painted hair. In the evening the dance reaches a feverish pitch as thousands of Toka dancers leap around in an absolute frenzy, sometimes forming small circles in which they try to trap women. When they catch one she is tossed up and down, fondled, and pinched by the excited males. (Note that female foreign visitors are allowed to watch the Toka dance, but are not off limits—stay well back if you don't want to be part of the action.)

The wild dance continues all night, and in the morning the chief or "bigman" of the host village produces a decorated ceremonial pole signaling to his men that they should begin the *Nao,* a line dance in which men beat out the rhythm with bunches of reeds tapped on the ground. Then the pigs are slaughtered and a feast is laid out on woven mats, featuring pork, *kava,* and *laplap.* The feast continues late into the evening.

DATE: Actual dates are announced a few days in advance, but there's always at least one and usually several Nekowiars on Tanna each year. August, September, and October are prime months. **LOCATION:** Any village on Tanna Island may host a Nekowiar. **TRANSPORT:** Daily flights serve Tanna's airport from Port Vila. **ACCOMMODATION:** Beach resorts and bungalows are available on the island, but depending on the location of the Nekowiar you may need to camp out with the guests. **CONTACT:** Vanuatu National Tourism Office (see *Resources*).

Resources

In Vanuatu: National Tourism Office of Vanuatu, P.O. Box 209, International Building #3, Port Vila, Tel 678-22515, 678-22889. **USA:** Vanuatu Tourist Information Office, c/o S.H. Enterprises, 520 Monterrey Drive, Rio del Mar CA 95003, Tel (408) 685-8901, Fax (408) 685-8903. **Australia:** National Tourism Office of Vanuatu, P.O. Box 4349, 37 Alexander Street, Crow's Nest, NSW 2065, Tel 2-792988 & 2-436-0566, Fax 2-438-5197.

SOUTH AMERICA

Land of tango and lover of illusion, Argentina offers one of the world's liveliest and cosmopolitan capitals and one of its most magnificently desolate wilderness areas. To explorers and outdoor sports lovers the country is a treasure chest of Andean cordilleras, mountain lakes, wild-west deserts, and the haunted coast of Tierra del Fuego—which is about as far away from civilization as you can get.

ARGENTINA

Culturally, Argentina is a melting pot. In a country overwhelmingly dominated by Europeans, the gringo visitor is both inconspicuous and, unfortunately, robbed of the indigenous culture that enriches the travel experience in neighboring countries. In northern areas where remnants of this culture survive, you'll find Argentina's most interesting events, which range from massive markets to carnivals and religious processions. At more European celebrations—wine festivals, *gaucho* gatherings, and snow carnivals—the friendly, gregarious Argentines are quick to invite visitors to participate.

National Vintage Festival (Vendimia)

Mendoza **February/March**

Open wide! The red wine flows generously (and mostly without cost) during Mendoza's annual festival honoring the ripening and harvest of the wine grapes. Events surrounding this week-long festival—one of Argentina's largest affairs—range from the blessing of the vines to folkloric music and dancing.

The main parade down Avenida San Martín features local bands, floats from each town in the province, and antique automobiles. The centerpiece is the image of the *Virgin de la Carrodilla,* patroness of Mendoza, which is carried on a cart preceded by the Bishop. The Bishop blesses the wine and a great fireworks and sound show takes place near the amphitheater. Folkloric events and concerts fill the week, which culminates in the coronation of the wine harvest queen.

DATE: Late February/early March. **LOCATION:** Mendoza, in western Argentina's Cuyo region. **TRANSPORT:** Daily flights are available from

Carnival in Corrientes: Shame on you if you can't play the clown on Fat Tuesday. *(Joe Viesti/Viesti Associates)*

Buenos Aires. The bus or train also will get you to Mendoza from most major cities in Argentina. **ACCOMMODATION:** Plenty of hotels and *casas de familia* (family homes with extra bedrooms for guests) are found in Mendoza, but the city is packed during festival week so reserve ahead. The tourist office on Avenida San Martín has listings of lodging. **CONTACT:** Argentina Tourist Information Office (see *Resources*).

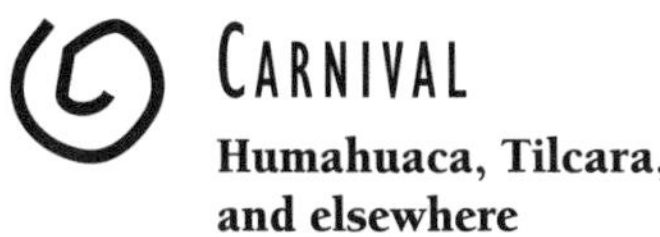

Carnival

Humahuaca, Tilcara, and elsewhere — **February/March**

Duck! It's Carnival Week in Argentina, and in one of many traditions celebrants pelt friends and visitors with water balloons. Two of the best cities in which to celebrate Carnival in Argentina are near the northern border. In picturesque Humahuaca, Carnival begins the Friday before Ash Wednesday with a *chicha* (corn beer) festival and Quechua Indian music. Musicians gather among the adobe houses and cobbled streets to play flutes and *charangos,* as circles of indigenous people move rhythmically in circles, sometimes waving handkerchiefs or corn cobs in a dance that goes on for hours. Drinking games are plentiful, and locals often insist that visitors chug a glass of *chicha* with them.

Just south of Humahuaca in the artists' colony of Tilcara, flowered statues representing the stations of the cross are displayed along the street, and processions come down from the mountains on Ash Wednesday. Nearby Corrientes has celebrated

Carnival for more than 30 years, but the festivities are decidedly European.

DATE: Carnival begins the Friday or Saturday before Ash Wednesday, depending on the town. **LOCATION:** Humahuaca, Tilcara, Corrientes, and elsewhere. **TRANSPORT:** Humahuaca is on the Rio Grande east of Route 9 in the Jujuy Province. Buses run regularly, and the town has a train station. Tilcara, about 50 km or 31 miles south of Humahuaca, can be reached by bus from Jujuy, Salta, Humahuaca, and La Quiaca. **ACCOMMODATION:** Hotels and camping are available in Humahuaca and Tilcara. **CONTACT:** Argentina Tourist Information Office (see *Resources*).

While you're there ...

- **Vuelta Ciclistica, Mendoza:** This summer bicycle race-and-ride moves through the villages and resorts of the wine country that lies in the shadow of Mount Aconcagua. (February.)
- **Snow Carnival (Fiesta Nacional de la Nieve), Bariloche:** Celebrate with local ski bums, international visitors, and competitors. A torch-bearing ski parade, races, and jumping competitions are all part of the European-style ski resort's week-long festival. (Early August.)

Festival of the Pot (Manca Fiesta)

La Quiaca **October**

Supposedly the oldest festival in Argentina, the Festival of the Pot (*Manca Fiesta* or *Fiesta de las Ollas*) has made few concessions to modernity. Local Indians still load their wares on llamas and burros, then make their way across the *altiplano* on steep trails. Watching them enter the market area is like taking a step back in time.

The festival attracts indigenous artists and traders from throughout northern Argentina and southern Bolivia. Perched high in the northernmost region of Argentina, La Quiaca is remote, but it's well worth the effort to get here if you're interested in a wide selection of native merchandise. Plus, there are outstanding opportunities to meet and observe the native population, which is mostly engaged in high-elevation subsistence farming.

DATE: Late October. **LOCATION:** La Quiaca is located in the northernmost nook of Argentina in the Jujuy Province. **TRANSPORT:** Buses and trains connect La Quiaca to cities south, including Jujuy and Salta. The town can also be reached via a bridge from Villazón, Bolivia. **ACCOMMODATION:** La Quiaca has its share of hotels, but the Bolivian side of the border offers a much better value on rooms. **CONTACT:** Argentina Tourist Information Office (see *Resources*).

While you're there ...

Gaucho Festival/Day of Tradition, San Antonio de Areco and elsewhere: Traditional events, music, and parades honor the *gaucho* (Argentine cowboy) in all ranch areas. San Antonio de Areco in particular has a wild-west feel. (November.)

Feast of the Immaculate Conception

Luján, Catamarca, and elsewhere **December**

Most Argentines (and most Latin Americans) are in love with the idea of virgin births, and on December 8 you'll find nearly every village celebrating the Immaculate Conception in one way or another. The most colorful festivities take place in Luján and Catamarca.

An image of the Indian-featured *Virgen del Valle* was found in a cave near Catamarca in 1620, and since then replicas of the image have been created in each village of the provinces of Catamarca, Salta, Jujuy, Tucuman, and Santiago del Estero. These are taken in procession to Catamarca, usually by pilgrims who march on foot. Some come in traditional costumes and since nearly everyone seems to be singing or playing the *charango* or *quena*, the festival is particularly lively. Bouts of drinking and dancing break out, climaxing on the day of the Immaculate Conception. As the original image passes through town in procession, spectators throw thousands of white handkerchiefs into the air.

At Luján the patron saint of Argentina, the Virgin of Luján, attracts four million people each year, who ask her counsel in matters of peace, health, and grief. During the days surrounding the feast, the neo-Gothic cathedral housing her shrine is a constant buzz of activity. The town's special procession on feast day is led by the truly devout—who've arrived in town by marching on foot or on their knees—followed by colonial carts and *gauchos* riding ornamented horses.

DATE: December 8. A similar festival takes place the Sunday after Easter. **LOCATION:** Luján (near Buenos Aires) and Catamarca (in the Andean northwest). **TRANSPORT:** Luján is 65 km/40 miles west of Buenos Aires on Route 7. Buses and trains depart several times a day from Buenos Aires. Catamarca is reachable by plane from Buenos and La Rioja, or by infrequent bus service. **ACCOMMODATION:** Many cheap hotels and *hospedajes* (large family homes where rooms are rented) are available, serving pilgrims who arrive throughout the year. **CONTACT:** Argentina Tourist Information Office (see *Resources*).

© Resources

In Argentina: Centro de Información Turistica, Santa Fe 883, P.O. Box 1059, 1368 Buenos Aires, Tel 1-3122332, Fax 1-3126834. **USA & Canada:** Argentina Tourist Information Office, P.O. Box 1758 Madison Square Station, New York, NY 10059, Tel (212) 765-8833 & (800) 722-5737, Fax (212) 582-7833. South American Explorers Club, 126 Indian Creek Road, Ithaca, NY 14850, Tel (607) 277-0488. **UK**: Argentina Tourist Information Office, Consulate of Argentina, 53 Hans Place, GB-London SW1X 0LA, Tel 71-589-314, Fax 71-589-3106. **Germany**: Consulate of Argentina, Adenauerallee 52, D-5300 Bonn 1, Tel 228-2280146, Fax 228-214809. **Australia**: Embassy of Argentina, MLC Tower, #102 Woden, Canberra, ACT 2606, Tel 6-2824555, Fax 6-2853062.

BOLIVIA

Little known and greatly underrated, Bolivia is a treasure chest of natural beauty and ancient traditions. The country was born of a monumental and catastrophic clash of cultures, and it remains hardly influenced by the values and customs of the developed world. The indigenous people who make up the majority of the population continue to live and celebrate as they have for centuries, with thriving traditions that abound in rich fiestas and celebrations. These events feature soulful music, outlandish costumes, and esoteric dances and rituals that mix the religions of ancestors and conquerors—creating some of the most culturally rich and precious spectacles on earth.

In terms of natural attractions, Bolivia offers a sampling of everything South America has to offer (except an ocean beach—which the government is still trying to get back from Chile). There are mountains, deserts, rainforests, beautiful lakes, and well-preserved colonial cities—all wrapped up in a social environment that's far safer and far cheaper than that of several of the country's neighbors.

Candlemas (Candelaria)

Copacabana **February**

About a week in advance of the big day, Aymará Indians begin to arrive, playing music and spinning yarn from great bags of wool as they walk. Other Indian groups follow, village by village, either dancing their way into town or beginning to groove as soon as they arrive—and not stopping until the end of the fiesta.

On the southern shore of Lake Titicaca, normally sleepy Copacabana becomes a pageant of sound and color as the festival revs into high gear. The town is decorated lavishly, and merchants set up markets to sell clothes, handicrafts, and food. Pilgrims ascend the steep hill to Calvary, where soothsayers and prayer chanters do a big business blessing people in Indian tongues and making wishes come true (for a price, of course). Inside the church the image of the Virgin is made up in jewelry and precious robes, and in a candle-lit passageway sorcerers crouch while making predictions based on the movement of the flames.

The main square is a 10-ring circus as *Chiriwanos* from the forests beat on huge drums and play long panpipes, surrounded by dancers in floppy black wigs who repeatedly bend forward from the waist and straighten up suddenly. Men crouch inside horned wooden bulls while "bullfighters" taunt them with whips and wooden swords. The scene gets rough when bulls are knocked down and jabbed, only to get up and charge into the crowd.

The fabulously costumed Incas of Oruro act out the entire conquest of the Andes, complete with the Incan god-king Atahualpa, the Spanish conqueror Pizarro, and plenty of sun virgins, priests, and royal messengers. In the end Atahualpa is executed, but in an optimistic plot twist he miraculously comes back to life—just like the Christian God.

On February 2 (the day of Candlemas), festival-goers carry a duplicate of the image of the Virgin in a huge procession (the real one let it be known that she doesn't wish to leave the church by sending a calamity down on the town every time she was moved). Priests dressed in gold and silver robes flank the statue, as confetti showers down and firecrackers are ignited everywhere.

DATE: The actual festival date is February 2, but celebrations begin up to a week in advance. **LOCATION:** Copacabana (La Paz Department) holds the biggest celebrations, but spirited fiestas are also held in Aiquile (Cochabamba), Challapampa (Oruro), Samaipata (Santa Cruz), and Angostura (Tarija). **TRANSPORT:** Copacabana lies about 150 km/95 miles west of La Paz on the southern shore of Lake Titicaca. It's accessible by bus from La Paz and nearby villages, and by ferry from lakeside towns in Bolivia and Peru. **ACCOMMODATION:** Although the town is filled with hotels, guest houses, and lodges, they fill up and double their rates during festivals. **CONTACT:** Dinatur or the Bolivian Embassy (see *Resources*).

© DEVIL'S CARNIVAL (LA DIABLADA)

Oruro **February/March**

What may be the world's most vibrant mix of ancient mysticism and high-spirited revelry takes place in a humble mining town on the high Bolivian plateau. Here, devils, she-devils, witch doctors, and llama shepherds converge for several days of dancing, worshiping, and romping through town.

Forty or fifty dancing companies—with 40 to 300 members each—begin rehearsing their diabolical moves in November, as they

Carnival raises the devil himself from the mines of Oruro, for eight fantasy-filled days of street music and costumed dancing. *(Joe Viesti/Viesti Associates)*

have for at least two centuries. The origins of the event are unclear, and are completely interwoven with Indian and European myths, traditions, and deities. Many locals point to an incident in 1789, when an unknown woman of beauty (later called the Virgin of Candlemas) helped a wounded outlaw. He worshipped her with candles in the cave where he lived, and later a church was erected on the site.

Since then, the Carnival has evolved into a celebration of almost anything of relevance in Andean culture. While it continues to honor the Virgin of Candlemas (who over time was renamed *Virgin del Socavón* or Virgin of the Mineshaft), it also variously lauds and derides the devil, the Spanish conquest of South America, Archangel Michael's defeat of the Seven Deadly Sins, and Inca

Yupanqui's triumph over the jungle tribes. The miners also like to have a solid connection with Satan, since they spend much of their time near the center of the earth. Altars to the devil (who is called *el Tío,* or Uncle), are erected inside the mines, and many Indian miners recognize him as *Supay,* the black god of the underworld.

The festival gets going the morning of Carnival Saturday, with the *entrada,* a spectacular entry march. You'll see Michael the Archangel, followed by groups of devils (*Diablos*) who burst onto the scene in an explosion of luxurious color and ingenious choreography. Lucifer is attended by Satan and *China Supay,* the devil's wife and carnal temptress. Surrounding them are dancing she-devils, bears, and condors, leading hundreds of other ferocious devils who leap, spin, and shout in a procession that stretches 20 blocks. Each wears a big, Tibetan-looking mask with light-bulb eyes, mirrored teeth, horns, and lizard or snake embellishments. Horse or ox-tail hair flies as the dancers leap in spurred boots through thousands of firecrackers in a series of sensual, acrobatic dance rituals.

A bizarre motorcade of cars and trucks (*cargamentos*) follows, each vehicle draped with forks, spoons, old coins, jewels, embroideries, and banknotes. This recalls both the treasures once offered in the worship of *Inti* (the sun god), and the wealth of *Tío* down below. Next come companies of Incas and historical personages of the conquest, who, upon reaching the stadium, present a series of dances in which good triumphs over evil.

At a mass in the church the dancers pray to the Virgin for pardon and sing hymns in Quechua, then move outside to continue leaping and cavorting to a vast variety of musical styles. You'll see *Tobas* wearing large tropical feathers on their heads to represent the jungle tribes conquered by the Inca. *Llameros* wield llama slings to symbolize the long animal caravans that plied the altiplano. *Callahuallas,* or witch doctors, dance with bags of herbs, while *Morenos* imitate black slaves.

These groups and dozens more perform all over town. Bleacher seats are available in the main plaza, which is wet during the day from hundreds of water bombs (note that gringos are favorite targets). At the stadium you'll get a glimpse of beautiful folk dances and the bright wool petticoats of local Bolivian women. Handicraft and food markets spring up everywhere, and in between processions there are dozens of allegorical plays which are also curiously Tibetan in theme and costuming. The whole thing ends on Temptation Sunday with *challas* (the sprinkling of drinks on all moving and fixed objects) and a trek out to the country to "bury" the festival until next year.

DATE: The carnival begins the Saturday before Ash Wednesday and lasts eight days (until the following Sunday). **LOCATION:** Oruro, 230 km/140 miles southeast of La Paz. **TRANSPORT:** There are trains from La Paz, Cochabamba, Potosí, or Sucre. A *colectivo* (rural taxi) takes two hours from the outskirts of La Paz. Day trips including transport, food, and seating are available from travel agents in La Paz. **ACCOMMODATION:** Hotels are found in Oruro, but either plan ahead or day-trip, since thousands of visitors converge for the carnival events. Beware of "gringo pricing." **CONTACT:** Dinatur or Bolivian Embassy (see *Resources*).

Phujllay

Tarabuco **March**

More than 10,000 peasants storm the community of Tarabuco each May to commemorate the 1816 Battle of Jumbati, in which an Indian woman led her forces in a rout of the Spanish invaders. One of Bolivia's most colorful and musical fiestas draws contingencies from more than 50 surrounding communities, who arrive on foot days ahead, loaded down with party clothes and supplies.

Perhaps the best part of this central Bolivian treat is the way it resounds with such unique music. Starting after a lively Quechua mass performed in an open field, peasants, residents, and travelers dance to the sounds of instruments like the *charango,* a stringed instrument usually made with an amarillo shell; the *pinkilló,* a reed instrument dating back to pre-Columbian times; the *zampona,* or bamboo panpipes; and the *pututu,* made from a bull's horn.

Since many Indian celebrations today feature brass bands, this is a rare opportunity to hear the traditional instruments played by both the Quechua and Aymará. The typical dress, which varies from village to village, is vivid and unforgettable. Men often wear festooned *monteras,* the leather hats imitating those worn by the conquistadors, as they stroll through markets selling musical instruments, ponchos, and weavings.

DATE: Usually the second weekend in March, but dates sometimes move to the Sunday after Ash Wednesday if there's a conflict with Carnival. **LOCATION:** Tarabuco, 65 km/40 miles from Sucre. **TRANSPORT:** An *autocarril,* or train/bus goes directly from Sucre to Tarabuco. Alternatively, it's a two-hour trip by *camión,* or open-bed truck. **ACCOMMODATION:** During Phujllay, it's next to impossible to find lodging. Bring your camping gear if you want to stay overnight, or day-trip from Sucre. **CONTACT:** Dinatur or the Bolivian Embassy (see *Resources*).

Feast Day of Gran Poder

La Paz **May/June**

The Aymará culture brings forth its festive best in the neighborhoods of La Paz, as thousands of native dancers gather to cele-

Ready with a charango *and feast-day costumes, a pair of Aymará Indians prepares to join the Gran Poder parade.*
(Bill Cardoni)

brate the "great power of Jesus Christ." Festival-goers prepare elaborately embroidered costumes and practice dances months in advance, debuting during the brilliant *entrada,* or opening parade. Throughout the festival, there are performances of masked dances like the *Morenada,* which relays the story of black slaves brought to Bolivia by the Spanish. Their loud, symbolic rattles represent the clinking of the chains—sure to send a chill through your bones. Some of the dozens of other dances include the *Suri Sikuris,* featuring dancers in ostrich feathers, and the *Incas,* a revival of ancient Inca ritual dances.

DATE: A moving date in late May or early June (the exact dates and parade route are available from Dinatur or the local tourist office each year). **LOCATION:** La Paz. **TRANSPORT:** La Paz can be reached by air directly from Miami in North America, and from all major South American capitals. From Europe, Asia, or Australia a change of planes in Lima, Buenos Aires, or Quito is usually necessary. **ACCOMMODATION:** La Paz has plenty of hotels, guest houses, hostels, and lodges, but during the fiesta you'll need to be flexible. **CONTACT:** Dinatur or Bolivian Embassy (see *Resources*).

While you're there ...

Holy Week (Semana Santa), San Ignacio: Easter Week in San Ignacio and nearby towns of the Eastern Lowlands is a bizarre and pious mix of theatrics, processions, and fire bombs, inspired by the local Indians' interpretations of Jesuit missionary teachings. (Easter Week, March/April.)

Day of the Holy Cross, Oruro and nationwide: Jula Jula women announce their marital status through the waving of flags, while costumed men court them with music and ritual fighting. If you get into town the eve before, take a stroll among the streets, where crosses are decorated with colorful confetti, streamers, and flowers. (May 3.)

Feast Day of Saint James the Apostle, nationwide: Saint James, the patron saint of many villages, is historically related to the Inca god of thunder and lightening. His day is celebrated in small towns around La Paz, and most vigorously in Quime. The towns of Cochabama and Potosi observe feast day with the *Tinku*, a ceremonial battle involving fists, clubs, and slings. (July 25 or the Sunday closest.)

Fiesta of the Virgin of Copacabana

Copacabana **August**

Although festivities honoring Bolivia's patron saint take place all over the country and in southern Peru, most Bolivians attempt to celebrate in Copacabana at least once in their lives. Nestled snugly between two hills on the southern shore of immense, deep-blue Lake Titicaca, Copacabana has been a site for religious pilgrimage for centuries. This festival, honoring the Virgin of the Lake, readily welcomes beer drinking, overzealous religious conviction, and greed with equal vitality.

Get up early and join the mob trying to get a glimpse of the huge, heavy statue of the Virgin emerging from the stark white shrine. A procession around the square follows, and since many miracles have been attributed to the Virgin, many of the devoted try to touch her or at least see her. Carrying miniature models of cars, houses, and cows around their necks, people pray for a blessing that will lead to possession of the real thing.

The steep, rocky trail leading to the Holy Sepulchre is packed with worshipers doing penance at the stations of the cross that dot the way. Vendors aplenty sell medical potions and plastic miniatures of desired possessions, but incredibly zealous prayer is the main visual attraction. Indians even hire blind men and beggars—who are said to have special powers—to chant prayers over burning incense. At the top, you can have your fortune told by a bird, have a drink, or visit the sepulchre, where hopeful visitors draw a picture of their desired possession in wax along the walls. Most people initial their picture to guarantee that the blessing is sent to the right person.

Along the lakeshore, those lucky enough to have cars line them up for blessings. Here the beer flows freely and swaying priests perform the ritual. At night, fireworks light up the sky while crowds revel in music and dancing while pledging their deep-spirited allegiance to the Virgin of the Lake.

Cavalcade of loot: Locals drape their vehicles with their families' most precious belongings and creep through town in a bizarre motorcade dedicated to the Virgin of Copacabana.

DATE: August 5, 6, and 7; coincides with Independence Day Celebration on August 6. **LOCATION:** Copacabana. **TRANSPORT:** The small town of Copacabana lies 158 km/98 miles west of La Paz on the southern shore of Lake Titicaca. It's accessible by buses from other villages, and by ferry from lakeside Bolivian and Peruvian towns. **ACCOMMODATION:** Although the town is filled with hotels, guest houses, and lodges, they fill up and double their rates during festivals. Prepare to be flexible! **CONTACT:** Dinatur or Bolivian Embassy (see *Resources*).

© Feast Day of the Exaltation of the Cross

Oruro and elsewhere **September**

The ceremonial acts of the Exaltation of the Cross that extend 15 days before and after feast day only hint at the magnitude of this event. Although you don't need to hang around a whole month—it's not a particularly friendly or welcoming place—you may want to pop in two days before to witness the "changing of the clothes," a ceremony involving the transformation of Christ's image. The ritual involves a weird combination of priests and military authorities who dance and parade to the music of regional bands.

The feast day itself is spectacular. Costumed *Diablada* dance groups depict the rebellion of devils against the Archangel Michael. This most famous of all Bolivian *comparsas,* or costumed dances, represents an epic duel between good and evil. During feast day, the dancing takes place at the Cala Cala tin mine in Oruro. Local folklore insists that *el Diablo* lives in the mine and can cause cave-ins and other ill luck. Bring your camera—the grotesque plaster masks of the devil feature horns, tusks, bulging eyes, and huge ears and mouths that you'll want to capture on film.

DATE: September 14. **LOCATION:** Best in Oruro, but also in La Paz, Obrajes, and Cochabamba. **TRANSPORT:** Located 230 km/140 miles southeast of La Paz, Oruro is reached by train from La Paz, Cochabamba, Potosí, or Sucre. A *collectivo* (rural taxi) takes two hours from the outskirts of La Paz. **ACCOMMODATION:** Hotels and other accommodations are available in Oruro. Make reservations early during festivals or plan to camp or day-trip from La Paz. **CONTACT:** Dinatur or Bolivian Embassy (see *Resources*).

While you're there ...

Festival of San Roque, Tarija: Tarija's barrio of San Roque fills with Bolivian folk dancers for this event. The *Chunchos,* who dress like jungle Indians, lead a spectacular parade, marking each step by putting chins on chests, then throwing their heads back. Musicians play traditional native instruments continuously during this eight-day affair. (Begins first Sunday in September.)

Resources

In Bolivia: Dirección Nacional de Turismo (Dinatur), Casilla 1868, Calle Mercado 1328, Ed. Mcal. Ballivian Piso 18, La Paz, Tel 2-367463, Fax 2-374630. **USA:** Embassy of Bolivia, 3014 Massachusetts Avenue NW, Washington, DC 20008, Tel (202) 483-4410, Fax (202) 328-3712. South American Explorers Club, 126 Indian Creek Road, Ithaca, NY 14850, Tel (607) 277-0488. **Canada:** Embassy of Bolivia, 77 Metcalfe Street, Suite 608, Ottawa, ON K1P 5L6, Tel (613) 236-8237. **UK:** Embassy of Bolivia, 106 Eaton Square, GB-London SW1W 9AD, Tel 71-2354248, Fax 71-2351286. **Germany:** Embassy of Bolivia, Konstantinstr. 16, D-5300 Bonn 2, Tel 228-362038, Fax 228-355952. **Australia:** Consulate of Bolivia, Penneys Building #517, 210 Queens Street, Brisbane, QLD 4000, Tel 7-2211606.

BRAZIL

Pulsing with irresistible rhythms, Brazil continues to confuse those who wonder how a country in such persistent distress can keep on dancing. Brazilians dance to spite their plight, and to transcend it—believing that pleasure is the only way to relieve pain. And if you doubt the prescription's effectiveness just plop yourself down for a minute in the mayhem of Carnival, or look into the rolled-back eyes of a drum-whacking cult priestess. Suddenly things like solutions and inhibitions get tossed aside in favor of fate and fun. Suddenly, you've turned Brazilian.

Brazil's indigenous people had their own festivals long before the Portuguese colonizers brought their traditions and special days. Next came African slaves, who added exotic rhythms and elements of their animist religions to the Iberian Christianity of their masters. Today, the fallout of this three-way culture clash is an ethnically scrambled, geographically huge nation that's incredibly rich in tradition. Brazil is a country where people constantly gather to sing, dance, and celebrate something—be it religion, sports, or life itself.

Carnival in Rio

Rio de Janeiro **February/March**

"Let the happiness begin," declares King Momo, igniting a fire of fantasy and rhythm so extravagant that the entire world feels the heat. "The world's greatest party" is a sleepless juggernaut of music, masquerade, magic, and madness—a gargantuan spectacle in which the spectators are intimately involved.

Where to start? First, there's the magnitude. Although the official holiday lasts only four days, almost nothing else happens for two weeks. Traffic comes to a halt and cabbies don't care; they can watch a beautiful girl—or boy—slither across the hoods of their cars. Thousands of transvestites parade in front of the Garota de Ipanema, and neighborhoods become rhythm machines as more than 600 block parties and street parades send up a cacoph-

Carnival in Rio: The world's largest party is also the world's largest transvestite gathering. (Cory Langley)

ony of drums, whistles, triangles, and yelping instruments called *cuicas*. At nighttime balls, Rio's rich and famous dance away in $10,000 costumes, while on the beach strolling samba bands attract throngs of writhing sequined bikinis. Helicopters spin overhead, broadcasting the event to a nationwide television audience concerned with nothing else.

Preceding page photo: *The skimpier the better: Thousands of plumed and nearly naked bodies form the ranks of Rio's amazing Carnival samba schools.* (Bavaria/Viesti Associates)

Although the balls cater to a rich, mostly white crowd, on the streets Carnival has the role of great equalizer in Brazil's highly stratified society. The samba beat penetrates all social levels in Brazil; secretaries become feathered dancing queens for the week, while bankers jump into the musical fray with street sweepers and petty thieves. The celebration also equalizes the sexes, since in addition to being the world's biggest party, it's the world's biggest transvestite gathering. And no matter what kind of scene they're into, Carnival's 300,000 or so overseas visitors find language gaps and cold-climate reserve melting away in a whirl of confetti, sexual ambiguity, and Afro-Brazilian percussion.

Rio's samba schools present the highlight of the city's organized activities, a two-day parade at the "Sambadrome" built especially for this purpose. The huge open-air structure has grandstands, party boxes, and largely unused chairs. Nearly everyone remains standing, dancing to the breathtaking pageant of massive floats, shimmying costumes, and infectious tempos. A burst of fireworks announces each school's entrance, then the *bateria*, a corps of 400 or 500 drummers, blitzes out a samba beat that whips the dancers—all 3,500 or so—into a frenzy of motion. At that point, one of the world's most dramatic spectacles of popular culture unfolds onto the promenade, a giant, dynamic mass of rhythm and color.

Each school is determined to drive the crowd wild and win acclaim as the best *sambistas* in Rio. The audience, sensing correctly that it's part of the show, responds to the visual and auditory rhythms with singing, hugging, and a massive free-form dance frenzy. Inside and outside the Sambadrome, the exuberant, infectious, and all-consuming fever is everywhere. In halls and streets packed way past capacity, all sense of decorum has long since evaporated into an orgy of dancing, singing, and exhibitionism, driven past all limits by the primal power of the samba beat.

DATE: The two weeks before Ash Wednesday. **LOCATION:** Rio de Janeiro. **TRANSPORT:** Rio can be easily reached by air from nearly anywhere in the world, but since incoming flights are jammed during Carnival, book well in advance. **ACCOMMODATION:** Book at least six months in advance and expect hiked-up prices and minimum seven-day stays. **CONTACT:** RIOTUR: Rua da Assembleia 10, 8/9-andares, 20011 Rio de Janeiro, RJ, Brazil, Tel 21-2977117, Fax 21-2527779. Also, EMBRATUR (see *Resources*).

While you're there ...

- **Holy Week, Ouro Preto and Minas Gerais:** Easter week is celebrated with a pious flair in these two cities and the surrounding area, which was once a center of gold mining and is now a living art treasure. Much of the mineral wealth was put into the construction of fine colonial buildings and dozens of breathtaking churches, whose dramatic sculptures and gold work are among the world's finest. (March/April.)
- **São Benedito, Aparecida do Norte:** Halfway between Rio and São Paulo, people come from all over the country to honor the patron saint of African people. Amazing dance groups perform the *congada,* which acts out old African stories, and the *moçambique,* which features swords, leg bells, and gracefully gymnastic feats. (The Monday after Easter.)

Carnival in Bahia

Salvador **February/March**

Whereas Rio's Carnival is famous for its grand balls and samba school parades, Carnival in Salvador is one of the world's great, spontaneous street parties. There's more grit than glitter, as giant sound trucks splash the ear-shattering Afro-Brazilian Carnival rhythms that drive the dancing pandemonium in the streets.

The center of all this participatory action is Praça Castro Alves, but the trucks, a uniquely Bahian phenomenon, are parked anywhere there's room. Sometimes they play taped music, but often live bands are set up on the flat beds. You'll see them moving slowly along the streets like giant, 20th-century pied pipers, stirring throngs of jumping bodies to chase along.

Groups called *Afoxé* societies parade through the streets in fantastic outfits, presenting the sacred music and dancing of Candomblé. These rituals are so close to their roots that participants still sing and chant in African dialects. The most striking society is the *Filhos de Gandhi* (Sons of Gandhi), whose thousands of members wear white tunics and turbans reminiscent of the original clothing of the East African slaves brought to Brazil. Projecting a completely outlandish appearance, these enigmatic marchers move through the streets to their mystical, percussive music.

DATE: The two weeks before Ash Wednesday. **LOCATION:** Salvador (Bahia). **TRANSPORT:** Salvador can be reached by air and bus from all big Brazilian cities, and by air from Miami, Frankfurt, Paris, and Buenos Aires. **ACCOMMODATION:** A large variety of hotels are available, but book in advance—lodging is tight everywhere at Carnival time. **CONTACT:** EMTURSA, Largo do Pelourinho 9, Travessa Ajuda, Edif. Sulamerica 2, 40000 Salvador, BA, Brazil. Also, EMBRATUR (see *Resources*).

© Carnival in Pernambuco

Recife and Olinda **February/March**

The economically poor but culturally rich streets of northeastern Brazil are particularly great places to experience Carnival. In addition to the usual all-day, all-night pandemonium, Carnival here offers astounding treats in the form of the regional *frêvo, caboclinho,* and *maracatú* dances, in which participants scoff at gravity and push the limits of human endurance.

The entire city of Recife knows Carnival is about to arrive when they hear the drums of the *maracatús* approaching. These groups originated when some slave owners let slaves elect their own kings and other officials, allowing them to stage ceremonious crownings. Stopping to dance in front of all the churches on their way into town, the *maracatú* groups are led by a small cart that bears the figure of an animal. Then come the king and queen, dancing under umbrellas as their entourage drums and chants a series of calls and responses in African dialects.

The *frêvo* vaguely resembles a wild Russian dance, with deep one-legged knee bends and gracefully flailing limbs. The *caboclinhos* are even more outlandish, with their traditional Indian garb of red feather headdresses, brightly colored anklets, beaded necklaces, and shiny medallions. Playing shrill native instruments, they precision-dance with leaps, spins, and backward hops, sometimes beating arrows against bows as they writhe around.

DATE: The two weeks before Ash Wednesday. **LOCATION:** Recife and Olinda are located about 830 km/515 miles north of Salvador, in the Pernambuco Dept. **TRANSPORT:** Recife can be reached directly by air from Miami, London, Lisbon, and Paris; and by train or bus from elsewhere in Brazil. Olinda is located about a half hour north of Recife. **ACCOMMODATION:** Both cities have plenty of low-budget and high-end accommodations, with a shortage of mid-range lodging. Prices rise and availability declines dramatically during Carnival. **CONTACT:** Contur Pernambuco, Rua Benfica 150, 50750 Recife PE, Brazil. Also, EMBRATUR (see *Resources*).

Festival of the Goddess of the Sea (Iemanjá)

Fortaleza and coastal Ceará **August**

Although guests often feel like intruders at authentic Candomblé ceremonies, Fortaleza's Festival of Iemanjá, the goddess of the sea, is large enough that visitors can attend without causing a stir. This is a great occasion to witness the impressive rites of Umbanda, as the Candomblé religion is often called in this area.

Believers begin arriving on the beach at noon from more than 150 nearby *terreiros* (churches), and each congregation stakes out a particular piece of beach. By late afternoon the celebration is in full swing, with *terreiro* members beating drums and chanting in their white-and-blue robes, or parading images of Iemanjá up and down the beach. Priests, both male and female, dance around in trances, sometimes foaming at the mouth and jerking spasmodically with their eyes rolled back.

Entering into a brief religious trance (*passo*) is part of the festival experience, and worshippers often welcome people into their circle for a brief trance with the help of a priest or priestess. Drummers lay down a spastic rhythm while the priestess takes the initiate's hand and begins to chant. She often puffs cigar smoke and spins the initiate around the circle in a slow dance that gets steadily faster, while *terreiro* members stand ready to steady or catch an entranced person who stumbles.

Since the goddess is said to enjoy carnal pleasures, she's honored with drinking, smoking, and a great deal of sexually ambiguous dancing, especially by the often-bisexual priests and priestesses. At dusk everyone moves to the surf, where wooden rafts are loaded with flowers, jewelry, perfume, and champagne. The rafts are launched into the sea, then symbolically overturned, thus satisfying the carnal desires of the goddess.

In Maranhão, costumed drummer/dancers prepare for a performance during Bumba Meu-Boi. (Suzanne Murphy-Larronde)

DATE: August 15 in Fortaleza. The festival is also celebrated on the beaches of Bahia on February 2, and in Rio on New Year's Eve. **LOCATION:** Futuro Beach (Praia do Futuro) in Fortaleza has the largest celebration, but other coastal cities in Ceará have similar celebrations. **TRANSPORT:** Fortaleza's airport handles flights from all over Brazil, and intercity buses serve the northeast and north. Take a Praia do Futuro bus from the city center to the beach. **ACCOMMODATION:** On the beach or in the city center, Fortaleza has plenty of hotels in all categories. **CONTACT:** EMCETUR, Rua Senador Pompeu 350, 60035 Fortaleza, CE, Brazil. Also, EMBRATUR (see *Resources*).

While you're there ...

Festas Juninas, Paratí and nationwide: Three festivals in June honor Brazil's favorite saints, Anthony, John, and Peter. Paratí's baroque churches, colorful fishing wharfs, and old-world atmosphere are particularly alive during the festivities. (June.)

Bumba Meu-Boi, São Luis, and throughout Maranhão: Cattle-raising areas celebrate the religious story of a slave who kills his master's ox and must resurrect it or be put to death himself. In addition to dancing and street processions, the folk tale is reenacted by costumed dancers, who are particularly colorful and talented in the island city of São Luís. (About 10 days, starting June 24.)

Círio de Nazaré, Belem: The Amazon region's largest annual festival features an extremely large procession in which crowds battle for the right to carry the "miracle car" holding the image of the Virgin. The church is decked out with lights, and bands play music non-stop. (15 days in mid-October.)

Reveillon, Rio: Iemanjá, the goddess of the sea, is worshipped at the Copacabana beach with dances, chanting, and the launching of small boats with offerings. (December 31.)

Festival of Jesus of Navigators, Salvador and Aracajú: Led by a decorated galley, hundreds of small, wildly festooned boats parade just off the Boa Viagem beach in Salvador, and through the Sergipe River in Aracajú. The festival includes four days of feasting, dancing, and drinking (December 29 through January 1.)

Resources

In Brazil: EMBRATUR, Brazilian Tourism Information Center, Rua Mariz e Barros 13, Cep. 20270-000, Rio de Janeiro, Tel 21-273-2212. **USA:** Brazil Tourist Office, 2441 Janin Way, Solvang, CA 93463, Tel (805) 688-8646, Fax (805) 688-1021. South American Explorers Club, 126 Indian Creek Road, Ithaca, NY 14850, Tel (607) 277-0488. **Canada:** Embassy of Brazil, 450 Wilbrod St., Ottawa, ON K1N 6M8, Tel (613) 237-1090, Fax (613) 237-6144. **UK:** Embassy of Brazil, 15 Berkeley St., GB-London W1Y 4RE, Great Britain, Tel 71-4990877, Fax 71-4935105. **Australia:** Embassy of Brazil, 19 Forster Crescent, Yarralumla, Canberra, ACT 2601, Tel 6-2732372, Fax 6-2732375.

CHILE

Slender, robust Chile is an anomaly in South America; it's a highly developed nation where the people look and act European, and the trains run on time. Little of the indigenous culture survives, and most people visit Chile to trek, bike, fish, or ski in its extreme landscapes. Not far from the Pacific coast—which stretches for more than 4,300 km or 2,666 miles—you'll find everything from deserts, volcanoes, and glaciers to mountain lakes, forests, glaciers, and fjords.

Although most public gatherings were banned during Chile's dark decades of dictatorship, a few religious festivals managed to survive. At the most colorful of these, you'll find medieval-looking horse processions, traditional music and dancing, and plenty of food and wine.

Cuasimodo Processions

Villages near Santiago **April**

An age-old tradition of piety and hostility is resurrected each Easter season as medieval-looking riders gallop around the countryside to "run Christ against the bandits." Originally a protective measure to guard traveling priests from banditry in the mid-1800s, the Correr is now a horsemen's pageant and religious pilgrimage.

In rural areas, lean Chilean horsemen called *huasos* dress in short jackets, cloaks, tight trousers, and fringed waistbands. With high-heeled boots and silver spurs shining, they ride their richly caparisoned mounts at the head of a procession of antique carriages decorated with flowers and palm leaves. Inside are priests and acolytes, traveling to deliver the host to bedridden parishioners. From time to time the group of horsemen will burst into a gallop, pulling ahead of the procession as they brandish crosses and wooden swords, then slowing down to resume a more solemn pace. The horsemen are often followed in the entourage by costumed bicyclists and motorcyclists who deck their humbler mounts with flowers and flags.

DATE: The first Sunday after Easter. **LOCATION:** Rural areas in the central region around Santiago, especially on the road north to Col-

Llamas just want to have fun: This fashionably festooned pack animal is attending the Fiesta de la Virgen de la Tirana. (Joe Viesti/Viesti Associates)

ina. **TRANSPORT:** Santiago's airport handles flights from all over the world. **ACCOMMODATION:** Hotels in Santiago range from low-budget to international class. **CONTACT:** Sernatur (see *Resources*).

While you're there ...

Fiesta de la Virgen de la Tirana, La Tirana: This authentic festival features indigenous dances with traditional costumes and devil masks—a well-preserved anomaly in Europeanized Chile. Thousands are drawn to La

Tirana village in the Atacama Desert, many walking on their knees to repay the Virgin for favors granted. In town the *tipicasque* dances, which go on for hours, are the centerpiece of an elaborate, masked pageant. (July 16.)

Independence Celebrations, Racagua and nationwide: There's plenty of drinking everywhere in Chile, as people sample the young wine and dance the *cueca* courtship dance around traditional makeshift huts topped with tree boughs. Racagua is known for its spirited festivities and rodeos. (September 18 and 19.)

Fiesta de la Virgin del Rosario

Andacollo **December**

Chile's most esoteric and picturesque festival draws pilgrims from all over northern Chile, Argentina, and Bolivia for ritual dancing, religious processions, and horse races. The music and costumes are a weird blend of pre-Columbian and East Asian elements—although the source of the oriental influence is unknown.

Team dancing by organizations called *chinos* is exceptional. Moving to the sound of strange, oriental-sounding instruments, the dancers whirl through the streets in vivid, Asian-style costumes of red, green, and blue. The image of the Virgin wears a crown of gold and emeralds, and is carried through the fray to the huge shrine on an elaborately carved frame decked with roses.

About 150,000 people attend the celebration, and most camp out on the surrounding hillsides. There are hundreds of open-air eating stands, amusement rides, Japanese pool tables, and other gambling stands. On the fringes, horse races and cock fights are staged. The area is a mining and grape-growing center, where cactus-covered plains and hills are overlooked by the snow-covered Andes.

DATE: December 24–28, climaxing on December 26. **LOCATION:** Andacollo, near Serena in the middle north. **TRANSPORT:** From La Serena *colectivos* run to the festival from Calle Benavente, near Colocolo, but many pilgrims walk. La Serena's airport has daily flights from Santiago. **ACCOMMODATION:** Since no hotels are available at the sight, most people camp on the hillsides. **CONTACT:** Officina de Turismo, Prat. Esp. Matta, Piso 1, La Serena, Chile. Also, Sernatur (see *Resources*).

Resources

In Chile: SERNATUR/Servicio Nacional de Turismo, 1555 Providencia Ave., Casilla 14082, Santiago de Chile, Tel 2-6960474, Fax 2-2361417. **USA:** Embassy of Chile, 1732 Massachusetts Ave. NW, Washington, DC 20036, Tel (202) 785-1746, Fax (202) 659-9624. South American Explorers Club,

126 Indian Creek Road, Ithaca, NY 14850, Tel (607) 277-0488. **Canada:** Embassy of Chile, 151 Slater St., Ste. 605, Ottawa, ON K1P 5H3, Tel (613) 235-2312, Fax (613) 235-1176. **UK:** Embassy of Chile, 12 Devonshire St., GB-London W1N 2DS, Tel 71-5806392, Fax 71-4365204. **Germany:** Consulate General of Chile, Leipzigerstr. 61/05-03, D-1080 Berlin, Tel 30-2292531. **Australia:** Embassy of Chile, 10 Cnlgoa Circuit O'Malley, Monaro Crescent Red Hill, PO Box 69, Canberra, ACT 2603, Tel 62-2862430, Fax 62-2861289.

COLOMBIA

Mention you're going to Colombia and the looks you get will make it clear why this country hasn't been overrun by hoards of gringo tourists. Its turbulent history and dubious exports notwithstanding, mythical Colombia is South America's big adventure-travel secret, a place where pleasant surprises seem to grow on trees—and in mountains, jungles, rivers, caves, beaches, and skyscrapers. Travelers who take the necessary precautions and venture to Colombia typically come back raving about a fascinating, lively, and culturally sophisticated country.

In addition to having some of the world's most diverse flora and fauna, Colombia boasts an ethnic mosaic that blends the old worlds of Europe and Africa with the new world of native America (some 50 indigenous tribes continue to live traditional lifestyles). Colombians love to party, and their fiestas reflect their famous love of the irreverent, the imaginative, and the absurd. These events are great chances to meet the witty, street-smart Colombians, and to hear their home-grown musical styles that mix African, Spanish, and indigenous elements in wild rhythms that fuel all-night dance parties.

Black and White Carnival (Carnival de Blancos y Negros)

Popayán **January**

Marking the end of the Christmas season, these two days honor the Three Kings with a rowdy mix of parades, masquerades, and face-painting that mimics the Kings' facial hues and puts everyone on even racial footing. The hijinx begin on the morning of January 5, the *Día de Negritos,* as youngsters dip their hands in black grease and chase each other around, decorating squealing faces with dark smears. At night the action moves to teenagers and adults, who also paint each others' faces and masquerade through the streets. Roving groups of musicians called *chirimías* play typical songs, with one member usually dressing up as the devil and running through the crowd with a whip or spear.

Racial flip-flop: On the Día de Negritos *everyone's painted black; tomorrow everyone will be white.* (Craig Duncan/DDB Stock Photo)

The next day, the *Día de Blanquitos,* turns everything white. Boys and girls chase each other around with flour and white powder, and groups of people parade by in cars and trucks pelting everyone in sight. Revelers throw water from balconies, and soon everyone is covered with the gooey white mix, ready to spend the night drinking and dancing to live music.

Popayán is a colonial gem that was once a main stop on the overland gold route between Cartagena and Lima. It's filled with churches and monasteries dating from the 17th century, and is close to both the volcanic, animal-packed Puracé National Park and the very traditional villages of the Guambiano Indians.

DATE: January 5 and 6. **LOCATION:** Popayán's celebration is the largest; Pasto also has a *Blancos y Negros* festival. **TRANSPORT:** Both Popayán and Pasto have airports, which handle flights from Bogotá, Ipiales, and Cali. Buses serve the entire southwest region. **ACCOMMODATION:** Both cities have a wide range of hotels. **CONTACT:** Colombian embassy or consulate.

Carnival in Barranquilla

Barranquilla **February/March**

Torrid, tropical, seedy, and undignified—what Barranquilla lacks in redeeming values, it makes up for in a Carnival so berserk that it's infamous throughout the hemisphere. During the "crazy days" just before Lent, *Barranquilleros* show themselves and the world that their city of dirty wharfs, industrial shanty towns, and clumsy skyscrapers has heaping helpings of what the rest of the world desperately wants—great style!

No extravagance is spared as crowds fill the streets day and night, dancing to the Afro-Caribbean beats of salsa, merenque, and the home-grown favorite, cumbia. The costumes are some of the best in the Americas, with masks alternating between high craftsmanship and almost sub-human gaudiness. Parades of floats whip through the streets packed with musicians and high-amp sound machines on buses and trucks. There's an aquatic festival in the harbor, several beauty contests, and a wacky "battle of flowers" on Saturday. On Sunday everyone takes to the streets in disguise, and on Monday there's a burn-em-up concert by Caribbean music groups. Finally, on the night before Ash Wednesday, the spirit of Carnival, "Joselito Carnival," is buried, and everyone tries to sleep off the effects of the more than 100,000 cases of *aguardiente* that have been consumed.

DATE: The five days before Ash Wednesday. **LOCATION:** Barranquilla's Carnival is the most extensive and famous, but spirited Carnival festivities also take place in Santa Marta, Cartagena, Buenaventura, and Tumaco. **TRANSPORT:** Planes and buses connect Barranquilla with the rest of Colombia, and direct flights serve the city from Miami and New York. **ACCOMMODATION:** Forget about finding a hotel in your desired price range if you haven't booked well in advance. **CONTACT:** CNT, Edificio Arawak, Carrera 54, 75–45, P-2, Barranquilla, Colombia. Also, Colombian embassy or consulate.

© Cartagena International Festival of Caribbean Music

Cartagena **March**

Set in Cartagena's fabulously off-balance world of smugglers, beaches, and all-night dance parties, this festival is the perfect spring break for fans of Afro-Caribbean music. More than 20 big-name bands converge in a tropical boil-over of salsa, soca, soukous, rara, reggae, junkanoo, and other styles. Throughout this five-day marathon, Cartagena's carnival atmosphere gets cranked up to its highest conceivable amperage.

There's hardly enough power to chill a beer in Cartagena, but sound systems are everywhere, blasting out of houses, bars, beach huts, and bright open-sided buses. The festival begins on the waterfront Wednesday night, with mock battles between conquistadors and pirates. Street vendors sell beer and rum to the rowdy mob, and erratic fireworks shoot overhead (and sometimes into the crowd) when the musicians arrive.

The concerts begin Thursday evening in the open-air bullring uptown. On a given night the lineup might include top bands from Colombia, Cuba, Panama, the Dominican Republic, Haiti,

Through the haze at Cartagena's music fest: A tropical boil-over of smugglers, beaches, and all-night dance parties. (Tom Clynes)

Jamaica, and one group from Africa. It's a disorganized affair but the sound is great and the crowd is always dancing. Most nights the ruckus lasts until 4 or 5 a.m. When it's over, die-hards head to the Boca Grande beach, where *vallenato* bands serenade the dawn with toasts of the local firewater known as *aguardiente.*

DATE: Five days encompassing the weekend closest to St. Joseph's Day (March 19). **LOCATION:** Cartagena. Events take place throughout town, but concerts are set in the new bullring, about three miles (five kilometers) west of downtown. **TRANSPORT:** Charter flights from New York and Toronto can be booked through the organizers. Planes and buses connect Cartagena with the rest of Colombia, and there are direct flights from Miami. **ACCOMMODATION:** Cartagena's Old Town has historic, interesting budget hotels and *pensiones;* the beach-front hotels at Boca Grande feature higher-end digs. **CONTACT:** For dates and bands, contact Modern World Music, 143 Avenue B, New York, NY 10009, USA, Tel (212) 529-5881, Fax (212) 529-5882. For transport, hotel, or package tour information, contact Above & Beyond Travel in New York City, Tel (800) 526-8539 or (212) 219-2299.

Colombian National Beauty Contest for Burros

San Antero **April**

In Latin America, beauty contests are still a part of most major celebrations. San Antero takes this tradition to its extreme with beauties who are actually beasts ... of burden. The contestants are burros, dressed in women's dresses and bonnets, and paraded in front of an adoring crowd. Highlights include the swimsuit competition and the crowning of the most beautiful veterinarian-certified virgin.

Don't come to this dusty town expecting to find a new breed of sensitive Latin men making a sophisticated, ironic statement about the objectification of women. Nope. The event actually started as a commentary on the hee-hawing sexual preferences of some of this region's rural *hombres*. It's evolved into a folkloric symbol of the irreverence in which the *costeño* culture revels, and an opportunity to satirize and criticize Colombia's appalling social and political conditions.

Both a king and a queen are elected, and contestants are often named after human public figures. One year a candidate for the mayorship of Bogotá was satirized with a braying namesake who ascended the stage ramp dressed in a dapper suit and tie. Once on stage he regarded the crowd silently, with a cold stare. Enraged at his superior attitude, the spectators responded with derisive whistles until the burro slowly turned and then dropped his trousers, showing off his bay butt to the crowd. The sophomoric stunt worked well with the humans, whose jeers quickly turned to a wild applause that didn't cease until the jury crowned him King of the Burros.

Considering the grand prize—no forced labor for the rest of the winners' lives—it's a wonder any female burros would risk disqualification for a night of passion. Still, handlers don't take any chances, and chastity belts are popular fashion accessories for hooved hussies who are hot to trot.

While most of Colombia is wrapped up in Holy Week's ostentatious piety, San Antero rounds out its parade of imagination with folkloric dances, art exhibitions, and other festivities. Nearby, Caribbean beach resorts cater mainly to middle-class urban Colombians, and just outside Arboletes there's a beach-side mud volcano. You can wallow and frolic in the bubbling, warm gray mud (good for the skin and hair), then run into the surf to wash off.

DATE: Festivities begin the Thursday before Easter and continue through Easter Sunday, with the beauty contest taking place on Saturday. **LOCATION:** San Antero is located about 150 km/93 miles south of Cartagena. **TRANSPORT:** The nearest airport is about 65 km/40 miles south, in Montería. Buses run from Montería, and along the coast from Tolú, Toveñas, and Cartagena. **ACCOMMODATION:** Beach-side hotels are packed during holy week, so book ahead. Other possibilities include nearby Tolú and Toveñas. **CONTACT:** Colombian embassy or consulate.

While you're there ...

Ibague Festival, Ibague: Featuring nearly all of Colombia's very diverse traditions of folk dancing, this festival brings performers from all over the country. (Usually the last week in June.)

Feast of St. Francis (Fiesta de San Francisco), Quibdó: In between processions and sporting events, the streets are filled with humans masquerading as devils, cats, and alligators. *Vacalocas* (crazy cows) made of wood with flaming horns move through the streets, propelled by drunken men. (September 26 through October 4.)

Resources

In Colombia: CNT/Corporacion National de Turismo, Calle 28 No. 13A–15, Pisos 17 y 18, Apartado Aereo 8400-240328, Bogotá, Tel 1-2839466, Fax 1-2843818. **USA:** Consulate of Colombia, 280 Aragon Ave., Coral Gables, FL 33134, Tel (305) 448-5558, Fax (305) 441-9537. South American Explorers Club, 126 Indian Creek Road, Ithaca, NY 14850 Tel (607) 277-0488. **Canada:** Embassy of Colombia, 150 Kent St., Ste. 404, Ottawa, ON K1P 5P4, Tel (613) 230-3760, Fax (613) 230-4416. **UK:** Embassy of Colombia, 3 Hans Crescent, GB-London SW1X 0LR, Tel 71-5899177, Fax 71-5811829. **Germany:** Consulate General of Colombia, Clara-Zetkin-Str. 89, D-1080 Berlin, Tel 30-2292669, Fax 30-2292743. **Australia:** Embassy of Colombia, 101 Northbourne Ave., Turner, Canberra, ACT 2601, Tel 6-2572027, Fax 6-2571448.

ECUADOR

Bounded by uneasy neighbors to the north, south, and east, Ecuador has been blessed with a relatively peaceful social and political climate. Visitors are often seduced by the country's easygoing Andean charm and friendliness, and by its wealth of natural attractions within a compact, easy-to-travel package. Although it straddles the line that gives the nation its name, the tall stature of its many volcanoes has endowed it with nearly every climatic zone, from snowy peaks to torrid jungle lowlands. In between the extremes are thousands of microclimates packed with endemic flora and fauna.

Ethnically and culturally, Ecuador is divided between the people of the Andean highlands and those of the Pacific lowlands. Although more than half the population is Indian, festivals and celebrations reflect the Spaniards' success at converting the Ecuadorian indigenous community to Catholicism. The colonial cities of the highlands host religious processions and rituals while jungle cities of the coastal lowlands carry on with their African-influenced celebrations.

Santos Reyes and Santos Inocentes

San Lorenzo **January**

If you manage to make it to San Lorenzo during the first days of the new year—and this is no easy stunt—you'll be blessed by a happening so unlikely that you'd be excused for wondering whether you've stumbled onto the wrong continent, or into the wrong century. San Lorenzo lies among the mangrove swamps of South America's Pacific coast, but the imagination races to pre-colonial Africa. Muddy streets are filled with black children in small groups, dancing and beating on makeshift drums. Their faces and bodies are painted in red and yellow, and their singing refers to Macumba (voodoo) spirits such as *el Rivel,* who steals corpses, or *la Tunda,* who frightens bad children to death.

Santos Reyes in San Lorenzo: With face paint and makeshift drums, children dance and sing of the Three Kings and the voodoo spirits of their African ancestors. (Tom Clynes)

The ostensible excuses for the occasion are Holy Innocents Day, commemorating Herod's massacre of children when Jesus was a baby, and Three Kings Day, when most Latin Americans give Christmas gifts to children. Yet in isolated San Lorenzo, Catholic rites are mixed and matched with Macumba and ancestor worship. The town, founded by slaves who escaped from the Caribbean in the 17th and 18th centuries, has retained much of its African identity, and spirits are regularly called upon to curse or cure.

The days between Christmas and mid-January are devoted to children's celebrations, and part of the low-key charm is that there are no organized events. Children simply run through the streets with their faces painted, often wearing makeshift costumes and beating on homemade drums. You'll also see men in black face paint wearing cones of rolled paper on their heads, setting up roadblocks and collecting "tolls" to support drinking. Known as *cucuruchos,* these foreboding figures descend from European-style marchers who protect the images of Jesus in Ecuador's highlands. On the coast the former slaves integrated the Christian holidays into their own celebrations, and now use the occasion to sing and dance to the wild *marimba* music.

DATE: Any time between December 24 and January 15 is a good time to visit. Most of the activity takes place around January 6 (Santos Reyes). **LOCATION:** Ecuador's Pacific coast, just south of the Colombian border. **TRANSPORT:** See *Getting to San Lorenzo* in this chapter. **ACCOMMODATION:** There are a few cheap and poor-quality thatched hotels. Creature comforts are limited to mosquito nets and bare bulbs; use the latter to check your bed for scorpions before you jump in! **CONTACT:** Ecuador Tourist Office or embassy (see *Resources*).

Getting to San Lorenzo

There are no roads to San Lorenzo. To get there, you can take either a *lancha* (a long motorized canoe) or the *autoferro* (a makeshift train/bus). Either way, you won't be bored.

By Lancha: From Guayaquil or Quito start with a steamy 10-hour bus trip to Esmeraldas, which is sometimes under siege by bandits. Tensions have cooled recently, but it's best not to travel at night. From Esmeraldas, hop onto an open-sided dune buggy heading north along the beach to La Tola (about three hours). There, a *lancha* is usually waiting to make the four-hour trip to San Lorenzo, with one stop at an isolated fishing village called Limones. This area is near the Colombian border, and there's plenty of *contrabando* activity that often prompts police searches of boats. If the *policía* pull away without finding anything, boatmen often trade elated high-fives. If they do find something, a "tip" usually takes care of the problem.

By Autoferro: The *autoferro* is essentially an antiquated Bluebird bus mounted on a train chassis and set on tracks. This unique contraption tackles enormous physical obstacles on its path from Ibarra, at 6,630 feet (2,210 meters) to coastal San Lorenzo. In the mountains it clings to cliffs and threads through more than 200 tunnels. In the jungle it's nearly strangled by vegetation. The scenery is spectacular and constantly changing; the hundreds of microclimates you'll pass through are home to some of the highest concentrations of endemic species on earth.

If the *autoferro* makes it all the way (and even if it doesn't), you're in for the ride of your life. Arrive at the train station early, as the ticketing process is crowded, confusing, and unruly (passengers unable to board have been known to beat up the driver). Double-booking of seats is not uncommon, but during the dry season the best views are from the roof. Then again, there are bats in the tunnels. At times the track is damaged and buses take over the leg between Ibarra and Lita. Be sure to take plenty of water and food since it's not unusual to be stranded by a landslide or derailment—sometimes for a day or two.

While you're there ...

Holy Week, Quito and elsewhere: Quito holds a huge procession on Good Friday, with flagellants, creepy men in purple, and men dragging crosses while being whipped by "Romans." (March/April.)

Feast of St. John the Baptist

Near Otavalo and elsewhere **June**

Coinciding with the winter solstice, St. John's day has been co-opted by Indians into a continuation of sun-worship celebrations. In the Otavalo area, several towns hold large-scale fiestas in which traditional music and dance play a large part. Satire runs through many of the dances, as Indians wear costumes imitating both mestizos and the tour-bus gringos who swarm Otavalo's marketplace. In town there are bullfights in the plaza, and just outside of town regattas are held on the Lago de San Pablo. In the nearby village of Iluman the festivities are a bit more traditional.

Otavalo itself seems to draw nearly every traveler to Ecuador to its famous Saturday Indian market—at least once. It's quite touristy, but for some apparel it's the best place in the country to buy. The surrounding area is full of stunning high mountain valleys dotted with Indian villages, mountain lakes, and volcanic craters.

DATE: June 24. **LOCATION:** Otavalo and other villages, including Iluman, Araque, and San Antonio de Pichincha. **TRANSPORT:** Getting to the Otavalo area is no problem, as buses run from Quito every few minutes. **ACCOMMODATION:** Otavalo is well-stocked with accommodation, but lodging is tight during the festival. **CONTACT:** Ecuador Tourist Office or embassy (see *Resources*).

Christmas and New Year Celebrations

Cuenca **December/January**

The extravagance of Cuenca's Christmas and New Year's Eve celebrations is known throughout South America. This beautiful colonial town spares no expense in decorations, and the bouts of drinking and dancing are legendary.

The morning of Christmas Eve brings the finest parade in all of Ecuador, the *Pase del Niño Viajero*. Indians and mestizos from all the surrounding villages stream into town in cars, trucks, and on donkeys decorated with tokens of prosperity ranging from strings of banknotes and bunches of bananas to bottles of booze and whole roasted chickens. Colorfully costumed Quechua musicians march through the streets, alongside children dressed up as biblical figures. The fun continues into mid-January, peaking on New Year's Eve with the burning of effigies of politicians, celebrities, and even fictional characters.

Cuenca is a relaxed town founded in 1557, and its cobblestone streets and old homes don't seem to have changed much

Cuenca: The Christmas season brings two weeks of costumes, parades, and one of South America's most notorious bouts of partying. (Donne Bryant)

since then. With a spring-like climate at Christmas and year-round, Cuenca and its unspoiled mountain surroundings are perfect for hiking. Nearby are pristine cloud forests and stretches of equatorial tundra called *páramo*.

DATE: Most of the action takes place between December 24 and January 6. **LOCATION:** Cuenca, in Ecuador's southern highlands. **TRANSPORT:** Cuenca's airport handles flights from Quito and Guayaquíl, and buses serve the city from all over the country. A train (with spectacular views) goes as far as Sibambe, but service is erratic. **ACCOMMODATION:** As a tourist city Cuenca has a wide range of hotels, but Christmas is high season, so book ahead. **CONTACT:** Ecuador Tourist Office or embassy (see *Resources*).

© Resources

In Ecuador: CETUR/Corporacion Ecuatoriana de Turismo, Reina Victoria 514 y Vicenta Ramon Roca, Casilla 2454, Quito, Tel 2-527002, Fax 2-568198. Also, South American Explorers Club, Toledo 1254, La Floresta, Quito. **USA:** Ecuador Tourist Office, 1390 Brickell Ave., 3rd Fl., Miami, FL 33131-3324, Tel (305) 461-2363, Fax (305) 446-7755. South American Explorers Club, 126 Indian Creek Road, Ithaca, NY 14850, Tel (607) 277-0488. **Canada:** Embassy of Ecuador, 50 O'Connor St. #1311, Ottawa, ON K1P 6L2, Tel (613) 563-8206, Fax (613) 235-5776. **UK:** Embassy of Ecuador, 3 Hans Crescent, GB-London SW1X 0LS, Great Britain, Tel 71-5841367, Fax 71-8239701. **Germany:** Consulate of Ecuador, Clara-Zetkin-Str. 89, D-1080 Berlin, Tel 30-2291258.

With Peru's economy and security on the rebound, the heart of the old Inca empire is again a traveler's hot-spot. In the highlands surrounding Machu Picchu and Lake Titicaca, native Peruvians still celebrate a great many pre-Columbian fiestas—albeit with Christian overtones added to placate Spanish colonists. These celebrations are a fantastic mix of piety and drunkenness, subtle beauty and over-the-top gaudiness.

PERU

Traditional music and dance always play a big role. There are more than 100 varieties of costume dances, in which masks and movements parody everything from bullfighters and conquistadors to jungle Indians, black slaves, and urban mestizos. In ancient Inca rituals, getting drunk on *chicha* (a corn-based home brew) was a religious obligation, and most modern festivals carry on with this tradition, deviating only in that the local Catholic church is now the most auspicious spot to fall down drunk.

Candlemas (Festival de la Virgin del la Candelaria)

Puno and elsewhere **February**

This town on the shores of Lake Titicaca becomes a 10-ring circus in the days surrounding Candlemas, as masked, costumed dancers mob the streets. Whirling to Andean panpipes and beating drums, the Indians from surrounding villages lay out a musical and visual feast that includes almost 100 varieties of the region's famous dances.

For several days, dancers roam the streets, often pausing to perform at the door of the church of San Juan, where the Virgin's image is housed. Aymará Indians swarm in, twirling each other by the elbow and swinging canes. *Llamero* dancers gracefully wield shepherd's slings, while *Sikuris* in matador suits and feathered headdresses mock the Spanish as they trot in circles around drums. Horned devil-men, sequinned conquistadors, and grotesque animals all play a role in the deeply symbolic dances.

Although there are official performances in the stadium, the nighttime street parties are much better. Bands from all over the

Candlemas in Puno: Lake Titicaca's 10-ring circus of music and incredibly costumed dancers. (A.S.K./Viesti Associates)

region play either brass and string instruments, or percussion and wind instruments that conjure the mysteries and glories of times long gone. Panpipes appear in an huge range of sizes and shapes (including man-sized bass pipes), and flutes are made of everything from bamboo to the wing bone of the condor. On the feast day itself, altars are set up on the four corners of the Plaza de Armas, and the image of the Virgin is carried through streets that are strewn with petals of yellow wildflowers.

DATE: Candlemas is February 2, but the festival usually extends to the weekend before and after. Check with the tourist office for actual dates each year. **LOCATION:** Candlemas is celebrated most fervently in Puno, but other places to see the action are Cuzco, Ayacucho, and Arequipa. **TRANSPORT:** Puno can be reached by train

Holy Week: Llamas ready for one of Ayacucho's many Easter processions. (Joe Viesti/Viesti Associates)

from Cuzco and Arequipa. The nearest airport is at Juliaca, about 44 km/27 miles from Puno. Bus trips are long and roads are bad. **ACCOMMODATION:** Puno has low and mid-range hotels, but very little at the top end. **CONTACT:** Peruvian Embassy or SAEC (see *Resources*).

WHILE YOU'RE THERE ...

Day of the Kings (Día de los Reyes), Cuzco: Fabulously dramatic depictions of the early events in Christ's life are staged. When Herod orders all male infants killed, horsemen storm into the crowd to snatch babies made of papier mache from women spectators, and dramatically behead them. Also, costumed Indian dancers reenact events from Inca history. (January 6.)

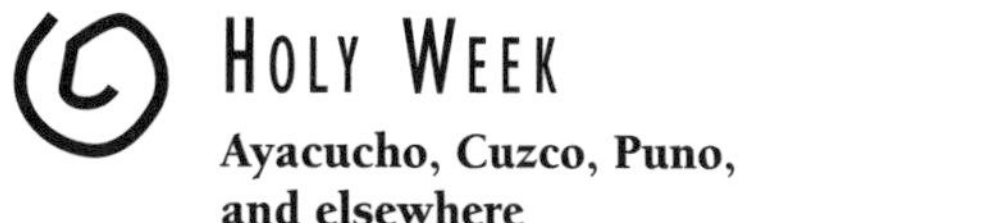

HOLY WEEK

Ayacucho, Cuzco, Puno, and elsewhere — **March/April**

Throughout Peru, Easter week is celebrated in lavish, often bizarre spectacles that range from processions of saints and mass prostration ceremonies to ceremonious hangings of Judas. Cuzco, the ancient center of the Inca world, puts on some of the best shows. On Monday of Holy Week a Christ-like statue of *el Señor de los Temblores* (the Lord of the Earthquakes) is dressed in special underwear and a wig and carried through the city on a carpet of

Catholicism, Cuzco style: Wearing shoulder pads to accommodate the weight of the sacred image, three men pause during the Corpus Christi procession in the Plaza de Armas. (Robert Frerck/Odyssey Productions/Chicago)

red flowers. First performed in 1650, the procession is a way of beseeching Jesus to spare the city from devastating earthquakes. As the procession makes the sign of the cross with the statue in front of the cathedral, Indians prostrate themselves, averting their eyes from the image in the belief that Christ is at that moment singling out who is doomed to die in the coming year.

On Good Friday in Cuzco and nearly everywhere else, effigies of Judas, politicians, and other unpopular figures are hung by the neck and set on fire. On El Calvario Chico (Little Calvary Hill) near Puno, people purchase miniature items in the belief that the real-life version of whatever is bought will come to the buyer during the next year. At Ayacucho, Christ's passion is acted out by the entire town, and the Holy Saturday festivities last all night. The town of Tarma lays beautiful flower carpets out on the streets for a nocturnal procession.

One popular Holy Week belief in Peru is that since Christ (God) is dead for a couple of days, He can't be offended by anything happening on earth. Thus, many people see Friday and Saturday as a time of complete license, indulging in sexual promiscuity, cheating, and robbery with a spirit of impunity, since Holy Week debauchers fear no possibility of divine repercussions from a God who sees no evil ... because He's dead.

DATE: Easter Week (March/April). **LOCATION:** Ayacucho, Cuzco, Puno, and nationwide. **CONTACT:** Peruvian Embassy or SAEC (see *Resources*).

While you're there ...

Feast of San Juan de Dios, Puno: Great traditional music accompanies a parade of decorated llamas loaded with firewood. In the evening the wood is set ablaze and *Suri Sikuri* dancers jump through the flames of bonfires. There's more dancing the next day as revelers parade the image of the saint through the streets. (March 7 and 8.)

Corpus Christi, Cuzco and nationwide: Masked dances, brass bands, feasts, and drinking bouts mark this fiesta, celebrated all over the Sierra. In Cuzco, people from outlying villages bring their statues of patron saints into town in a colorful procession. The images spend the nights alone in the cathedral, where they are said to dance and enjoy themselves just like the humans. (June; the Thursday after Trinity Sunday.)

Inti Raymi

Cuzco **June**

The full-day pageant of Inti Raymi is massive, colorful, well-choreographed—and like most sequels, not as good or as authentic as the original. Yet even though it's a mere shadow of the ancient spectacle of royal parades and animal sacrifices, today's re-enactment provides a glimpse of what ancient Peru must have looked like. More significantly, Inti Raymi's revival in the middle of the 20th century has returned to Peru's indigenous people some small measure of what was taken from their ancestors.

Although the gold has been long-since plundered and one of the earth's most productive empires has been reduced to poverty, this joyous, colorful pageant is an explosion of traditional costumes and rituals. Modern-day participants act out ancient roles as kings, courtiers, provincial chiefs, warriors, and others who once traveled from the far reaches of the empire to draw Inti, the Inca sun god, back to the southern skies.

Coming on the tails of Corpus Christi, and coinciding with the southern winter solstice and the Feast Day of St. John the Baptist, this spectacle of cultural continuity still draws more Indians than tourists. Most can't afford to sit in the bleachers (tickets must be bought in advance from the *Municipalidad* or a hotel), but standing places in the ruins of an Inca fort are free if you're there early.

The solstice day features a symbolic sacrifice to the sun (in the original a llama was sacrificed and its organs studied to predict the year's events). Participants dress in wild turkey feathers, scarves, and masks and carry palm lances. In rhythmic leaps they form elliptical figures, shouting in praise of the sun as bamboo flutes and lambskin drums provide the soundtrack. The proces-

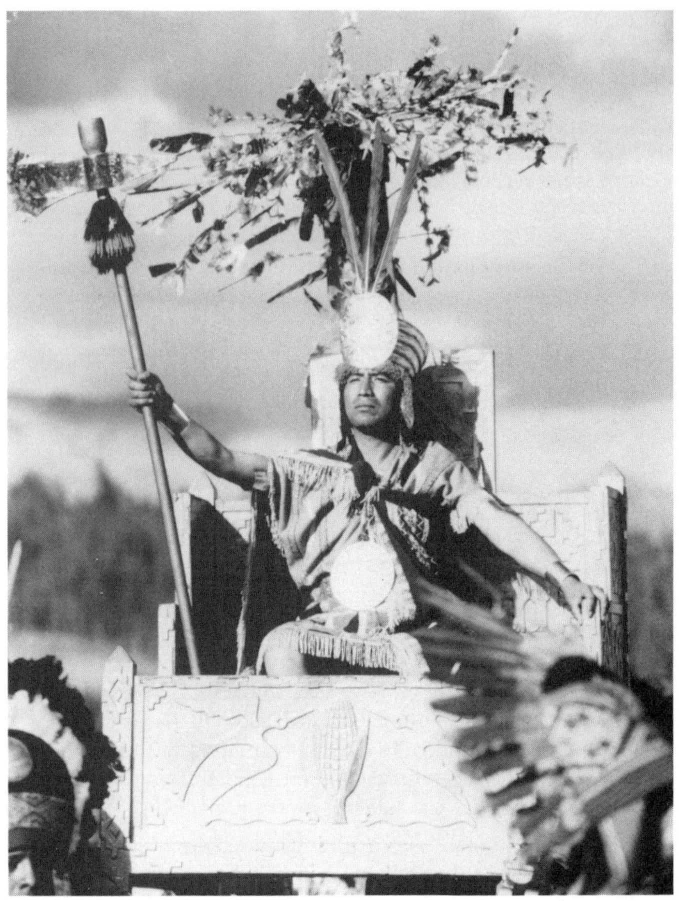

Inti Raymi: An epic reenactment of the ancient Inca solstice rituals. *(M.T. O'Keefe/Bruce Coleman Inc.)*

sion is truly spectacular, an epic of costuming, setting, and staging that—authenticity aside—is optimistic and energizing.

DATE: The entire week culminating on June 24. **LOCATION:** The ruins of Sacsayhuaman, on the northern outskirts of Cuzco. **TRANSPORT:** Cuzco's airport handles flights from Lima, Arequipa, Puerto Maldonado, and La Paz (Bolivia). Trains serve the city from Puno, Arequipa, Machu Picchu, and Quillabamba. **ACCOMMODATION:** Cuzco is well-outfitted for hoards of backpackers and higher-scale travelers, but Inti Raymi packs the town to its limits. Reserve in advance, or better yet get there early. **CONTACT:** Peruvian Embassy or SAEC (see *Resources*).

While you're there ...

Feast Day of Saint James (Santiago), Lampa and Santiago de Pupuja: Although James is the patron saint of Spain, Indians recognized him as the god of thunder and lightning. Worshipers make offerings to protect llamas and cattle, and parade the decorated beasts in the midst of markets and street dance parties. In Lampa, firemakers ride on horseback around the plaza dressed as ribboned colonial generals. *Ayarachi* dancer/musicians don exotic headdresses and play a tune believed to be the one played at the funeral of Monco Cápac. (July 25.)

Fiesta de la Virgen del Carmen

Paucartambo **July**

You never know what to expect next at this Andean jumble of strange dances and costumes. One minute an Indian man disguised as a woman is dancing with a bullfighter, the next a mysterious "doctor" in a top hat is dispensing advice to "patients" shivering with malaria and beating each other with cloth bags. Monkey men cavort with jungle warriors carrying stuffed animals on canes, while images of the Virgin are showered with confetti.

Each year in mid-July, sleepy, remote Paucartambo is transformed into a whirling fantasy world of sound, color, and religious fervor. The festival honors the Virgin of Carmen, whose image is carried from the church on the shoulders of 18 men as crowds throw confetti from white colonial balconies and set off fireworks. (Note the scar in one eye of the image, from an arrow shot during an Indian uprising.)

Because of the relative isolation of this colonial village (set in a beautiful valley at 2700 meters/9000 feet), the festival has remained one of the most authentic big festivals in the Andes. Each of several Indian dance groups represents an aspect of the colonial history of Paucartambo. The crazily hatted *Q'ollas* represent herders and merchants who travel through town, and as they dance and sing in the Quechua language they spin wool and lead llamas decorated with ear-tassels of red yarn. The *Chunchos* represent Indians from the jungle, and wear silk capes and wild headdresses made from wool and tropical bird feathers. *Waca Waca* dancers satirize the Spanish as they move up and down the streets staging hilarious mock bullfights.

For three nights these and other dancers—some in painted mesh masks, others in long-nosed ski masks, still others in huge, painted papier-mache devil masks—swirl through the streets drinking *chicha,* a homebrewed corn beer. One outrageous highlight is a mock war between the *Q'ollas* and *Chunchos,* during which they chase each other around the Plaza de Armas. The temporary warriors jump over small fires, squirt beer, and toss oranges in drunken, good-natured abandon.

DATE: July 16, 17, and 18. **LOCATION:** Paucartambo is located about 120 km/74 miles from Cuzco on a narrow, dirt road. **TRANSPORT:** Only a few buses and trucks make the five-hour journey from Cuzco's Urcos bus stop, but tour operators sometimes run minibuses from Cuzco for the day. **ACCOMMODATION:** Unless you day-trip with a group (in which case you can sleep on the bus), options are extremely limited. There are a couple of basic hotels which are usually full, and some locals let guests sleep on floors or camp in yards. **CONTACT:** Peruvian Embassy or SAEC (see *Resources*).

© Resources

In Peru: Direccion General de Tourismo, Avenida Corpac s/n, Calle 1, Oeste Urb., San Isidro-Lima 27, Tel 14-406119. South American Explorers Club (SAEC), Casilla 3714, Lima 100, Peru, Tel 5114-250142. **USA:** Embassy of Peru, 1700 Massachusetts Ave. NW, Washington, DC 20036-1903, Tel (202) 833-9860, Fax (202) 659-8124. South American Explorers Club (SAEC), 126 Indian Creek Road, Ithaca, NY 14850, Tel (607) 277-0488. **Canada:** Embassy of Peru, 170 Laurier Ave. W., Ste. 1007, Ottawa, ON K1P 5V5, Tel (613) 238-1777. **UK:** Embassy of Peru, 52 Sloane St., London SW1X 9SP, Tel 71-2351917. **Germany:** Consulate of Peru, Schadowstr. 6, D-1086 Berlin, Tel 30-2291455. **Australia:** Embassy of Peru, 197 London Circuit, Canberra, ACT 2600, Tel 6-2572953.

VENEZUELA

Just a two-hour flight away from Miami, Venezuela is a land of travelers and immigrants, a place where the cosmopolitan flair of Caracas contrasts sharply with the low-key cattle ranches of the west, or the jungled, primeval tablelands of the south. Despite oil reserves that are the envy of Latin America, the country is perennially on the verge of economic and political crisis—but Venezuelans rarely let little things like military coups get in the way of a good dance party.

With so many influences, it's tough to put a finger on the culture of Venezuela. Particular towns and regions specialize in distinct dances and musical forms, which are usually performed at religious festivals. The country's coastal African culture is especially vibrant, and even in the land of cowboys and matadors, the big drums and devil dancers are never far away.

The Devil Dancers of Corpus Christi

Nationwide **May/June**

When Venezuelans make a pact to dance like the devil they're not joking. During Corpus Christi in several towns, dozens of *Diablos* take to the streets in red outfits with horned and streamered masks, and spend the day banging on drums and shaking maracas. Moving through town, they dance and leap toward the church, then prostrate themselves on the steps as a sign of submission and inch painfully toward the church doors on their knees.

Each Devil Dancer participates in one of the country's most colorful and peculiar folk customs to fulfill a promise made when asking for divine intervention. Health issues are often the source of these religious agreements, and devil-dance pacts are made for a certain number of years and sometimes even for life. The dancers' profound faith in the tradition intensifies their belief that severe emotional penalties will result from not keeping a promise to dance. A man in Yare, for instance, danced on behalf of his brother for 17 years in an effort to protect him from harm for abandoning the vow.

Most prevalent in isolated coastal communities where there were once large concentrations of slaves, the devil-dance confraternities maintain a centuries-old tradition of portraying the submission of the devil to the Eucharist. The costumes of each group have distinct features, and dances range from free-form writhing to the beat of African drums, to elaborate double-files. Dancers joining the confraternities for the first time are often "baptized" by the other devils, who dance around the initiate and graze him with the magical ribbons of their masks.

In most towns, women don't get involved in the dancing, although the dancers of Naiguatá are a very notable exception. Here, female devils usually dance for the health of their children. Their costumes are particularly intricate, and are usually hand-colored with overlapping abstract designs.

DATE: Corpus Christi, the Thursday nine weeks after Easter. **LOCATION:** San Francisco de Yare (Miranda State), Naiguatá (on the beach near Caracas), Turiamo, Chuao, Cata, Cuyagua (all in Aragua State), and Patanemo (Carabobo coast). **CONTACT:** Venezuelan Information Center or embassy (see *Resources*).

WHILE YOU'RE THERE ...

- **Carnival, nationwide:** Carnival in Caracas is low-key, but El Callao (Bolívar State) throws a highly charged carnival that features the calypso music, dancing, and limbo of its once-Trinidadian inhabitants. Puerto Cabello (Carabobo State) performs a unique spectacle known as the Hammock Dance, and in Naiguatá, a kooky festival features men in drag and plenty of lively street theater. (February/March; the week of Ash Wednesday.)
- **Alma Llanera Fair, San Fernando de Apure:** The area where Venezuela's national dance and dress originated puts on a fair that features food, music, a cattle show, and a rodeo. (Mid-April.)
- **The May Cross (Crux de Mayo), Nationwide:** African drum beats and sensual dancing are backdropped by Spanish-style religious decorations at celebrations around the nation—especially in coastal areas. Private parties, parades, and maypole dances unite entire communities in a festive atmosphere of singing, dancing, eating, and praying. Best in Bailadores, Lagunillas, Boconó, and Jajo. (May.)

THE BIG DRUMS OF SAN JUAN

Curiepe and the Barlovento region **June**

The big drums erupt in dazzling polyrhythms for three days and nights, inspiring frenzied bouts of dancing. This cultural feast

The Big Drums of San Juan: Caught up in Barlovento's dazzling, Afro-Caribbean rave-up, two women throw inhibitions to the wind. *(Joe Viesti/Viesti Associates)*

reflects the African origins of the people in the Barlovento area, and brings people from all over the country to drink, socialize, and dance to the drums called the *mina* and *culo e' puya.*

The *mina,* which is named after the area in Ghana from which it came, is actually a set of two drums. The *mina* proper is a man-sized, hollowed-out tree trunk that is braced by two poles and straddled. The drummer uses sticks to play the body of the drum, its deerskin head, and the attached, smaller *curbata* drum. The *culo e' puya,* which may be Bantu in origin, is actually three long, double-skinned drums that the drummer places between his legs and plays with a stick in one hand and the bare palm of his other.

The music continues non-stop from noon on the 23rd until the night of the 25th. Drummers from all over Barlovento attend, and lay down overpowering, orgiastic rhythms. Special songs are played with various themes, including one for dead, unbaptized children, and several for Afro-Caribbean liberation. On the saint's night, an image of San Juan is placed in a position of honor, covered with flowers, and serenaded with all-night drumming.

DATE: June 23–25. **LOCATION:** Curiepe has the best-known and largest festival, but other towns in Barlovento between Curiepe and Patanemo also hold celebrations. **TRANSPORT:** The town is about two hours west of Caracas; special buses run during the celebration. **ACCOMMODATION:** There are no accommodations in Curiepe, but it's possible to day-trip from Caracas or stay in surrounding towns. **CONTACT:** Venezuelan Information Center or embassy (see *Resources*).

While you're there ...

Orinoco Fair, Ciudad Bolívar: The colonial gateway to the jungle and Angel Falls combines fishing contests with singing, calypso music, and horse racing to celebrate the sapoara fish that spawn abundantly in the Orinoco each year. (August 5–8.)

Resources

In Venezuela: CORPOTURISMO/Corporacion de Turismo de Venezuela, Avenida Lecuna, Parque Central Torre Oeste, Caracas 1010, Tel 2-5078831, Fax 2-5742220. **USA:** Venezuelan Information Center, c/o Venezuela General Consulate, 7 E. 51st St., New York, NY 10022, Tel (212) 826-1660, Fax (212) 644-7471. South American Explorers Club, 126 Indian Creek Road, Ithaca, NY 14850, Tel (607) 277-0488. **Canada:** Embassy of Venezuela, 32 Range Rd., Ottawa, ON K1N 8J4, Tel (613) 235-5151, Fax (613) 235-3205. **UK:** Embassy of Venezuela, 1 Cromwell Rd., GB-London SW7, Tel 71-5844206, Fax 71-5888887. **Germany:** German Venezuelan Society, Parkstr. 4, D-8000 Munich 2, Tel 89-5026531, Fax 89-5022311. **Australia:** Embassy of Venezuela, MLC Tower, Ste. 106, Woden, ACT 2606, Tel 6-2824827, Fax 6-2811969.

THE CARIBBEAN

ARUBA, BONAIRE, AND CURAÇAO

The polycultural ABC Dutch islands stand apart from the rest of the Caribbean in a host of ways. Just off the coast of Venezuela, the three islands feature a range of surreal, arid landscapes broken up by a mix of whitewashed villages, stray donkeys, elegant Dutch-style cities, and high-rise beach hotels. One of the few places in the Caribbean where Indian ancestry is still pronounced, the ABC islands have a unique ethnic mix that also reflects the influence of Africans, French, Jews, Spaniards, and, of course, the Dutch.

Wherever there are Dutch people, jazz can't be far away, and Aruba is blessed with the best jazz festival in the Caribbean. Aruba's Carnival has a Latin tinge, and it's during the pre-Lenten period that Aruba and Curaçao are at their most exciting and friendliest. Quiet Bonaire still beats to the drums of another era, and at its festivals you can often catch the Afro-Latino moves and rhythms of the *Kibrahacha* Dancers.

Carnival

Aruba **February/March**

On an island that appears at first glance to be solely set up for tourists, it's refreshing to see Arubans taking time to rev up a Carnival that's first and foremost a celebration of Aruban life. This is one of the finest Carnivals in the Caribbean, and for the two weeks preceding Ash Wednesday, the music, dancing, laughter, food, and drink seem endless.

The celebrations get going with a children's parade in San Nicolas, followed by island-wide competitions to choose district Carnival Queens. Bands move through the streets, and singers and costumed dancers are everywhere. In Oranjestad, days and nights are filled with formal balls and parades in which the best bands are selected, and on the Sunday before Ash Wednesday the Grand Carnival Parade gets going. Spectators are drawn into a moving frenzy of steel bands, floats, and costumes that lasts three days and includes a 4 a.m. pajama parade. Finally, the Grand Old Mask Parade signals that the festivities are drawing to a close, and King Momo, the effigy of Carnival, is burned at midnight.

DATE: The two weeks leading up to Ash Wednesday. **LOCATION:** Activities take place all over Aruba, but center in Oranjestad. **TRANSPORT:** Aruba is reached from other Caribbean islands by ferry or plane. Direct flights are available from Amsterdam and major North and South American cities. **ACCOMMODATION:** Aruba has plenty of pricey hotels and resorts from which to choose. **CONTACT:** Aruba Tourism Office (see *Resources*).

While you're there ...

- **New Year's Day, Aruba:** Although the welcoming of the New Year traditionally means doors are wide open around the islands, the racket of thousands of firecrackers has business owners closing up shop early on December 31. Midnight fireworks herald the New Year and ward off evil spirits, but the most interesting tradition is that of *Dandes* (strolling musicians) who travel from house to house, waking residents and singing songs of good luck and good cheer. (December 31–January 1.)
- **Tumba Festival, Bonaire:** Held to determine the official *tumba* (a local version of the Venezuelan *rumba*) song for Carnival, this authentic musical blast takes place just before the Carnival season begins. Contact: Festival Center, Tel 376368. (February.)
- **Sami Sail, Boca St. Michiel (Curaçao):** This small Curaçao fishing village pulls up its nets long enough to host a four-day sailing regatta. (Late April/May.)

Aruba Jazz and Latin Music Festival

Oranjestad (Aruba) **June**

Aruba celebrates her balmy nights under the stars with a monster summer festival that features some of the world's renowned jazz and Latin music performers. There's plenty of salsa, merengue, and jazz, and promoters wisely stretch the bounds to include reggae, calypso, soca, and other Caribbean music. The festival gets rave reviews not only for its lineup—past artists have included George Benson, Tito Puente, Dizzy Gillespie, Reuben Blades, and Celia Cruz—but also for its world-class sound and lights.

Carlos Santana at the Aruba Jazz and Latin Music Festival: The sounds of the Caribbean fill Aruba's balmy June nights at this exceptional concert event. (Aruba Tourism Authority)

The event is held in the open-air, 6,000-seat Aruba Entertainment Center, and the large crowd doesn't come close to scuttling the intimate ambiance and comradery of feverous fans from around the world, who dance in the aisles every night. During the day, noted musicians hold seminars.

DATE: Two consecutive weekends in mid- to late June. **LOCATION:** Oranjestad, Aruba. **TRANSPORT:** Aruba is reached from other Caribbean islands by ferry or plane. Direct flights to Aruba are available from Amsterdam and major North and South American cities.

ACCOMMODATION: Aruba has plenty of pricey hotels and resorts from which to choose. **CONTACT:** Aruba Tourism Office (see *Resources*).

While you're there ...

Hi-Winds Windsurfing Tournament, Aruba: More than 300 windsurfers from all over the world compete off the sandy shores of this windsurfing Mecca. The Around-the-Isle race is the most challenging, carrying a purse of $10,000; a race to Venezuela and back is also included. Bikini contests and sand-building competitions even manage to hold the attention of a few folks on shore. Contact: Aruba Hi-Winds Pro/Am Foundation, c/o BTA Group, L.G. Smith Blvd. 62, Oranjestad, Tel 35454. (Late May/June.)

San Juan Festival

Bonaire and Aruba **June**

Whether it's Juan or John, anybody sharing the name of the patron saint is considered special during this feast day of St. John. While musicians are busy serenading all the Johns, spry young men and women jump the traditional St. John's Fires while singing "Dina Baro," a ditty about a woman whose skirt catches fire as she hops flames.

If you're in Aruba on June 23, the day before feast day, go ahead and surrender to your burning urge to go out and bury a rooster. This tradition started out as a pagan agricultural celebration of the end of the harvest. Then some zealous Catholics got hold of it and reconciled the whole affair with a religious holiday; the result is a folkloric celebration honoring St. John the Baptist. Dances and music lead up to the "Deramento di Gai," or rooster burial ... which is now only simulated.

DATE: June 24. **LOCATION:** Aruba and Bonaire. **TRANSPORT:** Both islands are accessible from other parts of the Caribbean by boat or plane. Direct flights to Aruba are available from Amsterdam and major North and South American cities. **ACCOMMODATION:** Aruba and Bonaire enjoy a wide variety of accommodations. **CONTACT:** Bonaire Tourism Corporation and Aruba Tourism Office (see *Resources*).

While you're there ...

Caribbean Jazz Fest, Curaçao: Two days of world-class jazz heat up the beaches of this cosmopolitan island. Contact: Tel 612586. (Mid-November.)

Resources

In Aruba: Aruba Tourism Authority, L.G. Smith Blvd. 172, P.O. Box 1019, Oranjestad, Tel 2978-23777, Fax 2978-34702. **USA**: Aruba Tourism Authority, 1000 Harbor Blvd., Weehawken, New Jersey, 07087, Tel (201) 330-0800 & (800) 863-7822, Fax (201) 330-8757. **Canada**: Aruba Tourism Authority, 86 Bloor Street West, Suite 204, Toronto, ON M5S 1M5, Tel (416) 975-1950. **Germany**: Aruba Tourism Authority, Viktoriastr. 28, D-6100 Darmstadt, Tel 6151-23068, Fax 6151-22854.

In Bonaire: Bonaire Tourist Bureau, Kaya Simon Bolivar 12, Kralendijk, Tel 599-7-8322, Fax 599-7-8408. **USA**: Bonaire Tourist Information Office, 275 7th Ave., New York, NY 10001, Tel (212) 956-5911, Fax (212) 627-1152. **Canada**: Bonaire Tourist Information Office, 815 A Queen St. East, Toronto, ON M4M 1H8, Tel (416) 465-2958, Fax (416) 465-5846. **Germany**: Bonaire Tourist Office, Spaldingstr. 1, D-2000 Hamburg 1, Tel 40-230-967, Fax 41-230-473.

In Curaçao: Curaçao Tourism Development Bureau, Pietermaai 19, Willemstad, Tel 599-9-616000, Fax 599-9-612-305. **USA**: Curaçao Tourist Board, 400 Madison, Ave., Ste. 311, New York, NY 10017, Tel (212) 751-8266, Fax (212) 486-3024. **Germany**: Curaçao Tourist Board, Arnulfstr. 44, D-8000 München 2, Tel 89-598-490 & 89-523-2212.

Sitting at the crossroads of two worlds, the 700 islands of the Bahamas have a confused history that's seen its share of slavery, piracy, religion, and smuggling. Nowadays, roulette wheels and high-rises paint a velvety veneer over the spirit of the old Caribbean, which continues to thrive in back neighborhoods and outlying villages. And despite a reserved air that's typical of British-influenced islands, the Bahamas have a secret, African-influenced wild side that boils to the surface in a once-a-year frenzy called Junkanoo.

JUNKANOO

Freeport, Nassau, Family Out Islands | **December/January**

Unlike West Indian countries with a strong pre-Lenten Carnival tradition, the uniquely Bahamian celebration of Junkanoo (or Jonkonnu) is a masked madness that turns the islands upside down at Christmas. This expression of Afro-Caribbean culture is an explosion of color and rhythm that evolved from a slaves' day off, to a banned, underground tradition, to its modern incarnation as a combination Mardi Gras and mummer's parade.

Celebrated on Boxing Day (December 26) and New Year's Day, Junkanoo gets Bahamians from Freeport to Nassau out of bed at four in the morning for parades, regattas, and masquerading. Along the parade routes, you'll see (or better yet, wear) mysterious costumes made of crepe paper and gessoed cardboard, which bound and bob to the Bahamian beat. Cowbells, goombay drums (goatskin stretched over a wooden frame), whistles, and hardwood sticks complement the steel drum bands that give the event its infectious appeal.

The word *Junkanoo* may come from a French phrase meaning masked or unknown people, or from "John Canoe" (said to be an African king). Secret societies of masqueraders are headed by hereditary chiefs, who decide which masks members will wear to

Bahamian block party: Junkanoo's explosion of rhythm and color turns Nassau upside down on New Year's Day. (Joe Viesti/Viesti Associates)

represent their individual spirits. The masks and costumes are amazingly colorful, and neighborhood groups typically dress according to particular themes, while individuals in "scrap" costumes dart among the crowds.

The Junkanoo celebration has been heavily promoted by the tourist authorities, and thus has become increasingly commercial over the past few years. Yet even the influx of tourists can't overwhelm the essence of Junkanoo as a folk tradition—a boozy, colorful block party created by Bahamians, for Bahamians.

DATE: Boxing Day (December 26) and New Year's Day. **LOCATION:** Throughout the Bahamas. **TRANSPORT:** The Bahamas are accessible by air directly from the US and Canada; inter-island transportation is available via air or ferry services. **ACCOMMODATION:** As a resort area, numerous accommodations are available throughout the islands, but book well in advance during the high season. **CONTACT:** Bahamas Tourist Office (see *Resources*).

© While you're there ...

© **Great Goombay Summer Festival, Freeport and Nassau:** The tinkle of the cowbell and the thump of the goatskin goombay drums are heard throughout the summer as Junkanoo dancers parade through the streets for the entertainment of tourists. It's not authentic, but it's packed with fun stuff: Horns, whistles, and other noisemakers accompany the festival parades, beach parties, street dancing, and other special events. Goombay dancers, native revues, the Royal Bahamas Police Band, local calypso bands, Bahamian dishes, and arts and crafts displays vie for attention with water ballet, moonlit cruises, and parades. (June through August.)

Joe Billy Festival, Grant's Town (New Providence): This huge, informal party doesn't have anything to do with tourism; it gets the Christmas season moving in early December.

Resources

In the Bahamas: Ministry of Tourism, P.O. Box N-3701, Nassau, Tel (809) 322-7500, Fax (809) 328-0945. **USA:** Bahamas Tourist Office, 150 East 52nd Street, 28th Floor N, New York, NY 10022, Tel (212) 758-2777, Fax (212) 758-6531. 255 Alhambra Circle, Suite 414, Coral Gables, FL 33134, Tel (305) 444-8428. 800 Bryn Mawr, Suite 820, Chicago, IL 60631, Tel (312) 639-1111. **Canada:** Bahamas Tourist Office, 121 Bloor St. East, Suite 1101, Toronto, ON M4W 3M5, Tel (416) 968-2999, Fax (416) 968-6711. **UK:** Bahamas Tourist Office, 3 The Billings, Walnut Tree Close, Guilford, Surrey GU1 4UL, Tel 01483 448900, Fax 01483 448990. **Germany:** Bahamas Tourist Office, Moerfelder Landstr. 45–47, D-60589 Frankfurt, Tel 69-626-051, Fax 69-627-311.

DOMINICAN REPUBLIC AND PUERTO RICO

Sophistication, folkism, and big fun form a spirited punch in two of the Caribbean's large Spanish-speaking countries. Wherever you go, Dominicans and Puerto Ricans are celebrating something—be it a saint's feast day or a cultural tradition—and dancing the nights away to the region's homegrown merengue music.

Both Puerto Rico and the Dominican Republic are different, a little dangerous, and hip beyond belief. In Santo Domingo or San Juan, the best nightlife in the Caribbean is only a few minutes away from pristine rain forests and untouristed beaches. The weather is usually perfect, the people are friendly and enthusiastic, and for intrepid travelers on a budget, these Latin playgrounds are a Caribbean festival bonanza.

PATRON SAINT FESTIVALS

Puerto Rico **January/February/March**

Animist elements of African and native origin combine with Catholicism to produce a season of regional celebrations that include food, dance, games, and lots of music. Each of the *fiestas patronales* lasts about 10 days, and each is an important part of village life throughout Puerto Rico.

Festivities usually include religious processions in town squares or plazas, and revelry that extends past the particular Patron Saint Day to surrounding weekends and weekday evenings. Local celebrations of note include **Los Santos Reyes** in Aguas Buenas; **San Antonio Abad** in the town of Anasco; **San Patricio** in Loiza; **San Jose** in Ciales, Gurabo, Lares, and Penuelas; and **San Benito** in Patillas. **Nuestra Senora del la Candelaria** in

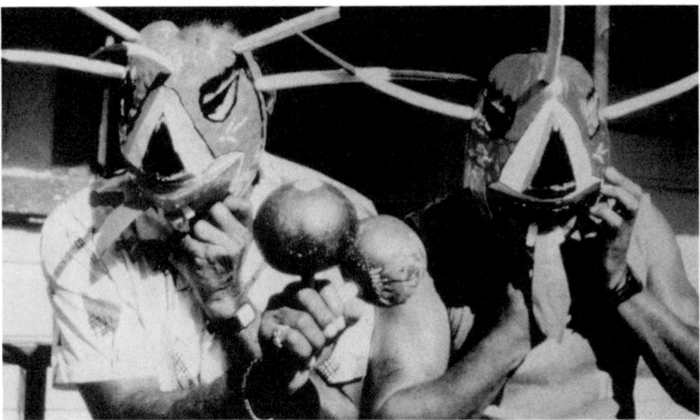

Maracas and masks: South-coast Ponce puts on the best Carnival in Puerto Rico. *(Fernando Marque/Puerto Rico Tourism Company)*

Coamo is celebrated in early February with the torching of left-over Christmas trees—a party that signifies the end of the Puerto Rican holiday season.

DATE/LOCATION: Los Santos Reyes in Aguas Buenas (January 6); San Antonio Abad in the town of Anasco (January 17); Nuestra Senora del la Candelaria in Coamo (February 2); San Patricio in Loiza (March 17); San Jose in Ciales, Gurabo, Lares, and Penuelas (March 19); and San Benito in Patillas (March 31). **TRANSPORT:** Puerto Rico's international airport in San Juan is accessible by air from most major US cities and several European cities. **ACCOMMODATION:** The island is full of hotels in a variety of price ranges. **CONTACT:** Puerto Rico Tourism Company (see *Resources*).

While you're there ...

- **San Sebastian Street Festival, Old San Juan (Puerto Rico):** Concerts, dancing, crafts displays, and delicious regional cooking are featured at this festival. (Mid-January.)
- **Carnival, Ponce (Puerto Rico):** The Thursday before Ash Wednesday brings out devil dancers in papier-mâché masks, who whack onlookers with inflated cow's bladders. Leading the parade is King Momo, the spirit of Carnival, who dances behind his huge mask. (February/March.)
- **Folk Festivals, Puerto Rico:** In Mariacau and Yaucao, coffee festivals are held near the end of February. February is also the time when Loiza hosts a festival celebrating the *buren*, a flat stone used for cooking, while *chapin* (small fish) are celebrated in Naguabo. Vaga Alta's Sugar Cane Festival in March has crafts exhibitions, regional foods, and local music. (February/March.)

Grand Costumed Dance (Gran Baile de Comparsas), Santo Domingo (Dominican Republic): In a festival that celebrates both Carnival and independence from Haiti, masqueraders dress like the devil and other characters to act out the struggle between good and evil. Merengue bands play and everyone goes wild in the street during this very musical celebration. (February 26.)

Festival de Merengue

Santo Domingo (Dominican Republic) **July**

To Latin dance fanatics the world over, the Dominican Republic can justifiably claim fame and status as the holy creator of merengue. This high-speed, highly danceable music is the national pride, the national pulse, and the dance sensation at Latin clubs around the world. It's also the guest of honor at the world's top merengue festival.

The Malecon—the wide, seafront avenue that borders the Dominican Republic's capital city—is colorfully alive as multitudes of orchestras offer the intrepid gringo plenty of opportunities to put his or her merengue skills to the test. Every few blocks there's an outdoor stage, and in between stages amateur DJs improvise seaside discos. Dominicans seem to be born knowing how to dance the merengue, and watching their whirling, hip-grinding shimmy is a lesson in erotic, spirited movement. Each year the rhythms get faster and faster, and couples execute ever more complicated moves at warp speed.

Top bands draw huge crowds who know the words to every song and leap into the air while singing along. Lesser-known bands beat out their polyrhythms on street corners, and there's higher-priced, all-night action in hotels throughout the city. Food and drink are in abundance: Barcelo rum and Presidente beer are among the favorites, and the fat pork sandwiches known as *chimichurris* are sold by the thousands at street-corner stands.

DATE: The last week in July through the first week in August. **LOCATION:** The Parque Litoral de Sur, better known as the Malecon, Santo Domingo. **TRANSPORT:** Santo Domingo, located on the Dominican Republic's southern shore, is easily accessible by air from large cities in North and South America. **ACCOMMODATION:** There are a variety of resort hotels and inns in Santo Domingo. **CONTACT:** Dominican Republic Tourist Office (see *Resources*).

While you're there ...

Fiesta de Santiago, Loiza (Puerto Rico): Saint James is honored with an Afro-Caribbean procession of revelers in painted, coconut-shell masks, and nine days of partying.

Malecon promenade: A parade of dancers puts the opening spin on the Festival de Merengue. *(Sullivan & Rogers/Bruce Coleman Inc.)*

© **Independence Day Celebration, St. Johns (US Virgin Islands):** A short jaunt from Puerto Rico, St. Johns whoops it up on July 3rd, the anniversary of the day in 1848 when the Danish West Indies freed its slaves, and July 4, the US Independence Day. Back-to-back independence celebrations end with Fourth of July fireworks and a gambol through town by the Mocko Jumbi stiltwalkers. (July 3–4.)

© **Summer Festival, Road Town (British Virgin Islands):** Half a month of culture brings a whole lot of steel bands, fungi, and calypso music to Road Town each year. Highlights include a prince and princess show and a showcase of calypso music. The festival encompasses the island-wide Summer Festival Days, three public holidays in a row that provide yet another excuse for a major party. Calypso contests, boat races, and parades make the short hop from Puerto Rico worthwhile. (Late July through mid-August.)

Festival de Puerto Plata, Puerto Plata (Dominican Republic): A great chance to merengue to the max, and we're not talking lemon pie. Top merengue bands play a seven-day marathon of the Dominican Republic's national music at one of the island's premier resort communities. (Second week in October.)

Malecon Boulevard New Year's Bash, Santo Domingo (Dominican Republic): Santo Domingo's seafront is lined with cafes and nightspots, and during New Year's Eve the Malecon becomes a Carnival unto itself. Music, dancing, and exotic food and drink welcome the Spanish Caribbean New Year in style. Contact: Santo Domingo Tourist Office. (December 31–January 1.)

Resources

In the Dominican Republic: Ministerio del Turismo, Av. México, esq. 30 de Marzo, Oficinas Gubernamentales, Santo Domingo, Tel (809)221-4660, Fax (809) 682-3806. **USA:** Dominican Tourist Information Center, Time Square Plaza, 11th Floor, New York, NY 10036, Tel (212) 768-2480, Fax (212) 944-9937. **Canada:** Dominican Tourist Information Center, 1650 De Maisonneuve West, Ste. 302, Montreal, PQ H34 2P3, Tel (514) 499-1918, Fax (514) 933-8450. **UK:** Consulate of the Dominican Republic, Royal Mail House, 6 Queen Mansions, Room 1, Brook Green, London W6 7EB, Tel 271-602-1885. **Germany:** Tourist Information Dept., Consulate of the Dominican Republic, Voelkerstr. 24, D-6000 Frankfurt 1, Germany, Tel 69-597-0330 & 60-590-928.

In Puerto Rico: Compañía de Turismo de Puerto Rico, P.O. Box 4435, Estacion Vejo San Juan, San Juan 00905, Tel (809) 721-2400, Fax (809) 725-4417. **USA:** Puerto Rico Tourism Co., 575 Fifth Ave., 23rd Floor, New York, NY 10017, Tel (212) 599-6262, Fax (212) 818-1866. **Canada:** Puerto Rico Tourism Co., 380 Ontario Street, Toronto, ON M5A 2V7, Tel (416) 969-9025. **UK:** Puerto Rico Tourism Co., 67—69 Whitfield St., London W1P 5RG, Tel 71-436-4060, Fax 71-255-2131. **Germany:** Puerto Rico Tourism Co., Kreuzberger Ring 56, D-6200 Wiesbaden 32, Tel 611-744-280, Fax 611-724-089.

FRENCH WEST INDIES

With a culture that's often closer to continental France than the Caribbean, Guadeloupe, Martinique, and the other French islands have great food and sophisticated, colorful traditions. High-rises and shopping centers contrast with open-air markets, and in the flowery countryside traditional women still dress in long, simple dresses. Of course, where there are French people, there's bound to be fantastic food, and festivals year-round offer great opportunities for visitors to sample the islands' amazing cuisine, while listening and dancing to the lively tamtam *and* zouk *music.*

CARNIVAL

Martinique and Guadeloupe **February/March**

The French brought the Carnival tradition to the Caribbean, and even though Carnival has evolved since then to resemble Trinidad's celebration, the elite masked balls of the French aristocracy survive. Carnival here also distinguishes itself by carrying on an extra day; while revelers elsewhere in the region are nursing hangovers, French island partiers are still going wild.

Sunday features a parade, while Monday sees zany burlesque marriages being performed in the streets. The red devils—especially children—take to the streets on Fat Tuesday, and on Ash Wednesday, the final day of festivities, the town is turned over to she-devils—either costumed ladies or men in drag—who wear black and white and smear their faces with ash. Finally, after an effigy of King Vaval (also called Bois-Bois) is burned, his coffin is lowered into the earth while rum flows and devilish crowds sing "Carnival don't leave us."

DATE: Celebrations build to full force beginning the weekend before Ash Wednesday. **LOCATION:** Hottest spots are Pointe-à-Pitre on

Carnival in Martinique synthesizes the traditions of African slaves and French aristocracy. (J.C. Carton/Bruce Coleman Inc.)

Guadeloupe, and Fort-de-France on Martinique. **TRANSPORT:** Flights from France and several spots in the Americas directly serve both Pointe-à-Pitre (Guadeloupe), and Fort-de-France (Martinique). The islands may also be reached from other islands in the Caribbean by plane or ferry. **ACCOMMODATION:** You'll find cities and towns heaving with hotels, but lodging is tight during Carnival season. **CONTACT:** French West Indies Tourist Board (see *Resources*).

WHILE YOU'RE THERE ...

- **Mi-Carême, Guadeloupe and Martinique:** Initiated as a break from the rigors of Lent, this day of wine, rum, feasting, and dancing takes place in the middle of the 40-day Lenten period. (March.)
- **Fête de la Musique Traditionelle, Ste. Anne (Guadeloupe):** This three-day get-down celebrates Guadeloupe's musical styles ranging from *qwo ka,* to *tamtam* and *cadence.* (Late May.)
- **African Festival, St. Martin:** African roots still have a stronghold during this showcase of arts, crafts, fashion, music, dance, and lectures on the island's African cultural heritage. (Early June.)
- **Jazz à la Plantation, Bass Pointe (Martinique):** The sounds of New Orleans soak up some French Antilles sun in concert jams featuring Creole and jazz music. Street bands, jazz lectures, and workshops contribute to the celebration. (Second weekend in June.)
- **Festival of Fort-de-France, Fort-de-France (Martinique):** The city and its suburbs make a two-week international spectacle of themselves with music, theater, and dance at the Place de la Savanne. (Late June/July.)

Fête des Cuisinières: Guadeloupe's revered cooks are honored at this colorful celebration of the island's French- and African-influenced cuisine. (Suzanne Murphy-Larronde)

© **Fête des Qwo Ka, Ste. Anne (Guadeloupe):** Leave your pacemaker behind and head to the beach! This festival of the big drums celebrates *qwo ka,* an African-derived form of rhythmic drumming. (Three days beginning on July 14, Bastille Day.)

© Chef's Festival (Fête des Cuisinières)

Pointe-à-Pitre (Guadeloupe) **August**

Food is the crowning cultural point in the French West Indies, and everywhere on the French islands you'll encounter immensely talented cooks who fill their pots with tradition, vision, and pride. The Fête des Cuisinières is the most palatable, mouthwatering, nostril-flaring event in Guadeloupe.

There are two styles of cooking on the islands. *Haute cuisine française* is traditional continental, while *cuisine créole* makes spectacular use of African methods and distinctly Caribbean ingredients. Both are featured at this festival, in which Creole-costumed cooks—women ranging from restaurateurs to mothers of six—make a quick stop at mass before parading en masse to a schoolyard bearing baskets of island specialties. These are used to prepare an extravagant five-hour banquet for hungry onlookers. You can't just sit down and eat—the cooks demand that would-be diners pay homage by singing and dancing for their supper!

DATE: First Saturday in August. **LOCATION:** Pointe-à-Pitre, Guadeloupe. **TRANSPORT:** Direct flights from Paris, Miami, Caracas, Montreal, Toronto, and San Juan will take you to Pointe-à-Pitre. The island may also be reached from other islands in the Caribbean by plane or ferry. **ACCOMMODATION:** You'll find the city heaving with hotels. **CONTACT:** Guadeloupe Tourist Office (see *Resources*).

While you're there ...

- **Festival du Marin, Marin Village (Martinique):** This week-long celebration of rhythm features folk, religious, and *chouval bois* (country fair) music, along with films and expositions. (Mid-August.)
- **Creole Music Festival, Pointe-à-Pitre (Guadeloupe):** Shine your shoes and head out for a day of Creole concerts at the local arts center. (First Saturday in November.)

Resources

In Guadeloupe: Office du Tourisme, 5 Square de la Banque, Pointe-a-Pitre 97110, Tel 82-09-30. **USA:** French West Indies Tourist Board, 610 Fifth Avenue, New York, NY 10020, Tel (212) 757-1125. **Canada:** Guadeloupe Tourist Office, 1 Dundas St. West, Suite 2405, Toronto, ON M5G 1Z3, Tel (416) 593-4717.

In Martinique: Martinique Tourist Office, Blvd Alfassa (bord de Mer), 97206 Fort-de-France, Tel 596-63-79-60. **USA:** French West Indies Tourist Board, 610 Fifth Avenue, New York, NY 10020, Tel (212) 757-1125. **Canada:** French Government Tourist Office, 1 Dundas St. West, Suite 2405, Toronto, ON M5G 1Z3, Tel (416) 593-4717.

JAMAICA

The diversity of laid-back Jamaica appeals to all types. For everyone from the tour-group crowds of Montego Bay to the hip and high set at Negril, Jamaica provides an exotic yet relaxing experience. Reggae and dancehall rhythms reign supreme, and many people plan their trips around one of the island's famous music festivals. Here you can experience the good times/protest music that sprang from African roots, through Trenchtown ghettos, and finally into the rhythmic hearts of the world. In addition to performance festivals, you can catch more spontaneous shows by Jonkonnu bands, which continue to thrill Jamaicans at Christmas with their outrageous dance routines.

Reggae Sunsplash

Kingston **August**

It's beach-blanket Rasta as dozens of top reggae and dancehall artists perform five nights of outdoor concerts. This is the hands-down mother of island reggae happenings, a huge festival with an international and local crowd, and a long tradition of starting late and mobbing steady.

The program rocks until sunrise most nights, and goes well beyond reggae. Monday kicks off the event with a beach party, and other theme nights include a World Beat Night, Vintage Night, Singers' Night, and International Night. Thursday night is always Dancehall Night, when well over 40,000 people, mostly Jamaicans, pack in to see local superstars.

Reggae's biggest festival has been a bit of a moveable feast in the past, and despite several assurances that permanent sites have been found, there's no telling where it will be from year to year. Starting in Montego Bay in 1978, Sunsplash has moved to Kingston, the Bob Marley Performing Center in Montego Bay, and back to a "permanent" location at Jamworld Entertainment Cen-

Reggae, ska, and dancehall step aside: Jamaica's most interesting music is made by the Maroon people, who celebrate their African and Arawak traditions at the Accompong Maroon Festival. *(Tony Arruza/Bruce Coleman Inc.)*

ter outside Kingston. Look for it floating somewhere between Montego Bay and Kingston.

DATE: First week in August. **LOCATION:** Probably Jamworld, about 15 minutes from downtown Kingston, but check on it. **TRANSPORT:** Kingston's airport handles flights from the Americas and Europe, and charters can often be found out of London and the US East and West Coasts. **CONTACT:** For packages from the US, call (212) 206-0048. Also, Jamaica Tourist Office (see *Resources*).

Reggae Sumfest

Montego Bay **August**

Only on a reggae-crazed island like Jamaica would there be enough soul to feed two humongous summer music festivals, planned intentionally on back-to-back weekends in August. Sumfest happens the second weekend, and there's plenty of people—both Jamaicans and outsiders skanking their way around the Caribbean—who are ready and willing to seize the scene for all it's worth.

Sumfest's four days happen at Montego Bay's Bob Marley Center. Like Sunsplash, there are theme nights covering Oldies/Soca, Roots and Culture, Dancehall, and International/Singer. Don't be scared off by the Oldies Night. It sounds like a dud but it actually includes a cool range of acts, from old American soulsters like Percy Sledge, to classic Jamaican ska and rocksteady bands, and even visiting soca bands. Roots and Culture Night features 70s-style, traditional Wailer-ish groups, especially popular with international visitors. Dancehall Night is what the locals save their energy for, as it features acts like Andrew Tosh, Michael Rose, Sugar Minott, and Jigsy King.

Not quite as together as her sister festival, Sumfest lacks organization but makes up for it with spirit and effort. Another plus: some of the Sumfest proceeds help local health and education projects.

DATE: Second week in August. **LOCATION:** Montego Bay is located on the north coast of Jamaica. **TRANSPORT:** Minibuses make the trip often from Kingston. **ACCOMMODATION:** There are a variety of resort hotels and inns in Montego Bay. **CONTACT:** Jamaica Tourist Office (see *Resources*).

While you're there ...

- **Accompong Maroon Festival, Cockpit Country:** This festival is a great way to experience the interesting culture and music of the Maroon people, whose isolation has allowed them to maintain African and Arawak traditions. (Mid-January.)

- **Bob Marley Birthday Bash, Kingston:** Protest singer, Rastafarian idealist, and reggae prophet, Bob Marley spoke poetically of the struggles of his people and Africans everywhere. He continues to be remembered with a yearly concert and memorial. Contact: Bob Marley Museum, Tel (809) 923-9380 or (809) 927-9152. (February 6.)

- **Negril Westend Reggae Festival, Negril:** Set against a backdrop of beautiful limestone cliffs in a tranquil part of Negril, this gathering of reggae artists includes both local and international talents, many of whom drop by nearby Mrs. Brown's to sample the mushroom tea and "special" cake. (Mid-March.)

- **Ocho Rios Jazz Fest, Ocho Rios:** Jazz is served up hot with an international flair in this week-long event featuring musicians from Great Britain, France, Holland, Japan, the US, and the Caribbean. Jazz and food are mixed to provide a mouthwatering musical repast, as jazz lunches, breakfasts, teas, barbecues, and cocktails are all on the musical menu. Contact: Jazz Hotline, Tel (809) 927-3544. (Mid-June.)

- **Christmas Jonkonnu, nationwide:** The Jonkonnu masquerade in its most traditional form is still practiced in Jamaica on Christmas Day and Boxing Day. Bands of 20 or 30 masked dancers parade through the streets, often accompanied by fife and drum. Each dancer plays a character in a traditional story. (December 25–26.)

Resources

In Jamaica: Jamaica Tourist Office, Cornwall Beach, Gloucester Avenue, Montego Bay, Tel (809) 952-4425. **USA:** Jamaica Tourist Office, 801 2nd Avenue, 20th Floor, New York, NY 10017, Tel (212) 688-7650, Fax (212) 856-9730. **Canada:** Jamaica Tourist Office, 1 Eglinton Avenue East, Suite 616, Toronto, ON M4P 3A1, Tel (416) 482-7850. **UK:** Jamaica Tourist Office, 1—2 Prince Consort Rd., London SW7 2BZ, Tel 071-224-0505. **Germany:** Jamaica Tourist Office, Falk Street 72—74, 600 Frankfurt/Main 90, Tel 69-707-4065.

TRINIDAD AND TOBAGO

Although the rest of the Caribbean keeps trying to reproduce Trinidad's Carnival on their own soil, the spirit of the Trinidadian people makes their celebration impossible to duplicate. Like some kind of genetic experiment gone fabulously wild, the island is a mishmash of East Indians, Africans, Carib Indians, Europeans, and even Chinese and Syrians. Such diversity generates a great energy on the island, which Trinidadians apply to creating the world's most participative big Carnival.

CARNIVAL

Port of Spain **February/March**

Not much else in the world compares to Carnival in Trinidad. This is the Caribbean's first, most artistic, and most musical Carnival—and its sexiest, by far. Unlike Rio, where you can watch the famous samba schools do their thing, or New Orleans, where heavy drinking blurs the edges, Trinidad's Carnival demands *participation*. You'll feel safe and welcome as you jump into the sweaty crowd and succumb to the gigantic power of the calypso beat.

Much of the "jump-up" is centered downtown south of the Savannah. In Independence Square and along Frederick Street, nearly every corner has a seriously huge sound system, and each "road march" packs dozens of speakers onto the top of tractor-trailer rigs. Music and masquerade are everywhere in the intense heat, and much of the action is competitive. There are calypso competitions, soca competitions, and the wild *Panorama* of marching steel bands.

The excitement begins just after the New Year as the new crop of calypso hits is released. Mas (masquerade) groups begin practicing in their mas camps, and steel bands start to work out in

Energy from diversity: The Caribbean's most participative Carnival is fueled by the roving power of the calypso beat. *(Joe Viesti/Viesti Associates)*

the "panyards." The steel drum, or pan, was invented after World War II in Trinidad (it's one of the few new musical instruments this century), and is made out of steel oil drums. Each one is painstakingly tuned to deliver its notes in one of four ranges, which are called ping-pong, guitar-pan, cello-pan, and bass.

In the week before Ash Wednesday the musical eliminations and king and queen competitions are held. *Extempo* is a hilarious competition in which calypsonians—the commentators and champions of the people—must pull a topic out of a hat and sing extemporaneously as the melody begins. In the semi-finals performers sing about their opponents, making the crowd roar with amazing on-the-spot blasts of insults, rhymes, and melodies. An *Ole Time Carnival* features exotic rhythms like those played by *tamboo bamboo* bands from Tobago, and in the final few days before Ash Wednesday, there's a head-spinning array of events. The amazing thing is that every single one of them is great, safe, and profoundly musical. Parties are everywhere, and everyone's invited (although some have small cover charges). At these events you'll notice how open and friendly people are, and you'll notice that everyone is happy when they get drunk; there are no fights or ugly scenes.

The *Panorama* begins on Saturday night, with marching steel bands, and on Sunday (called *Dimanche Gras*), the Calypso Monarch is selected in a raging epic of music, scurrilous lyrics, dust, and dancing at the Savannah. When you arrive at Frederick Street and get thrown into the amazing surge of bacchanalia, you'll accept the obvious—that you'll hardly sleep for the next few days.

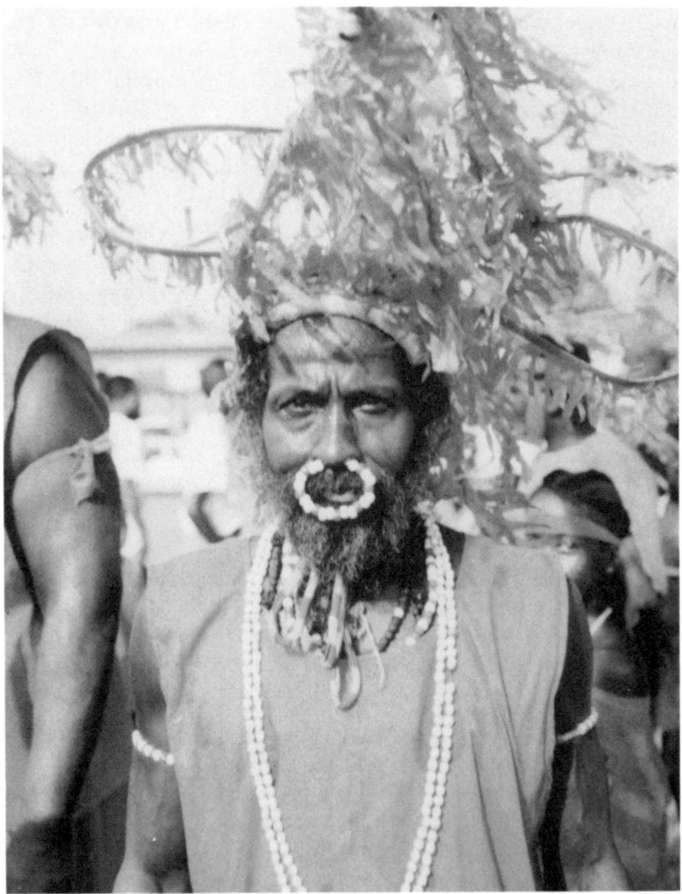

Polyrhythmic music and African-inspired costumes help Tobago celebrate its rich ancestry during August's Tobago Heritage Festival. (Joan Iaconetti/Bruce Coleman Inc.)

The craziness blends seamlessly into *J'ouvert,* or opening day. This day is less glamorous, less organized, and ridiculously fun: road marches start swarming through the neighborhoods just before sunrise, converging at the Savannah, where they are circled by wild crowds of revelers dressed in tattered clothes, who coat each other with mud (if you go out clean, you'll be quickly surrounded and smeared!).

Dancers fuel themselves with saltfish, black pudding, coconuts, rum, and beer, but by Carnival Tuesday everyone is running solely on Carnival energy. By early morning dancers are in full costume for the road marches that move down just about every street. Some of the mas bands (also called mas camps) are amazingly conceived and choreographed, with up to 5,000 dancers in wildly theatrical costumes and skimpy bikinis. The dancing continues all day and into the evening, and at 9 p.m. everyone converges on the Savannah for *Las Lap,* a final chance to go wild before organizers pull the plug on Carnival exactly at midnight.

DATE: The two weeks before Ash Wednesday, with the major surge of activity starting on the last weekend. **LOCATION:** Port of Spain. **TRANSPORT:** Trinidad can be reached by air from throughout the Americas, and directly from London and Amsterdam in Europe. **ACCOMMODATION:** Rates are doubled and rooms are scarce; book well in advance. **CONTACT:** Trinidad & Tobago Tourism Development Authority (see *Resources*).

While you're there ...

Hosein (Hosay), throughout Trinidad: This religious festival for Trinidadian Moslems commemorates the death of Mohammed's grandson, Hussain, and others who were killed by Sunni partisans in the year 680, irreconcilably splitting the two branches of Islam. It features processions of miniature temples of wood and paper, moon dancers, and beating of the *tassa,* a clay and goatskin drum that must be periodically tuned by heating it over a fire. (April–June; the 10th day of the Islamic month of Muharram.)

Tobago Heritage Festival, Tobago: This festival celebrates Tobago's quieter heritage with folk dancing, storytelling, and the *tamboo bamboo* bands. These bands use variously sized drums made from bamboo, creating West-African-based polyrhythms accompanied by call-and-response singing. (Early August.)

Resources

In Trinidad & Tobago: Trinidad & Tobago Tourism Development Authority, 134–138 Frederick St., Port of Spain, Tel (809) 623-1932. **USA:** Trinidad & Tobago Tourism Development Authority, Suite 1508, 25 West 43rd Street, New York, NY 10036. **UK:** Trinidad & Tobago Tourism Development Authority, 8A Hammersmith Broadway, London W6 7AL, Tel 081-741-1013.

MEXICO & CENTRAL AMERICA

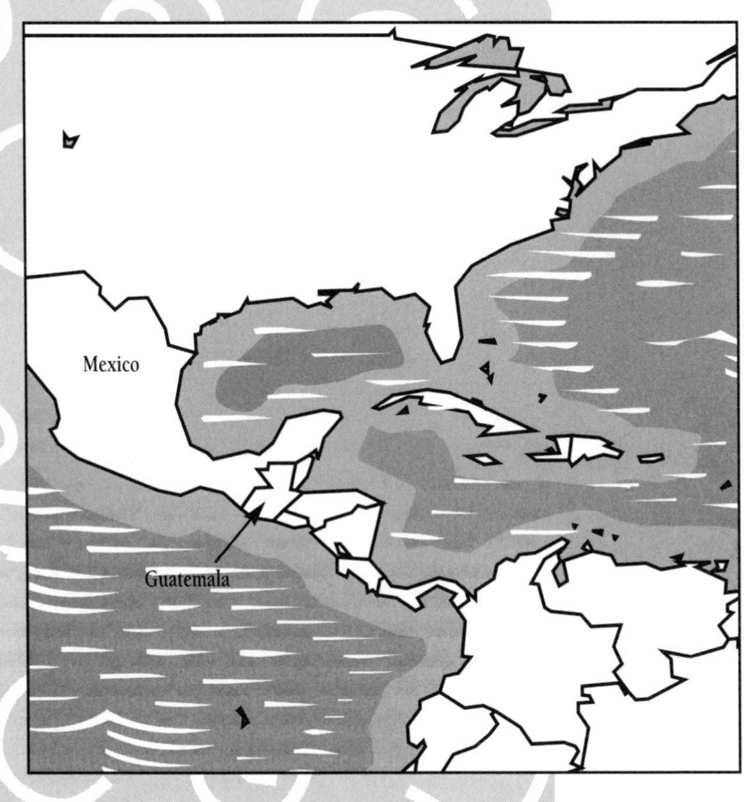

GUATEMALA

The Mayan world's most extensive ruins dot landscapes that range from volcanic peaks to jungled lowlands—yet Guatemala's indigenous culture is still very much alive. In mountain villages, each with its own distinct style of dazzling clothing, Indians celebrate fiestas and feast days in the shadow of white-washed colonial churches, and carry out their agricultural tasks much as they've done for centuries.

Guatemala's religious gatherings tell the story of a country with a lot to explain. Religion meant unity to the Maya, and today's peasants, when working in the fields, still have the gods of the soil enshrined in their hearts. In the processions and pilgrimages of the towns, the Indians and their conquerors carry images of the same god and saints, but beneath the surface the longest-running civil war in Latin America still simmers. Less publicized than the wars of neighboring countries, Guatemala's war has claimed far more victims—mostly poor, rural Indians killed or "disappeared" by their own government. Travelers should note that although Guatemala continues to offer one of the richest travel experiences in the hemisphere, visitors have been singled out as scapegoats, and should take appropriate care when traveling.

El Cristo de Esquipulas

Esquipulas **January**

The spiritual powers of the pine-forested valley that cradles the town of Esquipulas drew pilgrims even in the time of the Maya, but these days it's the image of the Black Christ that draws worshipers from all over Central America for one of the world's most colorful rounds of religious zeal.

In 1595, a carved mahogany Christ was commissioned by colonial authorities to help sell Christianity to the native population. The sales pitch apparently worked because the image is credited with hundreds of miracles, and today is the most popular religious site in the country. Many local residents and visitors crawl

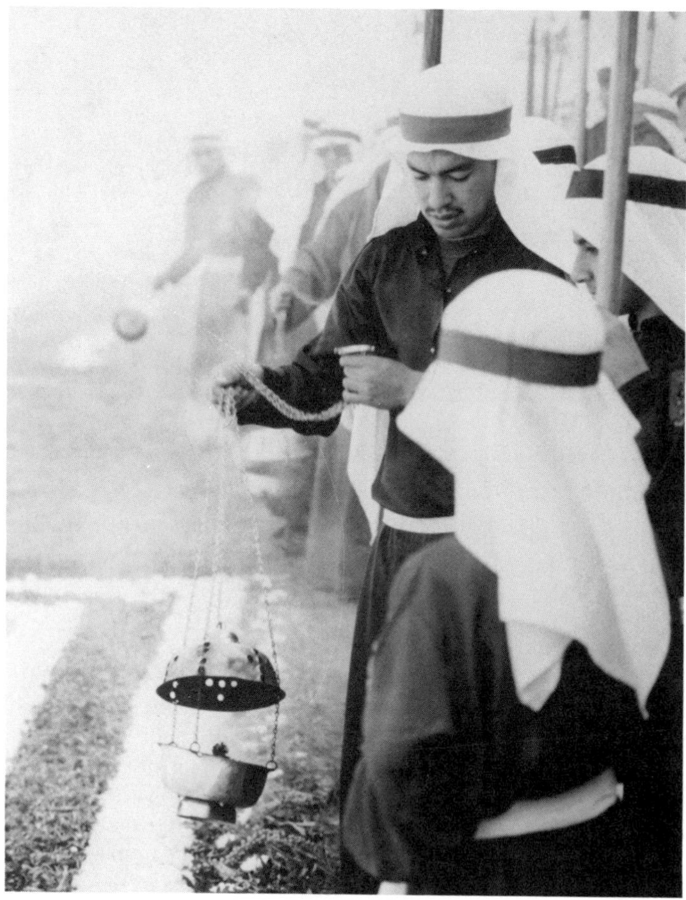

Good Friday in Antigua: A cucurucho scatters incense over a carpet of flowers in preparation for one of the grandest processions in Latin America. (Ken Laffal)

through town on their hands and knees to express piousness; people often help them by laying clothes and cardboard in front of them. You'll see pilgrims standing in line for hours to glimpse the twisted image or kiss the statues near his feet, then exiting the basilica backwards in supplication.

The Basilica is lit with thousands of candles, and outside after mass groups of monks sing Gregorian-sounding chants. Firecrackers are set off day and night, and the town is choked with people selling souvenirs—including the plastic Jesus gearshift levers that you see in all the buses.

Good Friday in Santiago Atitlán: In a pre-Christian ritual, Indians of Santiago Atitlán bring offerings to Maximón, a smoking and drinking god who grants favors to believers. Later in the day, Maximón's image is paraded around town next to Jesus. *(Robert Frerck/Odyssey Productions/Chicago)*

DATE: The week of January 15. **LOCATION:** Esquipulas. **TRANSPORT:** The town can be reached by bus from Guatemala city or Chiquimula, or by microbus from the borders of Honduras or El Salvador. **ACCOMMODATION:** Whether you stay in a flea bag or one of the posher hotels favored by rich Guatemalans, you won't have to pay more than US$5 most of the year. During the pilgrimage prices double and hoteliers see how many people they can pack into a room. **CONTACT:** INGUAT (see *Resources*).

© Holy Week (Semana Santa)

Antigua and Santiago Atitlán **March/April**

Guatemala's colonial gem and one-time capital lays out the carpet during Easter week—a carpet of colored sawdust and flowers, that is. The tradition began in the 16th century when rugs of pine needles and flowers were used for processions. Modern-day carpets showcase the talents of artists who stay up the entire night before Good Friday, using flowers and sawdust hand-dyed in bright colors to depict everything from religious scenes to geometric Mayan motifs and even scenes of Mayan gods sacrificing a chicken.

In the days before Easter, Antigua becomes a colorful, living theater. On Palm Sunday, vigils at major churches are interspersed with processions featuring 17th-century carvings of Christ affixed atop huge floats, or *andas*. As many as 80 float-bearers carry the *andas;* these *cucuruchos* pay for the privilege and switch places at every corner. Before dawn on Good Friday, men dressed as Roman soldiers ride through town proclaiming Christ's impending death. Starting just after sunrise, a procession bearing a sculpture of Christ on the cross departs from Escuela de Cristo across the carpets of ephemeral art, and hundreds of feet trod the patterns into obscurity. In a biblical twist that's unique to Antigua, the procession stops at the city jail, where two lucky prisoners are chosen to join the procession by shouldering heavy crosses. Later, they're allowed to go free.

In Santiago Atitlán, rituals are simultaneously Christian and pagan. Brilliantly dressed villagers carry an image of Christ together with Maximón (San Simón), the pagan saint who loves to smoke and drink. Wearing silk scarves, sneakers, and a hat, he has a heck of a day as villagers mob him for the honor of pouring hard liquor down his throat or lighting his cigar.

DATE: Easter week, beginning on Palm Sunday. Flowers are laid out Thursday night. **LOCATION:** Antigua and Santiago Atitlán. **TRANSPORT:** Antigua is easily accessible from nearby Guatemala City; buses leave every half hour for the 45 km (28 mile) trip. Santiago Atitlán is on lake Atitlán, and is best reached by boat from Panajachel. **ACCOMMODATION:** There are numerous accommodations in a wide variety of price ranges, but make reservations several months in advance as this is the city's biggest festival of the year. **CONTACT:** INGUAT (see *Resources*).

Christmas (Navidad)

Antigua **December**

Christmas Day in Antigua is closer to a riot than a religious holiday. Crowds liberally laced with *aguardiente* (cane alcohol) set the pace and firecrackers, rockets, and bombs are the order of the day. After a week of *posadas*—house-to-house travels to spread holiday cheer—the ceremonies begin on Christmas Eve with the noon ringing of the church bells. By mid-afternoon, the streets are filled with *gigantes,* giants whose ability to inspire awe depends on one's blood/alcohol level. *Gigantes* and *cabezudos*—men sporting large paper-mache heads—parade from Escuela de Cristo through the streets to the sounds of marimba bands. *Toritos,* men dressed as bulls and spurred on by fireworks laced to their backsides, race through the streets during the evening, ushering in a fireworks display at La Merced.

By nightfall, partygoers have lost their second wind and things quiet down enough to let a solemn procession of Joseph and Mary traverse the streets on its way to La Merced for the tra-

Fiesta de Santo Tomás: Chichicastenango's Dance of the Conquistadors reenacts the struggle between the Spanish and the Maya, a struggle that continues to this day in Guatemala. *(Joe Viesti/Viesti Associates)*

ditional mass at the Cathedral. By midnight, revelers have returned home to enjoy a traditional Christmas dinner. Noon on Christmas day sees church bells and rockets, and by mid-afternoon, all have assembled at Escuela de Cristo to celebrate the birth of Jesus Christ.

DATE: December 23–25. **LOCATION:** Antigua. **TRANSPORT:** Antigua is easily accessible from nearby Guatemala City; buses leave every half hour for the 45 km (28 mile) trip. **ACCOMMODATION:** There are numerous accommodations in a wide variety of price ranges, but make reservations in advance of the holiday season. **CONTACT:** INGUAT (see *Resources*).

Feast of St. Thomas (Fiesta de Santo Tomás)

Chichicastenango **December**

Although Chichi is known to most gringos as a place to shop for great Guatemalan clothes and doo-dads, it's known to Guatemalans as the Holy City of Quiché. Here, indigenous people actually have a measure of political power, and the syncretism of Catholic and ancient animist practices puts a funky spin on both the town and its nine-day festival in early December.

During the festival, near non-stop parades, dances, and games give Chichi a thoroughly wild atmosphere. Religious/political leaders known as *cofradías* can be seen with their elaborate costumes and headdresses, and plenty of locals are drunk from noon on. The *Baile de Conquista* is an elaborate dance skit representing the Spanish conquest, and the *palo volador,* or flying pole ceremony, features men who climb a six-story pole that's wrapped with rope, then fling themselves into the air while holding onto the rope, looping downward and outward as the rope unravels.

The church of Santo Tomás was built on top of a Mayan altar, and the people had no trouble converting their Mayan cross to a crucifix, or their pagan gods to Catholic saints. A small fire burns on the church steps all day, and people approach it to pray loudly in the Quiché language, then ritually splash alcohol on the steps as an offering. Inside, the floor is covered with pine boughs rather than pews, and through the incense smoke, you'll see the saints/idols covered with decorations of all types.

DATE: December 13–21. **LOCATION:** Chichicastenango, in Guatemala's western highlands. **TRANSPORT:** Buses serve the city from Guatemala City and points all over the western highlands. **ACCOMMODATION:** Although there are hotels in town, Chichi isn't known for its lodging selection. If you can't find anything there, you can try surrounding towns like Santa Cruz del Quiché. **CONTACT:** INGUAT (see *Resources*).

While you're there ...

- **All Saints/All Souls Day Kite Festival, Santiago Atitlán:** In an effort to communicate more effectively with the dead, the Indians of Santiago send massive, extremely colorful kites up to the heavens. (November 1 and 2.)
- **Burning of the Devil, Antigua:** It's one thing to light up a firecracker or two to scare the cat, but in Antigua, festival-goers set a match to the root of all hooliganism, the devil himself. At the Convent of Concepción, a large effigy of the unfortunate fiend is set ablaze while spectators stand atop the nearby Cerro de la Cruz to watch smaller fires spring up throughout the city. (December 7.)

Resources

In Guatemala: INGUAT/Instituto Guatemalteco de Turismo, 7a Avenida 1–17, Zona 4, Apartado Postal 1020 A, Guatemala City, Tel 502-2-311333, Fax 502-2-318893. **USA & Canada:** Guatemala Tourist Commission, 299 Alhambra Circle #510, Coral Gables, FL 33134, Tel (305) 442-0651, Fax

(305) 442-1013. **UK:** Embassy of Guatemala, 13 Fawcett St., GB-London SW10 9HN, Tel 71-3513042, Fax 71-3765708. **Germany:** Embassy of Guatemala, Zietenstr. 16, D-5300 Bonn 2, Tel 228-351579, Fax 228-354940.

For travelers both adventurous and lethargic, Mexico has it all. Posh resorts are sandwiched between turquoise Caribbean and emerald jungle, while the biggest city in the world is cradled by snow-capped volcanoes. Isolated Indian villages sit untouched at the bottoms of canyons, while ancient ruins hide in rain forests and colonial towns carry on a pace set in another century.

MEXICO

Mexico is big and so incredibly diverse that its festivals defy generalizations. In colonial, old-west Aguascalientes, bullfights and rodeos dominate. In hot, racially mixed Veracruz, the Carnival rages with a happy-go-lucky Caribbean beat. In Guadalajara mariachi bands and tequila fuel bouts of hat dancing, while in southern Chiapas ancient Mayan rites are mixed and matched with Christian feast days.

January Fiesta (Fiesta de Enero)

Chiapa de Corzo (Chiapas State) **January**

Some of Mexico's most unusual happenings stir up this small colonial city, and are known collectively as the January Fiesta. The action gets started January 9; for the next 14 days, a group of temporary transvestites known as *Las Chuntá* dance through the streets each night in colorful women's clothes, commemorating a colonial's housekeeper's gifts of food to the poor. Things get more bizarre on the 15th, 17th, and 20th, as *Parachicos*—dancers who wear masks of wood and mimick conquistadors—shake tin maracas and prance alongside lavishly costumed women.

On the 19th, everyone gets together for a big parade with plenty of music. The Combate Naval, a mock sea battle on the Grijalva River that recreates encounters between Spaniards and Indians, is enacted on the 21st. Canoeists "fight" to the sounds of fireworks shooting overhead, and over the next couple of days there are more parades and street dances to wrap up the party. Area arts and crafts specialties include colorfully carved and painted gourds called *jicaras*. The sheer walls and caves of the spectacular Sumidero Gorge offer some of the most impressive scenery in Mexico, and can be viewed from boats that leave from Chiapa de Corzo.

DATE: Mid-January. **LOCATION:** Chiapa de Corzo, on the Río Grijalva in Chiapas State. **TRANSPORT:** Buses serve the town from San

Parachico dancers take a break during the January Fiestas in Chiapa de Corzo. (Donne Bryant)

Cristóbal de las Casas and Tuxtla Gutiérrez; the latter city has the nearest airport. **ACCOMMODATION:** The town has one hotel; nearby Tuxtla Gutiérrez may be a better lodging option. **CONTACT:** Mexican Government Tourism Office (see *Resources*).

Opposite page: *Nuestra Señora Pilgrimage: The Dance of the Conquest pays homage to the Virgin of Guadeloupe, credited with uniting Aztecs and Christians.* (Robert Frerck/Odyssey Productions/Chicago)

CARNIVAL

Veracruz **February/March**

Like a volcano of color, a nine-day party erupts in this historic coastal city to prepare for the coming austerities of Lent. *Jarochos,* as locals are called, are known for their hard-partying, welcoming demeanor, and people from all over the country travel here to get a slice of the non-stop hedonism. This is the biggest mainland Carnival between Rio de Janeiro and New Orleans, and although it doesn't offer a particularly dramatic spectacle, it lets loose a wave of total madness—and is definitely one of the preeminent good-time events on the planet.

The city that gave the world "La Bamba" swings to the rhythms of the Caribbean—reggae, salsa, cumbia, and especially marimba—and in the *zócalo* (main square) there are so many bands set up that they compete with each other. Beginning the Tuesday prior to Ash Wednesday, wildly colorful floats (many of which present political or social themes) parade through the city every day, led by a procession devoted to burning an effigy of *El Señor del Mal Humor* (Mr. Bad Humor). Fireworks light the skies overhead during the night, and salsa music keeps revelers dancing in the streets at all hours. Children's parades, arts and crafts, tradi-

tional food, and storytellers provide entertainment during the entire fiesta, which ends with the traditional *Funeral de Juan Carnaval* on the day before Ash Wednesday.

DATE: Nine days, beginning Tuesday of the week before Ash Wednesday. **LOCATION:** Veracruz is located on the Bay of Campeche, 400 km (250 miles) from Mexico City. **TRANSPORT:** Veracruz is a major hub for buses running up and down the coast. It also boasts an airport and a train station that link with Mexico City. **ACCOMMODATION:** Hotels and inns are expensive by Mexican standards, and fill up quickly during Carnival. **CONTACT:** Veracruz Tourist Office, Tel 299-32-99-42.

While you're there ...

Carnival, Mazatlán: Mazatlán throws the best Mardi Gras bash on Mexico's Pacific Coast, and at this six-day celebration it's impossible to stay on the sidelines. Carnival includes parades with extravagant floats, mariachi bands, mock battles on both sea and land, a ceremonial crowning of the Carnival royal family, and some general partying down in the *zócalo*. Contact: Mazatlán Tourist Information, Tel 69-83-2545. (February/March.)

Spring Equinox

Chichén Itzá, Mexico **March**

One day each year, visitors to Chichén Itzá don't need booze or *hongos mágicos* to see apparitions. As the afternoon sun casts shadows upon the massive Mayan pyramid known as El Castillo, the feathered snake-god Kukulcán appears to slither down the pyramid toward the sacred *cenote*. The illusion is created by a shadow formed by the light hitting the balustrade, and it's believed that Mayan architects, so concerned with time and the seasons, positioned the temple to give the god of power and rebirth this springtime expression.

While the locals have always been aware of the serpent's springtime awakening, scholars didn't know about it until several decades ago. Once the word was out, travelers began flocking to the site and the spring equinox has become a major event. Folk dancers, musicians, and poets entertain thousands of visitors each year as they wait for the serpent to appear on the day of the equinox—the point when hours of sunlight exactly equal hours of darkness. While the serpent can also appear during September's equinox, the weather during the rainy season often obscures it.

Chichén Itzá is the largest and best-restored set of Mayan ruins in the Yucatan Peninsula. Built during the fifth century B.C., the temple of Kukulcán flourished until the 13th century. It was abandoned 300 years before the arrival of the Spanish conquistadors and fell to ruins, not to be rediscovered until an American explorer stumbled upon it around 1840.

DATE: The big party is on March 21, although the serpent can be seen up to four days before or after the equinox. Also September 21 (if the sky is clear). **LOCATION:** Chichén Itzá is 205 km (127 miles) east of Cancún on Route 180. **TRANSPORT:** Chichén Itzá can be reached by bus from Mérida, Cancún, and Valladolid; also, there are daily bus tours from the tourist hell of Cancún. **ACCOMMODATION:** There are three hotels within walking distance of the temple; more economical accommodations can be found a few kilometers away in Pisté, or in Valladolid. **CONTACT:** Mexican Government Tourism Office (see *Resources*).

Holy Week (Semana Santa)

Chiapas state and nationwide

Easter week is a big, big deal in Mexico, and dramatic processions, passion plays, and other displays of piety are held throughout the country. Some towns put on fabulous shows. In San Juan de Chamula and other villages around San Cristóbal de las Casas, Mayan-descended Indians spend Holy Saturday getting their children baptized in beautiful Catholic churches whose pews have been replaced by pine boughs and needles on the floor. The town's ruling elders, known as the *cargo,* make a periodic show of force, running around the square with their staffs and ribboned hats—lest any malevolent spirits get any ideas about scuttling the resurrection.

San Cristóbal de las Casas features Holy Week processions, complete with Roman soldiers whipping Jesus, and great parades through the narrow streets. (In a typical fiasco, sometimes floats are made too big to make it around corners; this prompts hilarious pile-ups that cannot be untangled until everyone behind the offending float backs up.) On Saturday in San Cristóbal, effigies of Judas and favorite politicians are set on fire, and when the flames reach the bomb-packed craniums, heads explode.

Outstanding reenactments of the passion can be seen in Taxco, Guerrero, and several other cities. In Aguascalientes and Merida, hooded celebrants walk in a beautiful torchlit procession marked by total silence. Elsewhere, music, dancing, and fireworks add a festive note to the religious observances. Be warned that traveling is particularly difficult as everybody jams buses, trains, and planes to make it either back home or to the beach.

In southern Mexico and Guatemala's highlands, pre-Columbian rituals of the Maya have merged with Christianity to form a rich and fascinating syncretism. (Robert Frerck/Odyssey Productions/Chicago)

DATE: Palm Sunday through Easter Sunday. **LOCATION:** The area around San Cristóbal de las Casas (Chiapas State), and elsewhere. **TRANSPORT:** San Cristóbal de las Casas can be reached by bus from Mexico City and surrounding towns in Chiapas and Tabasco states. The nearest airports are located at Tuxtla Gutiérrez and Villahermosa. Try to travel early to avoid the big squeeze. **ACCOMMODATION:** San Cristóbal de las Casas is packed with hotels. **CONTACT:** Mexican Government Tourism Office (see *Resources*).

While you're there ...

- **Spring Fair, San Cristóbal de las Casas:** The week following Easter is San Cristóbal's biggest shindig of the year, with bullfights featuring the best matadors in Mexico, and street artists, music, and food. (March/April.)

Feria de San Marcos

Aguascalientes **April/May**

Mexico's oldest and largest national fair is a 30-ring circus featuring everything that's great about northern Mexico. Some days, it's easy to pretend you're in Pamplona, Spain, as Mexico's best bullfighters demonstrate their toreadoric art and a running of the bulls adds a touch of dangerous illusion.

Holy Coca-Cola: Mexico's Religious Stew

The *zócalo* (plaza) in tiny San Juan de Chamula is dominated by what looks, from the outside, like a typical colonial Catholic church. A look inside reveals that it is typical—at least for the Indian-dominated Chiapas state—although the pope probably wouldn't be comfortable sitting on pine needles.

Pews have been removed, and amid smoke created by incense and thousands of candles, people huddle in small groups, clucking and praying in the Tzotzil language. Some are drinking, others socializing, still others lie asleep on the floor. On the altar an image of Jesus receives prayers that were once directed to the sun god, while in a corner an image of John the Baptist receives prayers once directed to Chac, the rain god. On the floor a shaman passes a small glass of Coca-Cola over a candle in the sign of the cross, counting on the mysterious bubbles to work their powerful magic.

At the time of the conquest, the lives of both the Indians and their Spanish conquerors were dominated by religions steeped in ritual. The Spanish considered it their duty to convert the "savages" they had enslaved, and the two religions were surprisingly compatible in many ways. For instance, both emphasized divine mystery behind all earthly and celestial events, and both taught faith and obedience rather than reliance on one's own reason.

Where conflicts arose, the Indians often disguised their pagan icons as Christian figures and carried on as usual, or a miracle might occur conveniently to resolve the issue. For instance, the Virgin of Guadeloupe was the first official dark-skinned Catholic image; she miraculously appeared to a converted Indian in the spot where Indians had worshipped the mother of gods.

In many places in Mexico, indigenous people were wiped out by disease and slaughter, or the old pagan ways succumbed to constant cultural oppression. In regions where there were no minerals to exploit, the Spanish influence was much less dominant, and over time the two religions converged in a rich and interesting syncretism. Areas like the hills around San Cristóbal de las Casas have held onto many pre-Columbian rituals, and religious authorities allow indigenous people to decorate churches to resemble the dark and comforting caves, cisterns, and mountains where their ancestors worshipped. Visitors (without cameras) are often welcome to come in and experience the rich traditions.

More than a million people show up over 22 days for rodeos, cockfights, and a folk-dance festival featuring regional dances. Ranchera and mariachi music by leading Mexican entertainers, formal balls, ballet, and theatrical performances are all part of the action that's been an annual occasion for nearly 200 years. The parade on San Marcos Day, April 25th, is spectacular, and don't forget to try some of the specialty called *charamusca,* a nut-covered taffy shaped into animals or people.

DATE: The fair starts the second week of April and lasts for 22 days, wrapping up in early May. **LOCATION:** Aguascalientes, south of Zacatecas in north-central Mexico. **TRANSPORT:** Aguascalientes is easily reached by train, bus, or air. **ACCOMMODATION:** The fair puts a big strain on the town's hotels, so book in advance. **CONTACT:** Mexican Government Tourism Office (see *Resources*).

Cinco de Mayo

Puebla **May**

In 1862 in Puebla, some 2,000 Mexican troops under the command of General Ignacio de Zaragoza defeated invading French forces of over 6,000 men (many of whom were "preoccupied" with stomach trouble at the time). Although the French returned to occupy the city a year later, the nation has chosen to ignore that fact to revel in the rare occurance of a Mexican military victory.

During this most important of national holidays, parades and sham battles—using fruit as ammunition—are the order of the day. Dances, parties, fireworks, and patriotic foods—including *mole* dishes, specialties covered in a sauce made from chile, spices, and chocolate—all celebrate the victory of *Puebla la heroíca.*

Puebla, Mexico's archetypal colonial city, is a great place to catch the Cinco de Mayo festivities, or to visit any time of year. With more than 70 beautifully preserved churches and hundreds of other colonial buildings with hand-painted tile work, prosperous Puebla is a huge, living museum of colonial architecture. Nearby Cholula also has a huge number of churches, and is the site of the Great Pyramid, one of the largest man-made structures in the world.

DATE: May 5. **LOCATION:** Puebla is 130 km (81 miles) from Mexico City. **TRANSPORT:** Buses run to Puebla from most major Mexican cities; plane service is available to Guadalajara and Tijuana. Train service is also available to Mexico City and Tlaxcala. **ACCOMMODATION:** The city boasts a variety of accommodations in all price ranges and many are centrally located. **CONTACT:** Puebla Tourist Office, Tel 22-46-12-85; or Mexican Government Tourism Office (see *Resources*).

Fiesta de Corpus Cristi

Papantla de Olarte (Veracruz State) **May/June**

This hillside town in the Sierra Madre overflows with visitors who come to watch the parades, dances, and unusual rituals of the Corpus Christi festival. A main procession kicks off the celebration on the first Sunday of the fiesta, and Totonac Indians line the streets in their traditional garb: flowing white shirts and pants for the men and intricately embroidered blouses and *quechquémitls* for the women.

The local people perform a wide variety of dances during the festival; some of the more common ones you'll see are *Los Negritos, Los Huehues,* and *Los Quetzalines.* Two or three times a day you'll notice crowds forming around a 30 meter (100 foot) pole on the church grounds. The *voladores,* or "flying dance" ceremony was done for religious reasons in pre-Columbian times, and today it's still quite a stunt. Five Totonac Indians climb the pole, and four of them bind their ankles with ropes that have been wound around the pole. The fifth plays a flute while the others dive head-first off the top, spinning around the pole as the ropes unwind them downward.

Peaceful, palm-shaded Papantla sits in verdant rolling hills in the middle of Mexico's leading vanilla-growing region, and the spice is available in many forms, including pods woven into the shape of flowers, birds, and insects. Nearby are the impressive ruins of the ancient religious complex of El Tajín, with ceremonial ball courts, the famous Pyramid of the Niches, and a statue of the thunder god, El Tajín.

DATE: Corpus Christi occurs eleven days after Pentecost, in May or early June. **LOCATION:** Papantla de Olarte, about 250 km (154 miles) north of Veracruz. **TRANSPORT:** The town can be reached by bus from Mexico City, Veracruz, and Villahermosa. **ACCOMMODATION:** During the fiesta the town's few hotels fill up quickly; Tuxpán and other nearby towns offer lodging options if Paplanta doesn't pan out. **CONTACT:** Mexican Government Tourism Office (see *Resources*).

While you're there ...

Fiesta de Tlaquepaque, Guadelajara (Mexico): City streets are filled with mariachis, dancers, and floats, as a carnival atmosphere prevails in Tlaquepaque, a Guadalajara suburb noted for its high concentration of artisans and craftspeople. (Late June.)

Guelaguetza

Oaxaca **July**

Also known as Lunes del Cerro ("Monday of the Mountain"), this festival of folk dancing has its roots in pre-Columbian times, when villagers honored an ancient goddess with song, dance, and gifts to win her blessing for a bountiful corn harvest. Today, dances and music draw on Christian and prehispanic themes.

From late morning to late into the night, dancers and musicians from seven indigenous villages surrounding Oaxaca don their most spectacular duds and perform traditional numbers in the city amphitheater. Dancing becomes an all-day marathon; among the highlights are the women's Pineapple Dance and the Zapotec Feather Dance performed by men reenacting the conquest of Mexico by the Spaniards. As part of the tradition, performers often throw little gifts (*Guelaguetza* is the Zapotec word for "gift") to the audience.

DATE: Third and fourth Mondays in July. **LOCATION:** The Cerro de Fortin, an open-air arena at the edge of Oaxaca City. **TRANSPORT:** Oaxaca, located 402 km (250 miles) from Mexico City, is easily accessible by car, train, bus, or plane. **ACCOMMODATION:** A variety of hotel and motel accommodations are available, but book well in advance of this event. **CONTACT:** Palacio Municipal Tourist Office, Tel 951-6-38-10.

Feast of the Assumption of the Blessed Virgin Mary

Huamantla (Tlaxcala state) **August**

Although observance of the Assumption—which commemorates the reunification of the Virgin Mary's body with her soul in heaven—has only been required of Roman Catholics since 1950, Mexicans have celebrated this feast day for centuries. In Huamantla, the Feast of the Assumption is the highlight of a two-week fair featuring native dances, arts and crafts exhibits, and markets.

At the center of the action is Mary, and it's interesting to see how literally people can interpret her journey to heaven: It's not at all unusual to see images of Mary borne skyward by homemade rockets. On the ground, visitors are treated to the vista of street after street carpeted with designs made from flower petals and colored sawdust, over which the figure of the Blessed Virgin is carried atop a decorated processional float. A midnight march through the city streets ends a day of devout celebration. The following morning, solemnity flies to the four winds in the face of an onslaught of bulls that rush the streets (à la Pamplona), totally obliterating whatever carpet remnants are left.

DATE: August 15. **LOCATION:** Huamantla is just east of Tlaxcala, about 120 km (75 miles) east of Mexico City. **TRANSPORT:** Buses regularly run to Tlaxcala from Mexico City. **ACCOMMODATION:** Several hotels in varying price ranges are available in Tlaxcala. **CONTACT:** Tlaxcala State Tourist Office, Tel 2-00-27.

While you're there ...

- **Fiestas de Octubre, Guadalajara:** During this month-long culture-fest, strains of medieval music are layered with mariachi serenades, and modern art mingles with pre-Columbian artifacts. (October.)
- **International Cervantino Festival, Guantajuato:** This world-class musical and theatrical event features an international cast. Contact: Festival Internacional Cervantino, Emerson 304, Piso 9, Mexico D.F. 11570, Mexico. (Mid-October through November 1.)

Day of the Dead (Día de los Muertos/Día de Difuntos)

Nationwide **November**

While death and decay send shivers up *Norteño* spines, most Mexicans barely give a shrug; to them, death is closer to a vacation than the end of everything as we know it. Like the Aztecs who once occupied the land, modern Mexicans see life, death, and rebirth as parts of a continuum; by celebrating with the dead, the living celebrate life. This tradition lives on in the Day of the Dead, a festive occasion that provides a link between the dead and the living, and a way for family and friends to devote special time to those who have passed on.

Festivities actually begin on October 31 as women clean house, make candles, and prepare large quantities of food, including tortillas, chicken, *atole* (a gruel made of sweet corn), hot chocolate, and special bread baked in the shape of small animals. Men build clay altars in the home and leave food and toys for *angelitos*—small children in the family who have died—on these altars overnight. The visiting spirits of children stay through November 1, the day of the *angelitos*, and remove only the essence of the gifts; what's left is fair game for living children on the following day.

Fiestas de Octubre: Guadelajara explodes with folklore and festivities during the entire month of October. Here, the Ballet Folklorico performs. *(Suzanne Murphy-Larronde)*

A spicier menu, liberally laced with tequilla or aguardiente, is prepared for the older deceased who arrive November 2. Candy *calaveras*—skulls fashioned of marzipan and elaborately decorated and monogrammed with the names of the deceased—are available from candy artists who crowd the streets alongside mariachi bands and small carnivals. In markets and everywhere, you'll see the folk art that's wildly popular both in Mexico and north of the border. There are *calacas* (dancing wire and clay skeletons); skulls that grin when jaws are manipulated; and elaborately decorated boxes with skeletons inside that perform everyday activities.

In Mixquic, huge cardboard skeletons stand guard all day at the gates of cemeteries, and are burned at night with great glee. The Zapotecs in Yalalag are more sober; with their white shrouds and torches, they make unearthly processions to the cemeteries, wailing all the way. Villagers in Oaxaca state make huge altars that can fill entire rooms. On Janitzio Island, beautifully dressed Tarascan Indian women go to the cemeteries with elaborate baskets of food and gifts. The scene is sublimely peaceful and picturesque (though tourists have definitely sniffed this one out), as the women and children sit quietly at the graves all night while the men sing Tarascan songs close by.

Everywhere, parish priests make their rounds and friends of the deceased pay their respects the living, being careful to speak well of the spirits who have come to inhabit the shadows for a short visit. The daylight hours of Day of the Dead itself are spent resting with loved ones, dead and alive. In the evening in many

Day of the Dead: In a cemetery near Patzcuaro (Morelia), family members stay up all night with their deceased loved ones. *(Robert Frerck/Odyssey Productions/Chicago)*

places in Mexico, a candle-bearing procession winds its way to the cemetery where candles and a picnic will be laid out on tablecloths. They're accompanied by musicians playing festive songs—and the dead who now return to their spiritual resting place until invited forth the following year.

DATE: All Saints Day or *Angelitos* (November 1), and All Souls Day or *el Día de los Muertos* (November 2). **LOCATION:** Nationwide. Prime spots are Janitzio Island (Lake Pátzcuaro), Mixquic and Toluca (near Mexico City), Amecameca (Oaxaca state), and throughout Chiapas state. **CONTACT:** Mexican Government Tourism Office (see *Resources*).

Nuestra Señora Pilgrimage

Mexico City **December**

Walking—sometimes even crawling—for days, people from all over Mexico make the trek to the nation's holiest shrine, the Basilica of Guadalupe, to honor the patron saint of the Americas and spiritual mother of Mexico. The pilgrimage is but a part of the national holiday commemorating the 16th-century appearance of the Virgin Mary before Juan Diego, a humble Indian. As he stood on Tepeyac Hill, where a shrine to the Aztec goddess Tonantzin had once stood, the peasant Juan witnessed the Virgin, who instructed him to tell the local bishop to build a temple upon that spot. His story was a hard sell; the bishop only believed it after

Nuestra Señora Pilgrimage: Celebrants carry a crucifix in the huge procession honoring the patron saint of Mexico. (Robert Frerck/Odyssey Productions/Chicago)

Juan produced a cloak miraculously marked with the image of the Virgin. The temple was built and the sacred location united Aztecs and Christians, giving Mexico a saint to call its own.

A dramatic new basilica was built in 1976, and the old one is now a museum. In the courtyard the mood is gleefully pious, with hundreds of musicians and dancers performing their art, and pilgrims from all walks of life approaching the basilica on their knees or eating Virgin-shaped corn cakes. Inside, a moving walkway takes people past the revered image. Most bring votive offerings to thank her for granting a wish, and huge piles of artwork, fruit, flowers, and candles lie all around.

DATE: December 12. **LOCATION:** La Basilica de Nuestra Señora de Guadalupe is located on Tepeyac Hill, at the northern edge of Mexico City. **TRANSPORT:** Mexico City is easily reachable by air from nearly anywhere in the world. Take the metro to La Villa or Basilica Station. **ACCOMMODATION:** There are numerous accommodations in all price ranges around Mexico City. **CONTACT:** Mexico City Tourist Information, Tel 5-525-9380.

While you're there ...

Noche de Rábanos/Night of the Radishes, Oaxaca (Mexico): As twilight approaches, farming families converge upon the city's *zócalo* (plaza) to set up decorated stalls displaying their intricate tableaux carved entirely out of radishes—either round red radishes or long ones specially grown for the festival. Nativity scenes are a favorite theme, and small birds made from everlasting flowers add a splash of color to the affair. The odd and unusual radish-art is accompanied by servings of syrupy *buñuelos*—deep-fried, sugared, and terribly healthy tortillas—served on clay plates that are then smashed in celebration of the impending birth of Jesus. (December 23.)

Resources

In Mexico: Secretaria de Turismo, Avenida Presidente Mazaryk 172, 11560 Mexico D.F., Tel 5-2508555, Fax 5-2073438. **USA:** Mexican Government Tourism Office 405 Park Ave. Ste. 1002, New York, NY 10022, Tel (800) 262-8900 & (212) 755-7212, Fax (212) 753-2874. Two Illinois Center, 233 N. Michigan Ave. #1413, Chicago, IL 60601, Tel (713) 880-5153. 10100 Santa Monica Blvd., Los Angeles, CA 90067, Tel (310) 203-8350, Fax (310) 203-8316. **Canada:** Mexican Government Tourism Office 181 University Ave. Ste. 1112, Toronto, ON M5H 3M7, Tel (416) 364-2455, Fax (416) 364-4337. **UK:** Mexican Government Tourism Office 60/61 Trafalgar Sq. 3rd Fl., GB-London WC2N 5DS, Tel 71-7341058, Fax 71-9309202. **Germany:** Embassy of Mexico, Adenauerallee 100, D-5300 Bonn 1, Tel 228-218043, Fax 1-47556529. **Australia:** Embassy of Mexico, 14 Perth Ave. Yarralumla, Canberra, ACT 2600, Tel 6-2733905.

CANADA & THE UNITED STATES

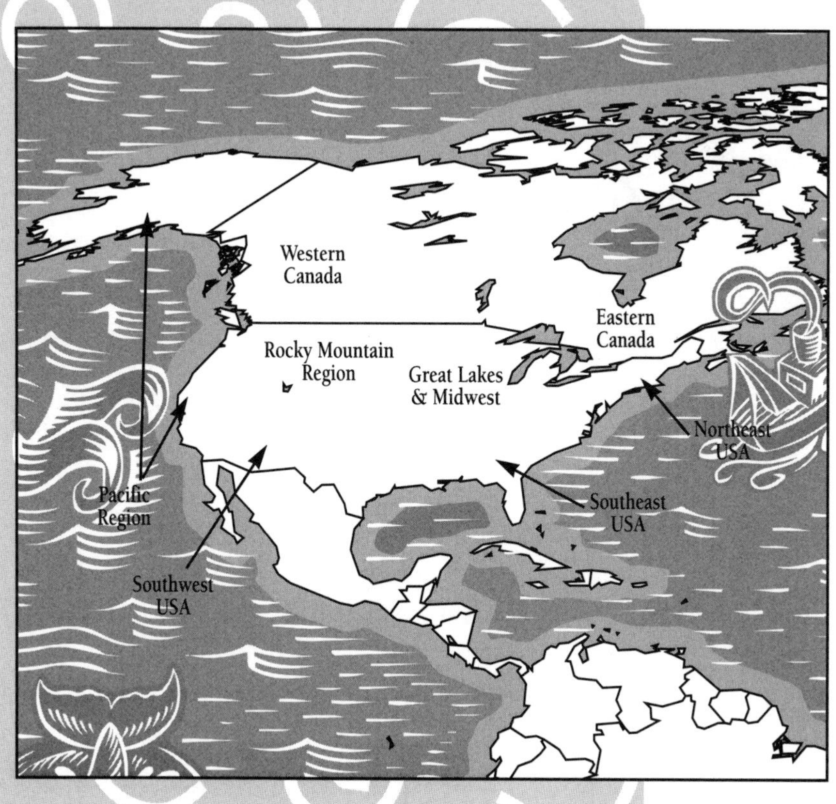

EASTERN CANADA

Eastern Canada's surprising festivals bring out the warmth and friendliness of the region's ethnically diverse localities. In Quebec, spirits soar as temperatures plunge and Carnival time provokes bouts of all-night snow-dancing. Conservative Toronto shows a wilder side during its summer ethnic events, while the cultural marvels of the Maritime Provinces showcase unexpected traditions that are always laced with a hearty sense of humor.

Labrador, Newfoundland, Nova Scotia, Ontario, Prince Edward Island, Quebec

WINTER CARNIVAL

Quebec City **February**

Merry, boisterous, indulgent, and at the same time genteel, this raucous French-Canadian street party brings out the wine, the fiddlers, and the entire city for 11 days of cold-weather madness. Celebrants jam the cobblestone streets of Quebec's Old City drinking "caribou juice" (wine and grain alcohol) from hollowed-out Carnival canes, and attending parades, snow-sculpture contests, and masked balls.

The world's biggest winter celebration reaches its most jubilant pitch on the second weekend, when a torch-lit parade moves through the fortified walls of the Old City, led by Bonhomme Carnival, the giant plastic snowman who serves as mascot for the festivities. Musicians and masked marchers dance behind him as fireworks shoot overhead, illuminating elaborate ice sculptures.

Bathed in the magic glow of the Ice Palace (which is lit from within), dancers cavort in the cold until the wee hours, keeping each other warm through rhythm and sheer numbers. During the day you can eat a steaming outdoor breakfast of pancakes and bacon, or bring the kids to a mini parade of cartoon characters. Sporting events are popular, and include the Chateau Frontenac toboggan slide, cross-country skiing, barrel jumping, motorcycle races on ice, and snowmobile racing. Young hockey players compete in the International Pee-Wee Hockey Tournament, and canoe races across the St. Lawrence River get interesting when teams of five men are forced to push and pull their canoes across ice packs. *Le Bain de Neige,* or snow-bathing, is for the hardiest hard-bodies only, since participants wear only skimpy bathing suits as they frolic in the snow.

DATE: The first Thursday in February through the second Sunday. **LOCATION/TRANSPORT:** Quebec City can be reached by rail or air from all over North America. **ACCOMMODATION:** A variety of accommodations for all budgets are available, but book ahead. **CONTACT:** Carnaval de Québec, 290 rue Joly, Québec, PQ G1L 1N8, Tel (418) 626-3716; or Tourisme Quebec (see *Resources*).

While you're there ...

- **Montreal International Jazz Festival, Montreal (Quebec):** What may be the world's biggest jazz blast turns downtown Montreal into an open-air concert hall for 12 days in early July. Streets are blocked off, eight outdoor stages are thrown up, and performers from all over the world lay down sounds that go well beyond the jazz diaspora. There's blues, African, bebop, and the super-diverse sounds of the Caribbean. Contact: Tourisme Quebec, c.p. 20,000, Quebec G1K 7X2, Tel (418) 692-2471 & (800) 363-7777. (12 days in late June/early July.)
- **Quebec City International Summer Festival, Quebec City:** One of the largest cultural events in the French-speaking world welcomes some 600 leading artists from all continents for more than 250 performing-arts shows. Contact: (418) 692-4540. (10 days in early to mid-July.)

Caribana

Toronto **July/August**

What does Trinidad have to do with Toronto? Carnival! Snaking in a giddy conga line through the city, Caribana creates a joyful roar. Calypso and soca bands on flatbed trucks stir up a frenzy as they move along, and some 40 mas (masquerade) bands with 10,000 members writhe away in an outrageous orgy of sound and color. About a million people show up—including more than 300,000 from south of the border—to partake in the activities and dance along.

Based on Carnival in the West Indies, Caribana is helping Toronto transform itself from a stiff Anglo outpost to a liberated, cosmopolitan capital. It started in 1967, when the West Indian community contributed the event to Canada's centennial celebration. It was so popular that the festival continued and has grown into a week-long folk gathering of music, art, and dance. Special embellishments include a couple of parades, three nights of ferry

Caribana: The Caribbean roars into Toronto for a week of music, dancing, and street parties. (Ontario Ministry of Culture, Tourism & Recreation)

cruises, a Friday-night ball, the Caribana Queen's Coronation, handicrafts, and distinctive food. But mostly it's just dancing in the streets.

DATE: A week in July and early August. The last day is always the first Monday in August, a civic holiday in Toronto. **LOCATION/TRANSPORT:** Toronto (Ontario) can be reached directly by air from anywhere in North America and Europe, and by rail from anywhere in Canada. **ACCOMMODATION:** A variety of accommodations for all budgets are available. **CONTACT:** Ontario Travel Information Centre, Eaton Store, 290 Yonge St., 2 Below, Toronto, ON M5B 1C8, Tel (416) 965-4008.

Acadian Festival

Caraquet (New Brunswick) **August**

In an effort to preserve the rich Acadian culture of east-coast Canada, this little town transforms itself into a 10-ring circus of diverse happenings. About 20,000 people attend the cultural, social, and athletic events each year, sampling French Acadian foods and participating in regattas, bicycle races, and mini-golf competitions.

"L'Acadie en Fête" is the festival highlight, a marathon variety show of Acadian actors, singers, artists, and musicians. Musical offerings include both Acadian sounds and modern rock, and dancing and theater pieces are presented for children and adults. Other festival highlights include art exhibits and concerts emphasizing the violin, accordion, and guitar.

DATE: Usually August 6–15. **LOCATION/TRANSPORT:** Caraquet is in northern New Brunswick on Chaleur Bay; the nearest airport is at Chatham. **ACCOMMODATION:** There are a few hotels in town, and camping is available on the outskirts. **CONTACT:** N.B. Dept. of Economic Development and Tourism (see *Resources*).

While you're there ...

Royal St. John's Regatta, St. John's (Newfoundland): Held since 1825, this rowing competition is North America's oldest continuing sporting event and draws the entire town to the shores of Quidi Vidi Lake. The picturesque Victorian port's excellent restaurants and pubs step up to the task of providing great food, drink, and companionship for the party afterward. Contact: (709) 576-8511. (First Wednesday of August, weather permitting.)

BuskerFest, Halifax (Nova Scotia): Performers from all over the world who make their living passing the hat converge on unlikely Halifax for 10 days of street entertainment extraordinaire. Curbs and sidewalks are front-row seats for the colorful doings of musicians, jugglers, acrobats, mimes, fire-eaters, contortionists, magicians, and clowns. Contact: Buskers International, 1652 Barrington St., Halifax NS B3J 2A2, Tel (902) 425-4329. (Mid-August.)

Toronto Film Festival, Toronto (Ontario): Though it's outgrown its "people's film festival" beginnings, Toronto is still more fun and better run than its more famous North American counterparts. More than 300 films are featured, with an emphasis on countries and genres that normally don't get much festival exposure. The movies and parties are great, and with a little planning the average Joe or Jane can get into most with few problems. Contact: Tel (416) 967-7371. (10 days in mid-September.)

Resources

In Canada: Tourism Canada, 235 Queen St., Ottawa, ON K1A 0H6, Tel (613) 954-3830, Fax (613) 952-7906. **New Brunswick:** Dept. of Economic Development & Tourism, P.O. Box 6000, Fredericton, NB E3B 5H1, Tel (506) 453-2964, Fax (506) 453-7127. **Newfoundland & Labrador:** Dept. of Tourism & Culture, Tourism Marketing Division, P.O. Box 8700, St. John's NF A1B 4J6, Tel (709) 729-2830, Fax (709) 729-5936. **Nova Scotia:** Dept. of Tourism & Culture, P.O. Box 456, 1601 Lower Water St., 4th Floor, Cornwallis Building, Halifax NS B3J 3C6, Tel (902) 424-5000, Fax (902) 424-2668. **Ontario:** Ontario Travel, Queen's Park, Toronto, ON M7A 2R9, Tel (800) 668-2746 & (416) 314-1727, Fax (416) 314-7574. **Prince Edward Island:** Dept. of Economic Development and Tourism, P.O. Box 940, Charlottetown, PEI C1A 7M5, Tel (902) 368-4444, Fax (902) 368-4438. **Quebec:** Tourisme Quebec, Case Postale 20000, Quebec PQ G1K 7X2, Tel (418) 643-2230 & (800) 433-7000, Fax (514) 873-4263.

USA: Tourism Canada, 501 Pennsylvania Ave. NW, Washington, DC 20001, Tel (202) 682-1740, Fax (202) 682-1726. **UK:** Tourism Canada, Canada House, Trafalgar Square, London SW1Y 5BJ, Tel 71-258-6346, Fax 71-258-6322. **Germany:** Tourism Canada, Prinz-Georg-Str. 126, 40479 Düsseldorf, Tel 211-072-170, Fax 211-359-165. **Australia:** Tourism Canada, 5th Level, Quay West, 111 Harrington St., Sydney, NSW 2000, Tel 2-364-3000, Fax 2-364-3098.

WESTERN CANADA

Canada's westerners know how to throw a party, and they're always sure to invite outsiders and treat 'em right from the moment they arrive. In super-sophisticated Vancouver, and in provincial centers like Winnipeg, Calgary, and Regina, locals find that the best way to seize the short summer is to celebrate it. Remnants of the old West mix with new-world cosmopolitanism in city festivals, and there's no dearth of a different sort of culture in the backwoods and tundras. While Native Americans celebrate ancient traditions, relative newcomers commemorate their own bygone era, paying homage to the miners, loggers, and settlers who blazed today's still hardly worn trails. The fun doesn't freeze up in the winter, and for those who like their good times hardy, this is a great part of the world for winter carnivals and snow sports like sled-dog races and ski races.

Alberta, British Columbia, Manitoba, Northwest Territories, Saskatchewan, Yukon Territory

Caribou Carnival and Canadian Championship Dog Derby

Yellowknife (Northwest Territories) **March/April**

An outdoor carnival in icy Yellowknife helps beat the northern Canadian winter blues and welcome the coming spring. This week of sports, entertainment, and contests draws thousands of visitors, and is highlighted by the Canadian Championship Dog Derby, which features competitors from across the continent. The biggest dog-sled purse in the Northwest Territories is at stake for the first musher who can finish the three-day, 150-mile race on Great Slave Lake. Other contests include igloo building, log sawing, snowshoeing, Indian wrestling, tea boiling, skiing, and a speed-skating

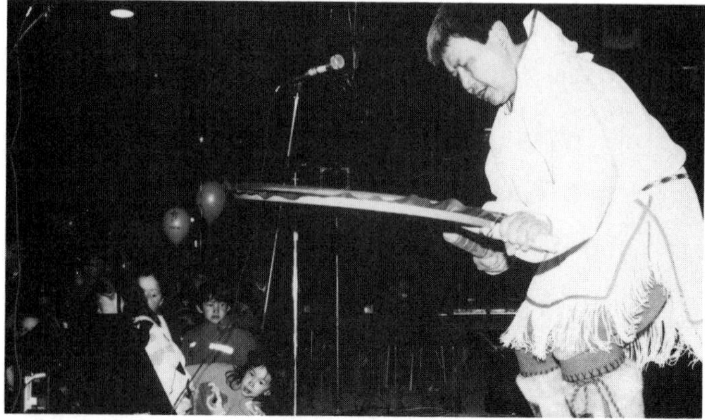

Toonik Tyme: The Inuit people demonstrate their unique traditional music at this far-north celebration in Iqaluit on Baffin Island. *(Baffin Tourism Association)*

derby. Local talent and regional celebrities are featured in the Carnival Capers variety show, and the Trappers Ball and Mushers Banquet are the social events of the year. Festivities are rounded out by a Miss Yellowknife Tournament, a cabaret, a casino, nightly fireworks, and an Ugly Truck and Dog Contest.

DATE: Five days in late March or early April. **LOCATION:** Yellowknife, Northwest Territories. **TRANSPORT:** Although the road up from Alberta is usually open it's a tough haul, and most people fly in. **ACCOMMODATION:** Several of the town's hotels open up especially for the event. **CONTACT:** Caribou Carnival Association, Box 1258, Yellowknife, NWT X1A 2N9, Tel (403) 873-9698.

While you're there ...

Toonik Tyme, Iqaluit (Northwest Territories): Nobody knows how long Toonik Tyme has existed since the event is based on the legend of a mythical race of people called the Toonik, who existed in Baffinland long ago. The revelry begins with Mr. Toonik's arrival by dog sled, and the festival queen's crowning. Competitions include dog-sled racing, beard growing, ice sculpting, ice fishing, tea brewing, igloo building, and "the toughest snowmobile race in the world." Hunters seek as many seals as possible throughout the week and then return with the raw materials for a seal-skinning contest. The event closes with fireworks, a barbecue, and a parade of floats. Contact: Baffin Tourism Assoc., P.O. 1450, Iqaluit NT, X0A 0H0, Tel (819) 979-6551, Fax (819) 979-1261. (Last week in April, sometimes spilling into early May.)

Nightly chuckwagon races are a romping, crowd-pleasing highlight of the Calgary Stampede. (Calgary Stampede)

CALGARY EXHIBITION AND STAMPEDE

Calgary (Alberta) **July**

The "Greatest Outdoor Show on Earth" brings Calgary rip-roaring back to its frontier past each July. In addition to great rodeo and exhibitions, the ongoing party is a hoot, drawing more than a million people from across the continent and the world to a town that is completely high on rodeo. You'll find mean broncs and friendly smiles, flapjacks and chuckwagons, painted shop windows, and locals everywhere urging you to yell "yahoo!"

Canada's largest rodeo was founded by a trick roper named Guy Weadick, who hailed from Cheyenne, Wyoming, home of the famous Frontier Days Rodeo. After visiting Calgary in 1912, he found the area suitable for cowboys (and there were already Indians), so he set out to start a rodeo. Since then, about a billion people have attended the event, which features a daily afternoon rodeo at Stampede Park just southeast of downtown Calgary. There's saddle bronc and bareback riding, steer wrestling, calf roping, and bull riding, all of which feature enormous cash prizes for the winners. In the evening, nine chuckwagons pulled by teams of four thoroughbred horses compete in a frantic, precarious dash for $50,000 in prize money.

Non-rodeo events include more than 40 rides and attractions, including agricultural and livestock exhibits, a fireworks display, and world-famous entertainers at the Grandstand Show. Visitors can also take a stroll through Weadickville, a hokey wild-West town with bad guys and a frontier casino. Around a thousand representatives of five neighboring Indian villages entertain guests at an "authentic" Indian encampment complete with tepees. This is also the best time of year to visit nearby Banff and Jasper national parks.

DATE: One week in early July. **LOCATION/TRANSPORT:** Calgary (Alberta) is accessible by several highways, including the Trans-Canada, and the airport handles flights from across North America. **ACCOMMODATION:** Hotels fill up in July, so book ahead. **CONTACT:** Calgary Exhibition and Stampede, Box 1860, Station M, Calgary T2P 2L8, Tel (800) 661-1260 & (403) 261-0101.

© While you're there ...

- **Winnipeg Folk Festival, Winnipeg (Manitoba):** Ten stages spread over 90 acres keep things interesting; you might hear gospel, Celtic ballads, country fiddles, or cloggers' shoes. The music continues well into the night at two of the park's three campgrounds. Contact: 264 Tache Ave., Winnipeg, MB R2H 1Z9, Tel (204) 231-0096 & (204) 982-6210. (A three-day weekend in early July.)
- **Vancouver Folk Music Festival, Vancouver (British Columbia):** One of the world's top folk and world music festivals is held in Jericho Park in one of the world's most captivating cities. Contact: 3271 Main St., Vancouver V6V 3M6, Tel (604) 879-2931, Fax (604) 879-4315. (Mid-July.)
- **Folk on the Rocks, Yellowknife (Northwest Territories):** Singers and performers come from all across the Northwest Territories, southern Canada, and the U.S. The most interesting are the famous Inuit throat singers, and the event also features Dene and Inuit folk singers, drummers, and dancers. There are also music workshops, arts and crafts, and a children's stage. Contact: Northern Frontier Visitors Centre (see *Resources*). (A weekend in late July.)

© Big Valley Jamboree

Craven (Saskatchewan) **July**

Quiet, picturesque Craven (population 300) is transformed each July as 40,000 country music fans hit town for Canada's largest country music festival. The beautiful Qu'Appelle Valley becomes a huge dance floor, as the continent's top performers whoop it up on a stage complete with video screens. Food concessions, a beer garden, and shops selling some of the tackiest souvenirs in North America ensure plenty of money-spending options. There are 300 acres of camping, and even with all the people, the park still has plenty of room—and eight lakes—for those who want to get away from it all.

DATE: Five days in mid-July. **LOCATION/TRANSPORT:** Craven (Saskatchewan), just north of Regina on Highway 11. **ACCOMMODA-**

In the same spirit that drove the gold rush, hearty souls raft across the river during the Dawson Discovery Days. (Yukon Government)

TION: There's camping in the park, or hotels in nearby Regina. **CONTACT:** (306) 525-9999 & (306) 721-6060.

© WHILE YOU'RE THERE ...

- **Buffalo Days, Regina (Saskatchewan):** Kicking off with the Pile O' Bones Parade, this rollicking event features music, art, livestock, and other local specialties. (Late July/early August.)
- **Fringe Theatre Festival, Edmonton (Alberta):** One of the world's top festivals dedicated solely to the fringe features local and international theater groups and individuals who perform comedy, tragedy, musical the-

ater, mime, and dance in indoor and outdoor settings. Contact: Chinook Theatre, 10329 83rd Ave., Edmonton, Alberta T6E 2C6, Tel (403) 448-9000. (Mid to late August.)

© **Dawson Discovery Days, Dawson (Yukon Territory):** The gold rush left this remote outpost with something to commemorate, and this three-day fest of sports and performances features a parade, raft and canoe races, a ball tournament, dances, and many other events. Contact: (403) 993-5434. (Late August.)

© Resources

In Canada: Tourism Canada, 235 Queen St., Ottawa, ON K1A 0H6, Tel (613) 954-3830, Fax (613) 952-7906. **Alberta:** Alberta Economic Development and Tourism, Box 2500, Edmonton, Alberta T5J 2Z4, Tel (403) 427-4321 & (800) 661-8888, Fax (403) 427-0867. **British Columbia:** Tourism B.C., 802-865 Hornby St., Vancouver, BC V6Z 2G3, Tel (604) 660-2861, Fax (604) 660-3383. **Manitoba:** Travel Manitoba, 155 Carlton St., Winnipeg, MB R3C 3H8, Tel (204) 943-3777 & (800) 665-0040, Fax (204) 945-2302. **Northwest Territories:** Tourism Information, P.O. Box 2107, Yellowknife, NT X1A 2P6, Tel (403) 873-7200 & (800) 661-0788, Fax (403) 920-2801. Northern Frontier Regional Visitors Centre, #4, 4807 49th St., Yellowknife, NT X1A 3T5, Tel (403) 872-4262. **Saskatchewan:** Tourism Saskatchewan, 500–1900 Albert St., Regina, Saskatchewan S4P 4L9, Tel (306) 787-2300 & (800) 667-7191, Fax (306) 787-0715. **Yukon Territory:** Tourism Yukon, P.O. Box 2703, Whitehorse, YT Y1A 2C6, Tel (403) 667-5340, Fax (403) 667-2634.

USA: Tourism Canada, 501 Pennsylvania Ave. NW, Washington, DC 20001, Tel (202) 682-1740, Fax (202) 682-1726. **UK:** Tourism Canada, Canada House, Trafalgar Square, London SW1Y 5BJ, Tel 71-258-6346, Fax 71-258-6322. **Germany:** Tourism Canada, Prinz-Georg-Str. 126, 40479 Düsseldorf, Tel 211-072-170, Fax 211-359-165. **Australia:** Tourism Canada, 5th Level, Quay West, 111 Harrington St., Sydney, NSW 2000, Tel 2-364-3000, Fax 2-364-3098.

NORTHEAST USA

Historic and civilized, the northeastern United States is packed with festivals that highlight each town's uniqueness through a standard program of music, food, and entertainment. The region's truly great events occupy extremes: At one end of the spectrum, exceptional music festivals draw swooning devotees of all genres to concerts set in the sublimely tamed countryside. At the other end, big-city fringe communities stage festivals and counterfestivals that break free of ethno-political restrains and urge participants—and spectators—to become part of the creative process.

Connecticut, District of Columbia, Maryland, Massachusetts, Maine, New Hampshire, New Jersey, New York, Pennsylvania, Rhode Island, Vermont

Kutztown Folk Festival

Kutztown (Pennsylvania) **June/July**

The anachronistic lifestyles of the Amish, Mennonite, and Brethren people are celebrated in this nine-day exposition of the Pennsylvania Dutch region's cultural heritage. Initiated in 1950 to preserve traditions and customs, Kutztown is recognized as the most authentic ethnic festival in the United States.

Special pageants are staged to show traditional Amish weddings and barn raisings (although the Amish don't actually participate, due to religious constraints). Sheepshearing, horseshoeing, ironworking, quilting, soap boiling, pewter making, basket weaving, and rug making are also demonstrated to the more than 110,000 people who travel here each year. Ethnic dances are performed and old-world foods like *Brodewarscht* (German sausage) are served.

DATE: Late June/early July. **LOCATION:** Kutztown fairgrounds and Main Street. **TRANSPORT:** Kutztown is 24 km (15 miles) southwest of Allentown on Route 222. **ACCOMMODATION:** There are accommodations in town and B&Bs and campgrounds throughout the area, but early reservations are essential. **CONTACT:** Kutztown Folk Festival, 461 Vine Lane, Kutztown, PA 19530, Tel (610) 683-8707.

WHILE YOU'RE THERE ...

- **St. Patrick's Day, Boston and New York City:** New York's biggest Fifth-Avenue parade features large helpings of puffery and politics, while Irish pubs around town rage into the wee hours. In Boston—a city that still draws huge contingents of Irish immigrants—the parade's good, but the dawn-to-dawn partying is even better (March 17 in Boston; the weekend nearest March 17 in New York City).
- **Easter Parade, New York City:** There's no band, and there's no parade ... at least not in a concrete, organized sense. Instead, Fifth Avenue between 49th and 59th streets is a spontaneously created urban spectacle—an occasion simply to go for a stroll, preferably in a new Easter outfit and an outrageous bonnet. If you're in town, be sure not to miss one of America's most precious people-watching opportunities. (Easter Sunday, March/April.)
- **Bang on a Can Festival, New York City:** At this adventurous gathering of the world's preeminent new-music composers and performers, consciousness-altering listening is the name of the game. Post-minimalist extravagance rules, as performers may simply stomp about on stage with their eyes closed or play everything from two pianos to a dozen boom boxes. Contact: (212) 777-8442. (Mid-May.)

TANGLEWOOD MUSIC FESTIVAL

Lenox (Massachusetts) **July/August**

Founded in 1934, the nation's oldest music festival is also one of the world's most esteemed. Concerts by the Boston Symphony Orchestra take place in the center of a 210-acre estate near Lenox, a beautiful New England town in the Berkshire Mountains. Guest conductors and soloists are common, and the event draws some of the top names in music. Concerts run almost nightly, and Saturday rehearsals are open to the public. Chamber music productions, music theater, choral music, jazz programs, and a Festival of Contemporary Music are also included in each summer's billing. Most concerts are performed in the Music Shed, which dates to 1917 and accommodates 10,000 under cover and more on the lawn.

DATE: Late July through late August. **LOCATION:** Tanglewood is located in Lenox, two-and-a-half hours west of Boston via the Massachusetts Turnpike. **ACCOMMODATION:** A summer resort area, Lenox boasts a number of inns, hotels, and motels in varying price ranges. **CONTACT:** Symphony Hall, Boston, MA 02115, Tel (617) 536-4100.

Russian pianist Mikhail Pletnev performs at the Breakers mansion in his North American debut at the Newport Music Festival. Three festivals covering classical, jazz, and folk make Newport America's most musical summertime city. (John Hopf/Newport Music Festival)

Newport Jazz, Classical, and Folk Festivals

Newport (Rhode Island) **July/August**

Three separate events make Newport the most musical midsummer city in America. Starting in mid-July, the Newport Music Festival is a rich and rare feast for lovers of classical music. About

45 separate concerts are played in the ballrooms and on the lawns of "summer homes"—actually the neo-classical and baroque mansions of millionaires. One of the most spectacular venues is the Great Hallway of the Breakers, a lavish mansion resembling a 16th-century Italian palace, which was built in 1895 by Cornelius Vanderbilt. The musical selection is diverse, but focuses on 19th-century chamber music—since it was written to make rooms like these come alive. In addition to about four concerts each day, the festival includes concert cruises in the harbor, brunch buffets, a midnight Clambake Club Cabaret, and a formal dinner and concert gala.

The Newport Jazz Festival is the world's oldest and best-known jazz festival, and is credited with launching luminaries like Count Basie and Duke Ellington into the big time. The array of outstanding jazz talent includes vocal and instrumental soloists, big bands, and combos. Stages are set up mid-August in the laid-back surroundings of the Fort Adams State Park, which overlooks Narragansett Bay and Newport Harbor. The three-day Newport Folk Festival is also held at the Fort Adams State Park, and features both top folk acts and up-and-coming performers.

DATE: Music Festival, mid-July; Folk Festival, early August; Jazz Festival, mid-August. **LOCATION:** Newport (Rhode Island). **ACCOMMODATION:** Weekend accommodation in hotels and B&Bs is booked solid at least two months in advance, so plan ahead. Write Newport County Chamber of Commerce, P.O. Box 237, Newport, Rhode Island 02840, Tel (401) 847-1600. **CONTACT:** Newport JVC Jazz Festival, P.O. Box 605, Newport, RI 02840, Tel (401) 847-3700. Newport Music Festival, P.O. Box 3300, Newport, RI 02840, Tel (401) 846-1133. Newport Folk Festival, Tel (401) 847-3700.

Pillar Polkabration, New London (Connecticut): One of the great musical and dance traditions of America's northern, blue-collar whites continues to flourish. At Ocean Beach Park more than 20,000 people turn out to get a slice of 40 meat-and-potato bands, at the longest-running polka festival in America. Contact: (203) 848-8171. (Six days in late July.)

Brooklyn (New York City) **September**

Known mostly for its amazing music and bouts of street dancing, this Labor-Day carnival also inspires some of the most incredible costumes north of the Caribbean. As reggae and calypso bands rage, people dressed as sailors, dragons, and long-beaked birds

Burning up NYC: A drag queen flirts with officialdom during Wigstock. (Catrina Genovese/Omni-Photo Communications, Inc.)

dance through the streets, and stilt dancers high-step confidently amidst the flamboyant finery.

Handicrafts and spicy-sweet foods like hot *roti* (barbecued goat) are sold by vendors, while political action groups hit the streets in force. In terms of magnitude, this Caribbean festival is on par with London's Notting Hill Carnival and Toronto's Caribana. About two million people show up over the long weekend, augmenting the half a million or so West Indians who live in Brooklyn. Short of taking an extended tour through the Caribbean, attending this event is probably the best way to sample the diversity of the West Indies through music, food, and late-night neighborhood parties.

DATE: First Monday in September. **LOCATION/TRANSPORT:** Eastern Parkway to Franklin Avenue in Brooklyn. **ACCOMMODATION:** Brooklyn is not known as a hotel hot spot; hotels, hostels, and other options are plentiful across the river in Manhattan. **CONTACT:** Caribbean-American Chamber of Commerce, Tel (718) 834-4544.

Wigstock

New York City **September**

What began in 1985 as a small gathering of bored and boozing drag queens is now one of New York City's biggest and most spirited events, drawing hundreds of thousands to a raging fete with a bandstand and big-name entertainment. Wigstock's dedicated chairman, hostess, and high priestess, Lady Bunny, acknowledges the event's now semi-approved standing, but prefers to describe Wigstock as "a hoot first and a cultural institution second."

This transvestite take-off on Woodstock has evolved into a montage of cross-dressing styles, including old-style impersonator drag, club-kid drag, half-drag, and low-cut dresses to show off bulging pecs. There's a lot of glitz, made possible by huge helpings of eyeliner, Fabulash, outrageous dresses, and wigs of all sizes, shapes, and colors. Lines between performers and spectators blur, with both categories ranging from hormone queens (those who live in drag) to weekend queens and the simply curious or bi-curious. Wigstock has featured some high-profile queens in the past, including RuPaul, Hedda Lettuce, Coco Peru, and Girlina. From time to time organizers run into problems acquiring permits for the annual shindig, so the event seems destined to wander around New York City like a lost tribe.

DATE: Sunday or Monday of the first weekend in September (Labor Day weekend). **LOCATION:** New York locale usually changes each year. **CONTACT:** NYCVB, Two Columbus Circle, New York NY 10019, Tel (212) 397-8222, Fax (212) 245-5943.

Halloween Parade

Greenwich Village (New York City) **October**

The magic and otherworldly drama of Halloween is unleashed on New York City as the streets of Greenwich Village host a nocturnal pageant of outrageous costumes, extreme politics, and spontaneous skits. This parade is completely different from any other in the city, in terms of location, time frame, participation, and mood. The mayor, of course, does not attend (unless he's in disguise), and little is planned. The tradition of free audience participation inspires some of the city's most talented artists and performers, who spend months creating personal spectacles designed to drop the jaws of New Yorkers who think they've seen everything.

The Halloween Parade is still the gay community's biggest camp fashion show. You might see Marilyn Monroe wearing handcuffs, cops wearing fangs, or "fashion police" writing out tickets for mismatched outfits. You could run across transvestites posing as nuns or Girl Scouts, or four fifties-style stewardesses known collectively as T.W.A.T. (Transvestites Will Attempt Travel).

Yet the parade's appeal increasingly extends to people outside the gay community. Like the city itself, the Halloween Parade has evolved, losing some of its intimacy as its popularity has forced it to move out of narrow side streets and into broad avenues. Both gays and straights wildly cheer any costume or act that shows exceptional creativity or craftsmanship. The parade provides a context for normally brusque New Yorkers to relate to each other one on one in a fantasy world that's both liberating and claustrophobic, joyful and sad, dreamlike and nightmarish.

The Halloween Parade has been transformed many times over, from a ritual of nature to an environmental protest, from an all-out drag parade to a life-affirming counterpoint to the tragedy of AIDS. After the main parade is over the romp continues (some say it just gets going) on Christopher Street, the city's wild gay mecca. The after-parade action is called the Promenade, referring to the traditional strutting of drag couples down Christopher Street. Much of the action takes place above street level, as exhibitionists go wild on balconies and fire escapes, creating scenes that vividly reinforce the obvious: that there's no place like New York on All Hallow's Eve.

DATE: Halloween Day. **LOCATION:** The route through Greenwich Village is periodically adjusted to accommodate crowds; in recent years the parade has ventured over West Houston, Sixth Avenue, and 14th Street, ending at Union Square. **ACCOMMODATION:** New York City is bursting with accommodations of all types, but don't expect bargains. **CONTACT:** NYCVB, Two Columbus Circle, New York NY 10019, Tel (212) 397-8222, Fax (212) 245-5943.

© Resources

In USA: United States Travel & Tourism Admin., 14th & Constitution, Washington, DC 20230, Tel (202) 482-4752. **Connecticut**: Tourism Division, Department of Economic Development, 865 Brook St., Rocky Hill, Connecticut 06067-3405, Tel (800) 282-6863, (203) 258-4368, Fax (203) 529-0535. **Washington (District of Columbia)**: Washington, D.C. Convention and Visitors Association, 1212 New York Ave. NW, Suite 600, Washington, D.C. 20005, Tel (202) 789-7000, Fax (202) 789-7037. **Maryland**: Maryland Office of Tourism Development, 217 E. Redwood St. 9th Fl., Baltimore, MD 21202, Tel (410) 333-6611, Fax (410) 333-6643. **Massachusetts**: Massachusetts Department of Commerce, Office of Travel & Tourism, 100 Cambridge St., Levere H. Saltonstall Bldg. 13th Fl., Boston, MA 02202, Tel (617) 727-3201, Fax (617) 727-6525. **Maine**: The Maine Publicity Bureau, PO Box 2300, Hallowell, ME 04347, Tel (207) 623-0363. **New Hampshire**: Office of Travel and Tourism Development, PO Box 856, Concord, NH 03302, Tel (603) 271-2598. **New Jersey**: Division of Travel and Tourism, CN 826, W. State St., Trenton, NJ 08625, Tel (800) 537-7397, (609) 292-2470, Fax (609) 633-7418. **New York**: New York State Department of Economic Development, One Commerce Plaza, Albany, New York 12245, Tel (518) 473-0715, Fax (518) 474-6416. New York Convention and Visitors Bureau, Two Columbus Circle, New York NY 10019, Tel (212) 397-8222, Fax (212) 245-5943. **Pennsylvania**: Pennsylvania Visitors Bureau, 1122 Transportation & Safety Bldg., Harrisburg, PA 17120, Tel (717) 787-4483. **Rhode Island**: Department of Economic Development, Rhode Island Tourism Division, 7 Jackson Walkway, Providence, RI 02903, Tel (401) 277-2601, Fax (401) 277-2102. **Vermont**: Agency of Development & Community Affairs, Vermont Travel Division, 134 State St., Montpelier, VT 05602, Tel (802) 828-3236, Fax (802) 828-3233.

Canada: United States Travel & Tourism Admin., 480 University Ave., #602, Toronto, ON M5G 1V2, Tel (416) 595-5082, Fax (416) 595-5211. **UK:** United States Travel & Tourism Admin., 24 Grosvenor Square, London, W1A 1AE, Tel 71-495-4336, Fax 71-495-4377. **Germany:** United States Travel & Tourism Admin., Bethmannstr 56, D-60311, Frankfurt 1, Tel 69-92-00-3617, Fax 69-294-173. **Australia:** United States Travel & Tourism Admin., Level 59, MLC Centre, King & Castlereagh Streets, Sydney, NSW 2001, Tel 02-233-4666, Fax 02-232-7219.

SOUTHEAST USA

The South's cities and towns serve up steaming platefuls of summer festivals that reflect both the region's many-layered past and its evolving diversity. Down-homey Appalachian weekends contrast with Miami's whirling Afro-Cuban dance-fests, and the genteel revelry of the Kentucky Derby is worlds away from the anything-goes romps of Key West.

Alabama, Florida, Georgia, Kentucky, Louisiana, Mississippi, North Carolina, South Carolina, Tennessee, Virginia, West Virginia

Everywhere in the South, music is probably the most exciting aspect of the festivals: the acoustic blues of Mississippi, the bluegrass of Kentucky, the salsa of Miami, the country twang of Nashville, the rock and rhythm & blues of Memphis. And then there's Louisiana. Drawing from a totally different cultural base from the rest of the country, the land of Creoles, Cajuns, and *Caribeños* is so bursting with romance and *joie de vivre* that Louisianans keep inviting the rest of the nation down to get some. The festivals they dish up are so refreshing they're almost un-American—great food is complemented by friendliness and the searing sounds of home-grown jazz, rhythm & blues, Cajun, and zydeco.

MARDI GRAS

New Orleans **February/March**

Although its parades and frat-party hype have become clichéd and touristy in recent years, Mardi Gras is still the nation's biggest and most elaborately perfect shindig. The action is non-stop as brass bands roam the streets, feathered Mardi Gras Indians "stomp some rump," girls pull up their shirts, and guys pull down their pants. There are black-tie social balls and dress-down neighborhood beer blasts, mid-morning parades uptown and all-night romps in the Quarter. Through it all, tourists from everywhere gawk and revel, while locals immerse themselves in social functions steeped in esoteric ritual and tradition.

What's so great about Mardi Gras? Basically, there's enough going on, and it's so diverse, that you can build your own party out of it. If you like out-of-control drunkenness and public exhi-

Carried away in New Orleans: America's biggest party breaks out in the last few days before Lent. (Tom Clynes)

bitionism, the French Quarter has plenty. There are also daytime parades tame enough for kids or bawdy enough for an S&M aficionado, and plenty of bars where jazz, blues, Cajun, zydeco, and rock and roll are on tap.

The week leading up to Fat Tuesday is the busiest tourist week of the year in New Orleans, yet Mardi Gras is first and foremost a bash put on by New Orleans *for* New Orleans—tourists just sniffed out a good time and started showing up as unofficial guests. The action reaches a frenzy on Mardi Gras day, with parades, walking jazz bands, and an electrifying crush of people swarming the French Quarter until midnight, when the streets are finally cleared by mounted cops.

What's not so great about Mardi Gras? It's crowded, it's claustrophobic, it's competitive, it's sometimes tacky in a corporate-sponsored way. It's not the best time to get a sense of the beautiful colonial city, and first-timers or even old-timers who miscalculate can get stuck in crosstown traffic for hours. At parades, anal-retentive dads set up sight-blocking ladders for their kids in *front* of the rest of the crowd. In the Quarter, frat guys high-five every time someone yells "show us your tits," and copycat idiocy is rampant. There's plenty of jostling and flashes of ugly territorialism, and fights can start at the drop of a name.

Still, Mardi Gras can be a great time—especially if you know someone local who can help you get an insider's experience. Nothing beats a French Quarter balcony, an uptown house near a parade route, or a party at a swank den or a riverside dive. Take the time to find out what's happening away from the French Quarter and the big parade routes, since every neighborhood has something going on. Events range from the biker and pickup truck parades of the Drieux Krewe to the street parties uptown.

The Bacchus and Rex parades usually have great floats, but the wildest costumes—by far—are at the gay parade on Mardi Gras morning. Be sure to check out the various tribes of Mardi Gras Indians, black groups whose incredible feathered costumes are based on Native American outfits. They prowl through the neighborhoods on Mardi Gras morning, with chiefs, spyboys, and flagboys chanting and beating Afro-Caribbean rhythms on drums and following elaborate and colorful protocol when meeting rival tribes.

DATE: The two weeks leading up to Ash Wednesday, with a concentration of action during the last four days. **LOCATION:** New Orleans, Louisiana. **TRANSPORT:** New Orleans is easily reached by air from throughout North America, but from Europe and elsewhere a change of planes is usually necessary. If flights to New Orleans are sold out, try flying into Baton Rouge and renting a car. **ACCOMMODATION:** To avoid frustration, try to reserve a year in advance, and certainly no later than January. The LHMA (see below) can provide lists of accommodations. **CONTACT:** Greater New Orleans Tourist & Convention Commission, 1520 Sugar Bowl Drive, New Orleans, LA 70119, Tel (504) 566-5095, Fax (504) 566-5046. Louisiana Hotel & Motel Association (LHMA), 330 Exchange Alley, New Orleans, LA 70130, Tel (504) 525-9326.

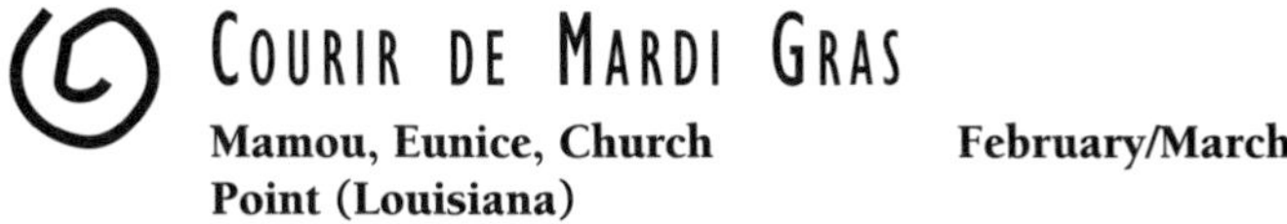

COURIR DE MARDI GRAS

Mamou, Eunice, Church Point (Louisiana) — **February/March**

In the small towns in the heartland of Cajun country, the wild ride of Mardi Gras is dramatically different from the New Orleans-style celebration. The Courir has its roots in medieval festivals, and Mamou, which was the first town to revive the tradition back in the 1950s, still has the largest celebration in the area.

Festivities begin the Monday before Mardi Gras (Fat Tuesday) with a street parade, and the bars that line Sixth Street swing their doors open wide and let the music and beer flow. On the morning of Mardi Gras, young men gather downtown on horseback, in flatbed trucks, and astride beer wagons. Noisy festivalgoers soon send them on their way out of town to scour the countryside for booty for the gumbo—money, food, even a live chicken or two—from cooperative residents. The riders whoop and holler as they ride away in masks and colorful capes, visiting farmers and friends while emptying the accompanying beer wagon. When the drunken procession staggers back to town in the afternoon with their loot in tow, a gumbo is made and all are welcome to partake. An evening dance follows for those still able to stand.

DATE: The Monday and Tuesday before Ash Wednesday. **LOCATION:** Mamou, Eunice, Church Point, and other rural villages around Lafayette. **TRANSPORT:** Mamou is 11 km (7 miles) southwest of Ville Platte on Route 13. **ACCOMMODATION:** There are accommodations scattered through the area in varying price ranges. **CONTACT:** Lafayette Convention and Visitor's Bureau, P.O. Box 52066, Lafayette, LA 70505, Tel (318) 232-3737.

© WHILE YOU'RE THERE ...

© **Mardi Gras, Mobile (Alabama):** The mother of all Mardi Gras in North America takes place amid Mobile's antebellum and colonial houses and tree-shaded, flowery streets. From its start in 1702, two weeks of parades and parties have culminated on Fat Tuesday as crowds chant the mystic words "Moon Pie!" to parading revelers. Contact: Mobile Tourism and Travel Dept., Tel (205) 434-7304. (First two weeks in February.)

© **Carnival Miami, Miami (Florida):** Little Havana's *Calle Ocho* goes wild during one of the largest street festivals in the country. The music is exceptional, with top bands from the Spanish Caribbean fueling non-stop dancing to salsa, merengue, mambo, and cumbia rhythms. There's a giant parade with floats, cars, and people in full regalia, as well as soccer matches, dog and bike races, cooking contests, a battle of the bands, and an 8K run. (Early March.)

© **St. Patrick's Day, Savannah (Georgia):** All of Savannah dons green for this festive celebration of everything Irish, and a three-day music fest features, rock, blues, and jazz in the City Market. The city is second only to Chicago in sheer numbers of Irish wannabes, and the crowds lining the streets for the parade can indulge in Southern hospitality Irish style: green beer with grits to match. (March 17 and the nearest weekend.)

© **Super Sunday, New Orleans (Louisiana):** The remains of Mardi Gras are swept up just in time to let the Mardi Gras Indians (black groups who have adopted the costumes of Native Americans) whoop it up in the city streets. Donning their finest feathers and beads, "Indian" groups compete to see which tribe tops the totem pole, marching through the streets while banging on drums and singing and chanting. This is one of America's most enduring, precious, and picturesque folk traditions. Contact: GNOTCC (see *Resources*). (Sunday closest to March 19.)

© Jazz and Heritage Festival

New Orleans, Louisiana **April/May**

It's been called everything from a low-key version of Mardi Gras to a victim of its own success, but the most diverse music festival on the continent continues to draw bigger crowds every year. The two-weekend Jazzfest is the American music lovers' rendezvous, an event where the spring comes early and the dancing comes easy. With simultaneous music on six stages, tons of great food, and New Orleans' all-night bar and club scene, the festival draws visitors from all over North America, Europe, and East Asia.

Jazzfest *is* big and it keeps getting bigger, mostly because everyone who attends once comes back the next year with more friends in tow. Some say the event is out of hand and old-timers mourn its origins in the early 1970s when 360 people attended, not 360,000. But today, the diversity of music draws all types: garden-variety rock and rollers, gospel devotees, jazz disciples, enigmatic world-beatniks, and plenty of new-breed eclectics from both coasts. Unlike Mardi Gras, the event is not widely embraced by locals. There are no parades, the French Quarter isn't the focal point, and shouts of "show us your tits" will provoke only beady-eyed scorn.

The $11 entrance fee for daytime events buys a lot more than jazz. At the Fais Do Do Stage, there's Cajun (the traditional music of rural white Louisiana) and zydeco (the traditional music of black, Creole Louisiana). The Ray Ban/WWL and Polaroid/WVUE stages feature bigger names like Bonnie Raitt and the Neville Brothers. At the WWOZ tent it's pure jazz; at Congo Square there's African, Caribbean, and R&B. And at the Rhodes/WYLD gospel tent you'll hear the soul-raising stuff of salvation. With so much happening at once, decisions are tough, and even during a great performance, it's often impossible to resist the urge to sprint over to the next stage and "discover" a Creole fiddler, a singing cowboy, or a soukous combo from Zaire.

There are crafts tents and plenty of other diversions, but much of the festival's draw is New Orleans itself, and all that comes with it. Official Jazzfest nighttime events take place in arena settings that are neither intimate nor cheap, and the unofficial offerings of the city's bars and clubs are much better. For many people, the daytime events are just a menu of appetizers, a prelude to the main course of music at night. Live music is everywhere, from bowling alleys to record stores to the bars of the Marigny District (Café Brazil, Café Istanbul, the Saturn Bar) or Uptown (Jimmy's, the Maple Leaf, Benny's, Tipatina's). In these humid barrooms there's no closing time—the bands cut loose, the people get giddy, and the possibilities get bigger in the swampy bottom of the American night.

DATE: Last weekend in April and first weekend in May. Friday through Sunday the first weekend, Thursday through Sunday the second. **LOCATION:** New Orleans, Louisiana. The festival's daytime events take place at the fairgrounds, about four miles (6.4 km) north of the French Quarter. **TRANSPORT:** New Orleans is easily reached by air from throughout North America, but from Europe and elsewhere a change of planes is usually necessary. Shuttle buses to the festival from the French Quarter and other locations are available. **ACCOMMODATION:** To avoid frustration, try to reserve a year in advance, and certainly no later than January. The LHMA (see below) can provide lists of accommodations. **CONTACT:** The New Orleans Jazz & Heritage Festival, P.O. Box 53407, New Orleans, LA, 70153, Tel (504) 522-4786. Louisiana Hotel & Motel Association (LHMA), 330 Exchange Alley, New Orleans, LA 70130, Tel (504) 525-9326.

Festival International de Louisiane

Lafayette, Louisiana **April**

It's smaller and the town's not as cool, but this musical feast ranks even higher than Jazzfest with world music buffs. In an intimate festival area in downtown Lafayette, Francophile rhythms and culture are highlighted with a week of concerts, plays, and culinary booths. The music is always great, as bands representing some 35 different nationalities around the French-speaking world—West Africa, Madagascar, Haiti, Quebec, Martinique, Guadeloupe, etc.—converge in Cajun and zydeco country to perform alongside the best of the locals.

The Festival International de Louisiane coincides with the first weekend of the New Orleans Jazz and Heritage Festival. Unlike its cousin, this two-stage event is free, and draws only a fraction of the crowd. The music (on two stages) lasts into the evenings, and alternative offerings include everything from a gourmet beerfest to plays, films, dance exhibitions, and street musicians. One of the festival's missions is to expose an international audience to southwestern Louisiana culture; along with cultural art forms, there's a wealth of Cajun and Creole cuisine for the sampling.

Diversity in the air: the Master Drummers of Burundi perform at Lafayette's Festival International de Louisiane. (Festival International de Louisiane/Philip Gould)

Even though Lafayette itself doesn't have the beauty and non-stop excitement of New Orleans, the surrounding countryside is a cultural treasure chest. The food's great, the prices are lower, and in roadhouses and juke joints local bands lay down searing boogie sessions as neighbors dance on springy floorboards. Organizers often fly performers in early so they can get together with local musicians, and the performances that result from these international musical friendships are part of what gives the event its precious and unique spirit. Where else in the world could you see a traditional band from Madagascar jamming with a fiddle and accordion duo from Opelousas?

Sidetrip: America's Coolest Tourist Trap

Approaching Mamou a few minutes after 9 a.m., the car radio clues you in: Fred's Lounge is already hopping. Carried over a live radio broadcast, the Cajun melodies generated at Fred's have the unmistakable lilt of good times, and your gang urges you to floor the rent-a-jalopy so you won't miss another minute.

When you pull up outside the concrete-block building, it's shaking with muffled waltz rhythms that surge to clarity when the door opens. Inside, there's hardly a chance to order a round of Falstaffs before some Cajun coots in bolo ties have whisked the women off to the dance floor. The band's separated from whirling dancers only by a thin piece of string, and as host Fred provokes the group with a hearty *"Laissez les bons temps roullez!"* your bleary eyes notice two signs that dictate the only rules of the house: "No substitute musicians," and "No standing on the juke box."

Fred's Saturday-morning Cajun dance is an American original, and despite international publicity, it hasn't been ruined by tour buses. The place is too small, too rustic, too authentic to interest the slick set. Locals still begin their weekends here, as they have for more than 45 years—though nowadays they might rub elbows with a handful of Japanese students, a group of visitors from France, or a gaggle of pale Northerners.

Around Mardi Gras or Jazzfest there are more outsiders than usual, but farmers in jeans and boots still start conversations with strangers in a French dialect, moving easily to English if necessary. And Fred Tate still works the bar when he's not at the microphone introducing the musicians, or organizing a contest to see who came the farthest to hang out at his humble hot-spot.

Fred's Cajun Dance and Broadcast happens every Saturday from 9 a.m. to 1 p.m. The bar is on Sixth Street in the center of Mamou (Tel (318) 468-5411). From Lafayette, take I-49 north, US-190 west, and Route 13 north. The dance is broadcast live on KVPI Radio (AM 1250).

DATE: Third week in April. **LOCATION:** Lafayette. **TRANSPORT:** Lafayette is 87 km (54 miles) west of Baton Rouge and is accessible by air from most major cities. **ACCOMMODATION:** All 4,000 hotel rooms within a 10-mile radius of Lafayette are fully booked by festival time, so reserve in advance. **CONTACT:** P.O. Box 4008, Lafayette, LA 70502, Tel (318) 232-8086.

Kentucky Derby: The "greatest two minutes in sports" is complemented by a two-week bout of "decadent and depraved" partying. (Churchill Downs)

Kentucky Oaks and Kentucky Derby

Louisville (Kentucky) **May**

One of the world's premier horse races, the Kentucky Derby is touted as "the greatest two minutes in sports," although Hunter S. Thompson payed it a different sort of compliment when he referred to it as "decadent and depraved." One thing is for sure: the hype and fun last a lot longer than two minutes. Louisville has stretched the Kentucky Derby Festival to encompass the entire two weeks preceding the race, and the town heaves with activities ranging from outrageously formal events like the Kentucky Colonels Banquet and Derby Festival Coronation Ball, to everyone's-invited events like country music concerts, fireworks, historic home tours, and square dance exhibitions. In between there's a hot-air balloon race, a mini-marathon, a steamship race, and the Pegasus Parade.

Louisville usually retains the aura of a kinder, gentler time, but the town gets completely flipped out during the days before the race. Plenty of locals avoid the crowds at the Derby, and the insider's line is that the more intimate Kentucky Oaks—a running of fillies the day before the Derby—is a much more rewarding experience that includes music and other entertainment in the infield.

On Derby day, the males take to the track for the first and most prestigious race in America's Triple Crown. Post time is

11:30 a.m., and the race for three-year-old thoroughbreds is run over a 1 1/4 mile-long track. The posh grandstand is packed with tens of thousands of the cream of Southern society, fueling their betting orgies with mass quantities of mint juleps and gourmet food. Seats are sold out months in advance, but the Clubhouse Gardens and infield are open to General Admission crowds.

The infield is like a rock concert without the music. Standing-room-only tickets go for $20 on the morning of the race, and inside a bizzilion beer-guzzling folks go wild in a Mardi Gras-like atmosphere of prolonged chaos. The scene is absolutely over the top; there's almost no chance of even seeing a horse, let alone the race (except on big-screen TV), but you will experience one of America's premier parties, a drunken bout of exhibitionism and high revel that would draw Hunter S. Thompson or any self-respecting gonzo journalist out of the press box.

DATE: The races are held the first Friday and Saturday in May; festival begins two weeks earlier. **LOCATION:** Louisville's Churchill Downs. **TRANSPORT:** Churchill Downs is located on Taylor Boulevard, near the intersections of Interstates 65 and 264 in Louisville. **ACCOMMODATION:** The city boasts a variety of accommodations in varying price ranges but be sure to book well in advance. **CONTACT:** (502) 636-4400.

© WHILE YOU'RE THERE ...

© **International Bar-B-Q Contest, Owensboro (Kentucky):** 40,000 folks' notion of where to get the best ribs can't be wrong. Tram-cooking, cook-offs, and bluegrass music grace the banks of the Ohio River in the self-proclaimed barbecue capital of the world. Contact: (501) 926-1860. (Mid-May.)

© **Spoleto Festival U.S.A., Charleston (South Carolina):** Sister to Spoletos in Italy and Australia, this art fest showcases classical music, opera, ballet, and theater amid posh surroundings. Meanwhile, a fringe fest showcases Southern and local talents—such as puppeteers, art exhibits, and music—in a more informal setting. Contact: 133 Church St., Charleston, SC 29401, Tel (803) 722-2764. (Mid-May/June.)

© **French Market Tomato Festival, New Orleans (Louisiana):** The locals keep trying to keep this one a secret, but the music and food are so great that the word's leaking out. The diversity of the tomato is celebrated, as is the diversity of music from Louisiana and the Caribbean. Contact: P.O. Box 51749, New Orleans, LA 70151, Tel (504) 522-2621; or GNOTCC (see *Resources*). (First weekend in June.)

© **Gonzales Jambalaya Festival, Gonzales (Louisiana):** Contestants must BYO 30-gallon cast iron cooking pots for this Cajun cook-off, and between tending the wood fire and stirring up some prizewinning jambalaya, cooks get to listen to live Cajun music and enjoy the small-town atmosphere. Contact: Jambalaya Festival Association, P.O. Box 1243, Gonzales, Louisiana 70737. (Second weekend in June.)

International Elvis Tribute Week

Memphis (Tennessee) **August**

Mention the King and it becomes clear that the word "fan" is short for fanatic. Elvis may or may not be dead, but his memory will definitely not be laid to rest any time soon. In honor of the anniversary of his supposed death on August 16, 1977, more than 50,000 fans from around the globe flock to his house to relive the golden years of rock and roll.

Concerts, art shows, laser light shows, dances, and banquets are hosted on the grounds of Graceland. Sporting contests include a 5K run and a karate tournament in Elvis's memory, and in between the special events you can take the standard tour of Graceland—not exactly a mansion, but more of a frozen tribute to 1970s kitsch. Choice spots on the tour are the Jungle Den, with its amazingly carpeted ceiling, and the TV Room, equipped with three screens to allow Elvis to watch three football games at once. The "dumpster of doom" is conspiciously off limits, but be sure to check out the Elvis Automobile Museum in Graceland Plaza, with a great reconstruction of a drive-in movie theater and a fantastic Harley-Davidson golf cart. In Memphis, local nightclubs host the inevitable Elvis impersonation contests, so don't be surprised if you're among the many who sight the King. A candlelight vigil on August 15th is the crowning requiem in honor of a man whose popularity continues to hold a nation captive.

DATE: August 9–17. **LOCATION:** Graceland Mansion. **TRANSPORT:** Graceland is accessible by car or shuttle-bus from points throughout the city. **ACCOMMODATION:** Memphis is home to a variety of hotels and motels in many price ranges, and not even an event of this magnitude can sell them all out. **CONTACT:** Graceland Mansion, P.O. Box 16508, Memphis, TN 38186, Tel (800) 238-2000.

Old Fiddler's Convention

Galax (Virginia) **August**

There are as many ways to play "Turkey in the Straw" as there are ways to rosin a bow, and old fiddlers are just the folks to prove it. For over 60 years, lovers of home-grown mountain music have come to this small town, bearing mouth-harps, bull fiddles, banjos, and dulcimers to add a suitable accompaniment to championship fiddling.

Hundreds of contestants from all over the world compete for cash prizes, trophies, and ribbons in categories that include guitar, mandolin, old-time fiddle, clawhammer and bluegrass banjo, dulcimer, dobro, old-time band, clogging, and folk singing.

Musicians and mountain music fans gather for three days of fiddlin' fun and authentic folk music at the Old Fiddler's Convention in Galax, Virginia. (Virginia Department of Economic Development)

The rules are strict: only acoustic instruments and authentic folk songs can be played, and no taps are allowed in the clogging contest.

DATE: Second week in August for three days. **LOCATION:** Felts Park, Galax. **TRANSPORT:** Galax is 96 km (60 miles) southwest of Roanoke. **ACCOMMODATION:** Camping is available at the park; hotel and motel accommodations are also available in the area. **CONTACT:** Old Fiddler's Convention, P.O. Box 655, Galax, VA 24333, Tel (703) 236-6355 & (703) 236-6473.

The World of Old Fiddlers and Other N'er-Do-Wells

If you don't happen to like toe-tapping, high-spirited, danceable music, then give a wide berth to fiddle conventions. Repertoires are typically restricted to pre-1900 dance music with certifiable roots in traditional European or American folk music, but old-time fiddlers are showmen at heart. Many contests even have a trick-fiddling award category; and fiddlers are notorious for throwing in flashy, crowd-pleasing stunts with every odd draw of the bow.

In the main event, fiddle-wielders compete by playing a waltz, a hoedown, and a tune of their own choosing, usually within strict time limits. Many fiddle conventions are a smorgasbord of traditional old-time music; in addition to fiddles, you're likely to hear accordions, harmonicas, dobros, banjos, guitars, spoons, bones, and even yodellers—if not on stage, then in impromptu jams out in the parking lot.

Here are a few of America's best places to fiddle around:

Mid-February: **Colorado Mid-Winter Bluegrass Festival**, Fort Collins, Colorado. Contact: Ken Seaman, Tel (303) 482-0863. • *Early April:* **Fiddler's Convention and Bluegrass/Folk Festival**, Stumptown, West Virginia. Contact: (304) 354-7440. • *Late April/early May:* **Merle Watson Memorial Festival**, Wilkesboro, North Carolina. Contact: P.O. Box 120, Wilkesboro, NC 28697, Tel (910) 651-8691. • *Mid-May:* **Old-Time Fiddler's and Bluegrass Festival**, Union Grove, North Carolina. Contact: (704) 539-4417. • *Late June:* **National Old-Time Fiddlers Contest**, Weiser, Idaho. Contact: Weiser Chamber of Commerce at (208) 549-0452. • *Early July:* **Old-Time Fiddler's Jamboree and Crafts Festival**, Smithville, Tennessee. Contact: Smithville Chamber of Commerce at (615) 597-4163. • *Mid-July:* **Official Kentucky State Championship Old-Time Fiddlers Contest**, Falls of Rough, Kentucky. Contact: (502) 259-3578. • *Mid-August:* **Old Fiddlers' Convention**, Galax, West Virginia. Contact: Oscar W. Hall at (703) 236-6355. • *Late September:* **Old-Time Fiddler's Contest and Festival**, Payson, Arizona. Contact: (602) 474-4515. • *Late October:* **Old Fiddler's Festival**, Sinton, Texas. Contact: Sinton Chamber of Commerce at (512) 364-2307.

While you're there ...

W. C. Handy Music Festival, Florence (Alabama): Although old W. C. is often credited as the "Father of the Blues," he was actually leading a vaudeville orchestra when he heard a ragged black man play what he called "the weirdest music I have ever heard." In this week-long celebration of Handy's legacy, parties and activities keep popping up all over Florence and in nearby Sheffield, Tuscumbia, and Muscle Shoals. Venues for the more than 100 events include churches, restaurants, the street, and the riverside, culminating in a headliner concert on Saturday night. Contact: (800) 472-5537. (Mid-August.)

Mississippi Delta Blues Festival

Greenville, Mississippi **September**

Although few locals show up, travelers who come to pay homage to the blues can count on a great day outdoors, in the foot-stomping land once haunted by Robert Johnson, Charley Patton, and Sonny Boy Williamson. Fantastic music, good food, and warm welcomes are in high supply, and the emphasis is on acoustic, Delta-style blues played on traditional instruments like guitars, jugs, harmonicas, and kazoos. A delectable spread of red beans and rice, catfish, and locally made arts and crafts provide a tangible reflection of Mississippi Delta culture.

DATE: Third weekend in September. **LOCATION:** Freedom Village, Greenville. **TRANSPORT:** The Festival grounds at the intersection of Highway 1 south and Route 454 are easily accessible by car. **ACCOMMODATION:** There are a number of hotels and motels in the area. **CONTACT:** 121 South Harvey St., Greenville, MS 38701, Tel (601) 335-3523.

While you're there ...

Zydeco Festival, Opelousas and Plaisance (Louisiana): The blues-based, accordion-laced music of black Creole Louisiana is featured in this great one-day gig at a country farm off Highway 167. There's also plenty of regional cuisine and African-American arts and crafts. Contact: Opelousas Tourist Info. Center, Tel (318) 948-6263 & (800) 424-5442. (Saturday before Labor Day; late August/early September.)

Festivals Acadiens, Lafayette (Louisiana): Twin-fiddling is just one of the musical highlights in this revelry revolving around Bayou crafts, food, and artistry. As the country's largest celebration dedicated to Cajun and Creole culture, it features two days of everything from ballads to dance band music from the '50s. Toes tap while netters and broommakers keep

Zydeco Festival: The music of Lousiana's favorite Creole sons is featured at this spirited blow-out on a farm near Opelousas. (Doug Bryant)

their fingers busy. Contact: Lafayette Convention and Visitors Bureau, P.O. Box 52066, Lafayette, LA 70505, Tel (318) 232-3737. (Third weekend in September.)

While you're there ...

National Storytelling Festival, Jonesboro (Tennessee): Mom used to call it fibbing, but when some folks got older, they turned it into a hobby

Tall Tales and Short Stories: Storytelling Festivals

With the popularity of verifiable, factual data on the rise, the storyteller's traditional role of informing folks of the goings-on around this vast nation wound up on shaky ground in the mid-20th century. No longer were people impressed with embellishment that made otherwise mundane events border on the fabulous. It seemed the only place a good storyteller could get a job was at a used-car lot, a TV newsroom, or Washington, D.C.

But no more. Societies like the National Association for the Preservation and Perpetuation of Storytelling have breathed new life and new respect into this formerly disreputable art. Now liars, embellishers, and embroiderers can openly practice their skills in front of adoring fans who gather to get a new twist on an old tale—or vice versa.

The **National Storytelling Festival** in Jonesboro, Tennessee is the granddaddy of them all, and meets in early October. Here are some other favored haunts of these masters of modern mythos:

Mid-April: **Gaston County Storytelling Festival**, Dallas, North Carolina. Contact: Cecilia Benoy, Tel (704) 922-7681. • *Late April/May:* **Annual Storytelling Festival**, St. Louis, Missouri. Contact: (314) 553-5961. • *Mid-August:* **Maine Festival of the Arts**, Portland, Maine. Contact: Maine Arts, Inc., Tel (207) 772-9012. • *Mid-September:* **Southwest Virginia Storytelling Festival**, Tazewell, Virginia. Contact: Historic Crab Orchard Museum, Tel (703) 988-6755. • *Mid-October:* **Alabama Tale Tellin' Festival**, Selma, Alabama. Contact: Public Library of Selma and Dallas, Tel (205) 875-3535.

and a few even went professional. Some 400 pro tale-tellers and their fans gather for three days of heavy-duty wool-pulling and other colorful embroidery in the oldest and most prestigious storytelling festival in the nation. Contact: National Association for the Preservation and Perpetuation of Storytelling, Tel (615) 753-2171. (Early October.)

☉ **Fantasy Fest, Key West (Florida):** By the time the morality squad decided this week-long Halloween romp was out of hand it was bringing in too much tourist revenue to stop it. Each year, letters to the local paper complain for weeks afterward about the nighttime costume parade's pseudo-flashers, bare breasts, and "preverted (sic) shimmying." (Late October.)

Professional storytellers and their fans gather for three days of tall tales at the oldest and most prestigious storytelling festival in America. (Tennessee Tourist Development)

Resources

In USA: United States Travel & Tourism Admin., 14th & Constitution, Washington, DC 20230, Tel (202) 482-4752. **Alabama:** Alabama Bureau of Tourism and Travel, 401 Adams Ave., PO Box 4309, Montgomery, AL 36103-4309, Tel (800) 252-2262 & (205) 242-4459, Fax (205) 242-4554. **Florida:** Florida Division of Tourism, 107 W. Gaines St., Suite 566, Tallahassee, FL 32399, Tel (904) 488-7598, Fax (904) 487-0134. **Georgia:** Georgia Dept. of Industry, Trade & Tourism, 285 Peachtree Center Ave. NE, Suite 1100, Marquis Two Tower, Atlanta GA 30303, Tel (404) 656-3545. **Kentucky:** Kentucky Dept. of Travel Development, 2200 Capital Plaza Tower, 500 Mero St., Frankfort, KY 40601, Tel (502) 564-4930 & (800) 225-8747. **Louisiana:** Louisiana Office of Tourism, P.O. Box 94291, Baton Rouge, LA, 70804, Tel (504) 342-8119 & (800) 334-8626. Greater New Orleans Tourist & Convention Commission (GNOTCC), 1520 Sugar Bowl Drive, New Orleans, LA 70119, Tel (504) 566-5095, Fax (504) 566-5046. **Mississippi:** Mississippi Division of Tourism Development, P.O. Box 1705, Ocean Springs, Mississippi 39566, Tel (601) 359-3297, Fax (601) 359-5757. **North Carolina:** North Carolina Travel & Tourism, 430 N. Salisbury St., Raleigh, NC 27611, Tel (919) 733-4171 & (800) 847-1862. **South Carolina:** South Carolina Division of Tourism, P.O. Box 71, Columbia, SC 29202, Tel (803) 734-0235. **Tennessee:** Tennessee Dept. of Tourism, P.O. Box 23170, Nashville, TN 37202, Tel (615) 741-2158. **Virginia:** Virginia Division of Tourism, Bell Tower/Capital Square, 101 N. Ninth St., Richmond, VA 23219, Tel (804) 786-4484 & (800) 847-4882. **West Virginia:** Travel West Virginia, State Capitol Complex, 2101 Washington St., E. Charleston, WV 25305, (304) 558-2286 & (800) 225-5982.

Canada: United States Travel & Tourism Admin., 480 University Ave., #602, Toronto, ON M5G 1V2, Tel (416) 595-5082, Fax (416) 595-5211. **UK:** United States Travel & Tourism Admin., 24 Grosvenor Square, London, W1A 1AE, Tel 71-495-4336, Fax 71-495-4377. **Germany:** United States Travel & Tourism Admin., Bethmannstr 56, D-60311, Frankfurt 1, Tel 69-92-00-3617, Fax 69-294-173. **Australia:** United States Travel & Tourism Admin., Level 59, MLC Centre, King & Castlereagh Streets, Sydney, NSW 2001, Tel 02-233-4666, Fax 02-232-7219.

GREAT LAKES AND MIDWEST

Most of the Midwest's celebrations fall into familiar patterns, marking seasons of small-town life with agricultural festivals, or bringing big-city folk together with tried-and-true music/food/ethnic/art festivals. The heartland's most amazing spectacles break the mold, and champion everything from UFOs, bikers, and country music to the region's wild weather. Cities use festivals to boast of their precious hogs and hobos, while in the wide-open country, lumberjacks, mushers, and other hearty sportsmen tackle the terrain in both summer and winter.

Arkansas, Illinois, Indiana, Iowa, Kansas, Michigan, Minnesota, Missouri, Nebraska, North Dakota, Ohio, Oklahoma, South Dakota, Wisconsin

St. Paul Winter Carnival

St. Paul, Minnesota **January/February**

These days the Twin Cities are probably a better place to live than to visit, but a century ago haughty easterners declared Minnesota unfit for human habitation. To prove them wrong, St. Paul residents decided to hold a rollicking carnival in the middle of Mother Nature's harshest season. The Winter Carnival was born and has since grown into a 10-day snow spectacular with ice castles, a Snow Sculpture Garden, torch-lit Sleigh and Cutter parades, and specialties like hot buttered rum.

Minnesotans, to their credit, don't get intimidated by winter, and make the most of it by participating in the cold-weather sports showcased by the festival. Carnival-goers stay warm in the Frozen 5K Run, and get involved in activities ranging from ice skating, snow volleyball, and pony rides, to that bucolic northern pastime known as curling. Snow golfing is always a hoot, and the

Chipping away: An ice sculptor concentrates on his craft at the St. Paul Winter Carnival. (Minnesota Office of Tourism)

big-time sporting highlight of the event is the International 500 Snowmobile race from Winnipeg, Canada, to St. Paul, a trek completed in two days. The "Legend of the Winter Carnival" is a pageant that features such characters as Astraios, god of starlight, Eos, goddess of the rosy-fingered morn, and Boreas, the king of the winds who discovered the winter paradise known as Minnesota.

DATE: 10 days beginning the last week of January. **LOCATION/TRANSPORT:** Downtown St. Paul, just east of Minneapolis off Interstate 94. **ACCOMMODATION:** St. Paul and Minneapolis have many hotels and motels in a variety of price ranges. **CONTACT:** St. Paul Festival and Heritage Foundation, 101 Norwest Center, 55 E. Fifth St., St. Paul, MN 55101, Tel (612) 297-6953 & (612) 297-6956.

© WHILE YOU'RE THERE ...

© **All-American Champion Sled Dog Races, Ely (Minnesota):** Beneath the swirling snows of January, Ely is transformed into Sled Dog City during the biggest sled dog race in the lower 48 states. There's a torchlight parade the Friday night before race weekend, and crafts markets, bingo games, and a flea market are in full swing during the competitions. Contact: Ely Chamber of Commerce, Tel (218) 365-6123. (Third weekend in January.)

© **St. Patrick's Day Parade and Party, Chicago (Illinois):** Prepare to whet your appetite for fun with some traditional green beer, in the town that's so kooky it dyes its river green (not kelly green, mind you, but a neon color that resembles engine antifreeze). In typical Windy-City fashion, the parade is politicized and commercialized, but you can erase memories of it in Chicago's famously warm neighborhood taverns, which are stretched to capacity by notorious afternoon and nighttime rave-ups. Contact: Chicago Convention and Tourism Bureau, Tel (312) 280-5740. (March 17.)

CHICAGO BLUES FESTIVAL

Chicago (Illinois) **May/June**

Chicago didn't create the blues; it just took the acoustic music of the rural South and made it into a northern, urban, electrified thing. Nevertheless, when Chicago gets the blues nowadays, it's an international event. For three days, lakefront Grant Park is packed with dozens of bands and thousands of listeners, celebrating the blues in the city that made them famous.

Unfortunately, if you only hit the main stage events you'd be tempted to say the whole thing is just dumb. Only a few spectators manage to get good seats in the Petrillo Music Shell, and tens of thousands have to watch the big-name performers from half a mile away—through a chain-link fence! On the lawn, urban professionals can be seen pulling cellular telephones out of pockets and giddily exclaiming, "Guess where we are!"

Luckily, there's a lot more than the main acts to keep your attention, and the sideshows really make the Blues Festival a great event. The Front Porch stage is downright intimate, and along Grant Park's sidewalks, musicians set up makeshift performance grounds and belt out both acoustic and electric sets. Fuzzy amps twist notes into weird sounds and spectators dance or pick up instruments and jam along. You never know what you'll come across—a big-name blues man or woman might stop by to do a song with an unknown friend, or a 10-year-old guitar sensation might leave an audience of 100 whooping in butt-kicked disbelief. Street performers peddle their itinerant howls, and drum-beaters transform bridges and tunnels into rhythm passages. Best of all, the performances are all free.

At night the show continues in Chicago's many blues bars, but again, the spirit of the blues isn't in obvious places. Famous north-side clubs are packed with well-heeled crowds who revel in the lazy bent-note clichés of the big names, while in grittier neighborhood dives you'll find up-and-coming or down-and-out bluesmen who care enough to actually try. Like the daytime festival, the best of the night isn't planned; it's found in the random, spontaneous moments ... just like the blues.

DATE: Either the last weekend in May or the first weekend in June. **LOCATION/TRANSPORT:** Chicago's Grant Park (Lake Shore Drive and Jackson Blvd.) **ACCOMMODATION:** Chicago is packed with accommodation options. **CONTACT:** Chicago Office of Special Events, Tel (312) 744-3315.

Bluegrass Festivals: Sunny Skies and Rolling Rhythms

Rumor has it around Nashville that if you want to play country music like you mean it, a degree from Bluegrass U. is a must. Bluegrass was actually one of the first steps out of the hills toward Nashville, but the evolution doesn't work in reverse—today's bluegrassers are quick to take a giant step away from anything with a cowboy hat on it.

The best place to experience bluegrass is at one of the many outdoor festivals that sprout around the United States during warm weather. Wherever the sun is shining and the hills are rolling, bluegrass fans will be picking their favorite tunes, on-stage and off. At any given festival, you'll see groups playing away in parking lots, on front porches, in parks and campgrounds—anywhere four guys and a fiddle, guitar, mandolin, and banjo can fit. Here are just a few of the top festivals:

May: **Ole Time Fiddler's and Bluegrass Festival**, Union Grove, North Carolina. Contact: Ole Time Fiddler's and Bluegrass Festival at (704) 539-4417. **Gettysburg Bluegrass Festival**, Gettysburg, Pennsylvania. Contact: Granite Hill Campground at (717) 642-8749.

June: **Bean Blossom Bluegrass Festival**, Bean Blossom, Indiana. Contact: Monroe Bluegrass Festival Headquarters at (615) 868-3333. **Telluride Bluegrass Festival**, Telluride, Colorado. Contact: Telluride Bluegrass Festival at (303) 449-6007.

Late July and early August: **Winterhawk Bluegrass Festival**, Hillsdale, New York. Contact: Winterhawk Bluegrass Festival at (513) 788-2526. **Grant's Bluegrass and Old-Time Music Festival**, Hugo, Oklahoma. Contact: Bill and Juarez Grant at (405) 326-5598.

September: **Thomas Point Beach Bluegrass Festival**, Brunswick Maine. Contact: TPBBF, Meadow Road, Box 5419, Brunswick, ME 04011, Tel (207) 725-6009. **North Iowa Bluegrass Festival**, Mason City, Iowa. Contact: (515) 423-3811. **I.B.M.A. Fan Fest**, Owensboro, Kentucky. Contact: International Bluegrass Music Association at (502) 684-9025.

Late October: **Country Rural Old-Time Music**, What Cheer, Iowa. Contact: (515) 634-2547.

Bean Blossom Bluegrass Festival

Bean Blossom (Indiana) **June**

Bill Monroe is considered to be the father of bluegrass, and his festival is the grandaddy of them all. Always attracting the top talents in modern bluegrass music, the event is held for five days each spring at Monroe's 100-acre park. Here, pickers and grinners as well as plain old bluegrass lovers from around the country stake their claim to five days in bluegrass heaven. In addition to concerts, the event features workshops and competitions.

Although the bluegrass music tradition extends back several centuries, it was Monroe, a high-mountain tenor and mandolin player extraordinaire, who put his stamp on it and made it into a unique musical form. Named after Monroe's band—the Blue Grass Boys, who began playing in 1938—bluegrass music has evolved to encompass a wide variety of styles that take their lead from Monroe himself. Small groups of virtuoso musicians—usually playing guitar, banjo, fiddle, mandolin, and bass—weave intricate, quick-tempo instrumental and vocal harmonies around traditional old-time melodies.

DATE: Mid-June. **LOCATION:** Bean Blossom Bluegrass Park. **TRANSPORT:** Bean Blossom is 72 km (45 miles) south of Indianapolis. **ACCOMMODATION:** Camping is available on a first-come, first-served basis; many campers arrive days ahead of the festival to settle in and start playing. **CONTACT:** Monroe Bluegrass Festival Headquarters, 3819 Dickerson Road, Nashville, TN 37207, Tel (615) 868-3333.

While you're there ...

- **Chicago Gospel Festival, Chicago (Illinois):** Two glorious days of gospel music fill Grant Park. Contact: Chicago Office of Special Events, Tel (312) 744-3315. (Mid-June.)
- **Days of Swine and Roses, Madison (Nebraska):** A hog-calling contest and the related husband-calling event are featured in this celebration of the off-beat and off-the-wall. Stay downwind of the Smelly Boot Competition, but line up for the mouth-watering pork BBQ, the challenging Farm Olympics, and the breathtaking Women's Chore Outfit Fashion Show. Contact: Madison Chamber of Commerce, Madison, NE 68748, Tel (402) 454-2251. (First weekend in June.)

Summerfest

Milwaukee (Wisconsin) **June/July**

If there weren't so many beer and soda company banners cluttering the stage views, you'd be more tempted to agree with promot-

Hog-Wild Holidays: Pigging Out in America

It's the stuff you can't quite figure out that keeps life interesting. Like how those stripes get in the toothpaste. The Internet. Or Michael Jackson. And why is it that humans are fascinated with pigs? Maybe it's the creatures' tendency toward excessive behavior that makes certain towns go hog wild enough to make pigs an annual *cause célèbre.*

Entire weekends are devoted to extolling the virtues of everything from ham hocks to rump roasts. Some porkoramas go beyond a rib barbecue or a modest hog parade to such things as greased pig contests, hog-calling, and porcine mud wrestling. One town (Kewanee, Illinois) even loudly boasts that it's the **Hog Capital of the World** at an early September festival. Contact: (309) 852-5672.

To celebrate pigs, you don't need to be the number one pork belly producer or rename your village Swinetown or Pigopolis. You don't even need a v-v-visit from a n-n-notable p-p-pig. Like the townsfolk that organize the **Days of Swine and Roses** (see previous page) and other festivals of *haute porkeure,* you just need to be able to carry a sense of fun to the outer limits.

In mid-September the **Possum Town Pig Fest** brings 20,000 pig-lovers to Columbus, Mississippi for great food, and blues, Cajun, and zydeco music. Contact: P.O. Box 2099, Columbus, MS 39704, Tel (601) 328-4532. In late September the **Marion Ham Days** in Lebanon, Kentucky features real country ham in the heart of bourbon country, with a "pigasus" parade, pig calling and tobacco spitting contests, country music, and a fantastic country ham breakfast.

The **Louisiana Swine Festival** exposes the secret lives of pigs for three days in late October or early November, in Basile, Louisiana. There's a swine show, a greasy pig contest, a carnival, and a human beauty pageant. Contact: P.O. Box 457, Basile, LA 70515, Tel (318) 431-5396. The **Big Pig Jig** in Vienna, Georgia is home of the state's Barbecue Cooking Championships—one of the tops in the U.S.—and serves up a squealing good time as the best BBQ-ers fight fork and tongue for the title. Livestock runs, crafts exhibits, and sporting events are just part of the goings-on in early October. Contact: P.O. Box 376, Vienna, GA 31092, Tel (912) 268-8275.

ers' claims that Summerfest is "the world's greatest music festival." This 11-day musical extravaganza *is* good, and despite its in-your-face commerciality it succeeds with an explosion of country, pop, rock, jazz, folk, bluegrass, and big band music. While performances sound continuously from eight stages, audience members can dance or sample international tastes from food courts dotting the lakeshore in one of the Midwest's most underrated cities. A comedy cabaret, a circus, sporting events, and children's theater are also featured, and between acts festival-goers can browse through displays of arts and crafts and other exhibitions.

DATE: 11 days usually beginning in mid-June. **LOCATION:** Milwaukee. **TRANSPORT:** Easily accessible by bus, plane, or car, Milwaukee is 145 km (90 miles) north of Chicago, Illinois. **ACCOMMODATION:** The area boasts numerous hotels, motels, campgrounds, RV parks, and B&Bs. **CONTACT:** Summerfest Office, 200 North Harbour, Milwaukee, WI 53202, Tel (414) 273-2680.

Lumberjack World Championships

Hayward (Wisconsin) **July**

Each year in late spring, muscle-bound sawyers, speedchoppers, chainsaw racers, tree climbers, and axe tossers gather in Hayward to decide who's the best lumberjack in the world. This backwoods event brings out a red-flanneled, suspendered crowd that loves wood and loves to square off amid the hearty smell of red cedar, bratwurst, turkey drumsticks, and roast pork.

In the old days, rivermen steered harvests from virgin northern forests through chilly waters to the mills. Nowadays, a sawmill turns great logs of cedar in preparation for the crowd-pleasing logrolling championships. Some of the best contestants in logrolling are women, and the sport's a bit like love in that all's fair except crossing the line or throwing a punch. Opponents can rock their end of the log, jump up and down, even aim a quick kick of water at the opposition's face—anything to keep dry the longest. Good rollers will whirl the logs so quickly that they propel across the churning water, paddle-wheel style, until one roller suddenly jumps up and "snubs" the log abruptly, hoping to throw the opponent off-balance.

DATE: Late July. **LOCATION:** Adjacent to the Lumberjack Village Pancake House in Hayward, Wisconsin. **TRANSPORT:** Hayward is located along Route 63, about 100 miles/160 km north of Eau Claire. **ACCOMMODATION:** There are several motels in and around Hayward. **CONTACT:** (715) 634-5115; also Wisconsin Division of Tourism (see *Resources*).

While you're there ...

© **UFO Days, Elmwood (Wisconsin):** In this town of fewer than 800 hardy souls, the reported sighting of a UFO more than a decade ago has provided cause for celebration ever since. Dances, parades, sporting events, and self-directed tours of UFO sighting spots are among the highlights in the town that promotes itself as the ideal landing site for otherworldly vacationers. So far, their efforts seem to have drawn more visitors of the human variety, but then again one never can be quite sure that the little old man in the next parking space is exactly what he seems. Contact: (715) 639-4501. (Last full weekend in July.)

© **EAA Fly-in, Oshkosh (Wisconsin):** The largest aviation event in the world features more than 12,000 planes—many of them outrageously experimental—in the air and on the ground. Although primarily a meeting of the Experimental Aircraft Association, this eight-day event is open to the public and features barnstorming and aerobatics displays by stunt pilots such as the Red Devils. Contact: EAA, Box 229, Hales Corners, WI, Tel (414) 425-4860. (Early August.)

National Hobo Convention

Britt, Iowa **August**

The carefree life of the free-wheeling freight-jumper is celebrated in what could probably be considered the Hobo Capital of America. Hobos—drifters who ride the rails and highways to get jobs here and there—get together in Britt's Hobo Jungle for story swapping and poetry readings around campfires. A memorial service at the Hobo Cemetery precedes the convention, and depression-era hobos come to recall their fellow rail-riders.

About 20,000 people join the hobos in a parade, a flea market, antique and classic car shows, hobo contests, carnivals, bicycle stunts, and a martial arts exhibition. The coronation of a King and Queen of Hobos is the highlight of the event, and to give crowds a taste of the hobo life, 500 gallons of Mulligan stew—the classic hobo meal made from whatever happens to be at hand—are dished up free of charge. The Chamber of Commerce also has a Hobo Museum where photographs and artifacts are on view.

DATE: Second Saturday in August. **LOCATION/TRANSPORT:** Britt, Iowa is 282 km (175 miles) northwest of Des Moines on Route 18. Hardcores can hop a freight. **ACCOMMODATION:** There are several motels in the area, as well as campgrounds and RV parks. **CONTACT:** Britt Chamber of Commerce, P.O. Box 63, Britt, IA 50423, Tel (515) 843-3867.

Sturgis Rally and Races

Sturgis, South Dakota **August**

The Black Hills are heavy with the sound of hogs as thousands of serious Harley-riders roar into town. Sturgis has become the top

Kickin' back: A biker takes it easy in the thick of thousands of comrades who roll into Sturgis for a week of racing and good times. (Kevin Fleming)

Harley-Davidson gathering in the United States, and it's a great place to see great bikes and great parts—both mechanical and human. Main Street is packed with tens of thousands of motorcycles, and on the outskirts of town there are hill climbs, races, short-track and half-mile sprints, and national-level drag racing events. Buffalo Chip Campground and nearby Rapid City feature rock concerts.

Some of the action is downright tame, such as the Top Gun competition (which showcases safe riding skills), but impromptu wet tee-shirt contests and beer blasts spring up here and there. Though the emphasis is on Harleys, don't fear that the good times will roll over you if you come in on a rice-burner—about a quarter of the bikes are foreign born, and folks like BMW and Honda host demo rides. In town, the National Motorcycle Museum is worth a visit, and for some biker kitsch, check out the hamburgers and Harley souvenirs at the Roadkill Café.

Some of the 200,000 folks who attend this event are definitely born to be wild; others get a thrill from ditching suits, ties, and the 9-to-5 status quo for one week each year. You'll see some true colors prominently displayed, as well as some polished and pricey designer leather jackets. But the spirit that moves these bikers is one and the same—a love of the open road and biker comradery.

DATE: Second week in August. **LOCATION:** Sturgis. **TRANSPORT:** By bike, Sturgis is 32 km (20 miles) north of Rapid City on Interstate 90. **ACCOMMODATION:** In addition to campgrounds, there are several hotels and motels in town to choose from, but they're booked far in advance. **CONTACT:** Sturgis Chamber of Commerce, Tel (605) 347-2556.

Bison Roundup: Modern cowboys coax the buffalo herd out of the Black Hills. *(South Dakota Department of Tourism)*

While you're there ...

WE Fest, Detroit Lakes (Minnesota): Mosey on over to Soo Pass Ranch for country music's answer to the rocking U.S. Festival. About 90,000 fans enjoy country-politan headliners like Reba McEntire, Tanya Tucker, and George Strait during 39 hours of live, foot-stomping, barn-burning music. Contact: P.O. Box 625, Detroit Lakes, MN 56502, Tel (218) 847-3992. (First weekend in August.)

Dally in the Alley, Detroit (Michigan): Detroit's foremost gathering of freaks and other folks commandeers a complex of alleys in the historic, run-down Cass Corridor, home to Detroit's artistic cutting edge since the sixties. What's basically an intimate street fair and gathering includes local bands on three stages, arts and crafts, food, beer, and old friends. This safe, magical event is Detroit at its Bohemian best. Contact: Anneliese Failla, Tel (810) 469-2968. (The Saturday after Labor Day—usually the second Saturday in September.)

Custer Bison Roundup

Custer State Park (South Dakota) **September/October**

The overwhelmingly scenic Black Hills provide the setting for one of the region's most thrilling spectacles. Brought back from near extinction through the park's efforts early in the century, the bison (popularly called buffalo) here now number 1,500. They're free to roam among the park's share of the Black Hills until each fall, when the herd is rounded up to be sorted, vaccinated, and thinned.

From several viewing points, you can watch as modern cowboys ride horses, jeeps, pickup trucks, and helicopters in an effort to coax the often unwilling herd into a six mile-wide corridor and then into pens. Cowboys who go one-on-one with a bison have to contend with a beast that's often taller than a man, and can run circles around a horse. Inside the pens the calves are branded and vaccinated, and the herd is sorted to select 500 for auction (a big chunk of the park's annual revenue comes from the sale).

The Custer State Park itself is a less-traveled gem near the tourist hell of Mt. Rushmore. Spectacular roads and trails for hiking and biking crisscross the Black Hills, where you can see elk, bighorn sheep, antelope, deer, and burros. There are plenty of campgrounds and comfy cabins, and in local restaurants you can sample a high-protein, low-fat buffalo burger.

DATE: Either the last Monday in September or the first Monday in October. **LOCATION/TRANSPORT:** Selected areas (inquire at any ranger station) of the Custer State Park, southwest of Rapid City, South Dakota. **ACCOMMODATION:** Campgrounds and cabins abound, both in the park and in nearby Custer. **CONTACT:** South Dakota Dept. of Tourism (see *Resources*).

RESOURCES

In USA: United States Travel & Tourism Admin., 14th & Constitution, Washington, DC 20230, Tel (202) 482-4752. **Arkansas:** Arkansas Dept. of Parks and Tourism, One Capitol Mall, Little Rock, AR 72201, Tel (501) 682-7777 & (800) 628-8725. **Illinois:** Illinois Bureau of Tourism, 100 West Randolph Street, 3-400, Chicago, IL 60601, Tel (312) 814-4732. Illinois Tourist Information Center, 310 Michigan Ave., Suite 108, Chicago IL 60604, Tel (312) 793-2094 & (800) 223-0121. **Indiana:** Indiana Tourism Development Division, One North Capitol, Suite 700, Indianapolis, IN, 46204, Tel (317) 232-8860 & (800) 289-6646, Fax (317) 323-4146 **Iowa:** Iowa Division of Tourism, 200 E. Grand Ave., Des Moines, IA 50309, Tel (515) 242-4705, Fax (515) 242-4749. **Kansas:** Kansas Travel and Tourism Division, 400 SW Eighth St., Topeka, KS 66603, Tel (913) 296-2009. **Michigan:** Michigan Travel Bureau, 333 S. Capitol Ave., Lansing, MI 48909, Tel (517) 373-1220 & (800) 543-2937. **Minnesota:** Minnesota Office of Tourism, 100 Metro Square, 121 Seventh Place E, St. Paul, MN, 55101, Tel (612) 296-5029. **Nebraska:** Nebraska Division of Tourism, P.O. Box 94666, Lincoln, NE 68509, Tel (402) 471-3796 & (800) 228-4307. **North Dakota:** North Dakota Tourism Division, Liberty Memorial Building, Bismarck, ND 58505, Tel (800) 437-2077. **Ohio:** Ohio Office of Travel & Tourism, Box 1001, Columbus, OH 43216, Tel (614) 466-8844. **Oklahoma:** Oklahoma Tourism & Recreation, 500 Will Rogers Building, Oklahoma City, OK

73105, Tel (405) 521-2409 & (800) 652-6552. **South Dakota:** South Dakota Dept. of Tourism, 711 Wells Ave., Pierre, SD, 57501, Tel (605) 773-3301 & (800) 843-1930. **Wisconsin:** Wisconsin Division of Tourism, 123 W. Washington Ave., P.O. Box 7970, Madison, WI 53707, Tel (608) 266-2161 & (800) 432-8747.

Canada: United States Travel & Tourism Admin., 480 University Ave., #602, Toronto, ON M5G 1V2, Tel (416) 595-5082, Fax (416) 595-5211. **UK:** United States Travel & Tourism Admin., 24 Grosvenor Square, London, W1A 1AE, Tel 71-495-4336, Fax 71-495-4377. **Germany:** United States Travel & Tourism Admin., Bethmannstr 56, D-60311, Frankfurt 1, Tel 69-92-00-3617, Fax 69-294-173. **Australia:** United States Travel & Tourism Admin., Level 59, MLC Centre, King & Castlereagh Streets, Sydney, NSW 2001, Tel 02-233-4666, Fax 02-232-7219.

ROCKY MOUNTAIN REGION

Reports that the Wild West is dead have been greatly exaggerated. At the many Rocky Mountain stampedes and rodeos, the rough sports and spectacles of a not-so-bygone era whip solidly into focus. This is Big Outdoors country, and you'll find events celebrating both the cowboys who made the Rockies a viable home for Europeans, and the Native Americans whom they evicted. In between the stampedes and powwows, there are plenty of excellent music festivals and beerfests that celebrate the region's newest flourishing tradition: microbrewing.

Colorado,
Idaho,
Montana,
Wyoming

TELLURIDE BLUEGRASS FESTIVAL

Telluride, Colorado **June**

The head count in this Rocky Mountain mining-turned-resort community surges as thousands of fans flock to the best bluegrass and country/folk music festival west of the Mississippi. Even with the leap in population, Telluride keeps the small-town good vibes—folks even form a roadblock to greet visitors on their way into town, and answer questions about where to go and what to do.

The festival and town itself are expensive, but camping makes the trip affordable and the setting is unbeatable. The road ends at Telluride, which is set in a box canyon in the craggy San Juan Mountains of southwest Colorado. While listening to some of the nation's finest bluegrass, folk, country, and gospel musicians, you can look up at snow-covered peaks on three sides. Many visitors combine the concerts with hiking and mountain biking in the region.

DATE: Thursday–Sunday over the nearest weekend to the summer solstice (usually the third weekend in June). **LOCATION:** Telluride Town Park. **TRANSPORT:** Telluride is located on the San Juan Highway, about a seven-hour drive from Denver or Albuquerque. Flights are also available from Denver. **ACCOMMODATION:** Camping is a must at bluegrass festivals, but stake your claim early in the week. There are also a variety of hotels and motels in town, but don't bother looking for anything cheap in this town. **CONTACT:** Planet Bluegrass, 500 West Main St., Lyon, CO 80540, Tel (303) 449-6007 & (800) 624-2422.

While you're there ...

- **Miles City Bucking Horse Sale, Miles City (Montana):** You know you're in cowboy country when the boots and hats have marks on 'em that you just can't get on an urban dance floor. This here's the real thing: professional cattlemen auctioning rodeo stock for the upcoming rodeo season. A rodeo and wild horse racing are part of the weekend events, and a parade runs through town on Saturday. Bring your dancing duds, so you can two-step the night away during street dances held on Friday and Saturday. Just be careful what you step in. Contact: Tel (406) 232-6585. (Third weekend in May.)
- **National Old-Time Fiddler's Contest, Weiser (Idaho):** This is the most prestigious fiddle contest in North America, and features the nation's best fiddlers performing throughout the city during the competition and informal jam sessions. Contact: Weiser Chamber of Commerce, 8 East Idaho Street, Weiser, ID 83672, Tel (208) 549-0452 & (800) 437-1280. (Late June.)

Great American Beer Festival

Denver (Colorado) **October**

The brewer's art occupies center stage at this showcase of the nation's beers. In a convention-hall setting, professional brewers, home brewers, and beer lovers get together to taste and talk beer. In addition to tasting hundreds of beers from America and around the world (one fluid ounce at a time), attendees have the opportunity to attend educational demonstrations, brewing seminars, and food courts.

Although the official judging is pretty much a joke (Budweiser walked away with a medal in 1994), there's plenty of interesting beer on hand for non-professional tasters. More than 200 American breweries present about 1,200 lagers, ales, bitters, stouts, porters, and wheat beers, made with everything from white chocolate and pumpkins to blueberries and chili peppers. Out-

Frontier Days: A bronc rider tries to maintain his seat at the world's classic Wild-West event. (Wagner Perspective/Frontier Days)

side the convention hall, metro Denver keeps beer lovers happy with six brewpubs—including the two largest in the nation.

DATE: Friday and Saturday of the third weekend in October. **LOCATION:** Currigan Exhibition Hall in downtown Denver. **TRANSPORT:** Denver's expensive new airport can be reached directly from the United States' big cities, and from Europe too. **ACCOMMODATION:** Denver sports plenty of lodging options. **CONTACT:** Association of Brewers, Tel (303) 447-0126 & (303) 447-0816.

FRONTIER DAYS

Cheyenne, Wyoming **July**

Rodeo's "daddy of 'em all" sports 10 days of bronc busting, parades, chuck wagon races, pancake breakfasts, carnivals, midways, and Indian events. Frontier Days is the world's oldest and largest rodeo, a going concern since 1897. It features the finest performers in rodeo, who ride, rope, and bull-dog their way through more than 500 head of brahmans, longhorns, and other livestock. Sideshows include military air shows and four parades featuring the world's largest collection of horse-drawn vehicles. Frontier nights are just as wild, with square dances, concerts, and lots of cowboy-style drunkenness.

In normally placid Cheyenne, an influx of more than 100,000 out-of-towners brings remnants of the wild West out of the woodwork. A stampeding hangover can be soothed with coffee and pancakes every second morning in the parking lot across

A Dude's Guide to the American Rodeo

All across the Rocky Mountains you'll see bumper stickers reading "There are no atheists in a rodeo chute." Rodeo is a rough, injury-ridden sport, and it draws a breed of men and women who see the rodeo circuit as their chance to go for the glory and big money.

The idea is not only to stay on the back of a beast that doesn't want you there, but to do so with style and finesse. Modern rodeos are organized around six principle events. Saddle bronc riding is the classic cowboy event, as the rider tries to maintain his seat on a wildly bucking horse for 10 seconds, holding on to a bucking rein with one hand while keeping the other in the air in proper style. How can you tell if a particular horse is a good rough bucker? It enters the ring in the air.

Bareback bronc-riding follows the same lines, sans saddle; cowboys must stay on for eight seconds. Bull-riding, a popular event in Cheyenne and elsewhere, is the most dangerous rodeo event as cowboys attempt to keep a bareback seat on a pissed-off Brahman bull flexing 2,000 lbs of muscle. Unlike the bronc, who simply tries to get the cowboy off his back, the bull wants revenge after he throws the rider, and desperately tries to gore or trample him. This is where rodeo clowns—those teams of former rodeo cowboys who rescue fallen riders—come into play. The barrel man tries to distract and annoy the bull, often jumping into a barrel to avoid a charge while his clown-mate spirits the rider from the ring.

Calf-roping and team roping showcase the cowpokes' lariat skills in a match of wits between man and horse. Men—singly or in pairs—work against the clock to lasso a free-running calf from horseback, then tie the rope to the saddle, dismount, throw the calf to the ground, and bind together three of the animal's feet. In bull-dogging, or steer-wrestling, cowboys must drop onto the horns of a galloping steer and work him to the ground while another cowboy, a hazer, rides his mount along side to keep the steer running straight. Barrel-racing, a women's event, didn't originate in practical cowboy work, but it has been added to many rodeos for its entertainment value.

from the Chamber of Commerce building. The food is free, so eat up, partner!

DATE: June 17–26. **LOCATION/TRANSPORT:** Cheyenne is located about 160 km (100 miles north of Denver). **ACCOMMODATION:** Rates double during the rodeo, but there's camping just outside of town. For a

Here's a list of some of North America's top rodeos:

Third Friday in January: **National Western Stock Show**, Denver, Colorado. The nation's largest livestock show features one of the top indoor rodeos during its 11-day run. Contact: Denver Metro Convention and Visitors Bureau, Tel (303) 892-1112.

July: **Cody Stampede**, Cody, Wyoming. A venerable classic, this Independence-Day rodeo is rich in prize money and features parades and street dances in the home of Buffalo Bill Cody. Contact: (307) 587-2297. • **Calgary Exhibition and Stampede**, Calgary, Alberta (Canada). "The greatest outdoor show on earth" makes Calgary completely nuts for 10 days. Contact: Box 1860, Station M, Calgary T2P 2L8, Tel (800) 661-1260 or (403) 261-0101. • **Wolf Point Wild Horse Stampede**, Wolf Point, Montana. One of the state's oldest rodeos, this three-day event features parades and a human stampede on Saturday morning. Contact: P.O. Box 293, Wolf Point, MT 59201, Tel (406) 653-2012. • **Snake River Stampede**, Nampa, Idaho. One of the top 25 rodeos in the country sees top action and professional-class rodeo events. Contact: Snake River Stampede, Tel (208) 466-8497. • **Santa Fe Women's Professional Rodeo**, Santa Fe, New Mexico. Women are making their mark on professional rodeo action, and this event is a forum for distaff buckaroos. Contact: Santa Fe Chamber of Commerce, Tel (505) 983-7317.

Early December: **National Finals Rodeo**, Oklahoma City, Oklahoma. The world series of the rodeo circuit, the National Finals are a nine-day ride-off of the top rodeo competitors—both men and women—from around the United States. Among the highlights is a Miss Rodeo America Pageant. Contact: Oklahoma City Visitors Bureau, Tel (405) 278-8912.

list of accommodations and restaurants, contact the Cheyenne Area Convention and Visitors Bureau, 309 W. 16th St., Cheyenne, WY. Tel (800) 426-5009 & (307) 778-3133. **CONTACT:** Cheyenne Frontier Days, P.O. Box 2477, Cheyenne, WY 82003. Tel (800) 227-6336, Fax (307) 778-7213.

WHILE YOU'RE THERE ...

Crow Fair Celebration and Powwow, Crow Agency (Montana): The "Tepee Capital of the World" hosts a six-day celebration of Northern Plains Indian culture with a rodeo, parades, Indian dancing, hand games,

More than 10,000 Crow Indians and other Native Americans converge for the ceremony and comradery of Montana's Crow Fair. (Jack Parsons/Omni-Photo Communication)

authentic costumes, and displays of crafts and food. While the event attracts more than 10,000 Native American participants from around the country, non-Indians are encouraged to attend as spectators. Contact: Crow Indian Tribe, Burton Pretty on Top, Crow Tribal Building, Crow Agency, MT 59022, Tel (406) 638-2601. (Mid-August.)

© **Testicle Festival, Clinton (Montana):** If you can't guess what a "Rocky Mountain Oyster" is, don't ask and just clean your plate. More than four tons of the stuff are served up alongside cowboy beans in this two-day gourmet spread. Live music day and night helps speed digestion. Contact: (406) 825-4868. (Third weekend in September.)

Resources

In USA: United States Travel & Tourism Admin., 14th & Constitution, Washington, DC 20230, Tel (202) 482-4752. **Colorado:** Colorado Tourism Information, (800) 265-6723. **Idaho:** Idaho Division of Tourism Development, P.O. Box 83720, Boise, ID 83720, Tel (208) 334-2470, Fax (208) 334-2631. **Montana:** Travel Montana, 1424 9th Ave., P.O. Box 200533, Helena, MT 59620, Tel (406) 444-2654 & (800) 847-4868, Fax (406) 444-1800. **Wyoming:** Wyoming Division of Tourism, I-25 at College Dr., Cheyenne, WY, Tel (307) 777-7777, Fax (307) 777-6904.

Canada: United States Travel & Tourism Admin., 480 University Ave., #602, Toronto, ON M5G 1V2, Tel (416) 595-5082, Fax (416) 595-5211. **UK:** United States Travel & Tourism Admin., 24 Grosvenor Square, London, W1A 1AE, Tel 71-495-4336, Fax 71-495-4377. **Germany:** United States Travel & Tourism Admin., Bethmannstr 56, D-60311, Frankfurt 1, Tel 69-92-00-3617, Fax 69-294-173. **Australia:** United States Travel & Tourism

Admin., Level 59, MLC Centre, King & Castlereagh Streets, Sydney, NSW 2001, Tel 02-233-4666, Fax 02-232-7219.

SOUTHWEST USA

Blue skies are usually a given at this region's many balloon festivals and musical gatherings, but reliable weather notwithstanding, there are plenty of surprises under the southwestern sun. This is a land where cowboy poets still roam and rhyme among the plains and valleys, and Indians commemorate their age-old presence in the mesas through spirited powwows and pueblo gatherings.

Arizona, Nevada, New Mexico, Texas, Utah

In counterculture festivals like Nevada's Burning Man Project, west-coast weirdness spills into the desert. And in Texas—once an independent nation and still culturally and ideologically distinct from the rest of the country—Texans proudly lay their unique heritage on the table during the state's lively music and food events.

COWBOY POETRY GATHERING

Elko (Nevada) **January**

Real men *do* rhyme, as if there were any question. Each January in the self-proclaimed "last real cow town in the West," favorite ponies are immortalized in iambic pentameter, while little doggies roam in and out of free verse.

Few would have dreamed when the event started back in 1985 that there would be such a consistent demand for doggerel. Yet year after year, rapt listeners come from around the nation to hear all about bad horses, bad men, wild rides, and rank cattle. God and women are favorite subjects, but plenty of cowgirls show up too, not only to read and listen to the poetry readings, but to hoot it up at the attendant Western dances, instrumental jam sessions, and concerts that are crammed into this week-long gathering.

DATE: Last week of January. **LOCATION:** Pioneer Hotel's Western Folklife Center. **TRANSPORT:** Elko, Nevada is about 100 miles from the Utah border. Both Amtrak and Greyhound stop in town. **ACCOMMODATION:** Traditional hotels and motels abound, but another option

Cowboy poets at play: Baxter Black (right) takes Wallace McRae for a twirl while slyly rifling through his vest pocket during Elko's Cowboy Poetry Gathering. (Sue Rosoff)

is to spend a couple of days on a local ranch as a working guest. **CONTACT:** Western Folklife Center, 501 Railroad St., Elko, NV 89801, Tel (702) 738-7508 & (800) 748-4466.

O'Odham Tash

Casa Grande (Arizona) **February**

Beating drums and thumping feet can be heard over the plains near the ruins of the Hohokam "Big House," as performers in

Home, Home on the Page: Cowboy Poetry Gatherings

Baxter Black, Bruce Kiskaddon, Badger Clark, and Curley Fletcher aren't household names, but the fact that these men spend very little time inside houses probably accounts for that. Their words echo with the solitude of life out on the range, and wax poetic about the endless night sky and a faithful steed. They humorously vilify bad horses and bad men, and recount range wars, wild rides, raw hands, and rank-smelling cattle.

Listeners can get caught up in the eloquence of their words and forget, but the worn leather of their boots is a reminder that most cowboy poets aren't duded-up college boys, but guys who have spent more time sitting in saddles or pickup trucks than standing on stage. Performances are sometimes interspersed with yodeling and other cowboy pastimes, and recitations are often attended by other forms of entertainment. Old-time string bands and Western tunes provide instrumental accompaniment for the Western dances that can accompany such get-togethers.

Elko, Nevada, is host to the annual **Cowboy Poetry Gathering**, probably the best-known of these events (see above). Others are:

Late April: **Cowboy Poetry Gathering**, Oklahoma City, Oklahoma. Contact: (405) 478-2250. • *Early July:* **Sunrise Festival of the Arts and Cowboy Poetry Gathering**, Sidney, Montana. Contact: Sidney Chamber of Commerce at (406) 482-1916. • *Early August:* **New Mexico Cowboy Poetry Gathering**, Silver City, New Mexico. Contact: Silver City Museum at (505) 538-5921. • *Mid-August:* **Montana Cowboy Poetry Gathering**, Lewiston, Montana. Contact: Lewiston Chamber of Commerce at (406) 538-5436.

feathers and beads recreate ritual dances to summon rain, heal illness, or prepare for war. One of the most authentic and entertaining powwows in America, O'Odham Tash draws more than 250,000 Native Americans and spectators.

The all-Indian rodeo attracts participants from all over North America. At the Saturday and Sunday dances Native Americans summon the heartbeat of Mother Earth in the drums, as dancers thank the Creator for a good harvest. Selectively screened craft shows feature hundreds of artists, including members of the local Tohono O'Odham and Pima tribes. The Maricopa tribe is known for its outstanding basket-weaving and pottery, and Hopis

Ready for an ancient dance: At powwows like the American Indian Exposition in Andarko, Oklahoma, Native Americans share their culture with visitors. (Fred W. Marvel/Oklahoma Tourism Photo)

carve beautiful *kachina* dolls from cottonwood. Peart Park hosts a traditional Indian barbecue in which meat is shredded and cooked underground for 24 hours.

DATE: Three days in mid-February. **LOCATION:** Casa Grande is located about half-way between Phoenix and Tucson, near the junction of routes 10 and 8. **ACCOMMODATION:** Although there are some nearby hotels, most visitors day-trip from Tucson or Phoenix, each about an hour away. **CONTACT:** O'Odham Tash, P.O. Box 11165, Casa Grande, AZ 85230, Tel (602) 836-4723.

Tejano International Conjunto Festival

San Antonio (Texas) **May**

Conjunto bands from Texas and Mexico converge on beautiful, mellow San Antonio for four days of accordion artistry, spurred on by legions of devoted and spirited dancers. Conjunto (pronounced "cone-HOON-toe") music has its roots in both Mexican and Germanic folk styles, and is popular in south and central Texas, as well as northern Mexico. In recent years, the addition of Cajun and zydeco accordionists has caused festival officials to consider broadening the top billing and changing the title to "National Accordion Festival."

INDIAN FESTIVALS AND POWWOWS

Caretakers of the land long before the arrival of European colonists, America's native people have managed to preserve some of their basic ways of life despite the fragmentation of tribes across the vast continent. The powwow, a traditional gathering that preserves Indian spirituality and traditions, renews customs and rituals through song, dance, and historical stories. Although some powwows are private affairs, most are occasions when the non-Indian public is invited to share and discover the bounty of the Native Americans' rich heritage.

The change of seasons is one of many causes for celebration, and tribes honor such occasions with bear, turtle, and buffalo dances. Some, like the mid-April **Yaqui Deer Dances** held near Tucson, are not meant to be tourist attractions, although outsiders are welcome. Others, like Albuquerque's **Gathering of Nations**, are full-blown extravaganzas, attracting more than 1,000 dancers who compete amid exhibitions of native foods, crafts, and culture, and a Miss Indian America contest. **O'Odham Tash** (see above) is one of the largest all-Indian rodeos, drawing more than 100,000 spectators to Casa Grande (Arizona).

Here's a run-down on timing and contact information for some of the best Native American Festivals in the United States:

New Year's Day: **Turtle Dance**, Taos, New Mexico. Contact: (505) 758-9593. • *Late January:* **Comanche Dance**, San Ildefonso New Mexico. Contact: (505) 827-0291. • *Early February:* **Buffalo Dance**, Picuris Pueblo, New Mexico. Contact: (505) 587-2957. • *Mid-February:* **O'Odham Tash**, Casa Grande, Arizona. Contact: (602) 836-4723. • *Early April:* **Ute Bear Dance**, Ouray, Randlett, and Whiterocks, Utah. Contact: (801) 722-5141. • *Mid-April:* **Yaqui Deer Dances**, Tucson, Arizona. Contact: (602) 622-6911. **Gathering of Nations**, Albuquerque, New Mexico. Contact: (800) 321-6979. • *Early July:* **Taos Indian Pueblo Powwow**, Taos, New Mexico. Contact: (505) 758-8626. • *Mid-July:* **Kickapoo Nation Powwow**, Kickapoo Reservation, Kansas. Contact: (913) 296-2009. • *Late July:* **Fort Totten Days Powwow and Rodeo**, Fort Totten, North Dakota, Contact: (800) 437-2077. • *Mid-August:* **Crow Fair and Rodeo**, Crow Agency, Montana. Contact: (406) 638-2601. **Inter-Tribal Indian Ceremonial**, Gallup, New Mexico. Contact: (505) 863-3896. **American Indian Exhibition**, Andarko, Oklahoma. Contact: (405) 247-3224. • *Early September:* **National Championship Powwow**, Grand Prairie (Texas). Contact: (214) 481-0454. • *September:* **Navajo Nation Tribal Fair**, Window Rock, Arizona. Contact: (602) 871-4941. • *Mid-October:* **Cherokee Indian Fall Festival**, Cherokee, North Carolina. Contact: (704) 497-9195.

Independents and up-and-comings have center stage at South by Southwest, while music lovers and major labels prowl the rockin' clubs of Austin. (Texas Department of Commerce/Elizabeth Grivas)

DATE: Second week in May. **LOCATION:** Rosedale Park, San Antonio. **ACCOMMODATION:** San Antonio has a wide range of accommodations. **CONTACT:** Guadelupe Cultural Arts Center, Tel (210) 271-3151.

While you're there ...

South by Southwest, Austin (Texas): This well-organized music convention focuses on up-and-coming rock, country, alternative, and other acts, with showcase performances, seminars, and schmooze-fests in the most happening town in Texas. Events are dominated by independents, rather than big-name labels and bands. (March.)

Burning Man Project

Black Rock Desert (Nevada) **September**

People who classify these things have to plunk this one down decisively in the category of "other." A proto-doomsday art gathering of high-tech anarchists in the middle of one of the emptiest places on earth, Burning Man draws a hodge-podge of "types" who come for an anti-program of arts, music, self-reinvention, and the fiery finale: the burning of a four-story wood-and-neon icon known simply as The Man.

Starting on Friday, freaks and freewheelers begin arriving from San Francisco and everywhere, setting up a makeshift circle-city—an "experiment in temporary community"—in the huge otherworldly plain that was once the bottom of a Pleistocene sea. In the "Inner Circle," people wander around pavilions in flowing robes or simpler short-and-tee-shirt ensembles, drinking beer or creating offerings to The Man in open-air clay workshops. Musicians play guitars, drums, hubcaps, and lots more, creating a marathon cacophony that forms a perfect aural backdrop to whatever is going on here. The motto is "no spectators," and to that end, everyone gets to work creating spontaneous institutions or unannounced performance art—look around and you'll find all-night raves, a makeshift tiki bar, a pirate radio station, a naked dancer with nipple rings, and a caravan of acidheads driving at 90 miles an hour through the desert (there's nothing to hit).

Larry Harvey is the founder of this underground hit, and he sees Burning Man as a solution to the American identity problem. "We have no culture in this country," he says, "just marketing." Burning Man, as "a monument to transcience," reminds people of their own mortality, and provides what Harvey describes as a sense of awe that used to be provided by religion. He started the event as a one-time-only solstice ritual in San Francisco in 1986, with the burning of an eight-foot human effigy on the beach. Harvey noticed a sense of spontaneous unity among those who worked on building and burning the Man, and decided to tap its potential with bigger and bigger events.

The event moved to the remote, cop-free desert after the police started breaking up the beach party, and each year more and more people make the drive and plunk down a $40 registration fee. Witches, CPAs, Druids, and bikini-clad teens are among those who drive or fly onto the site, and by Sunday it's rocking hard. A fashion contest, cocktail party, and several spin-off events take place under the towering, neon-lit anthropoid, and at the appointed hour his legs are set ablaze. As the flames rise flares and bombs rock the ground, and rockets shoot from his torso. Engulfed in fire, The Burning Man lights up the faces of the strange community at his feet, enraptured and howling in unison in the cool desert night.

DATE: Labor Day weekend (the first weekend in September). **LOCATION:** The temporary community of Burning City is located just north of the town of Gerlach, Nevada, in the Black Rock Desert. **TRANSPORT:** From Reno take I-80 east to Wadsworth, then take Route 447 north to Gerlach and follow the signs. **ACCOMMODATION:** Bring your own camping gear. **CONTACT:** Larry Harvey, (415) 985-7471.

Lighter than air-port: Spectacular mass ascents are the highlights of Saturday and Sunday mornings at the Albuquerque Balloon Festival. *(Albuquerque International Balloon Fiesta/Ferne Saltzman)*

© Albuquerque International Balloon Fiesta

Albuquerque (New Mexico) **October**

This is your chance to get up, up, and away as more than 600 balloons take to the air in one of the most colorful airborne spectacles on earth. The world's largest hot-air ballooning event covers two weekends during its nine days, and draws big crowds for spectacular mass ascents at sunrise on Saturdays and Sundays.

Aside from normal standards of conduct, there are no rules to dampen spirits. Spectators mingle, unhindered by "Do Not Touch" signs or off-limits areas, with pilots and crews, and they can even hitch hot-air rides. Highlights include the special shapes competition, with huge Harleys, polar bears, a cow, a dinosaur, and even Noah's ark complete with 28 animals. Thrill-seeking festival-goers have the chance to ride the skies, while on the ground there's live music and a parade. The U.S. Air Force Thunderbirds show up to dodge lighter-than-air craft, and the U.S. Navy sends its Leapfrogs parachute team. An awards ceremony and a gala grand ball crown the event.

DATE: Nine days in early October. **LOCATION:** Balloon Fiesta Park, Albuquerque, New Mexico. **TRANSPORT:** Albuquerque is 93 km (58 miles) south of Santa Fe on Interstate 25, and is easily reached by air from throughout the United States. **ACCOMMODATION:** There are numerous accommodations in all price ranges within the city. **CON-**

TACT: A.I.B.F., Inc., 8309 Washington Place NE, Albuquerque, NM 87113, Tel (505) 821-1000 & (800) 284-2282.

Resources

In USA: United States Travel & Tourism Admin., 14th & Constitution, Washington, DC 20230, Tel (202) 482-4752. **Arizona:** Arizona Office of Tourism, 1100 W. Washington St., Phoenix, AZ 85007, Tel (800) 842-8257, (602) 542-8687, Fax (602) 542-4068. **Nevada:** Nevada Commission of Tourism, State Capitol Complex, 5151 S. Carson St., Carson City, NV 89701, Tel (800) 638-2328 & (702) 687-4322, Fax (702) 687-6779. **New Mexico:** New Mexico Department of Tourism, 491 Old Santa Fe Trail, P.O. Box 20003, Santa Fe, NM 87503, Tel (505) 827-7400 & (800) 545-2040, Fax (505) 827-7402. **Texas:** Texas Department of Commerce, Division of Tourism, PO Box 12728, First City Centre, 816 Congress Ave., Austin, TX 78711, Tel (512) 936-0213, Fax (512) 936-0450. **Utah:** Utah Travel Council, Council Hall, Capitol Hill, 300 N. State St., Salt Lake City, UT 84114, Tel (801) 538-1030, Fax (801) 538-1399.

Canada: United States Travel & Tourism Admin., 480 University Ave., #602, Toronto, ON M5G 1V2, Tel (416) 595-5082, Fax (416) 595-5211. **UK:** United States Travel & Tourism Admin., 24 Grosvenor Square, London, W1A 1AE, Tel 71-495-4336, Fax 71-495-4377. **Germany:** United States Travel & Tourism Admin., Bethmannstr 56, D-60311, Frankfurt 1, Tel 69-92-00-3617, Fax 69-294-173. **Australia:** United States Travel & Tourism Admin., Level 59, MLC Centre, King & Castlereagh Streets, Sydney, NSW 2001, Tel 02-233-4666, Fax 02-232-7219.

PACIFIC REGION

The Pacific's large coastal cities are commonly thought of as the most important cultural points, yet this region's most eccentric and interesting festivals are often found in the hinterlands. Staged in spectacular settings, these events celebrate self-sufficiency in harsh environments, with wild sports and imaginative contests like Wilderness Women Competitions and Moose Dropping Festivals. And no matter where you celebrate on the Pacific Coast, you can count on local wines or handmade ales from the many wineries and microbreweries that dot the region.

Alaska, California, Hawaii, Oregon, Washington

Iditarod Sled Dog Race

Anchorage (Alaska) **March**

The longest, toughest sled-dog race on earth pits dogs and men against two mountain ranges, 150 miles of frozen Yukon River, the iced-in Norton sound, and countless grizzly bears on its 1,049-mile (1678-km) way from Anchorage to Nome. Leaders try to beat the course record of just over 10 days and 15 hours, while the rest just try to finish what's been called the Last Great Race on Earth. The route commemorates and duplicates part of the historic journey of the mushers from Anchorage who brought medicine to stop a diphtheria epidemic in Nome.

Spectators typically congregate at the start, but the finish in Nome (one of the few "wet" bush towns) is actually a bigger and better party. Another great spot to catch race action is Wassila, about 56 km/35 miles from the start, where an Iditarod Days Festival springs up, and where the Aurora Borealis light is particularly great at this time of year.

DATE: Starts March 5. **LOCATION/TRANSPORT:** Anchorage to Nome. Both cities are easily reached by air. **ACCOMMODATION:** Hotels fill up quickly and you wouldn't want to sleep outside, so book early. **CONTACT:** Anchorage Convention and Visitor's Bureau, 1600 A Street, Anchorage, AK 99501, Tel (907) 276-4118 & (907) 376-5155.

Into the wilderness: The cheering crowds of Anchorage are soon left behind in the Iditarod, which has been called the "last great great race on earth." (Alaska Division of Tourism)

While you're there ...

- **Snowfest, Lake Tahoe (California):** More than 120 separate events keep things hopping on Lake Tahoe's northern shore over a 10-day span, making this the largest winter carnival in the West. Parades, ski races, softball on skis, a model railroad show, a wild-game cook-off, and live music are just a sampling of the festivities. Grab your pooch for the Dress-Up-Your-Dog Contest, enter the man in your life in the Mr. Lake Tahoe Contest, and let whoever places higher ride home in the front seat. Contact: Snowfest, P.O. Box 7590, Tahoe City, CA 96145, Tel (916) 583-7625. (First week in March.)
- **Bebop and Brew, Arcata (California):** Enjoy some of the good life from 25 of the West Coast's best breweries as jazz music and handmade ales are served up right. Contact: Bebop and Brew, P.O. Box 400, Arcata, CA 95521, Tel (707) 826-2267. (Mid-May.)
- **Calaveras County Fair and Jumping Frog Contest, Angels Camp (California):** Let old toads grumble discrimination if they wish: this world-famous competition is for frogs only. A children's parade, 4-H competition, pony express, demolition derby, live rock bands, and a rodeo provide entertainment when the hopping stops. Contact: Calaveras County Fairgrounds, P.O. Box 96, Angels Camp, CA 95222, Tel (209) 736-2561. (Third weekend in May.)

Moose Dropping Festival

Talkeetna (Alaska) **July**

As the sun's rays give Denali (Mt. McKinley) a white glow that contrasts beautifully with the warm colors of the Alaskan sum-

Sled Dog Races: Mushers Away!

Remember those snowy days when you were a kid trying to get faithful Fido to pull you across the yard in your sled ... and he wouldn't budge? Well, there are some folks who met that challenge and went on to work and train sled dogs as a way of life. Years are spent breeding and training top Alaskan Huskies to compete in challenges ranging from weight-pulling championships to marathon races that span a continent.

Classes of dog racing are distinguished by the number of dogs pulling each sled, the length of the course, and the age and experience of the handlers. During the length of the race, which can be anywhere from a few days to a few weeks, both humans and dogs camp in the snow, following courses mapped out along trails, forest roads, and snowmobile runs. Sled dog races have sometimes served as a bridge between countries, as in the **Hope International**, where teams sledding off in Nome are helicoptered across the Bering Sea to complete the course in the Russian town of Anadyr, 1,200 miles away.

The **Iditarod Sled Dog Race** that traverses Alaska from Anchorage to Nome in early March is by far the most challenging of courses, with 1,049 miles of harsh terrain. Here are some of North America's other top sled-dog competitions:

Early January: **Copper Basin 300 Dog Sled Race**, Glennallen, Alaska. Contact: (907) 822-3663. • *Late January:* **All-American Champion Sled Dog Races**, Ely, Minnesota. Contact: Ely Chamber of Commerce, Tel (218) 365-2163. • *Early February:* **Yukon Quest International Sled Dog Race**, Fairbanks to Whitehorse, Alaska. Contact: (907) 452-7954. • *Mid-February:* **Wisconsin State Sled Dog Championships**, Wisconsin Dells, Wisconsin. Contact: Wisconsin Dells Visitor and Convention Bureau, Tel (608) 254-8088. • *Late March:* **Hope International Dog Sled Race**, Nome, Alaska to Anadyr, Russia. Contact: (907) 278-5783. • *Late March/early April:* **Canadian Championship Dog Derby**, Yellowknife, Northwest Territories, Canada. Contact: (403) 873-9698.

merscape, the snow-melt uncovers millions of moose leftovers. Residents of the small town of Talkeetna take advantage of the great weather and head outside to arm themselves for the annual Moose Dropping Festival.

Talkeetna's log cabins, dirt roads, and small-town feel are perfect for this celebration. You'll find dancing, drinking, and unusual sports where the town's biggest crop flies fast and furious. The Moose Nugget Toss is one of the most popular events during the weekend festivities, as well as one of the most challenging. The droppings are the size of a Milk Dud, but lighter and aerodynamically unpredictable as they fly toward targets made from antlers mounted on a large, moose-shaped board. Occasionally a throw is scuttled by a bush pilot making a landing on D Street.

The Mountain Mother Contest is open to certified mothers who exhibit such maternal skills as crossing the Susitna River on stepping stones while balancing two sacks of groceries and a baby doll. On the other side they're required to chop wood, walk a beam, change and wash diapers, and finally, prepare and bake a pie and ring the dinner bell. The winner receives flowers and champagne, but suburban housewives take note: the record here is under five minutes.

Talkeetnans hate to throw anything away. They coat moose droppings with varnish and make everything from necklaces and earrings to tie-tacks. In addition to stocking up on such doodads as moose-dropping swizzle sticks, you can dance and sample local food (just beware of anything suspiciously shaped), or hang around and enjoy one of Alaska's most friendly towns. You're sure to find lots of cosmopolitan company too, since this pleasant village is the climbing center for Mt. McKinley, at 6,164 meters (20,320 feet) the highest peak in North America.

DATE: Second weekend in July. **LOCATION:** Talkeetna. **TRANSPORT:** Talkeetna is at the foot of Mt. McKinley, north of Anchorage on Route 3. **ACCOMMODATION:** A wide variety of accommodations are available in both Talkeetna and nearby Anchorage. **CONTACT:** Box 76, Talkeetna, AK 99676, Tel (907) 733-1478.

© WHILE YOU'RE THERE ...

© **Haight-Ashbury Street Fair, San Francisco (California):** Once the center point of flower-child culture, the Haight withered during the 1980s. Nineties-style gentrification has caused the turn-of-the-century area to bloom again, but old-timers tisk at suburban dharma bum wannabes snoozing in doorways in $400 sleeping bags. It isn't the Summer of Love, but this famous neighborhood celebration features good music and food, and some truly outlandish clothes and handicrafts. Contact: (415) 661-8025. (Early June.)

OREGON BREWERS FESTIVAL

Portland (Oregon) **July**

Microbrewers from all over the country pour their finest beers here in the cradle of America's microbrewery revolution. Begun only a few years ago, this is already one of the biggest beer blasts on the continent. More importantly, it's the most fun.

Several secrets of success put the Oregon Brewers Festival hops and shoulders above other American beer festivals. First of all, you won't find any ridiculous "one ounce at a time" beer-tasting snifters. Beer is served by the mug and half-mug, and instead of an all-inclusive admission fee, you pay as you drink. (This limits overindulgence, since people don't feel like they have to drink a keg to get their money's worth.)

There's no judging, and instead of the usual convention-hall setting, the festival is held in downtown Portland's Waterfront Park, on the mellow banks of the Willamette River. When you get your beer (from one of more than 60 brewery booths in two beer tents), you can walk around the park, or relax at tables set up in the sun and shade. There's plenty of great food and entertainment by local folk bands, and the Oregon Brew Crew demonstrates home-brewing techniques at a special on-site brewery. Best of all, some of the nation's finest microbreweries fire up special brews for the event, so there's plenty of cutting-edge beer.

DATE: Friday, Saturday, and Sunday on the last weekend in July. **LOCATION:** Portland Oregon's Waterfront Park. **TRANSPORT:** Portland is easily reached by air from all over the US; the park is located in downtown, off Front St. along the river. **ACCOMMODATION:** Oregon has plenty of room at the inns. **CONTACT:** Widmer Brewing Co., 929 N. Russell, Portland, OR 97227, Tel (503) 281-2437.

◎ While you're there ...

◎ **Makawao Rodeo, Makawao, Maui (Hawaii):** Paniolos (rodeos) are an important tradition in Hawaiian life, and this one can't be beat for fun and demonstrations of the Hawaiian cowboy art. Contact: (808) 572-9928. (July 4.)

◎ **Logger's Jubilee, Morton (Washington):** The Northwest's anti-logging lobby would be appalled by everything but the beards at this axe-shouldering salute to lumberjacks. Lumber camp contests include wood chopping, crosscut sawing, chain sawing, horse pulling, log birling (rolling), and bucking in a jubilee that's been a tradition for half a century. Bed races, lawnmower races, carnival rides, a parade, dancing, a fiddling contest, and lots of food add to the weekend merriment. Contact: Morton Chamber of Commerce, Morton, WA 98356, Tel (206) 496-5123. (Second weekend in August.)

◎ **International Surf Festival, South Bay, Los Angeles (California):** Redondo, Hermosa, and Manhattan beaches host the world's best surfers, and put on two weeks of sideshows like a lifeguard championship, body boarding and body surfing competitions, and a fishing derby. Landlubbers can bump and spike in a sand volleyball tournament. Contact: *The Daily Breeze,* 5215 Torrance Blvd., Torrance, CA 90509, Tel (310) 540-5511. (Mid-August.)

Let the chips fly: Loggers go at it in the cross-cut sawing competition at the Loggers Jubilee in Morton, Washington.
(Washington State Tourism Division)

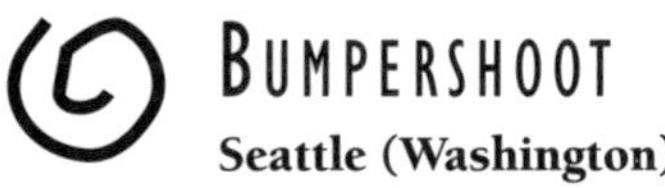

Bumpershoot

Seattle (Washington) **September**

The Northwest's most dazzling showcase of performing arts features dance, theater, literary arts, comedy, and visual arts. The four-day event distinguishes itself from similar festivals by its magnitude (15 indoor and outdoor stages on 74 acres), its diversity (local, national, and international performers), and its setting (in the middle of downtown Seattle right under the Space Needle).

Music is always a big draw in this city, and concert-goers can expect to see and hear everything from local grunge survivors and swampy zydeco combos, to bikutsi rhythm masters from Cameroon. The street-performer action is non-stop, and each year features several special off-the-wall projects. All in all, it's a lively scene that draws more than 230,000—many of whom are international visitors.

DATE: Friday through Monday, Labor Day weekend (usually the first weekend in September). **LOCATION:** Downtown Seattle. **TRANSPORT:** Seattle is easily reached from all over the U.S., Europe, and East Asia. The festival takes place directly under the Space Needle. **ACCOMMODATION:** There's plenty of hotel space in Seattle, but the tourist season is still in full swing, so book in advance. **CONTACT:** P.O. Box 9750, Seattle, WA 98109, Tel (206) 622-5123 & (206) 682-4386.

While you're there ...

Bankoh Na Wahine O Ke Kai, Molokai (Hawaii): Sorry, guys, this navigational challenge is for gals only. Six-woman teams launch their Hawaiian-style canoes on a remote beach on Molokai and set paddle for Honolulu's Duke Kahanamoku Beach, crossing the rough Kaiwi Channel. Paddlers come from around the world to compete for the championship title. Contact: (808) 262-7567. (Late September.)

Wilderness Woman Competition

Talkeetna (Alaska) **December**

Feminists, stay back 500 feet! In this competition for single women, the triumphant bachelorette must defeat a series of wintertime obstacles on her way to delivering a sandwich and a beer to a bachelor engaged in that most masculine of pastimes—watching a football game on TV.

On her way to servile glory, the eligible female—a rare species in Alaska—must snowmobile through an obstacle course, chop wood, and dispense with other chores before reaching the kitchen. There she's expected to cook up something that will find its way to the macho heart lounging on the recliner chair. Sponsored by the Talkeetna Bachelor Society, the event culminates in a gala Bachelor Ball and a Bachelor Auction (although some local women wonder why anyone would pay for a man after the Wilderness Woman gauntlet proves them to be pretty unnecessary).

DATE: First weekend in December. **LOCATION:** Talkeetna. **TRANSPORT:** Talkeetna is at the foot of Mt. McKinley, north of Anchorage on Route 3. **ACCOMMODATION:** There are a variety of accommodations available in nearby Anchorage. **CONTACT:** (907) 733-1727.

Resources

In USA: United States Travel & Tourism Admin., 14th and Constitution, Washington, DC 20230, Tel (202) 482-4752. **Alaska:** Alaska Division of Tourism, P.O. Box 11081, Juneau AK 99811, Tel (907) 465-2010. **California:** California Division of Tourism, P.O. Box 1499, Sacramento, CA 95812, Tel (916) 322-2881 & (800) 862-2543. **Hawaii:** Hawaii Visitors Bureau, Waikiki Business Plaza, 3370 Kalakaua Ave., Honolulu, HI 96815, Tel (808) 923-1811. **Oregon:** Oregon Tourism Division, 775 Summer Street NE, Salem, OR 97310, Tel (503) 378-3451 & (800) 547-7842. *Washington:* Washington State Tourism Development Division, 101 General Administration Building, AX-13, Olympia, WA 98504, Tel (206) 753-5600.

Canada: United States Travel & Tourism Admin., 480 University Ave., #602, Toronto, ON M5G 1V2, Tel (416) 595-5082, Fax (416) 595-5211. **UK:** United States Travel & Tourism Admin., 24 Grosvenor Square, London, W1A 1AE, Tel 71-495-4336, Fax 71-495-4377. **Germany:** United States Travel & Tourism Admin., Bethmannstr 56, D-60311, Frankfurt 1, Tel 69-92-00-3617, Fax 69-294-173. **Australia:** United States Travel & Tourism Admin., Level 59, MLC Centre, King & Castlereagh Streets, Sydney, NSW 2001, Tel 02-233-4666, Fax 02-232-7219.

Wild Planet Festival Finder

The *Wild Planet!* **Festival Finder** allows you to find and plan trips to events that fit your interests, your time frame, and your preferences for where you'd like to go. To make finding an event easy and fun, these three indexes comprise the **Festival Finder**:

- *What's It About?*
- *When Is It Happening?*
- *Where Is It & What's It Called?*

If you're interested in something special—like boat racing, kites, or zydeco music—consult the *What's It About?* **Festival Finder.** You'll find references to the countries that feature these types of events.

If you have a specific time frame in mind—let's say you have a vacation coming up in July, or you'll be in Singapore on business in October—check *When Is It Happening?* You'll be able to see exactly which events are happening where, during your window of opportunity.

If you know the name of an event—such as Art Deco Weekend—or the name of the country it's in (New Zealand), you'll find it in the multi-purpose *Where Is It & What's It Called?* **Festival Finder.**

Or if you simply want to browse through all of the offerings of any particular country, consult the **Table of Contents** or the map at the beginning of *Wild Planet!* and turn to the appropriate country chapter.

What's It About?

B

C

D

E

F

G

H

P

R

S

T

U

V

W

When Is It Happening?

January

Western Europe
France and Monaco:
International Circus Festival 32;
Monte Carlo Motor Rally 32
Italy: Carnival (Carnevale) in
Venice 61
Scotland: Hogmany and New
Year's Day 84; Up-Helly-Aa 85;
The Burning of the Clavie 86
Switzerland: Silvesterkläuse 112;
Vogel Gryff 112

Eastern Europe and Russia
Russia: Russian Orthodox
Christmas (Rozhdestvo) 141

Eastern Mediterranean & the Middle East
Egypt: End of Ramadan
(Eid al-Fitr) 156
Greece: Carnival 159;
Gynaecocracy 161
Israel: Id ul-Fitr 166
Turkey: Camel Wrestling 173

Africa
Ethiopia: Timket 178, 181;
Genna 180
Ghana: Addae-Kese 183

South-Central Asia
Afghanistan: Id-ul-Fitr 219
India: Spituk Festival 230; Pongal
(Makara Sankranti or Bihu)
231; Kite Festival 231; Elephant
March 232; Republic Day 232;
Float Festival (Teppam) 233;
Kumbh Mela 235
Nepal: Basant Panchami 270
Pakistan: Id-ul-Fitr 280
Sri Lanka: Duruthu Perahera 285

East Asia
China: Chinese New Year 299;
Ice Lantern Festival 300
Hong Kong: Chinese New Year
309
Japan: Toka Ebisu 315; Grass
Burning Ceremony 315;
Niramekko Obisha 315
Mongolia: White
Moon/Mongolian New Year
(Tsagaan Sar) 335
Taiwan: Lunar New Year (Sang-
Sin) 336

Southeast Asia
Indonesia: Pagerwesi Day 354
Malaysia: Thaipusam 363;
Birthday of Chor Soo Kong
365; Chinese New Year 365
Myanmar (Burma):
Independence Day 374
Philippines: Ati-Atihan 380;
Sinulog 382; Procession of the
Black Nazarene 383
Singapore: Thaipusam 388;
Lunar New Year 389
Thailand: Dragon and Lion
Parade 395; Chaiyaphum

© FEBRUARY

East Asia
China: Lantern Festival (Yúanxiāo Jié) 298
Hong Kong: Lantern Festival 308
Japan: Snow Festival (Yuki Matsuri) 313; Yah-Yah Matsuri Festival 315; Lantern Festival of Kasuga Taisha Shrine 315; Setsubun (Bean Throwing) 316; Eyo Festival of Saidaiji Temple 316
Taiwan: Lantern Festival (Yúanxiāo Jié) 337

Southeast Asia
Laos: Magha Puja 344
Malaysia: Masi Magham 366
Thailand: Chao Mae Lim Ko Nieo Fair 395
Vietnam: Mai Dong 405; Chu Dong Tu Festival 405; Huong Tich/Lac Long Quan Festival 405

Australia & the South Pacific
Australia: Compass Cup Cow Race 415; Adelaide Festival and Festival Fringe 416; Bindoon Rock Festival 417; Wind on Water 419
New Zealand: New Zealand International Festival of the Arts 431; Baldwin Street Gutbuster 432; Wildfoods Festival 433; Art Deco Weekend 434
Papua New Guinea: New Ireland Provincial Government Day 438

South America
Argentina: National Vintage Festival (Vendimia) 450; Carnival 451; Vuelta Ciclistica 452
Bolivia: Candlemas (Candelaria) 455; Devil's Carnival (La Diablada) 456
Brazil: Carnival in Rio 464, 466; Carnival in Bahia 467; Carnival in Pernambuco 468
Colombia: Carnival in Barranquilla 477
Peru: Candlemas (Festival de la Virgin del la Candelaria) 487
Venezuela: Carnival 496

The Caribbean
Aruba: Carnival 500
Bonaire: Tumba Festival 501
Dominican Republic: Grand Costumed Dance (Gran Baile de Comparsas) 510
French West Indies: Carnival 513
Jamaica: Bob Marley Birthday Bash 519
Puerto Rico: Carnival 509; Folk Festivals 509
Trinidad & Tobago: Carnival 521

Mexico & Central America
Mexico: Carnival 534, 536

Canada & the United States
Eastern Canada: Winter Carnival 550
Southeast USA: Mardi Gras (New Orleans) 569; Courir de Mardi Gras (Louisiana) 571; Mardi Gras (Alabama) 572
Southwest USA: O'Odham Tash 607

© March

Western Europe
Belgium: Mid-Lent Carnival 9; Dead Rat's Ball (Bal Rat Mort) 9
Iceland: Beer Day 49
Ireland: St. Patrick's Day 54
Italy: Easter 64
Netherlands: Breda Old-Style Jazz Festival 72
Portugal: Holy Week 76
Spain: Fallas de San José 92; Holy Week (Semana Santa) 95

Eastern Europe and Russia
The Baltics: Carnival (Uzgavenes) 120; Birstonas Jazz Festival 120
Bulgaria: March Music Days 123
Hungary: Budapest Spring Festival 129; Spring Festivals 130
Poland: Holy Week 132
Russia: Spring Festival (Maslenitsa) 145; Festival of

© April

© May

Roses 78-79; Festival of the Holy Ghost 79
Spain: Romería del Rocio 97-98

Eastern Europe and Russia
The Baltics: Skamba Skamba Kaukliai 120
Bulgaria: Rose Festival 122-123; Sofia Music Weeks 124
The Czech and Slovak Republics: Prague Spring International Music Festival (Prazke Jaro) 125; Bratislava Lyre 127
Poland: Juvenalia 135
Russia: Festival of Moscow Stars 147; May Day 147

Eastern Mediterranean & the Middle East
Greece: Anastenaria Firewalking Festival 162; Athens Festival 162, 165
Israel: Independence Day 168; Israel Festival 168
Turkey: Selçuk Ephesus Festival of Culture and Art 175

Africa
Ethiopia: Adbar 180; Festival of Sof Omar 180
Ghana: Deer Hunting Festival (Aboakyere) 184
Tunisia: Festival of the Sparrow Hawk 210

South-Central Asia
India: Dhungri Forest Festival 246
Sri Lanka: Vesak (Waisakka) 286
Tibet: Gyangzê Horse Racing Festival (Tamang) 295; Tshurphu Monastery Festival 295; Buddha's Enlightenment 296; Samye Dholdhe Festival 296

East Asia
China: Dragon Boat Regatta 302
Hong Kong: Bun Festival 309-310; Tin Hau Fisherman's Festival 310; The Buddha's Birthday 311
Japan: Hakata Dontaku 318; Cormorant Fishing (Ukai) 318; Hollyhock Festival (Aoi Matsuri) 319
Korea: Tano Festival 325-326; P'ungnam Festival 326-328
Taiwan: Dragon Boat Races 339

Southeast Asia
Indonesia: Waisak 350
Laos: Rocket Festival (Bun Bang Fai) 343; Sisakha Bu-saa 344
Malaysia: Kota Belud Tamu Besar 367; Gawai Dayak 367; Kadazan Harvest Festival 369
Myanmar (Burma): Kason Festival 374
Philippines: Carabao 385; Fertility Rites 385; Flores de Mayo and Santacruzan 386-387
Singapore: Dragon Boat Festival 391
Thailand: Rocket Festival (Bun Bang Fai) 395
Vietnam: Buddha's Birth, Enlightenment, and Death 407

Australia & the South Pacific
Australia: Camel Cup 421-422; Keppel Krabtastic World Crab-Tying Championships 421; Baycarna and World Smiling Championships 422; Melbourne Film Festival 422; Barunga Sports Festival 422

South America
Bolivia: Feast Day of Gran Poder 459; Day of the Holy Cross 461
Venezuela: The Devil Dancers of Corpus Christi 495; The May Cross (Crux de Mayo) 496

The Caribbean
Aruba: Hi-Winds Windsurfing Tournament 503
French West Indies: Fête de la Musique Traditionelle 514

Mexico & Central America
Mexico: Cinco de Mayo 540; Fiesta de Corpus Cristi 541

Canada & the United States
Northeast USA: Bang on a Can Festival 562

© JUNE

Western Europe

Eastern Europe and Russia

Eastern Mediterranean & the Middle East

Africa

South-Central Asia

© JULY

Eastern Europe and Russia

Eastern Mediterranean & the Middle East

Africa

South-Central Asia

East Asia

Southeast Asia

Australia & the South Pacific

South America

The Caribbean

Mexico & Central America

Canada & the United States

© AUGUST

Western Europe

Eastern Europe and Russia

© SEPTEMBER

Western Europe

Austria: Haydn Festival 6
Belgium: Breughel Festival 12
Denmark: Århus Festival 17
France and Monaco: Festival of Popular Music and Dance 38
Germany: Moselle Wine Festival 44; Dürkheim Sausage Market 45; Kulmbach Beer Festival 45; Oktoberfest 45-47; Cannstatter Volksfest 46; Berlin Festival 47
Iceland: Sheep Roundup (Réttadagur) 52
Ireland: Galway International Oyster Festival 59; Clarenbridge Oyster Festival 60; Belfast Folk Week 60
Italy: The Procession of the Thorned Men 70; Historical Regatta 69-70; Human Chess Match 70
Netherlands: Prinsjesdag 74; Brandaris Balkoppenrace 75
Portugal: Folk Music and Dance Festival 82-83; Vinho Verde Fair 83
Scotland: Braemar Royal Highland Gathering 87
Spain: La Merced 102
Wales: Festival of Music and the Arts 115

Eastern Europe and Russia

Bulgaria: Festival of the Arts in Old Plovdiv 124
The Czech and Slovak Republics: Zatec Hops Festival 127
Hungary: Savaria Autumn Festival 130
Poland: Wratislavia Cantans 137; Willa Atma 137
Romania: Wine Harvest Folk Festival 140; Cibinium Festival 140

Eastern Mediterranean & the Middle East

Egypt: International Folkloric Art Festival 157
Israel: Prince of Peace Music Festival 169; Sukkot 169
Turkey: Cirit Games 175

Africa

Ethiopia: Maskal 180-181; Ethiopian New Year 181
Tanzania: Cultural Celebration 192
Morocco: Moussem of Moulay Idriss 202; Engagement Festival 203
Zambia: Shimunenga 214

South-Central Asia

Bhutan: Thimphu Tsechu 222, 224-225
India: Dussehra (Ram Lila) 259; Festival of the Gods 260
Nepal: Bada Dasain/Durga Puja 273; Ganesh Charturthi 275
Tibet: Looking Around the Fields Festival 296

East Asia

China: Mid-Autumn/Moon Festival 306; Birthday of Confucius 306; Double Ninth Festival 307
Hong Kong: Mid-Autumn (Moon Cake) Festival 312
Japan: Nakizumo 321
Korea: Andong Folk Festival 330-331
Taiwan: Double-yang 340

Southeast Asia

Indonesia: Torajan Funeral Feasts 357; Erau Festival 359-360; Asmat Cultural Exposition 361-362
Malaysia: Papar Tamu Besar 370; Thimithi Fire-Walking Ceremony 370
Myanmar (Burma): Phaungdaw Oo Festival 376
Philippines: Penafrancia Festival 387
Singapore: Birthday of the Monkey God 390; Festival of the Nine Emperor Gods 390
Thailand: Narathiwat Fair 402
Vietnam: Mid-Autumn Festival (Trung Thu) 407

Australia & the South Pacific
Australia: Warana 427; Henley-on-Todd Regatta and Beerfest 427; Western Australian Folk Festival 428; Australian Football League Grand Finale 429
Papua New Guinea: Goroka Show 440-441; East Sepik Provincial Government Day 441; Malangan Festival 441; Hiri Moale 441

South America
Bolivia: Feast Day of the Exaltation of the Cross 462; Festival of San Roque 463
Chile: Independence Celebrations 474
Colombia: Feast of St. Francis (Fiesta de San Francisco) 481

Canada & the United States
Eastern Canada: Toronto Film Festival 553
Northeast USA: West Indian/American Day Carnival 564; Wigstock 565-566
Southeast USA: Mississippi Delta Blues Festival 582; Festivals Acadiens 582
Great Lakes & Midwest: Dally in the Alley 596; Custer Bison Roundup 596
Rocky Mountain Region: Testicle Festival 604
Southwest USA: Burning Man Project 606, 611
Pacific Region: Bumpershoot 620; Bankoh Na Wahine O Ke Kai 621

© October

Western Europe
Austria: Styrian Autumn Festival 6
Germany: Frankenstein Festival 47; Wine festivals (Moselle region) 47
Switzerland: Vintage Festival 111; Aelplerchilbi 111

Eastern Europe and Russia
The Baltics: Jazz and Blues Festival 120; Vilnius Jazz Festival 120; Bildes 120
The Czech and Slovak Republics: Bratislava International Jazz Festival 127; Pardubice Steeplechase 127
Poland: All Hallows' Eve/All Saints Day 137

Eastern Mediterranean & the Middle East
Egypt: Celebration of Ramses II's Coronation 157
Greece: Feast of St. Demetrius 165

Africa
Ghana: Great Yam Festival (Odiwera) 187
Kenya: Camel Derby 192
Morocco: Fêtes du Cheval 203; Fêtes des Dattes 203

South-Central Asia
India: Festival of Lights (Diwali/Deepavali) 261; Pushkar Camel Fair (Pushkar Mela) 264
Nepal: Festival of Lights (Tihar or Deepavali) 275

East Asia
China: Tan Ta 307
Japan: Festival of the Ages (Jidai Matsuri) 323; Marimo Matsuri 324
Korea: Shilla Cultural Festival 328; Paekche Cultural Festival 331; Halla Cultural Festival 331

Southeast Asia
Laos: The Festival of the Waters (Bun Nam and Awk Watsa) 344
Myanmar (Burma): Festival of Lights (Thadingyut) 377
Philippines: Zamboanga Hermosa 387
Singapore: Thimithi Festival 391
Thailand: Vegetarian Festival 396; Chon Buri Buffalo Races 397

© NOVEMBER

© DECEMBER

Where Is It & What's It Called?

A

B

C

D

E

F

G

H

I

J

K

L

M

N

O

P

Q

R

S

T

U

V

W

Y

Z

Dear Reader: We welcome your comments!

RE: Wild Planet! 1,001 Extraordinary Events for the Inspired Traveler

We would like to know what you think of **Wild Planet! 1,001 Extraordinary Events for the Inspired Traveler** and what you think would make it even more useful for you. Please take a few minutes to fill out and return this card. Thanks for your interest!

Where did you purchase this book? ______________________________

How did you become aware of this book? ______________________________

What feature of the book do you like the most? ______________________________

What feature do you like the least? ______________________________

How would you improve this book? ______________________________

____

Other subject areas of interest ______________________________

☐ Please send me information on other **Visible Ink Press** titles.

Name ______________________ Phone (_____) ______________

Street Address ______________________________

City ______________________ State ____________ Zip ________

Age _____ M _____ F _____ Do you own a PC? _____ Do you own a CD-ROM Player? _____

Visible Ink Press

In U.S. and Canada: 1-800-776-6265 Fax: (313) 961-6637